The Sopranos Sessions

To Susan Olds, Mark Di Ionno, Wally Stroby, Rosemary Parrillo, Anne-Marie Cottone, Jenifer Braun, Steve Hedgpeth, and the rest of the gang from the glorious '90s heyday of the *Star-Ledger* features section.

Love,
Kid & Genius

The Sopranos Sessions

Matt Zoller Seitz & Alan Sepinwall

ABRAMS PRESS, NEW YORK

Contents

The Foreword:
You Get What You Pay For

Before 2002, I had seen exactly one episode of *The Sopranos*, a chance encounter in an upstate New York motel room. I liked what I saw, but I had been raised by thrifty parents with a long list of things one should never pay for, and "premium cable" was at the top. Never mind basic cable; television was meant to be *free*. So in 1999, I watched that one episode, then let *The Sopranos* go. Three years and three critically acclaimed seasons later, all I knew was that Tony Soprano once took his daughter on a college visit and things did not go as planned.

Then I decided to buy a house with my then-boyfriend, now-husband, who happened to be making his own HBO show, *The Wire*. (In fact, he was so busy filming that I was alone on moving day; let's not revisit that old grudge.) Our new house had green laminate kitchen counters, just like Carmela Soprano's. More thrillingly, we had an HBO subscription and a nice cache of free DVDs. So when oral surgery sidelined me for a couple of days in spring 2002, I made myself a cheese soufflé and started my first binge watch, although that term was not yet mainstream. My hope was that *The Sopranos* would distract me from my pain until I could fall asleep.

I knew very little sleep over the next three days.

Like millions before me, I was hooked, showing up every Sunday night for the "three" seasons that aired over the next five years. (Like the writers of this book and David Chase himself, I count them as four seasons.) After it ended in 2007, I rewatched the series in full at least six times.

Serial dramas are now commonplace, yet few equal *The Sopranos*. One can watch it start to finish with enormous satisfaction, yet also enjoy single episodes with almost no context. Toward the end of my father's life, when his memory was failing, he happily watched the bowdlerized episodes on A&E the way his father had once watched *Perry Mason*. No matter that he couldn't remember the larger plot arcs; the individual shows never failed to entertain him.

I credit this quality to Chase's years on relatively traditional Hollywood fare, like *The Rockford Files* and *Northern Exposure*. He has an incomparable short-game/long-game approach to making television. There is a form in fiction that many claim, but few actually deliver: connected short stories in which the whole transcends the parts. *The Sopranos* works that way. Episodes we think are one-offs still carry important pieces of the story; plot-heavy installments can be enjoyed in isolation.

Consider "Pine Barrens." It may feel like a "bottle episode," but the animosity between Paulie and Chris will surface again and again—their secrets from that day endure. Or take "College," my first taste—as Matt Zoller Seitz and Alan Sepinwall tell us in this book, the episode where "*The Sopranos* became *The Sopranos*"— which makes the counterintuitive choice to have Tony in Maine while Carmela entertains the parish priest back in New Jersey. You can't subvert a genre until you understand it. Chase and his writers clearly knew all the ins and outs of Mafia movies, but they also recognized that their characters would, too. These wise guys were not only in on the joke—they *made* jokes.

Eventually, I became a little bit of a *Sopranos* obsessive. That might sound like an oxymoron, but when you read this book, you realize that there are levels of *Sopranos* obsessiveness. The trivia I so proudly identified during rewatches—*Look, there's Joseph Gannascoli, who will later play Vito Spatafore, as a civilian-schmo day player in season one*—are nothing compared to the details that Sepinwall and Seitz have mined here.

Speaking of our guides—while I have a vivid memory of my first *Sopranos* encounter, I am less clear when I started to read Alan and Matt's work, but I know it goes back more than a decade. It was probably through their excellent commentary on and recaps of *The Wire*. But I have continued reading them because of their intelligent overall enthusiasm for television. I *love* television. I have always loved television. Even as a child, I knew there was something fundamentally wrong with the snobby woman on *The Dick Van Dyke Show* who, upon meeting Rob Petrie, trilled, "Oh, I don't own a television machine." The number of good television critics in place when *The Sopranos* first aired is a testimony to newspapers (which I also love). But I think Alan and Matt are particularly exceptional in their approach to this groundbreaking show. It's hard to imagine that anyone has thought this long and hard about these episodes, unless it's David Chase, his writers, and the late James Gandolfini.

A burning question hangs over this enterprise: What about that finale? I don't want to give anything away, but I will say that *The Sopranos Sessions* provided me with—oh dreaded word—closure. I watched "Made in America" alone, my husband thousands of miles away in South Africa, filming an HBO miniseries. (Please note the motif of HBO taking my husband away when I need him most.)

When the screen went black and the sound cut out, I was convinced there had been an outage. In May 1998, there was a power failure in Baltimore just before the *Seinfeld* finale that knocked out cable to thousands, so perhaps I was oversensitive to the likelihood of it recurring.

Once I realized the dead screen was intentional, I felt, well, mocked. I had logged serious time with *The Sopranos*. I had even attended the premiere for season four's first two episodes, memorable because I sat in front of William Styron, who laughed heartily at the scene in which Adriana vomited so violently that her poodle ran for cover. I wasn't some bloodthirsty mook cheering for more whackage. I was a serious, thoughtful fan who could recognize William Styron at Radio City Music Hall. I wanted and deserved a great ending, like the montage to "Thru and Thru" in "Funhouse," the season two finale. By then I'd written seven books in a series of crime novels about a Baltimore PI, and I believed that if I ever chose to end my series, I would do it with a grand, reader-rewarding flourish. My feelings about the *Sopranos* finale joined a list of passionate grudges that includes the '69 Super Bowl, the '69 World Series, and the HBO executives who scheduled production of my husband's latest show to coincide with my book tour.

In all seriousness, this book helped me heal. I now understand that Chase was in a dilemma not unlike L. Frank Baum, who wanted to stop writing about Oz—the original Oz, not the HBO one—but faced an insatiable appetite from young readers. At one point, Baum went so far as to make Oz invisible to the world and had Dorothy Gale, now a permanent resident, send a note: "You will hear nothing more about Oz, because we are now cut off forever from the world." It didn't work; Baum would write eight more Oz books, and other writers continued the series long after his death. "Just when I thought I was out, they pull me back in"—sound familiar?

How does one resolve the problematic story of Tony Soprano, a monster that millions welcomed into their homes for eight years? It wasn't Chase who made a fool of me, but Tony, who had done the same thing to Dr. Melfi. But unlike Dr. Melfi, I was never going to have the resolve and discipline to turn my back on him. The scene in Holsten's, which had felt like such a fuck-you at the time, now seems like one of the more definitive endings in the history of television. *The Sopranos* deserved no less.

It also deserves no less than this thoughtful, engrossing compendium of recaps, facts, trivia, and analysis. When I heard that Alan and Matt were working on this book, I jokingly made one request: *Would you please explain the thematic significance of "The Three Bells," the 1950s song used in back-to-back episodes in season six?* They did, and with more detail than I ever anticipated. ("The classic Eisenhower-era arrangement with its marzipan harmonizing is a musical time machine, immersing listeners not in actual 1950s America, but in white, middle-class America's sentimental self-image of that time and place.") Nothing gets by these guys. If the FBI had brought this level of exhaustive investigation to the Soprano Family itself, Tony would have been locked up by the end of season one. And wouldn't we all be poorer for that?

Laura Lippman
Baltimore, Maryland
March 2018

The Introduction:
It Goes On and On and On and On

Guy walks into a psychiatrist's office. He tells the psychiatrist he's been having panic attacks and collapsing at work and home. "Lately," he adds, "I'm gettin' the feelin' that I came in at the end. The best is over."

Tough crowd. Who died?

I'll tell you who. Guy takes his daughter on a college tour. Runs into a traitorous ex-friend and strangles him to death in broad daylight. While they're away, his wife almost has sex with their priest but gives him a confession instead.

Thank you, try the onion rings . . . at Holsten's ice cream parlor. Guy goes there to meet his family for dinner. He selects a Journey song from the jukebox and watches as his wife and son arrive, while his daughter parallel parks outside (*forever*). He looks around, the door opens, and . . .

Did the mic just cut out?

What, you want a punchline to that? Or was *that* the punchline—not only to the most cryptic, most divisive, most debated ending to a TV show ever made but to one of the best shows ever made, period?

These are all jokes, and they aren't. First and foremost, they're famous scenes from *The Sopranos*, a show whose brilliance lay in the fact that you were never quite sure how to take it, all the way through that ending that could mean one thing, or another—or both.

It all sounded like a big joke before anyone had seen it, partly because *Analyze This*, a movie comedy with the same basic premise—wiseguy enters therapy—was debuting a few months later. As the show's hero, Tony Soprano, would later complain, that movie was a comedy. *The Sopranos* was strange, surprising, brutal and dark, and billed itself as a drama.

At the same time, though, it was as hilarious as any sitcom. Its humor ranged from hifalutin (mistaking Nostradamus for Quasimodo) to scatological ("Meeting's over!") to sickening (Phil Leotardo at the gas station). And the show's creator, David Chase, kept subverting our expectations. That cut to black in the finale really is a punchline to that scene, and to *The Sopranos* as a whole. It's just, like Tony Soprano's initial encounter with Dr. Melfi, or his reunion with Febby Petrulio, not the sort of punchline we expected, and we didn't know we wanted it until Chase provided it.

The show's mercurial unpredictability was electrifying. Pre-*Sopranos*, TV was widely dismissed as a medium for programs that didn't ask the viewer to think about anything except what was coming on next, and that preferred lovable characters who didn't change and had no inner life. The ideal network series was filler between commercials. It was hard to make art in this kind of environment, though some creators managed. There were lots and lots of rules. There were words you couldn't say, things you couldn't show, stories you couldn't tell. The number one rule: don't upset people.

The Sopranos wasn't the first show to break most of these rules: *All in the Family* gave us a bigoted (though not irredeemable) main character; *Hill Street Blues* pushed drama into more serialized, morally gray territory; *Miami Vice* belied the notion that TV shows couldn't look as good as movies. Nor was *The Sopranos* the first show to act like the rules didn't exist; see, among others, *The Prisoner*, *Twin Peaks*, and HBO's first original drama, *Oz* (featuring an actress named Edie Falco).

But it was the first show to do that and still become a massive, enduring hit.

Not since *I Love Lucy* had a show been copied as often and thoroughly, to the point where 2019 TV barely resembles the one into which Tony Soprano's SUV rumbled back in 1999. All the aspects of the series that once startled viewers have become accepted: serialization; narrative and moral ambiguity; antiheroes or villains as main characters; beauty for its own sake. That drama you just binged-watched on Netflix owes more to *The Sopranos* than to the rest of TV combined. The cell phones and references date the show to the turn of the millennium, but it still feels powerfully connected to what's happening now. But in 1999, it all felt brazenly audacious, from the way it handed its lead role to an unknown quantity—James Gandolfini—to the way it trained its audience to expect and even demand the unexpected.

It was a phenomenon almost from the start, and one we got to cover from the inside as the TV critics for the *Star-Ledger*, the hometown newspaper for both Tony Soprano and David Chase. Matt was on set when the first season was being shot and conducted one of the few interviews the famously press-shy Gandolfini ever gave. During the show's second half, Alan walked the streets of Hoboken with Joey Pants and got an extremely reluctant Chase on the phone the morning after the finale, for the only interview he gave about it for a long time.

We saw how much effort and attention-bordering-on-obsession to detail Chase and company put into the show. We fielded angry phone calls from Italian American anti-defamation activists who found *The Sopranos* a blight on their people and read delighted emails from other Italians who had never been prouder of their ethnicity or home state. We saw how the series, like *Lucy*, fundamentally changed both how TV was made and how the public at large felt about it. *The Sopranos* challenged TV to be better, and it challenged us to be better viewers. It didn't always succeed on either front—we heard plenty from the bloodthirsty hordes who wanted less yakkin', more whackin'—but it did more than even Chase himself could have possibly imagined when, fed up with the whole TV business, he was rooting for HBO to pass on the pilot so he could turn it into a movie.

We had previously written critical companion books for *Mad Men* and *Breaking Bad*, dramas that wouldn't exist without this one. *The Sopranos* wasn't nearly as fresh in our memories, and because it aired before the explosion of TV recap culture, we had to write most of this book from scratch.[1] Would it hold up after so many years and so many creative descendants, or would what was once shocking and bold now feel as clichéd as some of its most formulaic imitators?

Forget holding up—it often played better now. Freed from the shackles of having to predict its next plot maneuver, and fully prepared for Chase's love of anticlimax, we could see every aspect for what it was, rather than what we'd expected it to be. Much of the oft-maligned fourth season felt richer, more sure of itself, and other experiments, like Kevin Finnerty's trip to Costa Mesa, provided new treasures to unearth.

Best of all, we got to watch this remarkable cast at work again, particularly James Gandolfini. It's become easy since 2007 to put Gandolfini's performance on a continuum with the people who followed him, but with all due respect to the great Bryan Cranston, Jon Hamm, Elisabeth Moss, et al., our rewatch cemented his work as Tony as the best in TV drama history, as remarkable when acting opposite powerhouse costars like Falco and Nancy Marchand as when alone.

We wanted to call this book *The Sopranos Sessions* as a nod to Tony's relationship with Dr. Melfi, but also because we knew we would be sitting down with Chase himself for a new series of interviews that would revisit the show's origins, analyze nearly all of its most famous moments,[2] and even take one more go at that ending. What we didn't expect was how much like therapy our conversations began to feel—how, for instance, Chase's recall of specific details from two decades before wasn't always strong, but his memory of the emotions and instincts behind so many choices was, or how the conversation kept wandering down paths none of us expected—Chase included.

---

1 Even the episodic pieces we separately wrote during the final two seasons, and the ones Alan wrote a few years ago about the show's first season, had to be dismantled and rebuilt.

2 One notable exception we made: the Russian from "Pine Barrens," which may be *The Sopranos* subject Chase least enjoys talking about. Instead, we've included selections from a 2017 panel on the episode Matt moderated with Chase, writer Terence Winter, and director Steve Buscemi.

Those conversation were, like everything else about *The Sopranos*, a revelation and a confoundment at the same time. And they weren't even necessarily the highlight of the experience, since we got to rewatch the whole series and find new ways to write about Livia's diabolical grin, or Tony singing along in the car to the Chi-Lites, or Paulie and Christopher shivering in the Pine Barrens.

The Sopranos Sessions is broken into seven sections:

1. **The Foreword**, written by acclaimed novelist Laura Lippman;
2. **The Introduction**, providing a brief overview of our experience writing about the show when it originally aired and revisiting it now;
3. **The Recaps**, consisting of critical essays on every episode that aired during each of the show's seven seasons. These have been spoiler-proofed so that first timers can read them without fear of finding out what happens in later episodes and seasons.[3] They often look back, but never ahead;
4. **The Debate**, wherein our authors argue about what happened in the final scene of the final episode;
5. **The David Chase Sessions**, interviewing the show's creator. Although these try to focus on each individual season, they jump around a bit in terms of chronology and sometimes discuss foreshadowing, so you will probably want to avoid reading them until after you've finished watching all the episodes at least once;
6. **The Morgue**, a collection of excerpts from articles we wrote about the show for the *Star-Ledger*;
7. **The Eulogies**, covering the death and legacy of James Gandolfini, including the letter that Chase read at Gandolfini's memorial service.

Whether you're watching *The Sopranos* for the first time in the shadow of all the shows it influenced, making this book part of your annual "Bada Binge," or revisiting it like an old friend you haven't talked to in years, our hope is that the recaps will give each episode new insight and context, that our conversations with Chase will illuminate what it was like to make this amazing series, and that the *Star-Ledger* pieces will take you back to the days when *The Sopranos* was both the hottest and most divisive show on television, when the only thing all its viewers could agree on was that the Columbus Day episode was bad.

Enjoy, and don't forget to tip your waitress.

---

3 Although HBO broke the final run of episodes into two parts that aired in 2006 and 2007, and officially referred to them as "Season Six, Part One" and "Season Six, Part Two," Chase considers them to be separate seasons, bringing the grand total to seven. We agree, and that's why they're referred to that way throughout the book.

THE RECAPS

Season One

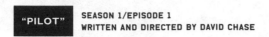

Woke Up This Morning

*"It's good to be in something from the ground floor. I came too late for that,
I know. But lately, I'm getting the feeling that I came in at the end.
The best is over."* —**Tony**

From its opening credits, through its introduction of its depressed gang-boss hero and his unflappable psychiatrist, to its unnervingly quiet closing song, "The Beast in Me," *The Sopranos* entered with a swagger, upsetting expectations and telling you to brace yourself.

The pilot episode of *The Sopranos,* created by TV veteran David Chase,[1] aired on January 10, 1999, with little advance fanfare outside the hermetically sealed world of TV critics who'd watched the pilot and the next three episodes on VHS tapes supplied by HBO the previous summer. Despite collective bullishness, reviewers had a hard time persuading people that the show was significant.

Skepticism was valid. Consider the cultural context: the 1990s featured numerous genre-upending series—*Twin Peaks, The X-Files, ER, NYPD Blue, Buffy the Vampire Slayer, My So-Called Life, Oz*—but people couldn't believe a weekly TV series could be art, or even something other than "pretty good, for TV." Self-contained theatrical films could be art; this had been common wisdom for forty years. TV? Not so much.

Plus, *The Sopranos* was about gangsters, and there'd been no shortage of gangster stories in preceding decades. The genre helped build commercial cinema, along with Westerns, musicals, and film noir, and kept producing popular and critical successes even as postwar movie attendance diminished. 1990 alone saw the release of six notable entries: *My Blue Heaven, King of New York, State of Grace, Miller's Crossing, The Godfather Part III*, and *Goodfellas*. That last one, a sprawling whack-fest set across Brooklyn and Long Island, was the most popular crime film yet by a master of the form, Martin Scorsese. Not only did it deal in some of the same notions as *The Sopranos*—mobsters posing as unremarkable suburbanites, and gangsterism as capitalism at its rawest—its style informed

---

1   Chase had written for some of the most acclaimed dramas of the '70s, '80s, and '90s, including the wisecracking private eye series *The Rockford Files,* the whimsical Alaskan odyssey *Northern Exposure,* and the Civil Rights–era drama *I'll Fly Away.* He was fed up with television when he wrote the pilot; he'd hoped HBO would decline it, so he could film a second hour for a movie and take it to Cannes.

Chase's show, including nasty shocks balanced with jocular humor, and an eclectic musical sensibility that mixed opera, show tunes, pop, and rock (including Muddy Waters' "Mannish Boy," an actual *Goodfellas* soundtrack cue). The *Sopranos* also shared cast members with Scorsese's classic, including Michael Imperioli, Tony Sirico,[2] Vincent Pastore,[3] and Dr. Melfi herself, Lorraine Bracco.[4] So already *The Sopranos* risked being dismissed as *Goodfellas: The Show*.

On top of all that, Scorsese regular Robert De Niro had just starred in a comedy called *Analyze This*, about a gangster in therapy. It was set to open in March 1999, less than three months after the *Sopranos* premiere, and trailers were already in theaters. Some writers generally assumed *The Sopranos* was a light comedy, too. Maybe it was the lingering whiff of the misfire *My Blue Heaven*, starring Steve Martin as a now-suburban mafioso in witness protection who can't give up his old ways. Maybe it was the title *The Sopranos*, which conjured prewar, whatsamatta-you Italians singing arias across red-checkered tablecloths.

But these misconceptions hid unimaginably richer depths. Written and directed by Chase, the pilot is a hybrid slapstick comedy, domestic sitcom, and crime thriller, with dabs of '70s American New Wave grit. It is high and low art, vulgar and sophisticated. It mixes disreputable spectacle (casual nudity, gory executions, drugs, profanity, and retrograde sentiments) with flourishes from postmodern novels, dialectical theater, and mid-century European art-house cinema. The series is sometimes as much about the relationship between art and its audience as it is about the world the artist depicts.

This self-awareness gives the opening scene, where Tony stares up at the statue in Dr. Melfi's office, another layer: this is a show that gives mass audiences the double-crosses and rubouts they expect from a Mob tale, but also psycho-therapy and dream analysis, economic and social satire, commentary on toxic masculinity and patriarchal oppression, and a rich intertextuality that posi-

---

2   Sirico played Tony Stacks in *Goodfellas*, one of the hoods who sticks a mail carrier's head in a pizza oven. If Paulie Walnuts seemed more authentic than some of the show's other crooks, it's because Sirico had a real criminal past. He was arrested twenty-eight times, starting at the age of seven when he stole nickels from a newsstand, and did prison stints for armed robbery and a weapons charge. Sirico claims he was inspired to try another profession when an acting troupe visited prisons where he was incarcerated. By the time he appeared in *Goodfellas*, he'd landed twenty-seven film roles and died in thirteen of them, including James Toback's *Fingers,* in which he perishes after a fist and knife fight with Harvey Keitel that sends both men tumbling down forty feet of stairs. He was shot in the leg and back when a rival hood caught Sirico kissing his girlfriend on the steps of a church. He used to don elaborate disguises before committing robberies, and once got busted for sticking up the same place twice while wearing the same blond wig.

3   A *Goodfellas* alum unceremoniously billed as "Man with Coatrack," Pastore's previous TV and film roles were almost all wiseguys.

4   The most prominent of the show's many *Goodfellas* alums, Bracco first gained fame therein playing Henry Hill's wife Karen, then struggled for worthy follow-ups in films like *Medicine Man* and *Radio Flyer*.

tions *The Sopranos* against the histories of cinematic and real gangsters, Italian Americans, and America.

The opening credits display this graceful interplay. They seem straightforward enough: here is the hero, this is where he lives. But they do at least five more things that dispel expectations and prepare us for something beyond the gangster-film usual.

Surprise #1: The man behind the wheel. If the overweight, balding, cigar-smoking driver who snatches a ticket from a toll booth is the show's protagonist and a Mafia boss (and we quickly learn that he is), the actor looks more like a henchman—one who'd get beaten up by a much smaller hero or shot by his boss to prove his ruthlessness.

Surprise #2: The music; "Woke Up This Morning," by Alabama 3, aka A3. Now universally recognized as the *Sopranos* theme, it was an unknown quantity in 1999. The song's rumbling bass line, warbling synthesizer effects, Leonard Cohen–esque vocals, and repetitive harmonica lament signal that this isn't the gangster story you're used to seeing. Notwithstanding oddball outliers like *King of New York*, post-1970 gangster pictures were usually scored with sweeping orchestral compositions (*The Godfather, State of Grace, Miller's Crossing*); playlists of postwar pop, blues, and rock (see any modern-day crime film by Scorsese), or some combination (*Donnie Brasco*). The pilot will use plenty of the second kind of music, but the present-tense newness of the A3 still throws the viewer off-balance.

Surprise #3: The filmmaking. Shot by series cinematographer Alik Sakharov with a handheld 35mm camera, on a route roughed out on videotape by series locations manager Jason Minter, the sequence is an assemblage of "caught" footage, taken in New Jersey locations without permits and edited in a jagged, unpredictable way. Eschewing the uninteresting technique of always cutting on the beat, the sequence holds images for unpredictable durations. It also avoids the cliché of showing cast pictures next to their names, instead going for a cinematic style that prizes journalistic detail and atmosphere.

Surprise #4: Immediately after the HBO logo is a shaky shot of converging perspective lines—actually a low-angle view of the ceiling of the Lincoln Tunnel, connecting New York City to New Jersey. If you know the Lincoln Tunnel and gangster movies, you'll be surprised when the light at the end of that tunnel coalesces to reveal Jersey instead of New York—not what's supposed to happen. East Coast movie gangsters only go to Jersey when going on the lam or dumping a corpse. Numerous classic gangster films are set in Manhattan and/or the surrounding boroughs of New York, because Manhattan is just more glamorous; it's where real people and movie characters go when they've Made It. East Coast gangster stories might move to Brooklyn, where the mid-level crooks live in duplexes with their aging mothers, or farther east to Long Island, where the bosses of bosses (and Jay Gatsby) buy palatial estates, but in Big Apple Mob films that's usually it. If the story travels farther, it'll probably beeline west to Chicago (historically the second most popular location for gangster movies), Las Vegas, Reno, or Los Angeles. Aside from some outliers (like the rare films set in small towns where gangsters hide out, or get entangled in film noir scenarios), the unspoken rule is to set the drama "anywhere but New Jersey"—except to depict the characters as losers.

So by entering New Jersey rather than leaving it, *The Sopranos* declares it intends to explore the characters' state as well as their state of mind, how each informs the other. The Cape Cods of East Orange immediately outside of Newark at least have some blocky, post–World War II anti-charm, but we fly past those, winding uphill through woods before parking in the driveway of a pale-brick house with no architectural personality.[5] It's the kind of place a man of no imagination whose regional auto-parts chain was just acquired by Pep Boys would buy for his wife.

Surprise #5: The mythic resonance of Tony's drive.

The American assimilation story has one component if you're a native-born WASP, two if you're an immigrant.

The first component is the migration from East to West, as prophesied by Horace Greeley ("Go West, young man!") and enshrined in Tony Soprano's beloved Westerns—films about rugged individualism and steely machismo. They depict the tension between civilization and the frontier, but also the reinvention of the self, American style. You go West to leave your old self (and sins) behind and become someone new. The first time we meet him, Tony is heading (roughly) West.

The second component is the movement from the big, bad city—where first-generation immigrants replicated rough versions of their home countries in neighborhoods prefaced with "Little"—to the boroughs or first ring of suburbs around the core city. The houses were small, but they at least had lawns. Second-generation immigrant families could live in places like the ones shown in *The Sopranos* credits and feel as if their family made it—or at least made it out. Their kids can play sandlot baseball, join civic organizations in Fourth of July parades down Main Street, and eat Chicken à la King, hot dogs, and apple pie in addition to spaghetti, lo mein, or lox. It's the kind of place where Giuseppe and Angelina or Murray and Tovah can raise kids named Ryan and Jane.

---

5   To lifelong Jerseyans, the route Tony takes from the Lincoln Tunnel to his house in North Caldwell makes no sense if he's going directly home, as he winds his way all around the Meadowlands, over by the Holland Tunnel, and into various other parts of Hudson, Passaic, and Essex Counties. But if the credits are meant to reflect a day where he's stopping by various Family-affiliated business (the sanitation company, for instance, is located in the shadow of the Pulaski Skyway, which he passes at one point), then it makes sense, even as most locals are inclined to yell at him to just hop on Route 3 West.

This abbreviated migration, in which ordinary car trips become reenacted journeys toward becoming "real" Americans, continues into the third generation, as the grandchildren of immigrants move still farther out, settling into remote housing developments carved out of fields and forests—communities without community, where deer snack on rosebushes, and you have to put chains on your car tires to get downhill when it snows.

It's here that the driver and his family live. A journey of cultural transformation starts with a shot of the Lincoln Tunnel's ceiling and ends with a man pulling into the driveway of a spacious house in hilly northern New Jersey[6] and exiting his vehicle. This sequence of shots compresses the twentieth-century East Coast immigrant experience into fifty-nine shots lasting eighty-nine seconds.

But the image of the driver shutting the car door and leaving the frame doesn't feel like a neat and comforting conclusion. There's an unstable, unfinished quality, conveyed by the needle scratch in the song (universal signifier of something cut short); by the unmoored and jittery way the filmmakers present the terrain; and especially by the character who guides us through it. The rings on Tony's meaty fingers, the thick dark hair on his forearms, the cigar between his teeth, the smoke trailing from his mouth as he checks the rearview mirror, the shots of the neighborhoods where he grew up but would never live today: these details describe a leader and father who was raised a particular way but aspires to be something more—or something else.

Cut to the driver, Tony Soprano (James Gandolfini[7]), sitting in a handsomely decorated waiting room, looking up at a statue. The first shot finds Tony in the background, between the statue's skinny legs. The second is a close-up of the statue from Tony's seated perspective, framed from solar plexus up: an inferior POV, looking up as if in awe, fear, or adoration. The statue is a female form, barebreasted. Her arms crossed behind her head. People don't generally hold their arms like that unless they're posing or stretching athletically. The outline of the arms evokes wings—angel or demon wings? The elbow points suggest horns. The body is lean but strong. It is an image of mystery and power, strong without seeming noble.

This is a woman of secrets.

The framing in the first shot makes Tony seem like a child gazing up at the opening from whence he came.

---

6 The Soprano house is located in North Caldwell, New Jersey. It was used for both interiors and exteriors during production of this pilot, but afterward for exteriors only. Interiors were reproduced exactly on a soundstage at Silvercup Studios in Long Island City, Queens. The backgrounds we see through the windows are high-resolution slides of the North Caldwell property projected on enormous screens.

7 Gandolfini's most memorable roles prior to the series tended to be small ones as tough guys: the *True Romance* thug who fights Patricia Arquette in the bathroom, one of the submarine crew in *Crimson Tide*, the bearded stuntman John Travolta beats up in *Get Shorty*.

This is also an image of biological elimination/evacuation: Tony is a human turd, shat out by a mother who treats her son like shit. Tony, we learn, is a "waste management consultant" who frequently feels like shit, or a piece of shit—because his uncle is in charge of the Mob Family Tony holds together; because his son is a doofus and his rebellious daughter hates her mother; because the Mafia is in decline and "things are trending downward"; and, most of all, because of his mother, Livia (Nancy Marchand[8]), whose profile vaguely resembles that of the statue Tony can't stop staring at.

Livia is a dour, relentlessly negative woman who cannot accept the love Tony gives her. She rejects the new CD player he brings over and the recorded music he knows she likes—What a good son!—and rebuffs his sad attempt to dance with her in her kitchen. She grouses that Tony isn't taking care of her in a loving, respectful way, even though he's supporting her in the house where he and his sisters grew up—a house that Livia suddenly treats as her own little Eden once it becomes clear that Tony is about to move her into a nursing home.

Between his emotional deprivation as a child, and the oppressively patriarchal culture of the Italian American Mob and gangsters, generally, Tony has issues with women, period. We see this between Tony and his wife Carmela (Edie Falco[9]), who knows he's a cheater and tells him right before his MRI that he's going to go to Hell when he dies; his daughter Meadow (Jamie-Lynn Sigler), who resents Carmela for posing as a righteous person after decades as a mobster's wife; and Tony's mistress (or *goomar*) Irina,[10] a Kazakhstani kitten who stubbornly dons JFK's yachtsman's cap. Then there are the dancers at the Bada Bing, the strip club/ money-laundering front Tony frequents: silent, sexually available, semi-nude, yet rarely ogled by Tony and the other gangsters, part of the decor.

Tony treats men and women very differently. With men like his protégé, nephew Christopher (Michael Imperioli[11]), he communicates through jocular banter that feels warm and knowing even when he's "breaking balls." He's clearly more emotionally accessible to men in, say, the pork store scenes. When he's with women, Tony alternates between courtly and protective, and peevish, possessive, and crude, depending on the woman. He's most likable around Meadow, who's not as cutting with her dad as she is with her mother. But Tony always shows a sup-

---

8 Marchand spent five seasons starring as *Lou Grant*'s wealthy newspaper owner Mrs. Pynchon and played Clara in the original live-TV version of Paddy Chayefsky's *Marty*, opposite Rod Steiger.

9 Falco had spent three seasons on HBO's first original drama series, *Oz*, playing the supporting role of prison guard Diane Whittlesey. *Oz* boss Tom Fontana graciously released her when a larger role on HBO presented itself.

10 In the pilot, Irina is played by Siberia Federico; thereafter, by Oksana Babiy (also credited as Oksana Lada).

11 Another *Goodfellas* alum (he played Joe Pesci's repeat victim Spider) and frequent Spike Lee collaborator, Imperioli is also the only *Sopranos* regular who got to write for the show.

pressed, volatile helplessness around women—an undertone of childlike delight, predatory anticipation, or beleaguered resentment—and it's captured in Tony's study of Melfi's statue.

The angles signifying the statue's dominance and Tony's inferiority continue in an exchange of dolly shots that move us closer to both. Tony is staring hard at the statue—as if that will help him figure out why he can't stop staring at it.

When Dr. Melfi opens her office door and invites Tony in for the first time, Tony is still seated, which means that when he acknowledges her, he's looking up at her just as he was at the statue, from an inferior, "awed" position.

Images matter here as much as words—not a common approach in 1990s television. Despite inventively directed predecessors like *Miami Vice*, *Twin Peaks*, *The X-Files*, and *Sex and the City*, dramatic information on scripted shows was conveyed mainly through close-ups of people talking. Critics noticed the evident care that Chase and his collaborators took in deciding what to show us, from what angle and for how long, and what to cut to next. This care proved crucial to the series' success: it invited audiences into the drama rather than spoon-feeding them exposition. The implacable wordlessness of images, scored to music or just ambient noise, sends the imagination pinballing from one association to another.

This is crucially important on a TV series concerned with psychology and therapy. Therapists look for connections and symbolism in the text of the patient's life story, analyzing it as scholars might parse a novel or painting. They find deeper meanings in dreams, fantasies, and seemingly random events, and uncover suppressed truths by perceiving patients' tone and word choices when talking about themselves, their relationships, and their thoughts.

As the pilot unfolds, we learn to read *The Sopranos* this way. We quickly notice the difference between Melfi and Livia in relation to Tony: Melfi is compassionate and Livia is not. Melfi listens because she's interested in her patients and works to help them understand themselves. Livia only listens for information she can use to improve her own position or inflict pain on others. Other people exist to Melfi; to Livia, they don't, except as extensions of herself or indicators of her power over others. Even though Melfi has been in Tony's life for less than half an hour (he storms out at the twenty-eight-minute mark after she presses him about his mother) she's already being positioned, in the viewer's minds if not his, as the anti-Livia: nurturing, caring. The sanctuary-womb of Melfi's office with its curved walls, integral bookshelves, window bands of sunlight, and tissue box give Tony a safe harbor to discuss subjects weighing on him.

Tony addresses several in his first session. The device of putting the hero in therapy lets Chase deliver reams of information about Tony, his crew, his bosses, his family, and their overlaps, along with the points where Tony's personal and professional distress are inseparable, all without the usual pilot-episode busy work. Tony's ruminations to Melfi start in therapy and then become voice-over narration, taking us in and out of Tony's consciousness. When we're in that room with them, we're hearing Tony speak, but when the episode cuts to the action he's recounting, suddenly we're feel as if we're in his head. The first such cut shows us the exterior of his house, then cuts to a God's-eye view of Tony lying in bed looking as if life has run him over with a garbage truck; there's even a tight close-up of one of Tony's bloodshot eyes, a composition more common to experimental films and science fiction epics like *2001: A Space Odyssey* and *Blade Runner* than gangster tales.

Voice-overs always risk becoming a crutch for storytellers to spew facts about the characters that we could have figured out given cleverer direction or dialogue ("That's Livia, my mother," a network version of the show would've told us). This episode mostly avoids this tendency through comical and often surprisingly placed interruptions. Time and again, Melfi or Tony stops the story, so the characters can decide how complicit Melfi might become, and Tony can modulate the hard truth about himself or shade things for sympathy. These moments of negotiation and retrenchment add droll laughs to an episode that otherwise derives its humor from aggressive displays of ignorance ("Czechoslovakian, what, that's a type of Polack, right?"), misquotes of famous movie lines ("Louis Brasi sleeps with the fishes!"), and hard-edged pay cable schtick (Carmela toting an AK-47 to investigate a possible prowler who turns out to be Meadow; Christopher and Big Pussy tossing Emil's corpse into the side of a dumpster).

These interruptions also illustrate a central problem with the gangster lifestyle. These criminals are constantly doing things that are morally and/or legally appalling, but to survive, they still have to present as a "regular" person. Tony entered therapy to understand himself better, so that he could stop having panic attacks, but from his first session it's obvious that Melfi wants to open doors he'd rather keep locked. Some of the patient–therapist misunderstandings are hilarious in an Abbott and Costello sort of way, in particular Tony mentioning that it's become harder to do his thing "because of RICO" and Melfi asking if that's his brother, and the exchanges that could be captions from an unpublished *New Yorker* cartoon. ("Hope comes in many forms." "Well, who's got time for that?")

As Tony describes his world to Dr. Melfi, we realize that there's barely a boundary between family and Family for Tony. When Uncle Junior (Dominic Chianese[12]), captain of a rival crew in the DiMeo Family, objects to Tony's attempt to stop him from killing Little Pussy Malanga[13] at Vesuvio, the restaurant run by

---

12 Where *Goodfellas* tended to be a more frequent casting well for *The Sopranos* to dip into, it did occasionally reach further back to the *Godfather* franchise, particularly with Chianese, who played Hyman Roth's henchman Johnny Ola in the second film.

13 Not to be confused with "Big Pussy" Bonpensiero from Tony's crew.

Tony's childhood friend Artie Bucco[14] (John Ventimiglia), he spits, "How many fuckin' hours did I spend playing catch with you?" One should have nothing to do with the other, but Junior feels entitled to Tony's unconditional fealty—even though, as Tony confesses to Melfi, "When I was young, he told my girl cousins I would never be a varsity athlete, and frankly, that was a tremendous blow to my esteem." In this small, interconnected world, where past slights are remembered and exploited forever, everyone seems blind to their true cost. When Tony expresses misgivings to Dr. Melfi about the current state of the Mob, it's not about the greater morality, just the inconvenience of so many wiseguys turning rat when arrested.

The pilot episode makes this point with blunt comic force. Tony literally drives over Alex Mahaffey (Michael Gaston) because Mahaffey owes him money. Christopher guns down Emil Kolar (Bruce Smolanoff) not because Emil poses an imminent threat to Chris or the Family, but because it's the simplest way to eliminate a competing bid from a rival garbage company, and to try to impress his mentor Tony. It's monstrous, all of it, and deep down perhaps these guys know that, but they squelch those feelings to get through the day, leaving Tony in such denial that he can complain to Melfi, "I find I have to be the sad clown" without a trace of self-awareness.

The first therapy session, like this entire episode, keeps circling back to Tony's relationship with his mother. She's not on-screen much—her presence is as sparing as Brando's in *The Godfather*—but when she is, her rocklike peevishness and furtive expressions pull focus from dynamic figures like Tony, Carmela, and Uncle Junior, who drives Livia to Anthony Jr.'s (Robert Iler) birthday party—a job she asked Tony to do—and implies that Tony should get whacked for interfering with the Malanga hit.[15] And when Livia's not on-screen, other characters talk about her, as in the infamous "So, what, no fucking ziti now?"[16] scene where Tony and Carmela talk with her "spiritual mentor" Father Phil Intintola,[17] and AJ reports, "She's not coming. Grandma just called. She started crying and hung up."

---

14 Both Artie and Silvio Dante are presented in the pilot as old friends Tony rarely sees anymore (everyone's surprised when Sil comes by the pork store). From episode two on, Sil is treated as a long-standing member of Tony's own crew, and Vesuvio as every local wiseguy's restaurant of choice.

15 After failing to sway either Junior or Artie—whose law-abiding wife Charmaine (Kathrine Narducci; Narducci auditioned her son for a role in A Bronx Tale and got cast as the hero's mother, her big break. Her mobster father died in a hit when she was ten.) won't allow him to use the sketchy cruise ship tickets Tony gave them while trying to close the restaurant at the time of the hit—Tony has Vesuvio blown up, figuring that will damage its reputation less in the long run.

16 AJ will have many memorable moments throughout the series—some, but not all, fart-related—but if you're new to the show while reading this, be warned that he definitely peaks with the ziti line.

17 Though Paul Schulze would play Father Phil for the rest of the series, the role here is briefly filled by Michael Santoro.

"She needs a purpose in life," Tony grumbles.

Anxiety about Livia triggers both of Tony's panic attacks. Cause and effect are obvious when he, Carmela, and the kids are touring the Green Grove Retirement Community with Livia and she spies its nursing home wing and accuses Tony of dumping her. But Tony's first attack has a more oblique connection. Near the end of the pilot, Melfi strives to steer Tony toward realizing he's doing better not because of his Prozac prescription, but because he's talking about his problems instead of holding them inside like Gary Cooper, "the strong, silent type." Then he tells Melfi about a dream he had about the ducks that, by flying out of Tony's yard, sparked his first attack: he unscrewed his navel until his penis fell off and a bird flew away with it. Tony describes the bird as aquatic in type, but resists calling a duck a duck even after Melfi pushes him to make this small breakthrough. The mother duck birthed its young and raised them behind the Soprano house, but in Tony's dream, the duck became an arbitrary destructive force. The life giver, the protector; the tormentor, the destroyer.

"It was just a trip having those wild creatures come into my pool and have their little babies," Tony tells Melfi. Then he chokes up at his own description. The sentimental tableau he's just described reveals his largely unrealized capacity for a gentleness that even waterfowl can sense, and that somehow survived within him, despite having a legendary gangster father and a punitive, withholding mother. But Tony would never intuit all this. "I was sad to see them go," he says, then moves outside of himself verbally, nearly mocking his own distress: "Jesus, fuck, now he's gonna cry!" Tony adored the ducks in the pool because they were guarded by a mother who protected and nurtured them in a manner free of ulterior motive, of deceit and manipulation, of the urge to annihilate. Livia, for all her evident helplessness, is the most actively destructive force in the pilot, a black hole vacuuming up hope.

But Tony can't or won't grasp this—not yet. He ultimately decided that he's crying because he's afraid he's going to lose his family. To what, though? A bullet? Prison? A heart attack from eating too much?

"What are you afraid of?" Melfi asks him.

"I don't know," he says.

But even if Tony doesn't know, *The Sopranos* is surely mulling it over.

Tony's two panic attacks were false deaths that felt like heart attacks or strokes. Near-death experiences often convince people to take stock and become emotionally or mentally healthier, stronger—more evolved. But Tony doesn't seem like that kind of man. Is there hope? Maybe Tony's distress is about his fear that there isn't—that maybe there's too much Livia in him, and it'll always be there no matter what he does, pulling invisible strings.

SEASON 1/EPISODE 2
WRITTEN BY DAVID CHASE
DIRECTED BY DAN ATTIAS

A Boy's Best Friend

"But she's my mother. You're supposed to take care of your mother." —**Tony**

The *Sopranos* pilot was shot in 1997, to be presented to the network as a proof of concept. The second episode, "46 Long," was produced in 1998 as part of a package of 12 more episodes. The elapsed time can be seen both visually (Gandolfini is heavier, Robert Iler taller) and dramatically, as Chase and company try to decide how much of a television series this anti-television series needs to be to survive. Some of "46 Long"—particularly anything involving Tony and Livia, the starting point for this whole endeavor—feels fully formed. For much of it, though, David Chase is still fiddling with the controls: how to balance the comedy and drama, how it should look. (Dan Attias, who would direct a few later episodes, leans harder on extreme close-ups than Chase did in directing the premiere.) It's an engrossing but occasionally awkward episode that alternates tones and modes.

In the scenes with Big Pussy and Paulie Walnuts investigating the theft of AJ's teacher's car, Paulie's obsession with the appropriation of Italian culture is on the lighter, at times sitcom-like end of the comedy spectrum, and seems to validate the idea that *The Sopranos* was *Analyze This: The Series*. The trouble that Christopher and his meth addict pal Brendan Filone (Anthony DeSando) get into when they start robbing trucks protected by Uncle Junior has more of a black comic spirit, and starts amping up the tensions among Tony, Junior, and Tony's own idiot nephew.[18] Silvio Dante (Steven Van Zandt[19]) convincing Tony to hang on to a suit or three before Christopher returns the truck speaks nicely to the hypocrisy of the whole endeavor: in this world, Tony and other authority figures lecture underlings about codes and rules that should never be broken, but flout them whenever it's convenient.

Christopher and Brendan's drug use and refusal to follow the rules recalls the cold open, where a wiseguy-turned-author on the Bada Bing's office TV explains that the golden age of the Mob is gone thanks to drug trafficking and other devia-

---

18 *The Sopranos* makes several references to Tony being the boss of North Jersey. "46 Long" walks that back a bit, to show that the ill Jackie Aprile Sr. (played by Michael Rispoli, the runner-up to Gandolfini for the role of Tony) is acting boss of the Family, even as Brendan notes that everyone knows that Tony is really running things since Jackie became "the chemo-sabe."

19 Van Zandt was the *other* runner-up to play Tony, but is far more famous for his other life as a core member of Bruce Springsteen's E Street Band and a prolific musician on his own.

tions from tradition. "The shoe fits," Tony says sadly, and of course he would: he told Melfi in the pilot that he feared he'd come in at the end. Tony's gesture of shooting a rubber band at the TV when a former foot solder turned state's witness appears is not only nonlethal, it's childish—the kind of thing a badly behaved kid would do to show off in class—and confirms the author's point. The fear that 1990s hoods are puny facsimiles of their predecessors is echoed in the scene where Brendan hijacks another one of Junior's trucks with two African American gangsters who are no more menacing or competent than he is.

When you look back across "46 Long," the cold open feels like a self-deprecating way of acknowledging that *The Sopranos* is anxious about following in the footsteps of classic gangster films, even while doing a new dance. Chase's characters react to the interview in the background either with sad nods or defensive bursts of derision. ("They pay this *chiachiadon*[20] by the word?" Paulie snarls.) The scene ends with Silvio impersonating Al Pacino in *The Godfather Part III*[21] at Tony's request, as if to say, *Well, if we are just imitating what came before, let's at least do it with gusto.* Not for nothing is Big Pussy reading a newspaper story about cloning. The Mob expert might as well be a TV critic complaining that the Mob movie genre, like the Mafia itself, is played out, and that even if it weren't, these small-screen hoods would still just be clones who couldn't live up to the example of their big-screen ancestors.

The pilot established that this show exists in our world and its people watch the same crime films we do. The dialogue includes movie quotations (and misquotations), and Father Phil even asks Carmela what Tony thinks of *The Godfather* trilogy (his favorite is *Part II* because of the flashbacks where Vito goes back to Sicily—fitting his mindset of nostalgic lament—but *Part III* was "like, what happened?"). But when he asks about *Goodfellas*—a rich source of this series' core cast—her reaction to the sound of Meadow sneaking home short-circuits whatever answer she was about to give: the screenwriting version of a record scratch. *The Sopranos* stays in active conversation with its own pop culture tradition, but its side of that dialogue is self-deprecating and playful, like an ambitious, smart-alecky young foot soldier who knows what happens to mooks that get too big for their britches.

Maybe the lowercase-family scenes are crisper and more potent than stolen trucks and cars because they're life-like and emotionally direct, and thus unafraid of judgment versus past depictions. Many of this show's predecessors and descendants portray the protagonist's work life more solidly than domestic life and parenting; but on *The Sopranos*, Tony's off-the-clock moments are more

---

20 Blabbermouth.
21 "Just when I thought I was out . . . they pull me back in!"

striking from the start, and the crime stuff is going to have to work to catch up. We've seen Mob violence like the Comley hijacking go awry in other gangster tales (Scorsese's in particular), but the Tony–Livia relationship, and the way Carmela and Melfi force Tony to discuss it, feels instantly distinct. Just check out Nancy Marchand's sour look when Carmela talks up Green Grove, or Livia's response to the kitchen fire—largely caused through her own paranoia—like it's another insult this terrible world has visited on her. Or the heavy-lidded, hangdog look—which James Gandolfini has by now perfected—as Tony surveys his childhood house without its most powerful resident. Tony and Livia feel lived-in from day one, but their dynamic is so tangled and damaging to Tony that he can't even see how destructive it is, and always was.

The show's sense that all its characters—civilians and gangsters—are living small, robotically materialistic lives is nearly unique in the Mob genre. "46 Long" presents lines and images about decline, decay, and the irrevocable passing of old ways, as well as an atmosphere of dissatisfaction anchored in the suspicion that things were better during some (largely unspecified) past. The Bada Bing's new phone system is more complicated than the old one. Presented with a truckload of stolen DVD players, Tony grills Brendan about their inferior visual quality versus laserdiscs and their paucity of good movies. "But the sound? Way improved," Brendan assures him.

"Good," Tony snarls, "because nothing beats poppin' up some Orville Redenbacher's and listening to *Men in Black*."

Paulie and Pussy's gumshoe routine at various coffee shops[22] evokes a line from Raymond Chandler's *Farewell, My Lovely*—"He looked about as inconspicuous as a tarantula on a slice of angel food cake"—but what makes it memorable is their realization that their heritage is being bastardized and repackaged by an international conglomerate and sold back to them at inflated prices. Pussy wearily accepts this reality; Paulie rages against it. "Fuckin espresso, cappuccino: we invented the shit, and all these other cocksuckers are getting rich off it . . . It's not just the money, it's a pride thing. All our food: pizza, calzone, buffalo *moozzarel'*, olive oil! . . . But this? This is the worst, this espresso shit." When Tony enters the kitchen in a bathrobe and tries to dance with Carmela (an image that echoes his awkward dance with Livia in the pilot), he sings Procol Harum's "A Whiter Shade of Pale," a song released thirty-two years earlier when he was in elementary school. Jackie Aprile, whom Tony says "crawled out of a sickbed" to meet with him and Junior, admits that his cancer is eating him up, then wonders aloud if he should just name a successor. "This day and age?" asks Tony, "Who wants the fuckin' job?"

---

22 "I'm fuckin' Rockford over here," Pussy complains about the assignment, as a wink to Chase's time on *The Rockford Files*.

Decline, decay, and the loss of potency and autonomy are all concentrated in Tony's distress over Livia. Mentally and physically, she seems worse off than in the pilot. She thinks her new Trinidadian housekeeper[23] stole a favorite plate from her. "You sure you didn't give it to one of the relatives? You keep forcing your possessions on people, thinking you're gonna die," Tony says. "I wish it was tomorrow," Livia replies.

Maybe Tony feels the same way.

This is a man who feels abandoned by his two sisters to take care of a woman who can't live with him because Carmela "won't allow it," but who can't live by herself anymore, either—and no matter what he does, Livia perceives him as an ungrateful son. Tony is so horrified by his mother's apparent cognitive decline that he grasps after any shred of evidence that she's doing well, such as her volunteering to drive her friends around—until Livia runs one of them over. This gives Tony the excuse he needs to move her into Green Grove. A later scene finds Tony packing up what's left in his childhood home, including pictures of his mother when she was young, and of himself as a child and a newborn. Overcome by conflicted feelings, he fights off another panic attack by forcing himself to sit. Freud would have a lot to say about a son whose feelings about his mother are so intense that they make him feel like he's about to die. Melfi's prodding in therapy seems to nudge him closer to profoundly dark realizations about Livia and, by extension, himself: the apple and the tree.

When Tony confirms Livia is physically healthy—"like a bull"—Melfi suggests that she be examined for depression, because "you know from your own life that depression can cause accidents, poor performance, or worse."

"What are you saying, that unconsciously she tried to whack her best friend?" Tony asks. Tony's depression is exacerbated by many factors, but his mother towers above everything else. Though she'd never characterize herself this way, Livia's still mourning her husband Johnny, whose death left her feeling emotionally and physically abandoned. She may miss Johnny for selfish and narcissistic reasons, but the ache is real. Part of her hostility toward her son might stem from the feeling that Tony, Livia's makeshift Johnny, is also abandoning her now, and she can't stop it. Viewed this way, the moment when Livia nearly kills her best friend feels like a form of projection. A boy's best friend is his mother.

Melfi finds it "interesting" that Tony would classify suppressed murderous rage against a loved one as another byproduct of depression, but she doesn't follow his remark to its logical conclusion. If the son is anything like the mother, he

---

23 Livia's casual racism comes out when she refers to her housekeeper as a *titsun*, the Italian equivalent of the N-word.

might be capable of the same subconscious mental calculus, and the same result: violence against a "best friend."

The episode's conclusion implies that Tony might have made this connection on his own. Fed up with Bing bouncer Georgie's (Frank Santorelli) inability to transfer a call, Tony goes berserk and smashes him in the head with the receiver.[24] One of the pieces of evidence that Tony presented to Melfi as proof of his mother's decline? "She can't manage the telephone."

<table>
<tr><td>

"DENIAL, ANGER, ACCEPTANCE"

</td><td>

SEASON 1/EPISODE 3
WRITTEN BY MARK SARACENI
DIRECTED BY NICK GOMEZ

</td></tr>
</table>

Protocol

"If all this shit's for nothing, why do I gotta think about it?" —**Tony**

James Gandolfini didn't quite come out of nowhere to star in *The Sopranos*, but he was obscure enough that, coupled with the titanic force of his performance, it was easy to view him as always having been Tony Soprano. The perceived lack of a border between actor and character back then worked to the show's benefit: no viewer thought, "Oh, James Gandolfini wouldn't really do that" because they had no other frame of reference. When revisiting the series, however, it can be difficult to resist projecting Gandolfini's death at the relatively tender age of fifty-one onto his most famous character—the protagonist of a series preoccupied with decline, waste, and missed opportunities, filled with images of death both unnatural and natural.

An hour like "Denial, Anger, Acceptance" is thus particularly tough to get through. Its core is about Tony confronting his own fragile mortality as he experiences the eponymous stages of grief over Jackie Aprile's impending demise. Gandolfini was a very different, and better, man than his alter ego, but in listening to Tony struggle with the meaning of life and death with Dr. Melfi, it's still hard not to imagine that it's the actor having the same conversation—or simply to think of him dying, like Jackie, far too soon. The *Godfather*-style sequence where Meadow's choral performance is intercut with the attacks on Christopher and

---

24 Another expression of the malaise affecting everyone in this episode: after Tony exits the frame, the camera refocuses on three dancers on the stage behind him, so uninterested in their present circumstance that they can barely bring themselves to move.

Brendan is particularly powerful beyond Chase and company's obvious intent. Seeing Christopher plead for his life, and then watching Mikey Palmice end Brendan's, is intense, and Brendan's death is the show's first real whacking of a notable character (Little Pussy Malanga was more talked about than experienced; we barely saw his face). But it's nothing compared to the moment in the school auditorium, as Tony's emotions find an outlet in the music, in the experience of seeing his daughter shine, and the brief realization of how much he needs to treasure these moments, for however long he has on this earth.

This is a great episode for both Tony and the actor who almost played him, Michael Rispoli. As consolation roles go, Jackie Aprile isn't a super-lucrative or long-lasting one, but Rispoli makes the most of his time. He nails the comic beats in the scene where Jackie doesn't realize that the "nurse" who visits him in the hospital was hired by Tony to give his day a happy ending, but also the dramatic ones, particularly where Tony wants to relive the mayhem at the motel while Jackie is obsessing over his temperature.

Gandolfini's performance and the struggle inside Tony that fuels it are strong enough to carry the episode. But although "Denial, Anger, Acceptance" is engrossing, it also feels unsteady. Livia appears only briefly and late, though it's notable for how casually she sentences Brendan to death, knowing what Junior will do with her advice; this is a cold, dangerous woman, not the warm maternal presence Tony keeps trying to convince himself that she is. The Mob Case of the Week, involving the Hasidic motel owner,[25] feels, much as Pussy and Paulie's stolen car investigation did in the previous episode, like Chase still experimenting: *Hey, wouldn't it be funny to see these tough Italian American wiseguys be stymied by a bunch of Jewish guys with strange hats and sideburns?* It turns out to be a bit more than that, partly because Ariel's willingness to die out of principle connects to Tony and Jackie's reckoning with their own mortality, but it's still less compelling than almost every other corner of the episode.

The hour's most welcome new development is Carmela's first dedicated subplot; it works both as a short story carved into the episode and as a new lens through which to view all the other narratives happening around it. Carmela invites Artie and Charmaine Bucco to cater her hospital fundraiser, to help them move beyond the trauma of losing their old restaurant and put money in their pockets while they wait for an insurance payout; but she winds up making her "friend" Charmaine feel even smaller about her status compared to the wealthy and powerful Sopranos. This subplot shows us that Carmela compels as much deference in her domestic sphere as Tony does on the streets.

---

25 Shlomo is played by Chuck Low, whose Hasidic accoutrements render him almost unrecognizable as wig salesman Morrie ("Morrie's wigs don't come off!") from *Goodfellas*.

It might seem odd to call a show populated by this many vulgar people a comedy of manners, but protocol, social status, and awareness of power dynamics are sunk as deep into *The Sopranos* as they are in the novels of Kazuo Ishiguro or Edith Wharton. Representatives of different cultures, classes, and levels of influence strive against one another for the upper hand. The Hasidim have a value system and code of honor as intractable and machismo-based as the one animating the Italian Americans hell-bent on rattling them. Carmela's desire to raise funds for the hospital is fueled by her wish to be seen as respectable. Chris is going against Junior largely because he feels the Family has denied him the promotion he believes he's already earned; by taking money out of Junior's pocket, he's denying Junior's power over him as a Family leader as well as being Chris's kind-of-uncle. "Him and his little friend, they're slapping me across the face, and they're hiding behind Tony," Junior tells Livia, tacitly seeking approval to crush the kid. No dice. Chris isn't a son to Tony, Livia explains, but he loves him like one. "And so do I, Junior," she adds, her widening eyes signaling that she's using her emotional sway over him to veto any retaliation in the works.[26]

The subplot about Chris selling amphetamines to Meadow to help her stay up longer while she's studying for finals parallels the bucking of protocol in the Carmela–Charmaine story. Meadow is leveraging her greater social status (plus sentimental family bonds) to pressure another character into doing something they'd normally avoid. Meanwhile, we see how Chris, the product of a virulent patriarchal subculture, looks down on his girlfriend Adriana (Drea de Matteo[27]) because she's a woman (ordering her to go answer the door while he smokes pot and watches TV). And we see how Adriana resents Christopher for earning stacks of cash through quick bursts of criminal activity and vegging out the rest of the time, instead of working a regular job like hers. ("Restaurant hostess, real tough work," Chris sneers, while Brendan does pull-ups in a nearby doorway.)

Charmaine's revenge is both effective and the kind of thing that only someone in her unique position—someone who grew up with Tony and Carmela but deliberately lives just outside their world now—could devise. The show has a great eye and ear for insults—particularly unintended ones—and this episode contains an especially wrenching example: Carmela can't even recognize that she's beckoning for Charmaine in the same haughty manner she used earlier for the housekeeper. In return, Charmaine sticks in the knife by revealing that she and Tony hooked

---

26 Then she adds, "He put up my storm windows for me one year." Classic Livia: her affection for Chris isn't about who he is, but what he does for her. That scene also returns to a recurring theme of the series: these people expect minor good deeds to pay dividends forever. Junior wants deference from Tony because of all the times they played catch.

27 De Matteo had a tiny role in the pilot as a restaurant hostess; when it came time to cast Adriana, she was brought back in and restyled, and a line of dialogue was later added to explain that Tony got her that hostessing job.

up back in the day and could have ended up together if she'd wanted, then twists it by adding, "We both made our choices. I'm fine with mine."

After the sting of this exchange fades, Carmela will still have her McMansion, and Charmaine and Artie will be living in their "cozy" fixer-upper and praying for their insurance money. But we've already seen in two episodes that Charmaine is determined not to be affiliated with Mob business. On a show in which almost every character is somehow compromised, she's an anomaly.

SEASON 1/EPISODE 4
WRITTEN BY JASON CAHILL
DIRECTED BY JOHN PATTERSON

The Casual Violence

"Here we go: the War of '99." —**Big Pussy**

After a couple of outings where the family material is notably more compelling than the Family material, "Meadowlands" strongly balances Tony's two worlds, partly because the lines separating them are so blurred. This blur is certified in the array of everyday household objects that become weaponized (a yo-yo, a woodchopper's axe, and a staple gun) and in Melfi's description of "the climate of rage in modern society . . . the casual violence"—the latter depicted repeatedly in this episode.

"Meadowlands" starts with Tony's nightmare about members of his crew learning that he's talking about his mother[28] in therapy, before he discovers that Silvio's dentist works in Dr. Melfi's building. These developments kick his paranoia into overdrive, to the point where he sends crooked, degenerate-gambler cop Vin Makazian (John Heard[29]) to investigate his therapist. Brendan's murder, followed by Jackie's death, forces Tony into a confrontation with Junior he was hoping

---

28 The one Tony–Livia scene this week (other than her brief cameo in Melfi's clothes in the dream sequence) is a delight, particularly when Tony notes that he visits her to get cheered up and asks, "You think that's a mistake?" Sadly, this is about the best he can hope for from an encounter with his mother: a minimum of yelling, and Livia in her incredibly roundabout way asking him to leave a few of the macaroons for her—not that she'd ever admit that is what she's doing.

29 Heard, who died the year this book was being written, was a great character actor who starred in a lot of small-scale, "best-kept secret" movies, including *Between the Lines, Cutter's Way, After Hours,* and *Rambling Rose.* Vin is one of the show's best-drawn recurring characters, made immediately vivid by the script and by Heard's performance as a self-destructive loser who can't admit what he's become.

to avoid. Jackie's funeral—with all the wiseguys in attendance, and FBI agents photographing them—is an eye-opening experience for AJ, who's only just been told what his father actually does for a living. (The titular word "Meadowlands" refers to a real area of northern New Jersey, a swamp near what was then Giants Stadium—now MetLife Stadium—that's been a dumping ground for murder victims through the ages; but it's also the psychological space where Meadow, who knows her family's secret, has been living for some time, and where she guides her brother in this episode. This is Meadow's Land.)

The Tony–Junior tensions that have been simmering for weeks hit a full boil here, though the only gun Tony uses is the staple gun he swipes from the hospital to let Mikey Palmice know how much he disapproves of Brendan's murder and Christopher's beating.[30] But for all of Chris's indignant demands for retribution, and the support of his fellow captains in calling for Junior's death, Tony instead—with some (maybe) unintentional help from Dr. Melfi—figures out a way to win the peace, by letting Junior think he's the new boss when he's really just a figurehead. The scene where Tony marches into Junior's favorite lunch place—armed, as Junior had suggested—and surprises his uncle with the offer is a series peak for tension. It's also a great indicator of what a savvy tactician Tony can be when he's not using phone receivers as cudgels: he doesn't just position Junior to take all the heat while Tony makes most of the decisions, but also exacts lucrative control of Bloomfield and the paving union.

As ways to learn your family's dirty secret go, AJ being spared a schoolyard beating because the bigger kid's father warned him not to touch Tony Soprano's kid isn't a bad one. The writers tend to let AJ be a profoundly spoiled but otherwise unremarkable boy: inarticulate, clumsy (his two hallway scuffles are among the most realistically ineffectual underage fights on TV), and slow on the uptake, even as Meadow patiently leads him to realizing their dad is a prominent mobster. AJ's dawning recognition as he surveys Jackie's funeral is a strong way to end an episode concerned with the crumbling walls between Tony's work and home lives.

And then there's the Dr. Melfi situation.[31] "It's complicated" would be an understatement; Melfi herself might need several sessions to dig through all the layers. Even before she backs into playing war consigliere in Tony's dispute with Junior, we see Tony battling three dueling impulses. First, he's attracted to his

---

30 The *Sopranos* tradition of acknowledging its screen-gangster predecessors mainly to show how the Jersey boys come up short continues here. The way Tony drops the staple gun on the street after using it on Mikey is a petty, nonlethal reenactment of the moment in *The Godfather* where Michael Corleone assassinates corrupt police captain McCluskey and his Mob ally Sollozzo. We also hear Christopher—a young hothead who, unlike the older guys, has never been "to the mattresses"—agitating for a hot war with Junior's crew (and misremembering details) "This is *Scarface*, final scene, fuckin' bazookas under each arm! 'Say hello to my little friend!'"

31 Tony continues his lie of omission to Carmela about Dr. Melfi's gender.

shrink. Second, she's helping him deal with his panic attacks and the ongoing emotional turmoil that comes from being Anthony Soprano. Third, if Silvio or, worse, Uncle Junior, finds out he's spilling his guts to an outsider—even someone bound by doctor–patient confidentiality—he could wind up in the ground with his friend Jackie.

That third impulse is the one that drives Tony to sic Vin Makazian on the poor doctor and her boyfriend. The beating at the traffic stop is fallout from Tony trying to protect himself, but the secret of his therapy is so potentially fatal that he can't even tell Makazian who Melfi is to him; Tony's evasiveness inspires Vin's faulty assumption that Tony's mistress is stepping out with another guy. When Melfi tells Tony about the incident—in a surprising instance of her own walls coming down in front of a patient—Tony's frustrated, but more because Makazian behaved recklessly (potentially exposing Tony's role in him being there) than from guilt over Randall's beating.

Another odd thing is happening here, and it's on Melfi's end of the relationship. Melfi's analysis of the deeper meaning of Tony's actions once again plays like a subtle, ongoing referendum on the intellectual and literary fascination with *The Sopranos*, a series about slobbish, nasty criminals and the women who enable them. Melfi is supposedly there to discuss what's roiling beneath all of the crime and violence, but she's as fascinated by these aspects as anybody who loves gangster movies (or true crime and autopsy documentaries, or the crime blotter in the newspaper). She insists on firm boundaries between herself and this patient—more so than her others—but the lure of the dark side is so magnetic that she still gets pulled into tactical discussions.[32] It's as if an especially eloquent viewer had been granted access to the *Sopranos* writers' room.

Equally fascinating is another Livia–Melfi blur. There are sections in "Meadowlands" where Melfi, who already offered Tony a maternal comfort his life otherwise lacked, seems on the verge of becoming a Livia, with all the sickness that entails. This is happening partly in Tony's head and partly on the show as a whole. The climactic image in the opening dream sequence underscores the connection to the point where even Tony gets it—thus his waking up in a fright. But then he forgets it, or perhaps submerges it but remembers it subconsciously: who knows how to explain the exact dynamics through which a therapist, poised between naiveté and complicity, becomes an associate strategist in a Mob war? However you explicate it, Melfi's relationship to Tony suddenly seems to mirror

---

32 This might be Bracco's peak thus far. Her performance in the scene where she and Tony discuss strategy lets us see that Melfi is becoming wrapped up in the crime drama that she insists she'd rather not be privy to, even as her measured demeanor and precise language stops just short of actively participating in Tony's schemes. Even the most inappropriate conversations can become permissible if you classify them as thought experiments.

Junior's relationship with Livia, whom he visits at Green Grove and treats as a combination therapist and consigliere.

It also connects with the potentially murderous resentment Tony expressed in "Denial, Anger, Acceptance." He bashed Georgie's head not long after nearly realizing a connection between his mother's "accidentally" running over her best friend and Tony wanting his own "best friend" dead, too (or exiled to Green Grove, a fate worse than death in Livia's mind). The shot from behind in the Melfi–Livia dream sequence evokes a famous moment in *Psycho*: Lila Crane in the cellar of the Bates house, approaching a seated figure that she assumes is Norman Bates's mother, then turning her around and discovering that she's been dead for years, her face frozen in a rictus grin. We later learn that Norman killed her and then kept her alive in his mind by absorbing and incarnating her personality. (The beast in Norman was caged by frail and fragile bonds.[33])

In the end, Tony decides to keep the relationship going because Melfi unwittingly makes him realize another benefit of therapy: her knowledge of human behavior, and how to manipulate intractable people like his mother and uncle, can come in handy as he rises to the top of the unofficial Family tree. "I get a lot of good ideas here," he tells Melfi.

SEASON 1/EPISODE 5
"COLLEGE"
WRITTEN BY JAMES MANOS JR. AND DAVID CHASE
DIRECTED BY ALLEN COULTER

The True Face

"Are you in the Mafia?" —**Meadow**

The pilot of *The Sopranos* built a world that was fresh and convincing enough to get viewers' attention, and the next three chapters were strong enough to hold it. But it wasn't until "College" that *The Sopranos* truly became *The Sopranos*—doing it, ironically, by separating three main characters, Tony, Meadow, and Carmela, from their carefully established community.

The audacity of the episode's structure is itself notable: it concentrates on just two narratives, sidelining everyone else (except for Christopher, in a performance that's literally phoned in). One plotline follows Tony as he tours universities in Maine with his daughter and spots Febby Petrulio (Tony Ray Rossi), a

---

33 Norman Bates was played by Anthony Perkins. Tony is short for Anthony.

Mob informant whose testimony jailed several of his colleagues and might have hastened his own father's demise. Tony's obsession with killing the rat erupts on the heels of Meadow grilling him about whether he's in the Mafia. His attempts to track and kill Febby with long-distance help from Chris are a source of farcical humor, with Tony taking an increasingly annoyed Meadow on a chase down a winding two-lane road, pawning her off on a group of local students in a bar, and constantly fabricating reasons for ducking into a phone booth.

The second story finds Carmela welcoming Father Phil Intintola (Paul Schulze[34]), a celibate flirt, into her empty house on the same stormy night she learns that Dr. Melfi's first name is Jennifer; distraught, she grumbles that Tony's refusal to volunteer Melfi's gender must mean he's sleeping with her. A dangerous dance ensues. (Their chosen film is *The Remains of the Day*, a 1993 drama about a housekeeper and butler who are too repressed and bound by their obligations ever to be together—sound familiar?) The connections between the plotlines emerge organically via juxtaposition, without excessive prompting. Whenever "College" seems to hand themes directly to the viewer, it does so in such a plainspoken way that they open new avenues of interpretation rather than close off existing ones. Meadow and Tony's discussions about honesty, Carmela and Father Phil's conversations about sin, guilt, and spirituality, and the scenes where both pairs ponder confidentiality and secrecy, refract off each other and illuminate the entire episode, and the series as a whole. "College" also gives us a clear sense of Tony's strengths as a father—he can be a good listener when he takes off the tough-guy mask—as well as the better qualities that Meadow might've absorbed from Carmela: her ability to recognize others' peace offerings (when Tony half-admits that he's in the Mob, she admits that she did speed to get through finals) and her willingness to call bullshit on men she catches lying or evading. ("You know, there was a time when the Italian people didn't have a lot of options," Tony weasels. "You mean like Mario Cuomo?" Meadow counters.)

But all this is a mere sideshow to the hour's bloody pièce de résistance, Tony's murder of the informant. It puts the *Analyze This* comparisons to bed forever, makes it clear that this isn't some cute series about a henpecked Mob boss with troublemaking kids ("Wiseguys: They're just like us!"), and announces that the evolutionary changes in TV storytelling that *Hill Street Blues* launched are about to be overthrown.

---

34 Schulze, who replaces Michael Santoro, was an old friend and collaborator of Edie Falco's. They attended SUNY Purchase together, and had acted together many times on stage and screen (and would continue to do so for years after *The Sopranos* ended, as toxic lovers on Showtime's *Nurse Jackie*). There's a shorthand and chemistry between them beyond the nearly romantic that's enormously valuable for a story that has to push their relationship to its outer edges at a point in the series when we barely know either character.

This might seem an excessive claim to anyone who grew up on television after *The Sopranos* and watched countless protagonists do horrible things, sometimes defensibly, sometimes not. But back in 1999, the effect of this particular killing was seismic. Four episodes in, viewers had seen murder and violent death attributable to negligence or incompetence, but Tony didn't commit any of the acts, nor was he directly responsible for their occurrence. Though he was way too free with his fists, Tony was a de-escalator: burning down Artie's restaurant so Junior couldn't have somebody whacked there, engineering Junior's ascent to the top slot to head off a war, and so on. And although it seemed unthinkable that he'd go through the series without ordering at least one person's death—he'd toyed with the idea—a killing like this seemed equally unthinkable, because TV protagonists didn't get down in the muck like that. That was what henchmen and guest stars were for.

Let's back up from the murder and examine its dramatic architecture to determine what made it so unusual. It's not the choice of target. Febby may have left the life years earlier, but he hasn't really reformed. Deep down he's still a criminal,[35] and he'll always be a rat, and because we've spent lots of time with Tony and none with Febby, and accept that this is the kind of thing mobsters *have* to do because of their code, of course we're going to take Tony's side. Also significant: this is a crime of opportunity. Tony didn't drag Meadow to Maine just to track down Febby and kill him, which would've been reckless and deranged versus merely impulsive. He isn't killing some random person for disrespecting him or to cover up some other offense. This is a former gangster—and a poor excuse for one. He sold out his friends (one of whom died in prison), then entered witness protection until the FBI ejected him. Now he's been living under an Anglicized alias, Fred Peters,[36] and lecturing about his former life to college kids. We already know (from the pilot and "46 Long") Tony and the others consider this sort of behavior a whackable offense.

All of this places Febby squarely in the category of "work problems." To frame things in terms of the *Godfather* films, as *The Sopranos* often does, Febby isn't that anonymous sex worker in *The Godfather Part II* who the Corleones killed to indebt a senator; he's more akin to Frankie Five Angels, the underboss in *II* who becomes a state witness and kills himself after committing perjury. The Corleones became American folk heroes despite being thieving, racketeering monsters because, with few exceptions, they only killed other mobsters and

---

35 We can see this in the scenes where Febby tracks Tony, visiting the motel and the restaurant and asking a garage worker if a man fitting Tony's description has been looking for him: those old mobster muscles are springing to life again.

36 A detail that dovetails with the gangsters' generalized disgust at Italian culture being watered down or erased.

their collaborators, and only ones that were coded as worse than the Corleones. That's the case here as well, though we feel for Febby's wife and daughter even if we don't care what happens to Febby.

No, Febby's murder was startling because of the context—a father-daughter road trip, mirroring Febby's life with the wife he'll never sleep next to again and the daughter he won't see grow up—and because of the joy Tony takes in doing the deed. There's no regret or distaste on his face as he twists those cords, only glee. The most frightening thing about Tony is the way he seems to trade depression for euphoria when hurting people. James Gandolfini's face splits into a predatory grin, practically a leer, and he throws his tall, broad frame into the action with the furious precision of a smaller, more graceful man. His arms and fists are a blur, his eyes blaze, and flecks of spittle fly out of his mouth as he curses the men he's battering and tormenting. He's never been scarier.

The lead-up to the strangulation reveals the scene's primordial essence: we're watching an apex predator stalk and kill its prey. We got a taste of this approach earlier in the episode when Tony visited Febby's home and watched him tell his daughter good night while sitting in a hot tub with his wife. Right before Tony sneaks up behind Febby in the woods, Febby hears a noise in nearby brush and looks to see what caused it, and we get a cutaway shot of a deer gazing at him, its curious face framed by the greenery. The sequence of actions that brought us to this point represents a journey backward in time: Tony and Febby arrive by car, a twentieth-century form of transportation; Febby loses his revolver, a nineteenth-century weapon, during the struggle, and there's a shot of the piece dropping onto the earth beneath his feet; then Tony strangles him and strangles him and keeps strangling him, an act of Shakespearean viciousness.[37]

The scene lasts much longer than you expect, until the audience feels assaulted as well. The editing cuts between tight close-ups of Febby's face, Tony's hands pulling the cords tight around Febby's neck, and Tony's face contorted in euphoric rage, his front teeth framed by his snarling mouth (like an upside-down smile) so that they evoke a carnivore's bared fangs. Close-ups of Tony's hands reveal that he's choking Febby so hard that the cords are cutting his skin.[38] After he drops Febby's lifeless body, he stands up and walks past the travel agency as insects whir and birds caw. He looks up to see a flock of birds—ducks, probably—in a V formation, a shot that resonates in multiple ways, none of them reassuring.

---

37 "Sweet soul, take heed, / Take heed of perjury; thou art on thy deathbed." Othello to Desdemona as he's strangling her; *Othello*, Act V, Scene II.

38 Tony is killing a version of himself here. When Febby and his wife call out to their child, it's a daughter who might've grown up to tour colleges with her own dad someday, as Meadow is doing. Tony's conversations with Meadow about his business, however guarded, give us a sense of a man who, like Febby, was born into a particular life and can't get out of it.

Shots of birds in flight after a character's death always evoke a soul departing. In this case, they also amplify the sense that we've just seen prehistoric savagery occur. These ducks harken back to the ones that left Tony's swimming pool, part of a narrative that we associate with Tony and Livia's relationship: her hold over his imagination, the genes that encoded half of the beast in him. And they stand in for the safe family and feelings of peace that seem to remain forever beyond his grasp.

Carmela's story is nearly as unsettling, partly because of how it fuses with Tony's. Tony's half of "College" is a scaled-down, two-character exploration of what it means to be Tony Soprano, a theoretically respectable man with a house, a wife, a kids, and a secret criminal life; Carmela's half is about being his complicit partner. We get a sense of how repressed she is, thanks to her acceptance of the contradictory sexual values of Mob marriages (men are expected, even encouraged to take mistresses; wives are supposed to be faithful) as well as the sexual politics of Roman Catholicism. Two of the movies that are name-checked in this episode, *The Remains of the Day* and *Casablanca*, revolve around great loves that cannot be. It's spot-on that she'd bond with Father Phil over these sorts of movies, and that she'd select a priest as the vessel into which to pour the specific desires, fears, and affinities that Tony would never entertain. There's (almost) no danger that the frisson of attraction will become physical.

Nevertheless, her evening with Father Phil unfolds like a date from the start—she even takes a pass at her hair before letting him in. Their interactions show that they genuinely like each other, and that each is getting something out of the relationship. Carmela gives the priest-plus an outlet for his intellectual curiosity beyond matters of scripture, plus imaginative fuel for fantasies of a life where he could have a normal relationship with a woman (thus their discussion of Jesus coming down off the cross in Scorsese's *The Last Temptation of Christ*). Father Phil gives Carmela a sympathetic ear, appreciation for her food and her personality, and a means to discuss religion, philosophy, and movies as art.[39] The script is clear on what's at stake for them: it's never a good idea to court a gangster's wife, or for a gangster's wife to step out. But the fact that Father Phil is married to the church adds another layer of taboo. When he rushes to the bathroom to retch after moving in for a kiss, it's not just the alcohol causing his body to rebel.[40] (The moment connects with the *Last Temptation* discussion, as well as with Tony's line while killing Febby: "You took an oath and you broke it!"[41])

---

39 Father Phil is a hardcore cinephile. You can tell because when Carmela mentions *Casablanca*, he goes immediately to the quality of the new print.
40 The camera tilts to one side as it follows the priest to the bathroom, as if the episode itself is drunk.
41 Another point of connection between Tony and Father Phil is the way they bring their values, their code, and even their rituals with them no matter where they are.

It seems fitting that "College" puts Carmela's confession to Father Phil and her subsequent taking of Communion—the moments when she's most emotionally naked—at the midpoint, where these characters' first sex scene might go were this a novel about two lovers. The close-ups of Father Phil pouring wine into a Communion cup and delivering it straight to Carmela's lips along with the Host are the true consummation of a storyline about sexual energy being teased out and shut down (or redirected). It's in these scenes that we move beyond the question of "Will they or won't they?" and enter darker territory. Carmela is in denial about her husband's affairs, but those pale in comparison to the other sins, the literal crimes, that she can't bring herself to confront. Her confession to Father Phil, delivered on the same couch where her family watches TV, sums up this series' fascination with evil and compromise, false faces and self-deception. "I have forsaken what is right for what is easy, allowing what I know is evil in my house," she says. "Allowing my children—Oh my God, my sweet children!—to be a part of it, because I wanted things for them. I wanted a better life, good schools. I wanted this house. I wanted money in my hands, money to buy everything I ever wanted. I'm so ashamed! My husband, I think he has committed horrible acts. . . . I've said nothing, I've done nothing about it. I got a bad feeling it's just a matter of time before God compensates me with outrage for my sins."[42]

Late in "College" there's a scene with Tony that explicitly connects the two stories. As Tony sits in a university hallway at Bowdoin College waiting for Meadow to be interviewed, he looks up at a quote emblazoned on a large panel hanging over a doorway: "No man can wear one face to himself and another to the multitude without finally getting bewildered as to which may be true."[43] It's a slight misquote from Nathaniel Hawthorne's *The Scarlet Letter*, about a minister who falls in love with a woman and breaks his vows.

---

42 Father Phil tells her exactly what she needs to hear about repenting and renouncing sin, even as we can suspect this is Carmela's momentary burst of remorse before she returns to enjoying the benefits of being a made guy's wife. By the next morning—after Father Phil is saved from a second moment of temptation by a stomach too full of pasta and alcohol—Carmela has, indeed, reverted to type. She couldn't have been more vulnerable in her confession, nor could she be any colder or more in control as Phil stumbles around in his undershirt trying to apologize for his behavior.

43 The correct quote is, "No man can wear one face to himself and another to the multitude without finally getting bewildered as to which may be *the* true"—as in, "the true face."

SEASON 1/EPISODE 6
WRITTEN BY FRANK RENZULLI
DIRECTED BY ALAN TAYLOR

Like a Mandolin

"I love you. I'm in love with you. I'm sorry. It's just the way it is." —**Tony**

In terms of plot advancement, "Pax Soprana" could have come right after "Mead-owlands," but its events register more strongly because we've seen how carefree Tony can be when he's away from the stresses and obligations of New Jersey and can just do whatever he wants—and more important, hurt whomever he wants. Remember how joyful and relaxed Tony seemed as he prepared to kill Febby Petrulio, tailing him around town like a private detective in an old movie, then emerging from the woods to garrote him: in five episodes, he'd never seemed less burdened by neuroses. This was not the put-upon husband, father, and Mob boss who trudges through life back in Jersey; this was a guy who *loves* when he gets to inflict pain independent of bureaucracy, politics, and their attendant headaches.

Tony's love of Mob action at its simplest illuminates "Pax Soprana." He's back on his home turf again, allegedly running things behind his uncle's back, with a wife, a mistress, and a therapist all catering to his needs in different ways—and he could not be more miserable, because he's back to worrying about the not-fun parts of gangster life. That stress is palpable throughout the episode, whether from Junior's high-handed leadership style or Tony's discomfort at dealing with demanding women.

In their first scene together, Melfi notes that she is a proxy for all the important women in Tony's life, and it's fascinating to see how they've started to blur in his mind. A few episodes ago, he dreamed that his mother was Dr. Melfi. Here his unconscious gives him Melfi as both his mistress (even speaking with Irina's voice) and his wife.

"What's the one thing your mother, your wife, your daughter all have in common?" Melfi asks him.

"They all break my balls," Tony says, making her laugh,[44] then adds, "They're all Italian, so what?"

"So, maybe by coming clean with me, you're dialoguing with them." Later, he pours it on by describing Melfi in terms that prize her gentleness (versus the

---

44 Tony's response to Melfi's question about a prostate exam to explore his erectile issues—"Hey, I don't let anybody wag their finger *in my face*"—is one of his most intentionally funny lines of the whole series, and Melfi's full-throated laugh in response is a delight. Tony wonders at one point why she took him on as a patient, but it's clear she genuinely enjoys his company much of the time.

confrontational qualities of Carmela, Meadow, and Livia) while comparing her demeanor very specifically to an Italian stringed instrument often heard in love songs. "You're gentle. Not loud. Sweet-soundin'. Like a mandolin."[45]

The problem is, he can't perform with any of the women he's juggling, physically or emotionally. He can't get it up with Irina, is barely interested in trying with Carm, and gets completely shut down by Melfi, who knows transference when she sees it. Tony can't get what he needs from them, any more than he can get Livia to be even the slightest bit affectionate when he visits her at Green Grove. He blames the Prozac and even floats the idea of "flushing" it to "see if the changes are real" because it "might be working a little overtime . . . a side effect."

"You know, not all impotence is the result of the medication," Melfi says; a few minutes later she points out that depression itself might also be a factor, and that if he still gets morning wood, the problem isn't the pills.

"You saying there's something wrong with me?" Tony says, flashing a scaled-down version of the predatory sneer we see on his face when he's inflicting violence. It's revealing that his fight-or-flight response would be triggered by such an innocuous comment; maybe it's because the implication, even before Melfi starts to elaborate on it, is that Tony might have to actually change, even a little bit, if he wants to get it up again.

Carmela's actions mirror Tony's in some ways. She's only slightly more willing than Tony to do the hard, tedious work of repairing relationships. Look at the way she behaves toward Tony not long after her confessional epiphany with Father Phil. She wants to have sex with him, probably to put that energy to productive use instead of bouncing it off the priest's vestments; but she has no idea that her husband's not doing any better with his mistress in this regard, and interprets his impotence as a sign that he's getting partner-type satisfactions from Melfi, sexual or not.[46] She tells Father Phil—in a smartly directed scene that includes a wide shot in which the cross literally comes between them— that she used to view Tony's girlfriends and mistresses as "a form of masturbation," satisfying a carnal appetite that, unlike Carmela's, seemed boundless. "I couldn't give him what he needed all the time. . . . But this psychiatrist, she's not just a *goomar.* For the first time, I feel like he's really cheating and I'm the one who's thirsty."

Carmela is right to call Tony out for ducking out on their anniversary to talk business with New York underboss Johnny Sack (Vincent

---

45 Lorraine Bracco's body language after she rejects Tony's kiss and then literally stands up to him is exactly right. She doesn't step back even though he's at kissing distance, because that would indicate fear, but at the same time, she gives him nothing that would indicate even a tiny chance of reciprocation.

46 Tony's impotent in his work life, too—unable to control Junior, and stuck having to absorb abuse for installing him, even though, as he points out, other members of the Family agreed it was good idea.

Curatola[47]), and her observations of how Tony neglects her for work and treats her as "someone you've just chosen to procreate with" are undeniably correct. But rather than push him toward the church, or trying to be a better person herself, Carmela tries to get his attention by spending his money on new furniture. Good-bye, brief guilt about enjoying the fruits of Tony's business, though at least she finally admits to Tony that she was jealous of Melfi's ability to help him, saying, "I wanna be that woman in your life."

Tony understandably develops fast qualms about the Frankenstein's monster he's created by making Uncle Junior the fake boss. The gambit was brilliant in theory but runs into the complicated realities of human beings, from Junior's pride to Livia's continued attempts to strike back at her son for putting her in a nursing home/retirement community.[48] At the moment, it's other members of the Family who are suffering—a buddy of captain Jimmy Altieri (Joe Badalucco Jr.) with the poker game, Tony's mentor Hesh (Jerry Adler[49]) having to pay Junior back taxes—and Tony is able to manipulate the Hesh situation into a scenario everyone can live with.

But you don't have to have watched the rest of the series to suspect that Junior's reign won't be peaceful for nearly as long as Octavian's—and that's even without our first significant appearance by the FBI, who take surveillance photos of everyone at Junior's coronation dinner. Junior has spent most of his life in the shadow of younger men—first his kid brother, then Jackie, now his nephew—resenting the lack of validation and respect he feels entitled to despite leaving people cold most of the time. After all these years, he has finally attained his birthright, but many of his business decisions seem punitive or nonsensical, generating so much chaos that Tony barely maintains the status quo by going behind Junior's back or hitting his uncle with shameless, transparent flattery—manipulations easily counteracted by Livia, whose hold over Junior is so powerful that she doesn't even need to draw attention to it.

---

47 Curatola is one of several notable *Sopranos* regulars with minimal prior acting experience. He was a masonry contractor who decided in middle age to audit *Law & Order* star Michael Moriarty's acting class, which led to a few small roles like Detective #1 in the *Law & Order* spin-off film *Exiled*. He almost missed the audition to play Johnny Sack because he wanted to have a smoke before going in; by the time he made it upstairs, the casting director was packing up for the day. "Then she looks up at me," he says, "reconsiders, takes out the [script] and says, 'Let's do this.' After I was done, she says, 'We want you to come back next week and read for the producers.'" He just had that kind of face.

48 When Junior visits Livia at Green Grove, she recognizes Johnny Boy's favorite cologne, Canoe, on him, and the two at times comport themselves like old lovers rather than in-laws.

49 A veteran of stage and screen perhaps best known pre-*Sopranos* for playing building superintendent Mr. Wicker on the sitcom *Mad About You*, Adler had acted in several late-period *Northern Exposure* episodes (when David Chase was producing it) as Joel Fleischman's old rabbi, who occasionally appeared to him in visions.

SEASON 1/EPISODE 7
"DOWN NECK"   WRITTEN BY ROBIN GREEN & MITCHELL BURGESS
DIRECTED BY LORRAINE SENNA FERRARA

White Rabbit

"My son is doomed, right?" —**Tony**

"Down Neck" is in some ways even more focused than "College," equally concerned with the handed-down values and codes that people honor or violate, but more preoccupied with biology and lineage. It revolves around AJ's precarious school situation after his suspension for stealing Communion wine, the memories the incident stirs up in Tony, and the possibility that AJ might be doomed to replicate the mistakes and miseries of his father. "I got in a little trouble when I was a kid," Tony told Meadow during their road trip to Maine; this is the episode where we get a taste of what he was alluding to.

"Down Neck" doesn't have an iconic moment like Tony strangling Febby or Carmela's confession, but it draws enormous power from showing the way Tony grew up, how the experience helped make him the adult he is now, and why he fears he may be making AJ into the same kind of man his parents made him. Father Hagy (Anthony Fusco) tells Tony and Carmela that attention deficit disorder is "an aggregate of symptoms" that may include inattention, impulsivity, and hyperactivity. "All he needs is a whack upside the head," Tony says, expressing the Old World mentality toward raising boys that helped make him the insecure, easily aggrieved, violent bully that he is today. "You'd hit somebody who's sick?" Carmela presses him. "You'd hit somebody with polio?" No, Tony says, but only because modern American society has deemed it unacceptable "to do a *tarantell'* on the kids every once in awhile."

His own father had a different attitude: "The belt was his favorite child development tool." His mother, apparently, was even more chaotic in her expressions of rage; an especially terrifying moment, shrugged off by Tony as "opera," finds a domestically stressed-out Livia accusing her young son of "driving me crazy" and threatening to stick a serving fork in his eye. With Melfi, Tony worries that the propensity for lawlessness and violence is "in the blood—it's hereditary," even though she reassures him "it's not a destiny written in stone. People have choices."

James Gandolfini is spectacular in the therapy scenes, as Tony vacillates between sharp clarity on his upbringing and willful ignorance about how truly dysfunctional it was. There's a powerful sense of Tony internalizing his father's toxic masculinity and exhibiting his own version of it; when Melfi asks how he felt after seeing his father beat a man for the first time, he says, "I didn't want him to do it to me," but then adds, "I was just glad he wasn't a fag." Asked if he's "concerned" that AJ is going to find out what he really does for a living, Tony retreats into deflections and rationalizations, and Gandolfini's expressions grow more resentful and petulant. "What about chemical companies dumping all of that shit into the rivers, and they get all of these deformed babies popping up all over the place?"[50] he says, avoiding eye contact as he rants. In earlier episodes, Gandolfini had such a handle on the role that he could seem to be acting with the back of his neck. Here he does a lot of acting with his eyelids, as the moments where he hides his expressive eyes provide the best window into Tony's troubled soul. When Tony tells Melfi, "He was a good guy, my father—he knew how to have a good time," Gandolfini glances down at his right pants leg as he's brushing lint from it rather than making eye contact.

Lorraine Bracco wonderfully expresses Melfi's reactions to these alarming details. Near the end, when Tony insists that he was "proud to be Johnny Soprano's boy," he looks Melfi right in the face, jabbing a finger at her, then at himself when she asks if his own son is proud of him: "Yeah, probably—and I'm glad! *Glad* if he's proud of me!" The good doctor tries hard to maintain her usual clinical distance, but simply can't once she appreciates all the ugliness Tony experienced while being led to believe he had a typical childhood. Her friendly curiosity while prodding and challenging her patient—like an old friend asking questions over coffee—makes you believe that Tony set aside at least some of his defense mechanisms.

The dialogue in past and present sequences links the choices (or predispositions?) of the grandparents, the father, and the son. "It's a crime to suspend that child from school with all the money you give them!" Livia declares during a family dinner, demonstrating the "money talks" attitude typical of so many *Sopranos* characters—and Americans. Young Livia tells young Tony that his father was arrested even though "he didn't do anything. They just pick on the Italians!" In the present, Tony asks the school authorities if they're testing Anthony's classmates, "the ones that aren't named 'Soprano'?" Junior says, "I bet that gym teacher shit a brick when your little friend puked on his boots, huh, Anthony?" making light of the situation that has Tony and Carmela so distressed, and making his grandson giggle. "Wanna encourage him, Uncle Jun?" Tony says, irritated. "Hey, whatever happened to 'boys will be boys'?" grins Junior, who's first seen in the flashbacks (played by Rocco Sisto) picking up Johnny Boy Soprano (Joseph Siravo) to go

---

50 If you're a James Gandolfini completist, this line has an extra-dramatic aspect: he costarred in *A Civil Action* as a man who blows the whistle on the owners of a Massachusetts tannery whose illegal dumping is polluting the local water supply and causing a high incidence of leukemia among residents. The film opened wide in North America on January 8, 1999, two days before *The Sopranos* premiered.

beat up a deadbeat debtor (Steve Santosusso). In a nifty bit of present/past mirroring, this scene echoes the very first act of violence in the series, down to the wide shots of a Sopranos paterfamilias chasing his quarry on foot and thrashing him in plain view of witnesses while a blood relative shadows him in a shiny new car.

The flashbacks bring new energy to the therapy scenes, partly because this is the first time since the pilot that *The Sopranos* has cut away from Tony and Melfi's discussions to show us Tony's recollections. Gandolfini and Bracco are strong enough actors that Chase might have gotten away with expressing these memories as a string of theatrical monologues. But there are virtues to showing instead of telling, in scenes that create a parallel *Sopranos* universe with juicy roles for actors we're meeting for the first time.

Laila Robins brings the younger Livia to horrifying life in a way that evokes but doesn't impersonate Nancy Marchand. Less effective is Siravo as Johnny Boy. He theoretically has the easier job, since he doesn't have to live up to an indelible present-day performance, but he comes in on the broader end of the *Sopranos*'s acting spectrum. Siravo does capture the wildly destructive energy and preening entitlement characteristic of so many of these neighborhood gangsters: you can believe Johnny would have been beloved by old-timers like Paulie Walnuts who sentimentalize alpha males that do as they damn well please, way out of proportion to their criminal skills. Civilians sometimes idolize them, too: the punch line of the flashbacks is seeing the same guy Johnny beat up leaning out of his window in casts to cheer him on.

It's fun to look at these scenes through the lens of the 1960s-era TV shows made before and after, including a great one by Chase's protégé Matthew Weiner, a writer-producer who joined *The Sopranos* in season five and went on to create *Mad Men*. Back in 1999, Jefferson Airplane's "White Rabbit" was already a clichéd choice to introduce a '60s flashback—especially given Tony's current pill regimen. But the story of the toxic Johnny–Livia marriage, and the specific Jersey-ness of the flashbacks (including news coverage of the 1967 riots elsewhere in Newark deployed as background, and as a comment on how white Americans were mostly unaffected by civil rights struggles), render "Down Neck" uniquely *Sopranos*, even if a music cue or two now seems too familiar.[51] The show's conflation of the familial and the professional continues in the '60s scenes: Tony is nearly as upset by

---

51 The Animals' "Don't Bring Me Down," which plays during Johnny's thrashing of the deadbeat, is an altogether better needle drop, less familiar than "White Rabbit" and with a title that reverberates with secondary meaning. Tony is depressed in large part because he's a mobster who routinely participates in evil. This flashback shows the roots of that part of his unhappiness, while in the present, Tony denies that his childhood was traumatic or that remembering it is unpleasant. The title could be Tony's unexpressed demand to his therapist.

remembering how his father favored his sister as he is with recalling his arrest at the amusement park for violating the terms of his parole. "He was using my sister Janice as a front," Tony explains to Melfi. "All the guys brought their daughters so when they did their business, it looked sweet and innocent."

The past and present stories also tie together neatly by having AJ inadvertently spill the beans to his grandmother about his dad being in therapy. Grandson and grandmother make a great comic combination here: AJ is so oblivious—whether from ADD, Sopranos genes, his questionable upbringing, or some combination—that he not only doesn't realize what he's telling Livia but is invulnerable to her usual emotional manipulations. Once Livia decides that Tony goes to a psychiatrist mainly to complain about her, she starts up the waterworks and loud self-pity, but AJ couldn't be less interested. Watching this malevolent old woman try to get inside this kid's thick head is like watching a master surgeon use a scalpel on a garbage can.

Of course, we've seen how dangerous Livia can be, even in the confined, monitored spaces of Green Grove, when she counsels Junior. We see it again here when Tony insinuates that his mother prevented his father from starting "a new book" and a supper club in Reno with an associate, reminding her that she said she'd rather smother her own kids with a pillow than watch Johnny take them away. "Well, if it bothers you, maybe you better talk to a psychiatrist," Livia says coldly. "That's what people do when they're looking for somebody to blame for their life, isn't it?"

SEASON 1/EPISODE 8
WRITTEN BY FRANK RENZULLI AND DAVID CHASE
DIRECTED BY TIM VAN PATTEN

Spring Cleaning

"Where's my arc?" —**Christopher**

As quickly as *The Sopranos* became a hit for HBO in the early months of '99, it also became controversial among some Italian Americans—many like Dr. Melfi's ex-husband, Richard La Penna[52]—who were tired of seeing movies and TV portray

---

52 Richard, the character most distressed by unflattering images of Italian Americans, is played by Richard Romanus, who portrayed a loan shark in Martin Scorsese's Mob drama *Mean Streets*.

them as gangsters. As TV critics for Tony Soprano's favorite newspaper, a major daily in a state with a robust and proud Italian American population, this book's authors heard early and often from citizens who resented the popularity of the show and accused it of once again casting a shadow over their people. Yet we also heard from Italian Americans who loved the series, and felt as much pride in having Tony as their pop cultural avatar as Tony does in this episode having Frank Sinatra as his.[53] This dichotomy of reaction to *The Sopranos* would soon become as much part of the show's fabric as Tony's dreams, as characters became stand-ins for anti-defamation protesters, and as the show engaged detractors head on.

These first-season episodes, though, were made in a vacuum—all written and produced months before any of them aired. Even if David Chase couldn't predict the audience's size, he and Frank Renzulli knew the reactions stories like this tended to generate from their fellow Italian Americans, and this installment at least partly tries to outflank the issue.

Reports of pending Federal indictments[54] for DiMeo Family members are all anyone can talk about in this episode, whether they're in the Mob or not. For seasoned wiseguys like Tony and Big Pussy, it's nerve-racking, but it's also the cost of doing business, and they focus on the practical:[55] hiding or destroying evidence, preventing the FBI from trashing too much of the house, or warning Dr. Melfi that some upcoming appointments may be missed due to "vacation."

For Melfi's loved ones, who are alarmed to learn that she's treating one of the mobsters from recent news reports, it's another opportunity to debate the enduring popularity of Mob stories, and the alleged harm they do to Italian Americans' image. The conversation waxes didactic, as Melfi's son Jason points out that the whole concept of Italian American anti-defamation was started by Mob boss Joseph Colombo (who did, indeed, found the Italian American Civil Rights League), while Richard argues that the number of Italian American criminals

---

53 Sinatra, who died during first-season production, is so present in season one that the producers might as well have listed him in the opening credits. His picture hangs in Satriale's in the pilot when Chris kills Emil Kolar; a bust of the singer (with inaccurately large lips) confirms Febby's identity in "College"; and this episode concludes with the Cake song "Frank Sinatra" as Chris steals a stack of *Star-Ledgers*.

54 The local FBI organized crime unit, glimpsed briefly earlier, finally gets a couple of faces in Agent Harris (Matt Servitto), who makes an effort to be polite to Tony (which Tony says makes him the worst of them all), and Agent Grasso (Frank Pando), who bristles when Tony insults him in Italian (and becomes the subject of yet another argument about Italian Americans' self-image). Most interesting about the looming FBI search warrants is Carmela's complicity in helping Tony hide criminal evidence—not just that she knows the money's source, but that she helps him stash both cash and guns in Livia's Green Grove closet.

55 The wedding hosted by captain Larry Boy Barese (Tony Darrow) for his daughter Melissa starts off resembling the kind of lavish receptions we've seen in other Mob films, but ends in a crueler, more *Sopranos* way, with Pussy taking back his present in case he needs traveling money, and all the other wiseguys and their families leaving early to do some "spring cleaning."

in pop culture is disproportionate to the number of Italian Americans actually involved in organized crime.

Amusingly, Richard has a kindred spirit of sorts in his wife's "Patient X," who responds to the FBI raid on his home by lecturing his kids about all the great Italian Americans (like Antonio Meucci) who had nothing to do with organized crime. Tony is in typical denial about many things—including the idea that spaghetti could have been invented in China, not Italy—but here, that tendency is presented as part of his larger desire (emphasized in "Down Neck," too) to keep his kids as far from the Family business as possible.

But where Richard is alarmed by the indictments because of the shadow they cast on law-abiding Italians, and Tony isn't happy because it endangers his business and freedom, the episode's title character is upset mainly because he's being ignored. As Christopher reminds Adriana, he loves movies, and seems to have joined the Family as much out of a desire to emulate his cinematic heroes as to be closer to his uncle. He's so young, cocky, and stupid that he doesn't even realize that he's better off not being named in the indictments or the newspaper, to the point where he becomes envious of his dead friend Brendan for being referred to as a "soldier" on local TV news.

This is the biggest spotlight on Christopher so far, but it's a melancholy one because everything he wants in life (besides the beautiful Adriana) seems so distant. He wants to write his own version of *Goodfellas* but can't even spell "managed," and doesn't realize screenwriting is work. (He thought the computer would do a lot of it for him.) Jimmy Altieri laughs at the idea that the Feds would care about Tony's glorified errand boy, who admits to his uncle later in the hour, "the fuckin' regularness of life is too fuckin' hard for me or something." If he's not clinically depressed,[56] he's certainly not taking any joy in the outlaw lifestyle he dreamed of as a kid.

From its opening nightmare of the murdered Emil Kolar returning from the dead to ask about sausages—the first *Sopranos* dream not from Tony's point of view—this episode is an outstanding showcase for Imperioli. The scene where Christopher confesses all his worst fears to Paulie is remarkable for how haunted and defeated he seems this early in the series, even as it illustrates the folly of trying to model your life on your favorite screen heroes.

"Legend" also happens to be the show's best argument against the charge that it glamorizes real and reel gangsters. The closest Christopher gets to living up to

---

56 Tony's conversation with Christopher in the car again illustrates how isolated Tony feels about his therapy. He suspects Christopher could be suffering from depression but can't come right out and ask him or discuss the condition in too-knowledgeable detail because he would risk exposure, and ultimately has to go along with Christopher's mockery of people who commit suicide.

his fantasies—when he pulls a gun on a baker who doesn't show the appropriate level of fear—is a moment that's doubly meta: not only is Christopher being thin-skinned and reckless like his favorite movie wiseguys, he shoots the poor baker in the foot, the same injury Imperioli's character Spider suffered at the hands of Joe Pesci's Tommy in *Goodfellas*.

The one counterargument neither Melfi nor the show bothers making is that Hollywood isn't biased against Italian Americans, but toward excitement. There have also likely been more Irish American gangsters in movies and TV than in reality, more Mexican and Central and South American drug kingpins, and so on. But that's what sells: the image of the brusque, tough outlaw who takes whatever he wants, in contrast to members of the "respectable" majority who have to be law abiding and considerate all the time. Not only does the general public find tales of crime and violence more interesting (at least in fiction) than representations of "regular" life,[57] but members of some of the same ethnic groups that get stereotyped regularly may feel empowered when the stereotype is scary, thrilling, or just socially unacceptable. Negative images notwithstanding, it's more fun to be seen as dangerous than dull.

It's useful to compare Richard's horror at his people being tarnished by a Tony Soprano with the way Jason's Jewish therapist Sam Reis (Sam Coppola, no relation to the famous cinema family) boasts of having a relative who was a wheelman for gangster Louis "Lepke" Buchalter.[58] "Those were some tough Jews," Reis says wistfully. If the go-to media depiction of Italian Americans is a cigar-chewing mobster, then the archetypal Jewish American character is a quick-witted nebbish, probably a stand-up comic or somebody played by one. For Richard, Italian mobsters are a stain on his people's legacy; seeing an Italian American actor play an educated white-collar professional like himself would surely brighten his day. But the existence of Jewish gangsters delights Reis because it proves that his people aren't all neurotic wimps. The grass is always greener.

---

57 A little over a year after *The Sopranos* debuted, CBS launched *That's Life*, a likable drama about an Italian American family who lived in the same part of Jersey as Tony and Uncle Junior but had no Mob connection; it limped along for two seasons and was canceled due to low ratings. During a promotional tour months before the show debuted, its star Paul Sorvino told one of the authors of this book that he would never appear on *The Sopranos* because it was defamatory toward Italian Americans. His most acclaimed movie role in the '90s was Paul "Paulie" Cicero in *Goodfellas*, the Mob boss who didn't have to move for anybody.

58 Leading New York City racketeer in the 1930s, and head of the Mafia hit squad Murder Incorporated, an independent consortium of contract killers that carried out hits for other mobsters while guaranteeing no footprints back to them.

The Devil He Knows

"I didn't hurt nobody." **—Tony**

In the grand scheme of *Sopranos* season one, the most important part of "Boca" takes place on a Jersey golf course, where Uncle Junior and Tony both say things they shouldn't, and Junior begins to ponder having his nephew whacked. His murderous thoughts are sparked by Livia, who complains to Junior about "my son, the mental patient" while tending her husband's burial plot in a graveyard overrun with "cemetery dogs."

But the episode's other major plotline is more striking: the transgressions of Meadow's soccer coach Don Hauser (Kevin O'Rourke), who secretly slept with Meadow's teammate Ally (Cara Jedell). This story shows how caring and morally upright Meadow can be when somebody she loves is in trouble. It also spotlights Artie Bucco, and treats his whiplash-inducing reactions to the scandal as a barometer of viewer reaction to *The Sopranos*, a show that sincerely warns of the spiritual consequences of the savagery it makes us crave.

Tony and Artie's debate over the coach's crime—and what it says about these longtime pals' very different attitudes about lawbreaking—is gripping, and addresses a larger point about our main character and the philosophy he shares with so many other characters. We've all seen stories about two childhood friends, where one grows up to be a cop or a priest and the other a crook—it's a staple of classic gangster films like *Angels with Dirty Faces* and modern crime thrillers like *The Indian Runner*—and *The Sopranos* could easily have done that with Artie. But this scenario is more original. Artie lives so close to Tony's world that he can practically taste it, but he's not a part of it, and he has Charmaine to pull him back toward the light when he's tempted to lean on the devil he knows. The ongoing temptation of an ordinary guy is powerful precisely because it's so small and yet so complicated.[59]

---

59 Ventimiglia had played a lot of cops and criminals (and sometimes both at once) prior to *The Sopranos*, and in interviews would joke about how he envied his costars who got to play tough guys while he was stuck playing sad sack Artie. But if it's not a flashy role, it's a complicated one that made him stand out more than if, say, he had been cast as Mikey Palmice. *The Sopranos* had a lot of mobsters, but only one Artie Bucco.

Already, Tony has made Artie offers he was wise to refuse but others that you couldn't blame him for accepting. (Had he taken Tony's cruise, the original Vesuvio would still be open.) It's hard being around these wiseguys and their obscene wealth and power, especially if you're a fundamentally decent person who struggles to stay afloat, and John Ventimiglia embodies Artie's inner struggle. It helps that Tony and Artie are so cleanly differentiated. They've known each other since childhood. They've both been married since their twenties. They like the same food and share many of the same values. Artie is just as angry as Tony to see a man wearing a baseball cap in a nice restaurant, even if he would never respond as Tony does to this lack of decorum. But as much as he wants to hurt Coach Hauser for what he did to Ally or let Tony take care of it, in the end he lets Charmaine convince him to do the right thing. Again.

And in the process, Artie does something impressive: he convinces Tony to do the right thing, too. This is still relatively early in the series; even after "College," Tony is presented more sympathetically than not. But we also know him as a man who's unswerving in pursuit of his own self-interest—and, as Charmaine tells Artie, having Hauser tortured and killed would make the dads feel better but not help Ally, Meadow, or the other girls on that team. Yet this one time, Artie and Dr. Melfi are able to steer Tony off this path. That he has to get fall-down drunk as a result speaks to how ingrained violence is for him, and how much these events forced him to examine his values, if only briefly, and it's poignant when he lies on the floor of his McMansion and tells Carmela that he didn't hurt nobody.

Meanwhile, the Uncle Junior plot helps illustrate why Artie is wise to steer well clear of Family business. Tony is seeing a headshrinker. His uncle gives head. Both these actions are unacceptable in the world of organized crime, where to be sensitive or giving is to announce oneself as unmanly. Junior warns his girlfriend Bobbi Sanfillipo (Robyn Petersen) against letting anyone in the Mob know that he's a willing and equal sexual partner, because "they think if you suck pussy, you'll suck anything." Bobbi rightly points out the insanity of this stance—he should be proud of his prowess, not ashamed—but the Mob doesn't always operate logically. Bobbi tells one person too many, and the news eventually filters to Tony, leading to that hilariously petty golf game. Once again, all the trouble starts because Junior has to insult Tony about his high school football experience—deeply attacking Tony's self-esteem—and you can see the bitter wheels turning in Tony's mind as he decides to go full Livia and mock Junior. Gandolfini and Dominic Chianese are wonderful here, as Tony revels in finding different ways to reference his uncle's activities while Junior slowly comes to a boil about it. As a result of those secrets being exposed, Junior (after harshly dumping Bobbi[60]) now ponders murdering his own nephew.

This is not a culture Arthur Bucco should want any part of, is it?

SEASON 1/EPISODE 10
WRITTEN BY JOE BOSSO AND FRANK RENZULLI
DIRECTED BY MATTHEW PENN

Mystery Box

"But I never really understood what he felt—to be used for somebody else's amusement, like a fuckin' dancing bear— 'til I played golf with those guys." —**Tony**

Even more than "The Legend of Tennessee Moltisanti," "A Hit Is a Hit" is concerned with Italian American self-image, ties between organized crime and popular culture, and the desire of disreputable outsiders to "go legit" without losing their cultural particulars. The new wrinkle here is the intersection of Italian American and African American gangster fantasies as Christopher crosses paths with Massive Genius (Bokeem Woodbine[61]), aka Massive G, a hip-hop mogul in the vein of Sean Combs or Jay-Z who loves the *Godfather* films so much that he'll even defend *Part III* ("It was misunderstood," he tells Adriana, but doesn't elaborate). One set of gangsters mistrusts the other, even though they're symbiotically linked, with the Mob maintaining a long history in the music business, and hip-hop culture taking cues from films like *The Godfather* and *Scarface*. Their point of collision is the $400,000 that Massive Genius claims Hesh owes the survivors of a "distant but deceased quasi-cousin" who recorded for Hesh's F-Note Records decades ago.

---

60 Junior smashing the pie into Bobbi's face is an homage to one of the most famous moments of the classic gangster picture *The Public Enemy,* in which James Cagney shows his displeasure with his girlfriend by smashing a grapefruit in her face.

61 A beefy, charismatic character actor, Woodbine has often been cast as drug dealers, assassins, cops, and other tough types, in the likes of *Strapped, Jason's Lyric, Dead Presidents,* and season two of FX's *Fargo.* The episode's themes of aspiration and assimilation are demonstrated in his character, a mogul in the making.

Christopher and Paulie are separately dismissive of Massive Genius's gangster credentials, even though the guy boasts his own link to Hesh[62] and owns a mansion and gun collection that puts Tony's to shame. The Italians and their associates (including Hesh, a wealthy suburban Jew who owns a horse farm that faintly resembles a plantation) are closer to mainstream acceptance than African Americans like Massive Genius, who are on a different track in the United States, with different obstacles and rules—a fact that Massive Genius seems to have accepted and resolved to work around, despite plainly resenting it.

One of the more striking features of "Hit" is the way it puts a previously incidental aspect of Tony's world—ingrained racism against black people—front and center, and examines it against aspects of American life other than crime. Like "Tennessee Moltisanti," "A Hit Is a Hit" is more didactic than the show's norm, with characters delivering speeches and trading accusations to underline the history and themes at play. This tends to work best in therapy scenes, where the entire point is to force the characters to talk through problems. But the script's determination to bluntly probe the issues from conflicting points of view is still intriguing because it sets the episode apart from the preceding nine. At times it feels as if Spike Lee had stepped in to guest-write certain scenes—not necessarily bad, because it shows that, even this early, *The Sopranos* is already confounding viewer expectations.

"Hey, whose fuckin' welfare check you gotta cash to get a burger around here?" Christopher shouts in a crowded takeout spot after taking Adriana to see *Rent*—a musical steeped in various forms of discrimination, including racism, homophobia and class-based snobbery. "Hairnet central," he adds a few moments later, then says defensively, "What am I, Mark Fuhrman?"[63] Christopher makes repeated racially tinged remarks as he and Adriana grab a post–Broadway show dinner. Both times, a black woman in the foreground turns around and glares at him, aghast, then returns her attention to the counter, more exasperated than furious; this obviously isn't the first time she's encountered such behavior. This is the context in which Massive Genius's life unfolds, whether he's negotiating deals with other rich men or ordering takeout burgers for his crew. In all of Massive

---

62 This is a strong Hesh episode. He's more in his element discussing rights and contracts with Massive Genius than Tony and his hangers-on, and less inclined to compromise than when Junior demanded a retroactive tax in "Denial, Anger, Acceptance." And yet, as he listens to the single that he took an undeserved writing credit on, and stares at photos of other acts from his old stable, you can see that Massive Genius at least temporarily forced him to think about whether his business practices were fair—even though he ultimately refuses to compensate G's relative.

63 Racist LAPD detective who found O. J. Simpson's bloody glove at the crime scene, but was discredited as a witness by Simpson's defense team after he lied on the stand about not having used the N-word during the preceding ten years. He pled no contest to perjury charges, which were eventually expunged from the record, and became a true-crime writer and talk show host.

Genius's scenes, we see him pushing to be accepted as a legitimate businessman (though with a somewhat overcooked "dangerous" edge, as when he intones "I do so love a good firearm in my hand" while laser-sighting Christopher's shoulder). His quest for legitimacy would mirror Tony's and Hesh's more closely if he weren't black and thus unable to pass for raceless, as non-WASPS are often able to do. The episode is aware of this defining difference and airs it through dialogue rather than pretend Massive Genius is on a level playing field with the others.

Despite his evident disadvantage, Massive Genius isn't afraid to push back when Hesh or the Italians try to out-alpha him. We see this in his very first scene as he confronts Christopher for his shabby behavior ("Your woman looks embarrassed."), emboldening a black police officer to tell another black patron, dismissively, "He's only bold because he's semi–hooked up with the Tony Soprano crew." This patron, Massive Genius's right-hand man Orange J (Bryan Hicks), invites Christopher and Adriana to visit the boss's crib, where "there's business to be done."

As it turns out, this "business" is only superficially about money; mostly it's about commanding respect, establishing a racial-ethnic pecking order, and using machismo and business smarts to pressure Hesh, an accused exploiter, to write a check for what amounts to cultural reparations. Hesh turns the negotiation into an ouch contest, telling Massive Genius, "You're talking to the wrong white man, my friend. My people were the white man's nigger when yours were still painting their faces and chasing zebras." (Hesh is white until someone who isn't white calls him white.) Hesh shrugs off Massive Genius's accusation that he stole from his relative, Little Jimmy, insisting, "Back then we were breaking all the rules," but Orange J counters, "You mean raping and pillaging." Massive Genius speculates that Hesh used Little Jimmy's royalties to buy horses, and Silvio says Little Jimmy ended up penniless because "he bought horse"—that is, his downfall was his own fault for using heroin, even though the Mafia might have supplied it. All of these scenes have an edge that belies their talkiness: it's as if the characters are engaged in an ongoing firefight with words.

"A Hit Is a Hit" also puts the biggest spotlight yet on Christopher and Adriana's relationship. Their scenes speak not only to the good eye David Chase had in spotting Drea de Matteo's potential in the pilot, but to Christopher[64] being more

---

64 Though Tony always refers to Christopher as "my nephew," Christopher here acknowledges that his actual tie to the family comes from being cousins with Carmela. An episode in a later season will clarify that the nephew thing is because Chris's late father Dickie was like an older brother to Tony, and also that Tony and Christopher's mother Joanne are related if you trace their ancestry back to the old country.

complicated than he's sometimes willing to admit. When the other wiseguys are celebrating the jackpot from the "Juan Valdez" murder with their girlfriends, Christopher just wants to go home to Adriana, and decides to invest his share of the money in her music-producing ambitions. His justification for her gifts in this area—"With how much you listen to the radio, you'd be good."—is as hilarious in its naiveté as Adriana's insistence that her ex-boyfriend Richie and his band Visiting Day (a whiny yet plausible Matchbox 20 wannabe) have what it takes to be big. But Adriana still comes out of the episode as more well-rounded and sympathetic than she entered it. She wants to be more than a mobster's girlfriend—or to be mother to Christopher's future children, spending all her time at the gym like Carmela "and her stretch marks." But, like Christopher with his screenwriting ambitions, she has only an outsider's dim understanding of how the music business actually works. Christopher's insistence that Massive Genius is only supporting her because he wants to have sex with her reinforces her doubts about her own gifts, as well as her fear that the rest of the world sees her as eye candy, too.[65]

As darkly funny as it is to watch Christopher order the recovering addict Richie to "spike up" and keep recording his monotonous single (right before hitting him in the back with a guitar), the episode is livelier when it focuses on Tony's side of things. Tony's encounters tease out different aspects of the episode's themes—like Massive Genius, Cusamano and his white-collar pals all love the *Godfather* films, and they're positively giddy to be playing a round of golf with a local crime boss—but they hit Tony hard. This subplot, too, is ultimately about assimilation, social mobility, and America's racial-ethnic totem pole. It dovetails with Massive Genius's quest for legitimacy as well as Hesh's nostalgia for the years when he made himself powerful.

The scenes between Tony and Cusamano's friends, and between Tony and Melfi, touch on the different ways Italian Americans have leveraged the social construct of "whiteness" from the mid-twentieth century through the end of the millennium—when they feel they have to, or when it's convenient. This is a subject rarely addressed on American television, in regard to any group: the internal jockeying for supremacy that mirrors the indignities a group suffers at the hands of the majority. We see how Italian Americans practice their own, intra-ethnic version of discrimination, by viewing some members of their tribe as more "white" than others, and thus more respectable; and how guys like Tony—whose ancestors

---

65 Massive Genius does seem interested in Adriana that way. Visiting Day is so plainly unremarkable that when G tells her that he could see them being filed under "Miscellaneous V" someday, it seems as if he's feigning interest because he'd like to file Adriana there, too.

hail from southern Italy, and often look less stereotypically "European" (white) in appearance than northerners—counter this soft bigotry by saying that their tormentors practice a neutered facsimile of Italiannness, like the coffee shops that vexed Paulie in "46 Long."

But this, too, can become a trap, as Tony concedes when he tells Melfi that Carmela is pushing him to get outside of his usual circle and "meet new people . . . Guys like me, we're brought up to think the *a Meddigan'* are fuckin' bores. The truth is that the average white man is no more boring than the millionth conversation over who shoulda won, Marciano or Ali."

"So am I to understand that you don't consider yourself white?" Melfi asks, underlining the idea at the heart of every other scene in this episode.

"I don't mean 'white' like Caucasian," Tony clarifies, then goes on to make the "respectable" Italians sound every bit as dull as he just said they weren't: "I mean a white man, like our friend Cusamano. Now, he's Italian, but he's *a Meddigan*. It's what my old man would've called a Wonder Bread wop. Y'know, eats his Sunday gravy out of a jar." Tony says he has mixed emotions about courting those sorts of Italian Americans because of "the guys"—his crew; men who, in Junior's words, would "be buried in their track suits."

His guys aren't wrong to be suspicious of the Wonder Bread types. Tony's misadventures at the private country club make him feel like a cartoon character, a deadly mook that well-heeled types can get a buzz from being around: the human equivalent of one of those illegal Monte Cristo cigars Tony gives Cooz. Tony genuinely tries to pump the swells for tips on how to invest his windfall, but they always steer the conversation back to the Mafia. You can see a little bit of the life go out of Tony's eyes each time this happens. That Cusamano, possibly the only other Italian American in the group, clearly has more in common with the non-Italians than with Tony makes things even more humiliating.

After a while, Tony decides to lean into the stereotype for fun, and tells the golf guys a ridiculous story about John Gotti[66] buying an ice cream truck. His prank on Cooz—giving him a mystery box to hang onto and obsess about—helps him reclaim his dignity, and sums up the gist of this rich episode. So much dehumanization is about fixating on externals—surfaces, categories, labels. Cooz just wanted a mystery box that he could show off to his rich friends. He never cared what was inside.

---

66 Boss of New York's Gambino Crime Family until 1992, when he was sentenced to life in federal prison for numerous Mob-typical crimes, including five killings he committed himself. He died behind bars of throat cancer in 2002.

	SEASON 1/EPISODE 11
"NOBODY KNOWS ANYTHING"	WRITTEN BY FRANK RENZULLI
	DIRECTED BY HENRY J. BRONCHTEIN

The Other Forever

"This is our friend we're talking about here." —**Tony**

After "A Hit Is a Hit" put most of the bigger season one stories on pause, "Nobody Knows Anything" presses play on one of the greatest home stretches of any TV season. It's an episode of portents and bad omens, death and destruction, and a tragic blurring of the lines between family and Family.

There's an early scene where Vin Makazian informs Tony that Big Pussy is now an FBI informant. It's notable not just because of Tony's utter contempt and dismissal for Makazian—a cavalier attitude that surely didn't send Vin jumping off the Donald Goodkind Bridge, but that contributed to larger feelings of hopelessness that put him there[67]—but because of the weather and the way the scene is shot. One of the more underrated aspects of the series is how well it captures the Garden State's extremes of weather. North Jersey heat is like being blinded and punched in the gut when you step outside, and the show's photography (by Phil Abraham) nails that. Here, the news that one of his oldest and closest friends has turned rat is among the worst things Tony Soprano could hear—at least until he finds out what his mother and uncle have been discussing at Green Grove—and the air around him in that scene looks and feels like doom, with the sky full of black clouds and the wind rustling Tony's shirt impotently around him.

The news sends ripples through Tony's entire crew, leading to uncomfortably tense moments like Paulie demanding that Pussy remove his shirt before their unscheduled schvitz.[68] But unsurprisingly, it weighs heaviest on Tony himself, particularly in a great therapy scene where he again turns to Dr. Melfi for unwitting management advice. As Melfi details why someone might have psychosomatic back pain, the camera pushes in on Tony, and you can see on James Gandolfini's face that Tony feels his friend's betrayal in his gut. He knows it, or

---

67 The most darkly potent moment of Makazian's suicide: he badges through the traffic jam—with the unwitting uniformed cop telling everyone in earshot that a police officer is coming through—so he can kill himself that much more quickly. Anyone who has spent much time in Jersey highway traffic can relate.

68 Paulie's often used as comic relief, but this is an excellent episode to show the serious side Tony Sirico could bring to the character and show. In addition to his locker room threat against Pussy, the earlier scene where he offers to unburden Tony of having to directly murder their friend lends the character more gravity than all previous episodes combined.

thinks he knows it, but he still needs to triple-check it, because friendships still matter deeply, even in the Family.

Livia has less equivocation about positioning Junior to order her son's murder. We've known going back to her Brendan Filone counsel that Livia has no qualms about arranging another human being's death. And we have ample evidence of how little she likes, never mind loves, Tony. Until now, she's viewed Tony's treatment more as an irritation that's given her license to enjoy complaining. But selling her house out from under her—seemingly keeping her imprisoned in Green Grove for life—is one sin too many, particularly right after Carmela bluntly labels her as a manipulator who's far more powerful than she wants anyone to believe. And Carmela is proven absolutely right in the scene where Livia walks Junior up to the idea of whacking Tony, even while acting pained to hear it discussed.

There's a lot of miscommunication here, but also situations where multiple things can be true at once. Makazian owing Pussy money, and even Jimmy Altieri being a rat, don't automatically exonerate Pussy. Tony surmises at the end that Vin's guy at the FBI "got his facts crossed" about the informant's identity because Jimmy and Pussy were arrested at the same time, but his theory has no proof. And while Tony isn't technically plotting a move against Junior when he meets with other wiseguys at Green Grove, that's only because he already made his move back in "Meadowlands" and has been secretly running the Family without Junior catching on.

The script and performances keep the viewer in an anxious state of not-quite-knowing. Pussy's back attack in the prologue might or might not be legit, but his display of agony is compelling enough to make us think Tony and Paulie would buy it. Vin's long close-up at the brothel as the guys help Pussy down the stairs sparks our suspicion, and the FBI raids a social club where Jimmy and Pussy are playing cards and finds guns and ammo there. As Pretty & Twisted's "The Highs Are Too High" plays on the soundtrack, the episode cuts between Pussy standing with his hands folded and an FBI agent futzing with a billiard ball at the pool table, and you may wonder whether Pussy is calm because he's been busted before or because he knows something the rest of the crew doesn't. Then he flees, which momentarily eliminates our suspicions. And then our feelings reverse again as Pussy gets instantly caught by a smiling agent who seems to have been waiting around the corner, handcuffs ready.

"Why the fuck would Pussy run?" Christopher says. "The guy's out of breath lifting his dick to take a leak." Right after that, Vin tells Tony, "He's wired for sound." A subsequent conversation between Tony and Pussy reestablishes the question of whether his back problems are legit and underlines Puss's concern about not being able to continue paying for his son's pricey college. It isn't until Silvio shades Vin's account because he owes Pussy tens of thousands of dollars that we begin to doubt he's actually a rat. Vin's suicide after his brothel arrest tragically cancels his debt, but also bars Tony from confirming Silvio's theory.[69] All he has now is his friend Pussy's word, plus fresh suspicions about Jimmy, who shows up at his house asking too many questions.

"You're a lucky man, Jimmy," Tony tells him in the basement, with an insinuating tone meant to flush out hidden motives. "Only a lucky prick like you would get pinched for a gun while he's out on bail for something else and still be out in time for dinner."

The episode's final scene—other than a brief glimpse of Tony contemplating the darkness that's coming beneath another ominous sky—takes us somewhere we've never been before: Mikey Palmice's house, as he fills in his wife JoJo (Michele Santopietro) on what's coming next for poor unsuspecting Tony, and Mikey's own position within the Family. Mikey's a goon and not nearly as clever as he thinks he is, but it's striking to see him come right out and tell JoJo what's coming. This level of either trust or recklessness has no equivalent in the Soprano household. Tony's machismo and street smarts demand this, but couples' *omertà* is a two-way street. We've already seen, especially during the evidence-hiding binge in "The Legend of Tennessee Moltisanti," that Carmela knows a bit of what goes on in her husband's business—at least where the guns and money are kept—and that she's good enough at interpreting context to avoid questions that could incriminate them both. Tony has never let her in on Family doings to to the degree that Mikey does here with JoJo.

Secrets are necessary in this line of work, but as Dr. Melfi notes, secrets can impose many burdens, physical as well as emotional. If all the members of Tony's family (and Family) were more open with each other, likely even more bloodshed would result, but there wouldn't also be this agonizing uncertainty—for Tony and the viewer—about what's actually happening, and what's coming next.

---

69 One unexpected and touching bonus in this episode is the revelation of Vin's apparently long-running affair with Debbie, the madam of the bordello (played by Karen Sillas of the great American independent film *What Happened Was...*). It illuminates Vin's personality in a way that makes him seem like a secret doppelgänger of Tony, and this makes Vin's earlier, fumbling attempts to be Tony's friend, rather than merely his fixer, now seem unbearably sad. The arrest, Debbie tells him, "was the straw" that made him kill himself, but he had a lot of problems, including his debt to Pussy. He was "not happy with how he turned out," and came to her for therapy as well as physical companionship. "Who wouldn't want to sleep with their shrink?" she asks.

SEASON 1/EPISODE 12
WRITTEN BY ROBIN GREEN & MITCHELL BURGESS
DIRECTED BY ALLEN COULTER

Tiny Tears

"To tell you the truth, I feel pretty good." —**Tony**

When the opening chants of Cream's "I Feel Free" play at the end of "Isabella," it's hard not to feel an electric charge. It's the perfect coda for one of the series' best and most memorable episodes, capturing not only Tony's elation and confidence after the botched hit knocked him out of his lithium-induced stupor, but also our joy at watching this show soar so high.

Despite its many moving pieces, particularly where we watch Junior and Mikey plot the hit on Tony while obstacles keep arising, "Isabella" is a simple episode. Between his feelings about Big Pussy's disappearance (and what it suggests about his old friend's possible betrayal) and Dr. Melfi's new drug cocktail, Tony's a zombie, shuffling around in his robe, sometimes barely verbal, numb to all feeling.[70] The depression and panic attacks were bad enough, but at least Tony still could function and feel occasional joy. "Tiny Tears" by Tindersticks becomes a great despondent soundtrack for his new stupor, and the sound department excels at putting us inside Tony's head by showing him distracted by a clock ticking and water dripping when he should be focused on Christopher discussing the Jimmy Altieri situation. Turning the camera ninety degrees and leaving it there throughout Tony's conversation with the family's housekeeper is a masterstroke, capturing in one image how deep depression shifts your perspective on life in a debilitating, unnatural way that eventually seems normal.

Tony's stuck in neutral, but he roars back to life when the two hitmen approach him by the newsstand. Time slows down further for a few moments as he spots them, making regular speed seem twice as fast when it resumes. The Tindersticks song recurs here—always a sign that a *Sopranos* music cue is commenting on the action rather than merely amplifying emotion or providing atmosphere—and the surging vocals, about letting the tiny tears making up a sea

---

70 Although Chase has said that no conscious reference was intended, there are points in season one where Livia and Tony both evoke the weird life in crime of Vincent "The Chin" Gigante, the boss of the Genovese Crime Family who ordered a failed hit on Gambino crime boss John Gotti in 1986. Dubbed "The Oddfather" by New York–area media, Gigante successfully avoided prosecution for thirty years by faking mental illness, wandering Greenwich Village in his bathrobe and slippers. Where Tony evokes him visually, particularly when puttering around at home, Livia's supposed dementia reminded some viewers of the arguments over whether the Chin was mentally incompetent or just a good actor.

finally pour out, reflect Tony's struggle between letting it all out to assuage his mental health, but also to hold it in, because that's what Gary Cooper (and most gangsters) would do. The chorus coincides with Tony crawling out of bed and going to the newsstand for orange juice and a racing form; the bridging image is a cinematic, low-angled wide shot, like something out of a Terrence Malick film or *Twin Peaks*, showing the wind raking through the kinds of old-growth trees that dominate suburban backyards like Tony's. But with the second botched bullet, the driver's side window shatters, the music cuts out abruptly, and the soundtrack becomes gunfire, curses, grunts, and squealing tires. Tony's murder of Febby showed he's not a man to be trifled with physically, but Tony's resistance is even more impressive given that he's being ambushed and has to emerge from a deep stupor to survive. It's animal instinct: Tony baring his fangs and growling, using the car as a weapon while exploiting his would-be assassins' bad aim. He crashes the SUV moments later, but we know from the cackle he lets out as he sees the second gunman tumble that Tony the bloody-toothed carnivore is back, and Uncle Junior—who already seemed very old, small, and powerless while cowering in the back of Mikey's car—is in big trouble. "To tell you the truth, I feel pretty good," Tony tells Melfi later. "Every fuckin' particle of my being was fighting to live."

Though Junior's ordered the hit, Livia set it in motion, but she seems unaware of having lit the fuse—or else is pretending not to comprehend the consequences. "Livia, you understand what's going on here?" Junior asks her, watching coverage of the botched hit on TV—that is, *Do you understand that Tony will figure out who ordered the hit?* "My son got shot, and he got away," she says, a factual report of what happened that takes no responsibility whatsoever. "What the fuck do we do now, Livia?" Junior follows up—*What's the next step now that there's a possibility of Tony moving against us?* "We go see him," she says, then bursts into tears: "He's my only son." Is Livia slipping into dementia, or only pretending to? "Who's that girl?" she asks Carmela at Tony's homecoming, referring to her granddaughter Meadow.

Sopranos fans who liked to romanticize the first season as more of a pure gangland saga than in later years remember moments like Tony fighting off the hitmen. But the episode also lingers on his pharmaceutical funk, the grievous and still-present wounds from his childhood, and his encounters with Isabella[71] herself, which turn out to be a pill-based hallucination. There's death and

---

71 That's Italian actress Maria Grazia Cucinotta as Isabella, probably best known for her role in *Il Postino*. The year 1999 was big for her in English-language productions, between this and playing an assassin out to get James Bond in *The World Is Not Enough*.

destruction galore, but the episode is largely about putting viewers inside Tony's head to appreciate how bad he's feeling about his life, Pussy, and his mother.[72] It's the first time the "objective" evidence we see and hear is contradicted by other characters' testimony—the first time the show tricks us into thinking we're seeing something we aren't. While it's easily explained by Tony's meds, the entire hallucination thread is presented with such quiet conviction, and is tied so intimately to Tony's suppressed knowledge that his own family is plotting to exterminate him, that it plays as *real*—and of course, emotionally speaking, it *is* real to Tony, because it's his subconscious screaming, *Your mother is incapable of real love, and she wants to kill you.* "Don't even go there," Tony warns Melfi, speaking of Livia's evident ill will, before Melfi has uttered even a syllable on the topic.

If Tony doesn't literally know of his mother's homicidal intent, and can't admit to himself that she means him no good, then deep down, at least, he's screaming for the kind of protective maternal figure he never had, and will invent one out of thin air if he must. Melfi, in her way, provides some version of that sort of support; therapists often nurture and listen as parents should, whatever our age. In the car with Melfi, Tony segues from denial of his mother's malevolence to an interpretation of a hallucination, guided by Melfi: in the early twentieth century, Isabella was suckling and comforting a newborn baby and calling it Antonio. "Even if it was the medication," Melfi says, "this fantasy of yours has meaning . . . Why the need for . . . a loving, caring woman now? . . . Your mother is always talking about infanticide." Tony tells her that he feels pretty good, and when he finds out who takes a shot at him, he's gonna feel even better.

But on some level, he already knows. Maybe he always has.

---

72 Having Tony hallucinate Carmela seeing Isabella is some nice misdirection for anyone starting to wonder if this woman was too good to be true. Later, at Tony's clandestine therapy session with Melfi shortly after the failed hit, Carmela gets her first look at her husband's mysterious, attractive therapist—and does not seem pleased.

SEASON 1/EPISODE 13

"I DREAM OF JEANNIE CUSAMANO" WRITTEN BY DAVID CHASE

DIRECTED BY JOHN PATTERSON[73]

Skyscraper Windows

"Cunnilingus and psychiatry brought us to this!" —**Tony**

"I don't die that fucking easy, Ma," Tony Soprano hisses at his mother as they wheel her down the hallways of her nursing home on a gurney. "I'm gonna live a nice, long happy life, which is more than I can say for you!"

It took him a long time to accept the truth. Denial will do that. Livia figured out her son wanted her dead before Tony figured it out. She believed he was onto her before he consciously was—or maybe she didn't know for sure, but decided not to take any more chances by siccing Artie Bucco on him, telling Artie through feigned Alzheimer's that Tony ordered the fire that destroyed Vesuvio. Tony initially takes Artie and his rifle as the next shot in his war with Junior, greeting him in Satriale's parking lot with, "You took their money?" He's still in denial, even after hearing it from Melfi and the FBI.

"I don't know what she told you, my mother, of all people," Tony says after Artie reveals where he got the information. Then he talks Artie into putting his rifle down, citing Livia's senility: "I swear to God, I didn't touch your place, Artie. My mother is confused." This may be the most impressive and difficult Tony Soprano lie yet. He sells it with total sincerity while trying to talk a tearful man out of shooting him, while grappling with the implications of his revelation: his mother not only wants to snuff him out, but took steps to have him killed.

When David Chase conceived this story as a self-contained feature film, he ended it with Tony suffocating his mother with a pillow. A version of "I Dream of Jeannie Cusamano" that ended with matricide wouldn't have lessened its power— if anything, it would've made the series even more of a 1999 conversation piece. But it would have deprived the show of a key source of conflict for Tony, and the audience of a great character and performance. And the fact that this oppressive monster once again manages to elude consequences gives the season undertones of futility and deep sadness. Tony can thwart every enemy in his life except the

---

73 This episode began a *Sopranos* tradition of John Patterson directing the finale of every season, which continued through the the fifth season. Patterson died during the long hiatus between seasons five and six, and the last two finales would be directed by Alan Taylor and David Chase. Patterson provides lots of memorable imagery here, like the extreme close-ups on Junior as he's being offered the plea deal; never have his eyeglasses looked larger, or sadder, than they do as he listens to evidence of his own insignificance.

most dangerous one—the one who brought him into the world and was supposed to love him unconditionally.

By this point, Livia has become so much larger than life—for us as well as Tony—that it seems plausible that she could have induced a mild stroke to avoid being murdered, or at least figured out how to fake the symptoms just as she did with dementia. "Dollars to donuts, this Alzheimer's thing is an act, so she can't be called on her shit," Carmela says. Livia's expression in her final scene is as open to interpretation as the artwork in Melfi's office and waiting room. Tony wails, "She's smiling!" as security pulls him away. Is she smiling at the anguish of her good-for-nothing son, or is it the curve of the oxygen mask, or the light in her eyes?

This delightful moment is all the more powerful because we had thirteen hours to build to it, rather than the two Chase would have had to play with in a feature. Small scenes like Tony bringing Livia the macaroons, or Dr. Melfi's many attempts to get Patient X to acknowledge his mother's danger, added up in the viewer's mind over time. Tony's struggle to contain his reaction as the FBI agents[74] play him the recordings of Livia and Junior plotting his murder, and his forlorn and self-loathing venting to Carmela, gain strength from all the time we've spent with these relationships. We understand Tony, and Gandolfini's performance, so well that all the actor has to do is blink a few times and shift the set of his jaw slightly to show just how badly all this hurts.

The architecture of the Tony–Livia relationship is astonishingly intricate in retrospect. It's driven not just by straightforward dialogue and definitive actions but subtle psychological and literary details, including the recurring talk of infanticide, Tony's two dreams about mother figures (the duck and Isabella), and the way that the idea of asphyxiation is woven through the season. Tony feels suffocated by his mother; the resultant panic attacks make him feel like he's suffocating; he now intends to deal with the problem by suffocating his mother (poetic justice), but arrives to find her lying on a gurney, a plastic mask on her face providing constant oxygen. ("That woman is a peculiar duck," Carmela tells Tony. "Always has been.")

In this whack-fest of an episode, which claims Jimmy the rat in a hotel room and Mikey Palmice in the woods,[75] Junior escapes Tony's wrath through sheer dumb luck: a U.S. attorney secures indictments against Junior and has him arrested along with fifteen other gangsters. The indictments are for white collar

---

74 A wonderful touch to that scene: Agent Harris looks mortified as the tapes play, not because he thinks they shouldn't be using them, but because he feels genuinely bad for a guy whose own mother would do this to him. Also, the finale introduces Harris's boss, Frank Cubitoso, played by Frank Pellegrino, yet another *Goodfellas* alum, and at the time also co-owner of New York restaurant institution Rao's.

75 Despite his brutal function, Mikey is essentially a comic character, but his final send-off in the newscast reminds us that he was a human being whose wife loved him. "He was so happy," she says. "He was going out to try out his new running shoes, you know. He told me that he loved me, and that he would be right back."

crimes that Tony wasn't involved in, and have nothing to do with the string of murders committed in his move against Junior, one of which (Chucky Signore) he carried out personally. But he's still an apple from a poisoned tree. The only reason we don't think he's as monstrous as his mother is because Livia is relentlessly sour and conniving (with occasional bursts of tearful self-pity), whereas the writers (and Gandolfini) keep indicating that there are redemptive qualities in Tony, such as his affection for his wife and kids (inconsistent and compromised as it is), his loyalty to his men (the loyal ones, anyway), his attachment to the ducks, his sharp sense of humor, and his vulnerability with Melfi.

It's Melfi, of course, who gets Tony to finally realize the true source of the plots against him. The two therapy sessions in this episode amount to a toxic explosion and a subsequent cleanup. "You don't want to go there," Tony warns Melfi at first, his voice and face leaving some doubt about who he's talking about when he says that he knows who hired the hitmen.

"Maybe *you* don't want to go there," Melfi says, shifting into that mode we first encountered in "Meadowlands" where she sounds like a literary critic looking for deeper meanings in her favorite show. She lays it all out for him, something therapists don't do except in extraordinary circumstances, such as, er, a patient's life being in danger. Tony's response when Melfi pushes him too far terrifies us and her, as this confident, smart, strong character seems tiny and weak with the bear that is Tony Soprano looming over her, profanely expressing his displeasure at her diagnosis of Livia. Here, though, as is always the case, Melfi keeps her composure. It isn't until Tony storms out that she lets her guard down and barricades the door.

The finale plays as if Chase and company spent months setting up an elaborate domino design, then began knocking them over to create something beautiful in the destruction.[76] Even the moves that don't work out for Tony—Livia's stroke, or Junior's lifesaving arrest—have a haunting twist, like Junior silently accepting that he was never actually boss of the Family. And as we've discussed going back to "College," it's striking how much happier and more at peace Tony seems whenever he's on the verge of killing somebody. Look at Tony during the meeting with the captains: a man who has just made small talk with two men whose murders he is in the process of arranging, and he couldn't be more pleased about it. Or look at how giddy he is—even his wife and kids make note of it—in the kitchen on the morning he thinks his guys are going to take down Junior's whole crew. This is the best part of his job, perhaps of his entire miserable life. Silvio torching Vesuvio, a scheme that could have been long forgotten, comes into play when Livia weaponizes Artie. The episode even climaxes Charmaine's arc when she tells Artie that

---

76 Tony pulling the gun out of the fish to kill Chucky feels very much like the product of a wiseguy—and a TV writer—who has watched many gangster movies and considered all the different places to hide a weapon.

she didn't go out and bury the hatchet with Carmela because she doesn't want the new Vesuvio to become "a Mob hangout" like the old one.

Artie's dilemma obviously lacks the dramatic heft of Tony's conflicts. But the episode ably uses him, Carmela, Father Phil, and even Dr. Melfi to illustrate what life is like living in Tony Soprano's shadow. Artie struggles at first with telling the insurance company about the arson revelation, but eventually chooses the path that benefits him most, letting Charmaine's happiness with the new place overwhelm his resentment, then mealy-mouthing about being a "yes" person rather than a "no" person. Father Phil seems dismayed by Artie's justifications, but any self-righteousness he might've felt is punctured when Carmela calls him out as a hypocrite, noting the joy he takes in acting as a surrogate husband for Mob wives (or, in Rosalie Aprile's case, Mob widows). That Carmela only is able to—or, perhaps, willing to—articulate this to Phil after seeing him touch Rosalie's hand shows that she's not without great flaws herself. But she also knows where her money comes from and where her loyalties must lie. When she's comforting Tony about the Livia news, she listens as he openly discusses his plans to take out Junior and Mikey—a Mikey-and-JoJo level of frankness—and doesn't flinch. This is the business she has chosen to marry into.

The season concludes with both of Tony's families, biological and professional, waiting out a torrential downpour at Vesuvio.[77] Tony makes a toast. In hindsight, it seems not just to celebrate his recent winning streak, but also to celebrate the impressive season of television that just concluded, and predict the wave of antihero-driven series that would appear in the wake of *The Sopranos*'s first year: "To my family. Someday soon, you're gonna have families of your own. And if you're lucky, you'll remember the little moments, like this, that were good."

---

77 If you thought one of the shots in the scene where Tony drives across the bridge seemed familiar, it's because it's also used in the opening credits: the eyes in the rearview mirror.

Season
Two

"GUY WALKS INTO A PSYCHIATRIST'S OFFICE"

SEASON 2/EPISODE 1
WRITTEN BY JASON CAHILL
DIRECTED BY ALLEN COULTER

A Very Good Year

"How many people have to die for your personal growth?" —**Dr. Melfi**

Throughout its first season, critics wrote about *The Sopranos* in terms that now seem condescending. One particularly notable piece was "From the Humble Mini-Series Comes the Magnificent Mega-Movie," written by lead *New York Times* film critic Vincent Canby in October 1999, six months after the first batch of episodes aired. Canby cites Rainer Werner Fassbinder's West German TV series *Berlin Alexanderplatz*, Dennis Potter's 1986 BBC series *The Singing Detective*, and season one of *The Sopranos* as "something more than mini-series. Packed with characters and events of Dickensian dimension and color, their time and place observed with satiric exactitude, each has the kind of cohesive dramatic arc that defines a work complete unto itself. No matter what they are labeled or what they become, they are not open-ended series, or even mini-series. They are megamovies. Such attitudes never entirely disappeared, thanks partly to the vestigial self-loathing of television writers, producers, and directors who still tend to describe any season of TV they're working on as as 'one long movie' and individual episodes as 'little movies.'"

This mentality resurfaced like a particularly virulent flu strain in 2017, during which half this book was written, regarding David Lynch and Mark Frost's *Twin Peaks: The Return*, an eighteen-part Showtime television series composed of one-hour episodes with opening and closing credits and an ongoing, serialized storyline that derived most of its power from two mythology-rich seasons and a prequel movie entirely dependent on them. Many film critics cited *The Return* as one of the year's best movies in the 2017 *Sight and Sound* poll and on personal lists. Why? Probably because it was directed by a "real" director rooted in quasi-experimental feature films, who filled the new series with surprising, horrifying, often mysterious artistic choices that still tend to be counted as "cinematic" rather than televisual. The notion that *The Sopranos* was notable because it was "really" a movie persisted throughout the run of the series. As late as 2007, film historian Peter Biskind (*Easy Riders, Raging Bulls*) introduced a *Vanity Fair* oral history of *The Sopranos*[1] by citing two long feature films, Luchino Visconti's *The Leopard*

---

1 "An American Family," *Vanity Fair*, April 4, 2007.

and Bernardo Bertolucci's *Novecento*, as comparison points, plus Norman Mailer's novels, before settling on "'personal' television writ large."

The "TV bad, movies good" mentality has proved especially durable. It's born of an era before *Twin Peaks*'s 1990 debut, which removed any lingering doubt that serialized TV made in the United States could be as innovative and revelatory as almost any feature. The reflexive dismissal of all of TV's artistic potential was never fair or fully informed—from the earliest days of television, every program format and length were bound by rules feature films didn't have to heed, yet still managed to amaze in ways films couldn't envision. Sneering at television seemed justified in the pre-cable, pre-streaming era of the 1970s, when American theatrical cinema's potential for personal expression was flowering, or at least catching up to international cinema a decade earlier, and TV was as much an appliance as an artistic medium. But it seems odd that the sneers have persisted, albeit diluted, among some cinephiles well into this century, despite the existence of *The Sopranos* itself, its countless would-be successors, and scripted TV's wholesale displacement of features as the centerpiece of American pop culture.[2] Despite the creative explosion in the past two decades, the medium's products still aren't allowed to rise or fall on their own merits, according to TV's innate characteristics; they are still judged against the best of other media and found lacking.

If Canby had waited to write his piece until he'd had a chance to watch the first episode of season two of *The Sopranos*, he might've cooled his jets. "Guy Walks into a Psychiatrist's Office" is engrossing, occasionally sublime, but mostly awkward, and its virtues and faults stem from its obligation to be a scripted, serialized TV show, rather than a "miniseries" or "mega-movie" or whatever. To intentionally mangle the network's slogan, *The Sopranos* is not just HBO, it's TV. As such, it has to deal with what professional TV writers call "housekeeping." Drastic plotline-driven character changes must make the show different but preserve familiar elements viewers have grown to love; otherwise you have to figure out how to walk the character back without seeming like you're rectifying a lapse in judgment.[3] The temptation to make grand, sweeping decisions is often too seductive to resist, because the resultant scenes are thrilling to write,

---

2   If this is victory, it's sure to be fleeting. Thanks to the ubiquity of electronic devices and streaming services like Netflix, Hulu, Amazon, Shudder, and Filmstruck, movies and TV are starting to blur together anyway, in a vast sea of "content." And increasing numbers of artistically ambitious filmmakers, such as Ezra Edelman (*O.J.: Made in America*) and Errol Morris (*Wormwood*) were riding the blur, releasing long-form works to theaters and television platforms simultaneously, which lets them qualify for Oscars and well as Emmys and get two distinct batches of reviews.

3   One notable example: *NBC's Homicide: Life on the Streets,* which gave its brilliant and eloquent detective Frank Pembleton (Andre Braugher) a catastrophic stroke at the end of season four to shake up the series and challenge the actor. Frank's rehabilitation was supposed to last a long time, but audiences complained that they didn't like seeing Frank struggle, so the writers had him recover with unrealistic speed.

shoot, act, edit, and ultimately share; afterward, the writers may realize that they actually alienated core fans, or create new constraints they must solve by cutting important characters or devising flimsy reasons to keep them.

The last two episodes of *The Sopranos*'s first season created all these problems and more. Nobody involved with the series worried about it much because they were busy meeting daily production challenges—plus, as Chase later said, he never expected it would last more than a season. Many of the show's distinctive elements, including its richly detailed sense of community and psychologically complex characters, would not have been possible in a movie, even a very long one. But as *The Sopranos* entered season two, it became obvious to the writers, and later to the audience, that the most pressing problem was how to make it work as TV.

At the end of season one, Uncle Junior, ostensible boss and Tony's most dangerous foe, was behind bars. Livia had been exposed as the mastermind of the recent moves against her son, and Mob associates as well as blood relatives were gossiping about the murderous secret behind their enmity. Tony came to Green Grove in the finale prepared to kill his own mother, only to back out after seeing that she'd suffered (or faked) a stroke. A rat had been exposed and snuffed out within Tony's crew, but another object of suspicion, Big Pussy, was still missing. Melfi, the hero's main source of insight and the closest thing to an ethical major character, had been driven from her practice. Tony's therapy was not a secret anymore, and in time could become common knowledge, a scenario that would make it harder for Tony to intimidate rivals and negotiate favorable terms. And, of course, the Family has to continue to find new ways to make money, even though, as Tony said in the pilot, they came in at the end of this thing.

Quite a set of conundrums for the writing staff. Our knowledge of them gives the opening of "Guy Walks into a Psychiatrist's Office" a hint of self-awareness, as if the series is tallying up challenges in the guise of scene setting.

Luckily for the show and for us, this is the finest music montage the series has staged thus far. A late-period Frank Sinatra classic, "It Was a Very Good Year," starts to play over the tail-end of an opening scene where a group of young people—including an Asian man impersonating Christopher Moltisanti—take a brokers' exam, and continues for the song's full length as director Allen Coulter moves through the world of *The Sopranos* in a manner reminiscent of the end of Federico Fellini's *I Vitelloni*.[4] The song's narrator recounts his entire life in a series of vignettes at different ages; the lyrics complement the elliptical nature of cinema and television storytelling, as well as the more basic fact of our jump forward in time. We pass Livia in her hospital bed as she stares at us defiantly,

---

4   In a series of gliding lateral tracking shots that evoke the movement of a locomotive, the film's hero leaves his small town by train while imagining his friends literally sleeping their lives away.

briefly (and unexpectedly) breaking the fourth wall. Tony plays cards in the back office of the Bada Bing and then accepts a cash tribute from captain Ray Curto (George Loros), whom Tony had approached as a potential replacement for Jackie Aprile Sr., early in season one. An orange-jumpsuited Uncle Junior walks in a single-file line behind bars, a once-powerful mobster now just another prisoner. A sinuous camera move that starts behind AJ's head reveals him staring into a mirror at a now visibly adolescent face, complete with the beginnings of a strong jawline, as Sinatra reminisces about being twenty-one. Melfi accepts patients at her motel. Paulie Walnuts mechanically fucks an unidentified woman who (judging from the block-glass backdrop, high heels, and fake breasts) might be a Bada Bing dancer. The FBI (seen only as hands arranging notecards on a corkboard) struggles to discern the true organization of the Family.[5] Wannabe screenwriter Chris watches the climax of the 1948 gangster film *Key Largo*[6] with seemingly rapt interest, until the camera, following his head, reveals no computer or notepad, just a line of cocaine.[7] Silvio gets a new suit and shoes. The brief scene of Tony teaching Meadow to drive is matched by Sinatra crooning about riding in limos with well-heeled girls. The dissolve from there to Irina riding Tony (with Frank mentioning the girls' chauffeurs) underlines the baseline sleaziness of Tony's existence, while tricking the viewer into thinking he went straight to his mistress's apartment after tutoring Meadow.

Then, as Sinatra winds down by discussing his autumn, the scene zeroes in on Tony and Carmela's marriage. The unfaithful husband sneaks into the house in the middle of the night, disposing of incriminating clothing and climbing into bed beside his wife. Carmela looks at Tony, who is pretending to sleep. Tony opens his eyes, not realizing Carmela was staring at him in an accusatory way, and is surprised to see her looking back. Carmela turns and faces the other way—an unmistakable rebuke. It's also reminiscent of Carmela's very first exchange in the pilot, when she alludes to Tony's unfaithfulness with a loaded remark. "I'll get home early from work," he says. "I'm not talking about work," she replies.

But then, so is this episode, the first proper scene of which has the deadpan timing of a joke setup: Tony goes to get the newspaper as he has so many times before, only to find Pussy lying in wait at the end of the driveway. Tony brings him down the basement, as he did while assessing whether Jimmy Altieri was a

---

5   This notecards-on-corkboard system is similar to how TV writers "break" stories while plotting out seasons of shows like *The Sopranos*.

6   Much of *Key Largo* is set inside a hotel just before and during a hurricane. The first season of *The Sopranos* climaxed with a storm that drove many of its key characters to seek shelter inside Vesuvio.

7   Christopher's drug problems seem much worse. He's clearly addled in most of his scenes, including the one with Adriana, Sean Gismonte, and Matt Bevilaqua at the bar where he asks his girlfriend to have a drink and slaps her after she complains that he left the gas burning on after "cooking your shit" and calls him a junkie.

rat. They reconnect awkwardly. Pussy insists that his back problems are real and berates Tony and his men for equating infirmity with betrayal. Tony draws Pussy into an embrace, then ruins a warm moment by getting too handsy, as if he's trying to pat Pussy down for a wire (and he is).

The subsequent dance between Tony (and Tony's crew) and the prodigal Pussy is unusually drawn out for a *Sopranos* subplot. But it's characteristic of an episode in which the storytelling is cleaner but also more minimalistic than season one's. The character moments are more leisurely and peculiar here than in any season one episode—Pussy's reintegration into the old crew is built around Silvio's Pacino-as-Corleone impressions, capped by the insinuating "Our true enemy has yet to show his face."—and the parallels between subplots are more glancing. Livia and Pussy's stories revolve around possibly faked health problems,[8] and both characters get a chilling moment in which they stare right into the camera, as if scrutinizing the spectator's attention—unseen in Livia's case; Tony's in Pussy's case—to assess whether their performance is believable. In a very long, initially unexplained sequence, the acting capo of Junior's crew, Philly Parisi (Dan Grimaldi), gets shot and killed by Junior defector and soon-to-be-Soprano soldier Gigi Cestone (John Fiore), as revenge for spreading stories about Tony's mother problems. Tony then calls Melfi to tell her it's safe to return to her practice; but despite this conversation and a subsequent encounter in a diner, Tony does not return to therapy with Melfi in this episode, and has to be content with discussing his problems with male friends and indulging in wordless domestic rituals with Carmela (like letting her heat him up some pasta).

As is typical in TV-drama season openers, important new characters get introduced. Chris becomes the boss of two low-level Soprano associates, Sean Gismonte (Chris Tardio) and Matt Bevilaqua (Lillo Brancato Jr.[9]), hapless meatheads who worship Tony and act as over-the-top enforcers in a boiler room operation selling worthless stock to gullible seniors. Tony's sister Barbara (Nicole Burdette), previously mentioned but not seen, shows up for a backyard party, along with Carmela's parents Hugh and Mary DeAngelis (Tom Aldredge and Suzanne Shepherd), who hate Livia and wouldn't be there if she weren't incapacitated, unavailable, and banned from the premises by Tony.

---

8   Janice's carpal tunnel isn't hugely convincing, either, so we might have a health fakery trifecta.

9   Before *The Sopranos*, Brancato Jr. had his breakthrough role playing the teenage version of the main character in Robert De Niro's 1993 directorial debut *A Bronx Tale*. Brancato Jr. had trouble with the law in the years after his Sopranos stint, culminating in a December 10, 2005, incident in the Bronx in which an off-duty police officer, Daniel Enchautegui, interrupted two men causing a disturbance in a vacant house next door to his and was shot and killed in a subsequent gunfight. Police arrested Brancato Jr. with another man, forty-eight-year-old Steven Armento—the father of Brancato Jr.'s then-girlfriend—and he was eventually convicted of burglary; he served almost five years. Armento was convicted of first-degree murder for firing the killing shot and sentenced to life without parole.

The most important new character by far is Janice—like Barbara, only talked about (and glimpsed briefly as a child in season one's "Down Neck"). As played by Aida Turturro,[10] she skips into the Sopranos's world and proceeds to dominate her kid brother. The script isn't shy about stating what's happening here psychologically. Janice, who had left Tony behind to care for their mother, is now consciously replacing her: claiming her unused car and house, waltzing into the Soprano home that Livia herself can no longer enter, and sticking up for Livia in talks with Tony and Barbara. Sometimes Livia even seems to be speaking through Janice. "Some family reunion," she tells Barbara at the barbecue. "The woman who birthed them all is barred from the premises."

"I'm still a little fat kid to her!" Tony rages. Maybe, but she's also an emotional infant whose presence further infantilizes Tony. "You look like a teenager," Tony says. "My therapist says I'm regressing," Janice replies unironically. The character's blend of hippie-dippie mysticism (she's calling herself Parvati), secondhand spirituality, and instinctive con artistry makes her the equal of the established characters, and gives Turturro—Gandolfini's physical and vocal match—a role so fingernails-on-a-chalkboard real that when adult Janice first appeared, the water cooler debate the following morning revolved around how much viewers could endure of her, how quickly she might be killed off, and by whom, and how painfully. No similar discussions ever happened about Tony, an actual murderer.

Janice's introduction gives *The Sopranos* a much-needed, perfectly timed jolt of energy. It also rectifies a storytelling problem: Livia is so far removed from the main action at this point that she can't sink her talons into Tony as easily anymore.

More pointedly than other episodes, "Guy Walks into a Psychiatrist's Office" fixates on generational changeover. At the party, Barbara and Janice agree that Tony reminds them of their father. Professionally, Tony is already the new Junior, and everyone but the FBI knows it. Christopher is becoming a low-level authority figure, even as he rejects Adriana's sincere concern and behaves irresponsibly while Sean and Matt carry on like his brainless overgrown sons. Janice could become a version of Livia eventually, but despite her powerful entrance, her mother's presence looms over family discussions and arguments—banished, but not forgotten. Tony talks about her as often as he did when they were still on speaking terms. "She's dead to me," he says twice in this episode, as if wishing could make a thing be true. Tony and Carmela visit Livia's house and find it vandalized, probably by teenagers from the nearby high school. "Fucking jackals," Tony says. Jackals feed on the dead and dying. Another wish.

---

10   The cousin of actors John, Nicholas, and Natalie Turturro, she'd previously appeared in the films *True Love, What About Bob?*, and *Sleepers.*

SEASON 2/EPISODE 2
WRITTEN BY ROBIN GREEN & MITCHELL BURGESS AND FRANK RENZULLI
DIRECTED BY MARTIN BRUESTLE

Pot Meets Kettle

"You don't know what goes through this mind of mine." —**Livia**

Viewed apart from "Guy Walks into a Psychiatrist's Office," "Do Not Resuscitate" feels very minor—a borderline placeholder.[11] But if you watch it back to back with the premiere, it feels like the second half of a two-parter. We learn that Pussy's back problems are real, and also that he's an FBI informant who flipped after getting caught trafficking heroin to pay for his son's college (his handler, Skip Lipari,[12] reveals that he's "been on our tit since '98"). Uncle Junior is allowed to leave jail for health reasons and wait for his upcoming racketeering trial under house arrest. And Livia draws Janice—her younger, shadow self—into her clutches through a combination of cutting negativity and quasi-therapeutic conversation, then hooks her deep by suggesting that her beloved Johnny hid money in their house.

The Livia–Janice/Tony–Junior duets are suffused with dark humor and intimate psychological manipulations. There's no love between Junior and Tony at this point: the nephew tells his uncle's caretaker Bobby Baccalieri (Steven Schirripa[13]), aka "the last man standing," that he's cutting Junior's income to "subsistence level." But Tony has enough of a shared, familial instinct for self-protection to order the disappearance of Green Grove's toupéed boss for daring to reveal that Tony nearly smothered Livia—information he wouldn't have had without Junior. His uncle is a treacherous, thin-skinned old man, but he's also his father's only brother, and the image of Tony carrying Junior out of his own home like a child (after his bathtub fall) has a primordial charge.[14] So does Junior's plea to "make things right with your mother," a request motivated by his desire to get

---

11 At the season two premiere at Manhattan's famed Ziegfeld Theater, HBO didn't even screen this episode, jumping from "Guy Walks . . ." to the third installment, "Toodle-Fucking-Oo," which introduced a significant new character.

12 Prolific character actor Louis Lombardi, often in crime and action films and TV shows, including *24*, *Mob City*, *The Usual Suspects*, and *Spider-Man 2*.

13 Formerly the entertainment director of the Riviera in Las Vegas, Schirripa was inspired to pursue acting after working as an extra in *Casino*. Although he's best known for playing Bobby, he gained a different following as Ben's dad on the ABC Family series *The Secret Life of the American Teenager*.

14 The music is Ella Fitzgerald and Benny Goodman's 1937 version of "Goodnight, My Love," which got radio play when Junior was young.

the whole family united before Junior's trial, but also by a sincere wish to give Tony and Livia the "Mother and Child Reunion" that Janice sings of during her weed-scented ride home from Green Grove.

Janice and Livia's scenes are fascinating for their mix of lies, confessions, and genuine vulnerability. Livia idolizes her late husband in ways that don't match the man Tony described to Melfi. But there are moments when Livia seems to acknowledge a grimmer reality that scarred her, to the extent that an ice-blooded manipulator with a borderline personality can be scarred. It's partly about raising three children she couldn't really love or connect with, but also about having a volatile gangster husband. "You think it was easy for me?" Livia asks Janice. "You don't know the kind of man your father was. Nobody knows. Nobody knows what I went through." But of course she eventually turns things back to her feelings of abandonment by Tony: "One thing I could tell you: it would kill him to see me now."

Janice is almost touching in her scenes with Livia. She really does crave a mother and child reunion, even though, by the end, she's hallucinating Livia's face on a stairwell sign in a matricide scenario sparked by Livia's citation of *Kiss of Death*.[15] But, like every other character, she can't see herself or others clearly enough to understand why such a scenario isn't possible. *The Sopranos* is a non-stop parade of egocentric oddballs who think they're the only person that sees the world and themselves clearly. "She's a complete narcissist, you know?" Janice, slags her mother. "Me, me, me." Pot meets kettle again in the scene where Tony rips into Bobby about his weight.[16] "Fat fuck," Bobby says, after Tony is out of earshot. "You should look in the mirror sometime, you insensitive cocksucker." Livia tells Carmela that she thinks she did "a pretty good job" raising two out of three of her children. Carmela replies: "They are all. Unhappy."

The script further fleshes out ideas of generational succession through a construction subplot that connects the Soprano Family more intimately with the northern New Jersey unions, introducing two African American community activists, the Reverends Herman James Junior (Gregalan Williams[17]) and Senior (Bill Cobbs[18]). The scenes involving the Jameses also build out the show's

---

15 1947 gangster film, the most famous scene of which finds gangster Tommy Udo (Richard Widmark) binding an associate's mother to her wheelchair and fatally pushing her down a flight of stairs.

16 Bacala's first appearance is shot to suggest that his stomach always enters a room well before the rest of him. Schirripa was actually wearing a fat suit at this point in the series, though he later put on enough weight that production felt comfortable with his natural physique.

17 Beach cop Garner Ellerbee on *Baywatch,* among other recurring TV roles; author of four books, including *A Gathering of Heroes: Reflections on Rage and Responsibility—A Memoir of the Los Angeles Riots.*

18 A bourbon-voiced scene stealer with over forty years' worth of acting credits, Cobbs makes such a powerful impression here as the World War II veteran and social justice warrior that it's a shock to realize that he only appears in two scenes.

complicated, unstable take on the relationship between Italian Americans and African Americans. The mobsters whose relatives hail from the Boot are often shown complaining about how mainstream society demonizes them while appropriating their culture, using victim language to gain sympathy. Yet they say racist things without fear of censure; subcontract felonies, including hits, to black criminals, while impugning their competence; and blame them for ills they had little to do with. This could be described as a symbiotic relationship if the two groups had comparable economic and social power, but they don't. The European immigrant experience is different from that of slaves' descendants for a lot of reasons, starting with the inconvenient fact that the Italian Americans (as well as Mob-affiliated Jews like Hesh, and recent emigrants from the former USSR like Irina) can label themselves as white to gain advantage in America, and blacks generally can't (see also "A Hit Is a Hit" on reparations).

The episode's racial tension is woven into a larger story about parents and children and the giving and taking of power. The elder James's "Never underestimate a man's determination to be free" is a Bible reference that resonates politically and racially. Both Cobbs's insinuating delivery and Gandolfini's conflicted but respectful reaction make it land hard enough to be remembered near the end, when the younger James talks to Tony about his recently departed dad and they bond over angst about the future. That the younger James is corrupt—playing both ends against the middle, as Agent Lipari claims Pussy is doing—gives the scene an edge of lament. Like nearly everyone else, these two men are in thrall to money. If he and Tony typify the next generation of power, the future will be as dire as the present.

"TOODLE-FUCKING-OO"	SEASON 2/EPISODE 3 WRITTEN BY FRANK RENZULLI DIRECTED BY LEE TAMAHORI

Old School

"There has to be consequences." —**Carmela**

"Toodle-Fucking-Oo" is the first genuinely scary episode of season two, thanks to the introduction of Richie Aprile (David Proval[19]), brother of the DiMeo Family's acting boss, the late Jackie Aprile Jr. Once a capo, he's now an entitled monster who's trying to get things going again with his old flame, Janice,[20] a "Vishnu-come-lately" (Tony's words) who's been away for a while herself. But the whole hour, including Richie-free scenes, has an undertone of dread, thanks to the pervasive feeling that order is fragile and chaos could engulf this world at any moment. "Let's not overplay our hand, because if she finds out we're powerless, we're fucked," Tony advises Carmela, commiserating over Meadow, who presided over the desecration of her grandmother's house. "See, that's what this is about: ego and control," Janice tells Tony and Carmela, addressing Meadow's situation but also summing up the hour.

While not a great *Sopranos* episode, it's a quintessential one. It draws connections between characters who anchor three very different, adjacent subplots (Meadow, Melfi, and Richie) without reducing them to case studies or turning this into a neatly labeled "theme episode." All the major players here want to save face. Authority figures like Tony—and Carmela, where their daughter is concerned—don't want to have to exercise it in ways that could make them seem unlikable. Comparatively powerless characters, like Richie and Meadow, try to grab as many indulgences as they can. But the episode doesn't oversimplify. There are points of overlap and contradiction, and places where the script seems to be of two minds on a moment or character. This is vastly more compelling than pinning every character to a designated psychological or philosophical spot, like the FBI's notecard-covered corkboards.

The title comes from "Toodle-oo," the phrase Melfi blurts out after running into Tony at a restaurant with his crew, and that she later describes to her own

---

19 Proval's breakthrough was in 1973's *Mean Streets*. He read for the role of Tony Soprano, played the menacing father Marco Fogagnolo on *Everybody Loves Raymond,* and was Eddie Murphy's acting coach on *48 Hrs*.

20 Janice and Richie are written as contemporaries who dated in high school, but Aida Turturro is twenty years younger than David Proval, and the age difference is apparent.

therapist, Dr. Elliot Kupferberg (Peter Bogdanovich[21]), as characteristic of "young girls [who] are not accountable for their behavior . . . 'Toodle-oo' was the action of a ditsy young girl, and I regressed into the girl thing to escape responsibility for abandoning a patient." Meadow evades responsibility in her own way, sloughing off blame for the house party disaster onto her buddy Hunter, playing on her parents' sympathies by reminding them how hard she's studying, and flattering them by describing how much worse things might have been if she hadn't exercised the restraint they taught her.[22] "I could've taken ecstasy, but I didn't!" Meadow yells.

It's hard to tell exactly how much power Meadow had to defuse the party. She sounds sincere when insisting things just got out of hand. But after her father busts her, she starts behaving like a classic older teen, testing limits, seeing how well she can game the system by making Tony and Carmela think they've punished her when they've done no such thing. (The smirk on Meadow's face as she leaves the kitchen after convincing her parents to take away her Discover card has a touch of Livia to it.) Jamie-Lynn Sigler's portrayal of Meadow is one of the most believable, unsentimental portraits of suburban teenage girlhood—a performance that captures the character's oblivious sweetness and her scathing disapproval (she has a magnificent eye-roll, and an even better "give me a break" eye-pop). This might be her best showcase yet, with her personal high point the scene where she and Hunter make grilled cheese sandwiches and hot chocolate, singing along with TLC's "No Scrubs" and turning the kitchen into a disaster area. This scene makes it easy to picture Meadow failing to notice Livia's house getting trashed. Among other things, *The Sopranos* is about consumption and waste, and failing (or refusing) to notice when you've made a mess of things. "When are they gonna realize that we're practically adults, responsible for ourselves?" Meadow whines to Hunter, as she pours hot milk into two mugs, spilling half of it.

Meadow punishes herself by cleaning up Grandma's house—a grand gesture, maybe for her alone, since Meadow doesn't announce it and Tony only sees it by chance. The key to Meadow's gesture might be the way she looks at the $20 Tony gives her: *this is dirty money*. Meadow calls her parents' punishment, which she herself devised, "so hypocritical, too, when you think how my dad makes a living." Maybe Meadow wouldn't accept punishment from her parents because of its hypocrisy. Dad's a gangster and Mom is content to spend his money and pretend

---

21 Though best known as director of '70s films like *The Last Picture Show* and *Paper Moon*, a young Bogdanovich studied acting under legendary teacher Stella Adler, and has periodically stepped in front of the camera throughout his career. Chase previously used him on *Northern Exposure*.

22 Don't lie. You did this, too. Admit it.

she doesn't know how he makes it. The lack of respectable authority figures could be devastating for Meadow because, as Janice correctly notes, she's embracing her biological destiny, acting out and testing boundaries—a pivotal time for her, and a terrible time to be living with parents who have no moral authority.

Richie reenters society to discover the world has moved on without him. He got ten years for dealing heroin, but his old pal Peter "Beansie" Gaeta (Paul Herman[23]), who used to help him move the drugs, escaped punishment, invested his gains, and now owns three pizzerias. Richie thinks he deserves a regular Saturday envelope as back pay—emotional as well as financial restitution from a former accomplice who never contacted him in prison—and won't take no for an answer. The violence Richie employs in this episode is sickening even by *Sopranos* standards, underscoring the show's commitment to physical realism as well as a half-horrified, half-mesmerized intensity; damaged bodies stay damaged for a long time.[24] Richie leaves Beansie bedridden, rods drilled into his bones. He might never walk again. Using Carmela's phrase regarding Meadow, there have to be consequences.

Unfortunately, often there aren't. On this show, as in life, not everyone who breaks a rule or exercises awful judgment suffers identical penalties; some don't suffer them at all. Beansie doesn't report Richie to the police because—to quote Beansie, Richie, and Tony at various points—they're "old school" gangsters. Tony doesn't punish Richie because Richie's a made man, a captain, and the brother of Jackie, a man Tony loved and admired. He warns Richie to never forget he's the boss. Richie's cobra stare and sarcasm confirm that he's not scared of Tony, just reined in by the power of Tony's office.[25] There's no logic or sanity to any of this. It's as if the story is being dictated by a sadistic God.

---

23 Herman has appeared in many notable American crime dramas, including *Once Upon a Time In America, At Close Range, Heat,* and *We Own the Night.* He also played Vince's accountant Marvin on *Entourage.*

24 This episode's director, New Zealand–born filmmaker Lee Tamahori, came to international attention for 1994's *Once Were Warriors,* a film about addiction, domestic violence, and toxic masculinity in Maori households that includes several beatings as stark as the one Richie inflicts on Beansie.

25 "I thought I told you to back the fuck off Beansie," Tony yells after Richie has run his car over Beansie multiple times. "I did," Richie sneers. "Then I put it in drive."

"COMMENDATORI"

SEASON 2/EPISODE 4
WRITTEN BY DAVID CHASE
DIRECTED BY TIM VAN PATTEN

Con te Partirò

"The 'tude, and the fucking medieval outlook." **—Janice**

"Commendatori," which sends Tony, Christopher, and Paulie to Naples, Italy, was widely considered the first bad *Sopranos* episode when it debuted. There's plenty of half-baked ziti on this plate, but the episode has its compensations, particularly its portrait of the Bonpensiero marriage and the strain Pussy's informant status puts on it. And it's worth asking what fans expected from the hour anyway, given what sort of show *The Sopranos* was shaping up to be—and considering how it prepares us from scene one for the Italy trip to be frustrating and mostly uneventful.

The opening finds Tony and his crew in the back room of the Bing trying and failing to watch the new DVD of *The Godfather Part III* with deleted scenes, and having to be content with Tony describing his favorite scenes from *Part II*,[26] the one where Vito goes back to Sicily: "The crickets. The great old house." Then Paulie beats the DVD player with his shoe.

The Italy trip itself is a disappointment for all concerned except Paulie, who's blissfully happy while uncovering what he thinks is his inner Italian. He's just a rich American tourist with a vowel at the end of his last name, repeating the same handful of phrases, but as far as he's concerned, he had a profound experience. Chris shoots up immediately and stays high the entire time, never goes to the topless beach or the crater like he swore he'd do, and buys Adriana a gift at Newark Airport after returning. Naples is portrayed as exotic only in that it's a place other than New Jersey with vague ancestral significance to the crew; it's depicted as just another semi-important European city with gorgeous old architecture but the usual problems, including corruption, crime, and dirty streets and beaches. "Listen, I've been to Italy many times," Janice tells Carmela, "and really, you're not missing all that much. The amount of sexual harassment that I was subjected to!" Series creator David Chase gets his first cameo here, playing the long-haired guy in the sidewalk cafe who reacts to Paulie's *"Commendatori . . . Buongiorno!"* with complete indifference.

---

26 While discussing *Part II*, Silvio again busts out his Michael Corleone impression, cracking most of the guys up as he snarls the film's famous lament of betrayal, "I know it was you, Fredo," while the camera cuts to the face of the traitorous Big Pussy.

The guys expect a *Godfather Part II*-style meeting with Zi Vittorio (Vittorio Duse[27]), an old don whose family is distantly related to the Sopranos, to cement Tony and Junior's new stolen-car export deal,[28] but feel disappointed and disrespected when the don doesn't meet them at the airport; it turns out that he is suffering from dementia, and (like Paulie) can only blurt handfuls words in a language other than his own. His daughter Annalisa (Sofia Milos[29]) briefly seems poised to become a flesh-and-blood version of Isabella, the dream woman from season one, but the episode can't decide whether to treat her as a three-dimensional character or a mysterious, smokin' hot object onto which Tony can project his issues (and sex drive[30]). Although they share a few obvious points of connection (e.g., they're both wrapped up in elder care issues; Annalisa's situation blends elements of Tony's relationships with both Junior and Livia), there's no chemical spark, or even of what Annalisa might represent to Tony, so when she announces a desire to have sex with him, there's no way to gauge if his "no" costs him anything (although his announcement that he doesn't shit where he eats rings true).

Mostly the trip seems useful to Tony as a means of getting outside of his own head and trying to think about his business in fresh ways. His idea of claiming Furio Giunta (Federico Castelluccio[31]), a long-haired enforcer with decent English and zero Jersey connections, is completely surprising, but makes sense in retrospect given the episode's other major plotline, Pussy's desperation and treachery, and the destruction it's wreaking on the local (criminal) community. It makes sense that Tony would clear his head a bit in Naples, ponder all the drama people he's known for decades are causing, and weigh bringing in completely new blood: an outsider with no connection to anything or anyone except the man who hired him. Of course, while he strategizes ways to protect himself and his end of the business, he overlooks how badly he hurt Carmela by not inviting her to Naples.

---

27 Played Don Tommasino in *The Godfather Part III*; a staple in both Italian and American cinema since Luchino Visconti's debut feature *Ossessione*.

28 The carjacking feeds into the show's fascination with how the Italian American Mob interacts with African American criminals. Two black criminals rob a white family of their SUV at gunpoint in Manhattan, and the father yells a racial epithet and adds, "Who else?" Cut to Tony looking at Polaroids of cars he ordered stolen. Strangely, the family is listed in the credits as the Sontags, presumably after Susan Sontag, author of numerous books of cultural criticism, including two that are particularly relevant to *The Sopranos: Against Interpretation* and *Regarding the Pain of Others*.

29 Half-Swiss, half-Italian actress with roles in more than twenty TV series, including Yelina Salas in *CSI: Miami*.

30 The dream image of Tony mounting Annalisa while dressed as a Roman centurion is the single worst filmmaking choice on the show to date.

31 Born in Naples, but mostly raised in New Jersey, Castelluccio had a few acting credits prior to playing Furio (including several episodes of *Another World*), but was primarily a visual artist.

The strongest moments happen back in Jersey. Pussy and his wife Angie (Toni Kalem[32]) are being torn apart by Pussy's informing, which Angie doesn't know about. She only knows that he disappeared for months, and that when he first returned home and she heard his voice again, "I wanted to vomit"; that she thinks about suicide now, and wants a divorce. Carmela, meanwhile, is being pushed by Janice (in a scene that makes Janice sound like Livia without malice aforethought) to see Tony as a poisonous exemplar of a patriarchal subculture: "These OG pricks especially, with their *goomars* and their prostitutes. Emotional cripples. And they expect their wives to live like the fuckin' nuns up at the Mount Carmel College . . . Madonna/whore's a full equation, I believe, with clothes, appliances, and houses."

"You *are* talking about me, about us," Carmela says.

"Carmela, no," Janice says, then says, "I dunno. That a woman of your intelligence is content to ask so little from life and from herself?"

Then this scene—maybe the strongest one in the episode, consisting of nothing more than two women talking in a kitchen—pivots as Carmela realizes she's being lectured on her lack of feminist virtue by a woman newly dating a made guy. "Marriage is a holy sacrament, " she says, "family is a sacred institution . . . and you, trying to fan the flames with Richie Aprile, of all people?" When Janice insists that Richie's prison experience gives him "a sensitivity to the plight of women," Carmela laughs in her face.

Despite many strong moments in the episode, "Commendatori" feels like a missed opportunity. The script keeps threatening to connect Carmela and Angie's disappointment in marriage to disappointment with Italy itself, perhaps to comment on the dangers of getting hung up on a sentimentalized ideal, or just to underline the sorts of experiences a woman like Annalisa has in Naples that Carmela could never have in North Caldwell; but the episode never quite comes together, despite the strategic threading of Andrea Bocelli's "Con te partirò"[33] throughout. Its seeming belief in the inevitability of disappointment and the importance of managing expectations feels like an insurance policy against viewer complaints. The Naples subplot didn't need to be a masterwork on the order of the Sicily flashbacks in *Part II*, but most of it isn't as memorable as the soggiest scenes in *Part III*. Just when you think you're in, it pulls you back out.

---

32 A veteran character actress whose career stretches from *Baretta* and *Starsky & Hutch* through *Picket Fences* and *The Sopranos*, Kalem also wrote and directed a thoughtful 1999 film adaptation of Anne Tyler's novel *A Slipping-Down Life*. A different, uncredited actress played Angie briefly in season one, just as Steven Van Zandt's wife Maureen begins playing Silvio's wife Gabriella here, after another actress played the role the year before.

33 The title translates as "I will leave with you." Bocelli recorded the song for his 1995 album *Bocelli*, a staggering international bestseller. The song remains in heavy rotation in Italian restaurants from Rome to Kalamazoo.

SEASON 2/EPISODE 5
WRITTEN BY TERENCE WINTER
DIRECTED BY TIM VAN PATTEN

"BIG GIRLS DON'T CRY"

Total Control

*"I'm making some changes." —***Tony**

"Big Girls Don't Cry" is the first great season two episode. It's Michael Imperioli's best hour as Christopher yet. It's a terrific showcase for Federico Castelluccio's Furio Giunta, exuding Old World charm at a party and Old World ruthlessness in a brothel rampage; and for Tony and Melfi, whose protracted denial that they need to be in the same room again has been this show's version of "Will they or won't they?" But more than anything else, it's proof that what David Chase and company have created here is a world unto itself, its history, traditions, and rules so clearly laid out that it holds our attention almost no matter who's on-screen. As mentioned regarding "Guy Walks into a Psychiatrist's Office," dramatic housekeeping is one of the most important and unpleasant duties of serial TV writers. Extending this metaphor, the first four episodes of season two saw the writers moving furniture around, throwing things out, maneuvering new pieces in, and sprucing the place up; this one is the open house where all that work shines. And it's a thing of horrible beauty.

Adding Furio prompts Tony to reorganize his crew: he promotes Silvio and Paulie, and Furio and Pussy report to them.[34] Tony's mainly trying to build a firewall between himself and street business—"Feds find an excuse, I'll do a dime for jaywalking." But the reorganization has the handy side effect of halting conversations with Pussy before they can start. Tony's been consistently distancing himself since Junior's indictment—remember "Toodle-Fucking-Oo," outside Satriale's, when he practically sprints away from Richie the instant he starts talking business?—but we can see that he's especially uncomfortable around Pussy, theoretically cleared of suspicion but still engendering mistrust. The ostracism stings in the scene where Johnny Sack has dinner with Paulie: Paulie makes Pussy leave but lets newcomer Furio (who's the same rank as Pussy, *and* dressed as kitchen help[35]) stick around. "This thing of ours,"

---

34 The scene suggests the two promotions are equivalent, but in time we'll see Silvio working as Tony's consigliere, while Paulie is captain of what used to be Tony's crew.

35 Tony cons Artie into hiring Furio as a cheesemaker at Vesuvio to help with the immigration details; our only glimpse of him actually working in the kitchen has him smoking a cigarette while he slices mozzarella. Charmaine knows instantly they've been had, even if Tony is paying Furio's salary.

Pussy tells his handler Skip at a diner, "Fuckin' joke. Thing of mine is more like it."[36]

The Tony–Melfi therapy relationship resumes after a quasi-comedic period of Elliot trying to get Melfi to admit she's attracted to Tony's world, and possibly to Tony himself, while Tony tries to use other people in his life as Melfi substitutes. This week it's Hesh, a charming, learned man who might be a decent makeshift therapist were Tony to tell him, "I need you to pretend you're my therapist and just listen." Unfortunately, Tony never makes that plain a request, and Hesh assumes they're just two old friends talking and that it's okay to bring up his own problems. Tony goes to Hesh after blowing up at Janice and Richie[37] and nearly killing a random Russian who dared to talk to Irina on the dock, but Hesh yawns in his face three times and recommends sleep, then launches into an anecdote from his record-industry past. But Hesh also drops a bombshell: Tony's father used to pass out, too. Clearly, a mental health professional is needed, and it just so happens that one calls to volunteer her services.

Adriana gifts Christopher a "Writing for Actors" class to support his screenwriting aspirations. His brief stint is written and acted with such a perfect balance of empathy and absurdity that if you compiled his scenes as a short film, you'd have a perfect picture of who he is and the crossroads he's reached. The implication here is that being an artist means being brave enough to publicly dredge up and use your deepest emotional pain. Christopher is fine with inflicting and even enduring physical pain, but he runs from the emotional kind, hiding behind hardboiled tough guy postures that don't always suit him, and lashing out physically and verbally at Adriana whenever she gets too close to the truth.

After struggling to see through another person's eyes in the first few classes, he commits to perform the most wrenching scene from *Rebel Without a Cause*. The James Dean–Nicholas Ray collaboration proves to be an unexpectedly perfect vehicle for catharsis because its hero, Jim Stark, is a wounded man-child who hides behind machismo, and, like Christopher, has father issues. Jim's dad is still alive but coded as oblivious and "weak"; Chris's father died when he was young. When Jim/Chris clings to his father's legs onstage, it has a different meaning

---

36 The more time we spend with Skip Lipari, the more clear it becomes that he's projecting a lot of his own professional baggage onto Pussy and the Soprano crew. At the diner, he answers Pussy's annoyance at being outshone by a fresh-off-the-plane Italian by grousing that he just got passed over for promotion in favor of "a Samoan."

37 Richie and Janice are reenacting an old history, but that of Livia and Johnny Boy rather than their own relationship. It's even happening in the house where Tony, Janice, and Barbara grew up, and there are times when Richie talks like a more meticulous Johnny. The show never mentions it, but maybe this is another reason why Tony is so spooked by this relationship, apart from the obvious familial-professional issues it presents.

than in the movie: Jim is regressing to boyhood and clinging to a daddy who has failed him, while Chris seems to be clutching the father he never knew to keep him from vanishing. (Like Tony with Hesh, the acting class becomes a substitute for the therapy Christopher badly needs.) The subsequent scene where Chris punches his scene partner in the face after he says a single letter ("A") steers the subplot away from poignance and back toward shock comedy, only to settle on poignance again, with a silent scene of Chris throwing his writing in the garbage.

This is also the episode where *The Sopranos* flat-out tells viewers that most of the violence is meant to be interpreted as physical comedy, except when it isn't. Tony tells Paulie about his promotion at the Paterson, New Jersey memorial for Lou Costello, half of the Abbott and Costello comedy team ("Who's on first?"), and the scene ends with a high-angled long shot of the duo embracing that's dominated by Costello's bronze head. Many of Tony and Paulie's interactions have a bit of a Bud- and-Lou feeling, because they often revolve around social protocol errors and fine points of inflection and language ("Mallomars" is one of those funny product names that might find its way into an Abbott and Costello sketch). In a grander sense, the image befits a series that often sets up explosions of physical violence like black-and-white-era comedy directors staging a slow-building sequence for Abbott and Costello, Laurel and Hardy, the Marx Brothers, or the Three Stooges—the kind that might start with two dunderheads ringing a doorbell and end with a house collapsing in flames.

Christopher's initial attempts to intimidate the brothel workers follow the familiar *Sopranos* pattern of spotlighting props that will be used for violence—the model car he forces the pimp to sit on, and the paintbrush Chris jams up his nose. We saw similar setup-payoff structures in "Commendatori," when Pussy murdered the Elvis-impersonating gangster in a house filled with Elvis memorabilia; and in Richie's first scene in "Toodle-Fucking-Oo," which lovingly introduces the coffee pot he'll smash against Beansie's head. These sequences are jolting, but their undertone of weirdness takes the edge off (as when Tony murders Chucky Signore with a gun hidden inside a fish).

But when the violence is intended as purely frightening or repulsive, the slapstick structure disappears, leaving raw, jagged mayhem—as when Furio rampages through the brothel with a bat, a gun, and his fists. We see a sadistic, bullying side of him he'd previously been hidden behind a cool, even dashing façade.[38] There is nothing funny about this scene, just as there's nothing funny about Richie run-

---

38 At Tony and Carmela's welcome party, Furio reveals he knows a bit about American culture already, explaining that his favorite TV show is *NYPD Blue*—or, as he calls it, "*The PD Blue*"—a show whose rough-edged but ultimately heroic main character Andy Sipowicz helped pave the way for more brutal descendants like Tony.

ning Beansie over. The question of how humorous a violent scene is depends on whose point of view it seems to adopt. The gangsters are jocular sadists, so when they're in full control of violence, it tends to have a grimly comedic edge. Furio's rampage is all about terrorizing people as an unstoppable monster, crashing through doors, breaking glass and bones. Director Tim Van Patten films the first section of Furio's assault from behind him, like Travis Bickle's brothel slaughter at the end of *Taxi Driver*.

The sliding scale of humor to horror in violent scenes evokes Mel Brooks's definition of the difference between comedy and tragedy: "Tragedy is when I cut my finger. Comedy is when you fall down an open sewer and die." In therapy, Tony expresses admiration for Furio's excellent work but also a tinge of regret: "I wished it was me in there."

"Giving the beating or taking it?" Melfi asks.

The scene ends before he can answer.

SEASON 2/EPISODE 6
"THE HAPPY WANDERER"
WRITTEN BY FRANK RENZULLI
DIRECTED BY JOHN PATTERSON

This Game's Not for You

"I don't know who the fuck I'm angry at, I'm just angry, OK?" —**Tony**

"Trust me, this game's not for you. I don't want to see you get hurt." Tony tells this to his old high school buddy Davey Scatino (Robert Patrick[39]), a sports store owner and gambling addict; but Davey wants into the Executive Game, a super-high-stakes poker game that Junior started decades ago, and takes Tony's warning as a challenge. Tony and Davey are at Meadow's school with their families (and the Buccos) for a college information fair, but ultimately Tony ends up schooling Davey on the ugly reality of what happens when civilians tangle with organized crime: one way or another, you end up owing the Mob favors for the rest of your life. After digging himself deep in a hole during an Execu-

---

39 The liquid metal robot in *Terminator 2: Judgment Day*, and David Duchovny's replacement on the original *The X-Files*, Patrick has appeared in dozens of films and TV series, often genre pieces dealing with action, crime, horror, or science-fiction. Davey Scatino was a huge departure from the cold killers and authority figures he usually plays; like John Heard as Vin Makazian in season one, Patrick channels every ounce of his character's delusional, then desperate, born loserdom.

tive Game marathon that includes Frank Sinatra Jr. (playing himself[40]), Davey ends up destroying his business and damaging his relationship with his wife and son.

This is one of the key differences between seasons one and two of *The Sopranos*: where the first focused on internal Mob-world action—what gangsters and their families and affiliates do to each other while battling for power—this one is more interested in the world beyond the Mob, in particular "civilians" who get a taste of gangster business practices and are ruined by them. While Artie Bucco's attraction to the Mob was core to several season one episodes, and we've occasionally seen regular citizens being traumatized by Mob-ordered crimes (such as the carjacking in "Commendatori"), Davey is the first such character whose story dominates most of an hour—including the subplot about Meadow and her musical theater partner, Davey's son Eric (John Hensley[41]), whose truck Dad confiscates as his first payment to Tony's gang. As such, "The Happy Wanderer"[42] is the first *Sopranos* episode that feels as if it's also a public service announcement.

Some of the characters in this episode don't need it. Elliot, who's constantly pushing Melfi to stay away from Tony, is one of them. There are a couple more at the poker game, including Sinatra and Dr. Fried (Lewis J. Stadlen[43]), both of whom cash out when Richie barges in, bringing a whiff of impending violence, and hassles Davey for his seven grand. Artie seems to have gotten the message, too, at least for the moment: when Davey comes to him for help, he begs off, especially upon learning that it's Tony Soprano that he owes. The very next scene is Davey stealing his son's truck back.

This is a key episode because it shows us the Mob world as the rest of the world (including anti-defamation activists) saw it: as a financial as well as moral black hole that swallows up everyone who gets too close.[44] It meshes with season two's strategy of coming at now-familiar characters and situations from different angles. But it's also a partial rebuke to viewers who, like Melfi, know that guys like

---

40 Sinatra Jr., a vocalist, songwriter and conductor, was the younger brother of actress and singer Nancy Sinatra and the musical director for his father during the last decade of his life. Throughout the elder Sinatra's life, he was dogged by accusations that he was too cozy with mobsters, but if his son had any misgivings about guesting on *The Sopranos*, he never mentioned them. Sinatra the elder died just under eight months before season two debuted.

41 Matt McNamara on *Nip/Tuck* and Gabriel Bowman on *Witchblade*, among other series. Also a fixture in horror films, including *Teeth* and *Hostel: Part III*.

42 The title comes from the durable German song so often performed by glee clubs and children's choirs, and from Tony and Melfi's discussion of the idea of people—like Davey Scatino, it turns out—who are able to move through life without the misery that weighs down depressives like Tony.

43 Longtime stage and film actor who made his Broadway debut in 1969 playing Groucho Marx in the musical *Minnie's Boys*.

44 Everything's a scam and everyone's a mark to these guys, as evidenced by Christopher putting a matchbook under a market scale to save money on seafood.

Tony are destructive and self-justifying but still find their criminal adventures intoxicating.

There is still a sense—a vestige of religious moralism, maybe—that low-level criminals "deserve it" when more vicious criminals bankrupt, terrorize, or kill them, because they "chose" to get involved in that world. "The Happy Wanderer" is of two minds on the matter. While it's true that that none of this would've happened if Davey didn't have a gambling problem, he's clearly established as an addict, different from Christopher only in the details. Tony's enabling this devastating meltdown might've been the spark for some of the viewer backlash that we witnessed firsthand at the *Star-Ledger* during the second half of this season. After readers had been delighted by all the scenes in year one of gangsters plotting to rob and kill each other, all of a sudden lots of them were complaining that Tony and the show had become too nasty and unlikable.

Not that Tony's having a lot of fun at the moment, either. Aside from fleeting pleasures like taking over the Executive Game,[45] or watching Silvio explode at poor Matt Bevilaqua for the egregious sin of sweeping up cheese from the floor while Sil is on a losing streak,[46] he's enjoying life a lot less than his happy-wanderer pal Davey, lamenting to Melfi early on, "I got the world by the balls and I can't stop feeling like a fuckin' loser."

Some of this is merely the headache of being boss. Richie continues to be a thorn in his side, particularly in light of Davey already owing Richie for losses in a previous game,[47] once again stirring up Richie's aggrieved belief that Tony is withholding what is Richie's. When the father-in-law of Tony's little sister Barbara dies, the funeral not only forces Tony to be in the same room with his hated mother (who puts on a big show of tears, despite barely knowing the deceased) but lets Janice glimpse her brother dressing down her boyfriend in public.[48] On

---

45 The relaunched Executive Game is conducted at the Hasidic-owned motel that Tony took an interest in during season one's "Denial, Anger, Acceptance." The dealer, Sunshine, is played by director Paul Mazursky (*Bob & Carol & Ted & Alice*), who, like Peter Bogdanovich, is an avatar of the sort of character-driven '70s filmmaking that inspired the makers of this show.

46 Sil, enraged: "Leave the fuckin' cheese there, all right? I love fuckin' cheese at my feet! I stick motherfuckin' provolone in my socks at night, so they smell like your sister's crotch in the morning! Alright? So leave the fuckin' cocksuckin' cheese where it is!" The bad-boy grin on Tony's face before and after implies that this is not the first time he's pushed this button of Sil's.

47 Glimpsed at that game, in his first appearance of the series: Aprile crew soldier Vito Spatafore (Joseph Gannascoli, who previously played a bakery customer in season one's "The Legend of Tennessee Moltisanti"). "He was good in [that] episode," explains David Chase, "and we were starting to run out of Italian American actors early on!"

48 Notice how, in this scene, Tony yells at Richie that "the rules have always been there," which is a variation of the sentiment Richie yells at Tony in "Toodle-Fucking-Oo": What's Mine Is Not Yours to Give Me. Like most of the Mob guys on this show, these two insist there's a preexisting structure of rules independent from any one person, when in fact it's all arbitrary and anyone with sufficient clout at that moment can do as he pleases.

the ride home to Livia's old house, she's more her mother than ever, fanning the flames of Richie's resentment toward Tony the same way Livia did with Junior in season one, but with the intimacy of lovers—cementing the notion that Janice and Richie are becoming a next-generation Livia and Johnny Boy.

Tony's dark mood isn't helped by the family secret Junior unwittingly reveals while negotiating the rights to the Executive Game: he and Johnny had another brother, Eckley (short for Ercoli), who was "strong as a fucking bull, handsome like George Raft," but developmentally disabled and institutionalized. Tony's not sure what upsets him more: that he had an uncle his parents never told him about, or that Eckley's disability, whatever it was, is another sign of something rotten in the Soprano genes.

Even Dr. Melfi's sensitivity toward Patient X seems at an ebb in this one, as she responds to this woe-is-me ramble by asking, "Now that you found out that you have a retarded family member, do you feel better about coming here? Is it permissible now? Is it enough of a sad tragedy that you can join the rest of the douchebags?"

Tony's not like the rest of the douchebags, though. He is predator, not prey, there to pounce on someone like Davey the moment the opportunity presents itself. And he's surrounded himself with people who think the same. Earlier, Meadow gets competitive about her performance spot in the school's cabaret night, feeling like a solo will be better for her college admissions than the duet she's assigned with Eric Scatino. When Eric bolts at the last second to protest the wreckage Meadow's father has made of his life, Meadow winds up rewarded with the exact thing she wanted, singing "My Heart Will Go On" from *Titanic*. Carmela, who knows enough of what's been going on between Tony and Davey to connect the dots, responds to this development by marveling, "That's a lucky break."

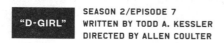

SEASON 2/EPISODE 7
WRITTEN BY TODD A. KESSLER
DIRECTED BY ALLEN COULTER

God the Father

"Even if God is dead, you're still gonna kiss his ass." —**Tony**

This is a story about loyalty to one's father and the anxiety that accrues when you consider rejecting him. Dramatically speaking, Tony Soprano is at the periphery of "D-Girl," but by the end you realize that he was the center of this universe the whole time, even when offscreen. He's not the godfather of the DiMeo Family, officially, but he's the closest thing to a fearsome Old Testament God-the-Father a lot of the other characters have. The final montage, set at the party following AJ's confirmation and backed by Emma Shaplin singing the title track from the trance opera album *Carmine Meo,* cuts (and sometimes dissolves) between three men who love, resent, and are terrified of Tony: AJ, Big Pussy, and Chris. By the end, all three appear unable to break from, or even oppose, Tony. We see his biological son standing with his family for a group photograph, after his parents catch him smoking pot in the garage, and mere days after scratching up his mother's car in a dumb accident; Pussy, bullied by Agent Lipari into wearing a wire to the confirmation party, sobbing in an upstairs bathroom after telling AJ what a great guy his dad is, and ignoring Tony's requests for him to join the portrait; and Tony's "like a son to me" cousin Chris, who spent much of the episode flitting around the edges of a Hollywood film shoot, sitting on the front stoop outside the gathering, thinking about Tony's menacing ultimatum to choose movies or him, then finally standing up and walking back inside.

AJ dabbles in newfound philosophy and tells his family God is dead and there's no point to anything. He's rejecting an abstract, symbolic, patriarchal authority because the one that raised him isn't going anywhere and will smack him if he mouths off too many times. "He's telling me he's got no purpose," Tony tells Melfi. "I told him it cost about 150 grand to bring him up so far, so if he's got no purpose, I want a fuckin' refund." Tony's unofficial surrogate son, Christopher, has a restless heart. He comes close to breaking into filmmaking, thanks to a connection with actor-director Jon Favreau[49] through his cousin Gregory (Dominic Fumusa[50]), who's engaged to Amy Safir (Alicia Witt[51]), Favreau's vice president of development. But even after Chris plays up his mobster status to impress the Hollywood tourists and enjoys a brief fling with Amy, he ends up feeling humiliated, used by both Amy and her boss. Favreau even steals an anecdote that Chris specifically asked him not to repeat and works

---

49 At the time, Favreau was best known as the writer and star of *Swingers*, a movie about young actors struggling with relationships that made stars of Favreau (who landed a stint on *Friends* as a result of it) and Vince Vaughn, and helped cement (or kill, depending on your point of view), the late '90s vogue for swing music and Rat Pack fashions. More recently, Favreau the director has gone mainstream with the likes of *Iron Man* and *The Jungle Book*.

50 After *The Sopranos* ended, Fumusa would play Edie Falco's husband on Showtime's *Nurse Jackie*.

51 A former child actress (she made her screen debut at seven as the terrifying Alia in David Lynch's *Dune*), Witt used "D-Girl" to transition into adult roles after spending four seasons as Cybil Shepherd's younger daughter on the sitcom *Cybil*. Post-*Sopranos*, she's been on *Friday Night Lights, Justified, The Walking Dead, Twin Peaks: The Return*, and many more.

it into the script for a star vehicle in which he'd play real-life gangster "Crazy" Joe Gallo.[52]

Like "The Happy Wanderer," "D-Girl" largely lacks the violence some gangster movie fans seem to require, unless you count Pussy grappling on the floor with Angie, Chris manhandling Favreau, and the cruelty (described but not shown) in Chris's story about a transgender woman disfigured in an acid attack by a homophobic wiseguy. The theme of men struggling with their loyalty to father figures strings the subplots together effectively, and there are a handful of exceptional scenes—Tony and Melfi's therapy session is particularly strong, focusing on how Tony's repudiation of his own mother might've stoked AJ's fascination with oblivion ("In your family, even motherhood is up for debate")—but the episode remains patchy. The showbiz portions[53] are especially dicey, and not just because inside-baseball showbiz satire was plentiful on HBO and elsewhere in 2000 (and still is). Specific industry portrayals are astute: Amy's tendency to compare everything in life to art typifies certain movie and TV people, and Favreau's character captures the "nice guy" persona of filmmakers who play sensitive and deferential so convincingly that outsiders fail to notice their self-interest and manipulation. But we never get a clear sense of what's driving Amy. Her sudden decision to seduce Christopher could be an act of rebellion against her boring lawyer fiancé or the result of a privileged woman's obsession with macho criminal alphas (similar to Melfi's obsession with Tony, or at least Elliot's description of it). But mostly she's a rough draft, though enlivened by Witt's nonjudgmental, deadpan performance. Chris' plaintive "I really liked you" only works if you think of Amy as a human female stand-in for the siren song of Hollywood forever pulling him away from Tony and the Mob life.

Still, there are many resonant images, including the anguished Pussy hugging AJ tight, distorting the transmission to eavesdropping Lipari; and Pussy on the bedroom floor with Angie, his tank top bloodstained where he shaved his chest to attach a wire. And the dialogue is exceptional throughout: for a minor episode, "D-Girl" offers lines quoted by fans to this day, including Carmela's "What kind

---

52 Gallo, a gangster with New York's Columbo crime family, was the subject of a 1969 novel by longtime *New York Daily News* columnist Jimmy Breslin that was made into a 1971 film starring Jerry Orbach. Breslin's gangsters are probably the closest to Sopranos gangsters from previous pop culture, aside from the losers depicted in the 1996 film *Donnie Brasco*. They're insular, petty, impulsive, lose fortunes on stupid schemes, hold dumb grudges forever, and make enormous, often fatal leaps based on incomplete or wrong information. Scorsese's gangsters are the Corleones in comparison.

53 The movie's director, we're told, had a film festival success with a "lesbian romantic screwball comedy," and here her juices have been watered down to direct a spy movie starring Sandra Bernhard and Janeane Garofalo. Christopher winds up contributing a line of dialogue, suggesting that Bernhard call Garofalo *buchiach* when Garofalo objects to the script's use of "bitch." *Buchiach*, Christopher explains, is Italian for every woman's least favorite word.

of animal smokes marijuana at his own confirmation?"; and Melfi's "Sounds to me like Anthony Jr. may have stumbled onto existentialism," and Tony's reply, "Fuckin' Internet."

SEASON 2/EPISODE 8
"FULL LEATHER JACKET" WRITTEN BY ROBIN GREEN & MITCHELL BURGESS
DIRECTED BY ALLEN COULTER

The Last of the Arugula Rabe

"Jean, you are a wonderful friend!" —**Carmela**

"Full Leather Jacket" ends with an act of violence so senseless and sad that it's understandable people remember it as "the one where Christopher gets shot." But it's strong and understated in its own right: a tightly structured riff on rebellion and its consequences, anchored to a close-up look at the dynamics of the Soprano marriage when it's in sync. Husband and wife exhibit mirrored behaviors that show their confident, nuanced rulership over their own worlds. The highlight is the kitchen conversation between Tony and Carmela about their dinner guest, Richie Aprile. "I want to compliment you on your behavior out there," she tells him, handing him a butcher knife. "Hey, I want him where I can see him," Tony says. "That's what we mean when we say family," Carmela says, kissing him on the cheek before he sinks the blade into the roast. This, more than any prior scene, best illustrates what Steven Van Zandt meant in describing *The Sopranos* as *The Gangster Honeymooners.*[54]

Tony and Carmela spend a lot of energy quashing rebellions here. Richie refuses to build a wheelchair ramp for Beansie Gaeta, and freely shows his core loyalty to Junior (and vice-versa; when Tony expresses reservations about Richie's plan to sell 10,000 stolen DVDs without a sign-off from New York, the old man, who's spent a season and a half pouting over not being feared enough himself, says, "Fuck 'em"). But he seems to realize the direct approach isn't working and plays nice, delivering a tripe and tomatoes to Carmela and giving Tony a leather jacket that he took off Rocco DiMeo, the toughest guy in Essex county.[55] Richie

---

54 See "Married to the Mob" in the Morgue section, page 416.

55 Junior's aside when Richie gives Rocco's jacket to Tony—"He later died of Alzheimer's."—illustrates how meaningless Richie's petty, long-ago victory was. When Rocco breathed his last, he didn't remember Richie's triumph or anything else.

hasn't been watching *The Sopranos* for twenty-one episodes like we have, so he doesn't really grasp what an ungrateful sod Tony is when it comes to this sort of thing. Richie's a sour, petty, arrogant, volatile hoodlum, but he's working overtime to signal peace, given his personal limitations and his affinity for Junior, and he credibly justifies his transgressions (as when he claims he pulled the construction crew[56] from Beansie's house to work on his future mother-in-law Livia's house). A line in the jacket scene partly explains his stubbornness over the ramp: "Beansie Gaeta would still be selling nickel bags on Jefferson Avenue if it wasn't for Jackie," he says, casting Tony's understandable display of dominance as disloyalty to Tony's late mentor/Richie's late brother.

As in "D-Girl," Tony is more a supporting character than a lead,[57] projecting power and inspiring fear and a craving for recognition, while secondary characters step into the foreground to win his approval. Tony is the gunbeam that all the cats want to sleep in, including Sean Gismonte and Matt Bevilaqua (now going by Drinkwater, a rough English translation of Bevilaqua), beefy nimrods who bounce between authority figures who might validate their nonexistent potential versus laughing at them (as during Furio's shakedown in their apartment) or yelling at them (as Tony does when Sean stupidly mentions business in the Bing restroom). If they hadn't shot Chris so impulsively, Richie, likewise craving respect, might've been a mentor. Matt and Sean's story also tenuously bridges the Richie and Christopher–Adriana subplots. The duo's snap decision to whack Chris, who just helped make them a lot of money cracking safes, comes after Richie trashes Chris in their presence, partly because Chris dared to hit Ade without marrying her first. "If there's anything you can do for me, let me know," he tells them.

This episode contains more examples of women in a patriarchal subculture twisting themselves into knots to excuse or explain domestic violence by their partners. The men resort to force whenever control over their mate is threatened, and coldly describe it as a fact of life that's not up for debate, governed by the same protocol that explains how much money to kick up to a superior and the circumstances under which a made man can be killed. Richie's first conversation with Chris in "Toodle-Fucking-Oo" contains a warning not to raise a hand to Adriana until they're married. Chris's fumbling proposal is partly an apology for having mistreated Adriana, in ways both obvious (physical and verbal abuse) and secretive (the fling with Amy in "D-Girl"), and partly a way to jump-start a respectable

---

56 Vito runs the operation, because construction is a major revenue stream for the Aprile crew.

57 In therapy, Tony masterfully analyzes his own behavior, surmising that he regifted Meadow Eric Scatino's car "to rub her face in shit," though he fails to understand Melfi's subsequent point that he was doing his part to separate from her in the run-up to college, something teens do to their parents through their own forms of hostile behavior.

life for himself.[58] Ade's mother Liz (Patty McCormack) recognizes Christopher as a threat, worries that he stole the ring, and warns Adriana that she can't seek shelter in her house if she marries him. Matt and Sean praise Adriana to Chris in blatantly sexual terms, and he takes it as a compliment.

This is one of the great Carmela episodes, illustrating how at peace she (usually) is with the moral compromises required to maintain her level of comfort. The polite way she turns the screws on anyone who dares to say no to her is perhaps more chilling than some of the show's physical brutality, because it shows how force can be exercised by people who've never raised a fist or pointed a gun. Carmela is fighting a two-front war here, against her daughter, who wants to go to school on the other side of the country, and her neighbor Jean Cusamano and her twin sister Joan (both played by Saundra Santiago[59]). Both are guilty of refusing to knuckle under and do what she wants. Meadow wants to move as far away as possible, a desire Carmela tries to short-circuit, first by trashing a letter from Berkeley warning of an incomplete admissions package, then by pressing the Cusamano twins for a letter of recommendation to Georgetown.

Carmela proceeds with naked self-interest—not with Tony's profanity-spewing rage, but calmly, cheerfully, with a smile on her face, or at least in her eyes. The line "I don't think you understand: I want you to write that letter" is as chilling a moment as the show has given us, climaxing a scene in which a woman stops by another woman's office with only a ricotta pie and a manila envelope. When Jean says Joan wrote the recommendation after all, Carmela says, "That's wonderful! Do you have a copy?"—making sure Joan didn't lie. The best bit of body language in this scene belongs to Santiago: when Carmela exclaims "Jean, you are wonderful!" and stands to embrace her, Jean recoils as if she's about to be enveloped by a python. And she is.

---

58 In retrospect, Chris's postcoital conversation with Adriana about how he wants to turn his life around is one of the only obvious, TV-style pieces of writing in the episode. TV characters often get their affairs in order, or state a desire to, right before the show drops an anvil on their heads.

59 Bronx-born actress who rose to fame playing Detective Gina Calabrese on *Miami Vice*.

"FROM WHERE TO ETERNITY"

SEASON 2/EPISODE 9
WRITTEN BY MICHAEL IMPERIOLI
DIRECTED BY HENRY J. BRONCHTEIN

The Admiral Piper

"That was a dream. Forget about it." —**Tony**

Spirituality has always hovered at the edges of *The Sopranos*, but it infuses every frame of "From Where to Eternity," the first episode written by a regular series actor, Michael Imperioli. His character spends the whole hour in the ICU, sleeping, being operated on, and engaging in delirious, often surreal conversations. The latter revolve around a dream Chris had when he was clinically dead for sixty seconds. He passed through a tunnel of white light and went to "our Hell," an Irish pub called the Admiral Piper "where it's St. Patrick's Day every day, forever." He saw Mikey Palmice and Brendan Filone there "playing dice with two Roman soldiers and a bunch of the Irish guys . . . the Irish, they were winning every roll"; his father, who kept being killed in exactly the same way again and again; and a bouncer who warned Chris that he was going to Hell, too, "when my time comes." Oh, and Mikey said to tell Tony and Paulie: "Three o'clock."

No explanation. Some dream.

But what makes this episode so sneakily strong is that it might not have been a dream. The episode never confirms or refutes Chris's interpretation of what he saw; we're left to decide. We could write off the characters' ruminations and snap decisions as community-wide panic attack sparked by violence, and treat their grapplings with sin and doubt as comical. But there's so much uncanniness here—from Paulie's girlfriend's[60] account of her own significant encounter with three o'clock, to the moment when the supposed quack psychic correctly names Paulie's first homicide, to the shot of a Jesus statue looming over Paulie leaving church after blasting his priest for running a useless spiritual protection racket— that the viewer may leave feeling unmoored, and perhaps convinced that Chris really did see the other side. Either way, the vision of the Admiral Piper explodes within the episode like a tiny-scaled Biblical miracle, shocking other characters into reexamining their lives, or at least considering it.[61]

---

60 Played by future *Scrubs* costar Judy Reyes.
61 The odd person out here might be Pussy, whom Skip Lipari keeps pressuring to really commit to his informant status, and who worries that Tony knows the truth about him on some level. "You're the one who's different now; you're the one seeing through different eyes," Lipari says. In the end, Pussy makes the grandest gesture a guy like him could make: he helps his boss revenge-murder a guy who helped shoot his figurative son.

Tony is in bunker mode throughout much of this episode, doubling down on every belief and characteristic that others criticize or question, playing devil's advocate in any conversation pertaining to the wages of sin, and coming off like the Devil himself in the scene where he and Pussy terrorize a beaten and broken Matt Bevilaqua (sulfurous cigar smoke pouring from Tony's mouth and wreathing his head throughout), then riddle his torso with bullets until he slumps in his chair like Christ crucified.[62] In therapy, Tony launches into one of his longest tirades, responding to Melfi's pressure to identify the immediate cause of his unhappiness (his crimes/his sins) with deflective rationalizations, from the notion that "We're soldiers. Soldiers don't go to Hell," to the Italian American Mob's century-old status as a preserver of old-world culture and a bulwark against exploitation by native-born WASPs. "The J. P. Morgans, they were crooks and killers, too," Tony says, leaning forward in his chair, "but that was a 'business,' right?"

"That might all be true," says Melfi, fuming, "but what do poor Italian immigrants have to do with you? And what happens every morning you step out of bed?"[63]

Even Melfi, who's at the fringe of the criminal world and understands it only through news stories and Tony's anecdotes, seems to be spiraling downward. We learn in her session with Elliot that she's been taking Ativan for depression and drinking alone, psychic fallout from deciding to take back Tony. And now she's ashamed of herself for twisting the morality knife at a moment when Tony's afraid of losing a young man who's like a son to him. Her job, she says, "is not to judge, but to treat. Now, I've judged. I took a position, goddamnit, and now I'm scared."

For the first time since "College," and mere days after scaring a woman into writing a recommendation to Georgetown, Carmela is frightened for her mortal soul, and for Chris's. When Chris survives surgery, Carmela credits her prayers in an empty hospital room. She admitted that she and her family[64] "[chose] this life in full awareness of the consequences of our sins" and asked God to spare Chris

---

62 *The Sopranos* is constantly getting compared to *The Godfather* and Scorsese Mob films, but this episode has more in common with an Abel Ferrara–directed Catholic-freakout crime dramas like *Bad Lieutenant* or *The Funeral*.

63 Not enough attention has been paid over the years to the idea that Melfi is not just trying to help Tony understand himself better or (as he accuses here) blame his outrages on a rotten childhood, but to awaken his latent sense of morality and improve him. This is something therapists aren't supposed to do—that's the job of clergy—but the fact that Melfi seems determined to do it anyway, sometimes half-consciously, speaks to Tony's deep impact on her life and work.

64 She could be talking about either her biological family or the far-flung Mob Family; the script never specifies, but there's so much category overlap that this might be a distinction without a difference.

and "deliver him from blindness and grant him vision, and through this vision, may he see your love and gain the strength to carry on in service to your mercy."[65] "You have to look at this experience as an opportunity to repent," she tells Chris once he regains consciousness. Her spiritual crisis is driven not just by Chris's ordeal but by Gabriella Dante delivering the news that a married gangster they both know fathered a child with his *goomar,* a Brazilian dancer. This leads Carmela to confront Tony about his continued cheating ("I can smell the CK One on your shirts")[66] and demand he get a vasectomy. "I had her tested for AIDS," Tony says, exactly the wrong thing to say. He grouses later that their own faith decrees that it's unnatural to prevent nature from taking its course (every sperm is sacred, as Monty Python sang) and besides, he's not cheating anymore.[67] Carmela's tenuous connection of Tony's infidelity and the overall sinfulness of This Thing of Theirs is symbolized by her fear of her gangster husband creating a child neither of them wants, but that they might have to live with for the rest of their lives: sin made sentient, consequences with a pulse.[68]

Woven throughout the episode's soundtrack is the Otis Redding hit "Lover's Prayer." It's used three times:[69] during the opening, underscoring Chris' surgery, and in the closing scene, after Carmela reconciles with Tony. Redding's classic is a straightforward torch song, with the singer in a defensive (kneeling) position, asking his lover to think well of him, forgive him, and stay with him through good times and bad, as Carmela does when she forgives Tony, and as Tony pledges to do in return. But in this context the lyrics take on a spiritual dimension, too. The last two lines return the song's meanings to earth, specifically to the bedroom, and seem tailor-made for the episode's closing scene: "My final prayer/You'll take this ring/and bear my seed."

---

65 There's a lot of talk of vision and seeing in this episode, from Lipari telling Pussy that he's seeing through different eyes now to Carmela telling her cousin she asked God to grant him "vision, sight, so that you can see your way to Christ clearly," and adding, "You saw, Christopher. You saw something. Something that none of us have ever seen."

66 This is a callback to that moment in the opening montage of "Guy Walks into a Psychiatrist's Office" when Carmela and Tony make uncomfortable eye contact in bed after Tony comes back from seeing Irina.

67 *Arrested Development* narrator: "He is."

68 Carmela's bedtime reading is Arthur Golden's 1997 novel *Memoirs of a Geisha*, about Japanese prostitutes in the 1930s and '40s. The novel and the subsequent 2005 film version were criticized for exoticizing and misrepresenting a subculture, a charge also leveled at *The Sopranos*.

69 Given the importance of the Holy Trinity in Catholicism, of course it would be three.

SEASON 2/EPISODE 10
"BUST OUT" WRITTEN BY FRANK RENZULLI AND ROBIN GREEN & MITCHELL BURGESS
DIRECTED BY JOHN PATTERSON

The Scorpion

"Well, I knew you had this business here, Davey." **—Tony**

Tony is a swirl of emotions throughout "Bust Out," one of the series' finest episodes to date. He is variously plagued by guilt over murdering Matt Bevilaqua (and also confused over why he feels guilt for this murder and not all the others), panic-stricken at the thought of going to prison for life because a witness saw him and Pussy near the crime scene, and smugly cruel as he systematically dismantles Davey Scatino's business and life. "I don't fuckin' deserve this," he insists to Melfi about the possible murder charge, even as the Davey story that gives the episode its title illustrates that Tony Soprano absolutely fuckin' deserves this, and a whole lot more.

The bust-out of Ramsey Sports and Outdoors—where Tony makes Davey use the store's credit to buy merchandise his guys will sell on the street, leaving Davey to face angry suppliers he can't pay—is another process-oriented look at Family moneymaking. Its ordinariness alone is depressing. The liquidation of Davey's store is conveyed in a single brief tracking shot of a truck being loaded up with merch, capped by guys pasting a "For Lease" sign across the doors. In some ways, it's scarier than the many murders the Family has committed: this bleeding of the store and the Scatino family proceeds in broad daylight and could happen to almost anyone. Davey's wife Christine (Marisa Redanty) thinks the family will get through her husband's latest meltdown because the store is registered in her name, while her contractor brother Vic Musto (Joe Penny[70]) thinks he can devise a payment plan. But like Davey himself, they have no idea what kind of man they're dealing with, and how coldly he can take everything away because—like the scorpion in the familiar parable he cites to Davey—it's in his nature.

Tony's arrogance, obliviousness, and monstrousness fill nearly every scene, except for the opening at the fairgrounds where he hears Richie's complaint about his share of the Family's sanitation business and feels guilty over the Bevilaqua hit (flashing to the young dolt's death after hearing a little boy call for his mother, just as Matt did when Tony and Pussy drew their guns), dodging the emotions by

---

70 In a much earthier mode than his suave TV leading-man roles on detective shows like *Riptide* and *Jake and the Fatman.*

slipping into ballbusting mode. He also threatens a disabled man into accepting a cash gift he doesn't want (to assuage his own guilt over being unable to control Richie, maybe[71]) and blatantly denies responsibility (to Melfi) for the murder we saw him commit, then walks out of therapy prematurely because he's so happy to be free. And when the witness recants, Tony fights back happy tears in the same bathroom where, unbeknownst to him, the wife he keeps taking for granted kissed Davey Scatino's brother-in-law. (Vic, a nice-guy beef-slab in mourning, distances himself instantly, and stays away forever after learning that Tony ruined Davey.)

As always, potentially cathartic realizations swim around in Tony's sub-conscious without surfacing long enough for him to identify and learn from them. Bevilaqua's murder probably nags at him because he's worried about the long-term prospects of his blood son A.J, a walking punch line, and his surrogate son Chris, who almost died on the operating table last week after being shot by, essentially, a couple of AJs with sidearms. Bad fathering[72] is a persistent dread of Tony's, though he shows little interest in improving. The outer limit of his imaginative empathy for AJ is a pizza and a six-pack of Coke. He's been negging the kid for weeks, even insulting him as a genetic mistake not fit to be his heir. When he decides to go the extra mile (which for Tony is the extra half-meter) and spontaneously take the boy fishing, AJ rebuffs him—not to be mean, but because he's a teenage boy who promised to go to the mall with friends. Tony tells Carmela he forgot about his son's swim meet because he was dealing with other things (the bust-out, though he doesn't say so), but this might be a case of forgetting an event accidentally-on-purpose, as petty revenge. He nearly admits as much to Carm. "What are you, six years old?" she asks.

Yes, he is. Everyone's a hostage to Tony's need to dominate. Watch how his mood goes from generous to menacing when Beansie says, "Fuck you, Tony," and how Tony smiles again when Beansie takes the money. If Carmela were an ordinary bored suburban housewife, her crush on Vic could've turned into a case of "what's good for the gander is good for the goose," with her serially unfaithful husband never the wiser.[73] But Tony's too famous for being deadly; and so Carmela takes off her apron and primps in the oven door, only to welcome Vic's assistant. Tony's movement through the world leaves wreckage in its wake, an image literalized

---

71 Janice has her own way of trying to control Richie, allowing him to hold a gun to her head during sex—in a darkly comic scene that ends with Livia descending into the living room on a power chair lift, demanding, "Are you smoking marijuana? I want to watch the TV."—even as she's telling an irritated Richie that he should be the boss.

72 He is, of course, a product of bad fathering, as "Down Neck" and Livia's anecdotes attest.

73 Notice the return of "Con te partirò," the official "Carmela's Romantic Delusions" theme, in the scene where she flirts with Vic on the phone in Meadow's presence. Interesting how Meadow just seems to know what's up.

in the final shot of the *Stugots* capsizing a rowboat after Tony gives AJ the helm. Those waves are the Soprano legacy.

SEASON 2/EPISODE 11
WRITTEN BY TERENCE WINTER
DIRECTED BY TIM VAN PATTEN

Alexithymia

"Whatsamatter, you still in mourning over the coming
of managed care?" —**Tony**

When we first met Tony Soprano, he wasn't the boss of New Jersey, but he was still highly ranked enough that he shouldn't have been getting his hands dirty as often, or as publicly, as we've grown used to by now. A captain shouldn't have tried to run over a deadbeat in a busy office park, and the head of this Family definitely shouldn't be killing Matt Bevilaqua himself. Some of Tony's literally hands-on attitude stems from the practical reality of making a TV drama about a gang boss. A Tony Soprano who delegates danger would be more responsible but far less exciting. Besides, Tony loves this stuff. The chance to inflict pain on other human beings, to brazenly take what he wants, to be utterly uncaged, are his best reasons to get out of bed.

Still, after his near-bust for the Bevilaqua hit, Tony finally attempts to follow the advice of his lawyer, Neil Mink (David Margulies[74]), to "insulate yourself from these shenanigans." He lets Silvio handle Family business while reporting to his front job at Barone Sanitation for the first time in years. It's the smart play. The safe play.

And Tony hates every second of it.[75]

Garbage is the business that brings him income, health benefits, and taxable income to pacify the IRS, but it is not the business Tony Soprano has chosen, and the longer he spends trying to lock himself away from the trash his crew pulls without him, the worse he feels. The continued insubordination of Richie "Manson Lamps" Aprile— who's still being egged on by Janice (or, as she's calling herself now that she's dressing and acting like a Mob wife, "Jan")—helps induce another

---

74 Long-working character actor, best known as the mayor of New York in 1984's *Ghostbusters*.

75 Okay, he may enjoy the "stress management" sex he has with Dick Barone's secretary—a peep show sight gag that, like the Roman centurion fantasy in "Commendatori," finds *The Sopranos* mistaking garden-variety crassness for audacity.

panic attack at the Garden State Carting Association Couples Invitational, in a daringly sustained piece of subjective filmmaking. The rash that appears on Tony's arm is an objective correlative for the "itch" he's been ordered not to scratch. "The things I take pleasure in, I can't do," he tells Melfi. She compares Tony to a shark, and suggests people like him suffer from alexithymia,[76] needing constant motion and activity not only to entertain themselves, but as distraction from thinking about the "abhorrent" things they do. Tony, proving her point, changes the subject to Richie, who's literally playing house with Janice.

Dr. Melfi is one of Tony's two mirrors in this episode. She's been spiraling out of control herself, thanks to the stress of treating a gang boss, crossing boundaries with him, and drinking to excess. Tony's panic attack finds its Melfi equivalent during dinner with her son Jason (Will McCormack) when she makes a scene while demanding another patron put out her cigarette.[77] Elliot again presses Melfi to end Tony's therapy—he's as relentless on this point as Melfi is with steering Tony to talk about Livia and his criminality—but Melfi denies her own shrink's reading as hotly as Tony denies basic truths about himself. Elliot's suggestion that she try Luvox—a drug for obsessive-compulsive disorder—annoys her until she realizes, with help from Elliot, that she is indeed "obsessed" with Tony. (Tony correctly deduces that his therapist is "on drugs," but she rolls right past the accusation.)

The second Tony mirror in this episode is Junior, whose inability to control his own life is illustrated by the starkest facts of his existence: the legal sentence confining him to his house, the monitoring bracelet, his gnawing loneliness (in retrospect, he regrets dumping Bobbie from "Boca"), and most of all his age, which makes him more vulnerable than he wants to admit. The sight of Junior standing at the sink from night until morning with his hand stuck in the garbage disposal is as inappropriately hilarious as it is sad. Richie and Janice chortle and tease, but this is agony for him. He only reaches a state of near-peace when he tells Catherine Romano (Mary Louise Wilson), the neighbor who's sweet on him, about his constraints, and their origin in "certain legal difficulties." An hour packed with impatience, frustration, and ennui glides to an unexpectedly placid, meditative finish, with consecutive scenes of Catherine massaging the sleeping Junior's feet and taking his glasses off (she puts his CPAP mask on for him) while *Diagnosis Murder* plays on TV, and Tony and his crew mingling with FBI agents outside Satriale's.

---

76 The subclinical inability to identify and describe emotions in the self. According to a 2014 *Scientific American* article, this condition "throws a monkey wrench into a person's ability to know their own self-experience or understand the intricacies of what others feel and think."

77 This episode aired six years before ten states, including New Jersey, finally banned indoor smoking in all bars and restaurants. New Jersey casinos were exempt until 2008.

Junior has, for the moment, accepted his house arrest. Tony flatly rejects his own unofficial version, going back to the pork store to hang with the crew and talk business, and it's by far the most relaxed and happy he's been all hour. Both men should take the advice of the closing Johnny Thunders song, "You Can't Put Your Arms around a Memory."[78]

"THE KNIGHT IN WHITE SATIN ARMOR"

SEASON 2/EPISODE 12
WRITTEN BY ROBIN GREEN & MITCHELL BURGESS
DIRECTED BY ALLEN COULTER

Pine Cones

"Gotta wonder where she is in all of this, my little niece." —**Uncle Junior**

The most famous moment of season two of *The Sopranos* happens here, and it's so unexpected that it takes a while to realize the writers spent almost twelve episodes setting it up.

Richie Aprile calmly continues his dinner after punching his fiancée Janice in the face; we cut to Janice, bloody-mouthed, wielding the same gun Richie holds to her head during sex. Forget the writing for a minute; the filmmaking itself is startling. Look at the timing of those two shots and the dozen or so shots leading up to it. We see Janice leave the kitchen, stunned and betrayed, but she seems to return much quicker than it would actually take to retrieve Richie's gun—a cheat that deprives you of the time required to anticipate the shooting. And when Janice is revealed, the shot isn't from Richie's viewpoint, who's still paying attention to his plate: it's for our benefit, to shock and delight us. We may wonder briefly if the gun is even loaded. ("I thought you were a feminist," Carmela says earlier, upon learning of their fetish. "Usually we take the clip out," Janice says. The most important word in that sentence is "usually.") But the scene answers this question, too, with abrupt speed. "The fuck outta here," Richie says, leaning back in his chair, "I'm in no mood for your—"

BLAM. One shot in the chest.

And a second as Richie struggles to rise from the kitchen floor. *BLAM*.

And the Manson lamps go dark.

Richie's death is one of the great televised examples of how a seemingly anticlimactic turn of events can be much more satisfying than whatever you

---

78 This 1978 song's title comes from a line of dialogue in an episode of *The Honeymooners*, which influenced the *Sopranos*'s East Coast sitcom sensibility and its Ralph Kramden–like protagonist.

expected. But careful study of the preceding eleven episodes confirms this wasn't an arbitrary twist designed to outguess the plot-guessers in the audience, but one that had been meticulously constructed to lead to a single, inevitable outcome.[79]

The first two episodes of season two are dominated by the return of Janice Soprano, aka Parvati Wasatch, aka the future not–Mrs. Aprile. She takes on both the narrative role and many of the personality traits of her mother so easily that we think of her as a comic irritant at best, a potential adversary at worst. Although she never asks explicitly for her brother's death—which would've made her transformation into the New Livia official—she spends a lot of time playing North Jersey Lady Macbeth, stoking Richie's resentment purposefully or accidentally (as in the sex scene, which is aborted because her pillow talk reminds Richie of his subordinate status). We keep thinking Richie and Tony are going to have it out at some point, perhaps after Janice eggs them on (or Junior, who dances around Richie all season before coming to his senses here), and that Richie, because he's not the star of the show, will become Tony's latest victim.

"This shit with your brother, it's been building since I got out," Richie tells Janice, while recalling the jacket. Richie's first free act was to mete out unauthorized punishment against a Soprano associate, and he only became more of a peevish, hateful wild card from there. Most of the Tony–Richie material in Richie's final episode is about the disposition of garbage routes and their profits, the biggest dispute yet because so much money is at stake (and because Jackie Aprile Jr., played by Jason Cerbone, has entered the picture now, and is constantly reminding Richie of his brother's legacy and his obligation to live up to it). Richie thinks he's not getting his fair share of the hauling business. He was already continuously pissed off by Tony's refusal to grant him his due respect, and now he's anxious over paying for a new house and renovating and decorating it to Janice's satisfaction. This is the episode where Junior, who's been toying with a Richie alliance all season, weighs the power struggle, decides he has to side with Tony,[80] and warns him that he's going to end up "lying in the street in a pool of [his] own blood." This episode is so sure we're expecting a standard gangster-movie exit for Richie that it ends the barroom conversation between him and capo Albert Barese[81]

---

79 This is true not just of the whole season, but this episode particularly. Notice how the opening shot of Richie's son and his dance partner waltzing in the new house sets up Janice's defense of the boy's decision to quit school, as well as Richie's panic over the prospect of possibly having a gay son. Richie's punch is an answer to Janice asking, "What if he was gay? What difference does it make?"

80 Bacala, after watching Junior do the mental calculations that lead him to realize he's better off with Tony: "I'm in awe of you."

81 Brother of Larry Boy Barese (his own nickname is Ally Boy), who was arrested as part of the same RICO case that took down Junior at the end of season one. The Barese siblings trade off appearances for much of the series, depending on Larry Boy's legal status.

(Richard Maldone) with what sounds like a tommy gun: a paint mixer, audio from the next scene with Carmela and Vic in the paint store.

This episode could've climaxed in other ways: Tony killing Richie; Richie accidentally killing Janice during sex; Pussy, suddenly a junior G-man, killing Richie preemptively to get back into Tony's graces; or a wedding, followed by Tony realizing he can't kill Richie because he's family now as well as Family. All these outcomes would've seemed justified considering all the seeds the writers had planted. But none would've been as startling, and retrospectively satisfying, as the one we got. The title comes from a phrase Irina uses while making Tony feel bad for dumping her, but it ultimately describes Janice, who tries on a white satin bridal gown during the fitting scene and rides unwittingly to her brother's rescue, right after Richie starts speaking openly about killing him.

Her shooting Richie also weirdly inverts season one's ending, which found the real Livia plotting to murder her son. Although Nancy Marchand didn't have much screen time in season two due to her health, we still learned information that complicated our sense of her as a purely malevolent person. She's still not nice and never will be, but we understand her better and feel sorry for her sometimes, especially when she talks about her brood's childhoods and seems sorry (as sorry as Livia can be) about failing them, nestling her acknowledgment of inadequacy within protestations that she did the best she could. She tells other characters, particularly Janice, that she had dark thoughts back then, and that her marriage to Johnny Boy was stressful and frightening; from what we've seen and heard of that period (including Tony's reports of the old man abusing him), it's a virtual certainty that Johnny Boy hit Livia. That electrifying moment when Janice shoots Richie represents the cathartic self-defense that Livia never made in the 1960s.

It is also an (incidental) display of protectiveness for Tony that the actual Livia could never muster. "Babies are like animals, they're no different from dogs," Livia tells Tony, after seeming to levitate downstairs the morning after Richie's murder. "Somebody has to teach 'em right from wrong!"

It's mother and son's first real interaction of the season, and though they briefly share a scene in the finale, this unknowingly turns out to be our farewell to the relationship, prior to Nancy Marchand's death two months after the airdate. It's a corker, with Tony witnessing the gamut of Livia's emotions as she blames Janice for what she thinks is Richie leaving her, refuses to accept any blame for how her kids turned out, tries to guilt Tony over his rising fortunes versus her own, then feigns senility again by acting hurt that he won't kiss her. Exasperated, Tony storms out of the house, only to trip and fall on the way to the car. He has accidentally recreated the moment he described to Dr. Melfi in the series' second episode—the only happy childhood memory he could conjure of Livia, of the two of them laughing at Johnny Boy when he took a similar tumble—and though Livia tries to wrestle her cackles back into crocodile tears, she can't help showing her true face to her son. This is who she is. As he screamed at the nurses when stroke victim Livia was being wheeled away from him in the season one finale, she's smiling, and he's the only one who can see it.

As irritated and exhausted as Tony is after disposing of Richie's body[82]— sarcasm dripping from his great phrase "pine cones all around" when Janice all but begs him to lie about Richie's final resting place—he radiates relief, even gratitude, as Janice's Seattle-bound bus turns the corner. His survival even briefly repairs the rift in the Soprano marriage, on increasingly shaky ground thanks to Tony's compulsive cheating, Irina's suicide attempt,[83] and Carmela's thwarted fixation on Vic (when Gabriella reveals the real reason for Vic's reticence, it ties together the Carmela and Pussy storyline: they're both hostages to circumstance). The episode's final scene is a reconciliation under duress. Tony sits on the couch next his wife, tells her Janice has returned to Seattle and Richie is "gone," and makes their mostly unspoken understanding explicit: "Carmela, after eighteen years of marriage, don't make me make you an accessory after the fact."

Within two minutes they're talking about Tony's responsibilities during Carmela's planned trip to Rome. Then she leaves him on the couch, alone but alive. The closing music is the Eurythmics' "I Saved the World Today." Vishnu may have come late, but her timing was perfect.

SEASON 2/EPISODE 13
WRITTEN BY DAVID CHASE AND TODD A. KESSLER
DIRECTED BY JOHN PATTERSON

Temple of Knowledge

"Isn't Pussy your friend?" —**Dr. Melfi**

The influence of David Lynch and Mark Frost's *Twin Peaks* was all over *The Sopranos* from the start, and as years passed, David Chase often talked about

---

82 The scene where Furio and Chris saw up Richie in the pork store kitchen testifies to how ordinary this extraordinary event seems when you're in this life. "It's gonna be a while before I eat anything from Satriale's," Chris says.

83 "You're putting me in a position where I feel sorry for a whore who fucks you?" Carmela yells at him. Well, sure—but that's the sort of thing *The Sopranos* does to its viewers constantly. There's no reason to care about almost any of these people, except for the fact that they're human, too, and, as Meadow puts it in "Bust Out," "We're all hypocrites."

the show, always fondly. The affinity was never as obvious as it is in "Funhouse." The episode understands that the most daring thing about *Twin Peaks* wasn't the way it mashed up different genres, its seesawing between satire, slapstick, melodrama, and horror, or even its surreal or expressionist imagery and sound design; it was the way that the show treated dreams, fantasies, intuition, and the uncanny as legitimate sources of information about our everyday world. The show's hero, Special Agent Dale Cooper, analyzed his own dreams for clues on how to solve Laura Palmer's murder, and even tried to deduce the identity of a person identified only as "J" in Laura's diary by having a deputy toss rocks at a row of bottles. The storytelling was rooted more deeply in the collected works of Sigmund Freud and Carl Jung than in any established method for writing a series.

The *Sopranos* one-upped even Lynch/Frost by devoting most of the first half of its season two finale to Tony uncovering the identity of a rat in his organization by decoding a series of food-poisoning-induced dreams. The original run of *Twin Peaks* never went this far. Not only do we get a solid twenty minutes of dream material, interrupted by brief scenes of Tony waking up long enough to belch, vomit, fart, shit, moan, curse, and argue with people; we also never see him discuss the dreams in detail with anyone else, not even Melfi, his dream sherpa. That means it's Tony who's doing the work of interpretation in "Funhouse." This is an indicator of real growth, even though it's not necessarily the kind Melfi wants (it seems to confirm her accusation that he's only sticking with therapy so he can become a better gangster).

"It's not my fuckin' head," says Tony, right before the dreams begin. "It's my stomach." Read as: *I'm not going to figure this out intellectually, I'm going to go with my gut.* Tony's actual guts—his digestive organs—are going to work through, process, *digest* the matter of the informant. Pussy is the toxin in the Mob's body politic that caused this allergic reaction. The organization's health will only be restored after he's been puked up or shat out.

It takes a while for Tony to figure out what we've known ever since "Do Not Resuscitate." Seven distinct sections of dreamspace are represented on screen, if you count Tony's conversation with Silvio and seeing himself whack Paulie through the binoculars as separate. And every time the episode plunges us into one of the dreams, their content and meanings are a bit plainer. It's as if Tony's subconscious keeps explaining things, Tony doesn't quite get it, and his subconscious tries again, in simpler language, until it finally abandons ambiguity and has the fish just flat-out tell him what he needs to know.

1. We see Tony meeting his guys on the boardwalk (plus Philly Parisi,[84] killed for being a blabbermouth), waiting for an unspecified "they" to show up. Tony tells them he's been diagnosed with terminal cancer (his life is in danger) by a doctor (like Melfi, the psychiatrist, who teaches him how to read himself, like the "open book" mentioned in the Stones song playing at the Indian restaurant). Pussy is the only one who never speaks or makes eye contact with Tony. Rather than wait for the inevitable, Tony decides to douse himself in gasoline and get it over with. Before he accepts the lit Zippo from Paulie, Tony asks, "Where's Pussy?" who by this point has disappeared from the dream.

2. We see Tony walking on the boardwalk again, this time in front of a real-life Asbury Park attraction called the Temple of Knowledge (although the name of the establishment is not visible on-screen[85]). Silvio glides into view, as if via conveyor belt, and tells Tony, walking in place as if on a treadmill, a variation of the same thing that he said in the season premiere, paraphrasing *The Godfather Part III*: "Our true enemy has yet to reveal himself."[86]

3. Then comes a segment where Tony peers through sightseeing binoculars and sees himself playing cards in an empty train station with Paulie, whom he suddenly shoots dead. The black "binocular" frame around the image evokes the type of surveillance that Tony knows the FBI has been running on his operation. The shooting has the sting of an out-of-nowhere betrayal, though it's hard to say for sure the "Tony" playing cards in the train station is a stand-in for the traitorous Pussy (a "known

---

84 Complicating matters, this episode also introduces Patsy Parisi, Philly's identical twin brother, now a semi-reluctant member of Tony's old crew. As writer/producer Terence Winter recalls, "When he saw how terrific Dan Grimaldi was in Episode 201, David immediately regretted having killed Philly Parisi off. Then he then said something like 'Well, you only get to play the twin brother card once per TV series, and I'm playing it now. This guy is too good not to bring back.'"

85 Although the mural seen in "Funhouse" was painted specifically for the shoot, it's based on the artwork on the side of a business operated by a psychic named Marie Castello who told fortunes on the Asbury Park boardwalk for sixty-five years. This is meaningless to anyone unfamiliar with southern New Jersey, but you still get the gist of what it means to the episode by looking at the art, the centerpiece of which is an all-seeing eye. Anyone who spent time in the lower half of the state between 1932, when Castello opened her business, and 1997, when she finally retired, will laugh at the rightness of this location showing up in a Jersey gangster's dream. It was mentioned twice in Bruce Springsteen's music, in "Fourth of July, Asbury Park (Sandy)," from the 1973 album *Greetings from Asbury Park, New Jersey!* ("Did you hear the cops finally busted Madam Marie for tellin' fortunes better than they do?"), and in "Brilliant Disguise," about his doomed first marriage, from 1987's *Tunnel of Love* ("the gypsy swore our future was bright . . . maybe baby/the gypsy lied"). Castello died in 2008.

86 The actual *Godfather III* quote is, "Our true enemy has yet to show his face."

quantity" suddenly turning on a colleague) or for actual Tony, who may have to kill a trusted member of his inner circle. Could be both.

4. The next time we enter dreamspace, with Tony and Melfi in therapy, we don't know it's a dream until we realize Melfi is acting strangely. Then we hear her voice coming out of the mouth of Annalisa from "Commendatori." She tells Tony he's the greatest threat to himself, a self-destructive force. Finally Tony asks, "You gonna make me eat something now?" (i.e., force Tony to take in something he doesn't want: in this case, pussy/the truth about Pussy), and Annalisa/Melfi replies, "If you keep this up."

5. Then we see Tony on the boardwalk in a tiny red car (like a clown car) with Adriana and Christopher; Pussy is supposed to be in the back seat. Furio, the new guy, replaces him, as he would presumably replace Pussy in the organization.

6. Tony appears in Melfi's waiting room with puffy eyes, wild hair, a dirty tank top, and a raging hard-on. Melfi invites him in for a conversation that leads him to admit that he's got "pussy on the brain." They discuss the two ways to interpret that word, followed by Tony fucking pussy/Pussy. This is the only dream in which Tony says he knows he's having a dream: it's a lucid dream, controllable to some degree. So when he "fucks pussy," it's by choice. He's also in coitus, or union, with the one person who's done the most to help him understand his subconscious—Melfi, who could be interpreted as standing in for that same subconscious. Tony and his subconscious have been playing "Will they or won't they?" since the pilot, and here they consummate the relationship. In a close-up of the dreaming Tony, he's smiling for the first time since he gave Carmela the fur coat.

7. Finally, we arrive at that astonishing moment when Tony finds himself on the boardwalk confronted by a row of fish on ice, and one of them opens its mouth and speaks with Pussy's voice. The slumbering Tony probably knows what this all means even before the conversation begins, because the symbolism of the tableau is laden with so many gangland associations: Pussy is a small fish being used by the FBI to land a bigger fish, and now that he's been marked a traitor, he has to get iced and "sleep with the fishes." But just in case Tony *doesn't* get it, his subconscious has the Pussy fish tell him, "Ya know I been workin' with the government, right, Tone?"

The material surrounding the dreams is pregnant with associations, too. The chain of dream sequences starts with Tony at a dinner meeting with Pussy and their partner in the phone card scheme, dining at the Indian restaurant he later thinks served him bad vindaloo. Scored to the opening section of The Rolling Stones' "Thru and Thru," the scene kicks off with a whole fish—as big as the ones that will show up on ice in the dream—being carried out of the kitchen, bypassing Tony en route to the table behind them. Then Tony and Pussy go to Vesuvio and have a second meal that includes mussels. Although Artie Bucco understandably obfuscates to save face, it's clear Tony and Pussy (who reports some mild diarrhea) got the food poisoning from his mussels, not the Indian joint.

What all this means for Tony's waking life is that he was absolutely convinced that the source of his distress lay outside of his circle, when in fact it was inside the whole time. He figures out that Artie's mussels sickened him before Artie is willing to accept responsibility. Turns out it wasn't the Indians (i.e., the outsiders) who laid him low, but an Italian: one of his own. By the time Tony and Silvio pay Pussy a house call and Tony finds wiretap gear in his bedroom, he already knows the truth. The confirmation is a formality. His subconscious has been warning him for a long time that Pussy was a traitor: he probably knew when Pussy looked into his eyes near the end of "Guy Walks into a Psychiatrist's Office." It just took a while for him to admit it to himself. And he couldn't have done without his distressed bowels, his rumbling subconscious, and the tools he got from Melfi.[87]

Pussy's execution is the melancholy counterpart to Richie's shocking death in "The Knight in White Satin Armor." In a sequence about half as long as the dreams that brought them there, Pussy's three closest associates take him out on the water and do everything they can to delay the moment when they'll have to kill him. All four know what's coming—the best Pussy can ask for is not to be shot in the face, and also to be allowed to sit before they kill him (he's granted the first request)—and all seem as nauseated by it as Tony was by the mussels. Beforehand, they share a drink, and Pussy tries to enjoy his final moments by spinning a tale of sexual bliss with the Puerto Rican acupuncturist who was part of his FBI cover story. Tony, irritated both with how long this is taking and the depth of his old friend's betrayal, won't even let Pussy have this moment, wiping the smile off his face by asking, "Did she even really exist?" It's up to him to fire the first shot when Paulie, Silvio, and Pussy himself all seem eager to drag things out. Then it's into the sea.

It was reasonable for us to assume, based on how pre-*Sopranos* TV dramas and gangster films handled things, that Richie would die in this season finale at Tony's hands, while Pussy would be dealt with earlier, or perhaps be kept around through season three to provide ongoing jeopardy. Instead we got a sensational

---

87 As if to offer more proof that Tony has been paying attention in therapy even while jousting with Melfi or storming out prematurely, the episode has Melfi make essentially the same observation at the end about the relationship between Tony's anger and sadness that Dream Melfi makes in Tony's food-poisoned mind.

detonation in the penultimate chapter followed by a surreal ramping-down in the finale. Both Richie and Pussy's deaths, indelible as they are, have an aspect of strategic anticlimax, or at least misdirection, that differentiated *The Sopranos* from all other contemporary TV dramas.

The relaxed denouement of "Funhouse" covers Livia's arrest for possession of airline tickets Tony got in the Scatino bust-out (which he impulsively gives her just to get her away from him); a Melfi therapy session in which Pussy is never discussed, even in coded fashion; and a closing montage focusing on Meadow's graduation,[88] scored to the rest of "Thru and Thru," concluding with series of dissolves from Tony smoking a cigar to the ocean where Pussy's remains are being eaten by smaller fish.

"You know that we do take away," Keith Richards sings the first time the song is used in "Funhouse," in the Indian restaurant. The song returns at the end and continues through the credits. *The Sopranos* never tells us why *this* song, in *this* episode, and if Chase's comments about music are any indication, he might've just included it because he liked how it sounded. But in context of the plot, it's powerfully resonant. The "open book" mentioned in the lyrics is a phone directory that can be used to reach out to someone (listed under "services") who can get you whatever you need, anytime, day or night—somebody who adores you and wants what's best for you no matter what occurs; a lover/protector whose motivations are selfless and pure, and will stick by you "thru and thru." Tony's subconscious played that role in "Funhouse."

It's the mother he never had.

---

88 After a season in which Meadow's college choice was framed as Berkeley (her preference) versus Georgetown (Carmela's), we instead find out she's going to Columbia, a more geographically convenient way to keep her on the show. But because it hasn't been mentioned before—Meadow previously considered Georgetown to be "a total reach," and Columbia's even more competitive—it seems to come out of nowhere, especially since it's introduced within one of Tony's dreams.

Season
Three

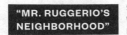

"MR. RUGGERIO'S NEIGHBORHOOD"

SEASON 3/EPISODE 1
WRITTEN BY DAVID CHASE
DIRECTED BY ALLEN COULTER

The Sausage Factory

"Ever go to tie your shoes and you notice your laces are wet?" —**Paulie**

"Mr. Ruggerio's Neighborhood" feels more like a self-contained overture than a standard season-premiere exposition dump introducing new business and characters. The title, riffing on the children's TV classic *Mister Rogers' Neighborhood*, could be the name of a never-produced comic opera based on *The Sopranos*. The main musical cue, segueing and sometimes combining the 1983 Police hit "Every Breath You Take" and Henry Mancini's *Peter Gunn* theme, makes sections play like a musical comedy, further amplified by director Allen Coulter's obsessively exact camera movements—constantly craning, panning, and zooming to follow characters and vehicles, with car windows and "binocular" camera mattes creating frames-within-frames. "Mr. Ruggerio's Neighborhood" is also the first episode that operates mostly in one mode, farce—although the depression and anger of Patsy Parisi, whose twin brother Philly Tony's had killed in "Guy Walks into a Psychiatrist's Office," gives parts of it a painful edge.

Much of it is told from the point of view of FBI agents, including Lipari, Special Agents Harris and Grasso, and boss Frank Cubitoso as they try to improve their surveillance on Tony's home and business operations. Although it's all played straight, much of the FBI stuff feels like a commentary on making or watching TV. The team assigns code names to major surveillance targets that evoke the nicknames that used to be given to characters and locations in turn-of-the-century TV recaps, like at the now-defunct *Television Without Pity*:[1] the Soprano home is "The Sausage Factory," Tony is "Der Bingle," Carmela is "Mrs. Bing," AJ is "Baby Bing." The opening scene of the agents gathered together around a long table, reviewing reports and making observations, could be a "tone" meeting of a TV show's writing staff, or actors' first "table read" of a new script. Surveillance experts perform a "sound check" in the basement when the family and housekeeper aren't home, to determine whether the air conditioning's ambient noise will prevent usable recordings. The close-ups of a replacement desk lamp being bugged, and the scene where two agents discuss whether they can move a work table one meter to the left without anyone noticing, echo the importance of scene-

---

1   As a result of Patsy's adventures in swimming pool micturition in this episode, the *Television Without Pity* recapper would later dub him "Patsy Pees-A-Lot."

to-scene continuity. Some of the FBI agents try their hand at acting, with varying degrees of success: the female agent spying on Meadow in her Columbia dorm is so convincing that a male student approvingly checks her out, while Agent Harris gets "made" by Tony even when he dons a fishing hat. Different "viewers" of this real-life "show" are watching for different reasons: some are interested in money changing hands, others in the relationships between criminal associates or family members; one agent is unreasonably excited to learn that Tony's "got the same Black & Decker as me," and another lives to ogle Adriana and her handsy tennis instructor.[2] The agents are also, like us, privy to developments the characters aren't aware of, and argue amongst themselves about when seeds that have been planted will bear dramatic fruit. The most blatant example here is the defective boiler in the basement of the Soprano home, hereafter known as the Richie Aprile Memorial Boiler because it pays off sooner than expected.

This episode also establishes how life, like TV series production, is built around routines:[3] you go here, you do this, you talk about that, and once in a while, problems arise requiring definitive answers to avoid long-term woes. Patsy is the wild card here, falling into deep gloom over the anniversary of his brother's death and trying to avoid flying into a rage and killing Tony. Dan Grimaldi gets a grand turn in the spotlight, expressing the character's soul-sick despair through tears, thousand-yard stares, and deadpan statements edged with simmering fury. When the armed, drunk Patsy wanders onto the Soprano property like a film shoot onlooker who slipped past the production assistant assigned to "lock it down" and ended up ruining a take, it gives the hour a momentary jolt of pain so intense that the episode can't suppress it. Tony's repeated, quasi-hypnotic command to Patsy to put the past behind him is likewise disturbing because of all the farcical rushing-about that precedes and follows it. In this line of work, not only do you have to accept that you or somebody you love could be killed at any minute, for any reason, by somebody you call a friend—you'll have to look the killer in the face and call him "boss."

---

2 As happens occasionally on *The Sopranos*, some of the surveillance of Adriana makes it feel as though it's the show that's getting off, not just the agent.

3 This episode has one of the funniest *Sopranos* meals yet: the Bada Bing office lunch anchored to Paulie's extended soliloquy on bathroom cleanliness. He's especially disgusted by men's rooms, consistent horror shows compared to women's restrooms, which he thinks are so clean that "you could eat maple walnut ice cream off the toilet."

"PROSHAI, LIVUSHSKA"	SEASON 3/EPISODE 2 WRITTEN BY DAVID CHASE DIRECTED BY TIM VAN PATTEN

Miles to Go

"What are you gonna do?" —**Tony**

"Proshai, Livushska" feels more like a traditional season opener than the hour that preceded it,[4] and not just because it deals with the offscreen death of series costar Nancy Marchand by officially giving Livia, pushed to the margins in season two, a proper send-off. The episode brings Janice back into the fold to stir up more trouble; casually reveals that aging Family captain Ray Curto (George Loros) is yet another FBI informant; and introduces important new supporting characters: Meadow's boyfriend Noah Tannenbaum (Patrick Tully) and not-quite-captain Ralphie Cifaretto (Joe Pantoliano[5]). The latter walks right into Tony's house and gives him a tearful hug as if he's been on the show from the start. We learn that he's taken over Richie Aprile's crew, and he comes on like Replacement Richie, down to his insistence on dominating a certain garbage route and his insubordination when Tony orders him to knock it off. We also spend more time with Livia's Russian housekeeper Svetlana Kirilenko (Alla Kliouka Schaffer), who clashes with Janice over possession of Livia's old record collection as well as the house that Janice still wants to claim (along with the fabled cash stash Livia told her about).

At first, there's no indication that this episode will write Livia out. Things kick off with an explosive act of garbage-related terrorism, then we cut to a shot of Tony lying on the floor surrounded by broken glass and what we might assume is his own blood, perhaps spilled by whoever detonated that bomb; it's actually the remains of a glass of tomato juice that Tony dropped after stuffing his face with capicola and fainting mere moments after driving his daughter's half-Jewish, half-African American boyfriend from the house in a racist snit. (This is another instance where Tony's bigotry, assumed most of the time, bubbles into view, with Tony using several Italian racial slurs in front of him, in addition to calling him a "charcoal briquette.") In one of the most brazen bits of formal playfulness yet seen on the series—right on the heels of the music-driven Keystone Kops absurdity of

---

4   HBO, in fact, aired it on the same night as "Mr. Ruggerio's Neighborhood," the only time two *Sopranos* episodes premiered together.

5   Jersey-guy character actor—known to friends and fans alike as "Joey Pants"—who followed in fellow Hoboken native Frank Sinatra's footsteps by playing Angelo Maggio in a TV remake of *From Here to Eternity* before breaking through as the pimp who loots Tom Cruise's house in *Risky Business*. Pantoliano's time on *The Sopranos* came as he was having another career moment thanks to his work with the Wachowskis in *Bound* and *The Matrix* and with Christopher Nolan in *Memento*.

"Mr. Ruggerio's Neighborhood"—the episode "rewinds" to the events leading up to Tony's collapse, in the manner of an old-fashioned VHS cassette; the "rewinding" noise continues on the soundtrack right up to the instant that Tony speaks with Meadow, who's sitting on the living room couch after screening the 1931 gangster picture *The Public Enemy*, the film that made James Cagney a star.

The film proves important not because of its hallowed spot in early film history, but because its emotional backbone is the loving relationship between the hero and his adoring mother (Beryl Mercer)—a bond Tony can only fantasize about. The episode cuts to *The Public Enemy* four times, and builds its final scene around Tony watching the horrifying finale where Ma Powers preps her son's bedroom for his return from the hospital, not knowing that he's been kidnapped and killed and that it's his corpse that's being brought home. What brings Tony to tears isn't the tragedy of Tom's death, but the simple image of a mother expressing joy that her son is coming back. It's never clear whether Tony is obsessively rewatching the entire film while dealing with his mother's death, or if it just takes him forever to get through it. Either way, it gains a talismanic power as this hour unreels, until by the end it transcends its plot function, illustrating a truth about how movies can explain us to ourselves even when we weren't looking for insight.

Much has been written about the questionable judgment behind bringing Livia back via then-state-of-the-art CGI, at considerable expense, and having Gandolfini and Schaffer act against a stand-in plus recordings of Livia's "dialogue"—a Frankenstein patchwork of phrases harvested from earlier episodes. Chase felt strongly that the show needed to have Tony and Livia speak face to face, rather than over the phone, or have Tony be informed of his mother's death after it happened and then deal with the relevant information in that scene (Livia possibly testifying against Tony over the stolen plane tickets) in some other context (maybe in therapy, where Tony deals with the legal and emotional implications anyway). The end product is distracting because the technology wasn't able to do exactly what Chase wanted. He was inspired by Ridley Scott's *Gladiator*, which similarly completed Oliver Reed's scenes after he died during production. But Scott had a much larger budget and could hedge his bets with high contrast lighting, smoke, mist, and other concealing devices, versus the Tony–Livia scene here, presented in a simple, brightly lit room that underscored distracting continuity problems like mismatched light sources and hairstyles varying between sampled shots.

But this defect proves minor, because the show understands its characters so well, and the episode's observations about grief and mourning ring so true.[6] From the moment that Tony reenters the kitchen after readjusting the backyard

---

6 The episode has an especially good ear for the non-sentiments people express after a loss when they can't figure out what else to say, like, "At least she didn't suffer," and "What are you gonna do?"

sprinkler (the water droplets on his face and shirt standing in for the tears he can't cry yet), "Proshai, Livushska" captures the awkwardness of publicly processing the death of a loved one you wanted to die.[7] Tony lashes out so ferociously in therapy that he calls his own mother the C-word. "I'm glad she's dead," he tells Melfi. "Not just glad—I wished she died. *Wished.*"

Livia's awfulness—or defectiveness, if you're feeling sympathetic—radiates outward even after her death. As Carmela says later, she knew who she was and deliberately requested no funeral because she thought nobody would come, but her children "ignored her wishes." Janice largely drives that decision, enabled by the funeral home owner Cozzarelli (Ralph Lucarelli, channeling the *Godfather* films something fierce[8]) and by Tony, feeling bad over not feeling worse and numbing his guilt with cash like always.

Without the viewing, burial, and reception, though, we would've missed moments like Junior laying into Tony in the back of the funeral parlor ("This economy's so robust, you get credit for shit you had nothin' to do with"); Svetlana telling Janice, "She was much work, but in end, she defeated me"; Janice hijacking the reception with what Tony terms "California bullshit"; Hesh being hassled to say something, and offering, "Between brain and mouth, there was no interlocutor"; the anonymous guest coming down the stairs in the background behind Tony, getting a quick read on the room, and going back up; Chris, coked and stoned, spinning his theory that everyone has a double ("Mrs. Soprano may have passed, but who's to say there isn't another Mrs. Soprano just like her?"); and Janice informing Tony that he was the only one of the children whose memorabilia Livia preserved, a revelation that he doesn't know how to take because it contradicts the idea that his mother was a harpy who couldn't express love and sought to have him killed.

This is also another episode that, like "Isabella" and "Funhouse," hints that undefined theological or cosmological forces are at work in the *Sopranos* universe. There's a brief reflection of Pussy, murdered in "Funhouse," in a hallway mirror that no one else in the shot could have witnessed, and a long scene in which AJ struggles over a "close read" of "Stopping by Woods on a Snowy Evening," a poem by "asshole Robert Frost" that's frequently used in eulogies. Meadow tries to help AJ figure out what "miles to go before I sleep" means, but without doing all the heavy lifting for him. "Just gimme the fuckin' answer so I can write this!" he whines.

Not only does Meadow ultimately refuse; her impromptu lesson in poetry explication raises more questions than it answers (it turns out that both white

---

7   "Grown children often secretly wish for an aged parent to die," Melfi assures him. "And it's not necessary for the parent to be a witness for the prosecution."

8   Cozzarelli: "I'll use all my powers, all my skills." Tony: "Don't go crazy."

and black can symbolize death). "He's talking about his own death," Meadow says of the poem's narrator, "which has yet to come, but will come."

That doesn't help AJ at all. The silent moments after his sister leaves briefly nudge *The Sopranos* in the direction of a horror film, with the boy hearing floorboards creak and calling out, "Grandma?" Was Livia's spirit visiting him, or was AJ's imagination playing tricks? Rather than provide answers, the show lets us sit in the quiet of the woods, snowy, dark, and deep.

 SEASON 3/EPISODE 3
WRITTEN BY TODD A. KESSLER
DIRECTED BY HENRY J. BRONCHTEIN

The Hair Apparent

"Yeah, but what's wrong with the kid? When's he gonna grow up?" —**Tony**

The legacy fathers hand down to sons, often without consulting them, binds a seemingly disparate collection of plotlines. There are four potential title characters in "Fortunate Son": Christopher, AJ, Jackie Aprile Jr., and Tony himself, whose childhood we return to as Dr. Melfi finally figures out what's causing his panic attacks.

The solution to that mystery comes with remarkable swiftness, relative to Tony having been her patient for two-plus seasons now: with Livia gone but the attacks continuing, Tony declares that Melfi needs to put up or shut up in this area, and she almost immediately does. Realizing that meat is usually present[9] when Tony collapses, Melfi probes his past until he conjures the story of how Johnny Boy wrested control of the pork store from old man Satriale, a degenerate gambler (like Davey Scatino) who had to pay debts not only with his business, but with the pinkie finger Johnny chopped off while eleven-year-old Tony watched.

As usual, Tony is bound so tightly by all the rationalizations and repressions necessary simply to function as a member of the Family that he tries to shrug off the story as no big deal—"What, your father never cut off anybody's pinkie?" he jokes with Melfi—but even he can see the link between Mr. Satriale's mutilation, Livia being aroused by the meat Johnny has brought home from work, and what in hindsight was his very first panic attack. Melfi compares the linkage to the

---

9   Though not always—the writers didn't settle on the idea until this season.

madeleines from Proust's *Remembrance of Things Past*—"This sounds very gay," Tony complains—before explaining that Tony's knowing the root cause of the panic attacks will make him less susceptible to them. The diagnosis is a huge turning point in the Tony–Melfi relationship. Before, he went to her because he labored under an omnipresent threat to his life and livelihood that only she could help fix; that problem mostly managed, doctor and patient have more latitude to explore his many other problems—and, as we've seen (say, leading up to "Funhouse"), for Tony to solicit help with work problems she should want no part of.

Tony was the son of a wiseguy who learned to ignore the terrible way his father put food on the table, and we've seen its psychological toll. Much of "Fortunate Son" illustrates how that same cost is being exacted on the next generation.

It's striking how much young Tony (Mark Damiano II) looks like AJ, and the resemblance carries through to the episode's final shot, where AJ suffers a panic attack of his own while his football coach appoints him defensive captain. Where Tony was always being groomed by Johnny to join the Family, he's never wanted that life for his own son. His namesake is spoiled and adrift. AJ's plans for his future change so rapidly that he can't even remember them all. And a visit to Columbia to see Meadow leaves him so intimidated by the very idea of college that he no longer wants to enroll anywhere. Football seems more like something he's doing to win Tony's approval—when he recovers a fumble in the game, the action slows down so Tony's cheers make him seem more animal than man—rather than a triumph of personal significance to AJ. The coach promoting him shouldn't be nearly as traumatizing as the finger/meat incident was for Tony, but AJ may feel locked into something he doesn't want, even if he still has no clue what he *does* want.

In contrast to AJ, the episode's other namesake, Jackie Jr., knows very much what he wants: to follow in his father's footsteps. Like AJ, he's keenly aware of his academic limitations, privately dismissing the desires of his mother Rosalie[10] (Sharon Angela) that he become a doctor. Christopher refers to him as "the hair apparent," but he's just a dumb, scared kid (when the two rob a college benefit concert together, Jackie pees his pants) whose godfather Tony is adamant that he won't be joining the uppercase Family.

Tony's two surrogate sons team up, despite their wildly different Mob standing, because Christopher is desperate for the cash to pay Paulie's weekly nut. The

---

10 Rosalie, a few years removed from Jackie's death, is now dating Ralphie, which only adds to the feeling of him being the Replacement Richie. He's angling to run the Aprile crew, he's dating Richie's sister-in-law and giving advice to Jackie Jr. He's a wholly new character in many ways, but in others, it feels like a writer's assistant went through every script and did a find-and-replace from "Rich" to "Ralph."

episode opens with Chrissie finally achieving his dream of becoming a made man. He worries at first that he might be taken out at the event, like Joe Pesci in *Goodfellas*, and when Adriana assures him that he watches too many movies, the episode winks at her, and us, by cutting immediately to Christopher all suited up in a parking lot, with a recreation of the famous *Goodfellas* push-in shot introducing the adult Henry Hill. This will be the last time in the episode Christopher's life resembles the kinds of movies that first made him want to join the Family. At the ceremony where he and Eugene Pontecorvo (Robert Funaro[11]) are made,[12] Chris takes a distracting bird on the windowsill for a bad omen. Paulie, now his direct supervisor, gifts him with a sports book, but insists on $6,000 a week, no matter how well or poorly business is going. Chris tries putting on airs—when Jackie Jr. and his buddy Dino (Andrew Davoli) get into a fight at Chris's favorite hangout, he warns them, "Don't disrespect the pizza parlor!" then quietly tells new underling Benny Fazio (Max Casella[13]) that he can't be seen in a place like this anymore—but has a lot to learn about his new role, particularly when he has a bad run at the sports book and comes up short paying Paulie. Everyone tells him that the promotion will make his life better, but instead it seems to weigh him down with more rules and responsibilities—all unshakable because, as Tony warns Chris and Eugene at the ceremony, "once you enter this Family, there's no getting out."

"This being made ain't working out the way I thought it would," he complains to Paulie.

Chris, like Tony, AJ, and Jackie, has grown up in this life, and been exposed to so much of its ugliness. He should be used to it by now. But, like the others, he's continually surprised by the depths of it all, where your brain turning itself off and your body collapsing seems less like a mental aberration than a sensible response.

---

11 An old friend of James Gandolfini's, Funaro was initially hired to play Ralphie. When Chase realized the actor and role weren't a good fit, he was recast as Eugene, a member of what used to be the Aprile crew.

12 Making his first appearance at the reception to celebrate Chris and Eugene's promotions: Carmine Lupertazzi, Tony's counterpart in New York and Johnny Sack's direct superior, played by yet another *Goodfellas* alum, Tony Lip.

13 One of the few actors to appear in both *Analyze This* and *The Sopranos*, Casella was previously best known for playing Vinnie Delpino, the best friend of Neil Patrick Harris's child prodigy on *Doogie Howser, M.D.*

SEASON 3/EPISODE 4
"EMPLOYEE OF THE MONTH" WRITTEN BY ROBIN GREEN & MITCHELL BURGESS
DIRECTED BY JOHN PATTERSON

Attack Dog

"No." —**Dr. Melfi**

The first ride-or-die episode of *The Sopranos* since "Funhouse," "Employee of the Month" inflicts catastrophic trauma on Dr. Jennifer Melfi, the major character least compromised by the show's criminal activity, then presents her with an opportunity to use Tony's dark powers to exact revenge, gives her time to think it over, and has her decide with a single word: "No." That lone spoken syllable, followed by the show's first-ever cut to black,[14] is one of the most powerful moments in the series to date, because "no" is the word that the man who raped Melfi in her office parking garage wouldn't accept, and that other men in her life, including her husband and son, consistently fail to respect.

The use of rape to "raise the stakes" on TV shows, or simply to jolt audiences out of any complacency, has rightly been criticized, thanks to so many subsequent dramas like *Game of Thrones, Sons of Anarchy, Westworld, Mad Men, Downton Abbey,* and *True Blood* employing it with wildly varying degrees of sensitivity. But sexual assault has been a staple of TV drama since at least the 1970s, when a newfound delight in brutality started to spill over from theatrical features to the small screen, and it became common during the 1980s—most notoriously on daytime and nighttime soaps, cop and crime shows, and legal procedurals. Among the most notorious instances was a two-part episode of the NBC series *Hunter* in which the show's female lead, Detective Dee Dee McCall (Stepfanie Kramer), got raped by a diplomat. The story ended with her partner Hunter (Fred Dreyer) killing the rapist in his own apartment.[15] The episode was praised for presenting the attack in a brutal but non-titillating manner, although a police officer committing vigilante violence left a sour aftertaste for some. *The Sopranos*, ever opposing the ingrained habits of traditional TV, leads us to think it's going to pull a *Hunter* here, and even carefully sets up intervention by Tony as desirable and seemingly inevitable. Melfi's attacker, Jesus Rossi (Mario Polit), is caught quickly but released on a technicality, and the police are made to seem indifferent or

---

14 This is first time that the show ever simply cut to black, as if somebody had pressed "stop." In every other case, the episode faded to black.

15 This plotline caused such a stir that the producers tried to repeat it again in season four, but Kramer objected to getting raped twice in the same TV show, so the script was rewritten to have her fight her attacker and escape before he could do the deed.

incompetent. Melfi's son and ex-husband rage against the attacker and express a desire to personally murder him but are clearly incapable of doing so, as confirmed in a cut from Richard's clenched fists (inadequate to the act he wishes he could commit) to a shot of a stump being split by a powerful blow from Tony's axe (a precise and confident display of force that's more in line with what "needs" to be done). The fact that Rossi is out in the world again, his mugshot hanging on the wall of a sandwich shop Melfi frequents, is so galling that it seems to validate the despair of Melfi's son Jason: "You know the whole world is a fucking sewer! It's nothing but a fucking sewer!" How will we viewers get satisfaction? The answer is, we won't—not right now, anyway; although the fact that the rapist is still out there would appear to promise some kind of traditional TV resolution further down the line.[16]

The awfulness of Melfi's predicament is amplified by the useless or toxic men in this episode who have to make themselves focus on her needs, and who are too easily distracted by their own feelings of emasculation (or in the mobsters' case, a craving for "respect"). Melfi had just taken Richard back, but the reconciliation is dashed as he keeps turning the attack into yet another referendum on the image of the Italian American people, and both he and Jason seem as angered by recognition of their own helplessness as they are by the attack itself.

So Richard is back briefly, and then gone again, as a result of the rape, while Tony is on the verge of being dumped by Melfi as a patient—"Richard was right," she vents to Elliot. "I've been charmed by a sociopath. Why didn't I listen?"—then gets a second chance[17] because he ironically makes her feel safer than Richard ever did.

On the Mob side of things,[18] Ralphie disregards Tony's orders not to draw Jackie Jr. into the thug life, and takes him along on a debt collection call that he deliberately escalates so that he can give Jackie what he craves (a chance to prove himself, like the robbery with Christopher in "Fortunate Son") and bond the fatherless young man more tightly to Ralphie. Ralphie's taunts include threatening to rape the target's wife. He promises that Jackie will "fuck your wife till she moans," terms that imply consensuality, or at least a woman ultimately deciding mid-rape that she "likes it," as Susan George did in Sam Peckinpah's 1971 thriller *Straw Dogs*.

---

16 Chase told *Entertainment Weekly* in 2001, "If you're raised on a steady diet of Hollywood movies and network television, you start to think, 'Obviously, there's going to be some moral accounting here'. That's not the way the world works. It all comes down to why you're watching. If all you want is to see big Tony Soprano take that guy's head and bang it against the wall like a cantaloupe . . . The point is, Melfi, despite pain and suffering, made her moral, ethical choice, and we should applaud her for it. That's the story."

17 From an extra-textual perspective, this story helps justify the ongoing therapy, even after Livia's death and the curing of the panic attacks in the two prior episodes, after which either party easily could have drifted away out of awkwardness or lessened urgency.

18 A bit of an afterthought here, but still noteworthy given the man's rank, is New York underboss Johnny Sack buying a mansion a stone's throw away from Tony's own.

Meanwhile, Janice gets beaten up by Russian mobsters for stealing Svetlana's prosthetic leg, but her brother doesn't take action: he doesn't want to provoke a war, and he sees the beating as fitting punishment for her greedy shenanigans.[19]

Tony's non-response to his sister's beating should make us wonder: Is this really the behavior of a loyal Rottweiler who would attack bad people on command, as Melfi's mind seems to believe? It's hard to say. In any event, for a Mob boss who prides himself on his ability to intuitively sense violence, Tony seems oblivious to the possibility that Melfi's wounds were inflicted by something other than a car wreck.

It's surprising to realize how brief the attack is on-screen: about ninety seconds, from Melfi passing her soon-to-be-assailant on the stairwell to the shot of an ER nurse sampling DNA from one of her fingernails. But the staging is so ugly and frightening, dedicated entirely to communicating Melfi's terror, that when you're watching it for the first time, it feels as if it goes on forever, like the sequence in *Straw Dogs* where George is beaten, raped, and sodomized, which lasts almost eight minutes; or the rape scene in Gaspar Noé's 2003 film *Irreversible*, which lasts nine, almost one-tenth of the movie's total running time.

This scene's impact is a matter of judicious writing and filmmaking:[20] you get enough of the act to absorb its heinousness and keep it in your mind as the episode heads toward its surprising ending, but not so much that it feels as if *The Sopranos* is rubbing your nose in Melfi's suffering (unusual restraint for a show that often presents violence as exceptionally brutal slapstick comedy).

Melfi's dream, which is worked out with an intricacy befitting a professional therapist's subconscious, arrives at the same conclusion, and it's only Melfi's self-psychoanalysis, coupled with her deep sense of ethics, that enables her to make the correct choice. Her dream presents Tony Soprano as a source of power (the electricity warnings on the box) and as a literal dispenser (thus the soda machine that accepts macaroni pieces, not legal currency) of lethal violence (the Rottweiler that Melfi initially perceives as the threat to her safety—remember all the times Tony has barked or snarled at her in therapy). But the dream also presents Tony as a nontraditional kind of protector, versus a police officer or security guard (the dog again—a breed that Melfi tells Elliot was "used by the Roman army to guard the camps"; the Mafia took root in the United States partly because Italian immigrants needed security and justice but felt they could not trust the police).

---

19 "I was supposed to be married at this point in my life," Janice complains after the beating, barely aware of the irony that she remains single because she killed the last man to punch her in the mouth.

20 Robin Green and Mitchell Burgess, a married team of screenwriters who worked with Chase on *Northern Exposure*, won the 2001 Primetime Emmy Award for Outstanding Writing of a Drama Series for this episode. Bracco was nominated as lead actress that year, but lost to costar Edie Falco for a different episode from this season, "Second Opinion." Green and Burgess went on to create the hit CBS police drama *Blue Bloods*.

Melfi's subsequent session with Elliot zeroes in on her ethical responsibility not to "use" a patient to solve her own problems. Such a scenario would be disturbing enough if Tony were merely an insurance agent and Melfi were pressing him for a better quote on term life. But it would cross the line into Biblical obscenity were she to deliberately push Tony's buttons (as she does physically when operating the soda "dispenser" in her dream) and turn him into a living manifestation of what Elliot calls "the forbidden part of [her] psyche: murderous rage."[21]

There's something else happening here: a more generalized warning by Melfi's subconscious that continuing to probe Tony's psyche could cause her further harm. She already had to go on the lam from her own practice at the end of season one, and has occasionally feared for her safety because of Tony's tantrums, but this dream seems to contain more dire warnings that she doesn't recognize because she's understandably thinking only of her present trauma. That warning on the side of the transformer(!) box cautions people "High Voltage: Call NJGE before Digging," and Melfi correctly deduces that Tony is the "dangerous" person that she "dig[s]" with. There's a similar, redundant warning in the dream along these lines: she tries to get a soda can to drop from the machine, and when it doesn't, she reaches up inside to force it out, and her arm gets stuck. These and other elements make it seem as if Melfi's subconscious is warning her about more here than the ethics of using a mobster to punish her rapist. Elliot is annoyingly relentless in pressuring Melfi to get rid of Tony, but he only wants what he believes is best for her—and he nearly succeeds by convincing her to move him along to behavior modification therapy. Yet she reverses when she sees how hurt Tony is by the prospect of rejection. She could walk away from this soda machine and save herself, if she could only make herself let go of that can.

Though *The Sopranos* helped jump-start modern TV drama's fascination with seriality, it was more often a collection of short stories featuring the same characters, and "Employee of the Month" in particular feels like an ugly tale with a beginning, a middle, and a definitive end—just not the one most in the audience wanted. Jennifer Melfi, a woman whose world is in contact with Tony's, but who still considers hers separate from his, has a clear chance to break every professional oath she's ever taken to do no harm, to violate all the written and unwritten rules of living in a modern society, and sic some Mob justice on Jesus Rossi. All she has to do, when Tony sees her obvious emotional stress and asks if she has

---

21 Here, as in other Elliot–Melfi scenes, it's striking how frequently he's off-base in his analysis. While he means well and obviously cares about her, he's much more one-note in pushing her to drop Tony than Melfi is in pressing Tony to confront his poor parenting and criminality. He also seems less sophisticated overall. She's usually at least a half-step ahead of him, and sometimes (as in this session, where he offers that unsolicited story about a soda machine falling on a motel guest in Gainesville, Florida) he seems like he's just talking to hear himself talk, versus deepening or expanding on Melfi's contributions.

something she wants to talk about, is to say yes—to choose, like her patient and the rest of his Family, what is selfish and easy over what she knows is right. Just say yes, and Rossi ceases to exist.

She says no.

<table>
<tr><td>"ANOTHER TOOTHPICK"</td><td>SEASON 3/EPISODE 5
WRITTEN BY TERENCE WINTER
DIRECTED BY JACK BENDER</td></tr>
</table>

Witness Protection

"We're trying to get to root causes." —**Dr. Melfi**

Remembered mainly for its gory scene of the retired, terminally ill hitman Bobby Bacala Sr. (Burt Young) killing his golf club–swinging brute of a godson and an innocent witness while coughing up pints of blood, this is an overstuffed grab bag of an episode, featuring numerous stories tied together, as on so many *Sopranos* episodes, by fear of physical decline and death, as well as anxiety over whether decisions were correct in hindsight. Most prove to be interconnected, not just by theme but in how their events have knock-on effects. In the end, "Another Toothpick" feels more like a housekeeping episode—though one that happens to be built around a main story (Bacala Sr.'s assignment to kill Bryan Tarantina's Mustang Sally) involving two completely new characters.

Said housekeeping involves:

- Mustang Sally's crime and punishment, the latter ordered by Gigi Cestone (in his first real leadership test since Tony promoted him instead of Ralphie to run the old Aprile crew) and approved by Tony;
- Bacala Jr.'s strained relationship with his boss Uncle Junior, whom he assumes is just being insensitive about his father's terminal lung cancer until he finds out that Junior has been keeping his own cancer diagnosis a secret;
- Ralphie's continued insubordination, which expresses itself in flagrantly disrespectful "jokes"[22] aimed at Gigi, Tony, and Vito, the brother of the man Sally rendered comatose;

---

22 This is a recurring thing on *The Sopranos*: verbal cruelty, followed up by a half-hearted protestation of "I was just kidding—can't you take a joke?" These insults are tiny, nonphysical versions of the beatdowns and gunshots—little eruptions of socially taboo impulses that people feel entitled to express until the person on the receiving end realizes they're being publicly dominated and decides to push back, as Chris does after Artie repeatedly insults him and makes inappropriate remarks about Adriana.

- The announcement of a project spearheaded by Assemblyman Zellman (Peter Riegert,[23] introduced as a guest at Livia's viewing in "Proshai, Livushka") to transform Port Newark into a standard-issue waterfront yuppie haven, with condos and yacht slips where shipping docks once were;
- Artie Bucco's pathetic meltdown after his crush Adriana quits her hostess job at Nuovo Vesuvio, and the midlife crisis that engulfs him as a result (he even starts wearing an earring) and causes Charmaine to ask for a divorce;
- The unsteady Soprano marriage, which takes another hit after they attend their first therapy session together and Carmela accuses Dr. Melfi of taking Tony's side;
- Tony's relationship with Meadow, already damaged by his earlier racism toward her mixed-race boyfriend, and not helped here by his "I told you so" attitude after a black man steals her new bike;
- Meadow taking the bugged lamp back to her dorm room, unwittingly foiling the FBI's surveillance plot in a hilarious anticlimax[24]; and
- Tony's resentment of an incorruptible patrolman named Wilmore (Charles S. Dutton[25]), who pulls him over for speeding after his couples' therapy session with Carmela, declines his offers of a bribe, then gets busted down and robbed of overtime pay as a result of Tony's phone calls to Zellman, and has to take a second job as a cashier at a fountain store.[26]

That last subplot intertwines with the Meadow–Tony scene: Tony, clearly feeling some regret at Wilmore getting busted, at first tries to give him $400—which Wilmore rebuffs—then snarls "Fuck him" when Zellman offers to get him reassigned. (A person with principles can have everything else taken from them, but they'll always have the security of knowing they did the right thing.)

This is an enormous amount of information to convey in one hour, and while "Another Toothpick" manages it, it's at the expense of the clarity and cleanliness

---

23 Character actor who first found fame as the exuberant Boon in *National Lampoon's Animal House* and was the star of the Bill Forsyth–directed cult classic *Local Hero*.

24 Seriously, imagine any other show devoting its entire season premiere to the FBI planting a bug perfectly designed to take down Tony Soprano, only for his selfish daughter to simply take the thing away with her four episodes later, without it having recorded anything of value.

25 An ex-convict who discovered a love (and talent) for acting while behind bars, Dutton was a star on Broadway (*The Piano Lesson*), television (the '90s Fox sitcom *Roc*), and movies (*Rudy*), and had a history with HBO, appearing on *Oz* and in the TV-movie *For Love or Country: The Arturo Sandoval Story*, and directing David Simon's *The Corner*, the miniseries that brought the future *Wire* cocreator to the pay cable channel.

26 Fountains of Wayne was a real place—a family owned store on Route 46 that sold lawn ornaments, outdoor furniture, and quirky Christmas decorations until closing in 2009. Owned and operated by the Winters family (no relation to *Sopranos* writer-producer Terence Winter), it inspired the name of the rock band, and was best known for its elaborate, lovingly curated holiday displays.

of expression that marks the series at its best. That said, there are a number of striking scenes. The murder of Mustang Sally and his friend—followed by Bacala Sr. coughing himself into a fatal single-car accident during his getaway—further escalates the season's graphic violence. Between that sequence and Tony's racism being foregrounded with Noah and Wilmore, the episode—like the rest of the season thus far—seems to be rubbing our noses in the depraved behavior we've come to vicariously enjoy.

Less gruesome but nearly as disturbing: Artie's drunken needling of Chris, his subsequent tearful confessions to his old friend Tony, and his mortifying dinner with Adriana; all of the scenes capturing Junior's horror and anger at the prospect of his own decline (his room-trashing explosion of rage might be the first time we get a modern-day glimpse of the street hood who used to be Johnny Boy's partner in crime); and Tony and Janice's wine-sodden commiseration. The latter ends with Janice asking Tony what happened to Pussy, and Tony responding, "Witness protection." By this point, the phrase seems like a euphemism for death itself, a void that swallows everyone up eventually.

Even by gangster film standards, this is a death-haunted series, featuring an unending string of funerals and memorial services (mostly for characters who died of natural causes); laments for the passing of old ways of life; intense discussions of spirituality, Hell, Heaven, sin and redemption, and observations of how indifferent people can be toward the pain of others. A genuinely empathetic character like Bobby Jr. stands out in this environment. The episode's most moving grace note is his: Bobby arrives at Junior's house to give him a ride to the funeral, admits that he's hurt by Junior's decision to stay home, then pivots to sympathy when he learns Junior has cancer, too. "I'm sorry," Bobby says, forgetting all about his justifiable grievance. "I don't know what to say."

"I'll say a prayer for your father," Junior mutters, still trying to peer around Bobby's hulking frame so that he can see the TV—an asshole even at his most vulnerable.

"My father. Now you," Bobby says, seeing only the vulnerability. Then, turning to leave: "What the fuck is happening?"

SEASON 3/EPISODE 6
STORY BY DAVID CHASE & TERENCE WINTER & TODD A. KESSLER AND
ROBIN GREEN & MITCHELL BURGESS; TELEPLAY BY TERENCE WINTER
AND SALVATORE J. STABILE
DIRECTED BY ALLEN COULTER

Work-Related Accident

"Why is other people's pain a source of amusement?" —**Caitlin**

"University" is one of the most intricate and complex *Sopranos* episodes, as well one of the hardest to watch. It follows two other rough episodes, "Employee of the Month" and "Another Toothpick," but outdoes both in violence, cruelty, and bleakness, stringing together humiliations and atrocities and climaxing with a twenty-year old single mother and stripper, Tracee (Ariel Kiley[27]) being beaten to death by the father of her never-to-be born child. This episode prompted television critics and cultural commentators, including one of the writers of this book, to ask if *The Sopranos* had stepped over the line separating anthropological frankness from pornographic obsession, particularly when it came to abuse of women,[28] and was terrorizing the audience as well.

The battered feeling stemmed not just from the scenes involving mobsters and dancers, but their juxtaposition with the lives of the kind of people who subscribe to HBO and send their children to private colleges and would get Dr. Melfi's madeleine reference in "Fortunate Son."[29] The latter are treated here as cleaned-up mirrors of what's happening behind the scenes at the Bada Bing: hypocrites practicing their own forms of misogyny (and denying it) even as they speak in euphemisms and the language of self-help and psychoanalysis to justify their shabby treatment of young women and everyone else. The episode also takes a jaundiced view of a nation, perhaps even a species, that ignores people like Tracee when it isn't busy literally or figuratively trying to fuck them. When Noah's father, a high-powered Hollywood agent, tells Meadow that one of his clients is Dick Wolf, creator of *Law & Order: Special Victims Unit,* he's name-checking a show that would've done an episode with a plot just like this one, but with a final scene of Ralphie being arrested for murder and the club being shut down, even though real life is sadly closer to *The Sopranos,* the kind of show where a stripper

---

27 This was only Kiley's second screen credit, after a *Law & Order* episode from earlier that year. After a handful of other jobs, she left acting altogether and is now a yoga instructor.

28 See page 357.

29 Where they might major in communications studies and perhaps write a paper on *The Sopranos.*

can be murdered behind the club where she dances and everybody just goes back to work.

The episode quietly identifies two counterparts of Tracee's on the college side: Meadow, whom Noah uses for sex, then dumps as soon as he realizes the relationship could prevent him from getting an A average; and Meadow's roommate Caitlin Rucker (Ari Graynor[30]).

Tracee's murder is merely the Everest in a range of abuse and neglect that also includes battery (Silvio beating Tracee), casual sexual degradation (Tracee in a rough three-way with a cop) and countless indignities, large and small, inflicted on young women, many of them abuse survivors who numb themselves with booze and drugs. Tracee's tragic story unfolds in the Bada Bing, a *Caligula*-like spectacle of cruelty, sexual exploitation, and random violence. This is a place where women earn baseline income by gyrating indifferently around poles and pick up extra cash in the "VIP Room," performing lap dances and sexual favors for high rollers and then kicking up a taste to Silvio, the owner and manager. The VIP room bouncer, George the bartender, further skims the women's take by demanding fifty dollars plus a free blow job for admittance. Chief among the high rollers: Tony Soprano.

Judging from this up-close look, the Bing isn't much different from the brothels depicted in "Nobody Knows Anything" and "Toodle-Fucking-Oo," save for the presentational bells and whistles it adds to a business that amounts to sexual slavery, or at least indentured servitude. We're told that the club paid for the $3,000 braces on Tracee's teeth that make her look like a busty child, and judging from Silvio's remarks as he brutalizes her outside of Ralphie's apartment (while Ralphie laughs at her through a window), she's paying it back on the installment plan by doing all the things a Bada Bing girl is expected to do. "Until you pay what you owe, that shaved twat of yours belongs to me," Silvio warns her, using the language of a pimp as he beats her as punishment for missing three days' work. It also seems likely that the club paid for the silicone implants on dancers who weren't, to quote Silvio's description of Tracee, "a thoroughbred"; such procedures cost a minimum of $4,000 in today's money.[31]

Befitting an episode that references both *Gladiator* and *Spartacus*, "University" turns the Bing into an arena of flesh, with dancers rather than fighters providing amusement, and no possibility of a slave uprising. The only woman who dares to fight back ends ends up lying near a garbage-strewn sewer pipe,

---

30 A phenomenal performance by an actress who came out of nowhere, without any prior introduction, playing a character who might have ended up in a ditch like Tracee, were she not upper-middle class, with caring parents, university-quality mental health care, and family friends who own a cottage in Vermont. Graynor has acted regularly as an adult, most recently as a lead on Showtime's drama about '70s stand-up comedians, *I'm Dying Up Here*.

31 The trio of dancers that open the episode are arranged on-screen from least-augmented to most, an evolutionary chart of a gender gradually progressing toward a Bada Bing ideal of beauty.

face pulped, skull smashed. "All we can do is choose how we die!" the *Gladiator*-obsessed Ralphie scream-quotes, but the final, sad irony of "University" is that Tracee was given no such choice, and in the end, she was just another problem to be disposed of. The final scene finds three more dancers casually discussing the fact that one of their coworkers went behind the club with Ralphie and disappeared, as if it were just another piece of workplace gossip. Which it is.

To say that *The Sopranos* takes a Darwinian view of social relationships would be putting it mildly. This is a world in which people celebrate their relative success in life by treating people lower on the social ladder as unfeeling servants. Meadow, after dropping in unannounced for mother-daughter bonding time—rightly assuming that Carmela's insecurity about being phased out will make her a willing audience anyway—signals to Carmela for more apple juice at breakfast by raising her empty glass, then rolls her eyes and sighs when her mother makes her get it herself. Paulie rags on Vito and Bobby for looking like "before, and *way* before" in a weight loss ad. Ralphie insults Gigi, whom he thinks of as inferior despite Gigi's superior rank, by suggesting his younger brother gave Tony a blow job, and smashes George's eye with a lock on the end of a chain in a coked-up *Gladiator* reenactment. Rather than file a police report, George goes to the emergency room and returns to work with an eyepatch, still demanding fifty dollars and a blow job for VIP room access because everyone, even the bartender, outranks the dancers. Tony needles Meadow for giving him the cold shoulder, practically sneering in her face as retaliation for hurting his feelings, and because he's her dad, she can't do anything in return but talk back and roll her eyes. Even the hateful sadist Ralphie has a hard-luck story that nobody is interested in hearing: "I had to quit school in the eleventh grade, help my mother. I was supposed to be an architect."

Meadow and Noah, meanwhile, are more appalled and inconvenienced by Caitlin's distress than moved to action, and treat her less as a soul in crisis than a problem to be managed or ignored. They take her out on her birthday because they're afraid she'll have a nervous breakdown or attempt suicide (note Meadow palming an X-ACTO knife) and become an even bigger problem. Noah doesn't hide his disinterest in being there, and tries to bail because he has an early class the next day. Caitlin glomming onto Noah after Meadow flees to New Jersey causes him to get a C– on a paper, prompting his success-obsessed father to file a restraining order against her. "Couldn't you try talking to her?" Meadow asks him. "She thinks we're her friends."

"We have to set limits," Noah says—nearly as chilling an innocuous sentence as Carmela's "You don't understand, I want you to write that recommendation" in "Full Leather Jacket." Tony said more or less the same thing in the opening scene where he refused Tracee's cake days before her murder.

Although Caitlin and Tracee differ diametrically, their narrative functions are similar: they're the human problem others would rather avoid than confront, testing the limits of their empathy. Tracee is more deliberate and insistent in her grasping because she's lived harder. Caitlin is a mentally fragile but financially comfortable kid from Bartlesville, Oklahoma, who's overwhelmed by her first exposure to a big city, while Tracee is a lower-middle-class abuse victim who paid the abuse forward onto her own son. She's reliant on mobsters old enough to be her father for affection, money, and insulation from the worst of life.

But where Tracee chases sympathy and sometimes dares to demand it, however stridently and naively, Caitlin's biggest problem is feeling things too deeply and not knowing anyone else who shares her fury at the very idea of suffering. This isn't just mental illness; her agony seems existential. Like a latter-day Holden Caulfield, she has a sponge-like ability to absorb injustice visited on others, even strangers, and feel it herself, in ways that seem performatively melodramatic but are nonetheless sincere. This is a young woman so insulated from the worst of life that she developed no emotional buffers between herself and experience. Now that she's moved into the largest U.S. city, she is so horrified by the existence of certain types of pain that she crumbles emotionally while talking about them. She's primally appalled by the Lindbergh baby's death, which she just now learned about, and is so determined to treat Meadow as her best friend and most important confidante that when Meadow goes home for a couple of days to get away from her and doesn't call, she assumes the worst: "I keep having this image of you in the hospital with your throat cut!" Caitlin watches Tod Browning's 1930 horror film *Freaks*—which used actual sideshow performers, including people with deformities, in its main cast, and has been a popular "ironic" college midnight movie for decades—and is repulsed and startled, not by the content of the film, but by the reaction of the rest of the audience. "You're supposed to sympathize with the freaks. This one guy had no legs. He just hopped around on his hands," she says. "Why is other people's pain a source of amusement?"

That her expressions of intense empathy strike us as comical, even ridiculous, says more about our own jaded numbness than the appropriateness of her reaction. Only upon our second or third viewing do we see through Caitlin's eyes, and realize that she's absolutely sincere (though obviously distressed) in every one of her reactions, not a brat as Meadow or Noah assumed. Just as we initially misread Caitlin's horrified reaction to *Freaks* as disgust with the freaks themselves when it was an expression of sympathy, and her disregard for Meadow's privacy as callousness when it was a projection of her fantasy of sisterly closeness, we mistakenly assume that her reaction to a half-naked homeless woman with newspaper pages in her crack comes from racism or class superiority when it's about her anger at society for letting people fall so far. "How can you be so *callous*?"

Caitlin asks Meadow and Noah, near tears not just at the spectacle on the street but also the others' indifference to it.

Although Meadow isn't as ice-cold to Caitlin as Noah, she's never truly empathetic, and remains largely oblivious to her roommate's suffering. She stings her own father by calling him "Mr. Sensitivity, who doesn't have any problems of his own" soon after describing a young woman who's having a breakdown purely in terms of the inconvenience she's causing Meadow. She keeps Caitlin at arm's length for the same reason Noah establishes "boundaries" and her father rebuffs Tracee: once you start looking at an annoying or difficult person as a human being who's not as strong or as together as you are, you start feeling guilty for disliking them.

"You gotta snap out of this, Caitlin," Meadow tells her, repeating a phrase her father uses whenever someone cries in his presence, and suggests that she needs to "talk to somebody" because her pill regimen is "not enough." Meadow's not motivated here by genuine interest in Caitlin's well-being. Like Tony grumbling as he aborts a blow job, Meadow is mainly annoyed at being interrupted while trying to have sex.

"University" splinters rooting interest among many different characters and makes them alternately sympathetic and abhorrent, so that we never get too comfortable with our read on anyone. There are minor linking devices, mostly visual, such as the match cut from Ralphie entering Tracee while she fellates the cop to Caitlin rising up out of the frame from a kneeling position and gasping, "Oh, my God—it was so horrible." But there's nothing so exact that it reduces and oversimplifies the meaning of what we're seeing.

Caitlin is a mirror of Tracee in some ways, but so is Meadow—particularly in scenes where we see the women relating to their boyfriends. Noah's attitude toward both Caitlin and Meadow—both threats to his GPA—is a lot like Ralphie's attitude toward Tracee: he uses her for sex when it's convenient (it's Meadow's first time, apparently; Noah shows no inclination to put on a condom until she insists on it) and casually dumps her as soon as she threatens to impede his life. Ralphie seems to want to marry into the Aprile family, continue grooming Jackie Jr. as a mobster and surrogate son, and regain the respect he thinks he lost when Tony passed him over for promotion—and when Tracee gets in the way of all that, it's the end of her, too. Both Ralphie and Noah fool their girlfriends into thinking they're caring people, but in the end, Noah gives about as much of a damn about Meadow as Ralphie does about his *goomar,* casually putting down their relationship the same way Ralphie puts down Tracee, in one shot, like an unwanted thoroughbred. Noah takes an unscheduled weekend trip with an old school friend rather than subject himself to more Caitlin, while Ralphie spends three days with his pregnant girlfriend—long enough to give her hope—then ignores Tracee's phone messages for three days and misleads her about marriage. One girl is removed with a court order, while the other simply disappears: both variations of Tony's ominous phrase "witness protection."

Almost every straight male in this episode, if not the show as a whole, views women other than their mothers, wives, and daughters on a sliding scale that ranges from bored condescension to homicide. Expediency rules every decision they make. When Caitlin announces she's done with pills while self-medicating with vodka, Noah bolts to get a good night's sleep instead of staying to help. Tony treats Tracee, in his words, "an employee," with an edge of exasperation that comes from feeling fatherly toward her, despite his better judgment. Thanks to the subtleties of James Gandolfini's performance, we get the sense that Tony is deliberately suppressing decent impulses when dealing with Tracee. Later—perhaps disturbed by her confession that she abused her son and was abused herself, and thinking of his own experience with receiving and meting out child abuse, and his fear of passing on those Soprano genes—he warns her, "You need another kid like you need a fuckin' hole in the head."

By the end, that's what she gets. When Tracee's corpse is laid out under the guardrail, Tony expresses the only thing close to a human reaction among the crew, shaming Paulie for making it all about Ralphie's insubordination. "That cocksucker was way out of line," Paulie says.

"Twenty years old," Tony says, "this *girl*."

"That, too," Paulie adds. But mere moments earlier, Tony beat down Ralphie while screaming at him for disrespecting the club, never saying a word about the human loss. When Melfi asks him why he's so quiet in his joint therapy session with Carmela later, he changes the gender and profession of the deceased and says "he" died in "a work-related accident."

The Kinks' song "Living on a Thin Line" is threaded throughout like a Greek chorus. The lyrics' evocation of an empire in decline evokes England specifically, but also Rome, by way of Ralphie's *Gladiator* fixation; This Thing of Theirs, the Mafia, in decline since the appearance of Tony's brother RICO; and the United States, a country whose original sin, building itself atop the boneyard of Native American genocide, is referenced via Ralphie's joke about Custer's last words. The song also underscores the ancient, cyclical nature of all the different kinds of cruelty we've witnessed, as well as individual and tribal indifference to it. The episode ends just where it began, on the stage, with silicon-breasted sirens barely writhing for an audience of men who barely seem to know what day it is. Different dancers, different verse, same song.

<table>
<tr><td>"SECOND OPINION"</td><td>SEASON 3/EPISODE 7
WRITTEN BY LAWRENCE KONNER
DIRECTED BY TIM VAN PATTEN</td></tr>
</table>

Blood Money

"One thing you can never say: that you haven't been told." —**Dr. Krakower**

"Second Opinion" sits at the middle of season three like the keystone of an arch. It follows a triptych of episodes so harrowing that some viewers felt brutalized, but the emphasis on talk here makes it feel like a midpoint reckoning—an opportunity to reflect on where Carmela is at this moment, morally and spiritually; where she's been in the past; and what we've seen on our screens over two and a half seasons. It's a chance for both Carmela and the viewer to take stock and decide whether to continue or bail.

Its heart is a conversation between Carmela and therapist Dr. Krakower[32] (Sully Boyar[33]), who cuts through all of Carmela's self-justifications, and ours too. Carmela is forced to acknowledge her role as an "enabler" in her marriage to Tony, living off his "blood money" and trying to avoid details of how he makes it. Not coincidentally, this is also the episode where both Tony and Carmela have to deal with Angie, slain informant Pussy's widow, who needs (or maybe just thinks she deserves) more money out of her secret arrangement with Tony—money that Carmela is convinced could be used to make a donation to Columbia, ensuring preferential treatment for Meadow. Carmela runs into Angie at the supermarket and invites her over for dinner, a passive-aggressive denial of the reality that they're both aware of on some level. She listens as Angie describes her financial situation, and brings the message to Tony, probably from guilt over whatever unacknowledged bad thing happened to Pussy. By contrast, Tony storms over to Angie's house, beats up her Cadillac with a baseball bat,[34] and warns her never to bring up money to Carmela again. With this and other hard facts weighing on

---

32 Krakower's last name is very similar to the last name of Sigfried Kracauer, the German sociologist, social critic, and film theorist who developed systems to analyze photography, motion pictures, circuses, dance, advertising, architecture, and tourism, and wrote about how modern technology seemed to be attacking or supplanting the normal mechanisms of human memory, to our detriment. Kracauer also wrote *From Caligari to Hitler,* a seminal text for film students—a book that treated post-World War I German cinema as a cultural premonition that foretold the rise of Nazism, and analyzed it the way Melfi and Tony might pick apart one of his dreams.

33 Subtle, piercingly intelligent character actor who appeared in *The King of Marvin Gardens, Dog Day Afternoon, Car Wash,* and *Prizzi's Honor.* Died March 23, 2001, at age seventy-seven, while waiting for a city bus in Queens, just two weeks before this episode aired.

34 As in the scene on the golf course where Tony and Furio confront Dr. Kennedy, this is a very public display of violence for the boss of New Jersey. But Tony can't resist when his temper acts up.

her, including undeniable evidence of Tony's adultery, Carmela tells Krakower that she wants to help her husband because "he's a good man, a good father." And Krakower dismantles her. "You're telling me he's a depressed criminal, prone to anger, serially unfaithful," he says. "Is that your definition of a good man?"

The remainder of this lacerating scene finds Carmela repeatedly running headfirst into the brick wall of Krakower's absolutism. He insists that the root of Carmela's problems is that she's married to a mobster, and she'll never have a chance to "quell [her] feelings of guilt and shame" and be truly happy until she moves out of the house, takes the kids ("what's left of them") with her, and files for divorce. His responses to her statements go right up to the edge of contempt, particularly when Carmela says that her priest urged her to stay with Tony and try to make him a better man, and Krakower asks, "How's that going?" When Krakower tells her he's not going to take her money, Carmela walks right into the statement as if it's a trap, speculating on the new financial arrangements she'd have to make with Tony until he cuts her off: "You're not listening. I'm not charging you because I won't take blood money. You can't, either."

Consider the motivations of the woman who sent Carmela to Krakower. It's more than a simple referral. Melfi doesn't just want Tony to understand himself; she wants him to understand himself so that he can get *better*, and it seems more obvious to us, and perhaps to her, by the week (thanks in part to her conversations with her own therapist) that Melfi doesn't think Tony can truly get better until he stops being a criminal. She's not judging Tony or feeling superior to him when she tries to steer him toward admitting the core truth about himself. Rather, she's treating his criminality as a health issue—the thing that's standing in the way of him and a life that's not just free from panic attacks, but murder.

Again, Melfi also represents the viewer as well as herself in her scenes with Tony. All the subplots about her empathy and complicity attest to how hard it can be to keep one's distance from a character as funny, charismatic, and chaotically exciting as Tony (there's also a chemistry factor; when Elliot asks if she's attracted to him sexually, her non-response, like her dreams, confirm that she is, at least a little). The show's attraction–repulsion to violence, intimidation, and degradation is the flip side of scenes like the ones between Carmela and the two therapists in this episode.

Maybe Carmela's one session with Krakower feels less like therapy than an aggressive one-man intervention because Melfi sent her there hoping that Carmela would get the stark ultimatum that Melfi herself keeps avoiding—and that even Elliot can't quite bring himself to issue, because, like Melfi, he believes that therapists shouldn't just tell patients what they should do. Notice that Melfi's first solo session with Carmela starts the exact same way as Tony's first session, with Carmela in the waiting room contemplating Melfi's art ("Country scenes"), including a replica of that famous shot of Tony framed between the legs of a statue of a woman with her arms bent above her head ("That statue is not my favorite."), and Melfi very quickly leading the patient to think about her life in relation to criminality. Carmela wonders if her husband's "mood swings" and silences are related to his mother's recent death and complains about "living with that twenty-four hours a day, seven days a week." Melfi mentions Tony's distress over the hypothetical "young man" (actually Tracee) who died in a "garbage compactor," which leads Carmela to point out that Melfi inferred the compactor part. "What is it *you* believe?" Melfi asks, her calm voice and gaze confirming that she knows Tony changed the details of that "workplace accident." After pointing out that "Tony reports to a strip club," which Carmela must know is a candy store for a gangster with fidelity issues, and that she might know was the real site of the "workplace accident," Carmela tells Melfi she's worried that nothing she's doing for Tony "can help him." And she begins to cry.

Melfi's very next act is to refer her to Krakower: a therapist who tells Carmela, "Many people want to be excused in their current predicament for something that happened in childhood. That's what psychiatry has become in America." He's describing absolution here—a therapeutic answer to confession, but without the incense, robes, and booth. Absolution of past sins, plus acts of penance and an unenforceable promise by the sinner to try and do better: Krakower doesn't provide that kind of service. It seems inconceivable that Melfi sent Carmela to see him without anticipating how he'd react. In effect, Melfi picks a therapist for Carmela who will give her a second opinion about her life with Tony that's identical to Melfi's but a lot more blunt.

For all her traditionalist belief in Freud's "talking cure," there is a secret, under-the-radar moralist in Melfi—somebody who believes in the social compact and wants everyone, including herself, to be better than they are, for everyone's sake. A number of her sessions with Tony, including their first one, have pressed him not just to talk about his mother, but to recognize his criminality as a root cause, perhaps *the* root cause, of his depression. Tony rarely confronts either subject directly because doing so would force him to consider turning his life upside-down and becoming somebody new. Not only is the very idea terrifying to everyone, not just mobsters, it's asking too much work of a man who's lazy about everything except eating, killing, stealing, identifying and murdering informants, and getting laid.

Plus, the social structure that enfolds these characters makes escape or reform almost impossible, short of turning state's witness or running away to live in obscurity (and probably poverty) while worrying that the next person who knocks could be a tall Italian man with a black leather jacket and a ponytail. In both Tony's world and the more civilized one he leeches off, there is an established order—a chain of command that no one is meant to buck, lest the whole system fall apart. "Second Opinion" illustrates the conundrums that occur when people try to break that chain.

Angie Bonpensiero pleads her case to a more sympathetic figure in Carmela, and gets her car smashed by Tony as punishment. Christopher complains to Tony about all the hazing and other indignities he's suffering under Paulie ("I guess you could call that a dick."), only to get threatened for squealing to the teacher. Uncle Junior, at Tony's urging, gets another opinion on his cancer treatment, leading his surgeon, Dr. John Kennedy[35] (Sam McMurray[36]), to petulantly dump Junior rather than deal with a patient who won't blindly accept his suggestions. Tony intervenes in Angie's, Christopher's, and Junior's storylines to reaffirm the status quo as he sees it: everyone needs to shut up and do what they're supposed to, according to the rules as set out by the Mafia and modified by Tony Soprano. It's understood that anyone who doesn't like his verdicts could find themselves on the receiving end of a golf swing or backing up into a pond.[37] The episode is bound together by scenes of characters questioning and ultimately accepting authority, be it Tony's (forcing Kennedy to give Junior some personal attention) or Kennedy's (notice how easily he pawns off Junior on Dr. Mehta by blessing him like a priest, disregarding Tony's orders by finding a cleverer way to dump him). Carmela escapes Tony's purview because she's the only character on the show (besides the New York bosses and the FBI) who has the where-withal to stand up to him, at least sometimes. She also—in a remarkable scene in which Edie Falco is acting mostly with her back to the camera—wriggles out of having to face Krakower's ultimatum by forcing Tony to give the full $50,000 donation sought by the "Morningside Heights gangsters" of Columbia University. It's a financial answer to a spiritual problem, and a means of avoiding the real question.

---

35 Junior, to Tony's annoyance, reveres the doctor mainly because he shares a name with his favorite president. Reminded by Tony that JFK's tenure struck the first serious blows against the Mafia as a national force, Junior says, "That was the brother"—Robert F. Kennedy, John's attorney general.

36 Film, television, and voice-over actor, perhaps best known for playing the swinger Glen in *Raising Arizona*, Neil's dentist father on *Freaks and Geeks*, and supervisor Patrick O'Boyle on *The King of Queens*.

37 Furio, finding an excuse to smack Dr. Kennedy upside the head: "You got a bee on you hat!"

SEASON 3/EPISODE 8
"HE IS RISEN" WRITTEN BY ROBIN GREEN & MITCHELL BURGESS AND TODD A. KESSLER
DIRECTED BY ALLEN COULTER

Early Retirement

"Rules are rules, otherwise what? Fuckin' anarchy." —**Ralphie**

"He Is Risen" feels like a transitional episode between whatever season three was and whatever it's about to become. The bulk of its running time is dedicated to introducing new business, most notably Tony's dalliance with Mercedes-Benz saleswoman and fellow Melfi patient Gloria Trillo (Annabella Sciorra[38]), and letting old business play out in an unhurried way—in particular Meadow's accelerating affair with Jackie Jr. right when he's giving up on college and refocusing on crime, and the strained relationship between Tony and the arrogant Ralphie following the latter's murder of Tracee in "University." Like Janice in her new guise as a born-again Christian, the season is reinventing itself on the fly.

The title is a quote from Aaron Arkaway (Turk Pipkin), the fundamentalist narcoleptic that Janice brings to Thanksgiving dinner,[39] but it ends up applying to the widely despised Ralphie. He's been obsessed all season with having been passed over as captain of Junior's old crew, and suddenly finds himself elevated to that position only because its previous occupant, Gigi Cestone, dies of heart disease during a bowel movement. "He'll be a fuckin' captain over my dead body," Tony had declared, only to make him one over Gigi's dead body. He bestows the title reluctantly, only because Ralphie's the most qualified candidate in a poor crop,[40] and notwithstanding their continuing bad blood.

Gigi's death is another example of *The Sopranos*'s skill at using anticlimax for different kind of surprise. We've been primed for several episodes now to

---

38 Striking and versatile New York actress of Italian American descent; costar of *True Love, Cadillac Man, Jungle Fever, The Hand That Rocks the Cradle*, and *What Dreams May Come*. Fans who wondered why her career never seemed to deliver on its early promise got an answer in 2017, when she said that accused serial rapist and sexual harasser Harvey Weinstein, cofounder of Miramax Films and the Weinstein Company, broke into her house and raped her in the 1990s and continued to sexually harass her for years after that, driving her away from show business. Sciorra's star quality is undeniable here: from the minute we first see her in Melfi's waiting room, working a potential sale on the phone and then joking that she's here because she's "a serial killer . . . I murdered seven relationships," she's got both Tony and the audience wrapped around her finger.

39 Janice, who usually responds to misfortune by shifting her persona, is now hanging with born-again Christians like Aaron, whom she met in her prayer group.

40 If this were a Martin Scorsese gangster film, Ralphie would be a Joe Pesci character.

expect the Tony–Ralphie rivalry to come to a violent head, perhaps with Ralphie engineering Gigi's death so he can replace him, or Tony ordering Ralphie's murder. "He Is Risen" initially leads us to think the situation will be resolved in this hour, escalating from Ralphie rebuffing Tony's offer of a drink at the casino. There's the intervention of Johnny Sack (who promised not to interfere in Tony's business, but who needs the Esplanade project, a Newark construction job that's a joint venture of the New York and New Jersey Families, to come off without a hitch); the melodrama over disinviting Ralphie and the Apriles to Thanksgiving dinner (probably the closest *The Sopranos* has come to acknowledging how sitcom-like it can be); and two separate scenes where Ralphie approaches Tony hat-in-hand, hoping for reconciliation and reciprocal apologies (for Tony thrashing him behind the Bing), as well as some acknowledgment that Tony genuinely respects him, only to be insulted. Ralphie is prevented from sitting during his first apology ("He let me stand there like a servant, scraping, bowing," Ralphie tells Johnny) and is denied the honor of sharing a drink with Tony at the second meeting, where he learns he's been promoted. Ralphie, ever-needy, tells Tony he needs to hear that the promotion was due to "merit," even though it clearly wasn't. Here, too, Tony thwarts his wishes. "If your opponent is of choleric temper, irritate him," Tony tells Melfi, quoting Sun Tzu's *The Art of War*.[41]

Throughout, the Ralphie matter is mostly treated as a workplace issue, with ego and face-saving mattering more than anything else. The conversations employ even more euphemistic language for gangsterism than usual. Johnny urges Tony to "keep a happy shop," while Tony describes the situation to Melfi as "a management problem" revolving around "a situation with an underling" who forced another employee (Tracee) to take "an early retirement."

But it's that last thing that makes the infighting over a promotion feel different from Tony's other "management problems." Ultimately, his hatred of Ralphie is about his grief and guilt over Tracee, a woman almost his daughter's age whom he kept at arm's length and failed to protect. As if trying to remove his own personal disgust, Tony uses variations on the phrase "he disrespected the Bing," making it

---

41 Tony describes this book as having been recommended to him by Melfi, but she never actually told him to read it. In "Big Girls Don't Cry," Melfi chastises him for not taking therapy seriously enough, and says that if all he wants out of the experience is to become a better gangster, he could just read *The Art of War*, an ancient Chinese text that's been embraced by CEOs as well as military tacticians. Although other fictional characters have cited it, including corporate raider Gordon Gekko in *Wall Street*, its repeated citation by Tony and his fellow gangsters made it a popular phenomenon. According to a May 13, 2001, article in the *Baltimore Sun*, publishers that put out translated editions of the public domain text saw ten times the usual sales figures that year and had to order emergency reprints to satisfy demand: "No question, the spurt is entirely because of *The Sopranos*," Sara Leopold, publicity director for Oxford University Press in New York at the time, told the *Sun*.

purely a matter of protocol[42]—interesting how he associates that physical location, a glorified brothel, with his authority and his personality—but it's clear to
everyone that he's treating this unauthorized killing as something different than
the Mafia usual. "If anything were ever to happen to you . . ." Tony tells Meadow
at Thanksgiving.

We may also worry about Meadow's safety during "He Is Risen," an hour
that starts with her at a college party taking ecstasy supplied by Jackie and getting
drunk on tequila, and continues with a furtive but hardly secret escalation of their
relationship, until Meadow steals Jackie's car and accidentally wrecks it rather
than let him bail to shoot another game of pool with his friend. "A Soprano and
an Aprile," coos Janice, still a romantic even after putting two bullets in Jackie's
uncle's chest. Meadow escapes serious harm, but the prospect weighs heavily on
Tony, and on us, because this season has been hell on women. The stories have
clarified what a repressive and frightening environment this subculture can be,
with traditional Roman Catholic beliefs becoming warped by gangster machismo
and an insular, tribal mentality. (The outside world is no picnic, either: Tony offers
to walk the recent rape survivor Melfi to her car after an evening session, and she
confesses to Elliot that she was so grateful she nearly fell into his arms and cried.)
Ralphie calls Tracee a "hooer" twice during a conversation with Johnny, and says,
"It wasn't my kid she was carrying," confirming that the only value a woman like
Tracee has to a guy like Ralphie is as a receptacle for seed or a bearer of children.
Ralphie uses the term to deny that Tracee's life had value. But Johnny uses the term
as well, without a hint of shame or self-consciousness. Even Tony's consigliere
Silvio—a cold-blooded character we view with affection because he's funny—tries
to steer Tony toward the idea that there was nothing special or important about
Tracee, despite his distaste for Ralphie, and that the real issue here, whether Tony
likes it or not, is that he assaulted a made guy. This is the same Silvio who acts as
a glorified pimp to the Bada Bing dancers, and who beat Tracee in plain view of
Ralphie three days before she was killed.

Jackie seems like the next-generation version of this mentality, sneaking a
peek down Meadow's shirt after she passes out, disapproving of her dating "a black
guy," and telling her he wants to ditch college and get into men's fashion—though
"not the faggy part of it," whatever that means. Although Meadow survives this
episode, her attraction to Jackie should set our teeth on edge. He's a dumbass
Hamlet who won't take no for an answer. An image in this episode sums up his
character: a long shot of Jackie peeling away from a meeting with Meadow and
blasting through a stop sign like it's not even there.

---

42 When he finally gets Ralphie to apologize for disrespecting the Bing, he pauses long enough for
his new captain to add, ". . . and the girl," though Ralphie quickly blames the latter on excessive
cocaine use.

"THE TELLTALE MOOZADELL"

SEASON 3/EPISODE 9
WRITTEN BY MICHAEL IMPERIOLI
DIRECTED BY DANIEL ATTIAS

Each Child Is Special

"I never met anybody like you." —**Tony**

The gorilla at the zoo in "The Telltale Moozadell" could be the Tony of primates. He's huge, hairy, with bloodshot eyes, and prefers to be sedentary, but after only a few seconds of looking at him, you sense the intelligence in his face, and the coiled power that could snap you in half. Zoo visits are great places for filmmakers to find incidental associations and grandiose metaphors. *The Sopranos* finds its share in this sequence, which pictures Tony and his new *goomar* Gloria sharing an afternoon. The main concerns in this episode are animal and spiritual; religion loosely ties the frameworks together. Both zoo visitors are wearing the skins of animals: Tony has his classic black leather jacket, while Gloria is wearing a long-waisted leather jacket with a fur (or "fur") lining. He notices she's wearing a Buddhist amulet of protection, which sparks a conversation. Tony says his "wack job" sister is a Buddhist, and gently teases Gloria about whether it's compatible with a job selling $150,000 cars. "The first noble truth is that life is suffering, but the Buddha preached joyful participation in the sorrows of the world," Gloria tells him, not long before leading him into the reptile house, where they have sex in front of a glassed-in yellow python—a rare instance of *The Sopranos* laying it on a bit thick with the Biblical allusions. The script at least acknowledges this by having Tony allude to an earlier conversation where Paulie told him that snakes "reproduce spontaneously" because they "have both male and female sex organs . . . that's why somebody you don't trust, you call a snake. How can you trust a guy who can literally go fuck themselves?"

"Don't you think that expression would come from the Adam and Eve story?" Tony replies, not having any of it, "when the snake tempted Eve to bite the apple?"

"Hey, snakes were fuckin' themselves long before Adam and Eve showed up, T," Paulie replies.

Tony doesn't eat an apple or find himself missing a rib in the reptile house scene, and Gloria is neither Eve nor Satan, but this episode gently parallels the Genesis story on one level: it's about pushing limits and going too far, until God brings the hammer down.[43]

---

43 It is also secondarily—through Jackie-Meadow and Tony-Gloria—about people diving into the deep end of a new sexual relationship without getting to know the other person first.

Chris, meanwhile, gifts his fiancée Adriana with the Lollipop Club, a bar seized to pay a gambling debt. She reopens it as a live music venue called The Crazy Horse,[44] only to have to deal with holdover headaches, including the drug dealer Matush (Nick E. Tarabay), who used to sell in the bathroom of the old place and assumes he still has privileges until Furio evicts him, underlining the message with a kick to the *testicoli*. Matush keeps pushing his luck with encouragement from Jackie Jr., a friend of a friend who still seems to want to skip to the top of the organization without proving himself. Their first scene together is a drily hilarious commentary on *Godfather* fantasies: Jackie hears Matush's hard-luck story and gives his blessing to deal drugs while feigning authority by resting his face on his hand in the same manner as Vito in the first film and Young Vito in the second. When Jackie goes to Chris to officially secure the permission he already granted, Chris shuts the younger man down and takes offense that he'd make such a request, considering that drug trafficking is a federal as well as state and local crime. Jackie tells Matush he can deal drugs in the vicinity of the club, another face-saving lie that lands Matush in the hospital. "They didn't give a shit," he hisses at Jackie through his smashed jaw, arm raised up by a pulley. "I don't think they like you."

Tony doesn't like him either. He admits that Jackie the younger has a certain charisma and feels protective of him because he's Jackie the elder's son, but he also can't help being turned off by his arrogance. Tony has repeatedly said that he doesn't want him getting involved in the gangster life because he promised Jackie Sr. he'd keep his boy out of it. But now he's doubly adamant because Jackie's dating Meadow, and Tony was recently reminded of the worst that can happen to the young girlfriends of mobsters.[45] Tracee's killer is the closest thing Jackie now has to a father figure. This subplot peaks with Jackie asking Ralphie if he can buy a gun "just in case," and Ralphie gifting him with his own .38 snub revolver—marking him as the paternal antithesis of Tony, who is so invested in the young man's survival and success that when he catches him in the casino, he orders him to leave immediately and "smarten up."[46]

---

44 The Crazy Horse is not officially The Stone Pony, the Asbury Park, New Jersey club where Bruce Springsteen and the E Street Band honed their craft, but the name is bound to make Springsteen fans think of it, especially when a character played by Little Steven Van Zandt holds forth on what a pain in the ass live performers can be. It's also the name of a club once owned by Vincent Pastore in New Rochelle, New York, and the name of the band Neil Young regularly plays with.

45 In the scene at the pork store, Tony dances around the idea that he won't allow a gangster to date his daughter, but he never explicitly says it to Jackie. It might not have made a difference with this thick, entitled kid, but Tony's often more direct in issuing a warning than he is here. Maybe there's a part of him recalling that he was once a gangster who dated a nice girl in Meadow's mother, and if he's condemning Jackie on this basis, he's somehow condemning himself.

46 Carmela has no idea of the depths of Ralphie's depravity. Talking to Rosalie Aprile, she calls him "a real find" and urges her to "hang onto him."

The Jackie story in this episode parallels the troubles of AJ, who likewise can't seem to stop indulging in grandly self-sabotaging behavior.[47] He has even less self-awareness than Jackie: pressed to explain why he abetted a Verbum Dei swimming pool break-in/party/riot with several other students,[48] he gives his parents the classic blank-faced-and-vaguely-constipated AJ expression while repeating, "I don't know." The subsequent meeting with school authorities is one of the sneaky high points of the season—a miniature referendum on the hypocrisy of the species. Just like the DiMeo outfit keeping a stripper-murdering cokehead on its payroll because he's "a good earner," the Verbum Dei headmaster and coach make it clear that AJ won't suffer any penalty. The meeting opens with a reminder of the school's "strict zero tolerance policy in cases of vandalism" requiring "immediate expulsion," then proceeds to subcontract discipline to the parents, to Tony's surprise and Carmela's mounting outrage.[49] AJ is given "a suspended sentence" as a reward for improving his grade point average to a C– (the lowest acceptable grade in most U.S. schools), and gets to keep participating in sports (directly contravening Tony's decision to pull him off the football team) because of what the coach calls his "skill" and "leadership qualities . . . We feel that it would be against his best interests, and the team's, to sever his relationship with the squad."[50]

Tony and Gloria's relationship is pushing limits, too. He drives right to her place of business, gives her presents in broad daylight next to a major road, and whisks her away for trysts. It's his deepest connection yet to a woman who's not his wife: "I've never met anyone like you," he says at the zoo after she explains her necklace. "I know why you lie, but you don't have to," Gloria tells him, in the scene where she asks him about the pistol he keeps in an ankle holster for "pickups in bad neighborhoods."

Both Tony and Gloria know this relationship isn't smart. In sessions, both express a similarly intoxicated satisfaction, but evade or lie whenever Melfi seems to be on the verge of discovering their affair. Melfi asks about the voice she heard on the other end of the line when Gloria called her to cancel in "He Is Risen" and

---

47 As if to make the parallel official, the episode cuts directly from Jackie playing junior godfather to the Soprano family meeting at Verbum Dei to discuss AJ's vandalism.

48 Look closely in the pool scene and you'll spot a young Lady Gaga, then a fifteen-year-old actress billed as Stefani Germanotta.

49 Edie Falco's delivery of "So it's not exactly 'zero' tolerance" is a master class in how to put sarcastic air quotes around a word without lifting any fingers.

50 There's a moment of possible moral compromise in this episode for Melfi as well: Tony overpays because he's in a good mood, then refuses to let his therapist return the overage, telling her "give it to charity." Moments later, Jason calls to check in with her ("I hate my patients . . . all of them," she admits) and request extra money to buy two textbooks. The scene ends with Melfi staring at the cash in her hand.

pushes for confirmation that she's seeing someone, a line of inquiry that makes her patient uncomfortable. "I think it's very unprofessional for you to confront me this way," Gloria says. Melfi replies she's keeping tabs because Gloria came in for treatment after attempting suicide after a breakup, but takes her word when it becomes clear that pressing further would upset her.

It's fascinating to watch Melfi skate twice along the edge of a realization she can't quite have yet.[51] She saw Tony and Gloria smiling at each other in her waiting room. She heard Tony's voice, a regular presence for an hour a week, while on the phone with Gloria. She knows Tony is happy verging on goofy, and expressing all manner of "go with the flow"–type thoughts, but she doesn't connect that language to Gloria—an openly devoted Buddhist—even after Tony paraphrases one of Gloria's lines from the zoo.[52] Here, as in her session with Gloria, Melfi pursues a line of thought right up to the precipice of identifying a lie, but stops short of confirmation.

"Your thoughts have a kind of Eastern flavor to them," she tells Tony.

"Well, I've lived in Jersey my whole life," Tony says.

"I mean 'Eastern' in terms of Asian, like Buddhist, or Daoist . . . "

"Sun Tzu," Tony says, a lie so transparent that even he can't sell it. "I told you about him."

Melfi stares at him for a moment, then says, "We have to stop now."

---

51 Tony has his own version of this: Jackie's repeated assurances that he's taking his studies seriously when he's doing no such thing. The scene where Jackie bamboozles Tony is another great example of James Gandolfini's ability to convey subtle gradations of self-consciousness just by doing certain things with his face and voice. His demeanor here communicates that Tony's not actually dumb enough to fall for something like this; it's more a case of him wanting and needing to believe it, because he doesn't want to make Meadow unhappy by killing the relationship, and because he's got so many other things going on in his life right now that he doesn't have the bandwidth for one more major drama. He's disabused of his optimism soon enough.

52 If the zoo is a place where warm and illuminating things happen for Tony and Gloria, does that make it the Sun Zoo? Thank you, you've been a great audience.

SEASON 3/EPISODE 10
WRITTEN BY ROBIN GREEN & MITCHELL BURGESS
DIRECTED BY JACK BENDER

".. . TO SAVE US ALL FROM SATAN'S POWER"

Ho Fuckin' Ho

"The boss of this Family told you you're gonna be Santa Claus,
you're Santa Claus. So, shut the fuck up about it!" —**Paulie**

A Christmas special for people who hate Christmas specials, ". . . To Save Us All From Satan's Power" is classic *Sopranos*, though it's comparatively light on violence and heavy on jokes, especially about heavy men. There's talk about the American mythology of Christmas, including Paulie's classic narrative on Santa and the elves, plus *The Grinch Who Stole Christmas* and *It's a Wonderful Life*. But by the end, Christmas cheer sleeps with the fishes. Tony watches a bit of *Life* on the bedroom TV after thrashing the livery cab driver who beat up Janice and trapping him under a sleigh in a store window. "Jesus Christ, enough already!" he mutters, as George Bailey dashes through the snow. On what might be the only afternoon of the year when a roomful of goodfellas get to publicly pretend to be jolly good fellows and get away with it, two wiseguys play Santa at Satriale's: Big Pussy via a 1995 flashback—probably wired for sound—and Bobby today, the replacement Saint Nick who warned everyone he had no aptitude for the gig and proves himself right. "Would it kill him to say 'Ho ho ho?'" asks Paulie, watching Bacala boss the kids around like a gym coach and call out a kid named Gregorio for going through the gift line twice: "You were on my lap five minutes ago . . . Now you're going on Santa's list and you're getting nothing!"

"Fuck you, Santa!" Gregorio shouts. And the room cries: "Hhh-*ohhhhhhhh!*"

Ultimately, though, Tony is the true Santa here—the Paulie Walnuts version, giving toys to good kids and throwing the bad ones beatings. His holiday to-do list starts doubling as a naughty list when he realizes Janice is still in pain after a Russian cab driver roughed her up for stealing Svetlana's leg. "JANICE'S RUSSIAN" he writes on his crinkled notepad, on the same page with "TRANS-FER CANNOLIS," a euphemism for laundering his money through different Russians. But he's also a skeptic's answer to George Bailey from *It's a Wonderful Life* and Ebenezer Scrooge from *A Christmas Carol*, an everyman who sees Yuletide ghosts but realizes nothing about himself except that he hates seeing ghosts. If the two characters were real people, the episode argues, they'd assume the ghosts were byproducts of bad plum pudding, or that the little fellow claiming to be an angel was a hobo who's not right in the head, and continue their accustomed sinning.

The episode starts with a 1995 flashback to Tony and Jackie on the Asbury Park boardwalk, talking to Pussy about brokering a diplomatic meeting between Jackie and Junior, who just hijacked one of the boss's trucks. We understand the show so well by this point that we're not surprised when a slow zoom into crashing waves segues to memories of Tony's old pal Pussy, the talking fish who ended up fish food, but it's still surprising to see Pussy in all his fleshy, bad-backed glory, Jackie looking hale and hearty, and Tony with more hair.[53] Tony, Paulie, and Silvio executed Pussy in "Funhouse," and this is the first full reappearance of the character in a flashback, aside from the brief glimpse in a hallway mirror in "Proshai, Livushka"—one of many indicators that *The Sopranos* might believe in a world beyond the material. The rush of memories of Pussy, Gigi, and Jackie Sr., colleagues whose loss weighs on Tony,[54] merges with the usual holiday pressures and brings him to the edge of another panic attack,[55] his first in a while: "I'm feeling like I got ginger ale in my brain," he tells Melfi. "Stressmas," she says.

But it's more than Stressmas. It's a potential moral reckoning brought about by revisiting a particular location where Tony dreamed of the fish-Pussy revealing his true self. Everybody's in denial here, including Paulie, who insists that he would kill Pussy again if he could. Tony plays Melfi with his friend, asking him why he went to a psychic last year when he supposedly doesn't "dwell on this shit," and why he isn't haunted by Pussy even though he sensed the ghosts of other men he'd killed at the psychic's office. "That was different," Paulie says, miffed. "Chrissie was shot. That was a paranormal event."

"Well, that was the difference between Puss and the others—him, you loved," Tony says, pressing Paulie.

"The world don't run on love," Paulie says, adding, "In the end, fuck Santa Claus."

In place of the traditional holiday fable of the cruel (or merely self-pitying) man who has a revelation and changes his ways, we get a story about a bunch of

---

53 This is one of the episode's many scenes that retro-engineer certain facts and associations and flesh out the *Sopranos* universe. "Funhouse" never explained why Tony kept dreaming of the Asbury Park boardwalk, but this episode names it as the origin of Pussy's future treachery: it's where he agreed to go to Boca Raton, Florida, right before Christmas. Tony's crew agrees that's probably where the FBI busted him for the heroin dealing that Tony cautions him about in 1995 and that ensnared him later. We also learn that Pussy's money and back problems dated back to at least 1995, that Tony's father acquired Satriale's in a bust-out that led to old man Satriale's suicide, and that he established the Santa tradition Pussy and Bobby inherit. Judging from the awkward thinning already afflicting Tony's hairline—What a fine job of toupee fabrication this is!—1995 might also be when he started seriously going bald.

54 The scene also resurrects Jimmy Altieri, whose own rathood deflected the question of whether Pussy was wearing a wire back in season one. Also, note that when the guys find Pussy's Santa suit at the pork store and start venting about Pussy's betrayal, the loudest and most indignant one is Ray Curto, revealed as yet another cooperator in "Proshai, Livushka."

55 No food is present for this one, suggesting even Melfi's brilliance only goes so far.

gangsters collectively trying to figure out when they should have realized that their old pal was a rat so they could have capped him and saved their future selves the trouble. Silvio dreams of a secret cheese thief[56] at the Bada Bing and finds Pussy's corpse in the strippers' dressing room, neck snapped in a giant mousetrap. "Ever since we found that suit, I been dreaming about the fat rat bastard," Silvio tells Tony, in the same basement where his boss interrogated two men who were later killed for informing.[57] Silvio and Tony deduce that Pussy probably flipped on the day when he showed up late for a sit-down Sil set up between Jackie Sr. and Junior. Tony thinks Pussy might've worn a wire for the first time under his Santa suit not long after that. Maybe he walked into Satriale's already wearing it. But who can say for sure?

Here, as elsewhere, Tony has several potential moments of self-revelation, but every time he catches a big fish, he throws it right back. Charmaine Bucco, newly separated from Artie and looking pulchritudinous, stops pretending she doesn't hate feeding gangsters in her place, and needles Tony and his boys by telling him a couple of FBI agents might be eating nearby; Tony doesn't read the obvious indicators in this scene that she hates his guts and wants him to be as uncomfortable as possible. It requires a return trip, with a more blatant telling-off, for Tony to become offended enough to take his business elsewhere. Even then, he seems more miffed at Charmaine's lack of fear than chastised by her disapproval of how he earns—and yet, this being *The Sopranos*, we can't rule out that the truer, deeper reason why Tony fled was shame—not that he'd admit it.

In the same episode where Tony openly discusses *goomar* gifts with Paulie and Silvio, and gives Carmela a $50,000 bracelet as unspoken compensation for the fact that he's secretly gotten a new mistress,[58] Tony explodes in rage at the sight of his daughter's boyfriend getting a lap dance, works him over in the men's room, and tells him "You hit rock bottom" twice—as if to force the kid to have the moment of clarity that has thus far eluded Tony. Here, as in the Jackie Jr. scenes in "The Telltale Moozadell"—and a lot of scenes where he's dealt with an insubordinate Ralphie or aggrieved Richie—Tony seems less offended by the other man's hypocrisy and moral turpitude than furious at the existence of the same sleazy, vicious, or self-destructive impulses in himself, if better suppressed. When Tony disciplines Jackie, it's like he's throwing his younger self a beating to

---

56 Judging from this scene and the prank Tony plays on Silvio via Matt Bevilaqua in "The Happy Wanderer," the owner-manager of the Bada Bing often has cheese on the brain.

57 If Meadow hadn't taken the lamp back to Columbia, Tony would be well and truly screwed here.

58 That Carmela decides to interrogate Tony about Charmaine's sudden va-va-voomness, accuse him of pursuing her, and tell him she knows that they had sex in high school suggests that she's already figured out he's cheating again, even if she can't prove it and is fixating on the wrong target.

flip him from naughty to nice. The bathroom attack is the closest the episode gets to a traditional Dickensian moral reckoning: Tony as leather-jacketed Ghost of Christmas Yet to Come, putting a boot in the ass of young Tony.

None of this registers because Tony understands his subconscious mainly as a trove of clues on how to run the business, augmented by a little Sun Tzu. Nevertheless, karmic payback comes on Christmas morning, when Meadow gives him the unexpected gift of a Big Mouth Billy Bass singing "Take Me To the River," forcing him to smile sweetly and say thank you instead of throwing up or passing out, and to agree to keep the toy on his desk where he can see it every day of his life. Cut to waves crashing at Asbury Park. Santa Claus is fucked.

SEASON 3/EPISODE 11
STORY BY TIM VAN PATTEN & TERENCE WINTER,
TELEPLAY BY TERENCE WINTER
DIRECTED BY STEVE BUSCEMI

Rasputin

"I lost my shoe." —**Paulie**

"Pine Barrens," aka "The One with the Russian," is the episode that *Sopranos* fans use to recruit new viewers. It works as a self-contained short feature about a Mob boss losing control of his business and his personal life, even as it advances key season-spanning subplots without resolving them and teases upcoming twists without promising specifics. It delivers all of the distinguishing characteristics longtime viewers expect—suspense, violence, and undertones of melancholy and mystery—while mostly erring on the side of comedy, be it slapstick-goofy (Paulie and Chris squabbling in the woods) or emotionally raw (Gloria hitting Tony in the back of the neck with his dinner). It's probably the best hour that great TV writer Terence Winter has scripted for any series. It's one of very best things that Steve Buscemi, a still-largely-unsung hero of indie film directors, has put his name on. It features two of Tony Sirico and Michael Imperioli's best comic performances, decadently satisfying entertainment that pulls the audience along from start to finish while leaving them with unexpected questions—like "What happened to the Russian?"

Now is not the time to resolve the matter of the Russian—we'll save that for the season finale recap—but it's not spoiling anything to say he was topic number one after this episode debuted. Tony's warnings to Paulie make it seem guaranteed they'll meet again: "If this cocksucker crawls out from under a rock, he's your problem, not mine. You deal with Slava,[59] you take the heat, you pay the price." Could there be war between the Russians and the Italians over the death (or wounding) of Valery (Vitali Baganov), the Rasputin of South Jersey, the vodka-swilling ex-commando,[60] the roaring giant who washes his balls with ice water?

Suffice to say that for a series that would pose such questions in dialogue, *The Sopranos* cares little about the particulars of what happened to the Russian, instead treating him like a force of nature turned loose in nature, presenting his fearsome power and wraithlike elusiveness as a test of Paulie and Chris's resourcefulness.[61] They utterly, haplessly fail, cursing themselves and everyone else the whole time. They fail before they've even gotten started. Look up "fail" in the dictionary and you should see Paulie and Chris in the snow, Chris bloody-headed and wrapped in the car floor mat, Paulie grimacing from the snow freezing his one shoeless foot, his typically immaculate salt-and-pepper hair poofed out like the wild mane of a German Expressionist dream figure. If these two were even a tiny bit less impulsive, confrontational, and self-defeating, they never would have ended up freezing in a van in the woods at night, eating half-frozen condiment packets and flinching at every snapped twig. The Russian is the punishment they deserve.

Maybe more Paulie than Chris. It was Paulie who picked up Valery's universal remote, then smashed it like the macho jerk he is rather than bend to the Russian's bluster and replace it. It was Paulie who strangled Valery seemingly to death with that floor lamp, Paulie who insisted on burying his "corpse" deep in the South Jersey woods so they could spend the night in nearby Atlantic City instead of somewhere closer, and Paulie who continually lied to the boss about who made most of the mistakes. Of course it was a joint decision to have Valery

---

59 The money launderer and Valery's best friend and war buddy; both introduced in "To Save Us All From Satan's Power."

60 Over a terrible cell connection, Tony tells Paulie that Valery killed sixteen Chechen rebels single-handedly, and was in the interior ministry, which Paulie translates to Christopher as, "You're not gonna believe this. He killed sixteen Czechoslovakians. Guy was an interior decorator." (Chris, confused: "His house looked like shit.")

61   There are multiple details that make it seem as if Valery has supernatural powers, from the sheer size of the gore cloud erupting from his skull when Paulie gets off his lucky shot, to the way his blood trail and footprints simply disappear, to the running creature Chris shoots that turns out to be a deer but might as well be a reincarnated Valery. Director Buscemi, long a favorite filmmaker of Chase's because of his debut feature, 1996's *Trees Lounge* (a film that stars many future *Sopranos* cast members), makes a lot of choices here that imply the Russian is something more than a mere mortal—including an overhead shot looking down on Paulie and Chris from treetops that initially seems from the point of view of Valery, who'd have had to climb like a squirrel to get that high. Every choice has plausible deniability while also being vaguely chilling, hitting that *Sopranos* sweet spot between the known and unknowable.

dig his own grave with a shovel he could use as a club, so that's on Chris, too. But mostly it was Paulie, the wing-haired, shoe-losing fool.

Then again, if we take Tony at his word that he's a "captain of industry" type, maybe he's the one who deserves the most blame. Stooge 1 and Stooge 2 wouldn't have gotten stranded if it weren't for Tony ordering them to go handle the Valery situation. It was Tony who assigned Paulie to pick up the $5,000 Valery owed Silvio rather than insisting Sil take care of it himself, and he could've intervened personally at any point if he'd so chosen—which we would've bought because we've seen how Tony loves to get his hands dirty. But he chose to delegate because he was so involved in his own melodramas, balancing a demanding new girl-friend against the needs of his family and the lingering bad mojo of his previous *goomar*, Irina.[62]

It's the section with Paulie, Chris, and Valery that people remember most vividly from "Pine Barrens," with good reason: from the minute Paulie opens up the trunk to reveal a living Russian, to the chaotic foot chase, to all the scenes of the woodland fools arguing and complaining, to the haunting cutaway of Paulie looking up through the window at the flock of birds flying out in a V-formation, these scenes are the comic heart of "Pine Barrens." But this is ultimately an episode about Tony, with Paulie and Chris's misadventures manifesting the chaos he's causing in his professional and private lives. The common thread binding every part of this hour is his unwillingness or inability to resolve demanding problems that are right in front of his face.

The episode opens with Gloria, just returned from Morocco,[63] visiting *The Stugots* right when Irina calls, and getting so angry at him that she tosses his gift to her into the water unopened. Tony's inability to admit what Gloria already knows (that it wasn't a school administrator calling) escalates the situation. Throughout "Pine Barrens," he does whatever he has to do to wriggle away from accountabil-ity and make it about him—the mentally, emotionally, and sometimes physically AWOL gangster-husband-father half-assing his way through life. He's chronically late to meetings and family gatherings, appointments, and dates, disrupts them by taking phone calls, and leaves them early, often with an excuse so unconvincing that it's an adjacent insult. He delegates inconvenient responsibilities to people

---

62 Everybody wants to know what happened to the Russian, but hardly anybody asks who slashed Gloria's tires. We assume it's Irina, based on Tony's past experience and the fact that she called his boat in the first scene, but the matter is never resolved here. To quote Melfi in this episode, "Read into things however you choose."

63 Still relatively new, Gloria is already so indelible a presence in Tony's life and on the show that she now gets entrance music: appropriately, "Gloria" by the Northern Irish garage rock band Them, which launched Van Morrison's singing career.

unequipped to handle them, and takes offense whenever anyone has the temerity to observe that he's not giving them a fraction of his full attention.

The A-story of this episode is Tony losing control of his life even as he experiences the bliss of infatuation with his volcanic new girlfriend. The B-story is Jackie Jr. carrying on like a younger, handsomer, much dumber[64] Tony, bailing on Meadow because she's sick and doesn't want to have sex or do ecstasy, then getting busted for being unfaithful. Every scene, including the ones with Valery, raises the question of just how badly people can screw up before being forced to fix things or suffering backlash from people they've hurt or inconvenienced. Tony is letting down everybody here, including the girlfriend that he tells Melfi is most responsible for his happiness. Tony's loved ones deserve a full meal of him, but they make do with half-frozen relish.

Gloria's the first to defy Tony, demanding and receiving better treatment (briefly), getting dissed again, calling him an "inconsiderate prick" and telling him, "If I wanted to be treated like shit, I'd get fucking married," then finally exploding in rage after he keeps her waiting three hours and throwing a slab of lukewarm London broil against the back of his neck as he's leaving to pick up Bobby. "You been eatin' steak?" Junior asks him right after, volunteering details of his suffering from chemotherapy but getting zero empathy. "You're having coffee, right? My father has glaucoma," Carmela says witheringly, when it becomes clear that Tony is angling to rush off from dinner rather than commiserate about her father's health.

Chris and especially Paulie feel the sting of Tony's neglect here, practically begging him to come rescue them as day turns into night, only to be met with one exhortation after another to *just handle it*. "He's living like a fuckin' king, and now all I hear about is cocksucker Ralphie!" Paulie hisses between chattering teeth. Tony starts to get things right again toward the end, apologizing to Bobby and thanking him for taking care of Junior, and asking Paulie to decide whether to go look for the Russian or head home.[65] But Paulie and Chris's relief and gratitude is more a matter of feeling grateful to be back inside a warm car again, eating sandwiches, than collectively feeling bad about resenting the boss. The entire world is Tony's wife, his *goomar*, his loyal but unappreciated servant.

Where did Tony learn to treat people this way? We already know the answer, and Melfi does her best to steer him into confronting it during the closing therapy scene; still, he denies the obvious. She invites him to speculate on what Irina and

---

64 Playing Scrabble with Meadow, Jackie assumes that "oblique" is a Spanish word pronounced "oh-BLEE-kay," while his own words include "poo," "ass," and "the."

65 This last gesture also has a self-protective edge, as outwardly considerate as it sounds: if Paulie made the decision not to go search for Valery, it's Paulie's fault if he turns up later.

Gloria have in common: "Depressive personality. Unstable. Impossible to please. Does that remind you of any other woman?"

Tony pauses for a second, then shrugs.[66]

SEASON 3/EPISODE 12
STORY BY DAVID CHASE, TELEPLAY BY FRANK RENZULLI
DIRECTED BY TIM VAN PATTEN

A Mofo

"I didn't just meet you. I've known you my whole fucking life." —**Tony**

The same aria, "Sposa son disprezzata," sung by Cecilia Bartoli, closes "Pine Barrens" and opens the next episode, "Amour Fou," making the latter feel like part two of an unofficial two-parter, or maybe a looking-glass world.[67] It at least plays like the punch line Melfi set up in "Pine Barrens": "Sound like anyone you know?"

The "anyone" is Livia, but it's also Gloria, who spirals into confrontational anger here when she realizes Tony will never put her first, and breaches enough boundaries (including taking Carmela home from the Mercedes dealership, then calling her to pitch a new car) to drive Tony to break up with her. The subplot's climax finds them battling it out in Gloria's cabin until she comes at him with a corkscrew and the much larger Tony nearly strangles her to death before coming to his senses (after her repeated gasps of "Kill me"). Recall that Tony almost smothered his own mother at the end of season one, and that his own panic attacks feel like asphyxiation. Talk about primordial—strangulation is one of the oldest ways of killing someone, predating every means of murder, maybe even rocks and clubs. And as a dream image it's charged with meaning: the subconscious often reaches for images of asphyxiation when dreamers are suppressing some important part of themselves, their needs aren't being met, or their truth isn't being seen and recognized. If Gloria hadn't exclaimed, "Poor you!" in response to

---

66 Twice in this episode, during the drive home and over the end credits, we hear Cecilia Bartoli's rendition (from the 1992 album *If You Love Me—'Se tu m'ami': Eighteenth-Century Italian Songs*) of "Sposa son disprezzata," an Italian aria written by Geminiano Giacomelli. It was used in *Bajazet*, Vivaldi's *pasticcio*, but composed for Giacomelli's opera *La Merope*. The lyrics particularly apply to Carmela, who knows her husband cheats; but it could also apply to Gloria and Irina, who likewise resent Tony's not fully committing to them and shutting them down when they ask for more; and to Paulie and Chris, loyal underlings who never seem to get their beloved boss's attention unless he's berating them.

67 "Pine Barrens" and "Amour Fou" have the same number of syllables, but the stresses are reversed. We're just saying.

Tony's self-pitying tirade, we could've inferred it from her language and behavior, which is born out of feeling abandoned, and wishing to destroy the abandoner by pushing him to destroy her first ("Suicide by cop," per Melfi's comparison in therapy).

Another key storyline here is also driven by feelings of disrespect, belittlement, and marginalization: Jackie Jr., frustrated by his inability to rise quickly in the organization, throws a Hail Mary that will force the Family to recognize him as a rising star: he will replicate Tony and his father's legendary robbery of the card game now run by Jackie's wannabe stepfather, Ralphie. The plan goes awry once his buddies Dino, Carlo (Louis Crugnali), and Matush join in. When Sunshine the dealer tries to reclaim control of the moment by quoting Rudyard Kipling's "If," Carlo shoots him twice, killing him and setting off a close-quarters gun battle that leaves Furio wounded and Carlo dead. By the end, Jackie Jr. is a fugitive, and—according to Tony, the boss—his status as Ralphie's unofficial ward means Ralphie must decide whether to pardon or condemn him.[68] The two stories run along parallel tracks, excluding almost every other major character. This invites us to see the Gloria and Jackie scenes as reflecting (or at least commenting on) each other. Their action even peaks almost simultaneously, Gloria's near-death followed immediately by Jackie botching the robbery and almost getting shot for his stupidity. Jackie's stumbling rise and immediate fall, with Ralphie as his enabling father figure, has been this season's counterpoint to stories about AJ screwing up and revealing a near-total lack of ambition, and his parents struggling to figure out how to cope with it.

There's a third story too, also paying off developments earlier in the season, about Carmela, and it leads her to accept, for now, the idea that she's not getting out of this marriage anytime soon, so she might as well make the best of it. She worries that she's pregnant again after spotting at the Metropolitan Museum of Art, cries at a painting of a newborn child and then a dog food ad (the dog being the kind of instinctively loyal protector that Carmela imagines herself to be), then finds out she's not pregnant after all, but has a meeting with Father Obosi (Isaach De Bankolè[69]), a priest recommended by Father Phil because he's studying

---

68 The scene where Tony and Ralphie debate Jackie's fate is one of the show's best-written scenes about two people trying to get each other to accept responsibility for making a huge but unpleasant decision. They keep pushing the matter across the table to each other like a poisoned meal that neither wants to taste. Ralphie tells Tony, "I want to give the kid a pass. . . . That's just me, though. I know you got bigger concerns, you're the boss, and I'll make sure your orders are done, whatever they may be"—as if already knowing what has to happen, but not wanting to be the one to name it. "I think you should go with your instincts on this, Ralph," Tony replies.

69 French-speaking actor from the Côte d'Ivoire; career hightlights include *Night on Earth*, *Casino Royale* and *The Limits of Control*.

psychiatry. Carmela's meeting with Obosi, moving from the confession booth to his office, continues a rich *Sopranos* tradition of characters taking a meeting that they expect and maybe hope will push them to make tough choices and set hard limits, only to realize that the authority figure is mainly there to help them take the easy way out, and preserve the status quo.

Obosi advises her to try to live within the good parts of her life with Tony rather than leave him and reject the evil he represents, which is exactly what a Roman Catholic priest, even an African one studying psychiatry, would say to a woman at risk of ending a marriage that, however flawed, is still sacred in the eyes of God. "Oh, the Church has changed so much," Carmela says, sounding relieved, having recalled Dr. Krakower warning her in "Second Opinion" that she can never be a good person while subsisting on blood money. "It's a complex world," Obosi replies warmly. This exchange is the logical endpoint of the scene where Carmela, Angie, and Rosalie discuss the lesson of Hillary Clinton (who stuck it out with a philandering husband and made something for herself). And it's more or less the same scene as the one in "Fortunate Son" where AJ wasn't punished for wrecking the school swimming pool, because the headmaster and coach wanted to win the football championship that year.

The most powerful storyline, though, is Tony and Gloria's, which starts spiraling from a peak of carnal and emotional excitement until it crashes on the floor of Gloria's house with Tony's hands around her throat. Gloria starts behaving like a character in one of those late-1980s/early 1990s films about agents of chaos. *Basic Instinct*, which plays during a pivotal scene in "Amour Fou," was the top grosser in this run of movies, but there were many, many more, all adhering to a template that studio bosses and entertainment journalists called "Fill-in-the-blank from Hell."[70] *Basic Instinct* is sampled in the scene where Jackie and Dino watch Sharon Stone's accused murderer Catherine Trammell rattle a roomful of male detectives by uncrossing her legs to reveal that she's not wearing underwear. Misogynist as the image might be, it speaks to something, well, *basic* in the story of men and women, an idea that's embedded in everything from film noir to blues songs: the woman as hypnotizing sexual force, causing men to act against their better judgment.[71]

What elevates the Gloria scene beyond reductive stereotypes is the care taken to set her up as a fully dimensional human being (including the detail that she was seeing Melfi to deal with suicidal impulses and relationship-destroying

---

70 See also: *Fatal Attraction, Disclosure, Unlawful Entry, The Hand That Rocks the Cradle,* Martin Scorsese's *Cape Fear* remake, et al.

71 It also reinforces the idea of Jackie and Dino as dumb, horny kids in way over their head, who would have been better off staying in to watch the rest of that movie.

tendencies). Gloria's litany of entreaties to die or be killed connects her with Livia, and, more importantly, with the constructed Livia that's taken up residence deep in Tony's mind.

When you look back over season three's arc, and the series to date, you see cycles of repetition in Tony's character development and his lack of development. He's held back, even trapped, by his inability to confront his mother's dominant role in his development, or deformity, as a person, but no matter how hard he tries to avoid the issue, it keeps erupting and nearly destroying him. You also see that Gloria, despite her flesh-and-blood realness as a woman, is also a quasi-mythological figure, representing aspects of Tony's psyche that he refuses to resolve. Season one ended with Tony nearly killing Livia. Season two climaxed with a Livia-like figure, Janice, killing Richie, a Johnny Boy–like figure, which set the stage for Tony's mixed feelings at Livia's death early in this season, in an episode that was literally haunted by ghosts. And then, a few episodes away from the finale, here comes Gloria, appearing in the waiting room of a psychiatrist's office, of all places, the result of Melfi's accidental double-booking,[72] that forces them to share space. Gloria and Tony have their first conversation while sitting on the bench where we first met Tony, framed between the legs of a sculpture of a woman who was later revealed to look eerily like the young Livia. Gloria doesn't so much enter the story of *The Sopranos* as materialize within it, as if summoned by incantation (in season two, Tony calls Livia a *strega*, or witch). As long as Gloria stays within a carefully delineated psychic space—like Isabella before Tony started talking about her—their relationship works. But once she breaches the edges of that space and impacts his family, Tony realizes the relationship has to be severed, or Gloria destroyed. In the end, we see an anguished, denial-prone son kneeling on the floor of a woman's bungalow, which could be a witch's lair–like cabin, trying to crush the life out of her by invitation—Remember Livia's wishes for others, including her son, and God, to take her now?—after she ignites his rage by saying, "Poor you!"

Tony's temper is often depicted as an uncontrollable force, which here leads him to grab a tiny woman by the neck and hurl her through the air—rarely has James Gandolfini's bulk been this terrifying—but he's able to arrest it this time, and retreat to think of a better solution. In this case, it involves sending a message tailor-made for a woman hoping Tony will toss her into a burning ring of fire.

---

72 If Gloria is a doppelgänger of the deceased Livia, it means Melfi double-booked a double.

"My face is the last one you'll see, not Tony's," threatens Patsy Parisi, the most milquetoast-looking guy in the crew. "We understand each other? It won't be cinematic."[73]

In therapy, Melfi clarifies to Tony that when she compares Gloria and Irina to his mother, she's not actually saying that he wanted to have sex with his mother—only that his desire to please these needy, self-destructive women derives from unresolved feelings and unmet needs that he hasn't explicated, because he's scared to face them. Nevertheless, she describes Tony's relationship with Gloria as *amour fou*, or "foolish love." Tony mispronounces it like "a mofo," an abbreviation of one of profanity's greatest hits: motherfucker.

SEASON 3/EPISODE 13
WRITTEN BY DAVID CHASE & LAWRENCE KONNER
DIRECTED BY JOHN PATTERSON

The Garbage Business

"How are we gonna save this kid?" —**Tony**

Almost no one shows up at the funeral home to say goodbye to the late Jackie Aprile Jr. It's two days before a Super Bowl pitting the hometown Giants against the Baltimore Ravens, and even the grief-stricken Rosalie understands that most of the wiseguys are out collecting bets. But the pitiful crowd at the funeral home, and the way that the reception at Vesuvio turns into a party where Ralphie tells dirty jokes and Junior sings old Italian love songs,[74] suggests a painful truth Roe might not want to acknowledge: few people in her life cared about her son.

If there's a flaw with the closing arc of season three, it's that Jackie generated as much enthusiasm among the *Sopranos* audience as he did among that crowd at

---

73 Though *The Sopranos* developed a reputation for putting its biggest developments in the penultimate episodes of seasons, this was largely unearned: no one notable dies in season one's "Isabella," and the death of Pussy—a bigger deal for season two than Richie's demise—comes in the finale. Because Gloria had become so memorable so quickly, "Amour Fou" fits this reputation better than its episode-twelve predecessors, feeling finale-ish to the point that the episode concludes with the sort of montage many dramas reserve for the end of a season: as Bob Dylan's "Return to Me" plays, we see Ralphie trying to console a terrified Rosalie, Carmela studying for her real estate license as a way to feel more independent, and Patsy calling his wife to tell her about the groceries he's bringing home for dinner. (His life isn't cinematic, either.)

74 Dominic Chianese is a gifted tenor, and the year before this episode aired, he released an album called *Hits*. Two years later, he named his second album *Ungrateful Heart*, after the Italian song Junior sings here.

Vesuvio. The season's more compelling antagonists were Ralphie and Gloria, but the latter was written off in "Amour Fou," and the former survives his beef with Tony, his punishment being that he has to order the hit on his girlfriend's son. "Pine Barrens" convinced some fans that the season would build to a war between Tony's crew and Slava's, but the Russians aren't even mentioned here; wherever Valery is, or isn't, is a mystery the series has no interest in solving.

The main work problem to be solved before the end is Jackie: a dumb kid with an overinflated sense of entitlement, good for a few jokes about his Scrabble abilities or his criminal ineptitude, but never a real villain in the mold of Junior, Livia, Richie, or Pussy. So devoting so much of "Army of One" to his murder and its aftermath can't help but feel anticlimactic: the wake for a dead man no one but his mother, sister, and former girlfriend will much miss.

But if Jackie himself doesn't seem enough to support a season-ending story arc, "Army of One" deftly uses his murder to illustrate the callus of lies and self-deception everyone in and around the Family has to build up to make it through the day, and what happens when someone like Tony or Meadow has to actually think about who they are and how they got here.

After Vito shoots Jackie outside the housing project where he's been hiding with Ray Ray[75] and his daughter,[76] Tony tries to appear mournful with Dr. Melfi—"In the end, I failed him. What the fuck you gonna do?"—who's unmoved by his transparent dissembling, and perhaps suspicious of her patient's role in this tragedy. Yet Jackie's death coming at the same time that Verbum Dei finally expels AJ for cheating on a test (and peeing in the boiler room[77]) ultimately forces him to be more introspective than usual about his life and the impact it has on his children.

Tony, like everyone else in his bigoted, self-preservational circle, quickly follows his crew's tactic of blaming the murder on anonymous black drug dealers, but he knows the truth: Jackie doomed himself by trying to imitate behavior that launched Tony and Jackie Sr. in the Family. Approving the murder of his daughter's boyfriend (even if he technically left it to Ralphie to make the final decision) doesn't sit well with him, and when Melfi asks what he wants for his

75 Played by Michael Kenneth Williams, a future HBO mainstay who played stick-up artist Omar Little on *The Wire*, gangster Chalky White on *Boardwalk Empire* (from *Sopranos* producer Terence Winter), and boxer-turned-convict Freddie in *The Night Of* (developed by James Gandolfini).

76 Jackie Jr.'s short, sad life, summed up in a single line: after he concedes defeat in a game of chess to the little girl, Ray Ray tells him, "See, you should've played that out. That's the only way you gonna learn."

77 The principal gets AJ and his friend to confess by convincing them his crack team has found a DNA match to their pee, but considering how the cops investigated the pool vandalism incident from "The Telltale Moozadell" like it was a high-profile homicide, maybe they're not that stupid for falling for the ruse. (Okay, they are.)

own children, his first impulse is to say of Meadow, "The important thing is, she get far away from me." He immediately clarifies that he means moral, not geographical, distance, but the fact that he would state it in such stark and self-aware terms feels like a breakthrough—or as close as a sociopath like Tony can come to one.

The details of Jackie's death fit the self-deceptive requirements of Mob life. Everyone in the Family knows exactly where he's hiding, but they have to pretend they don't, to allow Ralphie to save face while he's wrestling with this decision a gleeful Tony has forced on him. Even most of the spouses and children understand what really happened, though they all dutifully back the drug dealer lie. Meadow allows herself a brief period of candor, telling Carmela—a veteran at inventing bogeymen to blame for Tony's acts—"Look at who he grew up with. Look at who his father was. Look at everybody we know." But the honesty doesn't last—it can't if Meadow wants to in any way be a part of this family—and soon she closes ranks, scolding Jackie's sister Kelli for trying to speak the truth about what happened while a cousin is in the room.

Later, she gets upset at the reception when she sees how Junior and the others don't really care about Jackie: drinking heavily, throwing bread at her uncle while she sings Britney Spears's "Oops! . . . I Did It Again," then running out into traffic after telling Tony, "This is such bullshit!" She knows what really happened, knows that her father almost certainly was involved, but she can't do anything about it other than exactly what Tony wished for her in that session with Melfi: try to get as far away from him as possible. But we know from the Kelli lecture that even if she runs away, like her Aunt Janice did, her exile won't last. It can't. She's a Soprano.

So, even less avoidably, is AJ, who bears both his father's name and "that putrid, rotten fucking Soprano gene," as a tearful Tony describes it to Melfi after learning that his son also has panic attacks. In that earlier therapy session, he had laughed at the idea of AJ following in his footsteps the way he did with Johnny Boy—"AJ? In my business? Forget it. He'd never make it."—but much of the episode involves him struggling to find the kid an alternate path. Both AJ and Jackie were named for their fathers, and both were spoiled rotten. Meadow blames Rosalie and Jackie Sr. for being too permissive, the same accusation Tony lays on Carmela about how AJ thinks the world owes him everything. Jackie tried to be exactly like his father, and it got him killed; Tony's worked very hard to prevent AJ from doing the same, but the result so far is only better in that AJ is still alive. Military school seemed the last, best option for Tony to straighten the kid out,[78] but the

---

78 Tony may love his son, but he's also cruel to him, not just in the scene where he slaps AJ for saying "Sucks to be you," but in the moments right before the panic attack, where he starts making fun of the kid for wearing the cadet uniform for the very school that Tony himself is forcing him to attend!

panic attacks scotch that plan, leaving Tony and Carmela once again fumbling for the best way to make him even slightly less of a clown. Tony spends much of the episode reveling in the power he holds over Ralphie by forcing him to make the call on Jackie, but he's powerless as he asks Melfi how to save his own son.

The finale also deals with bits of uppercase-Family business: a cancer-free Junior preparing for trial, Tony freezing out Christopher for questioning his leadership over the Jackie situation, Tony favoring Ralphie in a financial dispute with Paulie[79] because Ralphie's the much bigger earner, and Johnny Sack trying to exploit this schism in Tony's crew by buttering up the frustrated Paulie with tales of Carmine Lupertazzi asking about him. But most of those stories—plus the FBI sending agent Deborah Ciccerone[80] undercover to befriend Adriana—are setting things up for the following season. "Army of One" is mostly interested in attempting to settle lowercase-family business—or at least acknowledging that, when you're part of the putrid, rotten, fucking Soprano family, the only thing that ever gets permanently settled is how much you have to lie to yourself and others to keep on going.

---

79 Paulie needs the cash because he's putting his mother Nucci (Frances Ensemplare) into Green Grove—and she's *much* more appreciative of the place than Livia ever was.

80 When this episode first aired, Ciccerone was played by actress Fairuza Balk. Between seasons three and four, Balk was replaced by Lola Glaudini, and—in a unique case for a show that occasionally had to recast roles, but otherwise preserved the original actors' work—Balk's scenes were reshot with Glaudini for future airings and home video.

Season
Four

"FOR ALL DEBTS PUBLIC AND PRIVATE"

SEASON 4/EPISODE 1
WRITTEN BY DAVID CHASE
DIRECTED BY ALLEN COULTER

The Halfback of Notre Dame

"Well, let me tell you something—or you can watch the fucking news—everything comes to an end!" —**Carmela**

Early in the fourth-season premiere, Tony smiles at a rustling in the bushes by the pool, assuming his beloved ducks have returned after a long absence. Instead, a squirrel emerges.

With "For All Debts Public and Private," *The Sopranos* was returning after nearly a year and a half away, and the show that emerged wasn't quite the same. Nor, for that matter, was the world it returned to, and that it had to depict going forward.

None of the series' characters died during the horrific events of September 11, 2001, but as anyone who lived in the New York–New Jersey area at that time can tell you, you didn't have to be directly affected by this tragedy to have it throw your world view off-kilter. The sidewalks were covered with impromptu memorials, commuter parking lots throughout Jersey were filled with cars whose owners would never claim them, and for a while everyone was either on the verge of tears or understanding of those who were. It was a shocking reminder of just how suddenly life could be taken away, even in a seemingly safe time and place.

So even though nearly a year has passed for Tony and company since 9/11,[1] that day's events are still very much on their minds as season four begins. "For All Debts Public and Private" doesn't lay this on too thick—the Twin Towers are no longer in Tony's rearview mirror in the opening credits,[2] Carmela alludes to what's been on the news, and Tony and Bobby Bacala briefly discuss the ter-

---

1   It's here that the series' timeline starts to get fuzzy. Jackie Jr.'s funeral was on January 28, 2001 (the day of the Giants–Ravens Super Bowl), while this episode is taking place at the end of the summer of 2002, even though Meadow and AJ are each advancing only a grade in school, and only months have passed in both the FBI undercover operation with Adriana and the cold spell between Tony and Christopher.

2   This was done by slightly lengthening the shots around the deleted shot of the towers, so that the timing of the opening credits wasn't affected. The decision to handle the World Trade Center this way fit in perfectly with one of the themes of the show: even when the historical context around organized crime changes, the Mafia itself doesn't change much.

rorist attacks while dining together[3]—but there's a sense, for both Mr. and Mrs. Soprano in particular, that an end could be coming at any moment, and they'd best prepare for it.

In the world of *The Sopranos*, everything is ultimately about money, even respect (which you demonstrate through money), and thus everyone's concern for their future (or lack thereof) is represented by cold hard cash. (The episode's title comes from a phrase printed on U.S. paper currency.) Carmela is stunned to see Angie Bonpensiero working as a supermarket sample lady and realizes that she—like any Mob widow (or, for that matter, any 9/11 widow)—could suffer a similar fate if she doesn't try to understand her husband's finances and have some say in their current and future distribution should she lose Tony. She pushes him to speak to her cousin Brian about investments she could easily access to in the event the worst happens. Uncle Junior's RICO trial is approaching, and with it more expenses from his lawyer than he's comfortable paying on Tony's allowance. Tony and Silvio hector the captains[4]—other than the absent Paulie, who's in jail in Youngstown on a gun charge[5]—over the Family's shaky finances,[6] and Bobby gets a promotion to run what's left of Junior's street crew.

To Carmela, Junior, and the captains, Tony projects smug authority. But his actions paint him as just as anxious about the future as the rest. He insists to Carmela that he has hidden money in overseas accounts she'll gain access to should the need arise, yet we see him simply burrowing cash in easily accessed places, including the bags of duck feed he keeps around in the event his feathered friends return.

This is deeply paranoid behavior, but sometimes people really are out to get you. Tony's annual waddle down the driveway to pick up the *Star-Ledger* is

---

3 In true *Sopranos* fashion, even that overt discussion of 9/11 is quickly derailed by Bacala's confusion between Nostradamus and the hunchback of Notre Dame ("You know, Quasimodo predicted all this.") and then his conflation of the Parisian church and college football team that bear the same name ("Hunchback of Notre Dame, you also got your quarterback and your halfback of Notre Dame . . . "). Even when *The Sopranos* is referencing a national nightmare, it's got room for jokes.

4 Introduced silently (and not referred to by name for some time after this): Carlo Gervasi (Arthur Nascarella), who has taken over Jimmy Altieri's crew, and is in charge of the Family smuggling business at the port. This scene also has Steve Van Zandt's spectacular delivery of Silvio's recitation of the two recession-proof businesses: "Certain aspects of showbiz, and our thing."

5 The writers had bigger plans for Paulie this season, but Tony Sirico needed back surgery. Leaving Paulie in jail for a while allowed them to film without Sirico, then shoot a whole season's worth of Paulie scenes all at once after he recovered.

6 Soprano hypocrisy in action: Tony is unmoved by Junior's pleas for more money for legal bills, yet when it's time to scold the captains, he tries to guilt them about the idea that "the boss of this Family" (technically still Junior) is "on trial for his life." Tony also has no qualms about buying property from Junior for a fraction of what, thanks to Assemblyman Zellman, he knows it will soon be worth.

accompanied by Afrika Bambaataa and John Lydon's apocalyptic "World Destruction," evoking not only the fragile state of the world but of Tony's empire as well. The FBI even gets an undercover agent inside his house briefly, when Adriana picks up Christopher with Deborah Ciccerone (aka "Danielle Ciccolella") in tow. Receipts are down, Ralphie is still alive to annoy Tony,[7] and Paulie is complaining about him to Johnny Sack.[8] Yet for all the stress—including things like the latest FBI infiltration attempt, of which he's unaware—and impulsive money moves, Tony seems to have a plan to deal with the potential conclusion of his own story.

"There's two endings for a guy like me," he explains to Dr. Melfi, in one of their more direct discussions of the nature of his business: "Dead, or in the can, big percent of the time."

Tony, though, sees a third way to wrap it up: "You trust only blood." Never mind that Christopher is only vaguely related to Tony—nor that his "nephew" has quietly been shooting heroin between his toes—he's the closest blend of family and Family available, and he's vulnerable to the mind games Tony has been playing with him since Jackie Jr. died. The whole thing is one long seduction, starting out with Tony negging Christopher for months, making him desperate for his mentor's approval, or even a non-grudging look. Instead, Tony goes much further by offering Chrissie a chance for revenge against the man who allegedly murdered his father: newly retired cop Barry Haydu (Tom Mason). We have no idea if this is true, or if Tony simply picked an easy target. Christopher is smart enough to acknowledge the possibility—but also pragmatic enough to realize that it doesn't matter, because if the boss of the Family wants this guy dead, then he's going to be dead.

It's a chilling scene, not least for the contrast between Christopher coldly executing a dirty cop and a *Magnum P.I.* rerun on Hadyu's television where Magnum and T. C. are pretending to be cops, to much more frivolous effect. Because of his father, this is a huge deal to Christopher—bigger than killing Emil Kolar or Mikey Palmice or anyone else so far—yet his manner is almost casual, because he wants to savor this long-awaited opportunity.

Money is once again a token of respect, as Christopher lifts a twenty-dollar bill from Haydu's wallet and pins it to his mother's refrigerator as a secret trophy, the end credits rolling over an extreme close-up of Andrew Jackson's right eye

---

7   Janice is back to her old habits here, snorting cocaine and making out with Ralphie in the guest bath of Tony and Carmela's house.

8   In the later meeting with Johnny and Carmine, Carmine tells Tony of a disturbing piece of information he heard about one of Tony's cookouts, and warns him, "Dons don't wear shorts." This is a long-delayed acknowledgment of various real-life wiseguys' grumbling after Tony wore shorts while grilling back in the pilot episode.

over "World Destruction" reprised. This feels like a triumph to Christopher, but he's just fallen hook, line, and sinker for Tony's gambit—a human shield against Tony's story having a bad ending.

"For All Debts Public and Private" takes *The Sopranos* into middle age. Chase didn't know at the time how long he intended the series to run, but its advancing years, and the shocking real-life reminders of how swiftly things can end, had him and the characters contemplating the conclusion like never before. It's hard to see things getting better for anyone from here.

SEASON 4/EPISODE 2
"NO SHOW"   WRITTEN BY TERENCE WINTER AND DAVID CHASE
DIRECTED BY JOHN PATTERSON

Mr. Mob Boss

"Wow. Listen to Mr. Mob Boss!" —**Meadow**

Early in "No Show," Silvio settles a dispute between Ralphie and the incarcerated Paulie Walnuts by awarding Paulie's crew five fake jobs at the Esplanade construction site: two are no-show, where you don't even have to turn up to get paid, while three are no-work, where you have to be physically present but are otherwise free to lounge around and do what you like. The no-show jobs are the more coveted, but the no-work jobs are pretty cushy, too. The episode finds most of its major characters opting for one approach or the other, including the ones who don't even work in construction: ignoring their current responsibilities while still enjoying the benefits.

This is most obvious with Meadow, who has been using Jackie Jr.'s murder as a blanket doctor's note to avoid a summer job, choosing classes for the fall semester, or even reading from the canon of great literature like she claims. Yet she still benefits from Tony and Carm's largesse, including a car they bought her as transportation to her very own no-show job. All she has to do to get out of anything is to mention Jackie's name, pout, and/or storm out of the room.

To try to get his daughter to start showing up to her life, Tony sends her to a therapist recommended by Dr. Melfi, but Wendi Kobler[9] turns out to have a different agenda from her paid one. Kobler's somewhat no-show herself (she keeps

---

9   Theater actress, cabaret star, and TV fixture Linda Lavin, best known as the star of TV's *Alice*.

calling Jackie "Jack" even after Meadow corrects her[10]), and Meadow is putting on an act at times, but what's fascinating is how much their interaction still mirrors many Tony–Melfi sessions, with Tony replacing Livia as the parent casting a shadow over everything. But he's more overtly threatening than Livia, and twice in the episode—the scene where the sound lowers and lowers until Tony explodes and dares Meadow to follow her year-in-Europe plan, then after her "Mr. Mob Boss" taunt—she gets a brief and terrifying glimpse of what her father is like at work.

Meadow ultimately abandons her Europe plan and registers for classes, but while her parents await the news, Carmela assures Tony that Meadow blames her, not him. Some of this stems from standard gender issues—teenage girls often turn against their mothers and rush toward their fathers—but given what else is going on with Carmela at the moment, it's easy to draw a link to her crush on Furio and her growing frustrations with Tony. No-working her own marriage,[11] she's more excited to talk to Furio about his plans to buy a house in Nutley than to interact with Tony. (And she clams up when Tony suggests Meadow could meet a guy like Furio if she takes the Europe trip.) Her concern about supporting herself if Tony disappeared, coupled with Meadow's emotional implosion—launched by the suspicious murder of the Family's previous boss's son—seems to have her questioning the status quo even more than usual. When she says Meadow blames her, is she projecting her own questions about why she's still married to Tony?

The more literal no-show and no-work jobs come into play with Christopher, temporarily promoted to run Paulie's crew.[12] Displeased with the decision are more senior mobster Patsy, and Silvio, who senses Tony's using his nephew for duties and confidences once his purview as consigliere. Christopher's out of his depth, approving Patsy's plan to steal fiber-optic cable from the Esplanade job site and

---

10   One of *The Sopranos*'s most striking contributions to TV drama is the way it redefined therapy more realistically, presenting it as a process that's not necessarily building toward an all-encompassing cure that makes the patient "better," and also as a job that attracts good, bad, and just okay people, all of whom differ on what constitutes good therapy. Dr. Kobler is very good in some ways and problematic in others, fitting right into a broadening spectrum of *Sopranos* shrinks that also includes the ambitious, danger-seeking Melfi, the passive-aggressively scolding serial-interrupter Elliot Kupferberg, and Dr. Krakower, who's equal parts advice columnist and disapproving rabbi.

11   Also no-working a long-term relationship: Ralphie, who is spending most of his time with Janice even though he's technically still dating Rosalie Aprile. Tony is understandably disgusted to learn of the affair—he shakes out his hand after touching one of Ralphie's shoes like he's afraid of catching a social disease—and even Janice seems to be regretting her decision after Ralphie cuts his toenails in bed and laughs at her when a stray clipping hits her in the face.

12   Paulie gets one of the coveted no-show construction jobs, allowing him to earn money even while he's stuck in Youngstown. Meanwhile, he's very much working Johnny Sack (or being worked by him) by gathering intel about what's happening in Jersey, particularly the off-color joke Ralph told about Johnny's plus-size wife Ginny: "I hear Ginny Sack's getting a ninety-five-pound mole taken off her ass!"

putting the much larger construction deal at risk, and turning to heroin again for emotional escape after Tony scolds him for it.[13]

But the greatest damage Christopher causes is something he's not even aware he's done. By making a move on "Danielle" in Adriana's view, he tears down the fake friendship Deborah Ciccerone[14] has worked so hard to forge with Ade, thus forcing the FBI to get more direct and brutal: they pull Adriana off the street and threaten her with prison time on drug charges if she doesn't actively cooperate.

Adriana is in way over her head here (it doesn't even occur to her to ask for a lawyer), and her response to the FBI's threats—particularly Agent Harris pointing out the ramifications of having brought an undercover federal agent into Tony's house—is to projectile-vomit across the table. She's been no-working her relationship with Christopher for a long time, enjoying the fruits of his criminal labor without having to confront what he does and who gets hurt by it. Now she has no choice but to be present.

No good can come of that.

 **"CHRISTOPHER"**

SEASON 4/EPISODE 3
STORY BY MICHAEL IMPERIOLI AND MARIA LAURINO,
TELEPLAY BY MICHAEL IMPERIOLI
DIRECTED BY TIM VAN PATTEN

Reservations

"Where the fuck is our self-esteem? That stuff doesn't come from Columbus, or The Godfather, *or Chef fuckin' Boyardee."* —**Tony**

Masterpieces can have flaws. The White Album has "Honey Pie." *The Godfather* franchise has *III.*

The Sopranos has "Christopher."

It is the nadir of the show's fascination with Italian American representation and self-esteem—and of the show, period.

---

13 Silvio's defense when he approves Patsy committing an additional heist from the job site—"Timeline got fucked up."—is vintage Sil double talk, and a prime example of the off-kilter charm of Van Zandt's delivery. Sil gets away with things no other member of the crew would, just as Van Zandt gets away with saying things no other actor in the cast could.

14 Our brief glimpses of Agent Ciccerone's home life provide a sharp contrast to the various Mob relationships. Ciccerone and her husband, fellow agent Mike Waldrup (played by a young Will Arnett) treat each other as equals, and he gladly takes their baby out of the room whenever Adriana calls for "Danielle."

Why does the hour—in which Silvio and the rest of the crew get offended by Native American protests of Columbus Day—stick out so glaringly, even compared to the show's other anti-defamation episodes?

For starters, it has nothing to do with season's arc, nor with Mob work at all. Season one's "Legend of Tennessee Moltisanti" is effective not only because it was the first time *The Sopranos* addressed defamation, but because Family business proceeded throughout. Here, save for the death of Bacala's saintly wife Karen (Christine Pedi) in a traffic accident, and Johnny Sack learning about Ralphie's "ninety-five-pound mole" joke regarding his wife Ginny (Denise Borino[15])—neither of which have anything to do with anti-defamation (other than the fact that Karen was last seen attending a lecture on the topic at the church)—the entire episode could be deleted without impacting any future storylines.

Second, it doesn't do anything to deepen our understanding of the characters or the world of the show.[16] "A Hit Is a Hit" is less successful overall than "Tennessee Moltisanti," but it still illuminates Chris and Adriana's relationship, contrasts the experiences of minorities in America, and has that great subplot with Tony at the country club. "Christopher" is a Silvio episode, but Silvio is a broad comic relief character, better on the periphery of scenes than their centerpiece. We learn nothing new about him, because the whole thing is played as a joke. Beyond that, Silvio's strident defense of Italian culture comes out of nowhere. Paulie Walnuts, not Sil, was always the guy bemoaning cultural appropriation and sentimentalizing the old country. "Christopher" would have been better if Paulie were the central character, as originally planned, before Sirico's back surgery forced a change.

Michael Imperioli's script has a few amusing flourishes, like the Indian casino being run by a "chief" who only barely qualifies for tribal membership, or Artie Bucco diving lamely into the back of a car after being hit with a Slushie when he helps counter a Native American protest. And the very final beat of the episode—Tony shrugs off Silvio's latest argument in defense of cultural pride by reminding him they have to call Frankie Valli to pay off the favor the chief did for them, followed by the soundtrack blasting The Four Seasons' "Dawn (Go Away)"— is a deft comic touch in an hour that's otherwise working way too hard to beat a

---

15 Borino got the part from an open casting call—attended by thousands of would-be *Sopranos* actors—she attended while missing part of her grandmother's wake. That's showbiz.

16 There's even an argument between Hesh and his old friend Reuben (Yul Vazquez) when Reuben compares Columbus to Hitler, offending the Jewish Hesh, which has no weight at all because we've never seen Reuben before, and never will again. It's just there to make the same satirical point as the earlier scene with Montel Williams' talk show: everyone draws the line of offense at a different place, always protecting their own culture over someone else's.

horse the series has long since killed,[17] dumped in the Meadowlands, then dug up again and transported to upstate New York.

Bacala's subplot is promising, and proceeds logically from his sensitivity. Karen had only appeared once before (bringing Junior food in the season four premiere), but that episode and this one efficiently turn her into a saint worthy of worship. The tragedy ripples outward. Janice[18] realizes that she wants nothing to do with a narcissistic pervert[19] like Ralphie, who dumped poor Rosalie Aprile because he couldn't take her perpetual mourning anymore. When he arrives at Livia's house, Janice shoves him down the stairs.

It's a fine story in and of itself, and works nicely in parallel with the indignation of Johnny Sack—who, like Bobby, doesn't step out on his wife—upon hearing about Ralphie's joke. But that material is an oasis in a desert of familiar material about old ethnic grievances, and occasional jokes about Iron Eyes Cody.[20]

When an exasperated Tony lays into Silvio in the episode's final scene about how all of this self-pity should be beneath them, it's hard not to feel like he's speaking for every *Sopranos* viewer who just sat through this hour of stereotype-busting, hollow rhetoric, and wacky hijinks, and would prefer that Silvio take these complaints up with Frankie Valli, rather than making us listen to them again and again and *again*.

---

17 The episode even brings in our old nemesis Dick La Penna for the sole purpose of his overwrought reaction to news coverage of the violence between Native and Italian protesters, suggesting it's so tragic, it "could be scored with Albinoni's *Adagio*."

18 An episode after Meadow goes to see Wendi Kobler, we finally meet Janice's own therapist, who buys into her lies and self-justifications in a way that Dr. Melfi rarely does with Tony.

19 You would think the show couldn't top Janice having sex with Richie at gunpoint for kinkiness, but there she is using a vibrator on Ralphie while pretending to be his pimp, only for the whole thing to be interrupted by the *Rocky* theme ringtone on his cell phone.

20 Cody, best known as the Native American brave crying a single tear over roadside littering in 1970s "Keep America Beautiful" public service announcements was, in fact, Italian American, just as James Caan is Jewish, a fact that gives pause to *Godfather* obsessive Silvio when he's reminded of it.

SEASON 4/EPISODE 4
WRITTEN BY TERENCE WINTER
DIRECTED BY JACK BENDER

All of Her

*"To me, she's beautiful—Rubenesque. That woman is my life.
To think she's being mocked?"* —**Johnny Sack**

Johnny Sack loves his wife.

This should go without saying, as it does for most of the married wiseguys. But the love most of these men give their spouses is compromised at best, guaranteeing neither fidelity nor honesty. Mistresses are understood as part of the deal; as Gaby noted at the wake for Karen Baccalieri, the other wiseguys made fun of Bobby for *not* having a mistress.

Bobby's unwavering love for his own wife was seen as a weakness, even though it didn't affect his work. But Johnny Sack's devotion to Ginny becomes an enormous Family problem in "The Weight," a black comic farce about stubborn pride, inappropriate humor, and how much one man is willing to endanger out of devotion to the woman he loves. It lacks the long build-up of "Cunnilingus and psychiatry brought us to this," but it's an effectively strange, scary, and very funny take on that old Corleone tune about keeping business and personal matters separate.

One of the episode's best running gags involves people like Junior and Carmine, who weren't at the dinner in question, being asked what's funny about the "ninety-five-pound mole" line to begin with. But even more potent is everyone's bafflement at Johnny's refusal to back down from his vendetta. Some of this is pig-headed pride—"We're talking about my wife's honor here!" he screams at Carmine, tellingly adding, "*My* honor!"—a quality even Tony can recognize. But nobody seem to understand why a man would risk business over an insult directed at his wife. Johnny takes things way too far—administering a harsh beating, and averting his own death and Ralphie's only after discovering that Ginny has been stress-eating hidden junk food—but the impulse to defend the honor of the woman he adores is nobler than anything the wiseguys are used to seeing.

The situation's so far outside everyone's comfort zone, in fact, that the episode takes a brief detour into the macabre, when Christopher and Silvio head to Rhode Island and hire three elderly retired hitmen to take care of Johnny, because no one in the Tri-State area can be trusted to handle it. The home they share is unsettling, gloomily lit, and filled with religious iconography. One is blind, one is on oxygen,[21] and there's a promise of Carvel birthday cake that Christopher—high and paranoid—has no interest in staying to sample. The show often plays Mob transactions for laughs, but rarely does the culture feel this bizarre.

In the end, both hits are called off. Johnny and Ginny's bond is somehow tighter, despite her lying, and he's kept his behind-the-scenes, pro-Ginny vigilantism a secret from her. It's a rare moment of pure spousal love on a show that suggests even non-Mob marriages are complicated at best. Johnny's feelings for his wife effectively complement Bobby's ongoing grief over Karen.

But the more striking contrast comes in the other major subplot,[22] as Carmela's interest in Furio goes from simmer to full boil when he invites her to dance at his housewarming party. Whether he means to seduce the boss's wife or not, it's working, thanks partly to Tony's indifference. Furio is a poetic man of the earth who hangs on Carmela's every word; Tony zones out during the meeting with Carmela's financial planner cousin Brian (Matthew Del Negro[23]), and later complains it was boring. He takes Carmela so thoroughly for granted that he doesn't even notice his smitten wife dancing right in front of him with a younger, more desirable man. This is dangerous territory for all involved. Tony's feelings for his wife will never be as uncontaminated as Johnny's are for Ginny. But if Johnny would go this far over a tasteless joke, how might Tony respond to finding out his wife is falling—hard—for a member of his own crew?

In the fight over the Cousin Brian meeting, Tony accuses Carmela of equating love with money, and she throws the idea right back at him. Yet the charge sticks to both of them. Tony solves marital problems via lavish gifts, and Carmela usually accepts the gesture. When he gives her an expensive dress from Saks,[24] she's almost as excited by that as she is by his agreement to go along with Brian's financial plan. It's Tony providing emotional and material support at once—even he usually figures out when he needs to do both—and it briefly seems to extinguish the Furio brushfire. But then we hear the same Italian song that was playing at the housewarming. At first it seems like it's playing in Carmela's imagination, but it's actually a CD that Furio loaned Meadow. And even after the music is turned off, it doesn't go away. Carmela's body is with one man. Her thoughts are with another.

---

21 One of the hitmen is played by Richard Bright, who was Michael Corleone's top henchman Al Neri in all three *Godfather* films. (The scene even mentions the hitmen taking out a character named Tommy Neri, Al's nephew in the *Godfather* books.)

22 There's a fourth, largely unrelated storyline involving the Soprano and Kupferberg families intermingling without realizing their connection, though it's ultimately about Elliot helping Melfi work through her ongoing feelings of powerlessness about her rape.

23 Giovanni Gilberti on *Rizzoli & Isles,* Michael Ambruso on *Scandal,* and Rafael McCall on *Teen Wolf,* among other credits.

24 The choice of store does not seem coincidental, given the marriage that dominates so much of the episode.

SEASON 4/EPISODE 5
WRITTEN BY ROBIN GREEN & MITCHELL BURGESS
DIRECTED BY HENRY J. BRONCHTEIN

"PIE-O-MY"

My Rifle, My Pony, and Me

"How's our girl?" —**Tony**

For all his enjoyment of ducks and other animal friends, Tony Soprano doesn't keep a pet of his own. Early in "Pie-O-My," Tony says he has never followed Hesh and others into horse ownership because "it's an animal. It's a commitment." This could well be true. But the thing about being a wiseguy—and particularly about being the boss of a Family—is that you can enjoy the benefits of owning things without the commitment that would bind anyone else.

If it's not love at first sight between Tony and the episode's eponymous race-horse, it's love at first victory, particularly since Tony's strategic advice helped it win. Ralphie owns the horse and pays all its expenses, but Tony very quickly acts like Pie-O-My belongs to him, taking bigger cuts of the winnings—originally offered out of friendship, to a man who has less than no desire to be Ralphie's friend—all without having to spend a dime on the horse. Given Tony's frequent preference for the company of animals to humans, it seems like his ideal relationship. By the time he goes to the stables in the middle of the night to sit with the ailing horse, it no longer feels like a burden, but a privilege. Tony usually gets what he wants: all he has to do is take it. So he takes Ralphie's horse.

Tony's sly takeover is paralleled in a variety of subplots about other characters muscling in on a possession or role that's not quite theirs. Carmela's is both the most justified and least successful. She doesn't want anything that isn't hers, just more control over and information about family finances, and more security via the insurance trust she wants Tony to arrange with Cousin Brian. Tony refuses after his accountant warns him that he'd lose the money in a divorce. He also denies her the cash she wants to invest in a medical stock, not permitting her any bit of financial independence. He has kept her in this lifestyle, and that's just how he would prefer she remain: kept. Even under better circumstances, she might be exasperated by him slipping out to tend to another man's horse, but after Tony's refusals? It's hard to blame her for rejecting Tony's explanations of how the horse now essentially belongs to him. ("It followed you home?")

Still, even if Tony infuriates her, Carmela's position is stable compared to her sister-in-law, who staked all her hopes on a different beautiful (at heart) creature: Bobby Bacala, her latest key to unlocking the happiness she knows lurks somewhere inside her. Bobby's house is revealed to be within binocular distance of Livia's, the better for Janice to thwart women moving in on the Family's most eligible bachelor. She claims one of Carmela's lasagnas as her own to give to Bobby (and routes the chicken marsala from Mikey Palmice's widow JoJo to Uncle Junior), and otherwise insinuates herself into Bobby's life, pushing him to release Karen and grab hold of her.

The results are mixed: she can't convince Bobby to eat Karen's last baked ziti, but her pep talk gets him off the couch so he can threaten a shop steward to stop campaigning against Junior's preferred candidate in an upcoming union election. It's the first time we've seen Bobby as a gangster rather than a glorified Family mascot, and while it's bad behavior on the whole—the shop steward decries the Mob's twenty-five years of pension theft—Bobby needs to do this to stay in Junior's good graces,[25] and by extension Tony's.

Janice isn't the only character spying on wiseguys. The hour opens with Adriana at the Crazy Horse, now taken over by Christopher and his colleagues in the same way Tony did Pie-O-My. The club was always meant to be a Mob front—Adriana's playing manager and booking bands, thus feeling like Christopher believes in her talents, is just a fringe benefit of being another place to hold meetings, launder money, smuggle goods, and assault people in private—but when Adriana observes Furio beating up Giovanni Cogo, it's as if she is seeing for the first time what kind of business, and man, she has gotten involved with.

Adriana's life has been doubly taken over: the FBI keeps pressuring her to squeal and stay out of prison. Even her case is reassigned without Ade's say, as regular handler Deborah Ciccerone is replaced by Robyn Sanseverino (Karen Young), who has no shared history with Ade and offers no pretense of friendship. Sometimes Ade is smart enough to keep certain crimes a secret—like Giovanni's beating—but then she'll turn around and volunteer information about one of Patsy Parisi's hustles, not understanding that giving even this minor bit of intel to the FBI would get her killed if the wrong people found out. She's far out of her depth, and it's hard to blame her when she shoots Christopher's heroin as a temporary, heartbreaking escape. By dating Christopher, Adriana's no less compromised than Carmela, Janice, or the other Mob wives and girlfriends, but she's still a relative innocent, trapped because she didn't know any better. (And because Meadow took the wrong lamp to school.)

Still, the episode's most striking tableau comes at the very end, with the titular horse, as Tony contentedly smokes a cigar and whispers reassurances

---

25 As often happens, Junior is distracted by minutiae: in this case, the official courtroom artist's unflattering sketch, which earns Junior's glower next time they're in court.

to Pie-O-My as the rain falls outside and a goat wanders in.[26] He seems more at peace here than in any scenes involving friends and family. He's now responsible for the horse emotionally, if not financially, but his face says this is fine by him.[27] This animal is just the thing he wanted, and he didn't have to pay a dime to get her.

SEASON 4/EPISODE 6
"EVERYBODY HURTS"   **WRITTEN BY MICHAEL IMPERIOLI**
DIRECTED BY STEVE BUSCEMI

Reflections

"What the fuck am I, a toxic person or somethin'?" —**Tony**

For a man in therapy as long as he's been by "Everybody Hurts," Tony Soprano has a remarkable knack for avoiding introspection. Dr. Melfi can poke and prod, but when Tony is confronted with an unflattering aspect of himself, he changes the subject before he has to gaze too deeply upon it.

Here he has no choice but to look in the metaphorical mirror—in the same hour where Artie and Christopher both stare at themselves in literal ones. The three of them, plus AJ, all end the episode displeased with what they see. The biggest development is Gloria Trillo's suicide by hanging. Like so much else about season three's denouement, it's deliberately muted: Carmela sharing half-forgotten gossip with Tony about a woman she has no idea he knows. It's not the death Patsy warned Gloria of, but it's not cinematic, either, just sad. Tony seeks answers at Globe Motors and from Melfi, but isn't satisfied by the idea that these tragedies rarely have one specific reason. This has to be his fault, and only his fault. Once he's decided that, he can't ignore the possibility that he inflicts only misery on his loved ones.

Certainly the pressure of being, respectively, Tony's protégé, and that protégé's FBI cooperator and fiancée, has wrecked Christopher and Adriana. Their heroin use has gone from occasional to constant. Christopher is high and barely functional when Tony tells him he's grooming him to take the Family into the

---

26   The scene leads into a reprise of "My Rifle, My Pony and Me," which Tony previously watched Dean Martin and Ricky Nelson sing in a scene from the classic Western *Rio Bravo* during the season four premiere. Not exactly Gary Cooper, but John Wayne did play the lead.

27   Gandolfini is great at everything asked of him as Tony, but he's always particularly striking in scenes like this, where Tony is alone—or at least not interacting with other people—and simply being in the moment. This scene also features one of the show's great closing shots, an image lit and framed like an Old Masters painting, with intimations of the Garden of Eden and Jesus in the manger.

twenty-first century. Our only other glimpse of Chris involves him staring into a mirror (after a junkie friend vomits in a toilet), as unhappy as Tony at seeing himself.

Although AJ is comfortable with the fabulous lifestyle his father affords him, the poor kid is too dumb to show it off. He screws up a trip to the Bing by confusing it with the pork store ("It's a gay strip club?" a friend asks). He can't find a private location to have sex with new girlfriend Devin Pillsbury (Jessica Dunphy). And his laments of the emotional burdens of being rich backfire when she takes him to *her* mansion, which makes the Soprano home look like a shotgun shack.

Tony, meanwhile, responds to the Gloria news by overcompensating with good deeds: signing a living trust for Carmela, getting Cousin Brian new suits and Billy Joel tickets, taking Janice out to dinner to compliment her on choosing Bobby, and arranging a loan to finance Artie's new Armagnac venture. Carmela and Brian have nothing but praise for Tony, but the other gestures bring him grief. Janice at first takes his comments about Bobby as an insult, which forces Tony to realize how much time he spends belittling her; she's only defensive around him because he has conditioned her to flinch whenever he opens his mouth.

Artie's own mirror stint, unfortunately, finds him in gangster-wannabe mode: making like Travis Bickle to rehearse planned threats against his would-be partner Jean-Philippe (Jean-Hugues Anglade), the brother of new Vesuvio hostess Elodi Colbert (Murielle Arden), whose flirtation with Artie started this mess. For once, Charmaine's not able to talk him out of a terrible Mob-adjacent business idea, so Artie goes to Ralphie, who's wise enough to realize he shouldn't shylock the boss's oldest friend. With fear of being a toxic person looming in his mind, Tony pouts because Artie didn't come to him first. The deal goes south, of course, and Tony gets a suicide-prevention do-over when Artie fails to collect the money he owes.[28] Tony forgives Artie's debt in return for Artie wiping his enormous Vesuvio tab, on top of the chance to more effectively collect from Jean-Philippe. But any relief Tony feels at saving Artie where he couldn't save Gloria vanishes when Artie suggests Tony was acting from self-interest, hoping to profit from his failure.

We know Tony well enough to know Artie's right: he had to know, even unconsciously, how this was likely to go, just as he knew what would happen if he let Davey Scatino into the Executive Game. Even when Tony thinks he's doing the right thing, he's still using people, and his concluding session with Melfi suggests he's had enough of examining this side of himself for a while. When your life is as ugly as Tony Soprano's, looking too closely at any part of it can make it impossible to function.

---

28 Jean-Philippe even tears out Artie's midlife crisis earring.

SEASON 4/EPISODE 7
STORY BY DAVID CHASE AND ROBIN GREEN & MITCHELL BURGESS AND
TERENCE WINTER, TELEPLAY BY TERENCE WINTER AND NICK SANTORA
DIRECTED BY JOHN PATTERSON

All the Girls in New Jersey

"You ever feel bad about any of this?" —**Assemblyman Zellman**

When you call an episode of your series "Watching Too Much Television" and build a subplot around a character being foolish enough to take legal advice from a TV drama, you are cloaking yourself in your channel's slogan from that era: "It's not TV. It's HBO." There was a clear gap then in quality and audacity between *The Sopranos* and the rest of television. Not this time; much of the episode doesn't work, and the failures are in areas that have nothing to do with how a traditional TV show might tell its story.

This is a rare instance of the series' approach of treating episodes as short stories failing. The idea of following a single scam (using a few frontmen to swindle HUD out of money for inner-city homes no one has any intention of fixing) from conception (Cousin Brian shooting the breeze with Tony and Ralphie after a Bing all-nighter) to execution (the money is secured, making Newark's worst neighborhoods worse off than before) is interesting, and digs deeper into Tony's business than we're used to going. But the process of it—specifically, the focus on Assemblyman Zellman recruiting his old activist friend Maurice (Vondie Curtis-Hall) as one of the frontmen—wanders too far afield from the show's world and characters. There's a stand-alone version of "former '60s radicals grapple with how badly they've sold out in middle age" that could be compelling, and Peter Riegert and Curtis-Hall have the dramatic chops to play it, but their conflict— particularly Maurice's regret at harming a community he's spent decades trying to help—feels shoehorned in. Some moments feel spliced in from a backdoor pilot[29] for a Zellman–Maurice spinoff that never got made. They have little screen time, but the absence of series regulars, or of concerns directly tied to them, makes their scenes feel long, and neither are substantial enough to carry the show during its Tony-less interludes.

The season three premiere "Mr. Ruggerio's Neighborhood" probably has the smallest percentage of Tony screen time of any episode, but it works because

---

29 Backdoor pilots are TV episodes that introduce new characters in the hope of building spin-offs around them. The *NCIS* characters debuted this way on *JAG*, for instance, and one of David Chase's final *Rockford Files* episodes was an unsuccessful backdoor pilot for a drama about Jersey wiseguys, including a boss named Tony. (For more on that, see the interview about season one.)

the FBI's actions are all about him. This episode, on the other hand, is about the collateral damage unleashed by Tony's crimes—and, other than the junkie who gets shot by the gang kids, it's comparatively minor. It's almost enough to make one agree with AJ, of all people, who—while rejecting the same nostalgic lesson about his great-grandfather that Meadow ate up in the series pilot—asks, "Who gives a shit about Newark?"

The parts of the hour that succeed do so as you'd expect of the show: by advancing subplots, deepening arcs, and exploiting our familiarity with established characters. The Adriana story that gives the hour its title does take a few cheap shots at network TV by having her push Christopher to get married after learning of spousal privilege from an episode of *Murder One*,[30] only to have a friend offer conflicting advice courtesy of *Murder, She Wrote*. But those jokes aside, "Watching Too Much Television" amplifies poor Ade's season-long nightmare, first with Christopher's enraged response to her fertility issues ("You knew you were damaged goods and you never fucking *told* me?"), then with the wedding shower that Carmela insists on throwing, wherein the Mob wives load her down with kitchen gear, consigning her to a retrograde domestic lifestyle she hated long before the FBI showed up. Adriana's a miniskirts, stiletto-heels, black-leather-couches sort of gal, somebody who needs to be able to stumble in at 3 A.M. and cook an omelette without worrying she's going to wake people up. She's being hemmed in from at least three directions here, and it's killing her.

Despite his many superfluous scenes, Zellman figures prominently in the highlight of the hour, a scene that ties him directly to Tony. At first the mobster seems okay with the crooked politician dating his ex-mistress, then realizes just how *not* okay he is with it. While driving at night, Tony hears "Oh Girl" by The Chi-Lites—a song played earlier in the episode, and discussed by Tony and Maurice right after Zellman breaks the Irina news to him—and begins to sing along as he often does with his favorite tunes. Within moments, though, the joy of recognition is replaced by a wave of tearful regret, vulnerability, and anger. Is it about Irina, whom Tony used and discarded? Is the song bringing him back to a younger, much happier time when he first heard it? Does it simply make him feel weak, and in desperate need of appearing strong? Or is he transferring his grief and guilt over Gloria onto Irina, who has "moved on" in a different way? Whatever the explanation, Tony barrels into Zellman's home, breezes past Irina, and belt-

---

30 An ABC courtroom drama from Steven Bochco that was a precursor to intensely-serialized cable shows like this, devoting its entire first season to a single case. Ratings were low, though—in part because network viewers weren't yet conditioned to watch every episode of a series—and the second season not only featured shorter story arcs, but swapped out leading man Daniel Benazali for Anthony LaPaglia, who if things had gone a bit differently, might have been otherwise occupied at the time playing Tony on a Fox network version of *The Sopranos*.

whips Zellman, channeling Rick from *Casablanca* as he sneers, "All the girls in New Jersey, you had to fuck this one?"

Tony's mood swing in the car is an extraordinary piece of acting from Gandolfini and an all-time *Sopranos* moment. It also offers further evidence that the easiest way for *The Sopranos* to prove its superiority to the rest of television wasn't to belittle it, nor even to experiment with its format and focus. All it had to do was simply be *The Sopranos*. As a whole, "Watching Too Much Television" isn't *The Sopranos* at its best, but its last five minutes sure are.

SEASON 4/EPISODE 8
"MERGERS AND ACQUISITIONS"
STORY BY DAVID CHASE AND ROBIN GREEN & MITCHELL BURGESS AND TERENCE WINTER
TELEPLAY BY LAWRENCE KONNER
DIRECTED BY DANIEL ATTIAS

The Boss's Wife

"For one thing, I already took his horse." —**Tony**

"Mergers and Acquisitions" is primarily a sequel to "Pie-O-My," reviving both the Tony–Ralphie rivalry and Carmela's quest for financial independence, then throwing in Furio's growing desire for Carmela and another subplot about Paulie's mother Nucci living at Green Grove, for an hour of takeovers—some stealthy, some amicable, some hostile. The stories all advance incrementally (the Nucci material is the only part largely confined to this episode, and it's comic relief[31]), but it all feels like we've been here before.

This is admittedly the point of the episode. Much of it revolves around Ralphie's new girlfriend, Valentina La Paz (Leslie Bega[32]), and Tony's struggle between his attraction to her and his revulsion at sleeping with a woman who's possibly done it with Ralphie Cifaretto. Valentina is Tony's type: brunette, professional (she boasts of working in an art gallery, but really it's a framing store with delusions of grandeur), and feisty (they spark after he watches her prank Ralphie into stepping in horse manure). She's not exactly the new Gloria Trillo—she's tackier and less emotionally damaged—but she's what might result if you photocopied Gloria enough times. The scene where they mess around with each other

---

31 In his quest to help Nucci make friends at Green Grove, Paulie has to send his cousin Little Paulie Germani (Carl Capotorto) and Benny to beat up the son of one of the more popular residents, as once again this peaceful little retirement community inspires Mob violence.

32 Played one of Howard Hesseman's students, theater-crazed Maria Borges, on the '80s sitcom *Head of the Class*.

after their first time in bed evokes two of Tony's indelible Gloria encounters: a threat of food being thrown, and Tony using his tremendous strength to hurl a tiny woman through the air—but playfully. His attraction to Gloria ran deeper, but so did the pain of being with her. Valentina seems like she could be lower-maintenance, provided Tony can get over the Ralphie issue. This turns out to be simple, once Valentina, then Janice, then Dr. Melfi (doing an armchair diagnosis based on what Tony feeds her from the other two) tells him about Ralphie's sexual proclivities, which we glimpsed briefly with Janice. Valentina says Ralphie "likes to bottom from the top." Once Tony feels satisfied there was no "penisary contact with her vulva," he's free to begin their affair.

But before he can even get started, one of Valentina's fake fingernails ends up in one of his shirts, and Carmela finds it. A few scenes earlier, Carmela had insisted to Rosalie that she'd made peace with Tony having *goomars*, but that painted talon drives her to break into the duck feed and steal cash to buy stocks in her own name.[33]

It's easier for Carmela to focus on money issues and Tony's adultery with Furio in Italy, dealing with his dying father. Although she fantasizes about him while watching ponytailed TV chef Mario Batali, her attention is fixed on domestic matters. But the distance only clarifies Furio's feelings for Carmela—as well as his awareness of how dangerous they are. Tony can take anything he wants from Ralphie—his horse, his mistress, a picture of the two of them standing next to Pie-O-My—without repercussions, because he's the boss. But if Furio wants the boss's wife, his only option is to follow his uncle's advice and kill the boss.

There's potential for great conflict here between Tony and his wife, his bodyguard, and his most hated underling, but it's all lingering below the surface, which is why the themes repeated from "Pie-O-My" make this episode fall a bit flat. Tony has so much time to obsess over matters of the penis and vulva because his lawyer has once again encouraged him to step back from day-to-day Family business, leaving Christopher to handle the big decisions largely offscreen. As we saw the last time Tony tried this (in season two's "House Arrest"), he doesn't do well being idle. Nor, at times, does *The Sopranos* itself.

---

33 Spending time around Cousin Brian is paying off, as she knows to invest slightly less than $10,000 at each brokerage firm to prevent the IRS from taking notice.

SEASON 4/EPISODE 9
"WHOEVER DID THIS"
WRITTEN BY ROBIN GREEN & MITCHELL BURGESS
DIRECTED BY TIM VAN PATTEN

Straight Arrow

"She was a beautiful, innocent creature! What'd she ever do to you?" —**Tony**

Off with his head.

And his wig.

More than a full season of *The Sopranos* (and more than a year and a half of our time) elapsed between Tony trying to beat Ralphie to death in "University" and actually succeeding in the instant classic "Whoever Did This." Both the delay and the resolution are vintage David Chase: deny the audience what they expect, and badly want, withholding and withholding while it appears that Tony and Ralphie's relationship has stabilized, then have them come to fatal blows during a slow mid-season stretch, over a dispute that seems unrelated to the heart of their feud.

What's more, "Whoever Did This" spends much of its first half—other than a subplot about Junior faking dementia in the hopes of a mistrial, only to start displaying symptoms of the real thing[34]—on humanizing Ralphie, to the extent that such a thing is possible.

We start with the Ralphie we know and loathe, but occasionally laugh at, as he puts two and two together about Paulie being the one who blabbed about the Ginny Sack joke, and prank-calls a dismayed Nucci (posing as "Detective Mike Hunt, Beaver Falls Police Department") with a story of Paulie being arrested for indecent acts. It's all fun and games as usual until—in a bit of a narrative cheat, since it involves a character we've never met before—Ralphie's son Justin is wounded while shooting arrows with a friend.

From this point until his final confrontation with Tony, "Whoever Did This" introduces us to a very different Ralphie: chastened, introspective, and profoundly regretful. Even the shape of his face looks different[35] in the moment when Ralphie shrugs off Tony's confession that he's now sleeping with Valentina—a move so self-serving and cruel in its timing (in the aftermath of Justin's injury, when he

---

34 To help facilitate what initially seems like a scam, Tony reaches out to Svetlana, who is still delightfully confident and unfiltered, dismissing Janice as a "boring woman" when their paths cross again.

35 Joe Pantoliano won the drama supporting actor award at the 2003 Emmys, the first *Sopranos* actor other than Falco or Gandolfini to be so honored, submitting "Whoever Did This" as one of his two episodes. Surprisingly, the other one was "Christopher," though this may have been an attempt to show the range of his performance. (Or because he thought the voters would laugh at the vibrator scene.) Whatever the reason, "Whoever Did This" was clearly enough, even though Joey Pants spends half the episode as a corpse.

knows Ralphie will be too grief-stricken to raise a stink) that the show's sympathies briefly flip from Tony to Ralphie.

This will not last, of course. Yes, Ralphie is thunderstruck by the near-fatal accident and Justin's long road to recovery. Yes, he can seek Father Phil's counsel, despite living perhaps the most sinful life of any major character. Yes, he can finally relate to Rosalie's own grief, which drove him away from her earlier in the season. But at his core, he is still the bitter, selfish lout who abused and murdered Tracee without a second thought, and who cheated on Roe and then cast her aside when her sadness bored him. His misogyny still comes roaring out of him when his ex-wife blames him for the accident, and after he proposes marriage as proof of how he's changed, Roe is sensible enough to decline.

Still, this is a more fully-formed and complex Ralphie than the one heretofore presented as the latest thorn in Tony's side. Even the decision to spend much of the episode in Ralphie's home—when we're used to seeing him at the Aprile crew's social club, or crashing with a girlfriend—feels deliberate, a means of illustrating that Ralphie had a life beyond his conflicts with Tony and the other wiseguys.

Tony has previously put up with Ralphie because he's the Family's best earner, and because it would violate Mob tradition to whack him over the death of an unaffiliated stripper. He had to find subtler means of revenge, like stealing his mistress and his horse. Telling Ralphie about Valentina shortly after Justin's injury not only avoids a fight, but also feels like Tony getting back at Ralphie for making him feel sympathetic in the first place. Tony Soprano never wants to be in a position where he has to feel sorry for Ralphie Cifaretto. This tragedy makes it impossible.

Then comes the fire.

Did Ralphie mastermind it? The episode never quite says so. Ralphie certainly has the motive—he even complains to Tony about the cost of caring for a declining horse—and the ruthlessness. But he's also adamant in his denials.

It really doesn't matter, though, because Tony believes he did it. Which makes the most important question about it this: to which "beautiful, innocent creature" is Tony referring as he smashes Ralphie's head against the kitchen tile and chokes the life out of him—Pie-O-My, or Tracee?

We have seen Tony swallow his rage before at people he hates, such as Uncle Junior and Livia. But they were family. Ralphie is not. Ralphie is just this obnoxious, repulsive *thing* who is at best perpetually annoying to Tony, even when they're making large sums of money together. Ralphie beat a young woman—one in need of help, whom Tony had repeatedly rebuffed, and who reminded him of his own daughter—to death, just because he could. But Tony hated him long before that. Plus, a lot of innocent people get hurt or killed in his line of work, and Tracee hasn't come up in a long time, whereas Tony's affection for Pie-O-My was recent, palpable, and untainted by guilt.[36] The horse was a beautiful, innocent creature that Tony loved, nursed through sickness, celebrated in victory. He felt more purely and deeply for Pie-O-My than for most of the humans in his life.

Earlier in the episode, Tony cautions an enraged Paulie against seeking vengeance for the prank call, because it would be bad for business and against the rules. Even in less criminal trades, we have to work with people we can't stand. But the rules of both polite society and the Mafia have never much applied to Tony Soprano, especially where his passions inflame his work. With Ralph a likely arson suspect, and definitely Tracee's murderer (a crime in which Tony feels complicit), the famous Soprano temper bursts out—leading to one of the ugliest and most intense fights of the entire series, despite the vast difference in size and strength.[37]

And there lies the body of Tony's most productive, if hated, employee.

The kitchen brawl happens so abruptly—after a long conversation about Pie-O-My and Ralphie's secret ingredient for eggs[38]—and with so little obvious foreshadowing that it lacks the cathartic power it would have summoned had it ended "University," or appeared later in season three. But it also shows how Tony, like his mother, never forgets perceived sins against him. Ralphie's life was over in the Bing parking lot, because it was inevitable that he would do something else to draw the boss's ire, just as it was inevitable that Tony would eventually succumb to his desire to put hand to throat and start squeezing.

There follows a prolonged corpse disposal sequence,[39] after which Tony and Christopher wait until dark to remove the remains. Tony, dazed from the fight, covered in blood, partly blinded from Ralphie's insect repellent attack, tells Christopher a laughably transparent lie about finding Ralphie dead like this—but Chris is so high on heroin, and so abashed about Tony seeing him like this, that he goes along without questioning it. The dismemberment sequence is, like the fight that led to it, graphic and stomach-churning, but also darkly comic, from Christopher being startled when the wig falls off Ralphie's severed

---

36 A few links between Tracee and Pie-O-My, via "University": Silvio refers to Tracee as "a thoroughbred," Tony tells another Bing girl that "I wanna show you where the horse bit me," and Tracee tells Tony that her mother held her hand over the stove when she was a girl; she and the horse both got burned.

37 At one point, Tony pins Ralphie against the wall in almost exactly the same fashion he does earlier in the hospital after Ralphie starts cursing out his ex-wife. In nearly every moment they are together, you can tell, Tony would very much like to put his hands on this guy and do what comes naturally to him.

38 Eggs, more than oranges, are frequently a harbinger of death on The Sopranos.

39 Breaking Bad—by far the best of the many antihero dramas that appeared in the wake of this one—famously elongated this even further by devoting two of its first three episodes to corpse disposal, and today the matter of getting rid of inconvenient bodies is among the most common tropes in TV drama.

head[40] to both of them realizing that the banging sound in the house is the bowling ball Tony removed from its bag so he could stow the head. Like Barry Haydu's murder, the disappearing of Ralphie Cifaretto is another event that brings mentor and protégé closer together, because now they have a secret to share—If the guys in the Family didn't understand Tony's desire to kill Ralphie over the death of someone they called a whore, how will they respond to learning he did it over a horse?—but Tony's uncontrollable temper and Christopher's drug addiction make neither partner particularly sensible.

After a trip upstate to bury the extremities at the farm of Mikey Palmice's father—where Tony again proves he's more capable than his underlings by driving the bulldozer they use to dig up the hard, cold ground—it's time to clean up and catch some precious sleep at the Bing, where the question of ultimate motive is answered.

Or not.

In the closing moments, Tony checks his inflamed eyes in the Bing dressing room mirror, which is decorated with photos of dancers past and present. In the standard-definition version that aired on HBO in 2002, the pictures were too fuzzy to make out. You could imagine that Tracee's picture was there, and that this was the show tipping its hand about that "beautiful, innocent creature" line, but you couldn't prove you saw anything unless you verified it with someone on the Sopranos crew, which nobody did.

The episodes are all high-definition now, though, and Tracee's face is very clear—at the center of the frame, no less. (She's a bit to the left of Tony's reflected jaw.) His eyes even fall directly on the picture before he turns to exit into the blinding morning light.

The enhanced focus is nice but inessential. The glimpse of the wall of photos was already enough to evoke Tracee, along with all the other incidental and purposeful pointers we encountered along the way, from the near-rhyme of horse and "whore" to the fact that Tony kills Ralphie as Ralphie killed Tracee.

But for all the mirroring, it's still possible that Tony kills Ralphie over Tracee without realizing why he's doing it. We know from his pathology that he has a gift for repression. He has huge breakthroughs with Dr. Melfi, then has no memory (or claims to) the next time she mentions them. Maybe in the kitchen, his thoughts are entirely about the horse, and it's only the following morning when he glances at the mirror that his other motivation nuzzles his conscious mind like a horse

---

40 Pantoliano went bald at an early age, but spent most of the early years of his career wearing convincing hairpieces on-screen. (The trick is that, unlike some other Hollywood toupee enthusiasts, he only wore them in character, not everyday life.) As a result, many Sopranos fans were just as surprised as Christopher to realize that was a rug.

taking a sugar cube. Or maybe he's bottled the memory up so tight that it can't escape, even with Tracee smiling right at him.

It doesn't matter. What does is that Ralphie is dead and gone, that *The Sopranos* did it in a way that no one would have expected going into "Whoever Did This," and that no one could forget when the episode was done.

SEASON 4/EPISODE 10
STORY BY DAVID CHASE, TELEPLAY BY TERENCE WINTER
AND ROBIN GREEN & MITCHELL BURGESS
DIRECTED BY ALAN TAYLOR

Intervention

"I'm like a visitor in my own town. Life went on without me." **—Furio**

There is one overt intervention in "The Strong, Silent Type," along with a bunch of characters either being confronted about their dangerous behavior or trying to curb it themselves. But the overt one is a doozy.

With the Tony–Melfi scenes, *The Sopranos* has always managed to thread the needle of pointing out the absurdity of a man in Tony's profession spilling his guts to a shrink, while treating their conversations very seriously. Melfi is genuinely trying to help Tony, and Tony occasionally makes an effort to be helped. The subjects they discuss in that room are real and raw.

Sometimes, though, the show can't help but have fun with the intersection of Family and family therapy, as we see in the black comic masterpiece that is the intervention Adriana and the wiseguys stage to address Christopher's heroin addiction. The people in that living room are not emotionally equipped to perform what recovering addict Dominic (Elias Koteas[41]) describes as "a care-frontation." Paulie attacks Christopher as weak and out of control. Silvio—in the best bit of intentionally stiff delivery of Steve Van Zandt's acting career—recalls finding Chris high in the Bing bathroom. ("Your hair was in the toilet water. Disgusting.") Even Tony, who has experience in a variation on this theme, gets angry and distracted the moment he learns that Christopher smothered Adriana's little dog Cosette. Within moments, we've gone from insults, to dirty little secrets (the Russian)

---

41 Earthy character actor, best known for his starring roles in Canadian art house puzzlers like *The Adjuster, Exotica,* and *Crash* (no, the other one), as well as *The Thin Red Line* and *Shutter Island* and *Let Me In.* Somebody should've cast him as Robert De Niro's son by now.

threatening to come to light, to Paulie, Sil, and Benny Fazio beating and kicking Chrissie into an emergency room visit.

Amazingly, this is one of the hour's more successful interventions, because at least Chris agrees to stay in rehab until he's better, albeit under threat of death from Patsy Parisi. Everyone else, whether talking to others or turning inward for counsel, is on the verge of succumbing to temptation.

The episode's title recalls Tony's original Gary Cooper lament with Dr. Melfi, which comes up again here even as his wife falls ever harder for a man who resembles Cooper far more than Tony does.

Melfi was absent from "Whoever Did This," so we get a belated opportunity here to see Tony grieving for Pie-O-My—moments after scolding Furio for crying over the death of his father, no less—and as full of self-pity as we've seen. It's a jarring enough display of emotion—what would seem performative if we hadn't seen how deeply Tony cared for the horse—that it prompts Melfi to do something she usually avoids: she confronts Tony directly, not only about how he's more depressed over losing animals than he's ever been over losing human loved ones, but about how his "sad clown" laments clash with everything Carmela told her during the joint sessions in season three, and everything Melfi herself has witnessed to date. Often, Melfi lets Tony's blatant lies and self-justifications sit there, because spotlighting them would threaten the intimacy and trust of their relationship. Here, though, Tony is so obviously lying—to both himself and his doctor—that Melfi can't help herself. When he bemoans the state of the world, invoking both 9/11 and the LA riots ("I feel like the Reverend Rodney King Jr.: Why can't we all just get along?"), she points out, "You've caused much suffering yourself, haven't you?"

Ultimately, Tony gives in to his own foreign strong, silent type, when visits to Uncle Junior's house lead him to see Svetlana for the kind of woman he goes for (give or take the blonde hair and artificial leg): assertive, independent, and, yes, beautiful. (She dismisses this compliment, especially compared to her cousin, but the way she's lit in that moment, it's like we're seeing her for the first time along with Tony.) Where Carmela is still trying to stop herself from giving into temptation with Furio, Tony roars right through this red light, only to experience an unwanted change of direction when the sex is done: Svetlana was using *him*, and has no interest in continuing things.

It's clear from Tony's expression that being rejected by a woman is a novelty for him, and an unwelcome one at that, and the episode's closing moments contrast Tony and Furio: the man Carmela has slowly grown to hate, even though she's married to him, and the man Carmela has fallen in love with, even though she won't let herself be with him. Tony is reheating leftovers that Carmela made, in a house she decorated; Furio is cooking his own meal, in a house he bought and then fixed up with his own two hands. Furio is who Tony fancies himself as, or at least wishes he could be;[42] is it any wonder that Carmela has come to feel so deeply for him, even though they've never kissed?

Both Furio and Carmela spend much of the episode trying to self-intervene to head off an affair that would likely destroy either themselves or Tony. Furio tries waiting in the car, and doesn't give Carmela the present he bought her in Naples, while Carmela keeps bringing AJ on her Furio visits, knowing that AJ's presence will keep her from doing or saying more than she should.

It's not an affair in the traditional sense, and sensible Rosalie tries to dismiss it as fantasy. But Carmela insists, "It is real. We communicate. He looks at me like I'm beautiful. He thinks I'm interesting when I talk. Just those few minutes when we see each other, I live for those. I feel like my life is slipping through my fingers, and I will never be happy."[43]

Succumbing to temptation nearly gets Christopher killed; Tony even says he's only letting him live because of their family connection. Tony can't stop himself from sleeping with Svetlana, just like he couldn't stop himself from killing Ralphie, which now has the entire crew suspicious and resentful of him (even as he tries to blame Johnny Sack, over the HUD scam). Tony's impulses tend to backfire and create new problems.

At least Christopher's locked away from his demons until his rehab stint ends. The others have to keep intervening for themselves, and that's not easy for any of them.

Whatever happened to Gary Cooper? He came over from Naples, and a lot of trouble followed with him.

---

42 Earlier in the episode, Tony orders the painting of himself and Pie-O-My destroyed, because it makes him too heartsick to look at it. Cheapskate Paulie knows a nice piece of free art when he sees it, but becomes so unnerved with the thought of the Tony in the painting watching him that he has it retouched so the boss is now costumed like Napoleon. He's trying to make Tony look European at the same time a visitor from the Continent is occupying the thoughts of Mrs. Soprano.

43 For a woman who was established early in season one as having an affinity for chaste romances like *The Remains of the Day*, Carmela's entirely nonphysical affair with Furio is beyond perfect, as if she'd stepped into a romance novel she wrote herself.

	SEASON 4/EPISODE 11
"CALLING ALL CARS"	STORY BY DAVID CHASE AND ROBIN GREEN & MITCHELL BURGESS AND TERENCE WINTER,TELEPLAY BY DAVID CHASE AND ROBIN GREEN & MITCHELL BURGESS AND DAVID FLEBOTTE DIRECTED BY TIM VAN PATTEN

Versales

"I'm sorry. I don't wanna do this anymore." —**Tony**

"Calling All Cars" isn't the shortest *Sopranos* episode ever, but it's close,[44] and it *feels* shorter—or, rather, thinner—than almost any other installment to date. It features some significant developments in the relationships between Janice and Bobby, the New Jersey and New York Families, and especially Tony and Dr. Melfi, but it's an episode almost designed to frustrate.

Dreams bookend the story, both involving Tony being haunted by ghosts: Ralphie and Gloria riding in the car with him in the first one (and the caterpillar on Ralphie's head transforming into a butterfly, even as Gloria transforms into Svetlana), then Ralphie leading Tony (now recast as an immigrant laborer like his own grandfather, with a poor command of English) to the home of a mysterious woman cloaked in shadow, whose aloof manner conjures up thoughts of the young Livia.

What do they mean? Well, Melfi figures out the first one, but she initially doesn't want to spell it out for Tony. "Can't you just tell me what the fuckin' thing means?" he grouses.[45] "I mean, you obviously know." We've seen Tony have dreams in times of stress; here, he is again under great duress due to the feud with New York over the HUD scam, but the dreams provide no insight into that. Instead, they seem to be meditations on people he's lost (or, in the case of Ralphie, rid himself of), and of transformation, amplifying his recent feelings about Gloria's suicide, Ralphie's murder, and Svetlana giving him the I'm Just Not That Into You treatment. (As Tony's kids might one day say, she's ghosting him.) His personal life is slipping away from him, too, not that he's aware of it. The dreams feel like a warning, even as the Miami hotel room he wakes up in at the end seems more nightmarish (down to the ominous red lighting of the bathroom) than the swampy home he visits in the second dream.

---

44 Season two's "Full Leather Jacket" is the shortest, at forty-three minutes. "Calling All Cars," in comparison, is forty-seven minutes. Season four's finale, "Whitecaps," is the longest at seventy-five minutes.

45 This wording nearly matches what AJ told Meadow in season three's "Proshai, Livushka" when she tried to help him explicate the Robert Frost poem and he got impatient with her.

Tony's not the only Soprano sibling battling ghosts, as Janice steps up her efforts to land Bacala by any means necessary—which first requires her to make him move past his grief over Karen. It's a rare Janice subplot where she's not being wildly unreasonable: leaving her own desires out of it for a moment, Bobby's wallowing and inability to let go are hurting him professionally, and young Bobby and Sophia personally. Still, you can't divorce her deeds from her true motive, and the extremes to which she takes it—cyber-stalking Bobby's son to make him scared of ghosts, and all but shoving Karen's final ziti down Bobby's throat—make it clear that altruism for the Baccalieri family has little to do with it.

That's a fairly low-stakes subplot, though, and the Carmela–Furio tension is on hold, which means the episode's most pressing plot is the growing argument over the HUD scam and Johnny's belief that New York deserves a cut. But even that conflict is primarily played for laughs, as the two Families focus their attentions on the appraiser whose work is central to the scam, Vic. ("'Vic the Appraiser,' they call him," Johnny explains to Carmine, in the most incisive parody of crime story nicknames ever written.) This leads to poor Vic being manhandled by guys from both sides of the Hudson, plus a new record for the number of times "appraise" and its variations are uttered in the same hour of a movie, TV show, or one-act play ("So go back inside, get your appraising shit, and start appraising!" Vito threatens him at one point). Even Tony's bank-shot solution to the feud is treated as a joke, since it involves going to Miami to speak with Carmine's son Little Carmine (Ray Abruzzo), a ridiculous, shallow figure who speaks in an overly formal manner while constantly dropping malapropisms and mispronunciations ("Versailles" comes out of his mouth as "Ver-SALES").

Tony's out of his element for much of the trip—the very un-*Sopranos* Beach Boys classic "Surfin' USA" plays over the final shot of him looking puzzled on the hotel balcony—which no doubt contributes to the second, stranger dream. But he no longer has Dr. Melfi to help him translate it, because he'd abruptly quit therapy a few scenes earlier, recognizing what the good doctor somehow can't: these sessions have provided no real value for either of them since she found the root cause of the panic attacks.

When she suggests they could go deeper on the sources of his pain and truth, he scoffs, "Pain and truth? Come on. I'm a fat fuckin' crook from New Jersey." It's a striking and direct scene in an episode that otherwise approaches things from unusual angles, and it's a stark contrast to the state of things between Tony and Carmela. There, he's ignored signs of trouble, acting like he always has on the assumption that he always can, while she's pining for Furio but unwilling to make things physical. Tony, though, sees the doctor–patient relationship with crystal clarity. He doesn't want to be judged by Melfi, doesn't want to contemplate his own inner pain more than he already does, and can't get into much detail about things that are tearing at him, like Ralphie and Tracee. And so he simply gets up to go, leaving a dumbstruck Melfi to leave the eponymous message (a staple of police dramas) for Elliot.

In their first session of the hour, Melfi tries to warn Tony about the danger signs in his own marriage, suggesting that his living wife behind the wheel of the car in his first dream is far more important than the dead mistress and associate riding in the passenger seats: "Whatever's gone on with the other two," she suggests, "you want to square it with Carmela." He's lost the ability to hear her, though, which explains why he walks out on therapy, but this means he has no one to help guide him through that strange second dream.

Who is on the steps? Livia? Gloria? Carmela? Vic the Appraiser in a really flattering dress? Tony has to puzzle that one out on his own, and so do we.

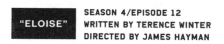

SEASON 4/EPISODE 12
WRITTEN BY TERENCE WINTER
DIRECTED BY JAMES HAYMAN

Meeting's Over

"You're standing too close." —**Furio**

Even by the standards of a series that made an art of the anticlimax, "Eloise"—and season four in general—seems to relish how frequently it subverts expectations. Several of the season's arcs spend the hour on the verge of collision, only to pull back at the last possible moment.

This is most obvious with the abrupt ending of Furio and Carmela's flirtation. They come the closest they've ever gotten to an actual date when she offers to go to Color Tile with him: "I would love to go with you there," says Furio, his voice aching for something more than just home decor. As Furio continues to endure Tony badmouthing and cheating on Carmela, the possibility of boss and bodyguard coming to blows, or worse, feels unbearably close—as close as a drunken Tony to a helicopter rotor, as Furio contemplates shoving him into it. It's late, no one else is looking, and Tony was publicly drunk at both the casino and the airport; one nudge would rid Furio of this man and perhaps allow him to be with the woman he loves.

Instead, Furio realizes he's the one who's been standing too close: to Carmela, to this country where he doesn't fit in, to this boss whose appetites and weaknesses mark him as unworthy of loyalty and respect. So he runs. No note, no call (unless you count an answering machine message he leaves at the Bing at

4:30 A.M., when he can feel confident no one would answer), nothing; he just lists the house in Nutley and flees the country without warning, leaving a stunned, devastated Carmela in his wake, wondering how foolish she was to stand so close to a man that could abandon her instantly, before anything had even happened.

Carmela's exasperation is perhaps meant to mirror what Chase, Winter, and company expected the audience to feel when the Furio arc ended in this way, though her method of channeling her frustration—causing an indignant scene at a dinner with Meadow's roommates and new boyfriend, aspiring dental student Finn DeTrolio (Will Janowitz),[46] over the question of whether there's gay subtext in *Billy Budd*—isn't likely how most *Sopranos* fans were dealing with it.

Where Meadow often turns a blind eye to what her parents do, both personally and professionally, she is for once able to see some of what's going on, as Carmela's anger continues through their birthday tradition at the Plaza that titles the episode, while AJ—oblivious as usual[47]—tells her about their mom's many trips to Furio's house.

Tony doesn't have much time to think about the puzzling disappearance of his top enforcer, because tensions with Carmine Lupertazzi's Family—and family—have gotten much worse. Here again we see the advantages and perils of getting too close to someone who's not quite yours, as Johnny Sack seethes over Little Carmine's insertion into this "de-buckle" when it's been Johnny at Carmine's side all these years, Little Carmine likewise resents his father suggesting he would be proud to consider Tony his own son, and even Carmine Sr. gets agitated over the suggestion that Tony presides over an actual Family, as opposed to "a glorified crew" that lives off of what Carmine allows them to have.

In the midst of the moves and countermoves—Tony's guys trashing Carmine's bar, Carmine having the Esplanade construction site shut down—Johnny Sack's seduction of Paulie Walnuts also ends abruptly when Paulie runs into Carmine at a wedding reception and is horrified to realize that, contrary to all of Johnny's talk, the boss of New York has no idea who he is. Like Carmela (who also has to flee to the bathroom while contemplating Furio's disappearance), he has risked his entire life over something even less real than Carmela's flirtations, and now has to scramble back to Tony's good side. An opportunity presents itself in the knowledge that Nucci's bossy friend Minn Matrone (Fran Anthony) hides her life

---

46 While Carmela is raising a stink about *Billy Budd*, Tony is at his most genial and charming with Finn, Meadow, and her roommates: a sharp and deliberate contrast to how he behaved around Noah Tannenbaum in season three.

47 "So, what, no fuckin' ziti now?" could never be topped as the quintessential AJ moment, but his sheer joy at at ripping out a noisy fart in mid-conversation with Meadow—then declaring, "Ah, dude! Meeting's over!"—comes amazingly close.

savings under her bed,[48] and when she catches him stealing it so he can give Tony a fatter envelope that week to appease him, he murders her with a pillow.[49] That death of a helpless old woman—the same death that Tony tried and failed to give to Livia at the end of season one—is the only casualty of the hour, though there's the promise of another one when Johnny suggests he's willing to go where Furio wouldn't, and invites Tony to take out Carmine for him.

Johnny's proposal leaves a threat of violence hanging over the finale. But the bigger threat seems to be right in Tony's house, from his profoundly unhappy wife, who can't let go of Furio, even after he so swiftly let go of her. As Tony points out the beautiful and independent woman Meadow has grown up into, he asks his wife, "Isn't that what you dreamed about?" The look on her face is that of someone who has been dreaming a lot about something else—someone else—altogether, then had the dream snatched away.

It's maddening on one level that *The Sopranos* spent a whole season on this emotional affair without consummating it physically, or leading Furio to a more direct confrontation with either Tony or Carmela. But studied anticlimax has been part of its toolkit since at least season two. And how better to put us in the shoes, and heart, of Carmela Soprano, then to leave us also wondering if, like the song says, that's all there is?

---

48 This revelation comes moments before a priceless bit where Paulie, Nucci, Minn, and Cookie—old and cheap, the lot of them—systematically clean out every free item (sugar packets, rolls, etc.) left on the table at the restaurant where they dined after seeing *The Producers* on Broadway.

49 For all the extreme violence served up in the first four seasons, Paulie's crime of opportunity here ranks with the show's most shocking acts, partly because the circumstances are so pathetic (he's feeling professionally homeless, and freaking out about money), but mostly because Minn is entirely harmless and a civilian. *The Sopranos* periodically steps up the awfulness in this way—as if to force viewers to understand the magnitude of the human monsters who populate a series they can't stop watching, and what it says about them that they'd rationalize such acts away on psychological or dramatic grounds, in order to keep experiencing all the pleasurable bits.

SEASON 4/EPISODE 13
"WHITECAPS" WRITTEN BY ROBIN GREEN & MITCHELL BURGESS AND DAVID CHASE
DIRECTED BY JOHN PATTERSON

Who's Afraid of Virginia Mook?

"Just go away, please! I can't stand it anymore!" —**Carmela**

Previous *Sopranos* years created the expectation that each season would climax with a significant death. Never mind that this was, other than season two, not true: Mikey Palmice at the end of season one was small potatoes, and the deaths of both Gloria and Ralphie were tabled from the end of season three until the middle of season four. (Jackie Jr. was only slightly more important than Mikey.) Perception has a way of feeling like reality, though, and by the conclusion of this, the show's highest-rated year, everyone assumed—practically demanded—some whacking. Even with Furio gone, there was still the New York feud, not to mention Johnny Sack's invitation for Tony to take out Carmine. Surely some bodies would drop by the end of even the show's most muted season, right?

"Whitecaps" delivers, just not in the way anyone might have expected. Carmine spares his own life when he settles the interstate dispute (despite Johnny's attempts to get Tony to proceed with the assassination anyway), and the hour's only corpses are the hitmen Christopher hired for the job, loose ends in need of elimination. But something more important, and shocking, seems to be dead by the end of the season:

The Soprano marriage.

No shot ever fired, no knife ever pulled, no garrote ever improvised so far in the show has cut deeper or done more damage than these two simple sentences Carmela hurls at Tony midway through the show's longest—and best-acted—episode to date:

"I don't love you anymore."

This is her thinking about all the women he's slept with while making a fool out of her, all the horrible crimes he has made her complicit in through his gifts and cash and this nice house she keeps ordering him to leave.

"I don't want you."

This is her thinking of the man she *does* want, but can't have, because his fear of her thug husband sent him running back from whence he came before he filled her life with false hope.

These are not the first harsh words Carmela fires at her husband in "Whitecaps," nor the last, but they are the simplest and most direct. She is as mad as hell, and she's not going to take it anymore, no matter the consequences.

For all of season four's other flaws—moving slower, wandering further afield of the show's most compelling characters, "Christopher"—it never took its eye off the rotting marriage at the series' core. From the first, Tony and Carmela were squabbling over money, and she was primping for Furio, and he was being distracted by a horse, a new mistress, *another* potential mistress on top of that,[50] killing and disposing of Ralphie, feuding with New York, and more. Other seasons toyed more with misdirection about what the ultimate conflict would be, but season four hides its primary arc in plain sight, because the audience has been conditioned by now to expect Family business to take precedence.

That part of the story is mostly a bust, by design. Carmine and Tony don't want a war—only Johnny does, as entitled and aggrieved as his would-be puppet Paulie Walnuts—and they shut it down before things go beyond vandalism and lost wages. But it's yet another brushfire that Tony has to put out, keeping him from noticing the inferno that's been building all season back home, and that finally bursts into a full rage when Irina calls the house to tell Carmela about Tony and Svetlana's affair.[51]

The Soprano marriage has always been built on a foundation of compromises and lies that both parties were willing to ignore. With few exceptions—usually when expensive presents are involved—Carmela has never been happy with Tony. She has contemplated cheating on him with Father Phil, Vic Musto, and Furio, but all three men lost their nerve before she crossed a line. She has contemplated leaving him before, wavering the most after Dr. Krakower's second opinion, but she has always stayed, because it was easier to do what she'd always done.

The Furio flirtation, though, lasted longer than the previous ones, and came at a time where Tony was being particularly high-handed, capricious, and mean. Furio was a way to escape this terrible life without having to escape Tony. It wasn't real physically, and barely even verbally, but it was just enough to keep her going: as she puts it to Tony in the most brutal of their many arguments throughout "Whitecaps," for those few minutes every day, Furio would make her feel like she had forgotten that she was terminally ill, only for Tony's daily arrival in the kitchen to remind her.

We are, like Tony, lulled into a false sense of security about the state of the marriage in the opening passages of "Whitecaps." Carm's sadness manifests as

---

50 When Carmela presents Valentina's broken nail as what she thinks is proof he had sex with Svetlana, James Gandolfini makes a meal out of the brief moment where Tony starts to defend himself, then realizes there is no version of the story that makes her less angry.

51 This pivotal phone call by itself nearly justifies the existence of the largely forgettable "Watching Too Much Television," since it's Tony's ending beatdown of Zellman, and Zellman and Irina's ensuing breakup, that piles the last straw on Carmela's back. "The Weight," meanwhile, was more effective on its own, but it takes on even more power as Tony suggests here that Johnny has never forgiven Carmine for not backing him up on the vendetta against Ralphie over the molo joke.

physical illness, but Tony's surprise gift to her of the eponymous Jersey Shore house is—like so many extravagant presents before it—enough to change her mood and suggest a happier future. They walk along the beach at sunset, talk about Whitecaps as a place to keep the family together, and if it doesn't all erase the Furio heartache, or Tony's cheating, it covers them over with sand and surf and peace.

Irina's call shatters that peace, and in its place is a series of arguments that are theatrical in their intimacy, their ugliness, and the sheer power that Edie Falco and James Gandolfini bring to them: *Who's Afraid of Virginia Mook?*

As exasperating as Furio's abrupt exit was in "Eloise," it primed Carmela to be as bereft as she is when Irina calls and tells her, essentially, that any woman Carmela has ever known could abruptly be revealed as Tony's newest mistress. She met Svetlana, drank with her the day Livia died, and liked her, and now finds out she's just the latest woman to make a fool of her.

And that, finally, is her breaking point.

The opening salvo, when Tony comes home to find Carmela throwing his possessions out their bedroom window, showcases Falco at her rawest and most vulnerable. Carm's anger and desperation as she hurls herself at her husband and wails for him to just leave her alone are almost feral, while Gandolfini gets to play Tony as more bewildered and annoyed, because he doesn't understand yet how bad and permanent this could be.

From there, it's rueful psychological warfare, not only between Carmela and Tony—who refuses to be kicked out of the home he paid for, and begins crashing in the pool house—but between Tony and Alan Sapinsly (Bruce Altman, a classic That Guy character actor), the smug attorney who owns Whitecaps and won't return the deposit even after marital strife scotches the sale. Sapinsly proves the easier opponent for Tony. When threats fail, he turns sneaky by loaning Benny and Little Paulie the *Stugots* and the pool house's speaker system to harass Sapinsly, his wife, and guests with *Dean Martin Live at the Sands*, at marriage-threatening volume.

Carmela, though, won't back down, and matters in and around the Soprano house grow increasingly toxic until every past slight and injustice comes flooding out: Carmela's comment from the pilot about Tony going to Hell when he dies, her growing up around Dickie Moltisanti and other wiseguys just like Tony, and, of course, Furio. It's the last that finally brings out the animal in Tony, who nearly takes Carmela's head off before putting his fist through a wall instead. Perhaps even scarier are the two words that come out of Tony's mouth moments after that punch: Livia's all-purpose taunt of "Poor you!" Tony once said that Livia wore his father down to a little nub, and it feels like this is what he's done to Carmela.

The fighters have to keep returning to their corners to deal with other Family and family issues. Junior scores a mistrial thanks to Eugene Pontecorvo threatening a juror. Paulie is still desperately trying to ingratiate his way back into the crew, Janice and Bacala are starting to get very flirty, while Christopher is out of rehab, sober, and through all of the steps but the amends. (In one of the finale's lighter moments, Tony suggests Chrissie might be better off skipping that part.)

But the episode keeps returning to this uncivil war between husband and wife, overwhelming predator and overwhelmed prey. Carmela can't do anything to Tony either financially or physically, but the emotional combat eventually proves too much for either to maintain, and even Tony's not stubborn enough to keep at it.

Each previous season had ended with the family together for a noted occasion: escaping a storm at Vesuvio, celebrating Meadow's high school graduation, attending Jackie Jr.'s memorial.[52] That tradition appropriately ends here, as the season closes on one last glimpse of Alan Sapinsly sitting next to the house that the Sopranos will no longer be buying, enduring the music of Dean Martin, because the family as we knew it has ceased to exist for the moment, leaving a trail of wreckage in its wake.

It's not the death anyone expected, or wanted. It's terrible, and it's spectacular.

---

52 That being said, this is the fourth time in a row that the final stretch of a season of *The Sopranos* has pivoted on a powerful contest of wills between a man and a woman. There was Livia and Tony in season one, Janice and Richie in season two, Tony and Gloria in season three, and now Tony and Carmela, the battle royale.

Season
Five

SEASON 5/EPISODE 1
WRITTEN BY TERENCE WINTER AND DAVID CHASE
DIRECTED BY TIM VAN PATTEN

Class of 2004

"Lotta changes since you went away, huh?" —**Uncle Junior**

"Two Tonys" begins in what feels like a postapocalyptic version of its own turf. We're in the Soprano backyard in North Caldwell, only the house seems abandoned: the lawn is covered with leaves, the grill is uncovered, and there's a puddle gathering in the pool cover reflecting an empty, lonely home. The *Star-Ledger* is still down at the end of the driveway, but no one's bothering to get it; instead, Meadow[1] runs over it in her car on the way to pick up AJ.

It's the same place, but different. The same show but different, too. Season five gets into Mob business quickly, brings Dr. Melfi back into the picture, and even gives us another subplot about Christopher and Paulie resenting each other. But Tony and Carmela's marriage, however flawed and phony it could be, was a major series foundation. Without it, Tony's life feels less sturdy.

Once the family separation has been reestablished—along with ancillary details like Janice and Bobby now being married (and taking over as hosts of the family's Sunday night dinners)—"Two Tonys" sets up a series of Family reunions, with a TV news report[2] about "the Class of 2004," a collection of wiseguys incarcerated in the '80s just being released. The focus is on four of them: Feech LaManna (Robert Loggia[3]), the legendary old-school gangster who ran the card game Tony and Jackie Aprile robbed as young men to get noticed; Tony's cousin, Tony Blundetto (Steve Buscemi[4]); New York underboss Angelo Garepe (Joe Santos[5]);

---

1 For this season only, Jamie-Lynn Sigler was credited under her then-married name, as Jamie-Lynn DiScala.

2 One of the talking heads in that report is author Manny Safier, played by new *Sopranos* writer Matthew Weiner. (The show occasionally put the writers on camera in small roles, like Terence Winter playing one of Dr. Melfi's patients.) Weiner got a job on the show because Chase was impressed with his spec script about an advertising agency in the early '60s—a script that would become *Mad Men*.

3 Loggia was in the home stretch of a career that went back to live television dramas of the 1950s like *Playhouse 90* and *Studio One*. He had his greatest success in the mid-to-late '80s, most famously as the boss who dances on the giant FAO Schwarz piano with Tom Hanks in *Big*.

4 A character actor best known for playing creepy thieves and murderers in films like *Reservoir Dogs*, *Fargo*, and *Con Air*, Buscemi was also an acclaimed indie film director (*Trees Lounge*) who had already been behind the *Sopranos* camera for season three's "Pine Barrens" and season four's "Everybody Hurts." He was family before he was Family.

5 Chase knew Santos well, having spent years writing dialogue for him as Dennis Becker, the decent cop forever doing favors for Jim Rockford on *The Rockford Files*.

and New York captain Phil Leotardo (Frank Vincent[6]). Feech makes an instant impression, strutting around the kitchen of Uncle Junior (who's back under house arrest after his mistrial) in an undershirt, with Loggia snarling out every insult and old story at the top of his lungs. Angelo has a more low-key introduction, explaining at a country club lunch with Tony, Johnny, and Carmine that he and Tony B were close friends in prison, but the scene's importance escalates when Carmine suffers a stroke that leaves the leadership of New York up for grabs.

The title "Two Tonys" suggests we're about to see the cousins get together, but Blundetto and Leotardo only appear in news footage. Instead, the title refers to a theory Tony proposes to Dr. Melfi, as part of his misguided attempt to seduce her now that he's not in a marital relationship with Carmela, nor a therapeutic one with her. "Forget about the way that Tony Soprano makes his way in this world," he tells her. "That's just to feed his children. There's two Tony Sopranos. You've never seen the other one."

Like a lot of what Tony says, this is self-serving nonsense. There may be multiple sides to Tony Soprano, but they're all him, and Melfi has seen most of them. A glimpse of the Barbra Streisand–Nick Nolte movie *The Prince of Tides* at Valentina's apartment convinces him to finally act on the feelings he's had for years.[7] It's not just emotional transference between doctor and patient—Melfi has a sex dream about Tony after he sends her flowers and asks her to dinner—but Melfi is neither unethical nor a dummy, so she declines. Whichever Tony claims to be standing in front of her, he's unused to taking no for an answer, especially for something he's desired for this long. And Melfi realizes she can only penetrate her patient's thick skull by being as blunt as possible:

"You're not a truthful person," she tells him. "You're not respectful of women. You're not really respectful of people. . . . You take what you want from them by force or the threat of force. I couldn't live like that. I couldn't bear witness to violence."

Whatever the nature of Melfi's attraction, it's nothing more than an impulse, and unlike almost everyone else on the show, she puts her values over her impulses, even when it triggers an outburst. She calls Tony out for who he really is and

---

6   Vincent was the runner-up to play Uncle Junior, but Chase declined partly because the cast already featured too many *Goodfellas* veterans. Vincent had played Billy Batts, the wiseguy who kept telling Tommy to go home and get his shine box. A frequent Martin Scorsese collaborator (he also sparred with Joe Pesci in *Raging Bull* and *Casino*), he was often typecast as hot-tempered mobsters, a fact he was pragmatic about: "It's better to be typed than not typed," he once told the *Star-Ledger*'s Stephen Whitty.

7   The little container of Tide in the gift basket, coupled with the note signed "Your Prince of Tide" (singular), is the entire *Sopranos* sense of verbal humor distilled to one gag: erudite and ridiculous.

accurately describes what their romance would be like, in a way that runs parallel to another fissure in the Paulie–Christopher friendship.

Their first scene this season finds them at the Bing, telling Patsy and Vito the story of "Pine Barrens" like it's an old joke, and not the nearly fatal disaster it was.[8] But even that genial moment deteriorates when Chris (rightly) blames Paulie for the whole incident, and soon they're back to their usual resentments: Paulie hates that Chrissie is Tony's pet, and Chris hates that Paulie still treats him like low man on the totem pole, sticking him with the enormous dinner check whenever they go out with other wiseguys. It's never been a healthy relationship—none of the Family relationships are, because they're all ultimately about making the most money possible—but the two of them can usually suppress their awareness of that. Here, it comes bursting out again until Chris sticks Paulie with one check, and Paulie sticks him with an even bigger one in Atlantic City, and when the waiter protests Chris' microscopic tip, they wind up killing him—and turning *that* into the newest fiasco to laugh about and bond over, at least until the next fight. It's as if they're acting out Melfi's entire speech to Tony, and not caring because they can always pretend to like each other again.

Carmela has already seen her relationship with Tony for what it was, and kicked him out of the house as a result, but he still hangs around, and even when he's not there, he's there. Following the separated-dad playbook, he lavishes gifts on AJ, including a noisy drum kit, hoping to buy the boy's love and loyalty. No need: AJ already blames Carmela for the split. Children of divorce often judge custodial parents more harshly, even when their sins pale in comparison to their ex's.

To emphasize the current state of things in North Caldwell, a big furry symbol in the form of a black bear wanders into the backyard, terrifying AJ and only retreating when Carmela bangs some pots and pans. It's not just that Tony is responsible for the black bear's arrival, since the animal control officers explain the great beast was attracted to the bags of duck feed. It's that Tony *is* the bear: the big, lumbering threat that hangs over this family, but is never so overt that anyone can justify taking a shot at it.

The bear is bad news for Carmela, but good news for a paranoid Tony,[9] who not only gets to use it as an excuse to have Benny and Little Paulie guard the house and keep tabs on who's coming and going, but gets to play bear hunter himself as an outlet for the frustration and self-loathing he feels after Dr. Melfi's final rejection.

---

8 In a retort to the many fans who were still asking what happened to Valery, Paulie replies, "Who the fuck cares?" when Patsy wonders the same thing.

9 He explains that he has turned Furio into a fugitive back in Italy, sentencing him to death should any of his Friends Over There get a look at him.

As he sits alone in the backyard at night, a lit stogie in one hand, an assault rifle in the other, looking more content than he has all hour at the thought that the bear might return, we are reminded that if there really are two Tonys, the truest Tony is the one who knows how to inflict pain, and enjoys doing it.

Carmela can kick that Tony out of the house, but she can never be rid of him entirely.

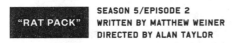

SEASON 5/EPISODE 2
WRITTEN BY MATTHEW WEINER
DIRECTED BY ALAN TAYLOR

Tony Uncle Al

"If things had gone different way back when, who knows?" —**Tony B**

Midway through "Rat Pack," Tony delivers a speech to his beloved cousin, Tony Blundetto, who's back in the world after two decades behind bars. When they were kids, our Tony explains, the two of them were like brothers, alike in so many ways, down to the name, that relatives differentiated them by referring to their fathers' names: Tony Soprano was "Tony Uncle Johnny" and Tony Blundetto was "Tony Uncle Al."

Now, though, Tony Uncle Johnny is the boss of New Jersey, has two thriving kids (well, one thriving kid and AJ), and is master of all he surveys. Tony Uncle Al is a laundry truck driver studying to become a certified massage therapist while living in his mother's basement—his marriage long over, his own daughter a runaway, a man so out of step that he wears a *Miami Vice* suit to his welcome home party and has "We Are the Champions" as his ringtone. When Tony gives an order, Tony B has to follow it, and when Tony Uncle Johnny calls in the middle of the night to ramble on about how difficult his seemingly fantastic life is, Tony Uncle Al has to listen.

Yet "Rat Pack" refuses to portray the reunion in such stark terms. Despite their divergent fortunes since Tony B got arrested on a night that Tony didn't, our Tony is trapped in the past almost as much as his cousin. Tony is also living in his mother's house, albeit without Livia (who was sister to Tony B's mom) around in person, but haunting him in spirit. He has gone back in time, and the return of Tony B is a bittersweet reminder of who he used to be, how much he's suffered, and yet how lucky he's been compared to his favorite cousin. We see

Tony watching a scene from one of his beloved World War II documentaries,[10] a tearful veteran explaining the tremendous guilt he carries: "All your life, you gotta remember what one guy did because he thought it was his job to do, and he took a shot for you." For a narcissist like Tony, it would be easier to let go of his own guilt if Tony B had died; back in Tony's life, he's both a visible reminder of how their paths diverged, and a disappointment for insisting on staying straight and studying for his massage license rather than becoming point man for Tony's used-airbag scam.

Compared to some prominent new characters of seasons past (or even of Feech in the previous episode), Tony B gets an understated introduction. We see that he's a reflexive ballbreaker, unable to resist making fun of, say, Artie for going bald, and the sensitive Tony can't help feeling mocked by Tony B's impression of Jackie Gleason's old Reginald Van Gleason III character[11] ("Boy, are you fat!"). It's only when the two Tonys are in the Satriale's parking lot—Tony Uncle Johnny getting high-handed about being the boss, an authority figure Tony Uncle Al should never joke about in public—that we get a hint of the dangerous man Tony B once was. "You're crowding me," Tony B says, with just the right shade of malice. But despite the insistence of Uncle Junior[12] that all the Class of 2004 graduates are "old rats on a new ship," Blundetto seems determined to chart his own course, to the surprise of both Tony and the audience.

The episode's title refers to its many non–Tony B subplots, as we get our most extended glimpse of the FBI's operation since the season three premiere. In one early sequence, we tour the New Jersey field office, where Ray Curto is meeting with his handler, Sanseverino is watching surveillance footage from the Crazy Horse parking lot camera, and Special Agent Cubitoso is listening to a recording of Tony made by construction company boss Jack Massarone (Robert Desiderio), who supervises work at the Esplanade. It's at once an impressive display of how far the Bureau's tentacles reach and a reminder of just how hard it is to make a case against these guys. Ray is clearly stringing the Feds along while trying to make money off the deal.[13] Massarone gets exposed as a rat and stuffed into the trunk of a car, and while Adriana's interest in cooperating vacillates

---

10 This one is closer to home than most: *We Stand Alone Together*, a companion film to the 2001 HBO miniseries *Band of Brothers*, about the paratroopers of Easy Company. Despite *Band* having a huge ensemble and the usual amount of cross-pollinated casting on HBO series (see Edie Falco moving from *Oz* to here), only one *Band* actor ever turned up in Sopranos country: Frank John Hughes, who appears in the series' last few episodes as Soprano soldier Walden Belfiore.

11 Playboy-lush character, one of many Gleason created on *Cavalcade of Stars*, his first variety series, which ran 1949 to 1952 on the soon-to-be defunct DuMont Network.

12 Hints of Junior's dementia continue apace, with him referring to Tony B as "Tony Egg" without realizing he did it.

13 In a sign of how slowly federal justice can move, they're still talking to Ray about the recording he made of Tony's lecture to the captains back in the season four premiere.

throughout the episode, she's so far removed from the action that her intel is only vaguely useful.

Massarone briefly gets in tight with Tony when they realize they both hate their mothers, and seals the deal with a painting of Frank Sinatra and his Rat Pack friends (Tony, as we know, is a sucker for art depicting things he already likes), but gets in trouble when a cop on the Family payroll tells Patsy that an FBI car was surveilling their meeting, and dooms himself through a nervous bit of flattery, asking a suspicious Tony if he's lost weight. Tony's already bitter about the whole thing—"Can't a guy be fuckin' nice anymore?" he asks, while thinking about the painting—and also on edge about his size thanks to Tony B's Gleason schtick. Tony may be self-delusional about a lot of things, but he knows he's not getting thinner, and that's enough—after some deliberations that baffle his underlings (Sil to Chris: "Tony's got his own process.")—to sentence Massarone to death.

Adriana's end of things involves her coming to grips with the consequences of her informing. Early on, she meets Sanseverino and another agent in a car and answers their questions about a murdered wiseguy; when one of her responses sends the second agent sprinting out of the car, it's the first time Ade has felt the tangible impact of what she does, and she spends the rest of the hour wrestling with guilt. Sanseverino tries to assure her that she's working for the good guys now, telling Ade that she joined the FBI after her sister was paralyzed by a stray bullet from an illegal firearm, and the story briefly does its job. But movie nights[14] with the Mob wives wear on her, particularly when mention of Angie Bonpensiero illustrates how despised both informants and their wives become. On the verge of confessing her sins—"I'm not what you think I am. I don't know what to do!"—she instead flees in tears, more alone than ever.

Easy as it is to sympathize with Adriana, she's not some pure soul being ruined solely by outside forces. She knows what Christopher does, and is excited whenever he brings home swag. And when she's displeased that her best friend Tina (Vanessa Ferlito) seems to be flirting too much with Christopher, and vice versa, she exploits her FBI connection to rat Tina out for a scam she and her father are running through her job. Tina was on no one's radar at the Bureau, and now she's in her own jackpot because Adriana was feeling jealous and powerless and decided to exercise the only control she has left.

This is a world that corrupts almost anyone who enters it. Adriana's more innocent than many, but even she can't resist. Is it any wonder Tony B would rather try to go straight, no matter how much it upsets his powerful cousin?

---

14 In a nice touch, Carmela and the others are forced to stare at the FBI warning about piracy before they can perform deep analysis on Citizen Kane. (Ade: "So it was a sled, huh. He should've told somebody!")

"WHERE'S JOHNNY?"

SEASON 5/EPISODE 3
WRITTEN BY MICHAEL CALEO
DIRECTED BY JOHN PATTERSON

Small Strokes

"I mean, don't you love me?" —**Tony**

The past can be a wonderful thing to contemplate. You were younger, your skin was smooth, your kids were small and adorable, you were at the height of your physical or creative powers, whatever. We see this all the time on *The Sopranos*, going back to the pilot where Tony lamented coming in at the end of something that had once been so much better, and lectured Meadow about his grandfather helping to build the church.

The past can also be a trap. Dwelling on history can not only interfere with enjoying the present, it can easily dredge up bad feelings best left alone. And few things are ever quite as great as your memories tell you they were; had Johnny Boy seen a therapist, surely he would have complained about not being around in Lucky Luciano's heyday.

Few characters on *The Sopranos* are more trapped in the past than Uncle Junior, who's forever bloviating about some caper he and his brother pulled, or what Angie Dickinson looked like, or how Tony used to treat him with more respect. Thus far, this was a conscious choice by a lonely old man who understood his best days were behind him. Late in season four, though, his phony dementia turned out to be sadly real, and in the haunting[15] "Where's Johnny?" his condition takes an aggressive leap that strands his mind in the past.

At first, this manifests itself in small ways, like Junior's repeating the old insult about Tony never having the makings of a varsity athlete, which comes up during a work meeting with Angelo Garepe and New York shylock Lorraine Calluzzo[16] about the growing feud between factions loyal to Johnny Sack or Little

---

15 Well, mostly haunting. The episode also features the funniest HBO crossover there never was, when Junior stumbles upon a *Curb Your Enthusiasm* repeat and mistakes Larry David and Jeff Garlin for himself and Bobby.

16 As Lorraine, actress Patti D'Arbanville was styled to resemble *New York Post* TV critic Linda Stasi, who had loudly complained about season four's lack of violence, and here Johnny Sack complains that Lorraine's solution to any problem is "'Whack this one, whack that one.' Never enough body count for Lorraine." It's a meta dig that goes too far, given that an earlier scene has a terrified Lorraine offering oral sex to Phil Leotardo and his crew to keep them from killing her.

Carmine, then at a family dinner at Bobby and Janice's attended by all three Soprano siblings.[17]

The latter comment is enough to make Tony—always sensitive about insults from anyone, but particularly from loved ones like Junior—wash his hands of his uncle and focus on work, where he's not only trying to intercede in the New York war (he proposes a power-sharing arrangement between Johnny and Little Carmine, with Angelo coming out of retirement to mediate), but also arbitrates a smaller feud between an indignant Feech and Paulie over the business of landscaper Sal Vitro (Louis Mustillo).[18]

Junior's dementia grows exponentially worse after a series of miniature strokes, only diagnosed after he's gone on a walkabout to the old neighborhood in Newark, where he can't understand why all the people and places he knew so well in the '60s are gone. However much misery Junior has brought others in prior seasons, it's still sad to see him so lost and confused. It's *The Sopranos* once again applying a slice of life, one that many people understand all too well, to a Mob context. The longer Junior's odyssey lasts, as he realizes he won't be finding Johnny Boy, the more childlike and afraid Dominic Chianese becomes. At one point, he winds up on a bench with a homeless woman who offers him sex in the backseat of the car he can no longer find: the memory of where he parked is as lost as the one about his brother's death.

Tony, still bitter over the varsity athlete comments, is unmoved by word that his uncle has gone missing. When Bobby and Janice tell him about the dementia, it turns into another argument between Tony and his sister about past slights and disappointments, including Janice observing how depressing it is that Tony is back in Livia's house, and Tony mocking Janice's sexual history in front of her new husband ("Roadies?!" a dismayed Bobby asks in response to one of the stories), until the siblings become violent.[19]

When Junior's neurologist—who also happened to treat Livia after her fake stroke—tells Tony how serious the condition is, and how the recent insults were

---

17 Barbara once again performs her primary function on the show: to appear confused about why everyone else is mad at each other, and to look relieved that she and Tom live far away from all this nonsense.

18 Where many civilians whose lives are damaged by the Mob invite the damage in some way (like Davey Scatino or Vic the Appraiser), poor Sal just has the bad luck to be mowing a lawn while Feech is driving Tony B around and gets the brainstorm to declare the neighborhood territory for his nephew Gary. After much back and forth between Feech and Paulie, Sal ends up with a broken arm, half his original territory, and a requirement to kick up to Paulie for his "help," as well as to mow Tony and Johnny Sack's lawns for free. And his son has to drop out of college because Sal can't afford the tuition on his drastically reduced income.

19 Artie, who has moved into the house at Tony's request, naturally takes an elbow to the eye during the fight. It's who he is. It's what he does.

surely a result of it, Tony relents and goes to the house in Belleville to find Junior's mind largely returned to the present. This allows Tony to address what he sees as the worst part of this whole unfortunate incident: it's not just that Junior's brain is forcing him to repeat the past, but that it's forcing him to repeat the ugliest parts of it—never all those times he and Tony played catch.

"Why's it gotta be something mean?" Tony asks, as vulnerable as we've ever seen him around his uncle. "Why can't you repeat something good? I mean, don't you love me?"

This is an unfair question, given that Junior has no control over how his condition manifests itself. But it's also true that the Junior we've witnessed all these years, and the one we've heard so much about in the past, rarely had a kind word for his nephew. Although he and Livia weren't blood relatives, they shared a congenital need to express their disappointment in all things Tony Soprano. Regardless of what year Corrado Soprano thinks it is, odds are it'll be one where he's saying something cruel to his brother's son.

The worst part is that, even in his fragile mental state, it's still not too late for Junior to try to correct all that's gone wrong in the past. All he has to do is respond to Tony's final question in the affirmative. But he can't. Whether that's from shame, or old-school reticence, or the dementia temporarily robbing his ability to speak, it ultimately doesn't matter.

SEASON 5/EPISODE 4
WRITTEN BY TONI KALEM
DIRECTED BY RODRIGO GARCIA

Steamrollers

"You don't know what it's like to have your son hate your guts." —**Carmela**

Imitation is the sincerest form of television, and *The Sopranos* is among the most imitated shows of all time, from fellow classics (*Breaking Bad*) to absolute stinkers (*Low Winter Sun*) to somewhere in between (*Brotherhood*). Most of these shows feature a charismatic antihero operating outside the law, and many also feature a wife whom the audience grows to despise, even though she's objectively far more sympathetic.

Despite setting up that template in the relationship between Tony and Carmela, *The Sopranos* largely avoided the misogynistic backlash that would greet many of Carm's spiritual descendants. Sure, there were fans who had less patience for family stories than Family ones—the "Less yakkin', more whackin'" crowd—and Carmela was the focus of a lot of their least-favorite subplots. But everyone other than the most hardcore Stockholm syndrome sufferers at least recognized that she was usually the wronged party in the Soprano marriage, someone capable of feeling guilt over the devil's bargain that she'd made of her life in a way her husband never could.

So what spared Carmela from the fate of *Breaking Bad*'s Skyler White or *Mad Men*'s Betty Draper? Why did even fans who could rationalize away the worst misdeeds of Tony or Christopher or Paulie Walnuts sympathize with Carmela?

It starts with the sheer force of Edie Falco's performance. Great as so many of the series' actors are, only Falco could fully match James Gandolfini for raw emotion, particularly in "Whitecaps." Carmela is a hypocrite and a user, and in many ways a much worse person than some TV wives who followed her, but when she's feeling vulnerable or self-aware, her work is so strong and so palpable, it feels like she's reaching through the TV to slap the viewer into tears.

Next, Carmela never objects to what Tony does for a living, only to the other women he sleeps with and the ways he treats her beyond the adultery. She doesn't know the full extent of what Tony is capable of, but she knows enough.[20] She's occasionally played accessory, helping him hide money, guns, or other contraband, and is largely unmoved by stories of people who have suffered at his hands (unless it's in a way that she feels she could suffer one day, like Angie Bonpensiero[21] working at the supermarket). It reflects poorly on her as a person, but if you tune in to *The Sopranos* partly to enjoy watching Tony and his crew run scams, you never have to worry about Carmela being the killjoy getting in the way of their fun, and yours.

Finally, the show makes it clear early and often that Tony is an awful husband, and that however much Carmela enjoys his spoils, no one deserves to be lied to and humiliated. Even in the pilot, one of her most memorable scenes is the one where Tony tells her he's in therapy—while on a date at a restaurant we just saw him take Irina to, making clear not only that Tony considers his own wife second best, but that the rest of their world knows it, and is complicit in making her a perpetual fool. True, Carmela knows how her lifestyle is funded yet does nothing about that. But Tony's cheating seems less like punishment for Carmela's complicity than another manifestation of his callous selfishness. And no matter how invested a viewer might be in seeing Mob action and Tony Soprano triumphant, episodes like "All Happy Families" illustrate how well *The Sopranos* insulated Carmela from most of the backlash that accrued to the spouses of subsequent antiheroes.

---

20 Remember how quickly Carmela absorbed and then moved on from Tony's strong implication about Richie's murder back in season two's "The Knight in White Satin Armor."

21 With this episode, Toni Kalem, who played Angie, became the only *Sopranos* actor other than Michael Imperioli to also get a script credit.

After a few episodes that treated the marital separation matter-of-factly, "All Happy Families"[22] brings the new status quo—and the many ways that it is *not* an improvement for Mrs. Soprano—to the fore, by focusing on how Carmela has become the villain to her own son.

Carmela has long been her kids' punching bag. Tony's behavior is always far worse, but no one expects any better from him, whereas even the smallest real or perceived maternal slight puts Meadow and/or AJ into attack mode. AJ still blames Carmela for kicking Tony out. He's struggling in school, despite the best efforts of guidance counselor Robert Wegler (David Strathairn[23]), and acting utterly disrespectful toward his mom. Tony is only making matters worse by lavishing the kid with gifts no matter how awfully he treats his mother: first with the drum set, and here with a new, fully loaded SUV as a half-assed bit of academic motivation, given without even a heads-up to Carmela.

It's exasperating for her, and Falco shoulders every last bit of weariness, even as the separation makes her free to lash out at Tony more brutally than in the past. When Tony refuses to pay to replace the home theater sound system he removed out of spite in "Rat Pack," she points out that she was using it to enjoy movies with her many friends, whereas he only has flunkies who suck up to him because they're scared of him.

It's an insult Tony shrugs off at the time, but it proves invaluable in helping him realize it's time to be done with Feech La Manna. Feech is once again nothing but an irritant for Tony, telling more of his old stories and stealing cars at the wedding of Dr. Fried's daughter, despite Fried[24] being a valuable friend of the Family. What triggers the decision to get rid of Feech is less the thefts than Tony recalling a moment earlier in the episode when he told a stupid joke at the Executive Game[25] and everyone laughed like a hyena except for Feech. Once Tony can admit that, as Carmela warns, the adulation is undeserved, he can see that

---

22 The title spins out of a famous line from *Anna Karenina*: "Happy families are all alike; every unhappy family is unhappy in its own way."

23 Strathairn is one of the show's most recognizable guest stars with no real history in Mob movies, having first won notice as part of the repertory company of indie director John Sayles (*Eight Men Out*) before taking memorable roles in more mainstream films like *A League of Their Own*, *Sneakers*, *L.A. Confidential*, and *Good Night and Good Luck*, which got him an Oscar nomination for playing Edward R. Murrow.

24 With Lewis J. Stadlen taking over the role as Max Bialystock in *The Producers* on Broadway around the time this episode was filmed, Fried is played here by John Pleshette.

25 Feech briefly takes over the game, in a callback to how Tony and Jackie Aprile first made names for themselves by robbing one of Feech's card games. Keeping with tradition, the Game has several celebrity players, including Giants Hall of Fame linebacker Lawrence Taylor and '80s rock star David Lee Roth, along with Hollywood manager Bernie Brillstein, the partner of *Sopranos* producer Brad Grey.

Feech's scowl even in this context suggests a genuine threat to his reign, and he has Christopher set Feech up with a parole violation.

This is an abrupt and disappointing end to the arc of a character seemingly designed for much greater importance, but it also illustrates the kind of growth Tony has experienced as a Mob boss that eludes him as a husband and father. The Tony of earlier seasons might not have realized he could eliminate the hot-tempered old thug by playing on his greed, machismo, and love of action, especially with so straightforward a scheme. As he asks Sil after his Executive Game epiphany, "Did I learn nothing from Richie Aprile?"[26] In fact, he did, and his nonviolent checkmate of Feech is proof.

Tony is also kept busy playing host to Tony B and his twin sons Jason and Justin (conceived during his long incarceration thanks to Tony helping to smuggle his sperm out of prison) and contemplating the increasing mess in New York, where Phil Leotardo and his brother Billy (Chris Caldovino) murder Lorraine Calluzzo[27] on Johnny Sack's behalf, prompting Little Carmine's advisor Rusty Millio (Frankie Valli[28]) to push for retaliation.

It's another reason why the separation is so much harder on Carmela than Tony. He has work as an outlet, even when everyone around him is being difficult. She has only her family, at the moment primarily a petulant teenage boy who treats her with nothing but contempt. Sick of playing the bad guy while AJ continues to worship at the altar of his cheating, cruel father, she ignores her better judgment and gives him permission to go to a concert in the city, provided he spends the night on Meadow's couch. Instead, he stays at a hotel with friends, where they get high and perform juvenile pranks on each other, like shaving off an unconscious AJ's eyebrows and gluing his face to the floor. Like Meadow was at first after being busted for the party at Livia's house in season two, AJ is utterly unrepentant when confronted about it, even saying "Fuck you" to his mother's

---

26 The shadow of Richie hung over almost every Mob antagonist who followed him (as Chase described them, "the asshole *du jour*"), to the point where even the actors were conscious of it. The penultimate season introduced Lenny Venito as Christopher's new sidekick Murmur, but on Venito's first day of work on location, neither he nor his costars knew anything about the character beyond his name. As the cast speculated, James Gandolfini wondered if Murmur was "the new Richie Aprile, the guy we yell at for nine months."

27 Lorraine is murdered after taking a shower, which means she runs around her apartment naked, screaming her head off, in her final seconds of life. It's one final humiliation for one of the series' few female gangsters, and an instance where the series seems like an advertisement for misogyny rather than an alternately grotesque and mordantly funny study of it.

28 Valli was the front man for the legendary—and Mob-adored—band The Four Seasons, and was a plot point in season four's "Christopher." As Rusty, he is very much presented as the Dick Cheney to Little Carmine's malapropism-spouting George W. Bush, an ally of Carmine Sr. pushing the son into a war neither seems prepared for. "We'll steamroll right over John," he boasts, "And I predict the guys on the street in Brooklyn and Queens, they'll welcome us as fuckin' heroes."

face, then walking away while she's in pain from falling while chasing after him. And again, like Meadow, he wraps Tony around his finger and makes him see his side of things, but the difference is that Carmela no longer has reason to play nice. Both Anthony Sopranos have been so awful to her for so long that she doesn't have to pretend anymore, and instead orders AJ to go stay with Tony over at Livia's house, despite objections from both father and son.

Even this could perhaps be framed by pro-Tony viewers as nagging behavior, but the episode's sympathies are strongly behind Carmela, who admits at dinner with Mr. Wegler that she's terrified of AJ going into the Family business. Given what happened to Jackie Aprile Jr.—just as spoiled and entitled and oblivious as AJ (but with better hair)—we share her justifiable fear.

Even the temporary victory over Tony and AJ feels hollow. Yes, she no longer has to put up with her son's insults and insubordination, and is even free to pursue an interesting man in Mr. Wegler, who couldn't be further from the world she knows. But she still goes home to a huge, empty McMansion, built for a large and happy family, now occupied only by Carmela and memories of better times. The hour opens with AJ practicing behind the wheel of the family station wagon in the driveway; it ends with a flashback to him as a toddler riding his Big Wheel down that same driveway, a worried younger Carmela calling after him. He didn't listen to her then, either, but he was still innocent and sweet. Not anymore. Now he's just another man who treats Carmela Soprano like garbage.

| "IRREGULAR AROUND THE MARGINS" | SEASON 5/EPISODE 5
WRITTEN BY ROBIN GREEN & MITCHELL BURGESS
DIRECTED BY ALLEN COULTER |

Telephone

"You know what? I might as well have fucked her. Thanks!" —**Tony**

We know that Tony Soprano lacks impulse control. We saw that throughout the string of events that led to Carmela evicting him in "Whitecaps." It was a bad idea to sleep with Ralphie's mistress, to beat up Assemblyman Zellman, and to sleep with Svetlana, but he did all three because he wanted to and couldn't stop himself.

We also know that Tony Soprano is a man with a particular type, and that Adriana La Cerva fits that type in many ways: sexy, assertive, eager to demonstrate her independence, and untroubled by the world of organized crime. Yet somehow, he never attempted to sleep or even flirt with his nephew's fiancée before the black comic events of "Irregular Around the Margins."

Maybe it's because they never spent any time together without Christopher and/or Carmela as chaperones. When they're alone in the Crazy Horse office, exchanging impressions of Christopher's "constipated owl look," Adriana confessing that she was scared of Tony when she met him, it's as if he's never really looked at her before—and realizing how many of his boxes she checks. But a bigger factor is Tony's survival instinct. He tells Melfi, who has taken him back on a probationary basis, that having sex with Adriana or starting a serious relationship with her would be a disaster for them both, ruining his relationship with his heir apparent, encouraging Carmela to seek a more brutal divorce settlement, and making Ade an outcast among heretofore welcoming Mob wives.

But we were there, so we know the real reason nothing happened in that charged air: Phil Leotardo's well-timed knock, and possible reluctance on the part of Adriana, who later insists to Agent Sanseverino that she would never cheat on Christopher with Tony. Without that knock, though, you just know Tony would have made a move, consequences be damned, because it's in his nature. No matter the danger, the man always gives into temptation.

But as Tony and Christopher both observe repeatedly through the episode's second half, perception has a nasty way of becoming reality in their business. After Tony and Adriana crash an SUV while looking to score cocaine, it doesn't matter that they didn't have sex, because the Mob has its own version of the Telephone Game that expands on what happened until speculation finally acquires a narrative, followed by humiliating, made-up details. Adriana sustaining "a severe blow to the head" becomes her giving Tony a blow job, and on and on until Uncle Junior is marveling, "Apparently, he came all over the sun visor!"

Gossip run amok puts Tony and Chris on a collision course until Tony B steps in with a pair of solutions that combine his knowledge of Mob culture and health care: first he gets the smug emergency room doctor to explain to Christopher that Adriana's injuries rule out her doing anything sexual with Tony at the time of the crash, then he arranges a very public dinner at Vesuvio where he, his mother, Christopher, Adriana, Tony, and Carmela all eat cordially while Vito and the other captains watch and come to pay homage. Christopher gets confirmation that Adriana was faithful, and he gets to save face with his colleagues.

Unfortunately, everyone knows that dinner is strictly ceremonial. Carmela isn't happy to be there, and even though she tells Tony earlier that she believes he wouldn't sleep with Adriana, she still sprints upstairs again, Meadow-style, just to get away from this man who piles so much misery on her. Adriana defends Christopher to Sanseverino, but her face (both the bruises and the expression) tell a different story. Christopher is convinced that Tony and Adriana didn't fool around at this particular moment, but he'll never entirely be sure they've *never* done anything. And everyone will be right to be mistrustful and pained about the whole situation, because Adriana knows Christopher was capable of strangling her, just as Tony recognizes deep down how easily he could have slept with Adriana if circumstances had been even slightly different.

Yet despite the darkness at the core of this foursome, "Irregular Around the Margins" is among *The Sopranos*'s most purely farcical episodes. The series doesn't often attempt primarily comic installments, though there are great jokes in even the most serious hours (e.g., Christopher's reaction to Ralphie's wig in "Whoever Did This"). The episode applies the series' core idea—"Recognizable family problems, but with Mafia-level stakes"—to the world of gossip and innuendo, letting the captains act like eighth graders passing notes while endangering Tony, Adriana, and Christopher. And since the jokes are often most potent when people are mad at each other, doing a whole episode where everyone is upset leaves greater room for comedy, like the bit of business where Carmela throws the pizza Tony brought as a peace offering onto the floor, followed by Tony scooping it back up before he leaves with his tail between his legs, or—after Tony B's quick thinking gets Christopher off the warpath—the most pressing issue suddenly being the fact that Chris threw food at Vito. (Tony: "That's got to be resolved.")

But the comedy comes from the same dysfunctional place as the drama: Tony Soprano's inability to stop himself from trying to take what he wants, when he wants.

"SENTIMENTAL EDUCATION"

SEASON 5/EPISODE 6
WRITTEN BY MATTHEW WEINER
DIRECTED BY PETER BOGDANOVICH[29]

Fish Out of Water

"You need to show resolve—a firm purpose to change." —**Father Phil**

David Chase likes to say that, contrary to critical consensus, *The Sopranos* isn't a show about how people don't change, or can't. In his view, personal change isn't impossible—just rare and incredibly difficult, particularly in a culture that rewards

---

29 Though Bogdanovich was an acclaimed director and a recurring *Sopranos* actor as Elliot Kupferberg, this is the only episode to put him behind the camera.

inertia and selfishness like the Mafia. In the series, people don't usually change, but only sometimes for lack of effort. For every wiseguy or Mob wife perfectly content with themselves, there's usually someone questioning how they got to this point in life and whether it makes any sense to stay. They try to alter either themselves or their contexts, but usually the world around them not only has no interest in this transformation, but actively conspires against it. Wherever you try to go, here you still are.

Rarely is that bleak but empathetic world view more elegantly or sadly articulated in the series than in "Sentimental Education," an hour in which Carmela and Tony B go to tremendous effort to broaden their horizons and be something other than what Tony Soprano assumes of them, only to be slapped down by some combination of how the world views them and their habit of following their subculture's rules.

After years of enduring Tony's serial adultery while refraining from reciprocating, Carmela finally has sex with another man. Mr. Wegler is using Carmela at least as much as she's using him, treating his efforts to improve AJ's college chances as currency in their burgeoning relationship, and he can be as stuck in his ways as Tony: despite knowing that Carmela didn't enjoy *Madame Bovary*,[30] he gives her a Modern Library first edition of it, suggesting if she tries it again, she might learn to love it as he does. But while he is far from a perfect catch, he's different enough from Tony to make Carmela feel different, too. Mr. Wegler is her estranged husband's diametric opposite: cultured, soft-spoken, and generous of spirit. Not only does he talk to Carmela after sex, their discussions of fine literature feel like ongoing intellectual foreplay. And he's willing to see potential in AJ that we doubt exists. She glows when she's around him, and as she thumbs through his copy of *The Letters of Abelard and Heloise* in the bathroom, she seems as carefree and immune from Tony's nonsense as she has at any point since the separation.

It's a lovely emotional oasis for her. Too bad it's doomed. Even before she and Wegler sleep together, Father Phil is already trying to box-block her. He's at his coldest and most judgmental when she discusses the relationship in confession. He insists his objections have to do with the sanctity of her marriage to Tony and the Church's aversion to spouses splitting, but he's not a disinterested party. They nearly had sex a few years back, when she and Tony were under the same roof. He seems less the strict priest than the jealous not-quite lover.

Carmela the sincere Catholic feels guilt over what she's done, but she also recognizes the change within her, telling Phil, "Something in me has been

---

30 Carmela's complaint that the story is slow and "nothing really happens" echoes some of the complaints about season four, or about Carmela stories in general, just as Wegler's defense of the book—"Outside, nothing happens. But inside, she has these extremes of boredom and exhilaration."—could also be the show's defense of the Carmela–Furio flirtations.

reawakened. And even if it never happens again with this man, just knowing that feeling of passion again, I don't know if it's ever going to go away. I'll need it." He scolds her and guilts her and tells her she needs to show the strength to change, when that's exactly what she's done in dating Wegler. If taking Carmela's confession during "College" rather than sleeping with her was Phil's finest moment of the series, this is his lowest, as he speaks for the part of Carmela's world that has no interest in her being anything but the wife of Tony Soprano.

And the worst thing is, Wegler thinks that way, too. Or, at least, he frames her every action as that of a Mob boss's ruthless spouse who will do what she must to get what she wants.

Wegler seems not so different from the men Carmela knows best when he agrees to, as he'll colorfully describe it later, put the arm on his colleague Tom Fiske[31] to boost AJ's grade, because he knows it increases the likelihood of more sex. But where a wiseguy would enjoy the spoils of his sin, Wegler instead is consumed with guilt over it, and shoves the blame onto Carmela, accusing her of the basest form of manipulation, telling her, "You strong-armed me using the only weapon you have: your pussy."

He's not wrong, based on what we know about Carmela's relentless pursuit of her goals, particularly where the kids are concerned. But he's still being unfair, in the knowing and deliberate manner of a wounded man. Carmela clearly enjoyed his company and conversation as well as the sex, and there were moments where we could envision their alternate reality as a real couple. Carmela might not have Wegler's literary schooling, but she reads constantly and can hold her own in a conversation about books, often making blunt statements or asking simple but cutting questions that the academic Wegler wouldn't have considered. Whatever conscious or unconscious agenda Carm may have had, her affection and respect seemed sincere; at worst, her emotions toward Wegler were "complicated." Wegler's formulation would seem crude and cruel coming from a wiseguy's mouth, but it stings worse coming from the kind man of letters that Carmela saw as her vessel to a better life. It conveys there's no way for her to trade up because so many straight men, regardless of social class, will describe women this way if they're feeling rejected or used.[32] Wegler's pettiness strands her back in the emotional cesspool. When Hugh comes by later to do some repair work, Carmela sinks into despair at the realization that, "Whatever I say, whatever I do, because I was married to a man like Tony, my motives will always be called into question."

---

31 Fiske calls it right not only in pointing out the unfairness of what Wegler is doing for AJ compared to what a hard-working student might get, but in dubbing AJ "Fredo Corleone," which is probably an insult to Fredo, but close enough for our purposes.

32 Contrast Wegler and Tony, and you're contrasting the Meadow and Tracee storylines from "University."

Whereas Carmela is hemmed in by other people's expectations, Tony B's problems come equally from how much he misses his old life as how much it misses him. He is achingly close to going straight: getting his massage certification, maintaining a relationship with prison pen pal Gwen (Alison Bartlett[33]), being picked out by his boss Mr. Kim (Henry Yuk) to be the front man for a massage therapy storefront business. All he claims to want is within his grasp, and he has the work ethic to get it. It wouldn't be a glamorous life like his cousin's, but it would keep him out of prison, or worse, and it would let him keep doing a thing he fell in love with while he was behind bars. It's all right in front of him . . .

. . . until, in an O. Henry–like twist, a drug dealer fleeing the cops throws a bag of cash right at Tony B, and suddenly he has the consequence-free means to live it up for a few days like the wiseguy he used to be. He buys everyone drinks at the Bing, outfits himself in a slick new suit and shoes, and spends hours blowing most of what he has left at the Executive Game.

At any other time, this might be a memorable adventure he could look back on wistfully whenever he saw the suit hanging in his closet. But it comes right as the massage parlor is about to open, and Tony B is overwhelmed with the need to make it work, both for his own sake and to reward Kim's faith in him. After a taste of Mob life, going straight feels suddenly *very* difficult, and the stress builds and builds until he releases it in a violent explosion against Kim that leaves his former employer bloodied and a koi from the parlor's pond flopping around on the floor.[34] There are three fish out of water in this scene: the koi, Kim, and Tony B. And a fourth in the episode as a whole: Carmela, who had a brief but blissful stay in the tweedy world of letters.

Tony Soprano is barely in this episode—physically, at least. He pops up a few times to argue with AJ and with Carmela over AJ's education, but mostly he casts a shadow over both of the hour's main characters, representing the past that Carmela can't escape, and that Tony B realizes he doesn't *want* to escape. In the closing scene, the two Tonys dine at Vesuvio, and Tony B belatedly agrees to run the used-airbag scam Tony had arranged for him. "It's hard doing business with strangers," says a delighted Tony.

---

33 Bartlett's a longtime *Sesame Street* cast member as veterinarian Gina, which can make for extreme whiplash for *Sopranos* viewers who sat with their kids watching her hang out with Big Bird and Grover.
34 This is one of the most impressive sight gags in the the show's run: an example of its commenting on its characters and framing the whole episode without needing a syllable of dialogue to make the point.

SEASON 5/EPISODE 7
WRITTEN BY TERENCE WINTER
DIRECTED BY STEVE BUSCEMI

Happy Birthday, Mister President

*"She made my father give my dog away." —***Tony**

In the opening scene of "In Camelot," Tony and Janice make peace over the argument they had when Junior went missing during "Where's Johnny," and the siblings reminisce about the past. Tony's beloved childhood dog Tippy comes up, and Janice is stunned to realize that even as a middle-aged man, Tony still believes that Tippy went to the country to live out the rest of his days after developing worms, when clearly he was put to sleep.

The truth about Tippy will prove more complicated, as Tony learns over the course of the hour that Livia hated the dog, so Johnny Boy gave it to his mistress Fran Felstein. But Tony's shock at the mere suggestion that Tippy was euthanized, when Janice and we know what a cynic he is about life and death,[35] is one of many blind spots that will be revealed in "In Camelot." We see the ways that Tony, Christopher, and Junior have learned to ignore fundamental aspects of their lives in order to function, and how painful it can be when the blinders are taken off.

Much of the episode revolves around Tony bumping into Fran (Polly Bergen[36]) while visiting his father's grave after an aunt's funeral. Tony remembers her as "the lady from Bamberger's, from the fur department," and it's clear that Johnny Boy's affair with her was no more a secret than most of the mistresses in Tony's era are. Rather than being ashamed, Tony, who's had many *goomars* of his own, is excited to spend time in the company of a woman who knew his father so well, and held a prominent place in his own youthful imagination.

But as Tony gets to know Fran, and attempts to do right by her by making Hesh and Phil Leotardo[37] pay the cut of the race track Johnny Boy left her, he's also forced to face some truths he's avoided about his own past. Dr. Melfi's ques-

---

35 Pine cones all around.

36 A television pioneer, Bergen acted opposite Robert Mitchum in the original *Cape Fear* and won an Emmy for playing the title role in *The Helen Morgan Story,* a *Playhouse 90* production of the musical drama about the torch singer's life and work. She was also an acclaimed stage actress, a regular on game shows and television dramas, and played Rhoda Henry, wife of Pug Henry, in the hit miniseries *The Winds of War* and *War and Remembrance.*

37 After Phil—who is utterly dismissive of Tony and the New Jersey Family in general—ducks Tony's early attempts to get his cut, we get a rarity for *The Sopranos*: an honest-to-goodness car chase, with Tony tearing after a fleeing Phil to talk payment terms. Like the series' other car chases (see Big Pussy trying to tail Christopher back in season two), it ends with a crash, as Phil bangs up his ride and his neck.

tions about Fran keep confronting him with realizations he'd rather suppress. It's not just that Tippy wound up living with Fran because Livia didn't want the dog around, or that Fran conjures mixed associations when she dons Tony's JFK captain's hat to imitate Marilyn Monroe's performance of "Happy Birthday." All the layers of Tony's discomfort combine in Fran's dance, a peerless example (by Bergen) of an actor selling the joke without seeming to be in on it, as well as a peak performance moment by James Gandolfini. It's clear that this combined evocation of the Camelot-era '60s and unwanted glimpse of his father's love life *does* turn Tony on, and that even beginning to admit this makes him so distressed that he falls into a stupefied daze.

In therapy, he denies being attracted to Fran, saying she's old enough to be his mother, which leads Melfi to hit him with a pricelessly smug expression. Tony, mortified, insists he never wanted to do *that* to his mom. As he's done so many times, he's misunderstanding the Oedipus complex again, seemingly on purpose; refusing to fully understand it allows him to avoid confronting what it means for his relationships with women. Melfi later gets him to recall how Johnny Boy was absent the night Livia[38] miscarried a post-Barbara pregnancy because he was catting around with Fran. For so long, Tony has viewed Livia as the alpha and the omega of all the misery in his life, lamenting all she did to Johnny Boy, and to him, never examining the effect his father's behavior had on mother and son. Melfi tries her hardest to get Tony to look at the full picture of his childhood and recognize that, even if Livia was a monster, she didn't become that in a vacuum—that she had help from the abusive and unfaithful man she lived with. But he can't accept that, because to acknowledge that Johnny Boy was a neglectful and destructive husband and father would require Tony (whose behavior is so similar) to admit that he is, too—and that this aspect of Soprano family history is repeating itself.

He's right on the precipice of taking Melfi's advice to forgive Livia and move forward, but within seconds, he's back to blaming his mother for everything. He can't admit that Livia wasn't the source of all his pain, just as he can't acknowledge how small and shabby Fran's life seems, given the legend he'd built around her in his mind. The episode ends with Tony at the Bing, regaling Artie, Sil, and Tony B with exaggerated stories about Fran's affair with JFK: he has to make her seem more important than she was so Johnny Boy's affair with her seems like a thing

---

38 After being played by Laila Robins in "Down Neck" and "Fortunate Son," young Livia here is portrayed by Laurie Williams—Chase recalls that Robins was unavailable—who expertly evokes both Robins and Nancy Marchand in her brief screen time, particularly the moment where Livia realizes that, by lying to her about Johnny Boy's whereabouts, her son has chosen his father over her, and turns against him accordingly. The way Livia clutches her robe is like a decades-early signal that she'll one day try to have Tony killed.

Johnny couldn't resist: *What was he gonna do? This was a woman so amazing, the president wanted her all to himself!*

Christopher doesn't even come close to recognizing his own blind spot, though his new pal, recovering-addict TV writer JT Dolan[39] (Tim Daly[40]), gets a look at the hypocrisies Christopher commits every day without realizing it. They became friends in rehab, and Christopher takes their Narcotics Anonymous work seriously. But he also doesn't hesitate to invite JT to the Executive Game when his sponsor expresses interest in gambling—even Tony tried to talk Davey Scatino out of playing at first—because outside of their respective sobriety, JT is like any other civilian to Christopher: a mark to be exploited. JT can't believe his friend would be so ruthless about a $60,000 debt, and brags, "What could you do to me that I haven't already been through?"

"I'm positive we'll think of something," says Christopher, right before he and Little Paulie knock JT through his coffee table and off the wagon.

On his way back to rehab, JT signs over his beloved convertible to pay part of the debt, then is aghast to hear Christopher spouting recovery clichés like, "There's no chemical solution to a spiritual problem." As a rational (if insufferable) human, JT can't believe Christopher would still try to act like a friend; as a man working in a sick business, Christopher has to think of all of this as perfectly normal. (If anything, he probably imagines himself as being much kinder to this guy than Paulie or Patsy would be.) When he explains how much interest JT will pay on his debt, he warns, "I will not fuckin' enable you," not comprehending that he did exactly that by inviting the poor sap to play.

Where Tony is able to beat down attempts to make him examine this part of him, and Christopher isn't even aware it's there, it's Uncle Junior who gets a devastating glimpse of what he's become—who he always was, really—at the end of his latest attempt to escape the boredom of house arrest. His current drug regimen

---

39 In earlier years, Christopher's writing ambitions allowed the show to have some fun at the expense of the movie business. The introduction of JT gave *The Sopranos* writers license to turn gleefully on their own medium. JT is presented as a hack who loves dropping the names of shows he's worked on (*Nash Bridges*) and producers he's meeting (Rene Balcer from *Law & Order*), and who can't get more than fifteen dollars when he tries to pawn his Emmy to pay Christopher. (The pawnshop owner: "If you had an Oscar, maybe I could give you something. An Academy Award. But TV? What else you got?") Among JT's past credits: the CBS Italian American family drama *That's Life*, which offers a belated opportunity to strike back at a series whose cast and crew used to brag that their characters weren't in the Mob, and whose star went on record chastising *The Sopranos* for being defamatory and announcing that he would never be on it. (Christopher: "What, that fake guinea-fest with Paul Sorvino? That was totally unrealistic!")

40 Daly starred in Chase's short-lived CBS drama *Almost Grown*, though at this point was more famous for his long stretch as one of the stars of the sitcom *Wings*. Like Frankie Valli, he's a season five addition to the recurring *Sopranos* cast who was already established as existing in the show's universe: in season three's "University," Daly himself is mentioned as a client of Noah Tannenbaum's father.

has made his memory sharper and his mood more upbeat. When the judge allows him to leave Belleville to attend the funeral of Tony and Janice's Aunt Concetta, it's the happiest he's been in forever—declining Tony's invitation to visit Johnny Boy's grave with him, Junior suggests, "I can pay my respects from the after party"—and he begins combing the obituary pages looking for any excuse to get out of the house and interact with people besides Bobby and Janice.

This starts out as comic relief, with Junior and his attorney shamelessly contorting Junior's relationships with the dearly departed for the judge's approval. But it quickly turns dark, with Junior raving about the deli platter at the funeral for his dry cleaner's seven-year-old son, oblivious to the devastated mourners. And when Concetta's husband Zio dies two weeks after his beloved wife, Father Phil's eulogy about all that Concetta and Zio enjoyed during their long life together utterly wrecks Junior, who has been alone for so long.

Junior's neurologist wonders if he had another stroke, while Uncle Jun insists the new meds have just stopped working, as he finds himself shuffling around like Tony on lithium back in "Isabella." A medical cause is plausible given Junior's condition, but more likely Father Phil's speech forced him to take a harsh but not inaccurate look at himself.

"My life is only death," Junior wails. "I'm living in a grave. I beat prison, and for what? I have no children. Will somebody please explain this to me?"

No one can, because what can you say? The funerals provided a brief distraction from his lonely, deteriorating existence, but only for so long. Christopher can focus on bleeding JT dry, and Tony can ignore his troubles at the Bing, but Junior's blinders, along with his dignity, have been stripped away. This is a life where the only way to function is to not look too closely at who you are and what you're doing. Tony and Chris can mostly succeed in that; Junior can't anymore, which is why they end the episode celebrating and he ends it sobbing.

SEASON 5/EPISODE 8
WRITTEN BY MICHAEL IMPERIOLI
DIRECTED BY JOHN PATTERSON

Truce and Consequences

"This is nice, no?" **—Tony**

From a Family point of view, "Marco Polo" is among the series' more minor episodes. There's continued back and forth in the New York civil war, with Johnny sinking Little Carmine's boat, and Little Carmine and Rusty trying to recruit Tony B to murder Phil's protégé Joey Peeps (Joe Maruzzo) in retaliation for Lorraine. But the most prominent Mob story of the hour is small and petty: Tony assigns Angie Bonpensiero, now running Pussy's old body shop, to repair Phil's car after the crash Tony caused during "In Camelot," taking pleasure in his dead rat friend's widow getting nickel-and-dimed by (as Tony describes Phil) "the Shah of Iran."

Lowercase family–wise, though, it's one of *The Sopranos*'s most charming and memorable episodes: a rambling, Robert Altman–esque hour, set primarily at the seventy-fifth birthday party for Carmela's father Hugh, so intimate, detailed, and cognizant of how well we've come to know these people, that it often feels as if we're in the Soprano backyard smelling the chlorine and grilled *salsiccia*.

Tony B spends much of the episode, and the party, fuming at being given such a thin slice of the Family pie after so many years away, and having to act like the hired help at his rich cousin's party. When he was pursuing his massage therapy dreams, it was easy to accept how little he had, but now that he's signed back up, he can't help but notice how drastically the two Tonys' roads diverged since that night twenty years ago. He covets the Soprano mansion, sees how well Meadow is doing (Meadow, more empathetic than most Sopranos, knows instantly that Tony B is thinking about his daughter Kelly), and can't deny how shabby his life is in comparison. His twins know nothing of the past (they'd been told throughout their childhoods their father was in the military overseas), but they see their diminished present as clearly as their dad does. Jason steals one of the many valuable items (a folder of '96 Olympics pins) that lies forgotten in the back of AJ's closet, and when Tony B scolds him for it, Jason protests, "I love where he lives" and says he doesn't want to return to Tony B's place anymore.

Earlier, Tony B had rebuffed Little Carmine and Rusty, wisely avoiding the New York war. But after a day as errand boy for both Carmela (helping with the party, then sitting way out on the fringes of it) and Tony (trying and failing to get Phil to ease off his demands for Angie), plus this outburst, he's had enough. He kills Joey Peeps, plus a prostitute unlucky enough to get a ride home from Joey, and limps from the crime scene on a run-over foot.

Tony B's gnawing resentment is but one thread developed before, during, and after the party that ranks with the *Sopranos*'s best evocations of how communities can poison shared milestones and rituals. Early on, it seems as if Hugh might not even make it to the party, as our first glimpse of him is when he falls off Carmela's roof while trying to lay shingles. This turns out to be another bit of classic *Sopranos* slapstick (Hugh falls past AJ's window; AJ, oblivious, keeps drumming), and Hugh escapes with minor aches and pains, which leaves open the question of whether Tony will be invited to the party now that he and Carmela are splitsville. Carm has good reason to not want Tony there, but it's really Mary opposing it because she fears Tony will embarrass her in front of her high-class northern Italian friend,[41] Dr. Russ Fegoli (Bruce Kirby). But Hugh—who has the surprise party spoiled early for him by an amusingly petulant Uncle Junior—suggests he won't come unless the man of the house mans the grill.

It's an inflection point for the Soprano separation. Tony is lonely[42] and miserable at Livia's, and Carmela's fling with Dr. Wegler left her pessimistic about finding happiness outside of the world she already knows. If ever there was a moment for them to better appreciate each other's company, it's now, during a long day spent with friends and family, with Tony on his best and most charming behavior, from the way he twirls the sausages around his neck to the Beretta shotgun he thoughtfully buys for Hugh. Throwing any sort of party is stressful for Carm—particularly when people like Tony B show up to "help" and wind up burdening her with more work—but the day still reminds her of what it was like to be married to Tony in better times. And looking at her own parents, who are still together after all these years, helps her appreciate the feeling of stability that comes from spending your life with the same person.

Despite early hiccups, this turns into a great party that continues well into the night, when a handful of guests convene to play the titular game in the Soprano family pool. Carmela has worked *so* hard to escape this marriage, to stay above the fray of all of Tony's nonsense, but she keeps being thrown back into the pool—literally here, when Tony and AJ toss her in fully clothed so she can join the game. (Edie Falco's resigned delivery of "Marco . . ." when Carmela is tagged is a

---

41 This is Imperioli's final *Sopranos* script, and not coincidentally the final episode to spend much time on issues of Italian American self-esteem, as Carmela lays into Mary, telling her, "There are Italians all around with their closet self-loathing. I just never wanted to believe my mother was one of them."

42 Despite Tony's newfound freedom to pursue any kind of sex he wants without being a hypocrite or having to hide his activities, Valentina has only popped up briefly in two episodes this season. With a different girlfriend, Tony might be giddy at all the time he can spend with her, but she's clearly just a placeholder for him. A big part of Tony's "meh" attitude is probably because his separation from Carmela has removed the thrill of the forbidden—a bigger part of the experience than he realized.

thing of minimalist comic beauty.) But if she's angry for a moment at getting wet against her will, it's not long before she's happy to realize she and Tony are the last ones in the pool and that he's making a move.[43] For so long, she's wanted to be wanted by Tony in this way, and not just because he's horny or lonely or atoning for his latest fuckup. Now here he is, acting like the man she once loved very much, looking at her like she is the only woman in the world for him, and soon they are doing what happy spouses do together.

Uppercase Family-wise, Tony B sticking his beak into the New York civil war is a big deal. But the more important piece of "Marco Polo" involves the cessation of hostilities in the civil war between Mr. and Mrs. Soprano.

"UNIDENTIFIED BLACK MALES"	SEASON 5/EPISODE 9 WRITTEN BY MATTHEW WEINER AND TERENCE WINTER DIRECTED BY TIM VAN PATTEN

Arch-Nemesis

"Is this what you grew up with?" —**Finn**

Almost every significant character on *The Sopranos* is either in the Mob or connected to it by ties of profession, family, and/or friendship. The major exception is Dr. Melfi, but she only knows what Tony tells her—a mix of truth, self-aggrandizement, and legal cover. If she could actually see the full extent of who Tony was and what he did, she might refuse to be in the same room with him again, let alone treat him.

Finn DeTrolio is far from the series' most charismatic figure, but as a civilian who grew up a continent away from all this, he has a distinct role in both Meadow's life and the series as a whole. None of this is normal to him. None of it is something to be shrugged off as just the way things are. And the more he learns about all the men Meadow calls Uncle, the more justifiably terrified he becomes of staying in a relationship with the daughter of Mr. Mob Boss.

After Finn fails to land a job on his own that might at least buy a new air conditioner in the middle of an oppressive New York summer, Tony hooks him

---

43 In an episode overflowing with lovely background details, the funniest may be Artie asleep on a pool chaise, a towel wrapped around his head like he's Audrey Hepburn rocking a chiffon turban in *Sabrina*.

up with the operation over at the Esplanade, where no-work guys like Vito and Eugene are amused by how hard he tries when he could lounge around with them. He soon learns to accept some of the spoils of dating the boss's daughter, but little about this environment seems right to him, even before he witnesses Eugene laying a savage beating on Little Paulie because he took offense to a joke implying he was gay.

Meadow has, like her mother before her, become inured to all of this. She has learned to tell the lie about who killed Jackie Jr.—one of several sets of nonexistent African American scapegoats who provide "Unidentified Black Males" with its title—as if she believes it, and she dismisses Finn's story of the Little Paulie beating because she only knows Eugene as one of her father's sweet friends.

But that beating helps to frame the next disturbing incident Finn witnesses Vito blowing a security guard in the Esplanade parking lot[44]—because he knows how dangerous even a joke about homosexuality can be. Vito is in grave danger if this secret ever gets out, which means Finn is in grave danger for knowing it, a situation made clear when Vito confronts him outside a Port-A-John—quipping, "Finn DeTrolio, my arch-nemesis," in a way that sounds much less jokey than intended—and ominously invites San Diego fan Finn to join him at a Yankees–Padres game in the Bronx that night.

Finn instead hides out at the apartment with Meadow, which turns out to be the more perilous locale. Where Vito simply looks disappointed and lonely as he stands in full Yankees gear outside the stadium, Meadow lures Finn into an endless argument about not only the Vito incident (She's in denial about this, too: "Vito Spatafore is a married man, Finn"), but the state of their relationship, given Finn's decision to take out a suitcase in the event he had to go on the run. The fight lasts only a few minutes across a pair of scenes, but it seems to go on *forever*, until Finn can hardly be blamed for proposing marriage to Meadow simply to end it.

The episode's title primarily applies to two sets of fictional black men in the past and present: the group Tony blamed for missing the hijacking that sent Tony B to prison, when he was really just suffering an early panic attack; and the group whom Tony B claim injured his foot, when it actually got run over at the end of the Joey Peeps hit. It is a racist lie coming full circle, so much so that Tony has

---

44 This was actually Joseph Gannascoli's idea, inspired by the nonfiction book *Murder Machine*, which referenced a gay Gambino Family hitman. "And when he got the script," *Sopranos* writer Terence Winter recalled at the start of the following season, "he called up and said, 'I said I'd be gay, I didn't think I'd be the guy giving [it].' I said, 'It doesn't work that way, Joe.'"

his first panic attack in years[45] upon realizing that his cousin was responsible for escalating the civil war in New York,[46] which could mark both Tonys for death.

The Peeps hit, and the connections Tony makes between the panic attack it causes while he's golfing with Johnny Sack and earlier attacks seemingly sparked by mentions of cousins, help Tony disclose to Dr. Melfi the guilt-ridden truth about that night when Tony B got pinched. It all started back when Meadow was a baby, not because of jealousy or bitterness, but because of the cycle of abuse and anxiety between Livia and her son that Tony barely recognized at the time. A screaming match triggered what Tony would recognize decades later as a panic attack, causing him to cut his head and miss the hijacking, ruining one Tony's life and leaving the other one on a path to take over the Family.

When Tony B was in prison, or even pursuing his massage therapy career, Tony could block out the memories and the guilt. With Tony B not only an active wiseguy again, but suddenly pushing New Jersey into the middle of New York's war, Tony can't avoid facing these feelings, and they're crushing him—to the point where he has another panic attack in the safe space of Melfi's office, just from discussing that fateful evening. This is the first time she has witnessed such an event—Gandolfini is so typically spectacular at portraying Tony at his most vulnerable that it's easy to overlook how deftly Lorraine Bracco balances Melfi's desire to help her patient in this moment of crisis and her professional fascination at finally experiencing what she's only heard Tony describe in retrospect—and though she pulls him through it, he feels no better. (Melfi compares sessions like this to childbirth, while Tony insists, "Trust me—it's like takin' a shit.")

Tony at least has a professional to guide him through these terrifying moments. Carmela spends much of the episode seeking a different form of counsel, deciding to hire a divorce lawyer after Tony is slow to follow up on the tryst at the end of her father's birthday party. But she discovers[47] that Tony has followed Alan Sapinsly's advice from "Whitecaps"—taking token meetings with top area attorneys so they're conflicted out of representing Carmela—and the few untainted ones are too afraid to tangle with the boss of New Jersey. It's brutal to watch, in many ways worse than Carmela's realization in "Sentimental Education" that everyone will always assume the worst of her because of Tony—at least she still

---

45 No meat is present for this one.

46 The Bush/Cheney parallels continue for Little Carmine and Rusty, with the latter discussing his recent heart surgery, and the former beginning to sport Texas-style belt buckles and delivering inspirational speeches that are just word salad, like, "The fundamental question is, will I be as effective as a boss like my dad was? And I will be. Even more so. But until I am, it's gonna be hard to verify that I think I'll be more effective."

47 She gets this bad news right as the black bear returns to her backyard. There are no coincidences on this show.

had a shot at her fair share in the divorce and carving out a life on her own. Tony smugly celebrates his victory by replying to her complaints with, "The only reason you have anything is because of my fuckin' sweat, and you knew every step of the way exactly how it works." He's trapped her in a life where she depends on the scraps he gives her to live on, always subject to his moods and petty grievances, knowing there is no way out.

The hour closes with Carmela watching Tony swim in the pool of the house where he no longer resides, listening to Meadow tell her about Finn's proposal. Carmela weeps not with joy for her daughter getting engaged to a nice guy who couldn't be more unlike Tony, but with despair at everything her own marital choice has—and will—cost her for the rest of her life.

Finn's prospects seem just as bleak. In popping the question, he proved himself unexpectedly fit to join this particular Family. His proposal prioritizes the short-term gratification of getting Meadow to *just shut up* about the damn suitcase over what is genuinely best for Finn, which would be to run away from all the people whose miserable stories fill the rest of the hour. This might be the only characteristic Finn has in common with Tony, an impulsive man with no long-term vision who momentarily undoes catastrophic marriage screw-ups by dropping small fortunes on gifts for his wife, some of which (such as the house that they ended up not buying) require years, even decades, of commitment. Finn spends much of the episode terrified of what Vito might do to him. Officially joining Tony's family is an easy way to become protected in the short term—just look at how differently Paulie Walnuts treats Finn once he learns out who he is—but he might want to have a long talk with his future mother-in-law about what you get, and what you risk, by marrying into this world.

SEASON 5/EPISODE 10
WRITTEN BY ROBIN GREEN & MITCHELL BURGESS
DIRECTED BY MIKE FIGGIS

On the Farm

"Tell me about the Soprano temper." —**Dr. Melfi**

A lot of old family stories get told throughout "Cold Cuts," perhaps none more potent than the one Christopher lays on Adriana while packing for a trip upstate to visit the farm of Uncle Pat Blundetto (Frank Albanese), where the remains of

Emil Kolar and a few other Family victims have been interred for years.[48] Chris recalls a summer he spent at the farm when he was eleven and the two Tonys were nineteen: as an "initiation," they tied him to a tree and left him there until three in the morning.

"I worshipped these two guys—Tony Soprano especially," he says, lamenting that when Tony was by himself, he was everything a younger cousin could have wanted, but that when peers like Tony B were around, he would show off and give in to his worst impulses.

The story suggests that, as Tony insisted to Dr. Melfi in the season five premiere, there *are* two Tonys: the good one only comes out when he's alone with the truly special people in his life, while the bad one is too easily influenced by people not worth caring about nearly as much.

The rest of the episode runs counter to Christopher's theory, because they show how often *Tony* is the one corrupting others, and not vice versa. The more he's in your life, "Cold Cuts" points out again and again, the worse your life is likely to turn out.

For all of Christopher's resentment of Tony B usurping his status as (to borrow Paulie's phrasing) the teacher's pet, when the two of them are up on the farm with Uncle Pat and his daughter Louise (Judy Del Giudice), they get along famously. They fish together, work efficiently side by side, bond over old vulnerabilities (the kids used to call Tony B "Ichabod Crane"), and crack jokes about their powerful cousin's shape (Tony B: "Our bodies are 86 percent water. His last blood test, he was 65 percent zeppole.").

Even though Chris and Tony B are on the farm to cover up murders, their scenes are bucolic and peaceful in a way *The Sopranos* almost never is, and it's not hard to see Tony's absence as a huge reason why. The moment he turns up at the farm—desperate to get away from Janice and Carmela and all the other sources of frustration back in Jersey—everything falls apart for poor Chris. Where Uncle Pat commended him on how he's done in recovery, Tony mocks him for it ("If you recover your fuckin' balls, give us a call."), and almost immediately, Tony B joins in a present-day reenactment of Chris's stories about how the older cousins used to laugh at at the younger one. Christopher drove up to the farm with Tony B, sharing stories and having a grand old time; he drives home alone, crying at the thought that he'll forever exist outside their club, even all these years later.[49]

---

48 Ralphie's remains were disposed of at a different farm, owned by Mikey Palmice's father.
49 Adriana, trying to cheer him up, suggests he return to screenwriting, or perhaps consider male modeling, which leads to one of the greatest pieces of delusional thinking of the whole series, as Christopher insists, "I'll get back to the writing someday, but from a position of great wealth. As far as male modeling, I'd probably be a success, but I wouldn't want to be around those fuckin' people."

Christopher gets off pretty lightly, though, compared to some of Tony's other victims. At the Bing, poor Georgie endures the most savage beating yet at Tony's hands, all for the minor sin of suggesting the value of living for today while Tony is in the midst of one of his rants about the terrible state of the world. Where his vision eventually recovered from the time Ralphie hit him in the eye, Paulie suggest Tony's beating may leave the bartender with permanent hearing loss, which finally inspires Georgie to quit the Bing and ask to never see Tony again.

As usual, Georgie isn't the one Tony's actually angry with, but he becomes a useful punching bag one last time, in an episode where Tony has abundant cause to feel mad. Johnny Sack continues to squeeze him over the Joey Peeps situation, simply because he can. Carmela[50] drains the pool to keep Tony from swimming in it uninvited, making clear she has no interest in taking him back.

And then there's Janice. When last we saw the siblings together, they had forged a tentative peace. Neither of them has ever been great at impulse control, though: Janice turns violent against a fellow soccer mom in an incident that ends up on TV, brings public shame and new fury to Tony, and forces him and Dr. Melfi to confront the roots of the famous Soprano temper.

"Depression is rage turned inward," Melfi suggests. Tony and Janice's parents were both angry people, but their rage pointed in different directions: Johnny Boy's out, and Livia's in, at least until she had absorbed so much of it that her anger could be expressed toward others in less overt ways. Janice's outburst against the soccer mom, and Tony's against Georgie, are pure Johnny Boy: let the fury build until it has to be unleashed on whoever's in front of you, whether or not they're the one responsible. The soccer incident embarrasses both of them, but proves genuinely useful for Janice, whose court-mandated anger management classes[51] have the desired effect of making her more relaxed and forgiving.

It's perhaps yet another Janice persona, like Parvati—even the world's best therapist couldn't pierce so many layers of emotional damage so quickly—but so long as she's trying, her motivation doesn't matter. She even manages to convince Bobby's daughter Sophia not to ruin her appetite for dinner by sneaking a can of Hawaiian Punch beforehand, simply by noting the child's behavior and staring at her until she complies. This is the kind of de-escalating approach to parent-child

---

50 Carmela also runs into Mr. Wegler, shrugging off his apology for how he acted in their last encounter and instead lying that she's getting back together with Tony, admitting later to Rosalie that she just got mad and wanted to hurt him. (She doesn't have Soprano genes, but she has her own version of the Soprano temper.) The scene ends with a very un-*Sopranos* freeze-frame of an embarrassed Carmela that fits the style of guest director Mike Figgis (*Leaving Las Vegas*), who follows it with an equally un-*Sopranos* wipe into the next scene with the guys up at the farm.

51 Evelyn, the most talkative woman in the anger management group, is played by future *Grey's Anatomy* star Chandra Wilson.

conflict that she and her siblings never experienced. "Mahatma Gandhi over here," says Tony, impressed yet also troubled.

If Janice's newfound restraint is indeed merely a performance, it's one convincing enough to fill Tony with anger and resentment at his own inability to calm down, which leads to a stunning display of anger owing much more to Livia than Johnny Boy. While eating with Janice, Bobby, and their kids, Tony deliberately brings up Janice's estranged *Quebecois* son Harpo, letting her discomfort build until he's openly taunting her by asking, "I wonder what's French Canadian for 'I grew up without a mother.'" And in one fell swoop, he's undone all of Janice's therapy, inciting her to come after him with a fork and curse at him in front of Bobby Jr. and Sophia. His work done, Tony flashes a smirk terrifyingly similar to the look we saw so often on Livia's face when she'd successfully pushed his buttons,[52] and he strides out of his sister's house to walk back to his mother's, insufferably pleased with himself.

Who would do such a thing? Who would look at a sister who has worked very hard to overcome her flaws—flaws that everyone, Tony included, has struggled to tolerate for so long—and tear down all that work in a few minutes out of petty jealousy?

Well, it's like The Kinks song says over the closing credits, which, in a *Sopranos* rarity, plays out while we're still watching the action (in this case, Tony walking home): "I'm Not Like Everybody Else."

 **SEASON 5/EPISODE 11**
WRITTEN BY DAVID CHASE AND MATTHEW WEINER
DIRECTED BY ALLEN COULTER

Three Times a Lady

"Our friend, he's gotta go." —**God**

One of the most divisive episodes of *The Sopranos* during its initial run, "The Test Dream" is often described as having the longest dream sequence in any episode of the show. It only feels that way because Tony's dream here lasts slightly more than twenty minutes and isn't interrupted by real-world scenes, as was the case with the equally long, but more fragmented, dream sequence in season two's "Funhouse."

---

52 See the end of "The Knight in White Satin Armor," when Tony falls down after leaving Livia's house and she can't stop herself from chortling.

This one is a lot more than a glorified retread, though, for three reasons:

1. It's not just about a particular problem or subject, it's about the totality of Tony.

   The dream shows how much has happened to Tony since season two, and how those events and others predating the series continue to affect him, making it a referendum on his entire identity; in "Funhouse," by contrast, the dreams were only about Pussy as an FBI informant. Much of what's weighing on Tony is in here, including the possibility of reconciliation with Carmela, and memories of all the people he was close to who've died (or been killed, possibly by Tony).

2. It demonstrates how much Tony has learned about himself and about how to interpret his own dreams.

   If, as we've suggested, "Funhouse" marks the first time where Tony Soprano truly learns from and correctly interprets the work of his own subconscious mind, then "The Test Dream" is the dream of a more sophisticated self-analyzer who has a stronger sense of who and what matters most to him. Melfi was Melfi in the "Funhouse" dreams, but she was also an all-encompassing stand-in for the largely unknown psychic depths of Tony Soprano, the part of himself that he's only somewhat recently learned to listen and talk to. Tony comes out of the dream knowing that Tony B shot Joey Peeps, which is something he suspected but was in denial about; he is proved right when Chris visits his Plaza Hotel suite to tell him that Tony B killed Phil Leotardo's younger brother Billy, officially dragging the New Jersey crew into New York's civil war and possibly sealing their doom. It feels like a premonition, that part of the dream—though in retrospect it could also just be a coincidence of timing, happening the same day Tony visited Tony B at his mother's house and felt certain that something was off.

3. This is the first dream in which real-world events reflect what's happening in Tony's mind nearly as they're actually occurring.

   While Tony B was killing Billy, Tony was asleep and dreaming of Tony B shooting Phil—a close symbolic match. All the dreams so far have been about what's happening in characters' lives right then and, sometimes, how the past informs the present; but nobody's dreams have correctly predicted something that could happen or was happening *while* they were dreaming.

The episode also offers a sophisticated examination of the dreamlike qualities *The Sopranos* can have even during waking moments. "The Test Dream" begins with two incidents that feel unreal or somehow mysteriously "off." One is Valentina becoming disfigured from an accidental grease fire. The other is Tony checking into the Plaza, including the sequence of dissolves as Tony kills time in his bathrobe, looking like the balding New Jersey silverback cousin of Dave Bowman, the astronaut who makes it to the end of *2001: A Space Odyssey*.

Then the episode officially becomes a dream. It starts with Tony waking up in his bed at the Plaza not next to the sex worker he hired, but rather Carmine Lupertazzi Sr., the deceased head of the New York Family now struggling to make sense of itself in a power vacuum.[53] Shortly before falling asleep in the real world, Tony learns from Silvio that Angelo Garepe's been whacked, probably by Phil Leotardo. He calls Paulie, telling him that Angelo's prison buddy Tony B was "acting all squirrelly" earlier, and that he might seek revenge. "Don't worry about it," Paulie assures him. "He ain't that stupid."

Tony might believe that, but his subconscious has its doubts. Moments after he scrambles out of bed with Carmine, the phone rings. Carmine fears it's "the man upstairs," looking to bring him back to his final reward. The voice on the other end is, indeed, a higher power: David Chase, the creator and god of *The Sopranos* universe. His word is law, and his word is, "Our friend,"—Tony B—"he's gotta go."

The anchor of the ensuing dream is its end, an apparently recurring conversation with Molinaro, his high school gym coach (Charlie Scalies),[54] which Carmela says is about feeling unprepared.[55] The dream is followed by a secondary character (Chris) appearing, as if summoned by the hero's psychic distress. The episode ends with Tony and Carmela unpacking the dream's contents. Their scene ends visually (with a cut to black) while the audio continues for two more lines of dialogue, suggesting what it feels like to drift off to sleep mid-conversation.

Throughout "The Test Dream," the flow between scenes, images, locations, and ideas is as sophisticated as anything that's been produced for American cinema or television. Looking back, it's difficult to remember what was real and what was a dream, and as the resolution of this one suggests, maybe the distinction was always more porous than we thought.

The part of the dream that most strongly affects Tony is where he imagines Tony B shooting Phil, first with a gun, then with his finger (perhaps an indication that Tony's mind somehow *knew* it wasn't Phil that got shot in real life; or a warn-

---

53 Right before Carmine suffered the stroke that killed him, he said he smelled burning hair. Shortly before the dream begins, Tony complains to Tony B that he can't get rid of the burning hair smell from Valentina's kitchen accident.

54 That Molinaro holds such a prominent place in Tony's unconscious mind speaks to why he gets so upset every time Uncle Junior tells him he didn't have the makings of a varsity athlete.

55 The whole sequence follows the classic test-anxiety dream, usually a nightmare about having to take an exam for which one hasn't studied. Losing teeth is another common event in these dreams, and Tony loses several over the course of his journey, before the bullets fall out of his gun, tooth-like, as he prepares to kill Coach Molinaro.

ing that Phil would be emotionally "injured" by what happened that night—not "ended" by Tony B—but would be back for revenge soon enough). Tony S gets chased through the streets by villagers, an explicit *Frankenstein* reference but also an expression of a general fear of mob/Mob retaliation (the Mob will hold Tony S responsible for Tony B's actions regardless). Tony's takeaway here is that his cousin is out of control, and at some point he'll have to fix the situation, and not with a stern talking-to.

But there's a lot more going on as well, stuff pertaining to Tony's current life and his psyche. The phrase "free-associative" gets bandied regarding nontraditional film storytelling, but here it fits. There are visual and verbal puns in "The Test Dream"; images and situations that connect many characters, plot points, or metaphors; and multiple plausible ways of interpreting the same moment—not canceling each other out but coexisting.

Just look at how it deals with one small aspect, the presence of Charmaine Bucco: Tony's sort-of-crush, an object of affection that'll never be reciprocal because of her outspoken disapproval of his gangsterism. Artie is connected to Charmaine, in the dream and in life, for many different reasons. He's there because he's Charmaine's husband (separated, like Tony from Carmela, but not yet divorced). But he's also in there because, like Tony B fresh out of prison, he represents the capacity to reform and improve. Past episodes have suggested Artie was a hellraiser back when he and Tony were running around the school hallways and Newark streets, a point reiterated here, with Artie replacing one person in a carload of individuals who otherwise all died violently, guiding Tony to the men's room, rescuing Tony from the angry villagers, and (wishful thinking on Tony's part) coaching him(!!!) through sex with Charmaine: "She likes it when you rub her muzzle."

Let's zero in on that "muzzle" line. It connects to the horses near the Plaza Hotel (which Tony notices and comments on) but also to Pie-O-My and Tracee "the thoroughbred." Ralphie, another character in the dream, definitely killed one of them, maybe both. The line also connects with a verbal near-rhyme that was driven home, via repeated use in season three, by all the gangsters who didn't think Tracee's death was worth getting upset about: they dismissed her as a "hooer"—a "whore," which sounds like "horse." And lo and behold, the dream cuts to Tony in the living room of his former home, high on his horse looking down at Carmela on the couch, animal and rider dominating the space (the equivalent of the elephant in the room—the obvious presence that's taboo to discuss). Carmela warns Tony that if he's going to move back in with her, "You can't have your horse in here."[56]

---

56 Possibly including Charmaine, whom, if Tony had an affair with her, Carm would see as another of his "hooers."

She pronounces the word like "whores": *You can't have your whores in here.* "I'll clean up after her," Tony promises. "You always say that," Carmela counters.[57]

This happens sometimes in dreams: a cascade of possible meanings you try to seize, only to see them bleed through your fingers and assume another shape on the ground: a row of droplets, or one large stain. One such bleed happens in the therapy scene where Melfi is replaced by Gloria (who sometimes speaks in Melfi's voice—Melfi was right to say that Tony has a thing for obstinate, dark-haired women). The conversation between therapist and patient becomes an admission of Tony's violence against women ("And then you choked the shit out of me!" yells Gloria).

Another occurs in the long sequence where Tony and Carmela get ready to meet Finn's parents and then share a meal with them at Vesuvio. He "awakens" in his home and goes downstairs to find Carmela in the kitchen, fully dressed for their meal, and says he can't go because he doesn't have anything to wear. He sees *Chinatown* playing on a TV in the kitchen bookshelf, next to a couple of *Better Homes and Gardens* cookbooks (corruption nestled comfortably amid the trappings of suburbia). Carmela chastises him for getting lost in the film instead of paying attention to her, telling him, "Your head is filled with this stuff."

"It's just that it's so much more interesting . . . than life," he says.

"This *is* your life," she replies, indicating the movie—an acknowledgment that, in certain ways, Tony's life *is* like the films he loves so much; but also perhaps that this particular story, *Chinatown*, fits Tony better than he would admit. (He probably thinks he's Jake Gittes, but he's more like Noah Cross, minus the incest: a man who can order other men killed.) The movie then changes to the 1951 version of *A Christmas Carol*, in which a greedy old rich man has a change of heart after being visited by spirits (as Tony is visited throughout this dream).

Television sets and movie clips recur throughout, connecting the dream with movies, television, Tony's life, and the notion of being under surveillance. The never-before-seen men's room attendant in this "Dream Vesuvio" watches a close-up of Tony and Vin Makazian's feet entering the lounge area outside the toilets. He could be either an FBI agent posing as help, or somebody on a film crew checking the framing of a shot on a monitor. *High Noon*, starring Tony's beloved Gary Cooper as a sheriff abandoned by townsfolk to face assassins alone, plays on the TV as he and Carmela enter the restaurant. It's a comment on the mental state of a man hoping to make a good impression on his possible future in-laws while realizing he's about to lose his little girl to adulthood. But *High Noon* also

---

57 Surprisingly assured horsemanship here by Gandolfini, who is not an actor you'd expect to see in a saddle.

speaks to the fact that, whatever happens with the New York–New Jersey Mob situation, Tony will likely have to face it alone, without allies.

It's all bleeding together here: multiple meanings or interpretations, blurred movie and dream realities. Vin Makazian is himself but also Finn's father (maybe because Vin rhymes with Finn), singing "Three Times a Lady" to his irritated wife, Annette Bening, costar of *Bugsy* (the title of which she mentions after watching Tony B shoot Phil[58]). Vin and Tony are both Michael Corleone, excusing themselves to go to the restroom to retrieve a hidden gun à la *The Godfather* (Bening worries that her husband is going to return with "just his cock in his hand" instead of a gun, paraphrasing a famous line from the film). At the urinals, Tony hands Vin a copy of *The Valachi Papers*, a 1968 nonfiction book about a mobster that was made into a 1972 Charles Bronson film that got buried at the box office in the wake of the far more popular *Godfather*. Perhaps the film's most memorable line is Bronson's assassin admitting, "I cannot bring back the dead. I can only kill the living."—a sentiment that resonates with this particular dream, and with *The Sopranos* as a whole. "Well, the piece wasn't behind the toilet," Vin says. "Well, this is real life," Tony tells him. "No, it's not," Vin replies, whereupon there's a tremendous explosion outside, and the dream shifts into Tony B shooting Phil and Tony Soprano becoming a monster hounded by a mob/the Mob.[59]

If we remind ourselves that every single thing happening here is a product of Tony's imagination, and compare this dream to past ones, we can see how much more sophisticated a dreamer Tony has become—almost certainly as a result of his regular conversations with Melfi, who (in various ways) stands in for Tony's subconscious itself whenever he dreams. He's aware that he's dreaming, as seen in the many conversations that discuss movies versus life and the screens strewn throughout, serving as transitions and bridging movies and reality. "You know, douchebag," he tells Mikey, "I realize I'm dreaming."

But what will he do with this dream?

---

58 The *Bugsy* quote is prompted by a question from Gloria, playing a TV newswoman, calling on Bening by name while reporting on the Tony B–Phil incident. It would be the strangest moment in the dream, except for all the others.

59 And being shot at by Lee Harvey Oswald, because JFK (and maybe Fran Felstein) is still lingering in Tony's head, too.

"LONG TERM PARKING" SEASON 5/EPISODE 12
WRITTEN BY TERENCE WINTER
DIRECTED BY TIM VAN PATTEN

Take Off and Drive

"How could you fuckin' do this to us?!" —**Christopher**

She was dead the minute she got in the car.

Not the car that Silvio uses to drive Adriana to the desolate woods where he murders her for ratting to the FBI at the end of one of the most devastating hours of the entire series. No, she was dead the minute she got in the FBI car, back in season four's "No Show," when Deborah Ciccerone outed herself as an agent and invited her target to come back to headquarters.

Once Ade got in that car, talked to federal agents, and didn't ask for a lawyer, it was over for her. Had she refused, she might have done a year or two in prison for the cocaine the FBI found in the club, maybe been shunned by Christopher and the rest of the Family, even had to start her entire life over from scratch. But she would have been alive. Even the sin of bringing an undercover Fed into Tony's house shouldn't have been a death sentence, because Tony *really* liked Adriana, as we saw in "Irregular Around the Margins"—and what did Ciccerone actually see for the two minutes she stood in the atrium?

But as soon as Adriana got in that car without protest, everything changed. She didn't know it, because she was too naive to think or do otherwise. Maybe Ciccerone and Harris convinced themselves that it wouldn't end the way it does. But for the two seasons where Ade was a reluctant FBI cooperator, that ugly scene in the woods—Adriana crawling through the fallen leaves, sobbing as Silvio (who has just tried to drag her out of the car while calling her a "fuckin' cunt") walks purposefully behind her and draws his gun—was sadly a matter of when, not if.

Adriana's slow-motion tragedy was unusual even for a series this dark. She wasn't wholly innocent. She knew what Christopher did for a living, and even assisted in some crimes out of fear, like covering up the murder at the club that finally goads Sanseverino to order her to flip Christopher or go to jail for twenty-five years instead of the original two. But she was also in way over her head, with no one to trust, trapped in a cycle of shame and abuse and addiction with Christopher, her handler pushing her to do things that would doom her. And because she didn't know better at any point—particularly on that fateful afternoon when she was just out walking Cosette—she kept doing them.

And it got her killed.

In the larger scheme of the series, Adriana's death isn't as important as several other developments in "Long Term Parking," chief among them the resurrection of the Soprano marriage. Carmela gives in not because she wants to, but because she's exhausted from failing to find another path in life besides the one involving the bear of a man she married. The Wegler affair suggested she would never be accepted as something more than a Mob boss's wife, and Tony made it impossible for her to get the divorce settlement she'd need to start fresh. "Marco Polo" showed she still has feelings for Tony, but she has no illusions. Tony can't even bother with the pretense that he'll stop cheating, promising only that his affairs won't publicly embarrass Carmela anymore. This is a business arrangement: Tony gets to come home, and Carmela gets the small fortune needed so she and her father can build a spec house. Though the two will eventually feel a bit flirty once Tony has moved back in, the resigned nature of the whole arrangement is conveyed in two shots: the perfunctory kiss on the cheek he gives her at Vesuvio once they've finalized the deal, and the way Tim Van Patten and director of photography Alik Sakharov shoot Tony from so far away when he finally returns to the house as a resident. He looks small and insignificant, even though he got what he wanted, because even he knows how empty the relationship is.

And as Tony reconnects with one old partner, another drifts further away. Billy Leotardo's murder leaves Phil out for revenge—conveyed in a haunting piece of acting by Frank Vincent, where we see Phil sitting at the bar flashing back on his brother's death, eyes burning with equal parts regret and rage—and Little Carmine looking for a way to keep this "fuckin' stagmire" from getting him killed, too. So he concedes the leadership to Johnny Sack, who takes to the job as if to the manor born, imperiously telling Tony their meetings at the usual spot by the river are over, because "it's undignified."

The civil war is over, but the Tony B matter remains unsettled. He's hiding at Uncle Pat's farm from "Cold Cuts," but calling Tony out of guilt, fear, or both, and then hanging up for the same reason. Finally he stays on the line long enough for Tony to confess the truth about his panic attack on the night Tony B got arrested. Like a lot of Tony's confessions (see also informing Ralphie about Valentina while Justin is in the ICU back in "Whoever Did This"), the timing is self-serving: Tony B's too far away and in too much trouble to do anything about it, and Tony is doing it to even the score between them so he'll feel less guilty about tracing the call and potentially turning him into Johnny and Phil. Instead, despite the threat that

Phil could take revenge on Christopher[60] in lieu of the Soprano cousin he wants to murder, Tony keeps stalling on giving Johnny the location, and refuses to do it outright because he's so offended by Johnny talking down to him after ascending to the throne. Although later he'll help arrange to murder the love of Christopher's life, when it's Tony's responsibility to facilitate the death of someone he cares more deeply about, he flinches.

This is the one bit of good news for Adriana in the whole doomed mess, because Tony's defense of Tony B at Christopher's possible expense leaves Chris disillusioned about "the guy I'm goin' to Hell for," and thus more open to the idea of going into witness protection when Adriana makes her pitch.

That is not his first reaction to hearing the news, though. Instead—in a scene that, by itself, probably won Michael Imperioli and Drea de Matteo their Emmys[61]—the information at first seems to break something inside him. Christopher gets twitchier throughout her story, the camera pushing in on his face, until the mention of the murder at the club—and what that means for the both of them—gets to be too much, and he turns pure animal: punching her in the face, choking her (as he did over the thought of her infidelity in "Irregular Around the Margins"), screaming in a guttural voice, "My God! What are we gonna do?!" And as many abuse victims reflexively do, Adriana apologizes for putting Christopher in this predicament, and they hug and weep together.

It's an astonishingly raw scene—closer to the intensity of some of the Tony–Carmela fights in "Whitecaps" than could be expected from any *Sopranos* scene not featuring them—and in the hours of offscreen conversation that follow, it appears the catharsis was enough for Christopher to realize how bad this is, and how their only salvation is to take the FBI deal and hide.

But like everyone in this world, including his cousin Carmela, the prospect of becoming someone different is more than he can handle. While clearing his head before agreeing fully to the FBI offer,[62] he stops to gas up his ridiculous Hummer and is struck by a glimpse of a poorer family traveling in a beat-up Chevy Citation: the life (mullet and all) that could be Christopher's if he flips on

---

60 *Sopranos* didn't reference Springsteen often, even with his guitar player at Tony's side for all those years, but Michael Imperioli gets to quote one of the most famous Bruce lyrics of them all (from "Born to Run") when Chris explains he was late for a meeting because the "Highway was jammed with broken heroes on a last-chance power drive." (To the show's credit, it is not followed with a winking close-up of Steve Van Zandt; he's shot from a distance, his expression impassive.)

61 Terence Winter's script also won an Emmy, and surely contributed heavily to the series finally winning its first Outstanding Drama Series Emmy.

62 For the most part, it's hard to blame the FBI agents for the various murders that seem to happen right under their noses. If there's a weakness to "Long Term Parking," though, it's that it seems very dubious that Sanseverino would allow Adriana to be alone and unmonitored for so long, given the risk of... well, of exactly what happens. Even if Ade wouldn't wear a wire, would it have hurt to have a few cars stationed near the apartment to see who goes where?

the Family. It's more than he can bear, and he not only rats Adriana out to Tony and Sil, but later helps cover up her murder, tossing a suitcase full of her clothes into the same clearing under the Turnpike where Tony nearly executed him in "Irregular Around the Margins," then ditching her car in a Newark Airport lot. Once he was willing to die rather than live in a world where his fiancée had slept with his mentor; here, he chooses Tony over Ade, and even if he's so broken up over the choice that he falls off the wagon after, he still made the terrible choice. (As a wise woman once said: Poor you.)

But back to Silvio's car. We never see Adriana get into it, and the episode briefly shows her driving herself down south, far away from people who have no real regard for her or her safety, the radio blasting Shawn Smith's "Leaving California," a song whose lyrics advise driving away as fast as possible—though that line ironically only plays after the daydream is revealed for what it is. Nor do we see the moment when Christopher fesses up to Tony and the others, nor even Adriana's actual death. That last choice led many fans to make like Sanseverino and try to concoct a version of the story where Adriana wasn't dead. Even the episode's final scene, with Tony and Carmela in the vacant lot where she intends to build her spec house, opens up with a shot of the trees designed to evoke the ones we saw when the camera panned up at the moment of Adriana's murder, teasing us with the possibility that we'd be returning to that first set of trees to witness Adriana climb to her feet, bloody but still very much alive.

None of these fake outs are really convincing, but we want them to be. And their cumulative power suggests David Chase, Terence Winter, and everyone else involved felt the same way. They didn't want Adriana to die any more than we did, and crafted an episode that tantalizingly suggested that she might not.

But this story only ever had one ending.

SEASON 5/EPISODE 13
"ALL DUE RESPECT" WRITTEN BY DAVID CHASE AND ROBIN GREEN & MITCHELL BURGESS
DIRECTED BY JOHN PATTERSON

Glad Tidings

"It's my mess. All my choices were wrong." —**Tony**

"Two Tonys," the first episode of season five, concluded with Tony Soprano sitting in a patio chair at night, awaiting the return of the black bear, assault rifle locked and loaded. He was the hunter. The bear was his prey.

"All Due Respect," season five's last episode, seems to resolve the matter of there being two Tonys, in that Tony murders Tony B in hopes of resolving the feud with New York. But does it really? Not only does Tony wind up as both the hunter and the bear at different stages of the episode—gunning down Tony B with a shotgun before his cousin is even aware he's there, and later emerging, bear-like, from the trees behind his house—but the episode, and the season, keep circling the idea that the two Tonys are really the same Tony, just manifested in different contexts.

We were told in "Rat Pack" that the two cousins—who were really more like brothers—were indistinguishable growing up, down to the first name, and the season made this manifest. They could've had each others' lives if not for circumstance. Tony's greatest weakness is his impulsivity, and how his temper often outpaces his rational mind. Tony B is presented as a more extreme example of that, as his death at his cousin's hands results from three unnecessary outbursts: beating Mr. Kim right when he's on the verge going legit, agreeing to the Joey Peeps hit after simmering in envy of his cousin, and gunning for the Leotardo brothers because he can't let Angelo's murder sit. All these tantrums lead to Tony B lying dead on Uncle Pat's porch.

The Tonys' name thing becomes impossible to overlook, too. Our protagonist gets to be just Tony, where this other man—completely new, but treated as a crucial piece of Tony's origin story, with whom everyone else on the show has a preexisting relationship—has to go by Tony B. He is the Plan B version of Tony, the Tony our Tony almost was, the chaotic not-quite-twin who brings out the "real" Tony's worst impulses (as Christopher insisted to Adriana back in "Cold Cuts"). It can seem like Tony dreamed him up as a way to see how a darker version of his life would have gone, just as he dreamed about Tony B going after the Leotardos as it was happening, as if he conjured the hit into reality.[63]

Tony B isn't a dream, nor Tyler Durden, nor any other literary device. Everybody sees him, everybody knows him, and episodes like "Sentimental Education" and "Marco Polo" lay out the small, messy quality of his life in a way that seems antithetical to dream logic. But there's something about him—or about any character introduced this late in a series who has such a shared history with longer-established characters—that isn't quite . . . right. Tony B exists, but it's almost as

---

63 Tony B and Gloria Trillo would have a lot to talk about. Both are fully realized, real individuals who also exist somewhere on the edge of metaphor, and seem to have materialized within the fiction of the show as manifestations of Tony Soprano's psychological issues. Gloria is an embodiment of Tony S's wish to both please and destroy his mother, while Tony B reflects Tony's easily bruised ego, his tendency to remain charming even as he bullies weaker people, his insatiable hunger for more, his inability to walk the straight and narrow, and the impulse control problems that impact everyone else in his life.

if he isn't meant to, and his continued presence in the narrative keeps causing problems for everyone else.[64]

"All Due Respect"—the title inspired by a marvelous (and Mob-ubiquitous) introductory phrase that allows the speaker to evade repercussions for any following insult—is all about Tony coming to accept that his cousin shouldn't be alive anymore, and that he has to be the one to kill him.

This is not an easy process for either him or his guys. He bolts early from a wiseguy dinner honoring Ray Curto because he knows all the captains and their lieutenants are seething over his reluctance to give Phil and New York what they want. His popularity in the Family is at such a low ebb that after Benny Fazio winds up with a fractured skull courtesy of Phil and his guys, Vito openly suggests it might be time for them to take out their own boss. Even Sil is willing to suggest this current mess came about because Tony's pride kicked in when Johnny started treating him like the hired help.

"You got no fuckin' idea what it's like to be number one," Tony replies, as oblivious to the Soprano crew's discontent as John was to his. "Every decision you make affects every facet of every other fuckin' thing. It's too much to deal with almost. And in the end, you're completely alone with it all."

It's a long-ignored member of the crew who gives him the final push toward a decision, the Pie-O-My painting improbably becoming a plot device. Tony pays a surprise visit to Paulie's home—with Paulie noting that Tony's increasingly rare stops there are one of the reasons he felt secure in putting the painting up—and is offended to see both that Paulie disobeyed his orders about destroying the thing, and had him retouched to look like "a goddamn lawn jockey."

"That's not a lawn jockey," Paulie insists. "That's a general."

Tony loves his military history (he's watching yet another documentary about legendary German officer Erwin Rommel when Carmela talks to him about the spec house), and as he stares at the painting one more time,[65] he considers what it would mean for him to make decisions that sacrifice men he loves for the greater good of the campaign.

We've already heard Van Morrison's "Glad Tidings" when Christopher meets with Silvio while hiding out from Phil. The song rises on the soundtrack again as Tony recognizes what he has to do. Tony B returns to the farm with groceries, and we hear the lyric "And we'll send you glad tidings from New York" as he exits the barn with his bags, and then "Hope that you will come right on time" just before

---

64 Those problems extended to *The Sopranos* writers themselves, who intended Tony B to stick around for the remainder of the series, only to realize they painted themselves into a corner, and that Tony B had to die after killing Billy.

65 And steps in rotten eggs, because eggs so often signal death on this show.

Tony steps out from another corner of the wraparound porch and ventilates his favorite cousin with a shotgun before he can defend himself or even recognize he's about to die. This is not the kind of rage-filled killing we've seen Tony commit on Ralphie or Pussy or Matt Bevilaqua; this is Tony the hunter stalking and killing prey. It's a clean, cold kill. Even Febby Petrulio got a few last words and a chance to beg for his life.

Though Tony B didn't exist for us before this season, James Gandolfini's performance makes it clear just how much his presence meant to Tony, and why he risked death at his cousin's hand rather than let Phil handle it. Tony B was, for a time, everything to Tony, and then he was gone, and then he came back like a specter of the past, to haunt our man for all the mistakes and regrets and lucky breaks he's made and felt over a lifetime. "I paid enough, John. I paid a lot," Tony tells Johnny Sack as they bring the feud to an end, and there is such pain on Gandolfini's face and in his voice that it's as if we'd also known Tony B all our lives.

The guys in the crew appreciate the sacrifice, too, but the finale mostly finds things far better for Tony at home, where he and Carmela are still making nice post-reconciliation—even if she dresses sexier for a snuggle session with the spec house blueprint[66] than she does for her husband—and where AJ and his friend Patrick (Paul Dano[67]) have such success throwing a party with their own money that AJ becomes excited about the idea of becoming an event planner. (Neither parent understands this idea, but both accept it as a fallback for their screw-up son that they can live with.)

Even the season's concluding minutes have Tony fleeing Mob business to get back to his family by any means necessary. Moments after he and Johnny broker a truce, armed FBI agents raid the house to bust the new boss of New York, sending Tony sprinting through the woods—fleeing prey in a very expensive suit. This turns out to be unnecessary, as Tony's lawyer explains when his client calls mid-flight that one of Johnny's captains has flipped, but only on other Brooklyn wiseguys. Tony's not at risk of arrest, but he's now so much closer to his own house than to Johnny's that it makes sense to keep walking home.

Before, it was Tony B who hid out in nature. Now it's Tony S—or perhaps we should call *him* Tony B now, since the finale ends with Tony emerging from the backyard tree line just as the black bear did in the premiere (the episode's chorus "Glad Tidings" rising for a third time on the soundtrack). Tony was always the bear as much as the hunter, but this last scene literalizes the Tony Bear of it all:

---

66 Hugh's old pal Ignatz, who has designed the spec house, is played by Bob Shaw, the series' longtime production designer.

67 Another of the show's innumerable cameos by future stars: Dano would become an indie film sensation in such features as *There Will Be Blood*, *Meek's Cutoff*, and *Love & Mercy*.

like the ursine interloper in "Two Tonys," more of a threat to this home in theory than in reality. Where once he turned up at the house without warning and drove Carmela mad, here his arrival instead invites her sympathy and concern: "What happened to you? Your shoes are soaking wet."

Tony has put his life back together, at work and at home, but he paid to do it—a lot. Now there's just the one Tony again, though he contains multitudes.

Season
Six

 SEASON 6/EPISODE 1
WRITTEN BY TERENCE WINTER
DIRECTED BY TIM VAN PATTEN

The Noose

"I don't care how close you are. In the end, friends are going to let you down. Family; they're the only ones you can count on." —**Tony**

Talk about starting with a bang.

"Members Only" breaks from *The Sopranos*'s traditional slow-building intro by jam-packing two hours of plot into sixty minutes and capping the episode with one of its most startling violent acts: defanged, housebound, senile Uncle Junior shoots Tony in the torso at close range. It's vintage *Sopranos*, expected yet somehow surprising, and twisted and pathetic rather than superficially exciting. You always figured Tony might get shot again, but not like *this*. It's downright humiliating, especially when director Tim Van Patten cuts to a God's-eye-view shot of fat, bloody Tony lying on the kitchen floor, laboring to hoist his bathroom-scale-certified 280 pounds high enough to grab the wall phone and call 911.

Heading into what was billed as the final season (but would later be split into two that aired across two years, even if HBO insisted on referring to both as "season six" for contractual purposes), the show's new-school version of classical filmmaking craft is at an all-time high. Every camera move, shot, cut, and line is charged with a sense of purpose. Van Patten and Winter weave symbolic images and lines into the narrative—elements that confirm the season's preoccupation with score settling, moral accountability, the need to confront one's own mortality, and the realization that joining the Mob is a lifetime commitment to evil—without being flashy about it.

"The bonefish are back in season," Tony tells Carmela while indulging their marriage-building habit of dining in fancy restaurants. The season's opening music montage—set to a dance club remix of William S. Burroughs reading fragments of his poem "Seven Souls," which describes a "director" who "directs the film of your life from conception to death"—shows a bit of a Carmela dream in which she hangs out in the bare wood skeleton of the spec house she's building on Tony's dime, and smokes a cigarette with the ghost of Adriana. It's significant that Tony and Carmela would externalize the idea of a new beginning for their dysfunctional marriage by building a new house. It's also significant that this house would be contaminated, in Carmela's dream, by the appearance of a woman who was "disappeared" for daring to go against the Family; and that Carmela would later run afoul of a building inspector because Carmela's supervisor dad cut costs with substandard material and assumed (wrongly) that Tony's government connections would get him a pass.

Not for nothing is the episode's organizing image a noose. Chase and company seem to be tightening the rope around every character's neck, forcing them to consider how their crime-funded personal adventures might end. Eugene Pontecorvo tries to leave Mob life and start over in Florida with his wife and kids; upon being told his blood oath will never permit that, he hangs himself in his garage. Van Patten's camera lingers in wide shot on Eugene's body as it dangles like the phone receiver Tony can't grab. As in *Macbeth*, the finale of *Deadwood*, and Steven Spielberg's *Munich*, the blood from bloody murder leaves a moral as well as physical stain. (The sight of Eugene trying to wipe a blood drop from his cheek after a hit is very "Out, damned spot!"—the result of the sort of act that yokes him to the organization forever.)

You can view Tony's shooting as near-death, but also as a chance for rebirth. People who survive this level of trauma sometimes go on to remake their lives. The overhead shot of Tony on the floor of Junior's kitchen is redolent not just of birth (or rebirth) but of the Hanged Man in the Tarot Card deck: a serene-looking figure suspended upside down from the Living World tree. "This is the card of ultimate surrender," a Tarot guide summarizes, "of being suspended in time and of martyrdom and sacrifice to the greater good. This is the archetype to meditate on to help break old patterns of behavior and bad habits that restrict you." But where can Tony escape to? His responsibilities leave him even less maneuvering room than Eugene.

As Tony once told Dr. Melfi, there are only two outcomes for guys like him: "Dead, or in the can." For now, everyone will fixate on the bullet he just caught, but this possibility of jail time looms, too. Judging from the sudden death of snitch Ray Curto[1] and the revelation that Eugene was a pigeon as well, there are as many rats in this Family as straight-up gangsters.

That the premiere devotes so much time to the life and death of Eugene, whose outdated wardrobe provides the episode with its title,

---

1 The episode wrings several dark laughs from Agent Sanseverino's increasingly gloomy mood. First she was Adriana's handler, and even she has to know by now that Ade's pushing up daisies. Then she's put in charge of Ray Curto, and he kacks right in front of her (just as he's finally starting to provide useful intel, after years of stringing previous handlers along). By the time she's introduced to Eugene, she may as well be wearing a black robe and carrying a scythe. This is the character's final appearance, so we have to imagine her response to learning of Eugene's suicide, but it probably involves an exasperated sigh and a sentiment like, "Yeah, that sounds about right."

only adds to the disorientation that kicks off with "Seven Souls" and the Adriana dream.[2]

If the audience knew Eugene at all, it was as the tall and skinny guy always seen with Vito in one of the show's easier running sight gags,[3] or perhaps they confused him with Cousin Brian a time or three. Now suddenly he's at the center of the action, trying desperately to let both Tony and his FBI handlers let him move his family to Florida in a bid to pull his son out of drug addiction, and we're expected to care about his hopes and dreams in a single hour?

Amazingly, this deepest of bench plays works, because the story's not *really* about Eugene. Yes, all the details are specific to his heretofore unseen life, including the miraculous news of an inheritance, and Robert Funaro effectively sells Eugene's despair at being trapped. But this story could have been about anybody from a regular to a guest star. It's about how hard it is for anyone in this life to get out alive, a lesson driven home not only by Eugene dangling from the end of a rope for what feels like hours, but by the agonizing cliffhanger, which leaves Tony on the brink of death partly because he forgot to charge his cell phone.

The past catches up to Tony throughout. Junior's dementia has him convinced that Little Pussy Malanga—the man responsible for Tony and Junior's feud in the pilot, when Tony conspired to prevent Junior from whacking Little Pussy at Vesuvio—is back and out for revenge. When he mistakes Tony for Malanga in the final scene, it's like the Alzheimer's is giving Junior a chance to rewrite history, wiping out Malanga and his nephew with one bullet.

Before the shooting, Junior's an obvious candidate for Green Grove, but Tony's still so damaged over what happened when he sent Livia there that he's completely turned around on the subject. Far from insisting it's "a retirement community," now he's saying the opposite to Melfi and opposing his sisters' attempt to move Junior. By refusing to do the thing that got him shot at in the first season, he sets events in motion to get shot at again. That, folks, is irony so pure even AJ might be able to recognize it.

Tony's centrality to the series' narrative and themes cloaks him in a kind of plot armor that takes some of the sting out of the cliffhanger, despite Van Patten and Winter's skillful staging. But the fact that the season gets to such a huge moment of violence so early is an ominous sign of just how close we are to the end.

As Carmela puts it during her dream, "I'm worried, Ade."

---

2   More disorientation: the meta touch of having Agent Harris's new partner Ron Goddard (Michael Kelly) paraphrase H. L. Mencken ("Nobody ever went broke underestimating the taste of the American public"), followed by an ailing Harris (who picked up an intestinal parasite on assignment overseas) lunging from the car and puking on the sidewalk. It's as if show is admitting that it's on the verge of getting sick of itself.

3   And even that sight gag loses its punch here, with Vito considerably svelter after actor Joseph Gannascoli lost a significant amount of weight between seasons.

Adriana's ghost assures her, "Everybody's worried."

"No," Carmela elaborates, "I am worried *all the time*."

And with good reason.

 **"JOIN THE CLUB"**
SEASON 6/EPISODE 2
WRITTEN BY DAVID CHASE
DIRECTED BY DAVID NUTTER

Heating Systems

"I mean, who am I? Where am I going?" —**Tony**

Once again zigging where the audience expects him to zag, David Chase follows up on Tony's grisly shooting with . . . another Tony? This one isn't boss of the Jersey Mob, but a precision optics salesman who speaks with James Gandolfini's everyday accent. He has a wife who is not Carmela (or at least is not voiced by Edie Falco when we hear her on the phone) and a pair of younger kids. And when, during a business trip to Costa Mesa, California, he has an opportunity to sleep with a fellow traveling salesperson, he loses his nerve, suggesting, "I could even be some other guy tonight and get away with the whole shebang. But no, I blow it."

Once again, we are somehow in the realm of two Tonys. Three, really: our man, who is eventually shown barely clinging to life in the ICU; the optics salesman who shares his name; and Kevin Finnerty, a heating salesman who apparently resembles both Tonys and inadvertently swaps briefcases and identities with this alterna-Tony.

The Tony we know appears at the eleven minute mark, pulling out his breathing tubes and repeating the salesman Tony's line about wondering who he is and where he's going.[4] Eleven minutes is an eternity in TV storytelling, particularly in the aftermath of such a messy cliffhanger, and it's easy to imagine the "less yakkin', more whackin'" contingent grumbling, "Of all the times to do another dream sequence. . . ."

But is that what this is? The Costa Mesa scenes are laden with symbolism, but they play out more coherently than anything in "Funhouse" or "The Test Dream."

What if this is not a dream? What if it's Purgatory?

---

4 This line—the whole Costa Mesa adventure, in fact—was inspired by something longtime *Sopranos* director John Patterson mysteriously said while hospitalized and dying of cancer in between production of seasons five and six.

Here Tony's stuck in Orange County,[5] with no way to leave (Purgatory). On one end of town is a shining beacon (Heaven), on the other, a raging forest fire (Hell). Over and over, he stops to assess the worth of his life. Then, having lost his own wallet and all the ID and credit cards needed to prove who he is, he steals the identity (sin) of Kevin Finnerty—a heating salesman who lives in one of the hottest states of the union (Arizona)—checks into another hotel, and falls down a red staircase, at which point he learns he has Alzheimer's (eternal damnation). While Carmela's busy in the real world telling him he's not going to Hell, Tony's in Purgatory, debating whether to tell his wife this is exactly the fate he has coming to him.

Granted, it may be splitting hairs to argue that this is a Purgatorial vision rather than a dream. Religious scenarios and dreams employ similar visual language; both bring us back to moral choice, and push us to ask big (often rhetorical) questions. When the Costa Mesa television asks, "Are sin, disease, and death real?," it flashes an implied answer, a yellow crucifix. (Translation: they are, so watch yourself.)

This is not a new approach for *The Sopranos*. In "Funhouse," a food-poisoned Tony understood the toxic truth about Pussy but couldn't digest it. Likewise, it hardly seems an accident that Tony sustained injuries to the pancreas, which neutralizes acid, and the gallbladder, which creates bile (he always had anger management issues). Nor does it seem accidental that the risk of sepsis is described as "an infection in the blood," since lots of other things are "in the blood" of a family, including Alzheimer's and a propensity for depression or violence (those "putrid" Soprano genes). Also worth noting: a bar patron, making small talk with salesman Tony, name-checks a specific type of car, the Infinity (without end); the bartender jokes, "Around here, it's dead," and pronounces "Finnerty" so that it sounds like, "finity" (finite, or limited). Of all the characters to rebuke Finnerty, Chase picks men of God—monks!—and has them be enraged over Finnerty's installation of a defective heating system. Tony has two job options: heating systems (Hell) or precision optics (clarity of vision).

But where Tony's subconscious mind would throw all these symbols into some nonsensical, ever-changing narrative (now Big Pussy's a fish, now Gloria Trillo's a TV reporter interviewing Annette Bening, who is both herself and Finn's mom), what we see in Costa Mesa is both more straightforward and more portentous. It feels like Tony is being judged for his terrible choices, and directed to pon-

---

5   The adjective "orange" is loaded with associations for *Sopranos* viewers. On an emergency preparedness chart, it's one level below red, the color typically indicating the worst conditions, and that happens to be the color of fire and most modern representations of Satan (when he's not pitch-black). Also, the *Godfather* trilogy has an entire mythology built around oranges, which usually herald an impending death or comment on greed and arrogance.

der the loss of identity that landed him in an ICU bed. First he's transformed into a more innocuous and meek version of himself, then forced to become Finnerty in order to obtain food and shelter, then told by a Costa Mesa doctor that he'll soon be losing himself altogether due to the Alzheimer's.

When asked for his name by the doctor, Tony/Finnerty laments, "What does it matter? I'm not going to know myself soon."

This is not merely a medical crisis but a moral and spiritual one. We can attribute these visions to trauma (and perhaps drugs). But it seems wiser to assume that the series, which periodically intimated the existence of other planes of being—remember Pussy in the mirror at Livia's funeral?—is tipping its hand here, and flat-out telling us that it believes in things the senses can't verify.

As both parallel and stylistic counterweight to the Costa Mesa scenes, everything happening in the reality we know better is slightly off—and significantly unvarnished—compared to the show's usual look and feel. Carmela goes without makeup. Silvio, temporarily in charge, conducts business out of the hospital waiting room (dealing both with fallout from Eugene Pontecorvo's suicide[6] and the captains' attempts to fill the power vacuum). AJ refers to his father by his full name and talks of murdering Junior,[7] Meadow shows more spine than she ever has in standing up to Tony's imperious surgeon Dr. Plepler (Ron Leibman), and the two siblings have a blunt conversation about how embarrassing they find this situation, and their family in general. This is the *The Sopranos*, stripped of artifice, every character an open wound just like the hole the surgeons left in Tony's stomach to help him heal.

This leads to two jaw-dropping bits of acting from Edie Falco. In the first, Carmela considers the latest report from the doctors and breaks down sobbing in a hospital corridor, as raw as we've seen her outside of "Whitecaps."[8] In the second, she plays Tom Petty's "American Girl," which she recalls as a recurring theme during a memorable trip from early in their relationship, hoping that the familiar song might help her reach her husband, wherever he is. Over the course of three and a half minutes—in a monologue beautifully designed to rise, fall, and crescendo right along with Petty and the Heartbreakers—her thoughts range from that trip and their carefree early days together, to the lust they used to feel for one another, to regret over her remark in the pilot about Tony going to Hell.

---

6   Vito, projecting about his friend's motivation for killing himself: "Maybe he was a homo, felt there was no one he could talk to about it. That happens, too."

7   AJ also hurls out a perfectly Livia-esque "Poor you!" in the middle of an argument with Meadow about hybrid cars.

8   Bonus credit to Michael Imperioli, who looks nearly as devastated as Christopher wraps his arms around Carmela to both show his support and find comfort over what he thinks is the impending loss of his uncle and mentor.

"That was a horrible thing to say," she confesses. "It's a sin, and I will be judged for it. You're a good father. You care about your friends. Yes, it's been rough between us. I don't know, our hearts get so hardened against each other, I don't know why. But you are not going to Hell. You're coming back here. I love you."

Our last glimpse of Tony, or Finnerty, or whoever he is now, finds him sitting in his hotel room, staring out at the beacon and debating whether to call his wife and give her the news about his condition. Moby's "When It's Cold I'd Like to Die" plays on the soundtrack. Like Carmela and all his loved ones back in the real world, Tony wants so badly to reach across time, space, and the barrier between here and there to communicate with them once more. But he can't do it, and hangs up the phone. This world isn't done with him yet.

SEASON 6/EPISODE 3
WRITTEN BY MATTHEW WEINER
DIRECTED BY JACK BENDER

Complicit

"Please, let me take that from you. Looks like it weighs a ton." —**Tony B**

"Mayham" is, as the malapropism-inflected title suggests, an episode in which many wild things happen, including a bloody heist run by Paulie Walnuts, asthmatic Silvio cracking under the pressure of being the top guy, Vito plotting a coup,[9] and the continuing adventures of Tony/Finnerty in Costa Mesa. Yet the hour's most important scene is perhaps its most down to earth and familiar: Carmela visiting Dr. Melfi to talk through her feelings about Tony's condition and the state of their marriage. Poring over her conflicted feelings toward Tony, Carmela admits that from the very start of their relationship, she knew he was a criminal. But she chose not to think about it. "I don't know if I loved him in spite of it, or because of it," she says.

Throughout the show's long run, fans were periodically forced to ask themselves that question—but rarely for long. These early season six episodes feel different, and not just because of the focus on previously marginal characters like Vito and Eugene and the long interludes in Costa Mesa. There's a sense of

---

9   We learn that Vito and Phil Leotardo are related via Vito's wife Marie (played by Elizabeth Bracco, Lorraine's sister), a familial connection no doubt emboldening Vito's talk of insurrection.

both the characters and the series reckoning with the morality of their actions, Carmela included.

She tells Melfi that over the decades, she'd confessed her fears of a compromised life to friends and advisors. And she admits that Tony's shooting, a local media event, has forced her now-adult children to "face all these years of façade-ing." Then she executes a typical about-face and suggests that Tony's gangsterism is a speck on the world's moral radar. Her admissions of guilt, she tells Melfi, are "bullshit, because there are far bigger crooks than my husband." Melfi keeps mostly silent during, but she does manage to interject what might prove to be the most damning three-syllable word in the show's history: "Complicit."

Complicit in what, exactly? Not just Tony's life of crime, but also a generalized (and, Chase suggests, very American) tendency to put self-interest ahead of everything and everyone else. To look out for Number One. Except for Melfi, whose Talmudic scrutiny of her patients' rationalizations makes her Chase's true dramatic surrogate, every major *Sopranos* character is supremely selfish, even when they present themselves as compassionate.

Silvio, reluctantly stepping into the boss's shoes, warns his wife not to ask self-interested questions about the future; but still she asks, and Sil listens. Bobby Bacala presses him to rule on how to distribute Junior's former proceeds, then arrives at Sil's house the next morning as he's being loaded into an ambulance following a respiratory attack, whining, "I didn't hear from you!" Slimmed-down Vito unsubtly bends Larry Boy Barese's ear about Vito being Tony's obvious successor, and collaborates with Paulie Walnuts, his partner in a robbery of Colombian drug dealers, to avoid giving Tony's Mob-mandated kick-up to Carmela. When Tony unexpectedly awakes from the coma, they cobble a bag of cash and hand it to Carm, making a big show of their generosity.

For that matter, Tony's exit from Costa Mesa is spurred on in part by the sound of Paulie's selfish drone, as the silver-haired capo blathers on about himself until Tony goes into cardiac arrest. Afterward, when the big boss is awake but barely functioning, Chris stops by to tell Tony he expects him to invest in Chris's first venture as a movie producer, a digital horror flick about an eviscerated mobster who reassembles himself and kills his killers with a meat cleaver.[10] Grotesquely invoking the memory of Adriana—whom Christopher himself gave up as a snitch—he says, "You owe me this."

The Keystone Kops antics of Silvio and company in Tony's absence—which includes Paulie taking a shot to the groin, a paranoid Vito anxiously gnawing on

---

10 Christopher's plans provide an opportunity for the show to bring back poor JT Dolan, who's pressed into writing the *Cleaver* screenplay in exchange for the erasure of his debts.

carrot sticks, and Sil being forced to conduct business while he's trying to go to the bathroom and read the *Star-Ledger*—illustrate how desperately these guys need Tony. But they also serve as a welcome respite from the strangeness of the Costa Mesa scenes, and occasionally bleed into them, as in the surreal bit where salesman Tony hears Paulie's voice droning through the walls.

The longer Tony stays in Costa Mesa, the more real his Kevin Finnerty identity seems. The monks from "Join the Club" sue him for his shoddy work on their heating system, in a twist recalling *North by Northwest* so thoroughly that one wonders if there's a Kevin Finnerty at all—or, as Tony asks the hotel bartender, "Is it possible I *am* Kevin Finnerty?" If we're thinking of Finnerty as salesman Tony's evil doppelgänger—when Tony asks if he really looks that much like Finnerty, one of the monks says, "To a certain extent, all Caucasians look alike"—then perhaps this meek, law-abiding version of Tony is starting to comprehend that the real him is a man who's done far worse than Finnerty has done to the monks.

An invitation to a Finnerty family reunion that he finds in his borrowed briefcase provides an opportunity to confront his counterpart, but the man who greets him outside the Inn at the Oaks has a different if very familiar face: it's Tony B, or at least a man played by Steve Buscemi, smiling and polite as he nudges Tony toward his final destination.

"Your family's inside," Tony B insists. "They're here to welcome you. You're going home."

He almost goes in. It seems so easy, so welcoming, to simply move on and leave behind all his concerns from the life of either Tony Soprano. But he doesn't. Earlier, Paulie's complaining voice from the real world nearly killed him; here, Meadow's voice appears over the sound of salesman's Tony's much younger daughter, both girls pleading for their daddy to come home.

The sounds of Carmela's voice and "American Girl" weren't enough, but Meadow (who, as Carmela points out to Melfi, didn't choose this life in the way Carmela did) and the clear threat posed by the portal to the Inn (containing another silhouetted woman who, like in the nightmare from "Calling All Cars," evokes Livia) are enough to finally shock Tony—our Tony, who has a thick accent, a long line of mistresses, and even longer line of thugs and killers who work for him—back to life.

Supposedly the dead know just one thing: that it's better to be alive. But the episode's closing scene suggests otherwise. As Carmela tends to her dazed, barely communicative husband, he doesn't look like a man who's happy to be here.

"THE FLESHY PART OF THE THIGH"

SEASON 6/EPISODE 4
WRITTEN BY DIANE FROLOV & ANDREW SCHNEIDER
DIRECTED BY ALAN TAYLOR

Kung Fu

"Supposed to be dead. Now I'm alive. I'm the luckiest guy in the whole world. Listen, after this, from now on, every day is a gift." —**Tony**

As Tony exits the hospital, he hears church bells and chirping birds, notices children going home from school, and feels the sun on his face. He grabs Janice's arm and insists that he is a changed man who will no longer take this life for granted. Janice, relieved that her little brother has survived this ordeal, indulges him for half a second, then goes to get her car, treating this epiphany as a speed bump on the road to Tony being Tony again. Given what we know about this family, is she wrong?

Janice is the ideal audience for Tony's newfound wisdom. Her life has been a never-ending pantomime of metamorphosis: she's been the yoga-loving hippie Parvati, an imperious Mob bride-to-be, a born-again Christian folk singer, Ralphie's sexually adventurous mistress, and Bobby's doting wife. She changes her name, her wardrobe, even her manner of speech, but remains an insufferable narcissist. And she knows herself more deeply than she would ever admit to Tony or anyone else. That's why she's so quick to shrug off this improved version of her brother, despite his seeming sincerity.

Which Soprano is right?

First, let's ponder the cynical Janice view: Tony thinks he wants to change, but is already much more himself than he recognizes. He's slowly recovering from an incident that should have killed him. He's talking a good game, chatting up the visiting evangelicals and the friendly scientist down the hall, telling a nurse he doesn't feel like his old self. And yet he's sneaking out of the hospital for stogie breaks, getting chesty with Phil Leotardo and basically ruining the life of the Barone family so he can protect his own interests by keeping his no-work job after one of Phil's guys buys the company. When he forgives the paramedic for picking his pocket (assuming the guy really did it), it feels like a pose he's trying on.

Everyone has a selfish agenda, it seems. Tony's being friendly to Janice's narcoleptic ex, Aaron, a man he once threw food at during a Thanksgiving dinner, because he's looking to acquire a Get Out of Purgatory Free card. The manager of rap star Da Lux (Lord Jamar) is happy his client got shot because it'll boost record sales (and his cut). Hesh's daughter is fond of born-again Christians, but only because they support Israel. The health insurance rep smiles and flirts with Tony, but she just wants him off the company books.

And here's Paulie Walnuts, who receives the kind of information that should fundamentally alter his sense of self—that the dying nun he thought was his aunt is really his biological mother, and Nucci the aunt who took him in to protect her sister's reputation—and responds with the same woe-is-me, the-world-owes-me-ice-cream-cake attitude he displays in the best of circumstances. He blames his own mother for the crime of raising him, and Jason Barone (Chris Diamantopoulos) for the bigger sin of having a biological mother who loves him more than she loves life itself. (The $4,000 a month shakedown he inflicts on Jason equals the cost of keeping Nucci in Green Grove.)

About the only person who's not blatantly looking out for number one is Bell Labs retiree John Schwinn (Hal Holbrook[11]), so of course he suffers a fate worse than death: a man who loves to talk (and is good at it) robbed of the ability to speak.

And now, evidence for the optimist's view of the capacity of Tony and the people around him to experience real, enduring change:

1. The repeated invocation of the Ojibwe saying, mysteriously posted on Tony's hospital room bulletin board: "Sometimes I go about in pity for myself, and all the while, a great wind carries me across the sky." It suggests that Tony, like most people, is so preoccupied with his own selfish concerns that he fails to take a larger view of life, to see himself as one atom in what *Deadwood* creator David Milch once called "the larger human organism." The "great pity" part gently mocks Tony's (and our) fixation on the visible part of life—the first-person aspect that we experience as individuals—while insisting there are larger forces at play, like destiny, fate, God, or some other mystical noun.

2. The second, third, and fourth episodes of this season contain more allusions to morality, spirituality, and eternal rewards than any three previous consecutive *Sopranos* hours. Besides Carmela's hospital bed apology and Tony's adventures in Coma Land, we've seen numerous appearances by characters who represent some version of a holy man expressing a vision of life that goes beyond self-interest. Tony's Coma Land ramblings put him face to face with monks whose lives he'd literally made more hellish via a defective heating system. Among other theological ambassadors, "The Fleshy Part of the Thigh" features Aaron's born-again evangelist friend, Pastor Bob (Rob Dev-

---

11 Legendary character actor Holbrook was yet another *Sopranos* guest best known for his work in gritty '70s cinema, most famously for portraying Deep Throat in *All the President's Men*.

aney), who was once addicted to cocaine and strippers; Paulie's biological mother ("How could you be a bad girl?" Paulie cries. "You're a nun!"); a cameo by a clean-shaven Father Phil; and a televised glimpse of David Carradine as Caine, the hero of *Kung Fu*, arguably the only network action series that doubled as a spiritual journey (Caine was a monk).[12]

3. Right after Tony's brush with eternity, Pastor Bob sells him on evangelical Christianity as a way to relate to Christ directly, without the intercession of liturgy. Pastor Bob is sincere, and the show treats his message with respect. But note that his word choice appeals to Tony's practical side; Bob is a theological salesman offering a prospective customer a better deal, a chance to get his guidance from the source.

4. Even John Schwinn comes across as one more holy man. In a memorable hospital room scene with Da Lux and his posse,[13] Schwinn regales Tony with Zen-inflected monologues. Among other things, he says that two boxers fighting on TV aren't really opponents, and aren't truly separate—that they're all part of the same continuum. The perception of individuality, of distinctness and apart-ness, is an illusion, he says: "The shape is only in our own consciousness."

5. Dinosaurs, dinosaurs, dinosaurs. Carmela[14] gives Tony a book about dinosaurs. Pastor Bob tells Tony (in a scene that undercuts his earlier salesmanship) that scientists are wrong, that dinosaurs walked among humans. Perhaps Tony, the twentieth-century gangster, is a kind of dinosaur, a species doomed to extinction by predators (other criminals, the FBI) and by failing to evolve and adapt. But according to the most recent science available as of this writing, dinosaurs didn't die out entirely; the survivors of the extinction event evolved into birds.[15] Is it possible that Tony could evolve into another kind of person, recognizably Tony

---

12 If Costa Mesa was just a product of Tony's unconscious mind, his childhood love of *Kung Fu* might explain the presence of bald monks as opponents of Kevin Finnerty.

13 The subplot that gives the episode its title involves Bacala offering to boost the career prospects of Da Lux's sidekick Marvin, played by Naughty By Nature front man Anthony "Treach" Criss, by shooting him in the leg to boost his street cred. This is played for broad laughs, as Bacala's usual expert marksmanship goes awry and he hits Marvin in the buttocks.

14 Carmela's behavior in the episode also shows that people can change, as she does something very out of character by warning Tony about Vito, when usually she's been content to stay as far out of her husband's business as possible while enjoying the spoils. Perhaps confessing to Dr. Melfi in "Mayham" that she had no illusions about Tony's career—and that she was attracted to that part of him in the first place—encouraged her to stop playing Kay Corleone and aspire for a moment to Lady Macbeth?

15 In the very first episode of the *Sopranos*, Tony and Carmela's marriage is introduced with a scene of the two of them in the kitchen, Carmela pressing him to commit to finishing work early and intimating that he'd better not stay out with his mistress while Tony's head is buried in a book. It's about birds. Carmela gets his attention by calling him "birdman."

despite being repentant and law-abiding, just as birds retained certain characteristics of their dinosaur ancestors?

6. The post-coma Tony seems more inclined to forgive and negotiate than hold grudges and fight for every scrap. After demanding $2,000 in cash from the paramedic he accused of ripping him off during a "wallet biopsy," he declines the cash with a wave of his hand. Later, he accepts Phil Leotardo's generally unfavorable terms of continued waste management employment with a sigh and a handshake. As Janice predicts, this state of affairs could be temporary, but it's still startling to witness.

He seems more aware of the world beyond his fevered mind. The combination of near-death experience and nonstop (if unasked-for) spiritual counseling appears to have made him subliminally aware of Schwinn's continuum. Both the dialogue and the filmmaking support this reading. Leaving the hospital, Tony basks in natural sound that he once would have ignored as background noise. Then, in the magnificent finale, Tony sits in his backyard listening to the wind in the trees, and the camera tracks from left to right over the treeline, echoing a camera move in the Coma World sequence that ended "Mayham." A crane-down reveals that the treeline isn't the one in Tony's backyard, but on the Passaic River, where Paulie Walnuts is about to enforce the terms of Tony's employment by beating down Jason Barone. The editing and camerawork collapse Tony's world and Paulie's, confirming they aren't separate. The left-to-right treeline pan is repeated a second time, gliding over the trees in Tony's backyard. Then it's repeated a third time, panning the treeline over Paulie as he exits the frame in the episode's final shot.

7. Put that Ojibwe saying into Sopranos language, and what does it say? "Poor you."

"MR. & MRS. JOHN SACRIMONI REQUEST . . ."	SEASON 6/EPISODE 5 WRITTEN BY TERENCE WINTER DIRECTED BY STEVE BUSCEMI

Jackals

"If they can make him cry and if he's that weak, what the fuck else can they make him do?" —**Phil**

Usually when this many *Sopranos* characters dress up to get together as appear in "Mr. & Mrs. John Sacrimoni Request . . . ," it's for a funeral. This time, in theory, it's for the wedding of Johnny Sack's daughter Allegra (Caitlin Van Zandt). But by the episode's end, it feels like a funeral for one boss, a reminder of how close another boss recently came to dying, and the moment when a third, wannabe boss is marked for death. John loses face with his men by crying while his federal escorts cuff him in front of the guests, the still-recuperating Tony fears he looks too weak after he faints on the way into the wedding, and fellow wiseguys spot Vito at a leather bar where he's gone to exorcise the feelings from a day when he was deep in heterosexual cosplay.

Vito has to play the straight family man more intensely than usual, amid a relentlessly heteronormative celebration of romance. He ponders his wife's ring while Allegra and her new husband say their vows, can't stop himself from complimenting Finn again ("And look at this young dentist, all handsome in his Calvin Klein"), and eventually feels so miserable at the lie he's living that he insists on leaving the wedding early so he can slip away from home to let his true self out.[16] The scene at the bar unfortunately winds up evoking a different Al Pacino movie, the cartoonishly homophobic 1980 thriller *Cruising*, with the image of Vito in leather gear designed to make him look silly after the rest of this season had so effectively made him a darkly complex figure.

But the episode compensates for that with the haunting use of "The Three Bells" by The Browns as Vito pulls up to the motel where he hides out while waiting to see how far the news of his "crime" will spread—a song that's also heard briefly in the previous episode's scene where Jason Barone gets educated in exactly what kind of business his father was in. It tells of the life of Jimmy Brown (no relation to The Browns) in three verses covering three major events in his life: birth, marriage, and death. The description of "a hidden valley" resonates with the memory of Tony wandering in Coma Land, as well as with the desire to escape expressed in the sto-

---

16 Though Joseph Gannascoli sometimes seems to struggle with the physical facts of Vito's homosexuality, the discomfort suits this moment in Vito's life, and something authentic and surprisingly sweet comes through in his performance—along with torment.

ries of Eugene Pontecorvo and poor Vito. The classic Eisenhower-era arrangement with its marzipan harmonizing is a musical time machine, immersing listeners not in actual 1950s America, but in white, middle-class America's sentimental self-image of that time and place. It's a dip in the reflecting pool that the country made for itself. The cycles of one man's life play out as nonjudgmental recitation of facts, each accompanied by a ringing bell[17] and a congregation's prayers to a God who may or may not be listening but seems like a decent chap. This is the idyllic American life that Jason Barone probably lived while shielded from the realities that are about to beat his ass on the dock. And it's the life Vito pretends to live but will never be able to truly appreciate. His façade starts crumbling here because the wedding reminded him that he has yet to find a valley he can call his own.

The episode references the famous *Godfather* wedding sequence several times, most notably in repeating the idea that a Mafia don has to grant favors on the day of his daughter's wedding,[18] but the feigned displays of strength showcased here are sad facsimiles of Vito Corleone's.[19] The stressed-out Johnny has to jump through legal hoops and spend a fortune (including repaying the U.S. Marshals for the costs of his one-day furlough) not only to give Allegra her special day, but to have what could be his last night out with both his family and his Family. But while Johnny is more powerful and polished than his Garden State counterpart, he shares Tony's temper and inability to let go of petty grudges, and Rusty Millio has become to him what Ralphie once was to Tony: an aggravation he wants to expunge. It's not a particularly smart move; as acting boss, and one easily swayed by events like Johnny's crying jag, Phil is the bigger threat, and it indebts him to Tony, while also arousing the suspicion that he's breaking his promise to the U.S. Marshals to not discuss business. Without those unsubtle confabs with Tony, the marshals might not have perp-walked him in front of the wedding party. Instead, he's mortified, and after lecturing Ginny and his girls[20] about staying strong in front of friends and Family, he breaks down, taking Allegra and Ginny with him, and leaves Phil and wiseguys from both Families questioning his manhood and viability as boss.

---

17 When Tony leaves the hospital, he hears church bells ringing.

18 An oblique *Godfather* reference, perhaps: the episode-ending song is "Every Day of the Week" by The Students, which runs through the names of the days in the proper order, rather than Apollonia's, "Monday, Tuesday, Thursday, Wednesday, Friday, Sunday, Saturday."

19 When Carmela picks up the *Star-Ledger* from the end of the driveway (sparing Tony the long walk in his condition), she sees a banner headline about Junior: "Cushy Psych Lock-Up for 'Don Squirrel-Leone.'"

20 Johnny's other daughter Catherine is played by Cristin Milioti, who would soon be a star of Broadway (*Once*) and television (she wound up as the title character on *How I Met Your Mother*).

Johnny's instantly reduced status isn't lost on Tony, who was already worried that his own guys think he's fragile. He collapses briefly from being stuck under the hot sun while negotiating the wedding security line, and conflates that incident and Johnny's with Melfi:[21] "They think you're weak, they see an opportunity. They're my friends, a lot of them, but they're also fucking jackals." Melfi, in a rare departure for her (perhaps feeling more protective of Patient X after his grievous injury), offers him some direct counsel on how to be a better Mob boss, telling him to "act as if" he's more confident and physically capable than he is. To do this, he tries the old prison-yard trick of finding a physically impressive opponent—his muscular new driver, Perry Annunziata (Louis Gross), who was once "first runner-up, Mr. Teenage Bloomfield"—to thrash in front of witnesses in Satriale's back office. Perry makes an easy target not only because he's an overgrown kid with biceps but no street smarts, but because he's the only guy hot-headed enough to fight back briefly, making Tony's victory seem more impressive. Tony lays a beatdown on him for an invented reason, then acts *as if* long enough to make it to the bathroom, where he pays the price for taxing his injured body by retching into the toilet.

Social-striving mobsters live in constant fear that their veneer of respectability will be torn away and they'll be exposed as parasites. Sometimes they're doomed to be exposed; no matter how circumspect the gangster and his family are, there will be days when the larger society (represented by cops or prosecutors) feels emboldened to call a gangster a gangster, and when it happens in public, it stings no matter how big a boss you are. *The Sopranos* has acknowledged this particular anxiety in the past, but never as frankly as it does here. Except for the prosecutor who fought the day pass, the government was generous with Johnny, yet somehow the day still became a mass public shaming in black tie. Terence Winter's script deploys these elements without fuss, and director Steve Buscemi deepens them with God's-eye view shots that physically diminish the gangsters at key moments (the wedding guests ascending a spiral staircase; Vito getting situated in the motel; Tony puking blood in the bathroom).

That men's room scene is a reminder of the sacrifices Tony makes to maintain the status quo. This life is destructive in every way: morally, spiritually, and now physically. He made his choice, and now he's paying in blood. After he vomits, he looks at himself in the mirror with a cocky-scary "I'm back" expression. Then a shadow of doubt crosses his face. Then he drops to all fours and vomits again. This is a different kind of cost-benefit analysis, conducted by the body, not the mind.

---

21 Tony, returning to the good doctor's care, again makes her laugh deeply by opening their first session of the episode with, "So let me ask you right off, is there any chance of a mercy fuck?"

SEASON 6/EPISODE 6
WRITTEN BY DAVID CHASE AND TERENCE WINTER AND
"LIVE FREE OR DIE"   ROBIN GREEN & MITCHELL BURGESS
DIRECTED BY TIM VAN PATTEN

Deep in the Valley

"This guy that got outed, look, the guys that work for me are asking for head. His head. What the fuck?" —**Tony**

Did you hear the one about the Jersey mobster who walked into a Norman Rockwell painting of New England? Neither did we, because usually you can't get there from here.

"Live Free or Die" ends in the state whose motto provides the hour's title, but it begins on home turf, with a wide shot of the still-recovering Tony shambling around the backyard in his bathrobe and having his reading interrupted by the grinding whine of a defective ventilation unit. He walks over to the unit, futzes with it, rips off the top and hurls it away in disgust, then resumes reading.[22] Moments later, the grinding noise returns, and rather than attack the problem again, Tony ignores it.

The final scene finds Vito in the fictional hamlet of Dartford, New Hampshire,[23] which seems to be filled with bourgeois gay men, as he strolls down the main drag and then ducks into an antiques shop. When he asks the clerk about a particular vase, the clerk compliments Vito's taste: "You're a natural." As the clerk walks away, Tim Van Patten's camera dollies in slowly on Vito as he continues to regard the vase. What makes this shot so potent is Vito's unselfconsciousness. For the first time in his history on the series, he seems completely at ease.[24]

These are gateway images that invite us to reflect on everything we've seen this season. In a sense, Tony's and Vito's stories are the same story. They're about men who want to change (or escape) the lives they have, and become different

---

22 Kevin Finnerty sold defective heating units, we were told.
23 The Dartford scenes were filmed in Boonton, New Jersey, a quiet suburb with a picturesque main street on a hill. In *The Sopranos* universe, Jackie Jr. was hiding out in the (wholly fictional) Boonton projects when he was shot—by Vito.
24 This closing shot also harkens back to many images on the show that feel like commentary on the show's mix of high and low art, starting with the pilot's opening scene in Melfi's waiting room. Vito, a tacky gangster who steals and kills, has an instinctive discerning eye.

people—or the men they always should have been.[25] The combination of the turn this character takes and the setting where it happens induces a magical feeling of suspension. It's as if Vito, like Tony, has briefly died and gone somewhere else.

Whither Tony? Or wither Tony? Hard to say. His near-death shook him up and caused him to adopt a live-and-let-live approach to Mob management. Here, Tony runs afoul of his crew by greeting news of Vito's orientation with a shrug. "I got a second chance," he says of Vito. "Why shouldn't he?" And a more poignant response to his crew: "You gonna take care of his kids after he's gone?" Notwithstanding his calculated public beatdown of Perry, he does seem softer and more reflective. As he lies in bed with Carmela, the vertical scar on his belly suggests a C-section; could we be privy to the gradual birth of a New Tony?

The defective ventilation unit illuminates Tony's present problem and his larger arc. Vito's exposure tosses a wrench into the gangster machinery, and Tony can't ignore that grinding sound. His ham-fisted jabs at enlightened thinking ("It's 2006! There's pillow-biters in the Special Forces!") don't work on this bunch, which views homosexuality as a graver sin than shooting a guy and grinding him up. Sooner or later Tony will have to give the order to kill Vito, watch helplessly while someone else freelances the deed, or take a stand and pay the price.

More significantly, though, that opening reminds us of Tony's failure to recognize the root cause of his psychic distress: he's a murderous criminal. Even therapy hasn't attacked the heart of the matter. Melfi's therapy is not making Tony a better man, but a better gangster. His dead mother isn't the problem; he is.

Vito, meanwhile, is enjoying his own version of the rustic yuppie life that Eugene Pontecorvo was denied when he escaped his Mob-ligations at the end of a rope. As Vito wanders around Dartford, he seems more relaxed—more himself—than ever. The masterful slow-build sequence depicting his flight includes eerie shots of Vito trudging through torrential rain after his car breaks down (abandoning the vehicle we'd seen him drive during his various Mob errands). Barely protected by a thin poncho, the drenched infant-doughy thug is reborn at a bed-and-breakfast, courtesy of an innkeeper who refuses to take a fistful of thank-you cash. For all she knows, he's just some traveler trying to get out of the rain. Vito awakes the next morning in an elegant four-poster bed, framed in a low-angled master shot that again reminds us of astronaut Dave Bowman's evolutionary stint in the white room at the end of *2001: A Space Odyssey*, a film whose

---

25 With four of the show's best writers getting script credit, you knew this one was going to bring the funny, and it delivered. Among the laughs: Christopher and Tony separately insisting they always knew Vito's secret, Tony's panic over whether Melfi believed he slept with men in jail, Paulie's disgusted reaction to the full Vito story ("How much more betrayal can I take?"), and Christopher rationalizing that his Arab clients can't be terrorists because one of them owns a springer spaniel.

main subject is evolution as both physical event and metaphor: what's gained and what's lost.[26] A baby-bodied mobster is reborn here. What will he become? Or, what will become of him?

It's surely no accident that Vito's stopover in Norman Rockwell country echoes Tony's sojourn in Coma Land, right up to his climactic arrival at a welcoming home. (Vito, unlike Tony, dares to step inside.) It also doesn't seem an accident that this episode sees Carmela chew out her pop for looting and dismantling the spec house. (Hugh counters that the house was a lost cause because she was supposed to wrangle the proper government permits to build with inferior material, and didn't do it; in other words, she neglected a problem that threatened a long-term dream, and now she has to accept the consequences. It's the Costa Mesa defective heating unit conversation transposed to earth.) This season is all about new beginnings (or reconstructions) and how they are thwarted by bad luck, poor judgment, conditioning, and genetics. It makes sense that Vito would feel safe in a place marinating in its own authenticity. His inability to reveal his hidden truth is what drove him out of Essex County. Dartford seems heavenly, and Vito is so happy there that he seems better off than anyone he left in Jersey.

Too bad bliss has a shelf life. How long will Vito's last? Eugene's corpse sways in the mind like a clock's pendulum, counting down the seconds. Newcomers to organized crime are promised a glamorous life where they won't be bound by the rules. What no one tells them is that they're trading one set of rules for another.[27] When Phil breaks the bad news to Vito's wife—having heard Finn's account[28] of Vito and the security guard—he sounds like a prosecutor: "The witness has no reason to lie." The disgusted reactions of the wiseguys back home suggest Vito can never return. The episode is called "Live Free or Die," but in Soprano country, it's not a choice but a sequence: live free *and* die.

---

26 Remember all that talk of dinosaurs and birds in this season's "The Fleshy Part of the Thigh"?

27 In parallel, we see Meadow working a pro bono case with an Afghan family facing a similar situation, having escaped the rules of one society for another that's not as free as it claims to be.

28 Not only is Finn shanghaied into testifying at the pork store, but he and Meadow now seem utterly miserable together. Their engagement was prompted in part by Finn's desire to insulate himself from Vito; with Vito now persona non grata in the Tri-State Area, the strongest bond these two kids had left has been dissolved.

"LUXURY LOUNGE" WRITTEN BY MATTHEW WEINER
DIRECTED BY DANNY LEINER

The Haves and Have-Nots

"Life's not fair, right, I know. But somehow, I believed my dad's crap about honest work. He used to say to me, 'You'll see. It pays off in the end.' What a joke." —**Artie**

One of the many plagues befalling Vesuvio throughout "Luxury Lounge" is the opening of a rival Italian restaurant, Da Giovanni, in a nearby suburb. When we see the place, with Tony looking like a guilty cheating spouse because he has to attend the confirmation of Phil's grandson, the buffet is as spectacular as promised: one amazing dish after the next, with ingredients to be analyzed and tastes to savor.

The first six episodes of season six were so rich and constantly surprising, they felt very much like that buffet. The thought of following them with an Artie showcase episode—even one where he splits time with another of Christopher's showbiz misadventures—and one that rehashes a similar episode's story beats ("Everybody Hurts": Artie gets too sweet on his hostess and learns his limitations as a tough guy)—sounds as appetizing as most of the wiseguys are finding Vesuvio's stale menu at this point. Instead, "Luxury Lounge" turns out more like the rabbit dish Artie improvises near the end of the hour: not what the diner might have ordered, yet simple and effective.

"Luxury Lounge" ties the story of Artie running afoul of Benny Fazio in New Jersey and Christopher and Little Carmine failing to impress Ben Kingsley in Beverly Hills with unifying emotional threads of envy and its twin, resentment. Or, as Christopher inadvertently sums up the theme while complimenting Lauren Bacall on her most famous role, "You were great in *The Haves and Have-Nots* [sic]"

Artie has always struggled financially doing things the right way, while his restaurant's most frequent customers profit from breaking the rules. Tony and Artie are childhood friends, and were even roommates briefly before Charmaine took Artie back,[29] but Artie is essentially the Family's hired help. He usually can swallow this, but when the mobsters get too invasive—which Benny does twice, first seducing Martina (Manuela Feris), the latest hostess Artie's smitten with, then using her to steal Vesuvio patrons' credit card numbers, costing Artie business—the chef with the prominent forearms has had all he can stands, and he can't stands no more. He goes to Benny's house and lays an impressive beating on Christopher's diminutive lieutenant. It's a rare triumph for Artie—which he

---

29 Loosely mirroring the Soprano marriage, the two reconciled between seasons five and six.

celebrates with some exaggerated Ali-style shadowboxing—and one he seems likely to get away with, because he's the boss's oldest friend. (Tony to Benny: "You don't shit where you eat. And you really don't shit where *I* eat.") But the same mouth that can't stop chatting up uninterested customers also can't stop from lording the situation over Benny when he brings his wife and parents to Vesuvio for an anniversary dinner, which leads an enraged Benny to plunge Artie's arm into a pot of bubbling sauce.

This violence is happening a continent away from Christopher and Little Carmine's attempt to get Ben Kingsley to play the Mob boss in *Cleaver*.[30] The Oscar-winning *Gandhi* star is, unsurprisingly, not impressed with their pitch, while Christopher winds up too impressed by, and envious of, a glimpse of the eponymous luxury lounge, where celebrities are gifted amazing swag in exchange for posing for the brands' publicity: *Ben Kingsley was spotted wearing an Oris timepiece while hanging by the pool at the Viceroy Hotel!*

Among Christopher's favorite perks of the job is all the free stuff he gets, but the garbage bag full of designer shoes he once brought home to Adriana seems pitiful compared to these lavish items that Kingsley couldn't be more jaded about. If Artie's a man whom Benny can assault and mutilate in his place of business without fear of repercussions, then Christopher is barely worthy of Ben Kingsley's notice at all. He is nothing to this man who represents so much of what he's always dreamed of being, and the recognition of that sends him spiraling, first on a bender that requires the intercession of sidekick/sponsor Murmur (Lenny Venito[31]), then by getting in on the swag action by mugging Bacall[32]—so he can abscond with her $30,000 ShoWest gift basket. But even that pathetic victory is short-lived, since he winds up on a cross-country flight with Kingsley, and has to see how irritated the *Sexy Beast* actor is to have to breathe the same air with him again.[33]

---

30 Also discussed by the creative team for this role, per *Sopranos* casting associate Meredith Tucker: Michael Douglas, Christopher Walken, Alec Baldwin, and Michael Gambon.

31 Kevin Gable's friend Duffy on *Kevin Can Wait;* one of those character actors with a tough guy face, a cocky grin, the East Coast bona fides to play a wide variety of character roles, and a résumé dating all the way back to *The Equalizer.*

32 The show considered several candidates to be the famous old lady Christopher punched, and at one point the script had Little Carmine singing the praises of Dame Maggie Smith's work in *Harry Potter and the Chamber of Secrets*. Bacall works perfectly, though, because she represents a very specific kind of old Hollywood glamour and toughness that would be particularly appealing to Christopher. Also, she's a great sport to endure such on-screen mortification in her eighties.

33 Also doing a lot of plane travel: the two Naples hitmen Tony brings over to take out Rusty Millio. On the trip back to Italy—seated opposite the Naples man David Chase played back in season two's "Commendatori"—the two marvel at how cheaply, thanks to the weak U.S. dollar, they were able to buy gifts for home, like a Mont Blanc pen. To them, the things that make Christopher sweat and despair are cheap trinkets.

Christopher comes out of "Luxury Lounge" with the gift basket and not much else. Artie fares a little better. He has to once again make peace with being the law-abiding grunt in the wiseguy world, but he can do it because he has this thing he loves, and he's good at it when he's not boring customers with ingredient lists or hitting on uninterested women ("You stare at me like food!" gripes Martina). John Ventimiglia is exquisitely desperate throughout the hour, Willy Loman via *Big Night*—a film referenced in the back-to-square-one cooking montage scored, naturally, to music that would sound at home in the old country.

Compared to their respective Bens this time out, Christopher and Artie are definitely the Have-Nots. But only one of them is able to accept what it is that he has.

SEASON 6/EPISODE 8
WRITTEN BY DIANE FROLOV & ANDREW SCHNEIDER
DIRECTED BY TIM VAN PATTEN

Imitations of Life

"Sometimes, you tell a lie so long, you don't know when to stop.
You don't know when it's safe." —**Vito**

"Johnny Cakes" is the biggest departure of season six, and possibly the series. "Join the Club" and "Mayham" may have brought us to an alternate reality, or the afterlife, but the Kevin Finnerty interludes still fit the overall style and mood of many of the show's dream sequences. Other episodes have traveled a much greater physical distance than New Hampshire, but still bring the show's atmosphere with them. You can take Paulie Walnuts out of New Jersey, but you can't take the New Jersey out of Paulie Walnuts, even when he's in Italy.

In "Johnny Cakes," though, it's not just that Vito isn't really being Vito anymore, posing as "Vince," a sportswriter working on a book on either Rocky Marciano or Rocky Graziano, depending on which lie he remembers to tell that day, and eventually falling into a romance with Jim (John Costelloe), the short-order cook whose breakfast specialty gives the episode its title. It's that the entirety of the affair plays out stylistically unlike anything the show's done before. The look and tone are somewhere between a *Twilight Zone* episode set in one of those classic Rod Serling small towns of the imagination, and a stubbly, two-fisted cousin of a Douglas Sirk movie,[34] about a couple of guys who could not be further removed from the quippy, college-educated, upper-middle class image of gay men so often presented on American TV at that time, notwithstanding occasional outliers like *Queer as Folk* and *Six Feet Under*. The opening intercuts Tony readjusting to "regular" life (for a gangster) and Vito in Dartford having an adventure of self-discovery that's about as dreamlike as can be while still feeling like it's happening in the *Sopranos*-verse. From the moment that Johnny, a Tom of Finland cartoon made manifest, rolls up on his Harley Davidson at a house fire and emerges moments later with an adorable blond child, we're in what we might imagine to be Vito's fantasy of the life he can never have back in New Jersey. The rest of this subplot is stocked with overt signifiers and melodramatic dialogue, from the classic 1950s diner that looks like a place where Rock Hudson might've nursed a hangover, to the tweedy types loitering in the parlor of the bed-and-breakfast, to lines like Vito's chapter-opening quote, which would fit on a poster advertising a pre-1960s melodrama about American souls in torment. Some of the details are unconvincing, and the performances feel a bit skittish even considering the storyline, but there are many unexpectedly right moments, such as the John Wayne–quality brawl outside the bar, sparked by the self-loathing Vito returning Joe's kiss with a punch, and the way he makes amends with a gesture—laying one hand atop another—that's probably the bravest thing he's done in his life.

Vito's scenes also provide an affecting mirror of Tony and AJ each grappling with their own fears that they're pretending, or fighting their true natures. But we're always reminded that Vito is worst off by far, because his fellow mobsters are so homophobic that they consider his existence a threat to their manhood. The parallel editing often makes it seem as if three major subplots are speaking to one another. We see Vito walk down the sidewalk in Dartford, his true nature kept under wraps, then cut to Christopher openly eyeballing women on the sidewalk in front of Satriale's; Tony gets up to leave the pork store right before Vito walks into the diner; AJ gets a backrub from a teenage hanger-on while her friend goes down on AJ's buddy, followed by Vito filching a fellow hotel guest's cell phone so he can call the wife and son who have no idea where he is, much less who he's evolving into.

Meanwhile, the Newark neighborhood where Tony grew up is undergoing its own transformation, and for better or worse, Tony decides not to fight it. The cash for selling the building that houses Caputo Live Poultry overcomes his fondness for being the Don Fanucci of the North Ward, and the realtor, Julianna Skiff

---

34 Sirk's 1959 classic *Imitation of Life*, about an white aspiring actress who befriends an African American widow whose daughter tries to pass for white as a teenager, plays on the Spatafores' TV after the Sacrimoni wedding.

(Julianna Margulies[35]), tempts him to revert sexually to the old self that Carmela (and perhaps Tony) believed that he'd outgrown. When Julianna offers to buy the building, Tony resists, partly out of attraction. Other than being Jewish instead of Italian, she checks all of his usual boxes—beautiful, intelligent, professional, brunette, damaged (her language suggests being in some sort of recovery)—and he wants an excuse to keep seeing her. He also genuinely likes the idea of a business like Caputo's enduring in that neighborhood: It fits his nostalgia-drenched ethos.

As usual, though, Tony prizes money above all else, and anticipates signing the papers at her luxury apartment in a converted glove factory. (Even her living space represents everything Tony claims to hate.) But despite having what he describes as "a baguette in my pants now 24/7" as his body recovers from the shooting, he can't go through with it, leaving Julianna frustrated and confused when he bolts. Tony's emotional calculus is conveyed nonverbally here through earlier shots of Tony fixating on Carmela's hands buttoning his dress shirt over the scarred belly whose innards she bravely stared into, and of her eyes gazing up at him adoringly, and rhyming images of Julianna trying to unbutton that same shirt later, a gesture that triggers guilty recoil in Tony. It's the first sign of genuine emotional change for him post-shooting, and one he's not particularly happy about, as evidenced by the closing scene where he yells at Carmela for failing to stock the fridge with smoked turkey—perhaps an attempt to retroactively give himself some justification, however absurd, for having almost stepped out on her.

While Vito is transforming himself with angst but high hopes, and Tony is mad at himself for doing the same, AJ is desperate to become someone else, and failing miserably. Where Meadow is the Soprano kid who knows what she wants in life and how to get it, AJ has drifted from plan to plan, identity to identity, never really fitting any of them. Here, he tries two—club kid and hitman—neither of which work out. The first finds him palling around with Hernan (Vincent Piazza[36]) and his crew and feeling important and valued, but he's just being used to pay the group's absurd bottle service fees, entertain them with Mob stories, and perhaps relay their problems to his father.[37] His feelings of inadequacy there, his boredom with life as a Blockbuster clerk, and his powerful memories of watching

---

35 Even a few years after she left her *ER* role as heroic nurse Carol Hathaway, Margulies was still among the most famous actresses on television when *The Sopranos* cast her. Julianna Skiff isn't exactly her playing against type (Carol had her problems, too), but Tony's world was so much grubbier and meaner than the well-meaning halls of County General Hospital that it was startling to see her pop up in it.

36 Piazza would later play legendary gangster Lucky Luciano on *Sopranos* writer Terence Winter's *Boardwalk Empire.*

37 Like Fredo in the first two *Godfather* films, a man whom others see as worthless except for his connections to power.

The Godfather with his dad inspire him to seek revenge on Uncle Junior, but it's bungled before it can even begin.

Tony's able to get AJ off the hook with help from Assemblyman Zellman, and their scene in the police station parking lot is a rare instance where Anthony Sr.'s temper over Anthony Jr.'s latest fuck-up transmutes to a more tender sense of concern for the danger his son just put himself in, as well as fear that AJ might follow in his footsteps. "It's not in your nature!" he insists, and when a defiant AJ claims his father doesn't know him, Tony presses on: "You're a nice guy, and that's a good thing, for Chrissakes!"

We've never seen AJ show interest in the Family business; here it seems he's drifted into the idea because nothing else he tries—not college, not clubbing—seems to fit. Pre-assassination attempt, Tony spends multiple therapy sessions asking Dr. Melfi[38] for advice on what to do with the kid, but she ultimately has no more idea than he does, beyond insisting that Tony and Carmela present a united front to AJ, whatever they ask of him.

Immediately after Tony disengages from Julianna, we see AJ back at the club, suffering another panic attack while studying his reflection in the bathroom mirror. Where the trigger for Tony's attacks tends to be meat, for AJ it seems to be trying on a new identity: football star, military school cadet, and now club kid. He doesn't know what he wants in life, but every change triggers something painful inside his rotten Soprano genes.

These stories all testify to how hard it is to fight tradition and conditioning, as well as the futility of resisting forces you know deep down overwhelm you, be it sexual orientation (Vito), an aversion to fidelity (Tony), a constitutional inability to be dangerous (AJ), or the rising tide of corporate expansion (the North Ward).

Tying things up in a non-*Sopranos*-like bow are the scenes with Patsy Parisi and Burt Gervasi (Artie Pasquale) trying to collect protection money in a neighborhood increasingly occupied by businesses whose parent companies aren't impressed by street-level strong-arming. A chain pastry shop's manager tells the mobsters that he doesn't have a line item for protection money, and that if someone were to throw a brick through their front window, the head office wouldn't even notice. Patsy's right: It's over for the little guy.

---

38 We get one of our longer and more amusing Melfi–Kupferberg scenes in this one, as she rightly scolds him for always trying to change the subject to Patient X no matter what she's interested in. ("I'm talking about my father, Elliot," she insists when he brings up Tony again. "I thought you were done," he shrugs.) Elliot cares about her as a patient and as a friend, but he's even more of an excited voyeur about the Mob drama than Melfi was when the series began.

SEASON 6/EPISODE 9
WRITTEN BY TERENCE WINTER
DIRECTED BY ALAN TAYLOR

"THE RIDE"

A Pair of Socks

"I was just thinking it'd lost some of its, you know, pop." —**Tony**

St. Elzéar was a French nobleman who died at thirty-eight, and who chose to honor his wife's lifelong vow of chastity. Which means that Tony, Paulie, Chris, and the guys spend much of "The Ride" paying homage to a man whose life they would do anything to avoid.

Not that their lives are much better. As Tony and Melfi discuss in therapy, people go on scary amusement park rides because they're bored, and the gangster lifestyle is essentially one long trip to Great Adventure. You wait on line for an hour, scream your head off for ninety seconds, then go to the back of another line.

Why do Tony and Chris try to hijack a hijacking? Because it's something to do, something to punctuate the tedium and hassles of a life that's a lot less glamorous than they had imagined. The two get drunk on the stolen wine and the retelling of the story ("We're with the Vipers!") for a while, but as time passes, the booze and the memories both lose some of their, you know, pop. And then it's back to another card game at Satriale's, another collection headache, another day of waiting for the next adventure.

As Tony puts it to Melfi in describing his post-coma attitude, "Every day is a gift. It's just . . . does it have to be a pair of socks?"

At least the old Tony could count on some excitement from his mistresses before those relationships went south. This new Tony doesn't even have that outlet; while he stands helpless on terra firma, his failed conquest Julianna is too busy laughing her head off on her ride to even notice him.

Throughout the series' run, its detractors complained that it glamorized the Mob, even as Chase, Winter, and company did everything in their power to show just how ugly and empty the lives of these characters were, how pathetic and selfish beneath the bravado. This one makes it plain.

Paulie Walnuts is not a man to be admired. He's a whiny cheapskate with a raging sense of entitlement. Even the other wiseguys can't stand him, and when his stinginess with the festival rides endangers kids, it gives them a long-desired excuse to shun him. Deservedly treated as an outcast and facing his own mortality with a prostate cancer scare, the only person he can turn to is the Lawrence Welk–loving adoptive mother whom he had cursed out and abandoned.

Then there's Christopher. Aside from a gift for attracting beautiful women with minimal self-esteem, he has nothing going for him. His Hollywood dreams will never lead anywhere, his position in the Family came from nepotism, and even without people like Tony goading him, he'll never have the discipline to stay sober for long. And by ratting out Adriana—which we finally see in flashback via a deleted scene from season five's "Long Term Parking"—he not only murdered the woman of his dreams, but has become so obsessed with her that the memory of her life and death seems destined to destroy him, whether through his own self-sabotage or Carmela's growing suspicion over Ade's fate.

A lot of major events happen in this episode—Christopher marries pregnant girlfriend Kelli (Cara Buono[39]) and falls off the wagon again, Tony and Phil cut Johnny out of the first of what will clearly be many future secret deals (eventually leaving Johnny, like Junior, boss in name only), Liz La Cerva (Patty McCormack) tells Carmela what she believes really happened to her daughter—but they're presented casually, as if these people are so bored with the business they have chosen that they can't even recognize momentous events right in front of them.

We meet Kelli only moments before she and Christopher get married.[40] While the series sometimes fumbles character introductions, we don't need to know much about Kelli, save that she's a replacement Adriana—less tacky with the makeup and nails, but seemingly more pliant, more submissive to her man and his moods. She's Adriana with most of her decency but without the fire that made Adriana so special and uniquely lovable: the Adriana Chris didn't know that he didn't really want.

All these characters are on a ride, all right, but it's not a roller-coaster with dips and curves and loops. It's the airport baggage carousel. They just keep going around in circles, seeing the same disappointed faces as they pass, waiting for someone or something to take them somewhere interesting. Someday that ride's going to crash like those teacups at the St. Elzéar feast, and when it does, the damage is going to be a lot worse than a kid with a bloody mouth.

---

39 Of the handful of *Sopranos* actors Matthew Weiner brought over to *Mad Men*, Buono wound up with by far the biggest role, as the eloquent and refined psychologist Dr. Faye Miller, who confesses to Don Draper that her father was "a two-bit gangster." In terms of tone and themes, Tony Soprano fathered everybody on that series, as well as on Terence Winter's *Boardwalk Empire*, Todd Kessler's *Damages*, the Edie Falco–starrer *Nurse Jackie*, and countless other series about sympathetic antiheroes.

40 When the crew throws Christopher a post-nuptial bachelor party at Vesuvio, Artie only talks about the food, and the guys seem genuinely interested in the specials. Perhaps Tony's advice from "Luxury Lounge" to focus on cooking has sunk in.

SEASON 6/EPISODE 10
"MOE 'N JOE" WRITTEN BY MATTHEW WEINER
DIRECTED BY STEVE SHILL

The Totality of Vito

"I'll take it." —**Johnny Sack**

And now, the end is near. Vito has lived free long enough, and now he wants to die.

The man is driving back to a place where all his old friends want to kill him, guzzling gin and listening to "My Way" on an endless loop. This is what you call a suicide mission. It's a much longer and more elaborate version of Eugene Pontecorvo tying a rope to a rafter in the basement—a self-contained, single episode story that in retrospect prefigured nearly every important moment of this season, but the tragedy of Vito most poignantly. And if you're wondering why Vito would bother killing that stubborn New Englander to escape the cops, it's simple: He's ready to die, but he wants to do it his way.

Vito's not the only one facing an end. In the space of one deceptively busy hour, Johnny Sack pleads guilty, Tony crushes Carmela's dreams of independence, Paulie reveals that he's battling cancer, Meadow edges closer to dumping Finn, and Tony finally makes peace with Janice's role in his life.

David Chase and company have been using the show's dwindling number of episodes to give each of their characters a few more moments at center stage before that final curtain. Three episodes ago, Artie got another star turn; the one after that, AJ. In "Moe 'N Joe," that curtain begins falling hard on Johnny, who's been disintegrating before our eyes.

Chase has hired a lot of acting diamonds in the rough, and Vince Curatola has shined brightest. A bit player in the first two seasons, he would become an essential part of the show, and it's painful to watch him portray how completely the Feds have broken Johnny. It's a masterful portrait of a once-powerful man who's had everything taken from him except his anger and sense of entitlement; now even that fire is dying. Johnny has smarts, a temper, and a love of family like Tony, but he's also what Tony aspires to be. He's the archetypal gangster, running New York and not New Jersey, dressed to the nines, always clutching his cigarette, calculating and ruthless in ways Tony can only occasionally be. Even a few episodes back, Johnny would've gone nuclear if someone tried to change the terms of a deal as Tony keeps doing in this episode. Now, he just shrugs it off.

To paraphrase Phil Leotardo, if the Feds can make Johnny Sack commit the cardinal sin of going on record about the existence of La Cosa Nostra, what can they make Tony do?

But rage, followed by resignation, is the mode of the hour. Johnny has fought and fought, only to realize he has no choice but to do whatever the Feds demand. Carmela earned every penny Tony gave her for the spec house (and then some), yet when he blows off meeting the building inspector who can keep construction moving forward—out of petty irritation that he's forced into awkward, rage-inducing small talk with Meadow (who objects to Tony's suggestion that she and Finn have been "living in sin") because Carm isn't home— she has no choice but to swallow her anger, even as she continues to enviously note the independence Angie Bonpensiero has achieved while running her body shop.

Tony's more full of anger than anyone this time out, not only over the Meadow argument, but a source of much older familial irritation: the older sister who always belittled him, then ran away and left him to care for their mother, then came home to seize Livia's house, car, and domineering position in the biological family. Though Janice has superficially changed from her debut, all her chameleon moves still serve the same needy behavior that persistently has her brother questioning her motives. "Janice only does acts of Janice," Tony insists. At the end of a particularly raw therapy session with Melfi, he snarls, "She took off. She laughed at all this shit. Then the trip's over and she's back and she's one of us. And she wants her piece. Well, let me tell you, she gets nothing! 'Cause I got the scars! So it's mine!"

Yet the same feelings of familial obligation ultimately push Tony to do an act of Janice himself, by agreeing to negotiate a deal on Johnny's behalf[41] in exchange for Johnny selling his McMansion to Bobby and Janice at an absurdly reduced price. It's a brotherly gesture so grand and unexpected, it cuts through all Janice's usual defenses and con artist personae. "Who knows what goes on in my head?" she weeps. (Carmela, baffled by this outburst, asks what's the matter. "She's happy—about the house," a resigned Tony explains, understanding his sister's moods better than his wife ever could.)

The allocution renders Johnny persona non grata within the Mob, and the plea deal strips away most of the fortune he spent a lifetime building for Ginny and his girls. But it feels to him like the only choice he has left, in the same way Vito decides to abandon the Gay Heaven of Dartford to go on his booze- and Sinatra-fueled suicide run back to Essex County.

The relationship with Jim is still mostly idyllic, at times even absurdly so: as Jim slips behind Vito in bed, we cut to one of Bacala's model trains going through

---

41 The brothers-in-law who negotiate with Tony are something of a mirror image of his own relationship with Bacala: in this case, the guy who married the other's (younger) sister-in-law is the one with a spine.

a tunnel, like the famous last shot of *North by Northwest*. But Jim and the other people of Dartford ultimately don't accept the totality of Vito any more than the Jersey wiseguys did. They accept the gay man with an eye for antiques and a taste for johnny cakes. But the guy with the Mob DNA is still there, too. The urges to drink, gamble, and mess around are too great, and Dartford is not only too sleepy a community for his appetites, but it's one where this former no-work job holder is expected to put in an honest day's labor.

Vito's internal monologue while playing handyman—agonizing over the slow passage of time even as he tries to avoid checking his watch—is, like much of the Dartford interlude, a stylistic departure for the series, but also the most efficient way to get across how temperamentally unsuited he is to the life he'd have to lead if he remained. Much as he may care for Jim and appreciate being able to live as an openly gay man, he knows he'd die a different death if he stayed. So, like Johnny and Tony and Carmela in this hour, he gives in to the inevitable, pointing his car toward Jersey and whatever fate awaits him.

SEASON 6/EPISODE 11
WRITTEN BY DIANE FROLOV & ANDREW SCHNEIDER AND DAVID CHASE
DIRECTED BY TIM VAN PATTEN

City of Lights

> *"He came out of the coma for a minute, and he said, 'Who am I? Where am I going?' At the time I didn't know what he meant. But coming here, I feel the same way."* —**Carmela**

Much of "Cold Stones" is spent contrasting Carmela and Rosalie's Parisian vacation with the escalating New York–New Jersey tensions. It is a tale of two cities, told in edits: Carm looks at a sculpture of a beautiful woman, and we cut to someone scraping bird splutz off the Bing sign; she looks at a Virgin Mary statue, and we see Tony getting a happy ending from a stripper;[42] she snaps a picture of a neon pig restaurant sign, and suddenly there's Murmur telling a dirty joke with a pig as the punch line.

---

42 Though Tony couldn't go through with it with Julianna Skiff, Carmela essentially gives him permission to cat around while she's out of the country—which fits with the deal they made when she took him back at the end of season five—and he takes her up on it.

Carmela is overwhelmed by both the beauty of Paris and how much more history everything has there versus North Caldwell. "This city is so old," she tells Roe during a sightseeing trip. "You think about all the people who have lived here, generation after generation, hundreds and hundreds of years, all those lives. God, it's so sad. I mean, it isn't sad, I don't know. It just makes you think—just makes you look at yourself differently."

History is at the heart of the entire hour, which features more callbacks to past episodes than any other in the run of the series: chopping up bodies at Satriale's, AJ's nihilist phase, Carm and Roe's aborted trip to Italy, Mr. Wegler's book about Abelard and Heloise, Richie Aprile's gay son, Tony's coma, and the deaths of Jackie, Jackie Jr., and poor Cosette and Adriana, who appear to Carmela in a dream.

Like Tony in "Funhouse" and "The Test Dream," Carmela has to travel to accept a truth that's long been staring her in the face: as the French policeman in the dream puts it while nodding toward Ade, "Your friend? Somebody needs to tell her she's dead." And like the alternate Tony in Costa Mesa, she looks out her hotel room and sees a beacon, this time for the Eiffel Tower instead of the house where Tony B wanted to send our Tony.

The trip is both dream and nightmare for Carm. She feels insignificant in this beautiful and ancient place. And as Rosalie laments after Carm brings up the deaths of her husband and son during dinner,[43] she can't help bringing New Jersey to the City of Lights. She's getting closer to accepting the truth about Ade, as well as her own complicity in evil for comfort's sake. But the stunning vistas can't heal the sickness inside her.

Those sharp cuts from the majesty of Paris to the muck of Essex County are about more than just sick humor. They show the roots of Carmela's unease. The Jersey violence ranks with the show's ugliest, particularly the gruesome sequence where Phil and his goons murder Vito, torturing him to death while he's bound and gagged[44] and leaving a pool cue jammed up his anus to remove any doubt as to why he was murdered. The murder is an especially theatrical production by Phil, not only with the pool cue, but with Phil literally coming out of a closet to let Vito

---

43 Despite the enormous tragedies life has handed her, Rosalie is perhaps the series' most level-headed and emotionally strong character. Life has to go on, and she always learns to go along with it. Where Carmela mopes through much of the trip, Roe is flirting with a much younger man ("They got a Belleville in France!"), and when Carm has her own AJ-esque nihilistic moment, Roe calms her down by humming a little Édith Piaf. Sharon Angela is always a delight in the role.

44 Phil's pushy, devout wife reminds him earlier about how sinners can repent on their deathbeds and still get into Heaven, so Phil puts tape on Vito's mouth to prevent him from doing that.

know just how screwed he is.[45] But Vito's fate is left to our disturbed imaginations, whereas the retaliatory murder of New York wiseguy Fat Dom Gamiello (Tony Cucci) by Carlo and Silvio gets play-by-play scrutiny. Tony's two top guys murder Fat Dom with pork store implements after Dom makes one taunt too many,[46] while also implying that the homophobic Carlo shares Vito's orientation.

Like most impulse killings in the series, it's chaotic, bordering on slapstick— Sil brains Fat Dom with a handheld vacuum, then leaps on his back—while also illustrating just what a mess Tony's entire Family is in now. Phil is powerful enough that he can brazenly murder a New Jersey Mob captain—a fugitive pariah, but still—and turn his corpse into an object lesson without fearing retaliation. Sil and Carlo are able to murder Fat Dom, but only by complete surprise (and Dom makes a better accounting of himself than you'd expect), and New Jersey is so beholden to New York that the body immediately has to be chopped up, Richie-style.

Tony doesn't know what those two did, but he *knows*. And more importantly, he knows exactly how deep he's in now. What's the first thing he does after performing mental calculus over why Sil wouldn't let him into Satriale's and what that means? He calls a construction buddy to get AJ a job, because he fears he may not have much time left to straighten out his reckless, insubordinate son.[47]

The sins of the past are catching up with everyone, and the future is cloudy at best. Carmela travels to Paris because with Meadow moving out[48] and her spec house business in ruins, she feels there's nothing to do at home. Melfi asks Tony how he wants to live his life, and he changes the subject because he can't imagine what he might want—or whether he'll be around to get it. We know the show is ending, but suddenly it feels as if the characters know it, too.

Realizing how big she felt in Jersey and how small in Paris, Carmela has an epiphany that she shares with Rosalie: "We worry so much. Sometimes it feels like that's all we do, but in the end it just gets washed away." When she goes home, one of the first things we see her do is take a load of laundry downstairs, to the very spot where Christopher ratted Adriana out to Tony. In the end, it all gets washed

---

45 Or is this Phil's way of telling Vito a secret about his own sexuality—and how Mob culture, a Catholic upbringing, and a controlling wife have forced him to suppress it (other than perhaps when he was in prison—because, as Tony told Melfi, you get a pass for that)—in the only way he can?

46 The scene owes more than a small debt to the famous *Goodfellas* moment where Tommy murders Billy Batts—played, of course, by Frank Vincent—after Billy tells him one time too often to go home and get his shine box.

47 The shakycam scene in the garage, where Tony's desire to help AJ battles mightily against his impulse to smash his face through that windshield, is one of James Gandolfini's finest moments.

48 Meadow, like her mother, proves to have a tremendous capacity for willful self-denial. When Meadow brings up the plan to go to California to be with Finn and his family, Carmela says, "I thought you two were having problems." "I never said that!" snaps Meadow—who had, in fact, said exactly that to Tony in the previous episode.

away, from the dirt on the clothes to the men and women murdered in unspeakable fashion. This, all of this, will someday be forgotten.

SEASON 6/EPISODE 12
WRITTEN BY TERENCE WINTER AND DAVID CHASE AND MATTHEW WEINER
DIRECTED BY ALAN TAYLOR

Least She's Catholic

"I got a guy." —**Tony**

"And I got a job." —**AJ**

At times, "Kaisha" functions exactly like a *Sopranos* season finale would.[49] It opens with a tribute to the late John Patterson, who directed the five previous season-enders. It closes, as most prior finales have, on a scene of the Soprano clan celebrating together. It's bookended by a Rolling Stones song ("Moonlight Mile"), just as season two's "Funhouse" used the Stones' "Thru and Thru" as a recurring motif, and as season five's "All Due Respect" used Van Morrison's "Glad Tidings."

Overall, though, "Kaisha" feels more like one of those episodes the series occasionally pulled out of the oven too soon at mid-season. Other than shelving the building tensions with New York[50]—and, in a deliberately anticlimactic *Sopranos* fashion, evoking the ends of seasons three and four, with Phil backing off after barely surviving a heart attack—it's not particularly interested in resolving various arcs, and largely retreads familiar character and thematic ground. Like the episode's title character—a fictional black girlfriend Christopher invents to avoid confessing that he and Julianna Skiff have been having an affair behind Tony's back—it seems to exist more as a promising idea than fully formed accomplishment.

Nowhere is this more obvious than in watching Christopher and Julianna inexorably pull each other off the wagon. Where previous episodes about Christopher's drug addiction managed to establish the depths of the problem without

---

49 There was a long production hiatus after "Kaisha" finished, and both David Chase and the authors of this book consider these to be two separate seasons.

50 Introduced in this episode: New York wiseguy Butchie Deconcini, played by Greg Antonacci, who starred in a pair of Chase-penned *Rockford Files* about two low-level thugs from New Jersey. The second episode, "Just a Coupla Guys," was a backdoor pilot for a spin-off about those characters, and even featured a Jersey Mob boss named Anthony with a shiftless son.

wallowing in it, this bender creates the illusion that we're sober people stuck in the room with these two, watching them get high and incoherent in real time. That Christopher's doing it with a would-be conquest of Tony's—payback, intentional or not, for what he believes happened between Tony and Adriana in "Irregular Around the Margins"—livens things up a bit in the light it sheds on the fraying relationship between mentor and protégé, but it still feels like a rehash, and not one that holds up to repeat dramatization as other *Sopranos* narrative loops have.

At one point the two addicts go to see *Vertigo*, and we're presented with a Hitchcock-ian double exposure of the two of them in the theater and getting high in Julianna's apartment. *Vertigo* is about a man trying to turn one woman into another, desperately attempting to redo a tragic event with a happy ending, to set the terms of a phenomenon no one can control: mortality. Kelli's no Adriana, and neither is Julianna, even if their names rhyme.

The injection of *Vertigo* into an episode featuring Julianna also reminds us of how subconscious repetitive drives have dictated much of Tony's sex life since we first met him. If Julianna is a re-creation of women the show has featured in the past, they're ones Tony has slept with (or tried to). Tony even acknowledges this tendency to Melfi when he vents about Christopher succeeding with Julianna (or so he thinks) where he failed. "You know what I been realizing: these women, they're all sort of the same," he admits, folding Melfi, Gloria, and Julianna under the same umbrella of "dark complexion, smart, they smell a little bit of money."

Melfi sees Tony's response to the affair—resigned rather than vengeful—as a sign of his progress, on top of his reluctance to sleep with Julianna in the first place. But the latter was at least as much a matter of biology as psychology. And Tony's unimpressed by the idea that he's getting better, suggesting that this lingering attraction to the good doctor is the only positive of their relationship at this stage. "Probably the reason I still come here," he shrugs, "[is] to hang out with you—'cause nothing really changes with the therapy part."

That sense of simply finding ways to fill time hangs over nearly all of "Kaisha." War with New York is averted only by Phil's heart attack and Tony's attempt to impart the lessons of his own hospitalization to his angry Brooklyn counterpart. And the spec house project comes back to life only so Tony can distract Carmela from investigating Adriana's disappearance. (Tony to Sil: "For all our sakes, my wife needs a career.")

The only one to break the cycle is, of all people, AJ. Pressed by Tony into a Mob-affiliated construction job, he takes his own stint with a hard hat more seriously than Finn ever did, and in the process catches the eye of job site receptionist Blanca (Dania Ramirez), a beautiful single mom. Her affections seem to do more to kick-start AJ's maturity than any of the tough love gambits Tony and Carmela have tried, and if he's too privileged to fully appreciate the kind of life Blanca has lived, his heart finally seems to be in the right place, as we see when he bribes a group of neighborhood loudmouths with his expensive bicycle so they'll leave and quit waking up Blanca's little boy Hector.

This newly responsible version of their son proves to be a monkey's paw situation to Tony and especially Carmela, who wanted AJ to start taking life seriously, but doesn't approve of the root cause of the change, complaining to Tony at the season-ending Christmas party, "She's ten years older than him, and she's Puerto Rican?"

"Dominican, maybe," Tony shrugs. "Least she's Catholic."

In that way, AJ's situation isn't that different from that of Tony's unofficial other son Christopher, who is also struggling to get better, while being dumped on for the methods he uses along the way. The wiseguys all mock Christopher's twelve-step activities, which only leaves him more isolated and more inclined to seek the comfort of someone like Julianna,[51] while the more Tony and Carmela look down on Blanca and Hector, the more likely AJ seems to prefer their company to those of his parents.

In the summer of 2006, when fans knew they wouldn't get more episodes until the following year, "Kaisha" felt exasperating. As part of a modern binge, it still feels like filler, but at least now a viewer can move instantly on to one of the great stretch runs any TV series has ever had.

---

51 The best moment of that whole plot may be the glimpse of Julianna telling her sponsor all the red flags about Christopher: that he's married, that he's in the Mob, and that Julianna nearly slept with his infamous boss, Tony Soprano. "I'm sorry, Jules," the sponsor confesses, "I don't even know where to fuckin' start."

Season
Seven

SEASON 7/EPISODE 1

"SOPRANO HOME MOVIES"

WRITTEN BY DIANE FROLOV & ANDREW SCHNEIDER AND
DAVID CHASE AND MATTHEW WEINER
DIRECTED BY TIM VAN PATTEN

Boardwalk Hotel

"You Sopranos! You go too far!" —**Bobby**

"Is this it?" Carmela asks Tony early in "Soprano Home Movies," after waking up to the sound of cops beating on their front door.

No, it's not quite "it"—if by "it," you mean the point where Tony's bad deeds finally catch up with him. He's rich enough to buy a good lawyer, and the charge that prompts his latest arrest is old and weak (possession of a handgun and hollow-point ammunition—fallout from the end of season five, where Tony fled from the Feds' arrest of Johnny Sack and chucked his piece in the snow, where it was discovered by a dumb suburban teen). But in another sense, yes, this is "it"— the final stretch for *The Sopranos*, the series. To answer one Carmela quote with another, from the season four premiere, "Let me tell you something: everything comes to an end."

The opening sequence of this episode—an off-kilter prologue, really, with an alternate narrative of that "All Due Respect" chase scene that opens like a hyper-text link—also echoes the lyrics of the show's theme: "Woke up this morning / Got yourself a gun." But this time, it's a gun Tony that didn't have anymore—and damn sure didn't want. The charge, though not quite resolved, looks like it won't stick, so it counts as a close call—one of many that Tony has endured over six seasons, the most drastic of which was his shooting by demented Uncle Junior.

"Soprano Home Movies" is largely a demonstration of Tony's inability to escape being Tony even when escape is the whole point. He and Carmela try to flee the anxiety surrounding Tony's gun charge and the irritation of AJ's new situation[1] by heading to Bobby and Janice's lake house to celebrate Tony's forty-seventh birthday.

It's a spectacular place to visit, and large chunks of the episode involve some combination of the four adults simply basking in the calming sights and sounds of the lake, with one scene dissolving peacefully into the next. But whether a Soprano

---

1   At the end of season six, a big deal is made of Tony getting tough with AJ and forcing him to take that construction job, and we're left with the implication that AJ has finally come within spitting distance of a work ethic. So, of course, we return from hiatus and now he's left construction to work at Beansie's pizzeria. So much for both his maturity and Tony's tough love.

goes to Naples, Paris, Miami, or an alternate reality, they are still a Soprano, and rot follows them.

While Tony and Bobby sit on a boat in the middle of the lake, for instance, the conversation inevitably turns to business. The two men speculate on what happens if you get whacked. "You probably don't even hear it when it happens, right?" Bobby wonders. The talk shifts to how Bobby has never actually killed someone on the job ("My pop never wanted it for me."), and Tony suggests that Bobby may be a more reliable number two than guilt-ridden junkie Christopher has turned out to be. (Chris appears for only a few seconds in this episode—trying to wish Tony a happy birthday before T hangs up on him—which is long enough to establish that Tony has yet to forgive him for Julianna Skiff and any number of other offenses.)

The episode's most important set piece takes place indoors, as we spend a long, drunken evening with the Soprano siblings and their spouses, first doing karaoke (Carmela has rarely seemed less guarded than when she's belting out "Love Hurts"), then playing an epic game of Monopoly that results in hurt feelings over the use of the unofficial Free Parking rule (when Bobby insists that the Parker Brothers put a lot of thought into the game as it should be played, his own wife snorts, "Fuck the Parker Brothers!"), over Janice telling an embarrassing (to Tony) but funny (to everyone else) story about Johnny Boy firing a bullet through Livia's beehive hairdo, and particularly over Tony's inability to stop making jokes about Janice's old ways. The scene is the most purely theatrical thing the series has done since "Whitecaps," a wiseguy riff on *The Man Who Came to Dinner*. It ratchets the tension and discomfort until Tony is warbling a version of "Under the Boardwalk" whose lyrics are about the sex acts Janice might have performed there.

This is too much for Bobby, who has already insisted that Tony is a guest in his home who should not be insulting his wife, and he sucker-punches his own boss, leading to an ugly, clumsy brawl that's like a sad comic mirror of Ralphie's death. Tony has always had the physical advantage in any fight we've ever seen him get into, but Bobby is younger and healthier (he hasn't been shot in the last year, at least), and is powered by a more righteous fury than the indignation Tony musters at the thought of one of his guys daring to strike him. In a shocking upset akin to Buster Douglas knocking out Mike Tyson, it's Tony who winds up on the canvas at the end of this bout,[2] though it's Bobby who then tries to run away, aware of the potentially fatal consequences of what he's just done.

---

2 Always perfect with the small details, this show: in the aftermath, Carmela notices a Monopoly hotel has gotten stuck to Tony's bloody cheek, and brushes it onto the floor.

"Tony is not a vindictive man," Carmela tries to reassure Janice the next morning. We know otherwise, and the events that follow prove her sadly wrong—albeit not in the way either she or we might expect. Tony has never been a gracious loser, and he stews over the various reasons Bobby had an unfair advantage, but he never seriously entertains killing his brother-in-law. That would be a Johnny Boy move, and as season five's "Cold Cuts" reminded us, it's Janice who inherited more of that form of the Soprano temper (witness Richie), where Tony is more like his mother than he'd ever want to admit. Janice killing Richie for punching her in the mouth (presented in a sad, funny alternate history to Carmela) was more a Johnny Boy reaction than a Livia one. Livia wouldn't have shot Richie. She would have henpecked him to death, or found something he loved and taken it from him. What Tony does to Bacala is exactly the kind of dish Livia would have served with cold cuts, where Johnny Boy and Janice both would have gone straight to blood.

A brother-in-law gets killed, but it's someone else's: while negotiating a deal with a Canadian crew, Tony offers to murder the troublesome ex-husband of one of their sisters, and insists that Bobby be the one to do it. This goes against Bobby Sr.'s wishes, and against Bobby's own gentle nature, but Bobby's in a vulnerable position where he can't say no to the boss. The hit mostly goes as planned, but the victim reaches out and rips open Bobby's shirt as the second bullet is fired, exposing his broken heart for all of us to see.

In the world of the Mob, Bobby has just improved his standing. From any other perspective, he's damned himself, and he knows it, judging by the look on his face as he returns to the lake to see Janice, baby Nica, and some friends all laughing and playing like they're in a laundry detergent commercial.[3] This is the life he wants, the one he will go to extremes to protect, but the cabin will be forever soured, because he'll remember the fight that happened here and what it forced him to do.

On *The Sopranos*, when a character compliments another character on bettering themselves, or simply changing, it's usually a sick joke. "The credit goes to you," Janice tells her brother, noting how mellow he's become. "You've really changed."[4] Of course neither Tony nor Janice has really changed—they've just become more powerful and loathsome over the years, and more tragic because of the glimmers of self-awareness that keep getting snuffed out. The sense that Tony had a chance to really change but missed his moment is indicated, subtly,

---

3 Tony sparks the fight by singing a dirty version of one Drifters song, and that closing scene is accompanied by another: "This Magic Moment," which matches the images but not Bobby's feelings.

4 This scene eventually turns into a riff on the "You're really funny" scene from *Goodfellas*, as an irritated Tony begins asking Janice, "I'm different how?"

when Carmela spots a jumping fish (probably the most important animal on this show, even more important than Tony's season one dream ducks) and Tony looks up too late to see it.

"You're a young man," Bobby tells Tony. "We both are. The world's still in front of us." But the episode's real message can be found in another Bobby line, when he tells Tony that he's glad he never had to do a hit because DNA evidence makes it so hard to get away with crime these days. You cannot escape your identity.

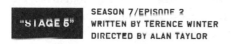

SEASON 7/EPISODE 2
WRITTEN BY TERENCE WINTER
DIRECTED BY ALAN TAYLOR

Spinning Wheels

"How will I be remembered?" —**Johnny Sack**

"Is it possible on some level you're reading into all of this?" Dr. Melfi asks Tony Soprano, after Tony says he suspects that his cousin, budding filmmaker Christopher, based a hot-tempered, spouse-betraying gangster boss on Tony.

"I've been coming here for years," Tony replies wearily. "I know too much about the subconscious now."

And on that note, let's dive into "Stage 5," perhaps the most self-reflective episode of a series that's already offered plenty.

The hour is remarkable enough for its richly detailed events, including the premiere of Christopher's splatterfest *Cleaver*; Carmela's confrontation with Tony over the implication, via Chris's movie, that Tony slept with Adriana; Silvio's survival of a Mob hit, apparently instigated by New York underboss Doc Santoro (Dan Conte), that kills Gerry "The Hairdo" Torciano[5] (John Bianco); Tony's admission in therapy that he fears Chris has forgotten Tony's big-brotherly love for him and wants him dead; and of course, the sudden decline and death of cancer-ridden

---

5   The Torciano hit is presented in a manner evoking Bacala's "You probably don't even hear it when it happens" theorizing from "Soprano Home Movies." Silvio is out dining with the Hairdo and two women when the sound drops out, replaced by a high-pitched whine, followed by blood spraying all over Silvio's face. It takes another moment for him to hear the sound of the gunshot and realize Gerry's been taken out right in front of him. Even a witness like Silvio doesn't hear it exactly when it happens.

Johnny Sack, who faces his final curtain with fear in his eyes.[6] He keeps smoking those coffin nails right up to the end, so stubbornly that even his wife Ginny, who was furious over his unwillingness to quit, busts out a pack at Johnny's bedside after hearing him call out for his mother. It's as if she thinks the promise of one more puff might inspire John to turn on his heel and walk away from the light.

On top of that, there's a persistent, at times suffocating aura of futility—a sense that individual hits, schemes, scores, and power plays don't mean much once you've accepted the fact that, as Carmela once put it, "Everything ends." "Stage 5" is the most literally and figuratively funereal hour the series has yet given us, a melancholy-to-depressive installment whose very title is a synonym for death—a reference to a nonexistent stage of cancer beyond Stage Four.

The characters, led by Tony, spend much of the hour going about in pity for themselves. Johnny dies of cancer. Phil Leotardo talks about his own heart attack, nurses an ancient family grudge against America's ruling classes (his family name got changed from "Leonardo" at Ellis Island), and worries aloud that he's compromised too much during his life. Shockingly, he even expresses doubts about the wisdom of staying mum while serving time, and about failing to personally avenge the death of his brother, Billy, at the hands of Tony B.

Tony himself seems stricken, battered, exhausted. Whether brooding over Johnny's fate or sweating Christopher's cinematic hit job ("All those memories are for what? All I am to him is some asshole bully."), you can tell his mind is elsewhere—most likely, on the prospect of his own demise and the question of whether he'll leave behind anything but money, grief, and fat jokes. (When the Bada Bing inner circle gathers to hear news of Johnny's death, a slow dolly into Tony's face in profile isolates; it's as if a dark thought has just snuck up on him.) Paulie Walnuts's toast to the dearly departed consists of bragging that he's kicked cancer; then he misquotes the Blood, Sweat and Tears song "Spinning Wheels," which, considering recent events, seems like a Top 40 omen. The Cleaver gets everyone eventually.

In a speech that turns out to be deceptively important to the entire series, given the man delivering it, Little Carmine meets Tony for lunch, where they discuss succession in an era of two-bit gang warfare and increased federal harassment (the FBI even busts Larry Boy Barese at the *Cleaver* premiere party). Tony—who wants somebody to step up and lead the New York Family just to end this bloodshed

---

6   It's a beautiful send-off for Vince Curatola, who went from masonry contractor to one of the most indelible members of the whole cast. One superb scene in particular is the first family visit, from the way Johnny gently breaks the news with an understated, "I'm very, very sick," to the daggers he stares at that prison guard who keeps telling them to stop touching (in freer, healthier times, Johnny would have had that guy's entire family killed), to the look of anticipation, when, after Ginny has gone, he smokes his first cigarette in a long time, because what can it possibly hurt now?

and his many headaches—asks Carmine what happened to his ambition. Little Carmine responds by describing a dream he once had. In the dream, his father turned 100, and Little Carmine gave his father "a mellifluous box," which the elder Carmine looked upon with "this gaze of absolute disappointment," because there was nothing in it. His dad told him, "Fill it up . . . come back when I'm 200." On the basis of that dream, and his wife warning him that she didn't want to be the wealthiest widow on Long Island, Carmine decided to seek happiness outside of the Family business. The dream "wasn't about being boss," Little Carmine explains to Tony. "It was about being happy."[7] It's also about the foolishness of pursuing wealth, power, and the approval of one's elders (or social betters) instead of actually living your life and enjoying each day as if it's a gift—even if it's occasionally a pair of socks.

As if that's not enough to chew on, "Stage 5" turns its mortality obsession back on itself, deploying so many images and lines of dialogue calling attention to *The Sopranos* as a TV series that the episode doesn't seem to be asking, "Will anyone remember us fondly after we're dead?," but rather, "Will anybody remember *The Sopranos* as anything but a blood-and-guts gangster show?"

There are warnings of the dangers of overinterpretation that seem like intentional retorts to Tony's remark to Melfi, and to critics like the ones who wrote this book. Christopher wriggles away from charges that he based the film's Mob boss villain (played by Daniel Baldwin[8]) on Tony by having JT Dolan attribute it to the Broderick Crawford character in *Born Yesterday* (who also memorably wore a robe). Whether Chris intended the comparison or not, he damn sure did it on purpose, yet he begs off responsibility, insisting that creativity is a mysterious thing. "It was an idea, I don't know, who knows where they fucking come from? Isaac Newton invented gravity cuz some asshole hit him with an apple!" he tells poor JT, before braining him with a Humanitas prize. Then there's the bit where an unseen viewer's TV reveals Geraldo Rivera interviewing Mob experts[9] about the current New York Mob madness. The panel bets on possible replacements for Johnny with the same jocular attitude you used to find in conversations during the original run of *The Sopranos* about who was going to get whacked next (which in turn echoes a comment about *Cleaver*, "These audiences today, they want blood."). The punch line: a reverse angle revealing that the TV belongs to none other than

---

7   Similar wisdom comes courtesy of Christopher's new twelve-step sponsor Eddie, played by Christopher McDonald, a good actor who's arguably much too recognizable (via *Happy Gilmore* and many other films) to be playing a random, never-before-seen character in an episode filled with C-listers playing themselves.

8   The Cleaver himself, meanwhile, is played by Jonathan LaPaglia, whose older brother Anthony was once a candidate to play Tony Soprano when the show was in development at Fox. Chase insists this is just a coincidence.

9   Including the return of Matthew Weiner's Manny Safier.

Elliot Kupferberg, who has gone full Mob fanboy over the years. ("This Santoro thing, I called it a year ago!") Carmine praises his own film's cleverness, particularly a close-up of a crucifix and a vaudevillian hanging from a rearview mirror. ("The sacred and the propane," Carmine malaprops.) And let's not forget Gerry the Hairdo's interpretation of Phil's heart problems as "a metaphor. He lost his balls is what I'm saying." (If so, it's a metaphor for a metaphor.)

Is this evidence that the writers sometimes worry that detractors are right: *The Sopranos* really is a whack-'em gangster soap gussied up in academic pretension? In scenes like the one with Little Carmine and Tony's lunch—where the gangster-gone-Hollywood Carmine orders seared ahi, mixed greens, and an iced tea, and Tony orders a Philly cheesesteak—you gotta wonder.

The self-reflexive aspect of "Stage 5" even shows up in the storyline about Johnny Sack's cancer—particularly when Johnny gets a second opinion from his orderly, Warren Feldman (Sydney Pollack[10] in a brilliant one-off supporting turn). Feldman's an incarcerated oncologist convicted of killing his cheating wife, her aunt who just happened to be there, and a mailman with bad timing. ("At that point, I had to fully commit.") Yet both Johnny and the episode seem clear in their conviction that just because the oncologist is a killer doesn't mean he doesn't have medical knowledge worth imparting. As Johnny's brother-in-law Anthony Infante (Lou Martini Jr.) notes, the blood on O. J. Simpson's hands doesn't make him any less of a great running back.

This is a self-justifying observation used by gangsters and those who write TV shows about them, but there's a strong hint of self-awareness to it, less an apology than a kind of coded self-excoriation. (For all the talk of Feldman's wisdom, he turns out to be wrong; Johnny actually dies more quickly than anyone foresaw.) This whole subplot is of a piece with Tony worrying that Chris only sees him as a bullying fiancée-banger, and Phil worrying that he muffed some of the most important choices of his life. Is *The Sopranos* judging itself as harshly as the harshest critics judged *The Sopranos*?

Maybe, but maybe not—and in any event, the Sopranos and *The Sopranos* both settle in a charitable place. "Whatever else happens, you made a movie, Christopher," Tony says, in a rare, tender moment between them.[11] "Nobody

---

10 Pollack, the director of *They Shoot Horses, Don't They?*, *Jeremiah Johnson*, *The Way We Were*, *Tootsie*, and *Out of Africa*, began his career as an actor in the early days of live TV drama and continued acting in his own films and others'. He would die a little over a year after "Stage 5" aired—killed, like Johnny Sack, by cancer.

11 Later, Tony attends the baptism of Christopher's baby daughter, taking the role of godfather more out of familial (and Familial) obligation than because either man wants it. The song playing is "Evidently Chickentown" by punk poet John Cooper Clarke, one of the show's weirder, more ominous musical selections. Legend has it David Chase heard the song only once before, while cleaning his garage in 1983, and made a mental note to use it in a show one day.

could take that away. Hundred years from now, we're dead and gone, people'll be watching this fucking thing."

SEASON 7/EPISODE 3
WRITTEN BY TERENCE WINTER
DIRECTED BY PHIL ABRAHAM[12]

Take Me Home, Country Road

"'Remember when' is the lowest form of conversation." —**Tony**

"Is this what life is like at our age?" asks Carmela Soprano, as Tony prepares to flee New Jersey while the FBI excavates the site of his first murder.

"The tomatoes are just coming in," Tony replies, a tad wistfully.

It's an odd thing to say, but it feels right. The tomatoes in his backyard are just one entry on a long list of things that he's never properly appreciated and maybe never will. The malaise that hangs over Tony like Pig-Pen's dirt cloud in *Peanuts* isn't a matter of fretting over the persistent unanswered question of whether he'll go out dead or in jail. It seems more unconscious—an incidental affliction, rooted in the curse of living in a perpetual state of disharmony with your own life. During Tony's eight years of therapy with Dr. Melfi, he's learned enough about himself to realize and admit that his life was fucked up from the start, and that he fucked it up worse with each passing year; yet he's never shown the insight necessary to seize that knowledge and break it open, much less change his circumstances. A bullet in the torso got the message across, but it didn't take. He's back to being beat-'em-up, bed-'em-down Tony, except more of an automaton, a bad boy reverting to type without reveling in it.

When Tony and Paulie go down south and hang with Beansie in Miami, Tony agitates to visit a motel and massage parlor they once enjoyed to get steaks, only to discover that it's has been replaced by a depressingly respectable hotel that only offers sandwich wraps after eleven. It's a smaller-scale letdown than the episode's parallel narrative of Uncle Junior in a group home for the criminally insane, where he goes from being a tin-pot dictator running a secret Poker Nation to a medicated institutional yes-man (joining in a sing-along of "Take Me Home, Country Road," for Christ's sake); it's a forced capitulation to a bland new world. In Miami, Tony

---

12 Abraham and Alik Sakharov traded off as director of photography for most of the series' run. "Remember When" was Abraham's first turn directing any TV episode, but he's since done that job on many prestige dramas, including *Mad Men*, *Breaking Bad*, and *Orange Is the New Black*.

gripes to Paulie about Johnny Sack's holier-than-thou attitude toward marital fidelity, and takes a young blond up to his room, but after he's spent himself inside her, he rolls over and makes chitchat, and you wonder: is it an alpha-male rutting urge he's satisfying, or does he just miss talking to Carmela?

Tony utters the episode's title (and this chapter's epigraph) when he grows disgusted by Paulie's nonstop glory-days yammering at dinner with Beansie and their lady friends, and leaves the table in disgust. Funny, though: three episodes in, it seems the final stretch of *The Sopranos* is about failing to remember and fully comprehend past choices, and having to face the consequences. If season six was about the difficulty, even impossibility, of altering one's life (much less one's nature, as if they aren't the same thing) then seven is about the past catching up with you, inflicting inconvenience and sometimes grave damage; how neither would be such a serious threat if you hadn't made the wrong choice; and (a corollary) how the consequences of a past bad choice wouldn't be so troublesome if they caught up to a changed person.

To face the past is to face one's essential nature, and ask how much one has grown or changed, or will change, and the extent to which one even can. Nobody likes to look in a mirror, except maybe a sociopathic narcissist like Paulie, who seems to think everything that ever happened to him is pure anecdote magic. Tony's flirting with preemptively whacking Paulie fuels a suspenseful sequence on a rented boat—a psychic return to Big Pussy's execution, without the aid of a flashback—but is it plausible? Paulie's a petty thug, not a novice meathead; even if he had been established as a diarrhea-mouthed dummy who dropped incriminating statements left and right, he surely would have been whacked by his own guys long ago, perhaps by Tony, who should have noticed this tendency earlier. Or maybe, like the state of his own physique, he's simply getting worse in his old age.

But like Paulie, we digress. The point is, bills that Tony thought he'd skipped out on keep coming due. When the cops in the premiere busted him for the gun he dropped while fleeing Johnny Sack's house,[13] the look of dumb astonishment on his face made clear he'd barely given that piece a second thought. In "Remember When," he runs from his cherry-pop killing, the 1982 murder of Newark bookie Willie Overall. Paulie reassures him that there couldn't be much left, but as Tony rightly observes, bones and teeth are all they need. True, Tony appears to have wriggled out of the gun charge, and he escapes responsibility for the 1982 killing as well, thanks to the incarcerated Larry Boy Barese pinning it on Jackie Aprile.

---

13 Johnny Sack's passing has no calming effect on affairs in New York, where Doc Santoro gets a Moe Greene Special, shot through the eye by soldiers working for Phil, who retakes his place as boss of that Family.

Either he's the luckiest Mob boss who ever lived or just another TV character, living in a blood-and-guts crime story that just happens to be structured like a sitcom: *Everybody Fears Tony*.

No murder or even gun charges for now. Instead, it seems Tony and everyone else are destined to suffer a fate worse than jail or even death: being forced to confront who they really are.

In "Soprano Home Movies," it was Bacala who had to abandon the pretense that he could be a made man without getting blood on his hands. In "Stage Five," Tony saw how much Christopher resented him, while Phil and Johnny Sack questioned how they had lived their lives. Here, Junior and Paulie—Tony's biological uncle and his unofficial one—come to terms with their devolution into sad old men.

Characters have been telling old stories all season, often about the resentment that grows between fathers and sons, or between mentors and protégés. Here, Junior recalls the day his father (Tony's grandfather) made him walk home eleven miles for turning down a 25-cent tip from a rich woman. Carter Chong (Ken Leung[14]), his behind-bars Bacala, loses his temper recounting the time his father dismissed a 96 score on a third grade spelling test because it wasn't a 100. Paulie notes that Johnny Boy gave Tony the Willie Overall hit when Tony was twenty-four, but Tony quickly and forcefully says that he was twenty-two.

It's those details they don't forget. Earlier in that conversation, Tony suggests that Johnny Boy never believed in him. Paulie counters that Johnny trusted him with the hit, after all, but Tony clearly resents that Johnny didn't believe he could become anything but a thug, condemning him to this life.

Tony's always been one to dwell on the past, but spending so much time with blabbermouth Paulie takes away his taste for it. Still, he at least has a present to hold on to. Junior and, to a lesser extent, Paulie, don't.

Junior tries to recreate the past in the hospital, enlisting Carter to help him run a funhouse mirror version of the Executive Game, with the patients playing for buttons and non-diet sodas. But he's not as strong as he once was, and faced with the threat of being transferred to a less cushy facility, he consents to a new drug regimen that leaves him a blurry, sleepy shell of himself.

Carter, bitter at the perceived betrayal by another father figure—and perhaps having read *One Flew over the Cuckoo's Nest* too many times—gives Junior a beatdown, leaving the official boss of New Jersey sitting in a wheelchair, cast

---

14 *Lost* cocreator Damon Lindelof recalls watching "Remember When" and thinking, "I've got to get that guy on *Lost*." Leung would spend the second half of the hit ABC drama's run playing depressed medium Miles Straume. He's worked steadily in TV and movies ever since, including a small role in *Star Wars: The Force Awakens*.

on his arm, a blank, depressed look on his face, and a cat from pet therapy as his only companion.[15]

Midway through their fugitive vacation, Tony and Paulie are shown a black-and-white photo of Paulie in his '60s heyday, flexing a bicep for the camera. What we realize instantly is that Paulie is trying to preserve that image all these decades later. He still pounds the dumbbells, even though the skin sags around his muscles. He still wears the same hairdo, even though the hair is gray and thin. He lives alone, has no real friends, is the least-productive, least-respected captain in the Family, and he Can't. Stop. Talking. The only real difference is the amount of TV he watches; in the '60s, he didn't know who Barney Fife was, while today he cackles hysterically at a *Three's Company* rerun.

Paulie's just self-aware enough to know that Tony's displeased with him. He has a flashback to Pussy's oceanic murder as he and Tony cast off in their fishing boat, is terrified throughout the voyage, and later has a dream (a very literal one by *Sopranos* standards) where he confronts Pussy the rat to ask, "When my time comes, tell me: Will I stand up?"

Paulie hasn't had to make that choice yet. None of the major surviving characters have. Right now, Paulie's punishment is simply having to be Paulie Walnuts, just as Tony's punishment is to be the boss of a decaying empire, and having to work with guys like Paulie.

The one characteristic that unites all the characters is a willingness to speak the language of self-knowledge without stepping outside of themselves and standing far enough from their own egos to gain perspective. Nobody on the series seems to have a conception of life outside of his or her own head, or a sense of history that goes beyond self-justifying factoid or self-pitying anecdote: Chris proclaiming that Lauren Bacall starred in *The Haves and Have-Nots*; Tony repeatedly whining, "Whatever happened to Gary Cooper?"; the hotel attendant who responds to Tony's questions about what happened to the old, sleazy, fun place by repeating, blankly, "I don't know."[16] One rarely gets the sense that Chase's characters understand that the world existed before they were born and will continue to exist after they're dead and buried (perhaps in a Newark basement). When *The Sopranos* is depicting Mob life or suburban life or the fine points of psychoanalysis, it's a compelling black comedy; but when it's showing us the distance between a character's self-image and the reality others see, it's a documentary.

---

15 Dominic Chianese shares James Gandolfini's gift for conjuring great acting moments opposite essentially thin air, here speaking volumes in silence while his scene partner is a cat.

16 Things would work out okay in the end for the hotel attendant—or, at least, for the actor playing him: future musical-theater titan Lin-Manuel Miranda.

SEASON 7/EPISODE 4
"CHASING IT" WRITTEN BY MATTHEW WEINER
DIRECTED BY TIM VAN PATTEN

A Pebble in a Lake

"Listen to me, OK? This is the gravy." —**Tony**

"What are you chasing?" Dr. Melfi asks Tony Soprano, whose compulsive gambling is destroying his life. "Money, or a high from winning?" The episode's title, "Chasing It," seems to promise an answer, but it's another evasion. Tony pointedly doesn't reply to Melfi in his session, but seems to respond later, when he apologizes to Carmela for belittling her adventures in real estate. She notes the illogic of Tony's betting over larger sums of money hoping to win his way out of debt, and he replies, "You start chasing it, and every time you get your hands around it, you fall further backward."

This is what Tony Soprano talks about when he talks about happiness. Not happy-wanderer happiness, but a deeper satisfaction that endures even during grim times. Six-plus seasons into *The Sopranos*, Tony never seems to feel deep happiness for longer than a few moments—maybe when he's taking pride in the accomplishments of loved ones or enjoying the company of old friends he can trust (for the moment). But even then Gandolfini's melancholy performance suggests that there's something gnawing at Tony, an unease more profound than the physical fear of ending up dead or in jail.

Since the shooting, Tony's unease has become palpable. He radiates unhappiness and instability in his everyday life and no longer seems able (or willing) to hide it. He says whatever's running through his head—impulsively proposing a politically impossible tactic, openly copping to his gambling debts in front of subordinates, and otherwise inspiring furtive "The fuck's up with Tony?" glances everywhere he goes. He's behaving like a man who isn't happy being a Mob boss, or a mobster period, and wants out. Because he knows he can't get out, he expresses that wish unconsciously, by doing and saying things that destabilize the life he's always known.[17]

---

17 Carlo, in Tony's doghouse for his failure to run the Family construction business as profitably as Vito, mentions an old *Twilight Zone* episode featuring a thug named Valentine. Tony cuts him off, but Carlo must be referring to "A Nice Place to Visit," an episode about Rocky Valentine, who dies during a robbery and wakes up in an afterlife where his every wish is granted. Every woman wants him, everybody thinks he's wonderful, and every bet he makes is a winner. Eventually, Rocky grows so tired of what he assumes to be Heaven that he asks to go to "the other place," only to be told, "This *is* the other place." Tony's existence isn't quite Rocky Valentine's, but it's close enough for him to sabotage it, just to make something different happen.

This is why Tony's all-consuming (and previously unremarked-upon) gambling addiction works, mostly, as something more than a standard network TV, crisis-of-the-week improv. When a character is convincingly drawn, the details of his self-destructive compulsion don't matter; what's important is that it makes sense given what we know about the character, and that it arrives at a critical juncture in the storyline. Both criteria have been satisfied here—and if it wasn't gambling, it would be something else. Tony has a lot of different nests—his marriage, his identity as a father, his relationship with his crew, his associates (including Hesh Rabkin, Tony's chief creditor), and his fellow bosses (notably Phil Leotardo, who officially takes the New York throne at a party where he's serenaded by none other than Nancy Sinatra)—and he seems determined to foul every one of them.

Late in the episode, there's a significant hard cut between two scenes—one of Tony's ugliest (and ultimately most pathetic) confrontations with Carmela, and a pivotal moment in the episode's B-plot, in which Vito Spatafore Jr. (Brandon Hannan), the goth-posing, profoundly troubled son of a slain gay mobster, responds to bullying in the boys' locker room at school by defecating in the shower. The Tony–Carmela scene builds on an earlier, more subdued confrontation, in which Carmela celebrates the successful sale of her first home—semi-successful, anyway, as she winds up unloading it on Cousin Brian and his pregnant wife—and Tony suggests betting most of the profits on a Jets game that he insists is a "sure thing." The second round finds a bathrobe-clad Tony sweepingly accusing Carm of ruthlessness and hypocrisy, which she's already heard many times and has clearly decided not to think about (just as Tony had decided, until fairly recently, not to obsess over the various sins he committed to amass the Soprano fortune). "The fact is, you're a shitty businesswoman who built a piece of shit house that's gonna cave in and kill that fucking unborn baby any day!" Tony bellows. "And now you can't sleep!" Carmela throws a vase at him and goes upstairs; in wide shot, Tony lumbers off into the background, leaving the vase shards untouched on the foyer floor.

We then cut to Vito Jr. being teased with homophobic slurs in the school showers. His mix of fuck-you indifference, goth affectation, and doughy sensitivity reads as way too sensitive for the macho zoo of high school. With his already innate alienation inflamed by his dad's being killed not for what he did, but for who he was, and the continued defamation of his dad's memory by the same thugs who rooted for his demise, he responds by facing his tormentors, squeezing out a deposit, and mashing it beneath his bare foot. It's social terrorism—a visual and olfactory assault that clears the room. It could only have been committed by a human being who cannot understand, much less articulate, the source of his unhappiness, but who has decided that if he cannot master or destroy his environment, he'll deface it.

It's the act of a young man who hates himself and everyone else so much that he just wants out, and doesn't particularly care how. Of course, the kid didn't anticipate getting rousted from his bed in the middle of the night by Idaho youth-camp goons—a scene that ranks as one of the most disturbing in the entire series, despite its absence of bloodshed, for the way that it syncs up with the previous episode's account of how Tony's dad Johnny Boy ordered Tony to perform his first hit back in 1982. In both instances—Johnny Boy forcing his son into a venal, violent lifestyle he might have transcended if left alone, and Vito Jr. being hauled off (on his mother's orders, and Tony's suggestion) to a brainwashing camp designed to force him to be the kind of person everyone around him would prefer—we're seeing a potentially free and unique soul brutalized by life and then reprogrammed into adopting, and potentially exemplifying, the mentality of his tormentors. (Marie Spatafore suggested a similar course of action a few episodes back, advising her gay husband to consider conversion therapy.)

After the shower outrage, we see Tony react to news of Vito Jr.'s action by deciding to pay the boy's mother, Marie, the $100,000 in relocation money she begged for in the episode's opening scene—money he failed to convince newly installed New York Mob boss Phil Leotardo that *he* should pay, because he's related to Marie and responsible for her husband's murder. Tony somehow assembles the money, then gambles it away—an act that destabilizes his home and professional lives. In both Vito Jr. and Tony stories, men liquidate assets, so to speak, to rebel against a life that's suffocating them, a life that forces them to embody lies. Tony is more self-aware, intelligent, and empathetic than almost anyone around him, including his wife and children, but favors his sadistic and violent streak, for survival's sake. Vito Jr. is rebelling, in his halting and inept way, against the macho straight mentality that contributed to his father's "disappearance," and the various institutions, from organized crime to the schools, that blandly continue its work.

Like many episodes from seasons six and seven, "Chasing It" follows thematically parallel narratives, and occasionally lets its plotlines converge, even collide, so that the stories seem to face and examine each other. The most obvious example is the scene where Tony, who cops to a long history of playing surrogate daddy, goes to Marie's house and confronts Vito Jr. only a tad less brutally than Phil did. When the man and the boy sit across from each other, it's like visiting hour at a prison, only we don't know which is the prisoner. When Tony urges Vito to step up and be the man of the house because nobody else will, he could be addressing himself as a boy—maybe even paraphrasing Livia, the dark shape lingering in the back of his mind, telling him what to do and say even when he's thinks he's not listening. Note that when Tony berates others, he seems to be talking about himself in code. His attack on Carmela accuses her of evading the facts of her own corruption—her willingness to compromise for convenience and profit, expressed in the construction of a shoddy house that could kill its inhabitants. Carmela later counters with a similar image, of Tony as a cartoon character blithely wandering through life oblivious to the piano dangling from a rope above his head. There's a difference, though: Tony is inarticulately accusing Carmela of complicity in corruption—a corruption he embodies. Carmela, on the other hand, seems to be warning him of physical rather than moral punishment: a value-neutral statement along the lines of, "You go in the water, you get wet."

What's Tony rebelling against when he fouls his nest? Probably none of the positive things in his life: a strong, if volatile, marriage to a woman who truly loves him, and who bore him two children who look up to their dad even as they see through him; the security of knowing that he rose higher in his profession (organized crime) than anyone could have predicted, and that he's amassed a fortune that allows him to drop $3.2 million on a yacht (according to Hesh) and bribe a building inspector so that his wife's probable-death trap home can launch her real estate career. But more than ever, he seems ill at ease around people who used to make him feel comfortable. When in groups, he still seems alone, and when he talks, even if he's in direct conversation, it's like he's talking to himself. Even the uncharacteristically (if deliberate) loose camerawork emphasizes this sense of volatility. Tony seems like a spiritual cousin of Eugene and Vito—guys who wanted out and got taken out; guys who unearthed their true selves too late, unbalancing their world and ensuring their demise. *The Sopranos* seems to be disintegrating as we watch it, like Junior's mind.

There's so much more to discuss here: Tony's anti-Semitic baiting of Hesh (more nest-fouling); Dr. Melfi's insistence that Tony attend sessions regularly, then ending the scene by standing up (she's the only character besides Carmela who seems unafraid of standing up to him); the abrupt death during her sleep of Hesh's girlfriend Renata, and Tony's astoundingly cold response (dropping off a sack full of cash to pay off his debt, and leaving as quickly as possible); the canny use, when AJ proposes to Blanca, of the main theme from 1978's *The Deer Hunter*, a movie about how men express emotion by not expressing it, referenced in a scene where a man defies gender stereotype and speaks from his heart. AJ's heart gets stepped on later when Blanca abruptly breaks off the engagement with minimal explanation ("All's I know is I just don't feel it."), but that's another story.

Do the characters themselves feel freer to not worry about consequences because they know the show is ending soon? Are they all, like Tony and poor Vito Jr., so fed up with the state of their lives that they'll do anything to break the monotony? Or are they all, as usual, just not thinking about how their actions ripple out far beyond the moment when they first occur?

It is, as Christopher notes at one point, "like a pebble in a lake—even the fish feel it."

SEASON 7/EPISODE 5
WRITTEN AND DIRECTED BY TERENCE WINTER

Hellfighters

"Chris, you're in the Mafia!" —**JT**

Early in "Walk Like a Man," Tony tries giving Christopher advice on grilling meat as Chris and Kelli host a backyard barbecue, noting that you can pull certain cuts off the flame and they'll keep cooking, thanks to the heat of the juices inside.

Later, when Tony orders a deeply depressed AJ to accept a party invitation from "the Jasons" (the sons[18] of Patsy Parisi and Carlo Gervasi, both of them Rutgers students and bottom-rung Family associates), the media room TV is playing *The Hellfighters*, a 1968 movie where John Wayne plays a firefighter who specializes in putting out fires on oil rigs—which might conceivably burn forever, depending on the size of the deposit below—by drilling deep into the earth and extinguishing the blaze with a well-placed explosive charge.

In the barbecue scene, Christopher stews in the juices of a very old beef, feeling ever-growing resentment toward Tony, Paulie, and all the other mentors who pulled him into this life that offers nothing but misery. *Hellfighters*, meanwhile, presents a macho metaphor for the more sensitive, feminized work done by Dr. Melfi and her colleagues, who dig into the heart of patients' histories and personalities to root out the sources of lifelong trauma—or at least, that's what Melfi's sessions with Tony ought to be. Unfortunately, Tony's right to say that Melfi has spent much of the past six seasons treating symptoms rather than probing root causes—though, to be fair, she might have dug deeper by now had Tony seemed more open to the idea. Tony refuses to work to put out his own fire, nor does he want AJ to put out his own, opting to toss him out of the frying pan of his own depression and into the low-simmering flame offered by the Jasons.

No one gets better, because no one is willing to do the dangerous work necessary to make that happen.

"Walk Like a Man" is another *Sopranos* parallel narrative, following Tony's biological and emotional sons to show the psychological toll of being related, by blood or by bond, to the Family in general and Tony in particular. AJ and Chris

---

18 Michael Drayer plays Jason Parisi, and Joseph Perrino plays Jason Gervasi, who join the series' ever-growing roster of Jasons, including Dr. Melfi's son, Jason Barone, one of Tony Blundetto's twins, Little Paulie's sidekick Jason Molinaro, and Lorraine Calluzzo's partner/lover Jason Evanina. It's like the twenty-first century version of the *Goodfellas* joke about all the Italian American kids of a certain age being named either Peter or Paul.

have both inherited unfortunate traits from their fathers: Tony's depression and Dickie's substance abuse. (Tony naturally goes about in pity for himself about the former and has no interest in hearing about the latter.) Both deal with their problems in their own ways—AJ by curling up into a weepy little ball whenever he thinks of Blanca, Chris by avoiding the Bing[19]—but Tony has no patience for coping mechanisms that don't live up to the episode's title. Chris may have a handle on his problem, but he didn't take the Gary Cooper approach, and Tony dislikes him for it.

(As he was when Janice's anger management therapy was briefly working, Tony's also jealous to see someone getting better when he never does. Witness his frustration when Chris calls him about Paulie trashing his lawn and verbally closes off any avenue Tony might have to yell at him.)

Tony may have a point about the face-to-face nature of their business, but he's also the one who guilted Chris into drinking some of the Vipers' wine in "The Ride." And, certainly, there are better ways for AJ to get over Blanca than watching bad James Franco movies, but what does Tony expect when AJ's been pampered his entire life? He and Carmela (who's privately happy about the break up because of "the culture divide" between her son and his one-time fiancée) are not equipped to meet AJ's needs—and, worse, don't fully understand this.

Chris has his problems with spelling and grammar, but he's not stupid. He can see that Bacala has taken his place in the inner circle (at the barbecue, Tony and Bobby discuss business—over two cold ones, versus Chris's alcohol-free beer, which Tony mocks), and he knows that his problems with Paulie (who begins stealing from the hardware store owned by Christopher's new father-in-law) wouldn't be nearly as bad if the two could go out for steak and a shot.

So he goes off the wagon again and sees the other wiseguys for what they really are: a pack of cackling animals who take pleasure in other people's misery. Having failed to find comfort among one clan, he turns to another, visiting former sponsor and frequent punching bag JT, seeking absolution for his many sins, which the Emmy-winning scribe has no interest in hearing about. JT doesn't just deny Christopher the empathy he seeks; he rebuffs him, supposedly because he's got a script deadline, but really because he doesn't want to get too close to a made guy hell-bent on sharing incriminating information.

Christopher wants an authentic connection: reassurance that he can finally tell the truth about who he is and what he'd done without being manipulated or punished or sold out, only to have JT tell him, simply but brutally, "You're in the Mafia!"—meaning that there is no way of staying sober, or feeling better, because

---

19 Not avoiding the Bing: Georgie, who has apparently resumed working there despite swearing the place off after Tony's beating in season five's "Cold Cuts." Even someone as peripheral to the life as Georgie can't entirely quit it.

of the business he chose. This is what Melfi keeps trying to help Tony see. It's what Dr. Krakower said to Carmela. It's the most honest thing anyone's ever said to Christopher. He shoots the messenger.

This world that's destroying his surrogate son is the same that Tony gladly pushes his biological son into, knowing full well that the Jasons are in the Family business. AJ needs real and lasting help, but Tony just wants the crying jags to end right this second, so he sends the boy to hang out with thugs who keep a vial of acid handy in case they should run across a debtor in need of torturing. (If Jackie Jr. had been a hair smarter, he'd be one of these guys.)

On a level of pure craft, "Walk Like a Man"—the directorial debut of longtime *Sopranos* writer Terence Winter[20]—is a marvel, not just because of the amount of information it contains, but also because of how it toys with audience expectations. So many potential "endings" for the show are teased out and then either defused or complicated, that at times it seems as if David Chase had ordered some intern to compile a master list from every article that speculated on the show's ending, then distributed it to the writers so they'd know what not to do. Could a Christopher–Paulie feud—which includes Chris shoving Little Paulie out a window and a vengeful Paulie tearing up Christopher and Kelli's lawn with his car—still bring down the Family? Maybe, but the peacemaking scene at the Bing seems to put a period to that. Might Tony or Christopher get in a jam and squeal to the Feds? It could still happen, but while Tony's gambling continues, and Christopher's stupidity leaves him with a conspicuous killing to deny, the only crooks who get ratted out are Ahmed and Muhammed, two Bing regulars of Middle Eastern descent whose names Tony gives to Agent Harris and his counterterrorism colleagues. Both the Chris–Paulie feud and Christopher's repeated attempts to unburden his guilt by confessing his role in Adriana's death—notice how each time he alludes to the event, he uses more specific, incriminating language?—seem less about "How do we end the story?" than "How do we force these characters to acknowledge the moral and psychological realities of their lives?"

More than some episodes, "Walk Like a Man" often indicates that *The Sopranos*'s true interest isn't gangsterism, but psychotherapy, and psychology's determination to unpack, define, and fix the roots of human unhappiness despite evidence that it's not possible to do such a thing, because people are just too complicated, and therapy's methods too reductive (despite their insistence on respecting the mysteries of the personality). There are at least five sequences in the hour that depict therapy or something like it. None are comforting. There's Christopher's group therapy confession; there's Chris's subsequent, coded one-

---

20 It remains, surprisingly, Winter's only directorial credit. He's also the only *Sopranos* writer other than David Chase to take a turn in the director's chair.

on-one in the stairwell, where he recasts his fiancée's murder as a dispute over a bad employee he happened to be sleeping with; and of course, there's Chris' final visit to JT. Then there's Tony's scene with Melfi and AJ's interlude with his own shrink; both prove equally useless in the short run but might eventually amount to something if therapists and patients would pledge to dig deeper.

Equally intriguing is Winter's examination of the destructive effect of macho culture, which is passed down the generations (witness the two Jasons) through a combination of nature and nurture. Building on the last episode's amazing use of the *Deer Hunter* theme, Winter teases out the Cult of Macho not just through numbing images of violence and sexual conquest, but through seemingly incidental touches that linger because of their metaphoric aptness. The old codes, defined in "Chasing It" when surrogate fathers Tony and Phil berated Vito Jr., are repeatedly likened to hazing. The Jasons torturing their customer in the woods has overtones of an initiation rite (for AJ). Tony himself invokes fraternities to Carmela as a justification for sending AJ to a party where he can drink and cavort with hookers even though he's not of legal age. The low end of hazing is represented in the party scenes with the Jasons: all male entitlement and apelike swagger. Previous episodes plumbed hazing's devilish depths: Tony being pulled into the life via his first murder, then punishing Bobby by forcing him into his own first hit.

Then there's the related matter of fathers and sons. Tony vocally obsesses over the idea that both criminality and depression are genetic, even as he rejects (to Christopher) the notion that alcoholism is an inherited disease like Alzheimer's. (If Chris' dad and Tony's hero, Dickie Moltisanti, was nothing but a junkie—as Chris says at the barbecue—then what does that make Tony? Nothing but an overeating, boozing, coke-snorting, stripper-banging fraud?) Tony tries to save his own son, who he fears will follow him into Mob life, by commanding him to attend a party at the Bing, a Mob-run flesh pit where, as Christopher notes, booze and sex are everywhere and half the strippers are cokeheads. Tony evinces a similar push-pull attitude toward Christopher. As Chris points out, Tony's the kind of guy who will pour a recovering alcoholic a drink and then judge him for taking it.

These codes are intertwined with straight male identity. Even men who have never gotten within a thousand miles of a fistfight or a brothel have entertained urges like the ones that are the *Sopranos* mobsters' stock-in-trade. Yet these impulses—and the industries devoted to satiating them—coexist with banal rituals of domestic life, wage slavery, and consumerist reflex. The episode's penultimate scene finds Tony and AJ—both hungover and trying not to act too guilty—joining the women of the house, Carmela and Meadow, for a family dinner around the kitchen table.

To walk like a man in this world, it seems, is to burn so slowly, you won't notice it until your soul has turned black.

SEASON 7/EPISODE 6
WRITTEN BY MATTHEW WEINER AND DAVID CHASE
DIRECTED BY ALAN TAYLOR

Comfort's End

"I haven't been able to tell anybody this, but I'm fuckin' relieved." **—Tony**

The most significant scene in the entire run of *The Sopranos* thus far occurs in "Kennedy and Heidi." It isn't the bloody car wreck or its disturbing aftermath. It isn't Tony's Las Vegas trip (in any sense of the word "trip"). It isn't Tony's two therapy scenes, or any of the scenes of mourning (or not mourning). It isn't even a scene, really. It's a five-second cutaway to the two title characters—the teenage girls in the car Christopher swerved to avoid.

"Maybe you should go back, Heidi!" says Kennedy.

Heidi's reply: "Kennedy, I'm on my learner's permit after dark!"

We all know David Chase's view of human nature is bleak. *The Sopranos* is set in a universe where good and evil have renamed themselves principle and instinct. Animals are not known for their inclination to act on principle. Nearly every significant scene enacts the same basic struggle, pitting the self-preservation instinct against the influence of what Abraham Lincoln called "the better angels of our nature." These angels have glass jaws.

That cutaway to the girls in the car makes Chase's central, recurring point more bluntly than seven seasons' worth of beatdowns, strangulations, and shootings, because the girls seem so "ordinary"—just a couple of students driving on the highway late at night, maybe thinking that when they get back home they might sneak a couple of glasses of wine and watch some TV. The difference between Heidi and Kennedy and Tony and Christopher is one of degree, not kind. The girls have a chance to do the right thing but don't. The exact reason for their decision not to help—by driving back to the scene or calling the cops—doesn't matter in the end. What's important, for Chase's purposes, is that they are presented with a moral test and they not only fail it, they don't seem terribly aware that it was a test. Tony Soprano and Christopher Moltisanti have failed too many moral tests to count.

Besides mirroring Tony and Chris at various stages of their lives, Kennedy and Heidi also represent the two identities inside so many *Sopranos* characters—especially Tony, whose deeply submerged decent self (the guy who dotes on his kids, banters with his wife, and idealizes young mothers and innocent animals) rarely emerges from his toxic cesspool of a personality. There have always been two Tonys. Kennedy is the voice in Tony's head that says, "Do the right thing." To which Heidi replies, "Fuck that."

Tony's murder of Christopher isn't about Tony's murder of Christopher: it's about the human impulse toward cold self-protection, illustrated with *Macbeth*-like viciousness both in the cutaway to Heidi refusing to go back, and then as Tony silences his compromised junkie of a surrogate son. (Tony starts to dial 911 but stops himself, punching all three digits only after Chris is safely dead.) Everyone is a threat to him now: garbage to be disposed of, just like the asbestos that one of Tony's guys spends most of the hour trying to unload. Asbestos, of course, is hard to eliminate completely, and Chris's presence in Tony's life seems destined to linger, even just as evidence of how little humanity Tony has left.

Just before the crash, during that long, beautiful, sad moment where Tony looks over at Christopher—perhaps realizing that he's high, or maybe fearing he could turn rat—Chris's stereo is playing Pink Floyd's "Comfortably Numb." That's the second time in two episodes that the writers have invoked that song (Tony quoted the lyrics at the start of "Walk Like a Man," coming down the stairs to find his depressed son sprawled out before the television). The most important word in the title isn't "numb," but "comfortably."

Numbness is the means to comfort's end. If you're numb to morality, to empathy, you can do whatever you want and feel little or no guilt. Comfortable numbness pervades "Kennedy and Heidi." It's there in the scene at the hospital where Tony is told that Chris is dead but can't muster the energy to feign shock or anger. It's tempting to rationalize Tony's non-response as a reaction to his physical trauma, but remember, he's lucid after the accident—lucid enough to abort his first 911 call and murder Christopher[21]—and he later mentions (incredulously, and perhaps with a glimmer of deep guilt) that he escaped the wreck with no serious injuries. As the episode unfolds, Tony can't even show a facsimile of authentic shock and grief; the best he can manage is paranoid touchiness about the fact that he's not dead, and unsolicited anecdotal nuggets. At Chris's wake, he tells the director of *Cleaver* about seeing the tree branch juxtaposed with Chris's daughter's car seat. His affable delivery is so inappropriate—along with the rest of his autopilot responses throughout the episode—that ironically, it could be interpreted as the

---

21   Tony finally smothers someone to death, and unlike his attempt with Livia, he doesn't even need a pillow.

behavior of a man in shock. Tony's expression as he kills Chris is horrifying because it's the face of a predator acting on instinct: inscrutable, mask-like, comfortably numb. (AJ had a similar close-up in "Walk Like a Man," while watching the Jasons torture the debtor. It was the most animated AJ had seemed in some time—and the most disconnected from his own emotions.[22])

The Sopranos is Comfortably Numbland. Only a comfortably numb person could begin a condolence call to the survivor of a car wreck as Paulie does, by noting that the deceased had a lead foot. Carmela[23] betrays her comfortable numbness by deflecting Paulie's anger over the fact that she and Tony arrived late to his mother's/aunt's funeral. In that same scene, Tony betrays his numbness in a small way, by cutting off Paulie's legitimate outrage over the Family's non-attendance ("It's a fundamental lack of respect and I'm never gonna fucking forget it.") by reminding him that Tony's the boss and a very busy man, and Paulie should be grateful that he showed up at all. Comfortable numbness enables men to kill again and again to protect money, property, and reputation. Comfortable numbness allows women like Carmela to live with deep knowledge of their husbands' viciousness while reassuring themselves that a disinterest in details equals a lack of complicity. Carmela knows Adriana didn't just "disappear," but she chooses not to think about it because doing so would cause her discomfort.

Surprisingly for an episode that spends half its time with Tony staying in a hotel and taking hallucinogens, the only actual dream sequence appears early on, as Tony imagines confessing his past killings to Dr. Melfi. (The dream turns out to be a useful rehearsal, as he later recreates most of his dialogue from it in less self-incriminating fashion.) But the entire episode has the air of a dream, or of Tony's trip to Costa Mesa.

Only this time, the imagery isn't of Purgatory, but the hotter place. Tony thinks he's going to Las Vegas to clean up Christopher's unfinished business—and to party away from all the people who expect him to be grief-stricken—but he winds up in Hell instead. He and Chris's stripper girlfriend Sonya (Sarah Shahi[24]) have

---

22 In this episode, AJ reverts to his depressed state after brief improvement, driven there partly by news of his cousin's death and everyone's reaction to it. "You know, people walk around like this is all something," he tells his shrink. "They're fuckin' laughin' and nobody takes even one second to think about what's really going on."(Moments later, considering all the meaningless violence in the world, he quotes Rodney King's "Can't we all just get along?" like it's the most profound thought he's ever had. In fairness, it probably is.)

23 Does anybody in the business play grief better than Edie Falco? Carm's reaction to Chris's death is almost as devastating as her hallway crying jag in the first Costa Mesa episode. Almost as brilliant, in a different way, is her delivery of the line about Julianna—who reeks of mistress to Carm—being a good-looking woman.

24 At the time, Shahi was best known for her work on Showtime's lesbian relationship drama *The L Word*. She's since become a familiar TV presence, with regular roles on dramas including *Life*, *Person of Interest*, *Reverie*, and *Chicago Fire*.

sex, take peyote,[25] then head down to the casino floor, where he's transfixed by a cartoon devil's head on a slot machine. (It's a smiling devil, of course, because right now Tony's enjoying his descent.) After breaking his long losing streak at the roulette table, Tony takes Sonya for a trip into the desert where the rising sun casts everything in a crimson glow. When the red sun flares at Tony for a second, it resembles the white Costa Mesa beacon, which seemed to signify Heaven.

As he watches the sunrise in the Vegas desert, he is as full of joy as we've ever seen him.

"I get it!" he shouts. "I GET IT!"

But he doesn't. Any righting of this universe's moral scales will be incidental. Tony's been living an expedient life for too long. If he was going to change, he would have done it. He's been going down this road forever, with too many close calls to count. Each time, he hears some version of Heidi and Kennedy in his head, Kennedy saying, "Let's go back," and Heidi saying, "No."

Heidi is driving.

They Are the Bus

"Where did I lose this kid? What did I do wrong?" —**Tony**

"The Second Coming" offers an interpretation of Tony's bellowing "I GET IT!" at the end of "Kennedy and Heidi" in one of his sessions with Melfi:

Tony: All I can say is, I saw, for pretty certain, that this, everything we see and experience, is not all there is.

Melfi: What else is there?

Tony: Something else.

[*Melfi stares, nonverbally pushing for him to elaborate.*]

Tony: That's as far as I'm gonna go with it. I don't fucking know.

Melfi: Alternate universes?

Tony: You're gonna be a fucking comedian now?

Melfi: I'm not.

---

25 For a few days, Tony gets to become Christopher, taking drugs and sleeping with one of his lovers, when he could never seal the deal with Adriana or Julianna, for one reason or another, while Chris was alive.

[*Tony pauses, nods.*]

Tony: Maybe. . . . This is gonna sound stupid, but I saw at one point that our mothers are the bus drivers. No—they are the bus. See, they're the vehicle that gets us here. They drop us off and go on their way. They continue on their journey, and the problem is that we keep trying to get back on the bus. Instead of just letting it go.

Melfi: That's very insightful.

Tony: Jesus, don't act so surprised.

[*Long pause.*]

Tony: You know, you have these thoughts, and you almost grab it, and then, *pffft*.

That's Tony in a nutshell—always pushing toward some realization greater than what his relatives, colleagues, and friends can muster, but invariably coming up short. In Walker Percy's novel *The Moviegoer*, the narrator touched on this dynamic. When he was on the battlefield in Korea in 1951, pinned to the ground and staring at a dung beetle crawling around in leaves, he likewise realized there was something else out there, something beyond what we can see. And then he forgot about it. He periodically remembers that he had that epiphany—every few pages of the novel's first chapter, in fact, and many times thereafter—but then he gets drawn into what he calls the "everydayness" of life, the familiar, comforting, numbing routines, and he forgets again. Unlike Tony, he has a developed enough psychological vocabulary to phrase his sensations more precisely—and even feel a bit smug about it, his narration lording it over the businessmen and working stiffs who lack his sophistication, his sense that there's Something Else Out There—but in the end, he and Tony are in the same predicament, the predicament we're all in, whether or not we realize it or care to admit it. Changing one's essential nature—one's entire world view—is not easy, even when, like Tony, you've suffered (and inflicted) trauma on an unimaginable scale, and have immediate life-or-death reasons for making a major change.

Tony tells Melfi that he knew he had a golden moment after Junior shot him, and that he let it slip away; the implication is that his Las Vegas trip was a half-assed attempt to create a new chance for epiphany. But is such a thing possible, for Tony or anyone else? Especially when it's just so easy to dwell on old grudges and feuds—to keep stewing in the juices, like the steak Christopher was cooking in "Walk Like a Man," long after the flame's turned off?

Phil is still after Tony about the ancient murder of his brother Billy; he makes a not-so-veiled reference to it when he says of Chris's widow that grief takes longer the closer the dead person was to you. AJ botches a suicide attempt, then tries to justify it with sob stories from seasons past. Carmela finally unloads on Tony, not only for passing on "the Soprano Curse" to their son, but because she's tired of hearing about his depression: "You have any idea what it's like to spend day after day with somebody who is constantly complaining?"

When talk of AJ's near-fatal plunge into the Soprano family pool leads some of the other Family captains to acknowledge their own children's shaky mental health, Paulie suggests it's all the toxins these kids have been exposed to for their entire lives (in an episode where Tony's guys are still dumping asbestos into the Meadowlands[26]). In this environment, it doesn't matter when the initial exposure or tragedy was; it stays with you for years, maybe your whole life.

AJ tries to kill himself—in the pool where Tony's beloved ducks once represented his desire for a happy family—after too much time studying the W. B. Yeats poem that lends its title to the episode. Yeats's bleak outlook on the future of civilization—"Things fall apart; the centre cannot hold"—applies to this whole season. The center of Tony's world—the men he loved and trusted most—is coming undone. Bacala. Junior. Paulie. Hesh. Chris. Either humiliated or marginalized or dead at Tony's hands. The episode after killing his surrogate son, Tony barely gets home in time to save his actual son's life, in one of the more harrowing sequences the show's ever done.

And then there's Phil. If you locked Phil and Paulie in a room together, whose air of entitlement and martyrdom would suffocate the other one first? But where Paulie's too dumb and relatively low-ranking to cause much pain and suffering through his woe-is-me routine (save to the odd civilian like Minn Matrone or Jason Barone), Phil is just clever enough and far too powerful to be dismissed. His man Coco (Armen Garo) would never be confident enough to sexually harass Meadow, the daughter of a boss—even of Jersey—unless he knew Phil had his back. Back in "Stage 5," Phil told Butchie he was done with compromises, and here he explains to Tony—who's never done any significant prison time—that in the can, "compromise" meant, at best, getting a very pale imitation of what you wanted: grilled cheese on a radiator instead of manicotti, masturbating into a tissue instead of sex with a woman. Phil won't compromise on the asbestos deal because he's itching for a war with Tony—a war he's willing to wage only because of his huge manpower advantage. (Witness the way he hides from Tony and Little Carmine in the little turret of his suburban castle; he's a coward at heart.)

But Tony's reaction to AJ's averted suicide mimics the dynamics of his post-shooting and post-Vegas reactions. He does what's right by diving in to save his son. Then he reverts to macho type, berating AJ for his stupidity and weak-

---

26 In an earlier scene with the crew, we see Silvio reading a book called *How to Clean Practically Anything*—both an incredibly useful text in their line of work and a reminder of how much wreckage they leave in their wake.

ness and perhaps resenting the vulnerability it made Tony feel. Then he turns nonjudgmental, purely empathetic. He cradles his weeping son and cries with him (maybe the most heartrending moment in the entire series, sharply acted by both James Gandolfini and Robert Iler). But then he reverts again, with both Melfi (admitting he despises AJ's sensitivity, his weakness) and Carmela (pushing her into an argument that pivots on who's genetically responsible for AJ's depression; blame he shifts, later with Melfi, to Carmela for "coddling" AJ). Here Tony admits his depression, and his family history of it, more frankly than at any other point in the show. But he ultimately pulls back, staunches his bleeding feelings, and tries to soldier on, a gangster Gary Cooper.

Melfi's own therapist, the smug Dr. Kupferberg, tells her of a study suggesting not only that sociopaths can't be helped by traditional "talk therapy," but that it can make them worse by helping them sharpen their skills at lying and justifying their worst traits. As omniscient viewers of the TV show, we know that Kupferberg has a point, that Tony usually lies too much to get anything valuable out of Melfi, and that he frequently uses her to map out strategy. Most times, he's scamming her, which is why he's able to spot AJ's lame excuse-making in that endless family session with Dr. Vogel (Michael Countryman).

But Tony—who's not even bothering to hide his newfound Livia-ness with multiple "Poor you!"s—does have the occasional moment of insight, as with his mothers-are-buses metaphor. Only someone with Livia for a parent would view motherhood that way, but the Family functions as a bus, too, one that everyone's either afraid or incapable of staying off for long.

Meadow reveals that she's dating another son of a wiseguy (Patrick Parisi, whom Patsy had earlier acknowledged "can be a moody prick sometimes") and has now given up on med school in favor of becoming a lawyer—two choices guaranteed to keep her involved in her father's lifestyle in some way. (Meadow being Meadow, she lets the man in her life talk her into it.)

Meadow had her chance to get off the bus for good, but instead she's inching toward a lifetime bus pass. Carmela had two chances—first when Dr. Krakower's second opinion told her to leave Tony, then when she actually threw him out—and both times she couldn't do it. Vito drove home to his own death, so great was the pull of his old life. Adriana couldn't leave Christopher and died because of him. Chris in turn couldn't leave Tony, and now he's gone to Hell for him.

Getting back to Yeats, one of the lines that transfixes AJ is the notion that "the best lack all conviction, while the worst are full of passionate intensity." On this show, "best" is a relative term, but there's no lack of contenders for "worst." And they're all filled with their own destructive, passionate intensity, even if what made them passionate happened so long ago that—like the Israeli–Palestinian conflict that vexes AJ so—they can't remember how the fire got started. But so long as those juices keep flowing, they'll keep cooking.

AJ's depression was, in every sense, a wake-up call. His long-delayed "loss of innocence" about his father's true nature, his father's business, dovetails with his sudden overwhelming awareness of all the evil and stupidity in the world—thousands of years of religious and ethnic feuds, how the profit motive trumps ethics and results in toxins being sprayed on food. "Depressed?" Dr. Vogel asks him. "How can anybody not be, when everything is so fucked up?" AJ replies.

His deep distress is mirrored by Tony's own dawning sense that his entire universe is decaying beyond repair, that he's helpless before realities he's only begun to acknowledge. Better to withdraw, ease back in the passenger seat, let Heidi drive. You believe, even hope, that some revelation is at hand; then you remember Tony's face as he pinched Christopher's nose shut: a gaze as blank and pitiless as the sun. Maybe the center holds just fine.

SEASON 7/EPISODE 8
"THE BLUE COMET"   WRITTEN BY DAVID CHASE AND MATTHEW WEINER
DIRECTED BY ALAN TAYLOR

Leadbelly

"End times, huh? Ready for the rapture?" —**Agent Harris**

So much for anticlimaxes.

After teasing—or threatening?—a war with New York all the way back to the HUD-scam beef in season four, *The Sopranos* finally delivers it in spades with the superb, scary, thrilling "The Blue Comet."

It is, unsurprisingly, a rout for New York, with Phil's guys murdering Bobby and putting Silvio into a seemingly permanent coma, while the only people Tony's guys are able to take out are their own turncoat Burt Gervasi and, in a case of mistaken identity, Phil's mistress and her Phil-lookalike father. It's an orgy of Mafia mayhem best characterized by a line from Ray Liotta's *Goodfellas* narration: real greaseball shit.

Tony even loses his other closest advisor in a bloodless but painful bit of business: Dr. Melfi, having taken Elliot's advice (and the study about talk therapy and sociopaths) to heart, fires him as a patient.

His inner circle gone, Phil's men still out looking for him, Tony ends the episode hiding out with what's left of his army, clinging to the assault rifle Bobby gave him for his birthday, literally gone to the mattresses. It's the worst spot we've ever seen him in, at the worst possible moment, with only one chapter of his story to go.

Earlier, after Silvio is gravely wounded in the Bing parking lot, while Patsy flees into the woods, Phil's button men cause an accident involving a motorcyclist, prompting the second of two "Run away! Run away!" reaction shots from a gawking crowd we'd assumed had gone inside for safety's sake. This is a good, mean joke—in the spirit of that cutaway to the girls driving the car that caused the accident in "Kennedy and Heidi," but with an undertone of audience criticism. The crowd outside the Bing runs like Tokyo extras fleeing Godzilla, then comes back to watch again, their rubbernecking impulse made plain when a gangland hit is followed by a car wreck.

Bobby Bacala's death is a companion to that Bing joke. He gets shot in a model train shop while coveting a scale model of a defunct train car that titles the episode. The prized toy is a very busy little metaphor. On an obvious level, it stands for any nostalgic impulse the gangsters have ever demonstrated; the lionizing of the Good Old Days when gangsterism supposedly had rules; Tony's criticizing the ongoing pussyfication of the American white man, and asking, "Whatever happened to Gary Cooper?" (For all his delusions, Paulie sees the past more clearly, remarking in a gravely distressed tone that he survived the New York gang wars of the '70s by "the skin of my balls.")

Also, Bobby's execution is intercut with a model train diving off a broken trestle bridge, which seems like a too-obvious *Godfather* borrowing (a murder intercut with something mundane) until you remember Phil's contemptuous earlier statement implying that the Sopranos aren't even a real family, but a pygmy clan that needs to be wiped out. They're scale models of gangsters, and Phil intends to smash them like a toy train set. As he crushes them, it's difficult to muster much sympathy for the vanquished because Chase has exposed their selfishness unmercifully. Thanks to the ever-more-conspicuously nasty behavior exhibited this season, often by characters we might otherwise be inclined to identify with (like Bobby becoming colder after making his bones), it's hard to get too choked up over the destruction (and self-destruction) of Tony or the members of his blood and crime families. The series has underlined, italicized, and boldfaced the fact that they're all killers or tacit enablers of killers. As we watch them go down, we might as well be watching a toy train derail.

Last, Orson Welles once called *Citizen Kane* "the greatest electric train set any boy ever had." The train-shop scene is a jokey admission that filmmakers are overgrown kids playing God with life-size toys. As the series chugs toward its final destination, Chase is staging one collision after another. We shudder in revulsion, then try to guess what he'll smash next. Bacala's death (a virtual boss sprawled across a pile of model trains) ties in with the sight of those rubberneckers at the Bing recoiling from horror, then going back for more, all the while drawing no apparent distinction between a gangland hit and a car accident. They're drawn to pain like flies to shit. It's as if Chase is both celebrating and condemning his ability to mesmerize with suffering.

Especially striking throughout are the parallels between Phil and Kupferberg, two men saying the right things for the wrong reasons. When Phil lays out all his problems with how the Jersey crew conducts its business, is any of it inaccurate? Especially after we see how badly they bungle whacking him?[27] We know Phil's really orchestrating this war because he's mad about his brother and resentful that Tony never did any significant prison time, but again, is he significantly wrong to characterize Jersey as a bunch of bumblers?

Kupferberg, meanwhile, is absolutely right about Tony using therapy to become a better criminal instead of a better human. But he's badgering Melfi to dump Tony—in the most obnoxious, unprofessional manner possible, turning a dinner party into an intervention and revealing Tony's identity to the other guests as a trivia question ("The answer is a female opera singer *and* gangster.")—not because he's concerned about her ethical well-being, or about what Tony might be doing to other people thanks to his therapy. Kupferberg's just a snob—and, like Phil, a bully—who can't tolerate the thought of a well-heeled colleague regularly interacting with a criminal. He can enjoy the Mob saga as an abstraction—as his favorite TV show, as it was for much of the audience—but it's never sat well with him that Melfi was associating herself with "Leadbelly." And the more violent and exciting this soap opera has become for Elliot, the more disdainful he finds the idea of her direct involvement in it.

Across these final two seasons, the show has gotten progressively grimmer, and Chase has made it tough to mourn his principal characters for any reason besides their stillborn human potential. The episode's bits of meta-commentary—on violence as entertainment and suffering as spectacle, and on the morality of those who watch—gain context in the scene where Melfi decides she's had enough of Tony's charismatic intransigence and kicks him out, using his theft of a magazine page from her waiting room as the pretext. This is the doctor–patient equivalent of Al Capone going to prison for income tax evasion, rather than his more serious crimes, but it gets the job done for Melfi, a mostly ethical person who

---

27 Tony, Sil, and Bobby are so overconfident about their ability to take out Phil that they playfully shadowbox after Tony makes the call, in a moment presented in slow-motion and scored to Mascagni's *Cavalleria rusticana*—famously used in *Raging Bull*, which happens to be the movie where Frank Vincent first made a name for himself.

has indulged a monster for far too long because she thought she was helping him, but also because—like Elliot—she got a vicarious thrill from his world.

The final Melfi–Tony scene—which ends with her closing the door on him like she's the Godfather and he's poor Kay Corleone—might be the most explicit acknowledgment of Tony's brutishness since killing Christopher. As he talks to Melfi about his son's botched suicide and subsequent treatment, and his daughter's decision to give up medicine for prelaw, he isn't saying anything new; if we're not moved, than we're at least sympathetic. But because we're seeing Tony through Melfi's eyes, it looks like crocodile tears. Melfi wonders, as we're supposed to, if this burly killer with a soft spot for pets and children feels anything, or if his emotionalism is overcompensation, a means of lying to himself and the world about his cauterized soul. (When AJ breaks down and starts to weep after learning of Bobby's death, Tony drags him off his bed and callously hurls clothes at him.) Melfi has occasionally spoken bluntly to Tony, but never so disdainfully: "You miss appointments because you don't give a shit, about commitments, about what I do, about the body of work that's gone into building up this science. Go ahead, tell me again I sound like your wife." It's just tip of the iceberg of what Melfi now fully understands of her complicity, but it's all she can directly confront him with, and the anger in her voice is enough to make up the difference for us, if not for Patient X.

If Tony is Chase's surrogate, Melfi is (or is supposed to be) ours. She's saying she feels deceived and manipulated, that she's had it, that this relationship isn't really going anywhere, and for the sake of her mental health and personal honor, it has to end.

And it will—with Tony outgunned, outmanned, outmaneuvered, and now lacking all the people whose counsel he depended on most, Jennifer Melfi included.

 **"MADE IN AMERICA"** SEASON 7/EPISODE 9
WRITTEN AND DIRECTED BY DAVID CHASE

No Encore

"It's so amazing that it was written so long ago.
It's about, like, right now." —**Rhiannon**

In hindsight, maybe we should have seen it coming.

Even for a series infamous for its anticlimaxes, "Made in America" proudly defies the notion of explosive endings. Long before the ice cream parlor door opens,

Tony looks up, and . . . *something* happens—or nothing at all—the series finale sets us, and Tony, up for the idea of disappointment and confusion.

Every time "Made in America" seems to be building to something big, even basic emotional closure, it falls apart. The war with New York ends swiftly once Butchie realizes Phil's vendetta has gone too far and permits Tony to whack him. AJ's SUV ignites while he's in it with teen-model girlfriend Rhiannon (Emily Wickersham[28]), but both escape long before the ridiculous car blows up over a pile of burning leaves. Tony makes final visits to Silvio and Junior, but both their minds are essentially gone: the comatose Sil's to bullet wounds, the childlike and paranoid Junior's to dementia.

Even the plot that consumes more screen time than the Mob war doesn't so much end as stop, as Tony and Carmela are able to talk AJ out of his plan to enlist in the military, instead landing him a job as a development executive for Little Carmine's production company[29]—a solution no one seems particularly thrilled with, even if it's better than the alternative.

Tony wins the war, but it's a Pyrrhic victory at best. All his top guys are gone. Paulie reluctantly agrees to run the Cifaretto crew—the Family's most profitable outfit, but also its most cursed, going back to Richie Aprile—because there's no one else to run it, and the only reliable soldier he seems to have left is Walden Belfiore (Frank John Hughes), who kills Phil only a few episodes after his debut. Tony is able to return to his life, but his sister is now a widow,[30] his daughter is marrying Patrick Parisi, and AJ is still AJ. And Uncle Junior's sorry state—a shell of himself, barely subsisting at a dingy state-run mental hospital—reflects a sad alternative to Tony's long-ago speculation that a boss like him will likely end up either dead or in the can.

By the time Tony, Carmela, and the kids are all on their way to Holsten's for the last supper we'll ever share with them, it feels like the series is looping back in on itself, but in a deliberately more opaque fashion than we're used to from *Sopranos* season finales.

The show's season-ending scenes always reaffirm certain core values, such as community and family, but with an edge of mystery or disquiet or a bitter ironic undertone. Season one ends much like season seven, with the Sopranos taking shelter from a storm (literal in "I Dream of Jeannie Cusamano," figuratively in

---

28 Rhiannon (introduced in season six as Hernan's girlfriend) was Wickersham's first significant screen role. She has since spent 100-plus episodes on *NCIS* as investigator Ellie Bishop.

29 His first assignment: *Anti-Virus*, a script *Cleaver* star Daniel Baldwin gave Tony, involving a detective who "gets sucked into the internet through his, uh, data port" and has to "solve some murders of some virtual prostitutes." Too bad JT Dolan's not available to punch it up.

30 Have some pity for the poor Baccalieri children. At least Bobby Jr. and Sophia will remember their biological parents, where Nica will grow up only knowing this narcissist.

"Made in America") at a restaurant (Vesuvio then, Holsten's now). Tony ends season one nearly killing his mother and then being unable to discuss it with his mother-substitute, Dr. Melfi, after scaring her into the shrink equivalent of witness protection. Season two ends with a party at the Soprano house celebrating Meadow's high school graduation, intercut with glimpses of sanitation and other Mob business being conducted; the final shots are Tony's face as he lights a cigar and exhales, then an image of the ocean where Pussy's remains are being picked apart by fish. Season three ends with Uncle Junior singing to much of the show's core cast at Vesuvio; Meadow, distraught over Jackie Jr.'s death, storms out onto Bloomfield Avenue, and for a moment seems in danger of being run over. Season four ends with a shot of the *Stugots* anchored by the Jersey Shore, blasting Dean Martin to intimidate Alan Sapinsly into returning Tony's cash deposit on a home that his wife no longer wants because she's divorcing him. Season five ends with Tony emerging from snowy woods and walking through his own backyard—the happy wanderer, returned to a restored marriage that briefly seemed over. Season six ends with the extended Soprano family gathered in their home at Christmas. These endings all feel solid, settled, even as they provoke reflection. Against this pattern, season seven's capper doesn't feel like a proper ending. It feels like what a show might give us if it couldn't decide on an ending. Or one that veers away from the idea of endings. A denial of endings. An attack on endings. A record scratch. A flipped switch.

This is not what we wanted. It's puzzling and infuriating. Like expecting a conversation and getting a sucker punch or a shrug instead. It is not what we expected. It's something else. It's not something you just watch. It's something you grapple with, accept, resist, accept again, resist again, then resolve to live with.

It's absolutely in character for this show.

Since season two, at least, and maybe before that, *The Sopranos* excelled at subverting our expectations. Sometimes it gave us what we didn't know we wanted. Other times it gave us what we definitely didn't want and over time we either grew to like it, rationalized our way into believing it was something else, or pretended it never happened. The show made us laugh at its audacity, its invention, its careful tending of expectations for an outcome it never had any intention of giving us. Other times it seemed to be regarding us with cool disinterest and proceeding with whatever it was going to do anyway, like David Chase snubbing Paulie in "Commendatori" after Jersey greets Italy with the episode's title. There was never any question who was in charge of this experience. If *The Sopranos* were a band, it would be the kind that favored new material whether it resonated with the crowd or not, played its greatest hits only when it felt like it, and was fronted by a singer who turned his back to the audience. The final performance of a band like that might end with the musicians striding off the stage in the middle of what you know in your bones is their last song, the guitarist and bassist intentionally forgetting to unplug their instruments on the way out. Feedback. Sparks. Blackout.

No encore.

And here's the thing: if you look back over everything leading up to the scene at Holsten's, it's impossible to claim that we weren't warned the gig would end like this. This is Richie Aprile being set up for a showdown with Tony only to get shot at the dinner table by Janice. It's Pussy's treachery being uncovered not through careful detective work, but through dreams brought on by food poisoning. It's the Russian who might or might not have made it out of the forest. It's the employee of the month. It's Gigi Cestone having a heart attack on the toilet, Ray Curto plotzing in the front seat of Agent Sanseverino's car, Tony Blundetto getting ambushed on the porch. It's Ralphie living through "University" at the end of season three and making it halfway through season four before finally being killed for a crime that had nothing to do with Tracee's death, and that we'll never know if he actually committed.

As goes *The Sopranos*, so goes "Made in America." While it's structured like most of the previous finales, from Tony outmaneuvering one last enemy to the family gathering for a celebratory meal, nothing gets neatly wrapped up. Meadow's wedding is discussed, but only in the abstract. We hear Carlo flipped to protect his son Jason, but we never see him flip, nor do we know whether his evidence could prove damning enough to bring down the Family. We hear twice that subpoenas are being handed out, but despite Tony's depressed reactions, we never learn if they will lead anywhere. There are indications that the gun charge might finally bring Tony down, but there's no closure on that, either. Tony visits Sil in the hospital, but we never learn if he'll die soon or remain in that vegetative state for years. We hear Meadow had to go to the doctor to change her birth control pills. Did she have a pregnancy scare? Did she switch medicine to be extra-certain that she didn't perpetuate the family/Family legacy with the son of a known gangster? Unlikely, since she tells her dad she went into law after seeing his treatment at the hands of cops and FBI agents—but we don't know.

Tony's lawyer Mink sits there whacking that bottle of ketchup over and over until Tony grabs it out of his hands and tries to do it himself, and the ketchup still doesn't come out.

But if nothing works out quite how we, or Tony, might want it to, this seems part of the point of the episode, and the show. We go about the show in pity for ourselves while a great wind carries us across the sky. We all came in at the end, and can't shake the feeling that the world (and our art reflecting it) should make more sense than it does.

The pilot episode started with Tony telling Dr. Melfi that he feared the best of his business (and by implication, America) was over. The creeping sense of numbness and despair; the sense that the best (whatever that meant) was past; the concurrent sense that no experience that feels important to us is as important to history, or even to our friends and relatives, as we'd like think; that when we're gone we'll probably be forgotten, like 99.99999 percent of the human race: this is encoded in every second of "Made in America," and was foretold throughout the run of the series, most notably in Carmela's Paris monologue about individual woes being obliterated in the sweep of history, and in the gradual erosion of Junior's memory, which reaches its piercing conclusion here.

Junior doesn't remember anything about his long, colorful, nasty life, including shooting his own nephew; he doesn't even recognize that nephew by the time Tony consents to visit. As goes Junior, so goes the world. The widowed Janice seeks refuge in a house that used to belong to Johnny Sacrimoni. It's surrounded by McMansions; Tony informs her that when Johnny built the house, the area was all cornfields—there's no indication they ever existed. We learn that the key to finding Phil is locating a gas station with a pay phone in front of it; an attendant explains that few gas stations have pay phones anymore. It's as if pay phones never existed. One of the Little Italy scenes begins with a shot of a double-decker tour bus zipping through the neighborhood, and we hear an announcer telling the tourists that Little Italy used to be a huge, thriving neighborhood, but now it's been reduced to a handful of restaurants and stores. The scene ends with Butchie realizing he has wandered deep into Chinatown without even noticing. Where did Little Italy go? It was right there.

"Fuckin' A, I'm disappointed," Phil exclaims at one point.

To quote another episode title, join the club.

Almost nobody gives a damn about your life but you, and according to Chase, there's a good chance you don't even give as much of a damn as you think. If you did, you'd already have done the hard work necessary to change yourself to match your idealized image. Most people aren't capable of that. It's too hard, we're too lazy as a species, and life is just too long and too filled with problems that need immediate solving. And then, at some point, you're not in the picture anymore, and it's all a moot point, for you anyway.

At Holsten's, Tony looks up at the sound of the door opening. Cut to black. Wait, then roll credits. The story continues. You, the audience, are not around to see it.

"When you go to a place you've never been before, it's like all the people were imaginary until you got there," Carmela told Rosalie in "Cold Stones." "It's like until you saw them, they never existed. And you never existed to them."

Tony's final encounters with his sister, best friend, and uncle are all appropriately solemn, even if none provide quite what Tony is looking for. The Junior scene in particular—in many ways, the last proper scene of *The Sopranos*, before whatever occurs at the ice cream parlor—is hauntingly sad and beautiful, like the "Don't you love me?" conversation that ends "Where's Johnny?" with the pathos cranked up. Junior has been dead to Tony since the shooting, but the Junior that Tony knew has vanished into snowy woods. When Janice comes to tell him about Bobby's death, he recalls just enough of his life to assume that she's Livia, Nica is baby Janice, and the murdered Bobby is Robert F. Kennedy. By the time Tony finally deigns to visit (in hopes of safeguarding Junior's fortune for Bobby's kids), even that speck of memory seems gone for good, until Tony has to take pity on the uncle who tried to murder him twice by telling him, "You and my dad. You two ran North Jersey."

Whatever's in control of the vessel that was Corrado Soprano Jr. ponders this a moment and says, "Well, that's nice." His body isn't dead yet, but his mind is.

This is the road mercifully not taken by Tony Soprano. For all of his many failings, he has a wife who loves him and two children who will mostly turn out okay. He may die in that ice cream parlor. If he doesn't, he may soon go to prison as a result Carlo's ratting, or for the gun charge, or some old piece of evidence from the Scatino bust-out. If this is the end of his story, he's been blessed with far more than he deserves. If it's not, the tentacles of his life stretch out wide enough that he seems insured, Alzheimer's chances aside, against sharing his uncle's crushingly lonely fate.

But "Made in America" is a story of familial disappointment for Tony, too. He never had a choice about going into the Mob, thanks to Johnny Boy, but he never wanted it for his kids: he figured Meadow could do better, and deserved to, while AJ was too lazy and dim to survive it. Yet the bulk of the finale is about Tony accepting Meadow's decision to literally marry into the Family, and to pursue a law career inspired by witnessing her father's treatment by law enforcement; and about Tony and Carmela coming to terms with the idea that a job working for Little Carmine is the best of a bunch of bad options for their dead-end son. Tony has tried to change both himself and his family, working—well, not hard, exactly, but a little bit, when he could spare the time, because you know how busy he is. And here he is, years later, basically in the same place. His family, too.

Chase, returning to the director's chair for the first time since the pilot, paints the closing stages of the war against New York with an apocalyptic brush to suit the end-times reference Agent Harris[31] made in "The Blue Comet." The safe houses down the Shore, Tony's airport meeting with Harris, and the interstate sit-down at a truck depot all seem to take place in a winter designed to make humans go the way of the dinosaurs discussed in "The Fleshy Part of the Thigh." AJ and Rhiannon listen to Bob Dylan's "It's Alright, Ma (I'm Only Bleeding)" like they're the first people to discover it and understand its ominous message; the song serves as a fitting final shiv in the flank of the Baby Boom generation that Chase and company have been jabbing at for seven seasons. It also provides a perfect soundtrack to the fiery destruction of the ridiculous car that Tony bought AJ specifically because he thought it would keep him safe, by being heavy enough to roll right over other cars without the driver spilling his Red Bull. (Gasoline is made from refined fossil fuels, so you could see the detonation of this guzzler as the dinosaurs' revenge.) Phil's murder is one final bit of deadly *Sopranos* slapstick, as Walden pops him while he and his wife are at a gas station, their infant grandkids secure and oblivious in the back seat, the car rolling forward to crush Phil's skull as a concluding indignity to the Leotardo line, the rubberneckers once again stand-ins for *The Sopranos* audience—thrilled and horrified almost within the same breath. Same as it ever was.

Which brings us to the dinner. The last supper for the *Sopranos*, or maybe just for us.

By the time Tony Soprano enters Holsten's to meet his family for dinner, the Mob war has receded and life has begun to return to something like "normal"— whatever that means for this bunch. Tony sits down in a booth and flips through the jukebox trying to pick a song (a great self-referential joke for a show that prides itself on picking exactly the right song for a scene). He chooses Journey's "Don't Stop Believin'" (the refrain "Don't stop" expressing the feelings of *Sopranos* fans who didn't want the show to end); the little bell on the restaurant's front door as Carmela enters, and Steve Perry sings about a small-town girl just as she sits with Tony. They exchange chitchat. "What looks good tonight?" Carmela asks. "I don't know," Tony replies. When she asks if he's spoken to his lawyer again, he tells her, "It's Carlo. He's gonna testify"; Carmela's grave expression indicates that this could mean trouble down the road.

The bell rings again, Tony looks up, and a middle-aged white guy in a Members Only jacket (so named in the final credits, and another nice extra-textual

---

31 *The Sopranos*'s final belly laugh: Harris, having already crossed several ethical lines in feeding intel to Tony, gets much too excited to hear about Phil's murder, cheering, "Damn! We're gonna win this thing!" Now that he's no longer working directly against Tony, he's become a *Sopranos* fan, just like everybody else.

gag)[32] enters the restaurant and heads offscreen, AJ coming in right behind him. AJ sits with them. More chitchat; the Members Only Guy, now seated at the counter, looks toward their table, drumming his hands. He glances again after we watch Meadow attempt to parallel park.

AJ discusses his new job, and Tony affirms his callback to the season one finale: "Isn't that what you said one time? 'Try to remember the times that were good'?" as Meadow continues desperately trying to park. The guy eventually gets up from his stool; Tony glances up at him as he passes the family while heading for the bathroom. Is he an assassin, sent to kill Tony and maybe his family as well, or is he just someone who recognized Tony from media stories? Is he pulling a Michael Corleone? Is there a gun taped to the back of a toilet tank? We don't know. Moments later, two young African American men ("unidentified black males") enter the restaurant. Tony was almost killed by a couple of young black men in season one; are *they* assassins, or just a couple of friends going out for dinner? We don't know.

Meadow is the last Soprano to approach the restaurant. The final scene of the final episode of *The Sopranos*, and David Chase is spending a solid minute on Meadow's poor parking skills. And yet the tension is unbearable. So often on *The Sopranos*, when a character or characters spend a lot of screen time shooting the breeze or fixating on some mundane bit of business, the non-drama is followed by a beatdown or a bullet in the brain; your attention starts to wander and then WHAM.

We expect the same dynamic this time. But no:

Meadow successfully parks the car.

She runs across the street.

We worry that she might get run over.

She does not.

Cut to the inside of the restaurant.

Tony looks up at the sound of the bell ringing.

Cut to black.

The sound cuts out, too.

After about ten seconds of nothing, the credits roll.

There is no music.

The Sopranos ending is so structurally daring and fundamentally frustrating that audiences openly rebelled against it at the time, and have argued about its meaning and intentions ever since. It aired in the summer of 2007, after three seasons of ABC's *Lost*, a show that taught viewers to look for patterns and clues

---

32 "Members Only" is the title of the season six premiere, in which Eugene Pontecorvo—who wore a Members Only jacket himself, and bore a passing resemblance to this Holsten's customer—hangs himself because he's unable to escape Mob life.

in order to understand or predict story elements that the writers weren't ready to divulge. The internet therefore roared to life with theories that would account for the cut to black, explain it, diagram and footnote it, and file it safely away. True to form, much of the audience became fixated on the question of whether Tony had been shot, as if that were the be-all and end-all of the matter, and tried to "solve" the final scene as if it were an acrostic, then exclaim, "I got it!" Never mind that for every piece of evidence cited to support this idea, such as Bobby's statement that you never hear it coming, and that first silent bullet that strikes Gerry the Hairdo, there were other moments that could complicate such a reading that had to be studiously ignored, such as Carmela's description of, in essence, a television show of life that continues after the spectator (us, not Tony) stops watching it, or the Journey song itself, which warns of a story that never ends, but "goes on and on and on and on."

And to be fair, *The Sopranos* was dense enough in its references, motifs, and "mythology" that it was impossible not to want to scrutinize it in this manner. The series was filled with elements that could mean everything or nothing. Take the matter of the eggs, which, as we've noted here, feel like Chase and company's answer to oranges in the *Godfather* films: Richie makes eggs at Livia's house, in the same house where he later dies; Ralphie is making eggs when Tony comes over and kills him; Tony steps in rotten eggs right before he makes the decision to kill Tony B; a senile Junior calls Tony B "Tony Egg" while Bobby is making eggs, and moments later gets the call saying that Carmine has died; Carmine suffers his ultimately fatal stroke while eating egg salad; Adriana offers to make Chris eggs right before he leaves and decides to betray her to Tony; Valentina gets horribly burned while making Egg Beaters; Janice makes a frittata before Tony instructs Bobby to commit his first murder, and on and on and on and on.

The number seven comes up just as often as eggs. There are, according to Chase, seven seasons of the show, one of which opens with "Seven Souls"; the names Anthony and Carmela both have seven letters, as does Vesuvio, as does Soprano; seven dream fragments expose Pussy's deception in "Funhouse"; Gloria tells Tony she murdered seven relationships, while Amy in "D-Girl" starts to tell Chris about the hierarchy of seven needs, and the rapper Da Lux gets shot seven times. There are seven episodes dealing with *Cleaver*, about a murdered mobster who becomes a Grim Reaper figure, and the seventh episode of every season deals with Tony's past and the possibility that he's cursed by his genes. And when Dr. Krakower describes a fate for Tony (in a seventh episode, no less), it's to be sentenced to a jail cell and made to read *Crime and Punishment* every day for seven years. You could make spreadsheets of this stuff and use it to prove all sorts of things. No doubt many people have. But none of that explains the

The Debate: Don't Stop Believin'
You Know **Exactly** What Happened
at the End of *The Sopranos*

*After several unsuccessful attempts to reconcile
our many contradictory feelings and theories about the final scene
of* The Sopranos, *we decided to talk it out.*

ALAN: Tony Soprano is dead.

MATT: Wait, what?

A: He's dead, Matt. It's obvious.

M: Well, this isn't how I thought this would go. To quote Tony, the floor is yours, senator.

A: "Made in America" opens on Tony asleep in the safe house. His eyes are closed, he's not noticeably breathing, and the camera angle makes it look like he's lying in state at the funeral parlor, waiting for his friends, family, and viewers out here in TV land to pay our respects. He jolts awake within moments, but we begin our final hour in Tony's company with this image of him suggesting that he's already dead, and that he just—like Silvio watching the Gerry Torciano hit—needs some time to catch up with the finality of the situation.

That coffin-like image isn't the first major allusion to death of the final season, nor the last of "Made in America" alone. In the season premiere, Bacala raised the idea of what happens when you die, speculating, "You probably don't even hear it when it happens, right?"—a line so clearly important to the end of the series that the conversation is replayed at the end of the penultimate episode, after poor Bobby had that question answered. Images of death—or a Hell frozen over from overcrowding and neglect by management—abound throughout the series finale, as the show's usual fascination with the extremes of weather in the Garden State gets amped up to an almost supernatural degree. When Tony's meeting Agent Harris by the airport, or Butchie is wandering through the last remaining scrap of Little Italy while talking to Phil on the phone, or when Tony and Butchie and Little Carmine sit down to broker a peace in that cavernous truck depot, the cold and wind and snow are all so palpable that the only truly applicable phrase is, "You'll catch your death."

And that's even before we get to Holsten's, a scene shot and edited unlike anything else in the history of this show.

M: Yes, but why does a preponderance of imagery related to death and decay mean that Tony had to be shot dead at that diner at that exact moment? This is what I keep coming back to. I don't believe it's necessary to establish that to discuss the ending of the show, nor do I think the evidence necessarily points to that.

Whenever the *Sopranos* ending is discussed, and somebody starts with the presumption that Tony is dead, I ask the same follow-up question: "Why do you need for Tony to be dead?" Because you have to need him to be dead to insist not only that he got shot right there in the diner, but that him being dead is in fact the entire point of the scene, and that no other approach is permissible. Because nothing in that scene says, "Somebody just killed him and that's what the cut to black is about." The only objectively true statement that can be made about that ending is that it's ambiguous. Spending long hours trying to prove Tony was shot at the diner becomes a substitute for meaningful engagement with the show's themes, which are disturbing not just because of their implications, but because Chase and the writers present them in an open-ended, mysterious, or deliberately opaque way, like a brutal reminder us that we can't absolutely know certain things, and it's delusional to insist we can.

The final close-up of James Gandolfini's face contains no note of fear or apprehension. He's just looking up at the sound of a bell ringing, and if classical continuity editing is to be our guide here, the person entering is Meadow, last seen in the third-to-final shot of the scene, walking toward the diner. I suppose you could argue that somebody snuck in from the side, out of frame, and shot Tony. But again, that seems like a reach to me, especially since Members Only Guy hasn't come out of the bathroom yet. And, as I said, it proceeds from the speaker's *need* to have Tony die at that moment, not from any evidence in the scene itself.

A: I hear what you're saying. But the very fact that Chase devotes so much time to what seems like nothing makes the whole scene all the more nerve-racking. To paraphrase one of the Four Questions from the Passover seder, on all other nights we don't watch Meadow attempt to parallel park even once; why on this night do we watch her attempt to parallel park over and *over* again? Why is this night different from all other nights?

Chase lingers on the parking job to raise the question of what terrible thing will happen because it's taking her so long. Chase provides glimpses of all the other customers—a scout troop, two unidentified black males at the jukebox, a man in a Member's Only jacket like Eugene Pontecorvo's at the counter—because he wants us to wonder if one of them might be there to take out Tony. (Well, maybe not the scouts.) Chase lets the tension build and build and build—including Members Only Guy walking past Tony and into the men's room—so that we'll be primed for something awful to happen as Meadow sprints across Broad Street and into the restaurant. Chase replayed the Bacala death line and laid down so much death imagery throughout the season and this episode, so we will understand that when the scene jarringly cuts to black, it's because Tony has just died, either via a bullet from Members Only Guy or a coronary from one onion ring too many.

Death is what happens, end of story, right? We can all go home now. Frankly, I'm not even sure why we're still debating this.

M: All right, let me back up for a second and say that at no point during my now ten-plus years of arguing about the meaning of this scene have I said that "Tony died" is an inconceivable or unacceptable interpretation. It's not *wrong*. In fact, it's the most obvious interpretation, given that Tony's pissed a lot of people off over the years, and in the overwhelming majority of gangster stories, the main guy dies at the end. Plus, that last stretch of twenty-one episodes does have a persistent chill, visually and plot-wise—a series of deaths and declines, with a lot of the color bleached out. So absolutely, the show is putting us in a frame of mind to anticipate a death.

But I don't think he *has* to be dead for us to think about all that related stuff, and I don't think that's the only possible interpretation. He could've had a coronary or another panic attack. Or it could be, as I wrote in my original recap hours after the finale aired, that the character who died there was us, the spectator. We don't get to watch the show anymore. He whacked the viewer. Or maybe nothing happened in that scene, but Tony went on being Tony and maybe died of heart disease or Alzheimer's, which, given all that we've seen him go through, is a sadder outcome.

I think we're supposed to be thinking about death, or the finiteness of life, during that last scene, but not necessarily that Tony died right then and there, and that's the end of the story.

Because, while you're right to point out how Chase and company have very deliberately put us in a death-obsessed frame of mind during this final run, during the preceding seasons he showed us time and time again that he was never interested in doing the obvious thing. And the single most obvious thing to do in a gangster movie is to kill the main character—out of reflex, or because the storytellers want to express that crime doesn't pay.

Remember, too, that Tony is the Homer Simpson of crime bosses, miraculously avoiding death or prison even as it claims other characters. Think about the randomness of him seeing the FBI agents coming over the hill and escaping even as they arrest Johnny. Or him surviving three car wrecks, one of which fatally wounded Christopher. This guy lives a charmed life. So does AJ, who luckily fails to kill himself—Tony happening to come home at that moment is a Tony-caliber stroke of good luck—and in this very episode, the kid survives a truck explosion. What's more in character for *The Sopranos*, to kill a magically charmed character in the final scene, or to refuse to do so?

A: I don't know the answer to that hypothetical, because either one seems like the kind of thing *The Sopranos* might do.

M: The point is, *The Sopranos* resisted all the usual gangster movie reflexes for seven seasons. I can't imagine that it would succumb to them in its final moments, no matter how great the temptation—and as our conversations with Chase confirmed, that temptation did exist. There has to be something else going on here, otherwise the scene wouldn't end as it ends, in such a studied "inartful" way.

I hate that when you ask, "What happened at the end of *The Sopranos*?" and people just shrug and say, "Well, he died!" A better question is, "What did that ending mean?"

A: Yeah, I would say the circumstantial evidence of death in the scene is overwhelming. But is that enough to convict Chase for murdering his main character? I mean, if you step back and think about it, killing Tony this mysteriously does defy *Sopranos* modus operandi in multiple ways.

M: Aha! Doubt.

A: Other than maybe the revelation that Big Pussy was an FBI cooperator—a plot idea conceived in the show's embryonic stages, without Chase expecting anyone would care about him resolving it—*The Sopranos* tended to keep its plot cards face up. You knew virtually everything important that was going on, not only with Tony, but with all his enemies and allies. At this moment in "Made in America," nobody that we know of wants Tony dead. Phil is gone, Butchie made peace with New Jersey, and anyone else who might wish Tony a violent end is out of the picture.

A man in Tony's business will always have enemies—Eric Scatino probably still nurses a massive grudge—so it's not outside the realm of plot logic that some rando or long-forgotten character could have hired Members Only Guy to do the deed. (For that matter, Members Only Guy could be the loved one of a Soprano victim himself.) But it's an enormous leap from how the series told stories in every scene, and episode, up until this one.

M: Yes. And I would argue that, if the main takeaway from that scene is, "Oh, they shot him," then either the show has failed and suddenly decided to give up and be a typical gangster story in its final four minutes, or there's something else happening here.

I vote that there's something else happening. And if it helps to move the discussion beyond the question of whether he's dead or alive, I'll just say, "Fine, he's dead." And now what? What does that leave us with, if that cut to black means somebody somewhere shot Tony? What is this ending *saying*? Or if we can't discern that, what is this ending trying to make us think about?

A: Maybe we should ask the cat.

The show absolutely dabbled in the supernatural throughout, from Paulie being haunted by Mikey Palmice, to Tony dreaming something that Tony B was actually doing, to whatever and wherever Kevin Finnerty was. There's a reason *The Twilight Zone* keeps coming up, whether in conversation or on the safe house TV in the finale. The cat turns up at the safe house and gets brought back to Satriale's, much to Paulie's horror—"You can't even put them near a baby; they suck the breath right out!"—particularly once it starts fixating on a photo of Christopher from the set of *Cleaver*. Is this, the superstitious Paulie wonders, just a cat, or his late colleague returned to life? Sometimes, a cat is just a cat, but it's hard not to consider this one within the context of what happens, or doesn't, a few scenes later at Holsten's.

The Austrian physicist Erwin Schrödinger famously theorized that if you place a cat into a box with some kind of hazardous material, the cat may live or die, but until you actually open the box to check, the cat is simultaneously dead and alive.

Maybe the wiseguy who has turned into a cat—Schrödinger's cat, to be precise—isn't Christopher, but Tony?

M: What do you mean by that?

A: What I mean is, maybe that cat is Christopher reincarnated, or maybe it's just a cat that won't stop hanging around Satriale's and staring at a photo of Christopher. We don't know, and will never know. And thus, that cat is Christopher and *not* Christopher at the same time.

M: Just like the Holsten's scene. And the Russian. And the matter of whether Ralphie was responsible for the fire. By telling other people what we think happened, we are revealing ourselves. We're admitting who we are.

A: Yes, the Holsten's scene is about death—specifically, about the idea that we are all here on borrowed time, and our lives can be snatched away at any moment, without warning or explanation or the slightest hint of fairness.

M: "Death shows the ultimate absurdity of life." —AJ Soprano, Fuckin' internet.

A: There's no way around that, and even David Chase says as much in the sixth interview later in this book. And it's true that, the longer the Holsten's scene and the parallel parking go on—and on and on and on—the harder it becomes to shake the feeling that Tony, or Meadow, or maybe everybody, is about to get whacked.

But the scene can be about the *idea* of Tony's imminent demise without actually featuring it—and, if we're being stubbornly pedantic, it *doesn't* feature it. Meadow runs to the door, the bell rings, Tony looks up, and . . . nothin'. You can interpret that cut to black any way you want it (to quote the other Journey song featured on the jukebox right below "Don't Stop Believin'"), but maybe Tony is the cat: dead and alive at the same time, because we can't see into the box to know for sure.

M: Well, that's been my overall point in these arguments from the very beginning, and I'm glad you framed it in those terms, because it does a nice end run around the whole "Tony Soprano, dead or alive?" question, which I've always thought was an attempt to change the question mark at the end of the sentence to a period. I think "Tony died at that moment" is a valid interpretation. But I also think it's fair to say that he lived beyond that moment, even to a ripe old age, because ultimately this scene is making us ask, "What have we learned?" or "Where have we been?" and "Where is Tony, right now, as a person?" These are reckoning questions, and they can occur at many different points in a person's life.

Of course, these questions occurred to Tony after Junior shot him, and that his response was to absorb rather shallow lessons—like, make better choices in the moment, and try being a better listener—while ignoring bigger ones like, "Maybe you're depressed all the time because you're a gangster." Melfi steers him toward this realization throughout the series, even in the pilot. But he always manages to avoid going there. I think the ending is sadder and more powerful if you think, "All those people he killed, all those people he loved that died, all the stuff he's been through personally, including getting shot and being in a coma—none of that really made much of a dent in this guy's thick skull."

A: Okay, but then, why the cut to black? Why the ambiguity at all?

If the scene's about the fragility of life, and the omnipresent specter of death that leaves us all fumbling about for meaning in this cold, cruel world, why leave even a trace of ambiguity? Why cut to black on that shot of Tony's uninflected face, as opposed to a glimpse of Members Only Guy raising a pistol, or even Tony looking distressed as his body deals with a gunshot, a coronary, a stroke (like the one that killed Livia), or some other cause of sudden death?

It could be that Chase simply likes ambiguity and confusion. *Blow-Up* is one of his favorite films, and it has a famously non-definitive ending that invites the viewer to project their own meanings. He was never interested in the Russian, the rapist, the stable fire, or any of the other characters and threads that he left dangling over the life of the series, except as forces that test the main characters and reveal their essence.

Or it could be like the decision in "Long Term Parking" to not only provide a glimpse of Adriana's daydream where she just gets in her car and heads south on I-95, but to deliberately stage her death scene so that she's off-camera when Silvio fires the fatal shot. Maybe, after spending a decade telling stories about this man—and having spent a whole lifetime thinking many of the same thoughts as Tony, particularly where their mothers were concerned—Chase just couldn't bring himself to direct a scene explicitly killing him, or even one where he asked James Gandolfini's face to point us more blatantly in that direction.

M: Well, that's interesting, because it brings Chase himself into the mix, and I think we both should admit that our interpretation of the ending is affected by our conversations with him while writing this book.

And by that, I don't mean he handed us the answer, because *The Sopranos* was never the sort of show that made you hunt for answers in that way. I just mean that Schrödinger's cat is useful if you're applying it to a story that could end either in a radical, art-house movie way, or in a traditional way, but with a fancy wrapping.

A: It's hard to play dumb about what we discussed with Chase, but the great thing— or the maddening thing, depending on your point of view—is that even with all he ultimately told us, there's still no definitive answer to the dead/alive question.

We know what the scene *means*, but we don't know what *happened*.

M: An important distinction.

Yeah, I was thinking that, too—that despite the hours we've spent talking to Chase about the ending, I don't think it's necessarily been "explained" in any meaningful sense, in terms of what happened next, and I get the impression that Chase can't really explain it either. It's not an insult to say that he doesn't really know why he did what he did, because all through our interviews with him, we kept trying to get him to explain the reasoning behind certain choices, only to discover that there wasn't any, and he and the writers and directors were just doing what felt correct.

That final scene is something he felt was correct, and that came out of his desire to subvert or amend the traditions of the gangster film, while perhaps coming to terms with the fact that he was unable to escape them. This is a show that's very interested in dream language, psychoanalysis, and the contradictory, mysterious forces that make us who we are, and it's inevitable that this series, perhaps more than other works of art, would have become a Rorschach test.

A: Tony's situation as he enters Holsten's is complex however you look at it. Professionally, he has just survived a war with New York—has, in fact, enough juice that he was able to kill a rival boss with the tacit approval of Phil's successor—but his organization is in a shambles. Paulie, long the most useless captain on the payroll, is the only major ally he has left.

Personally, he's on good enough terms with his immediate family that they'd all happily join him for onion rings and more at their favorite ice cream place. And, other than a couple of ugly fights, he has been getting along much better with Carmela since she took him back than he ever did during the first six seasons of the show. But Meadow is marrying into the extended Family by getting engaged to Patrick Parisi and becoming a lawyer—two things Tony never wanted for her—and AJ recently survived a suicide and is so lacking in direction that this low-level job working for Little Carmine feels like a salvation.

So when he walks into the restaurant, judgment has already been passed, or maybe suspended. He is either an enormous success or a pitiful failure.

M: Or he can be both.

A: The cat.

M: Yes.

A: Let me ask you this, then: If, during one of our many conversations with Chase, he had invited us to lean in close, and whispered, "Guys, Tony's dead," how would that change your feelings about the ending?

And, flipping that, what if he'd whispered, "Guys, Tony's alive"?

M: If he'd said, "Yeah, I killed him," I would've been deeply disappointed in Chase. Because it would've meant that he did the most obvious thing and then tried to hide it by making it seem as if he was creating an ambiguous or art-house type of ending.

And I think I would have been equally disappointed if he'd said, "Tony is alive." And that's because I *like* not knowing, and to me, everything about this ending says, "You're not supposed to know, you're supposed to live in the not-knowing." A lot of characters live there and have to make peace with it. The loved ones who lost people to "witness protection" or because they "ran away" suspect they were murdered but can't prove it, even though we viewers saw it happen. This ending puts us in their shoes. We make up stories to reassure ourselves that we have control over life, and we really don't.

I'm reminded of that moment in "D-Girl" where Dr. Melfi summarizes existentialism for Tony. "When some people first realize that they're solely responsible for their decisions, actions, and beliefs, and that death lies at the end of every road, they can be overcome with intense dread . . . a dull, aching anger that leads them to conclude that the only absolute truth is death." I think the insistence on "proving" that Tony died is a means of reasserting control over the show, and over the life of the person doing the proving. Death is the only absolute truth for everyone, and if you read that ending simply as "he died," you can wash your hands and walk away from it and not have to think about anything else that might be raised in that scene.

This is a show about either accepting that you're not in control of anything, or making a conscious decision to deny that. The idea of presenting the ending as a thing that can be mastered and explained is philosophically the opposite of everything that led us to that point.

I know this is a minority reaction, but I like being baffled or challenged or frustrated by art. I like having to make a case for a particular interpretation or just throw my hands up. It's fun for me. What I don't like is any kind of conversation that seems to be leading toward, "He's dead, end of discussion." Because that should *not* be the end of the discussion when you're talking about a show like this one, a show about psychology, development, morality, and all these other deep and tangled subjects.

The way the ending teases audiences by seeming very definite while denying us answers and closure makes it the ultimate *Sopranos* moment. And it throws all the other things we've been discussing, here and throughout this book, into sharper relief. Because it's taking the question of whether Tony lived or died off the table.

A: I spent many years after the finale as a card-carrying, vocal member of Team Tony Lives. I made arguments like the one above, about how a secret assassin repping an enemy we never heard of before would clash with every narrative rule the show ever followed. More recently, I found myself swaying over to Team Tony Dies, not only because of the death imagery throughout the season—including the way so many episodes open, as this one does, with Tony waking up from a deep slumber—but because some of my initial, long-hardened impressions of the scene didn't hold up under further scrutiny.

I had thought, for instance, that the sense of paranoia instilled in the viewer by the rapid editing style Chase uses for the scene was shared by Tony himself— that, perhaps, the point of it all was to finally put us in the mindset of the main character, to make us realize, "*This* is how miserable it is to be Tony Soprano: to spend every minute of every day worrying about who could be coming through a door to kill you."

But all that stuff exists outside the text, not in it. Gandolfini's playing it as Tony enjoying a peaceful night out with Carmela and the kids, up to and including that final look on his face in between when the bell rings and the screen goes black.

M: Yeah, he's checking out the scene in there for self-protection, but he does that everywhere he goes.

A: So for a while, it seemed easier to just go with the idea that he dies—that the cut to black follows on Bacala's line from "Soprano Home Movies," Silvio's reaction to the Hairdo's death in "Stage 5," and all that death imagery. I thought about Tony's entrance into Holsten's in the context of the earlier scenes where he visits Janice and then Junior. In both of those, Chase employs an unusual editing style, cutting directly from a shot of Tony looking out at the space he's just entered to a different point of view where he's already crossed most of the distance to the relative he's come to see.

M: Yes! And the music is continuous throughout. Bits of time are elapsing in terms of the physical motion of Tony in that space, but that's not indicated by the music, which never stops. That's one more reason why this scene feels dreamlike, along with all those incidental characters, like Members Only Guy and the uniformed Boy Scouts, who feel like people you'd meet in an '80s music video.

I think you could make a better case for Tony Dies if you assume he's dead before this scene even starts.

A: The distance he walks is shorter each time, and when he gets to Holsten's, we just cut from him looking at the restaurant to him in the booth, in a way that suggests he's seeing himself—really, that he's seeing the whole scene play out, like he's already left his body and is just envisioning what might come next back on this mortal plane.

So it felt better to go with "Tony died." It was An Answer, in a way that "Tony lives" never entirely felt like one to me, and when Chase wrote that article about the scene for *DGA Quarterly*, and talked about the fragility of our mortal existence,[1] I was able to smile and say, "Aha! That's it! I know now, and I don't have to worry about this anymore."

Except the longer you and I talked about it, both on our own and with Chase, the less substantial that idea felt, too, until by the end, I wasn't entirely sure that even *Chase* knows if the guy's dead or alive.

And does that matter?

M: You mean does it matter if Chase knows what happened? No. It's become increasingly clear to me as we've worked our way through the entire series again, with over ten years of perspective on that finale and nearly twenty years of living with the show in some form, that Chase is an intuitive writer, somebody who's not trying to send messages or create puzzles for people to solve, but is just trying to make people feel and think and question themselves.

It's also easy to see that Chase is of two minds on the last scene. Which is perhaps something he telegraphed by bringing that cat into it.

This is an artist sorting through contradictory impulses, in hopes of reaching audiences in a deep way. There are no cookies for figuring things out.

A: Okay, so a hypothetical: Either way you lean, what happens after that cut to black?

If Meadow just walks in and the family enjoys the rest of their onion rings, a nice meal, and some ice cream, what happens to Tony Soprano after? Does he sweat and strain rebuilding the Family after the damage Phil inflicted upon it? Do the Feds show up a week later to arrest him, Carlo having finally given them the missing piece of their RICO prosecution? Is the Daniel Baldwin script a huge hit at the start of AJ's shocking career as a Hollywood tastemaker?

And if Tony drops dead after the bell rings, whether from a bullet or (like poor Gigi Cestone) internal distress, obviously the next few moments involve Carmela, Meadow, and AJ being horrified and grief-stricken, but what comes after? Does Tony's death alter the career plans of either kid? Did he really leave enough money in overseas accounts to take care of Carmela after his passing, or will she soon be taking Angie Bonpensiero's old job passing out supermarket samples? Does Paulie freaking Walnuts somehow become boss of the Family, or

---

1   "This Magic Moment," by James Greenberg. *Directors Guild of America Quarterly*, Spring, 2015. Chase: "I thought the possibility would go through a lot of people's minds or maybe everybody's mind that he was killed. He might have gotten shot three years ago in that situation. But he didn't. Whether this is the end here, or not, it's going to come at some point for the rest of us. Hopefully we're not going to get shot by some rival gang mob or anything like that. I'm not saying that [happened]. But obviously he stood more of a chance of getting shot by a rival gang mob than you or I do because he put himself in that situation. All I know is the end is coming for all of us."

does Butchie throw up his hands at this point and decide to put his own guy in charge of the gang that couldn't shoot straight?

I ask this not to spoil the details of the many pieces of *Sopranos* fanfic I have saved to the cloud, but to consider the larger question: Which ending is more interesting? Whether we get to see what comes next or not, which is a more entertaining, exciting, and/or thematically fitting conclusion to the story of *The Sopranos*: Tony's abrupt death or his continued existence?

M: I think it's more interesting if he lives. I think it would fit with the cycles of experience depicted on the series. This guy has much more self-awareness and sensitivity than other people in his line of work, but is still a prisoner of his conditioning and maybe his genes, and always seems to fall far short of enlightenment. And if, to quote *Mad Men*, the greatest predictor of what somebody is going to do is what they have done in the past, Tony's always going to basically be Tony, the loquacious gangster who puts himself first.

I think it's also interesting if he dies, though that's a less disturbing ending to me, because it's the standard gangster story ending, and no matter how you read it, for reasons of genre history it always comes back to "Don't do crime, kids."

A: Back in the day, I felt like death was an easier sentence for Tony to take, because so much of his life—thanks to genetics, mental health, and the monstrous business he has chosen—brings him so much misery. But in rewatching the series and writing this book, it's clear that among Tony Soprano's greatest gifts is his ability to live in the moment, shrug off the overall pain and paranoia of his life, and enjoy the many fruits that come with being the boss of New Jersey.

M: "If you're lucky, you'll remember the little moments, like this, that were good." The end of season one.

A: Right. So maybe he'd have a relatively fine old time drifting into old age.

The day James Gandolfini died—in sudden, startling fashion that sadly evoked the very themes Chase was trying to convey with this scene—I wrote that, "as horrible a human being as Tony was, it gives me a small bit of comfort on this surprising, terrible day, to imagine Tony still alive, waddling out of his SUV and into the pork store, or calling up Dr. Melfi for one more shot at therapy."

Now? Now, I'm Schrödinger's critic: equally intrigued by the idea of Tony living and Tony dying. I understand what the scene was about—and, more importantly, I know how it made me feel the first time I watched it, every time since, and through all these conversations I've had with you and the rest of the *Sopranos*-loving world about it over the last decade. I felt then, and now, afraid for Tony Soprano, and painfully aware of both his fragile mortality and my own, more keenly than any other piece of art has made me feel. That matters much more to me, ultimately, than a definitive answer.

M: There was a moment a few years ago when a journalist[2] reported that Chase told her Tony lived, and he got mad at that—as mad as he's gotten at all the people who keep saying Tony died. But what he said, specifically—and he was directing it toward everybody—was, "'Whether Tony Soprano is alive or dead is not the point. To continue to search for this answer is fruitless. The final scene of *The Sopranos* raises a spiritual question that has no right or wrong answer."

I think the most important two words in those two sentences are "spiritual question." And if we fixate on anything other than that, we're missing the point. When people ask me, "Do you think Tony died?" I sometimes answer, "Of course." And then I pause and add, "Sooner or later, everybody does." Which admittedly is a dickish thing to say—but you know what I mean? That bell, to me, is a tolling bell, as in "Bring out your dead." It rings every time somebody goes through that door. I'm not saying "Holsten's is Heaven!" or anything like that. I mean it's a prompt for us to think about death and life, and what we've done with our lives.

Maybe the ending is moralistic, but not in the way that some of the people who need Tony to be dead might frame it. Maybe the ending is saying, "This guy never got it. Are you gonna be like him?"

A: This is all-important, and we'll see what happens to the conversation now that the phrase "death scene" is out there. We only have this one life, and precious little control over how long it lasts. How do we choose to live it? Tony Soprano has clearly made many bad choices, as have the other people at that table with him, as have nearly all the characters with whom we've spent these eighty-six-plus hours of television.

I think you and I are in agreement on the larger point of the scene, right, Matt?

M: What point is that?

A: Obviously, he's alive.

M: ALAN.

---

2   "Did Tony Die at the End of *The Sopranos*?" Martha Nochimson, *Vox*, August 27, 2014. "When [Chase] answered the 'Is Tony dead?' question, he was laconic. 'No,' Just the fact and no interpretation. He shook his head. 'No.' And he said simply, 'No, he isn't.'"

THE
DAVID CHASE
SESSIONS

These conversations took place between the authors and
Sopranos creator David Chase in a series of French
and Italian restaurants (and one hotel bar) on
the Upper East Side of Manhattan between
September and December 2017.

Session One:
"Why would I want to do that?"

On the origins of Chase's career and The Sopranos, *finding James Gandolfini and Edie Falco, "College," and more.*

ALAN: Tell us about your mother.

DAVID: I said a lot back in the old days, about depression and my mother, stuff like that, and I kind of oversold it. The reason I talked so much about her and about the pressure is because I knew that's what the show was about, and I wanted there to be a connection, so that people would say, "Hey, gee, that sounds interesting." Over the last maybe eight to ten years, I really have to come to the conclusion that in many respects, I had a very happy childhood. My mother was nuts, and she obviously did not have a happy childhood. I have a hunch that she might have been abused. And my father was a different kind of guy altogether, although he was also an angry person. But my mother? My mother was very funny.

A: How far in Caldwell did you grow up from where *The Sopranos* house was?

D: As the crow flies, a mile. To actually get there? Ten or twelve minutes.

MATT: How much did the world of the Mob overlap with yours?

D: A little. My father had a hardware store in Verona, New Jersey, and he knew these two guys who had a tailor shop in Verona. They were connected. I think a lot of them lived in Hanover. As I was leaving New Jersey and the East Coast, some guy had his garage got blown up in North Caldwell, and the guy in Roseland got shotgunned to death.

I was interested in the Mob probably mostly because I was Italian. My father and I used to watch *The Untouchables* every Thursday night. I think that's the reason the Mob really grew on me. When I was watching that show, I was watching my father. He knew all those gangsters' names, Frankie Yale and all those people. I was interested in my father's youth, where he came from and what he did and what it was like then.

An even better example of that was William Wellman's *The Public Enemy*. His [Cagney's] mother in there looked my grandmother. It all started with *Public Enemy*, even before *The Untouchables*.

So he watched *The Untouchables* every week. But he and my mother especially hated the Italian Mob, the gangsters. They were ashamed of them, thought they were terrible people. From watching *The Untouchables*, a friend and I got the idea to shake down the president of the school class in eighth grade for lunch money, and he went and told the principal! [*Laughs*] I got in a lot of trouble for that.

My father said, "You're imitating the most horrible, the worst kind of people on the planet!" He didn't say it that way, but he was furious. It was further confirmation that I was a bum and a punk and all that.

But he'd watch *The Untouchables* anyway. So many people were like that.

A: That makes me think of Richard La Penna. Did your father object to the idea that there were so many depictions of Italians as wiseguys?

D: There were fewer depictions back then. I mean, this is pre-*Godfather*, which really kick-started all that stuff, and *The Godfather* was *so* Italian. Before that, as I recall, in the original *Scarface* you had Tony Camonte, but there weren't Italian actors playing the roles, either. It all came due with the advent of *The Godfather*.

A: What do you remember of the first time you saw it?

D: I was disappointed in it because I'd read the book. The book had the whole story in there, two movies' worth. And Marlon Brando wasn't Italian. I liked it—I'm not saying I *didn't* like it—but I remember the book just blowing me away, so in comparing it to the book, as I was, they weren't the same thing. I've seen *Part I* since then, and I like it a lot better, though I still to this day like *Part II* better than *I*.

A: How and when did you decide you wanted to write for TV and movies?

D: When I was in film school. I went to film school because I wanted to be a director, and that's where I learned that films had to have a script. Writing a script was cheap in comparison to making a film. Going to graduate school, film school—it cost money to make films, even small ones. But all you need to write them is a paper and pencil, so that's when I started thinking about it. I was twenty-one, twenty-two, something like that.

I had written scripts for small films that I made, but I can't remember the name of this first one I wrote. I was inflamed by Jean-Luc Godard and stuff like that, not knowing what the hell I was even talking about—or what Godard was talking about. [*Laughs*] Stanford Film School had a documentary department, and I was there because I got in, and because I got a fellowship, so I went there because it was open to me. So over a period of two years, you could either write a thesis about . . . I don't know, what's that famous thing where they show an impassive face and then a baby crying?

M: The Kuleshov Effect.[1]

D: Yes. The Kuleshov Effect. You could write about something like that, or you could make a film. I decided to make a film. It was called *The Rise and Fall of Bug Manousos*. It was about a grad student who has a fantasy of this alternate universe

---

1   In 1918, Soviet film theorist Lev Kuleshov demonstrated how editing could create meaning by juxtaposing identical, uninflected close-ups of actor Ivan Mozzhukhin's face with shots of a child lying in a coffin, a woman on a couch, and a steaming hot bowl of soup, then showed the results to onlookers, who concluded that the man was sad, horny, or hungry, depending.

where he's a mobster. It wasn't very good. [*Laughs*] Although I did get $600 from a student film distributor! My father loaned me the money, about a thousand [dollars], and then I got the $600 and he never let me pay him back!

A: What was the first thing you sold on a more adult, legitimate scale?

D: An episode of a TV series called *The Bold Ones: The Lawyers*. The producer was a guy named Roy Huggins.[2] Our teacher had sent him our script . . . and he read it and wanted to hire us. So he hired me, but by that time, the friend I wrote it with had given up and gone back to Chicago, so I wrote this episode, and that was the first thing I did.

A: Huggins then went on to create *The Rockford Files*. Was that how you wound up on *Rockford Files*?

D: No, it was more circuitous than that. I was under contract at Universal almost that whole time.

A: So you had gone to film school, wanted to be a director, been into Godard, and now you're writing episodic hours of TV for Universal. How did you feel about that at the time?

D: I was excited by it. I was actually inside a major studio. I went there every day, I had a parking spot, and I got to work with really talented people. I then became terrified of directing, and didn't want to do it anymore because I saw how they were treated—"Hey asshole, look what you did!" So I thought, "I could never do that." I had worked [on TV] before *The Rockford Files*, but that wasn't as stirring to me. *The Rockford Files*, to me, had a feeling of real place and real time, and I felt it was taking place somewhere other than its time slot, that it was really Los Angeles.

A: You wrote a couple episodes late in the run of *The Rockford Files*, both with Greg Antonacci: one where the two Jersey guys come to LA, the second where Jim goes to Jersey, with a Mob boss named Tony who has a son named Anthony Junior!

D: The son was a drummer, he took drumming lessons.

A: And in the episode before that, there's a reference to a Carmela.

D: That's right: "Say hello to Cousin Carmela."

A: Was the second Mob episode conceived as a backdoor pilot?

D: Yeah. [NBC president] Fred Silverman in action. It was ahead of its time. In fact, how could they have possibly made a TV series at that time like that? I didn't expect it to get picked up.

A: Around when would you say you went from that excitement you felt before, when you were going to Universal every day to work on *Rockford*, to your later feelings of being done with TV, and wanting to get out and make movies?

---

2 Creator of TV's *The Fugitive*. The show's last episode became the top-rated single episode ever aired up to that point, and jump-started a cultural obsession with series finales that continues to this day.

D: Well, I had always wanted to make movies. When did the thrill of TV wear off? I don't know. I think after enough network meetings. I can't stand talking to these people. I can't stand what they want to do. What a paucity of entertainment.

M: What kind of notes did they give you?

D: Just . . . the *worst*. I had worked on a show before that that I had liked a lot called *The Night Stalker*. I was very excited by the medium at that point. But that show was kind of absurd. If there was anything in an episode that could possibly have disturbed anyone, you'd get a note saying "Take it out." And I guess it was a good thing, because it taught you to find another way to do what you wanted to do.

A lot of what I disliked about the job was broadcast standards, not the people in programming so much, but what you could say or couldn't say, and how long you could hold a shot.

A: You told me back in the day that *The Sopranos*, as an idea, started more as you telling your friends stories about your mother, and them saying, "You should do a show about that."

D: My wife was the one who told me. She didn't say what kind of show it should be, but she said, "You should do a show about your mother. She's hysterically funny." I agreed with her, but I didn't know how to do it. And given what we're talking about now, what TV network back then would do a show about David's mother?

A: *The Sopranos* premiered in January '99, so it was in development for a long time, but do you remember when you started getting serious about the idea of, "Oh, it should be a Mob boss"?

D: I changed agents, and I signed up at UTA. When I went in to meet them, they said, "What kind of ideas do you have?" I told them the idea that was *The Sopranos* and my agent said, "Forget that. It's never going to happen. Not going to work." But I pitched it as a movie then, and he said Mob movies were out of date, especially Mob comedies. I think maybe . . . what's the movie with Alec Baldwin?

A and **M:** [*Simultaneously*] *Married to the Mob.*

D: I think it had not done too well. Because of that, he said a feature with the Mob wouldn't work. I was going to cast De Niro as the character who became Tony, and Anne Bancroft as Livia. I think it could've been very interesting, but he told me to forget about it as a feature. And then, when I went over to Brillstein-Grey on a development deal, they suggested doing *The Godfather* as a TV series. And I said, "Why would I want to do that? It's already been done."

Then I was driving home that night, and I started thinking about the fact that the guy had a wife and a son and a daughter, and the shrink could be a woman, and that network TV drama was very female-oriented, so I thought, "Maybe that feature idea could work as a TV series." It had home life in it, it had . . . women's points of view, kids, all of that.

A: Do you remember the first network you took *The Sopranos* to?

D: Fox.

A: They wanted Anthony LaPaglia to play Tony?

D: That came later. They had nobody in mind. They got the scripts and maybe a month or two [passed] . . . I hadn't heard from them, and then I got a call from a woman who's still in the business. She said, "Listen, we're getting to the time now when we're going to be making our pickups, and I want to get in touch with you and tell you before you talk to anyone else that I liked your script a lot. It was really, really good." And I said, "Great, when do we get started?" And she said, "Let me think about this for a while, because I'm not sure this is something we still want to do. I'm not getting the feeling we may do this for a certainty. But I want to tell you as one human being to another, I really liked what you did." So I knew I was dead. [*Laughs*]

M: Did you ever get a sense of why they didn't want to give you a green light?

D: Anything that would offend anybody was not wanted on network television.

A: At that point did it go to CBS, or other places first?

D: I think it went to CBS, and then the other usual suspects.

A: And you told me once CBS wanted to take out all the psychiatry.

D: Yes.

A: Did they say why?

D: They didn't have to. I knew why—"Psychiatry, yuck! The lead goes to a psychiatrist? That makes him weak!"

At that point I said to the people at Brillstein-Grey, "Why don't we take it to HBO?" My deal at Brillstein-Grey was just about up, two years of it. . . . Brad Grey called my agent and said, "David's deal is about up here, and he did what he said he was going to do. He wrote two really good pilots, and we couldn't get them on. But I'd like permission to extend the thing, maybe, and take it over to HBO to see if they might be interested, because I think they might be." I met with [HBO president] Chris [Albrecht] and that was good.

M: So then you get the green light to do the pilot of *The Sopranos* for HBO. How did you [cast it]? What was the process? Did you have particular people in mind?

D: I never write with people in mind. We hired Georgianne Walken and her partner, Sheila Jaffe. What happened was, I saw Steve Buscemi in *Trees Lounge* and thought, "Who cast that? That's an amazing cast." I found out, called them, and they said they wanted to do *The Sopranos*. In the process of meetings, they would say to me, "Have you heard of that person? Do you know who this person is?"

It was a two-people casting process, and they were the ones who introduced me to Gandolfini.

A: You talk all the time about Steve Van Zandt being in the running for Tony. How seriously was he ever considered for that part?

D: To my mind, he was pretty seriously in it. It was a completely different show. The whole show changed—I saw it as a live-action *Simpsons*, and I was pretty serious about it. Once Gandolfini showed up, it was pretty obvious that his face and his words helped direct me to what it should be.

M: That's quite a compliment to him.

D: Oh yeah, absolutely. Absolutely. Then I recognized him from *Get Shorty*, but in that he'd been a sweetie pie, holding the baby.

M: Can we back up for a second and talk about James Gandolfini's audition, or his reading? Can you put yourself back in that room and describe what you were seeing and feeling?

D: He came in and he started to read and he was very good. All of a sudden, he stopped, and said, "I have to stop. I can't . . . I can't focus. Something's up here. I'll come back in Friday." So I said, "All right," and then Friday came along and he couldn't come in. I swear this is what we were told: his mother had died. It turned out his mother had died *years before*!

A and M: [*Laughter*]

D: So he never came back, but he'd done so well, and [the casting people] were really pushing him, too. He finally came to my house in LA and we went to my office at the house there, and we taped him doing it. He did it and it was great. After that, I had to bring the three of them over to HBO to read for Chris and Carolyn and I forget who else. And Cathy Moriarty as Carmela. I remember Jim reading with Cathy. It was great.

A: Did he read with Lorraine Bracco as Carmela, or had she said by that time she didn't want the part?

D: Lorraine never said she didn't want to play Carmela. Maybe she said it to her rep, but she never said it to me. I said, "I think she's really good . . . but I've seen her do this role. I might be interested in seeing her do Dr. Melfi." Lorraine might have been amazing as Carmela, too, but you would've had this feeling of, "I've been here before."

A: One of the most important scenes in the pilot, from your perspective, was Tony grabbing Christopher. How was it written, what did Jim do that was different, and how did you react?

D: It was written that Christopher says something like, "Hey, what are you talking about?" Then Jim would go [*jabbing a finger*]—*da da da*—like a love tap. I wouldn't call it a love tap, but hey, just like that: *Wake up!*

But when when we shot it, Jim grabbed him by the collar, yanked him up out of his chair, and I remember Christopher had a bottle of beer in his hand, and it fell accidentally. While Tony was talking to him, you heard the bottle skidding along the concrete, and it was great! It was the bottle that sold me on this.

I thought to myself, "Yeah, that's the real Tony. He's not love-tapping anybody. That's the real guy."

M: Right before I think season four or five, when everybody was renegotiating their contracts to come back, I said, "Do you want to come back?" He said, "I want to come back, because it's the greatest part I've ever had, but I also don't want to come back because no matter how long I spend in the shower, I can't wash the stink off me from this guy." How much of that stink came from the character as written, and how much was the darkness he dredged up for himself as he played the guy?

D: I had questions myself about Jim Gandolfini. I've always asked myself, he's such a *big* guy, and yet he's such a sweetie-pie. But he could really be nasty and unpleasant if he had to be. I've always asked myself, is Jim such a sweetie-pie because there's a tendency there to be a bully, and the ability to be one, because he's so big? Does he overcompensate and be this nice guy everyone loves so he won't come off like a bully? I never got an answer.

M: He was a *big* guy.

D: Huge.

M: And he seemed even bigger. Something about his physicality was almost overwhelming. He reminded me of Zampanò, Anthony Quinn's character in *La Strada*, or King Kong.

A: And other than when he's incapacitated by something else, there's not a single fight in the run of the show that Tony does not win.

D: Well, that's probably true. There were none that he lost?

A: He may have been sucker-punched once or twice,[3] but physically he could not be beaten, and that was a part of the legend of the character as he goes along.

D: Seemed realistic to me. That guy was enormous. Even when he was in high school. What do you think his sport was?

A: Football?

D: Basketball.

M: Really? [*Laughs*]

D: Everybody says football. He was thin and tall.

A: What do you remember of Edie [Falco] coming in? Had you seen her on *Oz*, or did casting people bring her to you?

D: I didn't see her on *Oz* until after she read for us. She came over on skates [*Laughs*] at HBO headquarters out here in NY, and that's all she wrote. I felt so lucky all the way through, for however many years it was. I felt so lucky with that cast. I can say that without feeling I'm being sentimental or anything. There wasn't anything they couldn't do.

---

3 In "Soprano Home Movies," Tony will blame both a sucker punch and his post-shooting physical condition for losing the brawl with Bacala. You make the call on whether either excuse counts.

A: What was it like writing for Edie and watching her work over the years?

D: Watching her work was great. You could stay down there on the set twenty-four hours, just watching what she did. Never missed *a* line. Not one. I don't know how somebody does that. She didn't hide herself or do anything like that. She was there, she came in, did her work and went home, and it was always faultless.

A: There's not a lot of Carmela in the first few episodes. Had you planned for the role to be as big as it became?

D: Yes. That's what I said from the beginning; the reason I thought this whole thing might work as a family show. Family shows were a women's medium, and this was a family show. I thought this might be successful, or at least keep its head above water, because it would attract, unlike most Mob pictures, a female audience because of the family show aspect.

A: Can you recall the first time you realized what she was fully capable of?

D: The thing that comes to my mind is the audition. She was just so good! I mean, there couldn't have been anybody else. In the audition, she went pretty seamlessly between comedy and drama, or the mixture of the two.

A: Did you know Nancy [Marchand] before this?

D: I knew her as Margaret Pynchon [the publisher on *Lou Grant*], so when I saw her show up, I thought, "What the fuck is this?" [*Laughs*] Then she started, and that was it. That was really something, because the character was my mother, and it was like looking at my mother all over again. And she later said to my wife, "Honey, I trust that this entity that I'm portraying is deceased?" She channeled it, I'm telling you. I can't explain it.

A: At what point did Nancy tell you that she was sick?

D: She was coughing when she came in for the initial reading. Coming up the stairs. We were on the second or third floor of this little building on 79th Street or something, and she was coughing then. She was very straight up about it. She didn't say, "I only have a year or two to live," but it was passed on to us that she was ill.

A: Did it give you any pause?

D: No, because at that time I had no belief this thing was going to go anywhere but the pilot.

A: Knowing what you know now, would you have thought about somebody else?

D: There was nobody else. I think over 200 women came in, and they all did this crazy Italian mama thing, but when she came in, she did what you see . . . she got my mother's inflections right, she got everything.

M: I've seen season one so many times, but I'm still not sure how much of her malice in manipulating Tony and Junior is conscious and how much of it is simply instinctive. There are times I don't even know if *she's* aware of what she's doing, and I wonder how much of that is in the scripts and how much of it is in the way she delivers the lines.

D: I don't know, but I do know that if I was to think about my mother, my mother did not consciously manipulate anybody. She was incapable of having a plan. But I will say that it's more like that than it is that she's a conscious manipulator, or an evil person.

A: In the third episode, where Brendan dies, there's a scene where she's talking to Junior, and Junior is basically asking her without asking her if it's OK to kill Christopher and Brendan, and she says that she likes Christopher, because, "He put up my storm windows one year," but she tacitly gives her approval for Brendan. And Junior goes and kills him. Is she conscious of what she's doing there?

D: I believe that's the kind of thing that comes right from my mother's mouth. "I like him because he put up my storm windows one year." She was always getting cousins to do things for her, coming to adjust the antenna on her TV . . . Her relationship with Junior . . .

M: It seems like there's a little connection happening between the two of them even when Johnny is still alive. There's something about the way he looks at her, the way he talks to her. And then, when they're elderly and Johnny's no longer in the picture, he is constantly coming to visit her. There's talk, and it's kind of semi-scandalous. There's a sense in which the brother is moving in on Johnny's woman!

D: Right, right.

M: And yet it's an entirely platonic relationship?

D: Completely. He's also asking for her advice.

A: She becomes his consigliere, certainly more than Mikey is.

D: Well I think he saw something in her, that she had an ability to—this is an interesting question. Do people do things with intention or not? I mean, was John Gotti a really intelligent guy who thought everything through, or did he just do it out of something innate in him?

A: You'd wanted to direct forever, and you got to direct this pilot—what did you have in mind in terms of what you wanted it to look like, to sound like, to feel like?

D: I wanted to open it up. I wanted it to be expansive, to be wide. I didn't want it to feel indoors-y and TV-ish. All I remember wanting to do was, I'd always been completely taken by the Meadowlands, and I wanted it to have that feeling. That's as far as I took it.

A: One thing that struck me was when they're outdoors, the weather is such a present factor: the sunlight outside the pork store is so harsh; when Tony's by the water, the wind is so harsh it's like his shirt is almost floating. The weather in the show is always very severe, even when it's a nice day.

M: There's an awareness of the elements that's unusual.

D: Part of that was just the desire to do something different than any typical downtown New York gangster movie: put it out there, with the trees and wind and all that stuff, in New Jersey. I think most people in America would not think of New Jersey as a Mob place. And part of it was wanting to give a kind of a spiritual feeling of the woods, because I remember that's what it was like when I lived there. We used to play in the woods all the time as kids. There were a lot of animal sounds out there.

Clifton, New Jersey, where I grew up, is sort of urban. Then we moved from there to North Caldwell, which was a lot of woods, and I spent a lot of time in the woods, playing in the woods. So that figured into my feeling for the show before it was written. When I was in college, I took a year-long course in American literature: Hawthorne, Poe, a lot of James Fenimore Cooper, woodlands stuff. I just love that. I kept thinking about New Jersey as a lost paradise.

M: I want to detour here and talk a little more about that experience of nature as a kid, because that's important to the show.

D: I really grew up in Clifton in an apartment complex, and there weren't a lot of woods around there, but my father and his business partner used to take me and his son to this cabin out in the New Jersey woods somewhere. It was owned by the Boys Club of Newark or something. My uncle, who was an officer in that club, also used this cabin for bringing boys up to get them to nature. I went there several times. It had no water, no nothing, but it was a cabin. I just really loved it. I loved camping out and I loved all that stuff.

When I moved to North Caldwell, New Jersey, as you know, it was woodsier. It was right across the street from my house, and I was always tramping through the woods. I had muskrat traps and a .22 rifle.

M: Do you know how to shoot?

D: No. My mother had my father pull the firing pin out of that because she was afraid I was going to kill him.

M: By accident or on purpose?

D: On purpose! She told me that at his wake

M: Wow. It's a good thing you never ran into any bears carrying that .22!

D: Yeah! I went to a lot of summer camp, Boy Scout camps and stuff like that in New Jersey. The woods are very mysterious to me, both spooky and beautiful. They inspire me quite a bit.

M: The first time you saw *Twin Peaks*, you must've thought, "Oh my God, somebody understands me." There's so much of the woods in that.

D: Yeah, something like that. I always felt to myself that there's something about David Lynch—we're born, like, six months apart—that made me think to myself, "Somebody understands me," or "I understand that." I know that feeling he's going for.

A: So you finished making the pilot. At that point, you didn't want HBO to pick it up, correct? You just wanted to be able to take it and [get] some funding and complete it as a movie?

D: Yes.

A: What would the second half of the movie have been? There's twelve more hours of plot that ended up unspooling on TV.

D: There would have been a couple more incidents of violence. It probably wouldn't have had as much family in it—as much of the kids or Carmela.

M: It would've still included Tony putting a pillow over his mother's face?

D: No. I had never gotten that far when I was thinking about it. The original story, the Anne Bancroft–De Niro version, he was going to go up to her and smother her with a pillow. But [Nancy] worked out so well. And she said to me at the end of the season, "David, just keep me working." She was pretty sick by that point, but she was so good [that] I just couldn't kill Livia, so we had to invent this whole thing where she was left alive, and "Look at her, she's smiling!" That had to go in. And then she really wasn't as germane to the second part of the second season.

A: A year passed between when they picked up the pilot and when you started making episode two. Robert Iler's a foot taller, there's a new pork store, a new Father Phil . . .

D: Silvio's part of the gang now! He really wasn't in the pilot!

A: In that year, what did you see, looking at the pilot, that made you go, "We should do more of this," and "These other things need tweaking?"

D: We had to figure out what the permanent sets would be, how to do it economically, who had worked out really well in the pilot. Almost everyone in it was pretty good.

M: How open were you to actors adding or changing lines?

D: Not open at all.

M: You never let something through?

D: A couple times I did, especially a little bit more toward the end. But I felt that if we started having actors changing lines, we couldn't let it go on like that. Those guys were so, so desirous of getting their faces in front of the camera, telling each other what to do— all the guys in Tony's crew, especially. Tony Sirico was a part-time director all the time. "Stay, stay, stay over here! Come on over here with me!" [*Laughs*]

A: Dreams were obviously a big part of the show, as much as certain people wished they weren't. When you first started doing them, were there certain stylistic rules or ideas that you wanted?

D: There were, and I'm sure we talked about this before: no moving camera. Just recently I read that there were two rules, but I forget what they are.

M: Why no moving camera?

D: Because if you push in on somebody it means, "This is important," especially in TV.

That's why there were no music cues in the shrink's office, because in a typical network TV show, when patients start to get down to business and reveal themselves about why he's so happy or what the truth really is, they'd push in really slowly and you'd hear a synthesizer, you know?

I hated that stuff. And I didn't want to punctuate what was important in the scene and what wasn't.

M: Did you have a model for the Tony–Melfi relationship?

D: Yeah, a shrink that I'd had in LA.

M: What was your relationship with that therapist like?

D: It was like a re-mothering. She's probably dead now, and I haven't called her. Yeah, it was mostly kind of a re-mothering. She was very good at making me feel better about myself.

A: Melfi does some of that with Tony, but a lot of their relationship is her calling him out on his behavior to varying degrees. Sometimes she dances around it and sometimes she can be confrontational.

D: There were things Tony did that really offended her.

A: How did you figure out, over time, what those boundaries were, and where she'd be more willing to say, "What you are doing is bad?"

D: You know what's odd? To a certain extent, and this is only a slight bit, but it's there—with certain issues, it would be hard to tell the difference, in my head, between Lorraine Bracco and Melfi. If I felt "Lorraine would probably hate this," a little bit of that would seep into Melfi. I tried to avoid that, but I couldn't always do it.

M: Was it just a matter of knowing Lorraine as a person and her value system?

D: Yeah.

A: Let's talk about "College." At what point did you become conscious of the fact that Tony hadn't killed anyone yet?

D: When we were trying to write the fifth episode. I had shied away from it when I wrote the pilot the first time, when I handed it in to Fox. I was thinking, "Network TV won't let you do that kind of thing anyway, so don't put in any murders or bombings or anything like that. Just do gangster tropes." Then, once Fox turned it down, I thought, "You stupid asshole, that's what people *watch* these things for."

M: "Less yakking, more whacking."

D: Right! So when HBO bought the show, I knew that we had to get to it sooner or later. But I also didn't want to be dependent on that stuff. I've said it a million times: *The Sopranos*, in one season, had more gangsters in New Jersey than there had been in twenty years, and more whackings! And when it was time to do "College," I was starting to get bored with [the killing]. I was bored being there in New Jersey all the time. I said, "Let's take them out of town, on vacation," which turned out pretty well.

A: One of the reasons it hits us as hard as it does is that Febby's not a threat to him, he's just a guy living his life.

D: That was intentional. The network didn't start complaining about that episode until after we'd shot it, and it was because that murder was really great. I don't think a lot of TV actors would've done that, or given their all for that, the way Jim did. He had spit coming out of his mouth.

When HBO read the script, they didn't see any of that. Once they saw it and he was schvitzing and everything like that, that's when Chris Albrecht called. He said, "We gotta do something about this," and I said, "If he doesn't kill that guy, he's a scumbag. He's a traitor and an informant. He has to be killed."

Then I came up with the stupid idea of the guy selling drugs to kids in high schools, which was, to me, a terrible cop-out.

A: Junior is a housebound adviser and is increasingly senile in the later years, but he's very proactive first here as a captain, and then as the on-paper boss. Did you miss that in the later years when you couldn't do that anymore—because if he was active, Tony would've killed him?

D: No. I was always very satisfied with the stories about Junior, what Junior became and how it started. He was everybody's favorite character to write.

A: Really? Why?

D: I don't know. Well, first Livia was. I guess it's because they're so outspoken. They're senior citizens, so they just say whatever's on their mind. They never pull their punches, they're always very direct and outrageous.

Christopher was another one we had a soft spot for, even though he was monumentally stupid. The characters who were the most fun to write were the ones who took themselves very seriously.

The line people always quote to me is Livia's, "Psychiatry? That's just a racket for the Jews!" [*Laughs*]

A: Speaking of psychiatry: the idea of doing this long bit [in "Isabella"] where Tony's hallucinating and we don't know it, and it ends up being a big part of the plot—where did that come from?

D: I don't know. I just dreamed it up, I think.

M: It's the first instance of Tony having a dream or fantasy that leads him to a conclusion about his waking life—with Melfi's help, of course. There's a chain of realizations that leads him to figure out that his mother never loved him and wants him dead. I feel like "Isabella" and "I Dream of Jeannie Cusamano" are two halves of a two-parter. You have this psychic eruption in the first one that is analyzed and resolved in the second one.

D: Yeah. You might say that Roman Polanski's *Repulsion* is kind of a precursor, although I suppose people have done psychotic episodes, breakdowns, in movies and TV before where you didn't know if it was the real thing or not. I think it was just *sui generis*.

A: Was there ever a point where you wanted to leave the question of whether Isabella was real unresolved?

D: No.

M: Okay, because later on you *do* leave things unresolved.

D: I caught that disease. [*Laughs*] I wasn't a spoiled baby at that time!

M: Tony has a long history of being in situations where he has to decide whether or not to kill a guy, and the answer is usually, "I'm going to kill him."

D: And he's killing people he shouldn't be killing personally.

M: The failed hit on Tony in "Isabella" is another instance where, in reference to "College," he seems more alive, more emotionally connected to the world, happier, when he's killing somebody or fighting for his life.

D: I totally believe that. I think that would happen to any of us. We'd feel elated on some level. Or maybe not—maybe we'd be so blown away by the fact that we just came out of a near-lethal experience. But in his case, on a biochemical level, I believe that whatever those natural drugs are, they'd be kicked in by that happening.

M: You mention drugs, and in this show, a lot of drugs are used and a lot of people have issues with them, or are in recovery and should be, or they go into it, come out—

D: And then they go back in.

M: Is violence a drug for Tony?

D: I guess I'm gonna say yes.

A: The orange juice—is that meant as any kind of *Godfather* homage?

D: Not that I knew about!

A: That just makes me think of all the theorization of the meaning of eggs in *The Sopranos* and how eggs represent death, and Valentina makes Egg Beaters so she only gets burned and doesn't die! Was the egg thing something you were conscious of?

D: Absolutely! [*Laughs*]

M: So the egg thing in *The Sopranos* is what oranges are to *The Godfather*!

D: [*Sarcastically*] Exactly!

A: Was the entire first season in the can when the show premiered, or was some of it still being made?

D: It was in the can.

A: I ask because there are a couple of episodes, "The Legend of Tennessee Moltisanti" and "A Hit is a Hit," that feel like they were written in response to the anti-defamation complaints you got.

D: I knew that stuff was coming. When I was working on *The Rockford Files*, we used to get shit all the time. You weren't allowed to give people an Italian name at that time—anybody who was a gangster had to be "Mr. Anderson" or some shit. That was a constant problem. It was right around the time when Joe Colombo got killed, I think. When I was working on *Northern Exposure*, after John Falsey left the show, we did one in which there were five families in Sicily, like, not Mob families, but they were "the Five Families," and they had these conventions and stuff like that, sit-downs and all that shit. Man, that caused a huge, huge uproar.

So I knew this was going to happen. When we first got started, I said to HBO, "Should I change my name back to my father's name?" and they said, "No, don't do it. You're known as David Chase, so let it go." I thought it would go better if people saw I was Italian, and that it was my right to do what I want with my heritage.

A: The first season ends with the torrential rainstorm. Everyone winds up at Vesuvio. Almost every season after that ends with the family at some kind of dinner gathering, up to the last scene of the show. When you did that first one, did you look at it and say, "This would be a nice way to tie things up," or was that just how it kept happening?

D: That's how it kept happening. It was part of my belief—and I think it's correct, actually—that food is so important to Italians as a subculture.

I had really good cooks in my family. My father's mother was really good. My own mother was so-so. She did some things well. My father was a good cook. I had a couple of aunts, like, I had a total of maybe fifteen aunts, between my mother and my father. There were three or four in there who were really, really good. Those women would gossip about each other. My Aunt Edie, for some reason, would put sugar in the Sunday gravy, and my mother and her sisters would make fun of her behind her back about that—and not like gentle teasing, either. It was serious business. "Can you imagine putting sugar in that?"

A: Did you know back then, because it's not really revealed until season three, that meat is one of the big triggers for Tony's panic attacks?

D: I had no idea.

A: Was Jimmy Altieri also a rat, or did Vin Makazian just confuse the two fat brunette guys?

D: He was a rat.

M: Did you know Pussy was a rat when you were making season one?

D: No. I never thought we were coming back for a second season, so I was in no way prepared for that.

M: So was this a case of, "Oh, we already had a rat on the show and we killed him off, we gotta come up with a different rat"?

D: I don't think so. We were told a while ago that those guys were all ratting on each other, all the time.

What happened was, in show number eleven, Pussy disappears. Then the season ended after thirteen, and I went on vacation, came back, and I knew the show was liked a lot but I didn't know whether they'd renew it or not. I knew nothing about anything. And I came back and all I knew was that everyone was saying, "Where is Pussy?" I thought, "Now what?" We had to have a plot, and they're already going "Where's Pussy?" so we have to figure out where he is, and then we got interested in the whole question of Stockholm syndrome, and Pussy becomes a junior G-man, inflated by his own stuff. That's how it came about, because we had to do something, and it was that plus the Richie story.

A: Artie Bucco occupies a unique moral space within the show. He's not part of the Mob; he's sometimes tempted to be part of it, but he either resists on his own, or Charmaine talks him out of it. But he grew up with these guys, and his and Tony's and Silvio's kids all go to the same school. How important was having a guy like that be a significant part of the world to the show?

D: Not important. We just liked him.

M: The character or the actor?

D: Both, but we liked the character a lot. Johnny [Ventimiglia] was great. When he'd get all emotional and overhyped and teary-eyed and stuff, he was great. But the character wasn't necessary at all. You could have made the show without him. You couldn't have made it without Livia, for example.

A: What percentage of the characters were on the show more because you liked the character or the actor than because they were essential?

D: A lot. As actors, they were all just so good. All the writers had the same feeling: they loved writing for those characters.

Session Two:
"I never knew whether we were coming back or not."

On Janice, Richie, Furio, Italy, renewal, and painting yourself into corners.

ALAN: Did you have any trepidation about doing a second season? Or once the show was on the air, did you want it to come back?

DAVID: You don't like to sound self-pitying, it sounds ridiculous. But it's really hard work. With that show, when I heard it had been bought, I was almost destroyed. I said to my agent, "Oh my God, they bought the show." So every time we were picked up—and you can talk to any showrunner and they'll tell you the same thing—it's mixed emotions you'd feel.

A: So, you had this whole idea of the arc of Tony and Livia for years. Now you're coming back and you have to start over from whole cloth. How terrifying was it? Or wasn't it?

D: I recall I jumped in with both feet and just got to work. I don't think I was terrified. That's from all those years of episodic television: that's the job, so you just do the job.

MATT: You went from not knowing if they would make a pilot, not knowing they'd pick it up and let you make a whole season, and not knowing how the public would receive it or whether audiences would respond, to having the hottest show on TV. That's quite a change in fortunes.

A: *The New York Times* was saying, "It just may be the greatest work of American popular culture of the last quarter century."[4]

D: Exactly, right. That's crazy.

M: The *New York Post* columnist Jack Newfield did a sit-down with you.[5] I remember thinking, "Oh, it's official, David Chase is a big deal." It was like reading an *Esquire* interview with Francis Ford Coppola in about 1979.

D: I remember doing the Jack Newfield interview. Yeah, it was a real kick, and I began to warm to the whole idea of doing serious television. Then I did get to the point where I wanted it to go [away], and by the time the last season came around, that was enough.

A: Each year when a season ended, there would be speculation on the outside: "When is it going to be the last season?" and "When does David want to end it?"

---

4   "Sympathetic Brutes in a Pop Masterpiece." Stephen Holden, *New York Times*, June 6, 1999.
5   "Even Wiseguys Get the Blues." *New York Post*, April 4, 1999.

Were you not sure of when you wanted to end the show, or did you have a better idea?

D: Here's what would go on: I got into the frame of mind that unless the show was going to be done exactly the way I wanted it done—and that includes money [to make the show], and my money, too—it would be okay if we were canceled.

A: So if the show had ended with season four, with Tony and Carmela separated, and the last image was Little Paulie blasting Dean Martin at the lawyer on the dock, you'd have been okay with that?

D: Yeah. That's a great ending, actually.

A: Besides Big Pussy being a traitor, the other big idea that year is Janice and Richie. Where did those characters come from, and who did you look at other than Aida and David to play them?

D: The only one I remember is Annabella [Sciorra], who we looked at for Janice. As far as Richie's concerned, there were quite a few guys.

M: What was it about Aida Turturro that made you think, "This is Janice?"

D: She's just a miraculous actress, she really is. She gets so deep into it. Like, if there's a sad thing, Aida can get to crying and it's just not a problem. And it's so believable, because she really is crying!

M: Offscreen, is Aida like Janice at all?

D: She's not mean like Janice at all. In fact, she's very effusive and she laughs a lot.

You know what it was, though? In talking to her, and seeing her read and everything like that, I saw my Italian aunts. I saw my father's sisters, who weren't really like that, but they were like that enough.

A: Janice had been mentioned a couple times in the first season. We'd seen her in the flashbacks to the 1960s as Tony's older sister. Why did you bring the character into the present and add her to the regular cast?

D: I don't know. Maybe she was there because we didn't know how much we could push our luck with Livia, and we needed another thorn in the family. I think that's how it came about.

With every one of those new actors, there was just no doubt about it once we read them. David Proval is not a big guy. He's a small guy, and obviously no threat to Jim Gandolfini. But there was just something so threatening about that guy on-screen, where there isn't at all in real life.

A: Some people look back on season two and think, "This is the season of Richie Aprile and he comes in and he's the antagonist." But he dies in the second-to-last episode, and he's not even killed by Tony, whereas Pussy is reintroduced right after the Sinatra montage, and the finale is all about him. Did you view Pussy as the more important threat to Tony that year?

D: I'd say a different kind of threat. I probably saw him, in a sense, as the more important story, whether he was the bigger threat or not. Having one of your best friends go through that change was really low-hanging fruit, and we went for that a lot. I mean, that story was very, very important—especially because Vinnie was such a good actor. I just loved working with him and letting him do his thing.

A: Janice shooting Richie is a famous *Sopranos* moment because it was so unexpected in the timing of it, who did it, and how it happened. Where did that idea come from?

D: We were sitting in the writer's room one day and I said, "How about if Janice does it in episode twelve?" I was thinking about their relationship and the whole thing. That makes me sound gimmicky—like, "Oh, they'll never see this coming." It wasn't about that. It was about, "Oh, this will be really good. If Aida does it, this will be really good."

M: What would've happened to Richie if Janice hadn't shot him?

D: I guess he would've gone another season or something. I don't know what he would've done in that season. I didn't think about it that way.

M: This might be a good time to clarify something I've been hearing for almost twenty years, which is that Richie Aprile and Ralphie Cifaretto are the same guy, and if Richie had continued, he would've turned into Ralphie. Is there any truth to that at all, or is it just something that fans made up?

D: That's something the fans made up. If that's the way it seems, I have to plead guilty.

M: So you never seriously considered keeping Richie going until season three, season four, whatever?

D: I never thought about things that way. I thought, "We're doing this season now." Partly because of the way HBO conducted themselves, I never knew whether we were coming back or not.

M: It's so interesting to hear you say that, because there's this perception of *The Sopranos* after season one not just as a network-realigning show, but as a medium-realigning show, and one that HBO was willing to back up the Brinks truck to keep.

D: Yeah, that surprised me, and maybe I'm wrong—maybe I'm hot-headed and I have to be pissed off at somebody, it could be that—but it always seemed that it took forever for them to push the button. People would ask me if the show was coming back, and I'd say, "I don't know."

A: You've said you weren't satisfied with how the Italy episode turned out. Why not?

D: I wasn't happy with the cast. It just didn't seem real. Annalisa did not really seem like a Mob housewife, or a Mob wife, and in the end, she was just too sexy, too young.

M: Too much of a fantasy?

D: Yeah, another one of those. That was basically it.

A: I remember when I heard they were going to Italy I thought, "Oh, this will be epic, the Mob show goes to Italy," and the episode is, by design, not that at all.

D: Yes. In reality, those guys don't really travel. They don't really leave their neighborhoods. Maybe they go to Florida or Vegas. I wanted to do more what their trip to Italy would be like. Maybe it's because we had too much fun making it, that's another thing it could have been.

I should look at it again, maybe it's not what I think it was.

[*Pause*] Nah, I don't want to look at it again.

A: What made you want to add Furio to Tony's crew?

D: I believe it came about because we saw him in that episode and we wanted to bring another guy into the crew, someone who was a tough badass, and we remembered him.

A: But Federico wasn't even an actor, he was an artist.

D: Incredible, yeah. I mean, I bought everything he did. I had a lot of luck with people who weren't actors. I'm marveling to myself that we had such good non-professional actors on that show.

A: You also got a lot of mileage out of Peter Bogdanovich, who I think had done some acting before.

D: He studied with Stella Adler. We had used him in *Northern Exposure*, which is why I remembered him. And Joe Gannascoli, whatever else you believe about him, was really something as Vito. I wonder what it is. Maybe Italians are just natural thespians.

A: In season two, Christopher's screenwriting ambitions started giving you an excuse to do episodes like "D-Girl," where he interacts with Hollywood people playing themselves, as well as the Alicia Witt character, and Tim Daly as the writer who they paired him up with. Was that fun to be able to take the piss out of the business?

D: Oh my God, it was delightful! My favorite bit was when Tim Daly tried to turn in his Emmy for money at the pawn shop! They were like, "Well, an Oscar, maybe—but fifteen bucks!" [*Laughs*]

A: [The Webistics pump-and-dump scheme] introduces us to Matt and Sean, the only people lower on the totem pole than Chris at that point, and probably the only people dumber than him. Sean has to keep going to the bathroom every time they're on a heist! [*Laughs*]

D: It's a phenomenon! You know that, right? There's guys who'd go in for a robbery and they'd have to take a shit!

M: Any theory as to why that happens?

D: More than just nerves, or having to leave a talisman? I've heard both of those theories. But it's a thing.

A: "From Where to Eternity" is the first *Sopranos* script by Michael Imperioli. How did he end up becoming an occasional contributor to the show?

D: We were always looking for new people, and I saw *Summer of Sam*, which he cowrote, so I thought, "Well, let's give him a try." He's a smart guy. We all liked him.

A: That's a memorable episode just because it's one of the first times the wiseguys are really confronted with these questions of Hell and evil and what do they do, and Melfi just comes at Tony about it.

D: You know, that storyline was based on a true story from my hometown. It was the second time that I used it on a show. I used the basic story in *The Rockford Files* for "Jersey Bounce."

There was this guy in my hometown in Caldwell, Michael, a house painter who was one of those Johnny Boy types from *Mean Streets*, only worse than that—just a fucking asshole. He would get in fights with people. Like, in a nice restaurant, a crowded restaurant, he'd look at a guy across the room and be like, "What the fuck are you looking at?" And the guy would just be eating. If he said something, he'd go over to him and start trouble. Even if the guy looked away, same thing would happen. He was just a bad, bad fucking guy. There was a concert at Montclair State and he got up on stage in the middle of the concert and was fucking around, took an instrument away from somebody.

But he had a girlfriend and he beat her up, and the girlfriend was the sister of a really low-level mobster. There was another kid in the town who knew him—two other guys knew him, and they wanted to get the attention of the Mob and become mobsters. So they got Michael to come over and give a bid about painting the garage while the parents were out. They were going to kill him to win the love of this low-level mobster.

So he came over to the garage. And they shot him in the back of the head, put him in the trunk of the car, and took him to Newark Airport.

And then they began to worry about the fact that he might be discovered, so they went *back* to Newark Airport, and they were going to take the body to Eagle Rock Reservation to bury him. But they went back to the airport like a month later, and they got the car and they were driving it out and they got caught with the supplies to use for burial. And that's where the idea for "Long Term Parking" came from.

A: You eventually used every part of that story! In season two, Carmela flirts with a house painter!

M: Speaking of Vic: eventually Carmela has sex with a man who isn't Tony, but it takes her until season five. Did you ever have discuss having it happen sooner?

D: We did have those conversations, but—how can I put this? There were always some sort of personal issues having to do with Carmela and what she would do, or not, or what she was going to do. I was in conflict with Robin [Green] very often about Carmela and what she was doing or what she would be capable of, what she should be, and I would get very frustrated with the whole argument, and finally I was like, "Fuck it, I don't want to talk about it anymore."

And I began to grow concerned, after five seasons, about that aspect of Carmela. In the same way I got concerned later about how long it took Tony to kill Christopher, I felt that way about Carmela taking a lover. I thought, "This should've happened a long time ago, what is she, a dishrag?" or something like that.

M: Was there a sense of whether it would be realistic for a Mob wife to step out?

D: We considered that all the time, and asked everyone we could about it. Most people said "no," but it's hard for me to believe that that's the case.

A: She never actually sleeps with another man until Mr. Wegler, and that's during the separation, so it's not an affair at that point, except as far as Father Phil is concerned. But in season four, for instance, was there ever a point at which you were going to have Carmela and Furio consummate their feelings for one another?

D: It came up. We did contemplate it. But we didn't, and looking back on it now, I'm sorry we didn't do it. But who knows? What happened happened, and if we'd gone down that road, we wouldn't have had "Whitecaps."

M: My guess was that it didn't happen sooner because she has a very strong guilt about cheating, and she doesn't want to be like her husband.

D: Yeah, and she's afraid she's gonna go to Hell when she dies.

A: Vic Musto might've slept with her until he realized how dangerous her husband was.

D: We figured that anybody who knew who her husband was would react like that. Wegler was outside of that world.

A: We talked before about "Isabella" helping Tony come to a revelation about Livia. A good chunk of "Funhouse" is Tony having dreams while suffering explosive diarrhea, and the dreams force him to finally admit to himself that Pussy's a rat and he needs to go. How confident did you feel, at that stage of the series, that you could build such a big moment out of Tony's subconscious?

D: Confident enough. I thought about, how are we going to get Tony to find out that it was Pussy? And I said to myself, "I just don't want to do a procedural, him going around from place to place, asking questions with a pad and pencil." And then I said to myself, "It's totally believable that he would know this somewhere already," and I thought, if things had a reality to them, I never question it. And I believe the psychology of that, and I believe that if it had come up with Melfi, she would have maybe enlightened him about that. If things were based on real dynamics, I never doubted it. And I always felt we were safe. I can't think of anything else. There were times things were so outrageous, you'd think, "Is that real?"

A: There was no way Pussy could live once Tony found out, was there?

D: No, unless he was sent to prison for some reason.

A: The season was always heading toward his death no matter what?

D: Yeah. Our technical advisor, Dan Castleman, told us about the fact that Stockholm syndrome played a big part in Mob–police relationships. Mobsters, once they flip, they become real junior G-men, and that's what we loved.

M: Like in Pussy's relationship with Skip Lipari.

D: Yeah. Pussy was always going a little bit too far.

Session Three:
"I shout things at them in the privacy
of my house."

Goodbye Livia and Tracee, hello Ralphie and Gloria

ALAN: You had to reconfigure the entire series as a result of [Nancy Marchand's death]. When you found out, do you remember, beyond the grief over Nancy, what you were thinking about in terms of, "What do we do now with the show?"

DAVID: Sure, I did think that.[6]

A: In the Livia funeral episode there's the digital Livia, and I believe her hair is different in every single shot she winds up in, because you had to take bits and pieces from all over. Why did you decide you wanted to do that, and in hindsight, is it something you would've done, knowing what the result would be?

[*Chase hangs his head and rubs his brow*]

D: I would not have done it over again. I would try it again now, but things are different now. I convinced myself it was going to be fine, even after I saw it. And, dare I say it, it was a mistake.

A: Their last significant interaction is at the end of season two where he storms out of the house and trips on the steps and falls and she laughs at him. In hindsight, that's a very good final interaction between the two of them.

D: That just didn't occur to me. I thought, "Oh God, I gotta play her off."

---

6 Terence Winter: "My recollection is that we had just begun to write season three when Nancy died, and we were only in the process of mapping out how Tony would get back in her good graces. I also recall that originally David wasn't set on writing "Proshai, Livushka" himself, since he had just written the season opener. I, along with Todd Kessler, Robin, and Mitch, lobbied and told him he was the only one who could possibly write it, and of course he did. I don't think anything else we were planning changed significantly as a result of Nancy's death."

A: How much do you think the show changed as a result of Livia no longer being a physical part of it?

D: I don't think it changed tonally. None of the relationships were affected by it. Tony was affected by it for a short time. She was an asset, so we lost an asset. But I don't think it changed the direction of the show at all.

A: With Gloria, Tony realizes at the end of the relationship that she's the ghost of his mother coming to haunt him. Would that character have existed in a season which actually featured Livia, or was she someone you came up with afterward?

D: Afterward.[7]

A: Do you think Livia would've been a character for the whole run of it if she had held on, or do you think at a certain point you might've written her out anyway?

D: We might've written her out anyway, because you don't want the guy to be too close to his mother and be accused of being obsessive about her, or of [the show] being too close to *White Heat*.

A: In season three, you have stories about Ralphie, Gloria, and Jackie as different foils for Tony at different points. Who do you think is the most important of the three to that particular season?

D: It's hard to say. I mean, Jackie was definitely not. Not at all. They had different functions. I guess I'd have to say Ralphie, although Gloria was very important.

A: What would the season three story have been with Livia?

D: "Tony has to be nice to his mother."

A: In the Livia funeral episode, there are two bits that people like to talk about.[8] One bit is someone opening up the cabinet with a mirror on it and you see Big Pussy's reflection for a moment. His ghost popped up a few other times over the course of the series, but that's a really brief, blink-and-you'll-miss-it moment. Why did you feel Pussy might make an appearance there?

D: I don't know. Maybe he was there to greet the dead? Something like that. Nobody really notices, right?

A: They don't.

MATT: That's a particularly interesting spectral visitation. It's not from the POV of one of the characters. Nobody in that scene is positioned in a way that they can see it. But that's a very death-haunted episode, generally.

D: Yes, it is.

---

7 Terence Winter: "I recall that David came in with the idea that Tony would begin an affair with a woman he met in Melfi's office, and she naturally would have the same traits as Livia somehow, but I'm almost certain the idea of Gloria and the affair predated Nancy's death. The character was not created in any way to be a replacement for Livia, but we came to rely on her in that way in terms of her relationship with Tony."

8 The other is the man who, as Janice is forcing people to say nice things about Livia, appears briefly in the foyer, then slips back up the stairs. He's not a ghost, per Chase, just a guest "who didn't want to be involved with that!"

M: You've also got AJ hearing noises in the house.

D: Yes. "The woods are lovely, dark, and deep."

M: Meadow talks to him about his poetry assignment and is trying to help him discover his own answers, but he keeps saying, "Just tell me the answer." At the time, we had no idea what was to come on the show, but watching this episode again I thought, "Oh, this feels like David Chase and the writers already getting frustrated with the audience."

D: [*Laughing*] Right, right.

M: Were you getting frustrated at that point at all?

D: Yes.

M: With what?

D: When people misinterpret something—look, it's there to be interpreted, and you the artist may not even know what you're doing, but somebody else may see it because it's coming from your unconscious, or your subconscious. What's irritating is either when they complain about it, or they act arrogant about it, like they know better than you in some way—although I just said that maybe they do.

Since the internet, or maybe before that, there's a certain kind of propriety people have about TV. Like they're in the writer's room. They actually seem to sometimes fantasize that they *are* in the writer's room.

A: If viewers ascribe an intention to you that wasn't really your intention, does it bother you?

D: Are we talking about the last scene of the show?

A: Yes. About people saying, "The last scene must mean *this*," but it's not what you intended.

D: It's a tough thing, because I think it's good that people interpret it. If they interpret it wrongly, they're not stupid—unless it's really stupid! [*Laughs*] And you think to yourself, "Why did I bother writing this scene if that's what you take from it? It's so far from what it meant." Or, "Have you never watched the show before?" That's another one you can say to yourself.

But theoretically, for the most part, I like it when people debate the show.

You know what it is, I think? When people are arguing with each other, I get angry because they're not arguing with me, they're arguing with each other! But when they argue, I get defensive. So I'm confused in that regard.

M: Do you want to jump in and be Marshall McLuhan in that scene from *Annie Hall*?[9]

D: No.

M: You've never even attempted to?

---

9   Overhearing a loud, pretentious professor in line for a movie mischaracterize McLuhan's work, Woody Allen's character produces Marshall McLuhan, who tells the man, "You know nothing of my work. You mean, my whole fallacy is wrong. How you ever got to teach a course in anything is totally amazing."

D: Well, I shout things at them in the privacy of my house. [*Laughs*] I use bad language!

M: Is there part of you that is just uncomfortable with interpretation generally, or the idea of "What did the artist mean? What is he trying to say?"

D: No. I have a liberal arts English degree, so I was brought up thinking that's what it was all about, and I had to learn that sometimes, or oftentimes, art just *is*. It's not attempting at anything. It's not providing answers. But I had to grow up a little bit before I got to that.

M: At the risk of implicating myself and Alan in this, when you read the sorts of pieces we as TV critics write about a show like this, are you more likely to find yourself going, "Huh, that's interesting," or "Guys, you're completely missing the point of this?"

D: The question you should be asking me is, "Which do you like better? The negative reviews or the positive ones? Which do you go for first?"

M: All right, David. I withdraw my question and substitute yours: Which do you go for first?

D: Negative.

M: Why?

D: Because it'll get me charged up! Why do you like to pick fights? Why do you have an argument with your wife? This is not only me, but it's friends of mine in the business and people you know! We scan those things for negative reviews so we get pissed off!

A: But when you find someone reaching and they completely miss it, that doesn't bother you as much?

D: No.

A: Well, this season has the two most famous "unresolved" plotlines in the show: the rapist and the Russian. You intended neither of them to be any kind of continuing thing?

D: No.

A: So when you started hearing people saying, "When is Melfi going to tell Tony about the rape? When is the Russian going to come back?" what was your response?

D: "People, aren't we all trying to escape network television? What do you want from me?" You know, "Is that what you really want?"

A: Is there anything you could've done with "Employee of the Month" to more clearly spell out, "This is it right here, don't expect any more"?

D: No. And that goes to the point you make when you say you have to learn how to watch a show. As the writer, you think to yourself, "God, can't you bring something to the table? Can't you know that that 'no' meant 'no' in that case?" Or, "We don't know for sure, of course, but can't you see that *probably* means 'no'?" A definite "no?" By the way the acting was done, the timing, everything? You think to yourself, "Can't you bring something to this table? Why does everything have to be laid out for you?"

M: If the question of whether the rapist will ever be caught is not the point of the storyline, then what is? What is your interest in that storyline, if it's not about crime and punishment?

D: There are people who don't make deals with the devil. We have a few characters like that. Most everybody on the show made a deal with the devil.

Of course, Melfi had made a bigger deal with the devil, still.

M: You mean, in continuing to have Tony as a patient?

D: Yeah. "Technically," that's what she says to him in the first episode. I asked a shrink in my neighborhood, "What would you do if you had a Mob boss in there and he'd be telling you things and violence is involved? Would you treat him?" He said, "Yeah, I'd treat him, but if I knew physical harm had taken place, I'd go to the police." The look on his face and everything was very cagey, and I thought it was an interesting viewpoint, or an interesting place to be in your head, that people could get hurt and you're a doctor and you're still more loyal to self-justification or narcissistic concerns. I thought that was an interesting thing for Melfi.

M: In talking to mental health professionals in the context of writing the show, did you ever talk about this idea of the mental health professional as someone hoping to correct or solve the patient's behavior so as to prevent that kind of thing from happening in the future? And was that ever offered as justification for treating a probable criminal like Tony?

D: We got this award and went to this ceremony in the Waldorf-Astoria. About eight shrinks talked on a dais about it, and some of them glanced at that reading. They said, theoretically, of course, there's the hope that therapy would make a better person of Tony, or make him more content with himself or whatever. But not much.

A: At any point in season three, did you ever ask, "Would Melfi still have Tony as a patient at this point?"

D: Yeah. If you had to hide in a motel for a while to practice therapy, why would you ever go back to that situation?

A: Did you ever come close sooner than in that next-to-last episode to terminating the relationship for good?

D: Yes, but I can't tell you when. I know a couple of times it came up. We talked about how, as an intelligent woman, she's putting herself in too much danger and compromising her morals, her safety, everything, by continuing to hang out with this guy.

It was similar to my feelings about Carmela: How long is this woman going to be made a fool of? That was the reason for cutting it off.

M: At several points in the run of the show, I'd think, "Oh, this'll be the season where Melfi cuts him loose," or "This'll be the season where Carmela divorces him." But you never did either of those things—until the end, with Melfi.

D: Well, there was a season where he hardly saw Melfi at all, so I guess I thought we *did* do it in her case. With Carmela, I didn't want to break them up. Just emotionally, I didn't want to see it. And I felt, given that she's an Italian American girl, this and that, and she's a mobster's wife, it would be very hard for her to do that. So we fought about that for quite a while.

A: Did Edie, Jim, and Lorraine, as three of your more prominent actors, give you pushback on story ideas?

D: Edie, no. Lorraine, some. Jim, all the time.

A: What in particular did he tend to object to?

D: Brutality, I think.

A: Did he say why?

D: Because it was so dissonant with his own values. I could say, "Well, Jim was a big guy, an angry guy, and he was concerned about that. He didn't want to be taken for a bully or a thug, even before the show." It was for the obvious reasons: he didn't like what the characters were doing and he didn't want to portray that.

A: So what would you tell him?

D: We'd go around and around, I'd say this and he'd say that. It depended on the case. In the end, he'd always do it.

M: I watched a documentary about Jim. It included a part about just him acting. Working on the set, working with the lines, the blocking and so forth. There were snippets of behind-the-scenes footage of him getting frustrated, like if he felt like a scene wasn't working for him, if he didn't think he could play it or it just wasn't right. You'd actually see him snap and go like, "Goddammit! This doesn't work!"

D: He did that a lot.

A: The confrontation between Tony and Gloria, when they're in her house and he picks her up—

D: That was a scene Jim objected to. That was an all-day sucker, to get him to do that.

M: Why didn't he want to do it?

D: He just didn't want to do that. And we don't know what it's like to have to pick up a woman and throw her. I mean, I hope you don't know. He didn't want to be seen that way, thought of that way—he probably didn't want to experience it, because he has to go there to do it. It has to be believable, and he actually has to be doing it. He didn't want to be thought of as a beast, you know?

A: One of the oddities of this season is that Robert Funaro is credited as a cast regular in every episode he's in, which did not happen in later seasons, even though he was more prominent in later seasons than that. Was there some Eugene Pontecorvo story you'd planned that got cut?

D: Eugene was going to play Ralphie.

A: Really?

D: Yeah, that was Jim's suggestion. He'd worked with [Funaro] as a young actor, and then we tried it and began to realize it wasn't going to work, so before we started shooting, we replaced him.

A: Had Joey Pants ever come in for anything before?

D: No, he hadn't . . . I knew Joey Pants socially, and he'd come in to read for me on other things. We were also getting down our list of Italians! My impression of Joey Pants was always that he was a feature actor, and he wouldn't be interested in doing this. I'd never seen him do—he'd done a TV movie or two, I think.

A: We've talked about Richie versus Ralphie. Richie gets a prominent introduction. Ralphie just walks into Tony's kitchen in the middle of the Livia funeral episode as if he's always been there, and then he winds up being hugely prominent. Do you think that was in part because you thought, "People will recognize Joey Pants, we don't have to do a lot of work here?"

D: I'm working on a script now where I think the same thing: every time you introduce a new character, you don't have to play "The Star-Spangled Banner." It's just, here's another person in this universe.

A: It's a more violent season, graphically, overall than the previous two, especially the three-episode run of "Employee of the Month," "Another Toothpick" and "University." At the same time, the mobsters are more overtly racist than before. It's not just dealing with Noah Tennenbaum, it's also the Charles Dutton cop. There's an increased amount of racial epithets and commentary. And there's the bit where Carmela goes to see Dr. Krakower and he's blunter than Melfi has ever been in telling her to get away from this life. You talked before about the number of times over the years you just tried to scream at the audience, "These are evil people, this is a show about evil." Did you feel you were trying that a little more consciously or unconsciously that year?

D: Did I say it was a show about evil?

A: Not necessarily—you talked about evil. I don't know if you used those exact words, but you talked about these characters as making deals with the devil.

M: You did use that phrase, and I'm not talking about using it at the exclusion of others, but certainly one of the topics of the show is evil.

D: Yes, and a deal with the devil, for sure. Cheap compromises.

It might've been subconsciously there, when I think about the Krakower thing. But I wasn't looking to be didactic. I had entered, knowingly or willingly or not, into a dialogue with the audience. I'd say something, and they'd say something back, but I always tried to distance myself from that as much as possible so that I wasn't concerned with what they thought. I think, by and large, I was pretty successful.

A: What would you say the overall, most important story of season three wound up being?

D: The Ralphie story. [When Ralphie killed Tracee], we were right at the boiling point with some of the audience. People were saying, "How can they kill that girl?" and I said publicly, "It's funny, nobody complains when they kill a guy." And I really saw it that way. There was a lot of criticism from feminists who complained about the fact that they killed this girl. But they watched the show every week when men were being killed. That just didn't compute for me. Do I need to say, "They're all human beings?"

M: I remember there were a lot of complaints during season three, because I heard them, about violence against women. That was the season not only with Tracee dying in "University," but with Dr. Melfi's rape in "Employee of the Month." And also, related images like Silvio manhandling Tracee by the car in "University."

A: And Ralphie laughing while he's doing it.

M: I don't think we'd ever seen Silvio commit violence before. There was this sense that the characters were . . .

D: Uncaged.

M: Yeah. They were animals toward women, they were brutal. It was as big a shock to the system as hearing the unbridled racism in the back half of season one.

D: I'm only saying, the only thing I ever read about it at that time was feminist complaints about the death of Tracee. I never heard anything about Silvio or any of that stuff. It's interesting that they all got clotted in that one season, though. Melfi's rape, that was the same season?

A: She's raped in episode four, Tracee dies in episode six. And in between, Burt Young coughs himself to death. It was a happy stretch of the show. [*Laughs*]

M: It was. I remember having conversations with people at the *Star-Ledger* about the level of violence on the show.

D: Really?

M: Yes, and the blunt sexual humiliation and violence, the stuff with Tracee, the rape. There was one writer Alan and I both knew who said, "I can't watch the show anymore, it's become pornography." Everybody's breaking point is different with regard to that.

D: But here's what I don't understand: If Melfi's rape had not happened in tandem with Tracee . . . how would it have been *outré* to do a story about rape? Because it was so graphic?

A: I think, to a degree, people were protective of Dr. Melfi. Like, she's this "strong woman" in the context of the show, and here, she's brought terribly low.

D: Oh, I see.

M: Here's what I was trying to get at with these violence questions: Was there ever any frustration on your part, or the part of the other writers, that the audience loved these gangsters so much?

D: Yes.

M: Was there any element in this stuff we're talking about—violence against women, racism, escalating levels of brutality, the sadism of characters like Ralphie—where this was your response to these viewers? Like, "You can't like these guys! Goddammit, what's wrong with you?"

D: Yes.

M: So you were trying to answer the question, "What do we have to do to make you people not like these guys?"

D: Yeah—to make you see what this show is about. It's about people who've made a deal with the devil, starting with the head guy. It's about evil. I was surprised by how hard it was get people to see that.

I mean, you only have me to trust about this, but I can tell you, there would've been a limit as to how far we'd have gone to make sure people got that.

M: In "University," the show parallels the tragedy of Tracee and her death at the hands of Ralphie with Meadow and Noah. What was the thinking of intertwining those two stories?

D: I think it was just to compare the upbringing of Meadow with the upbringing of Tracee, like Tracee's mother burning her hand on a stove. It went back to this TV movie I had made called *Off the Minnesota Strip*,[10] about teenage hookers from Minneapolis. I remember when I went out there, I began to see how to some that was about class. I wanted to compare Meadow's soft upbringing with Tracee's. Meadow thought her life was full of drama, but Tracee's was *really* full of drama. I think I included Noah because he was such a soft guy, a decent man.

M: I wonder if one of Tony's main sources of guilt over Tracee is that he didn't want want to hear about her problems.

D: Tony never wants to hear about people's problems, and that was a big one. I think he was aware, on some level, that he had one kind of daughter, and then there were lots of other daughters running around this country—strippers, prostitutes, the women that he preys on.

A: After Tracee dies, Tony attacks Ralphie and Ralphie screams out, "I'm a made guy! You can't do that!" We've seen Tony do that to made guys before. He stapled Mikey, he's done a number of things. Did you have a sense of what the rules were and weren't for somebody like Tony?

---

10   1980; written by Chase, directed by Lamont Johnson (*The Last American Hero*), and starring Michael Learned, Mare Winningham, and Hal Holbrook, who would work with Chase again in "The Fleshy Part of the Thigh" twenty-six years later.

D: It's all horseshit. [*Laughs*] Ralphie was citing horseshit, and he knew it.

It's all about money. Didn't we say there were monetary problems because they'd fallen out? That's the reason Tony has to make good with him. Another deal with the devil.

A: Rosalie, despite being a Mob wife, is one of the better human beings on the show.

D: She is, yes. She was good.

M: And Ralphie really is the devil.

D: We did that whole scene [in season four's "Whoever Did This"] with "Sympathy for the Devil," where we quoted the lyrics, in the hospital and in the scene with the priest. That was a lot of fun.

A: By the time we get to "Employee of the Month," Melfi is looking to offload Tony to another therapist. Was there any concern in your mind of, "If she solves the panic attacks, why does he keep going to see her, and how do we maintain this relationship over the life of the show?"

D: No. I thought by that time, he was in it. He was hooked on therapy, like so many people.

M: What kind of progress do you think Tony thought he was making?

D: "I bought my wife a nice fur hat, I'm not yelling as much, I'm a better listener." I'm sure he thought all that. [*Laughs*]

M: But not the deeper stuff that Melfi wants him to think about.

D: No. These things would pertain to the deeper stuff, but if you're a better listener, ergo, you're a better person.

M: You have a lot of characters on this show who are in therapy, or at least have occasional visits there, or who speak in the language of self-help. Sometimes even Paulie!

D: That stuff is all around, that's why. It's all over the place. And Christopher's "I gotta be a better friend to myself." [*Laughs*] But it's always self-justifying.

A: Melfi sometimes turns out to be a better consigliere to Tony than Silvio. She'll give him advice without realizing its context, like when she tells him to read *The Art of War*. How complicit do you feel she actually was?

D: Not complicit. Or at least not consciously complicit.

A: You talked before about how she made a deal with the devil to continue treating him.

D: That's the whole thing: "This is my patient." When have you ever heard of a therapist yell at a client and say, "What are you doing? That's terrible! You shouldn't do that!" When have you ever heard them go that far? I think to therapists, the parents are automatically at fault—which they are! Everything results from parents' mistakes. But they can't help it most of the time.

M: A lot of time the parents are just repeating the mistakes that were made [with] them.

D: I guess it's just that. You know—why is the world still a fucked-up place? It's generation after generation after generation after generation.

Session Four:
"We were having troubles."

The Soprano marriage falls apart, Ralphie's gotta go,
and Silvio has thoughts about Columbus Day.

ALAN: You came back after 9/11 had happened. How did 9/11 impact the show?

DAVID: I think in ways we really don't know. You know, we went to work every day at Silvercup Studios, and our windows were against the East River. We'd sit together each day looking at the skyline of Manhattan, and the World Trade Center was gone. There was a lot of tension. People would come in and be like, "Did you see the news today?" It was a lot like what we do now with Trump: "You hear what he said today?" It had a great impact on me.

I've read people say that they saw the show grow darker and darker, and that Tony got worse and worse after that. I don't agree with that, but I may be blind to it. But if it did, I think 9/11 had a lot to do with it. I think the direction of the country was getting darker and darker.

MATT: Whose idea was it to end this season with, essentially, *Who's Afraid of Virginia Woolf?* It's really like a two-hander by the end of it.

D: The impetus for ["Whitecaps"] was she had put up with too much of Tony's misbehavior, and it had gone on too long for me to feel it was credible. At least for someone that intelligent. Couldn't it have been that they had split up overnight or something, over a weekend? It just didn't seem real. And I just felt that that story would have tremendous resonance.

A: Across the whole season, you see the slow disintegration of the marriage that Tony doesn't even notice. How did you figure out the elements you were going to use to make her realize she had to go?

D: I don't remember if I decided that the season should be about their breakup. I think I did. I tried to give each season a theme. Season one, Tony as a son, that was the theme. Then Tony as parent, then Tony as a husband. It went like that.

A: And season four is the marriage as a whole?

D: Yes, you're right.

A: When I went back and rewatched "Watching Too Much Television," which ends with Tony beating up Zellman, I remember the scene where he listened to the song and beat him up, but I forget that that's the reason Irina places the phone call, because he humiliates Zellman, Zellman dumps Irina, Irina calls Carmela as revenge, bye-bye Tony. It's a whole Rube Goldberg thing going on.

D: Those two were incredible. That last scene where he punches the wall, they shot that at four o'clock in the morning. It was really great.

A: You've talked about how Jim didn't like accessing that part of himself. This is one of those times where Carmela's in the room where it happens, on the receiving end of Tony's rage. What was Edie's demeanor over the course of filming that?

D: She didn't have any! [*Laughs*] No, she was just herself! I don't remember her having an issue. Edie never gave anything away about how she felt about what she was doing.

And Jim, even though he was Tony's angry, fuming self—I don't recall that he put up that much resistance to it because it involved Carmela, or it involved Edie, so he wasn't going to fuck the scene up for her, you know what I mean? He was being a professional actor, and very generous. So, he knew that she had come prepared, and she was ready to do this, so I think he felt he had no choice.

A: Where did the idea come from to use Furio as one of the wedges in the marriage?

D: When Federico came to the show, he brought a certain vibe with him. He is an attractive guy, and he was coming up there every day to drive Tony, so it just seemed realistic.

A: In this season, was there ever a point where she and Furio would consummate, or was it always going to be this frustrating, unrequited thing?

D: I think it was going to consummate, but it seemed out of character, at least at that time in their lives. One thing we usually put into action was the fact that, if you step out on a guy like Tony, there's the usual thing that would happen in that kind of relationship, and I think maybe she was afraid of it.

A: For herself, Furio, or both?

D: Good question. Really good question.

M: You think Tony would've hurt her if she'd cheated on him, if he found out about it?

D: Depending on the day, yeah, I think he would've slapped her around.

M: You think Tony is capable of committing violence against his wife?

D: I think so.

A: Furio's abrupt departure after he decides not to shove Tony into the helicopter rotor is often held up as one of the show's more notable anticlimaxes. At any point, was there thought of having a direct conflict?

D: It was never interesting to me. I never found it particularly interesting because of the [possibility of a] fight scene. It just seemed so expected, to have those two guys fight it out.

M: The cliché of what the audience of a TV show would want would be, "Carmela sleeping with Furio and then a fight with Tony and Furio, maybe ending in Furio's death," and you didn't do any of that.

D: Because you know it's going to end with Furio's death! So what's the point in going through all that?

M: There's a lot going on with relationships and marriages in this season. In addition to this thread with Furio and Carmela, obvious fractures begin to appear in the marriage as early as the first couple of episodes, and eventually, it all builds to "Whitecaps." But you've got more tension between Artie Bucco and Charmaine, and you've got Bobby losing his wife, which I'd completely forgotten about.

A: Which happens in "Christopher," of all episodes!

M: And that comes out of nowhere. I never in a million years would've thought something like that would happen on a show like this.

D: Why is that?

M: I've learned how to watch the show now, but at the time, I'd been mentally trained by other forms of TV to not expect it, especially the way it happens, with him finding out from a phone call. You mostly learn about their marriage through Janice over the next few episodes, which is also not something you expect. And with Ralphie, there's a lot going on with him and Rosalie, and then with Janice. Both of them basically decide that he's human garbage and they don't want anything to do with him, and Janice physically kicks him down the stairs, which is pretty funny.

A: And also, Christopher and Adriana. This is a huge season for the two of them.

M: It's like "the marriage season," in a lot of ways.

D: It was going to be about Tony and Carmela's marriage, but until you mentioned it to me now, I never took stock of the fact that so many other marriages and relationships were center stage in season four.

M: This, too, illuminates to me how much of this process is instinctive. I'm looking at this series like it's a stained-glass window in a church, like, "Oh, look how nicely this fits with that," and it turns out that you and a lot of other writers were independently pursuing your own strands, but somehow it all came together.

D: What other writers?

M: Well, you have other people in the room besides you, is what I mean.

D: Yeah, yeah. But I have to say, they didn't pursue strands on their own. The direction of the show was up to me. They executed it really well, but it wasn't up to them to decide things like, "Should this be about marriage?" or "How should this scene in this episode turn out?" That wasn't the way it went. It usually isn't. The showrunner decides the architecture.

M: Could we talk about that process? That's something that I think would be illuminating to the readers. When you look at an episode of *The Sopranos*, you see "Written by David Chase and Terence Winter," or "Robin Green and Mitchell Burgess." What do those credits actually mean? Did they write the whole script? A piece of it? Is it a situation where you all work on it together and you say, "Okay, I'll put your name on episode five?"

D: You meet in the room and you break the story. That's what we call it: "breaking the story." [My wife] Denise and I would go away to our house in France, and I'd think about it for a couple of months, and then I'd talk to her about it to straighten it out in my head. She'd offer me ideas, or I'd see what made her laugh, or what didn't. I'd come back with the whole season plotted out, and I had a big chart of one to thirteen. If the chart was here, it would say, "Tony." I don't remember what the Mob story was, so I'd figure that out first. I would write down, or plot out, the story of that for thirteen episodes. It started out with season one being "Tony vs. his mother." There was only like three movements in that orchestral piece. As things went on, it got more and more complicated, so it wouldn't be just one Tony story, there'd be like three Tony stories, a Chris story, two Carmela stories.

M: You're talking long-range plotting, not just within a single episode.

D: Yes. I'd explain all that and write it down on the board, and pontificate about it. Then I'd say, "Okay, that's what I got. Now we gotta figure out what episode one and two are." We would touch on some of the things in that long form, but I can't remember what the episodes were about—they were really about something else.

Like, for example: let's just take Tracee. I don't think she was part of the long-term plan. That came about as we got to episode six in season three, and I said, "OK, what's this going to be about?" We had the animosity between Tony and Ralphie, Meadow being her usual snarky self, we had all these elements. And from that came the story of Tracee. It didn't come about until we were on it and actually had to write it.

So, all the long-term stuff, most of that usually played out, but not in the detail I thought it would, because we'd come up with something else, or something would happen.

The easiest one to understand is—remember the one where Feech took over that gardening business? That was a Terry Winter thing. Terry knew somebody who lived in Brooklyn with him—his cousin, I think—who got muscled out of his gardening business by a local wiseguy, so I said, "Let's do that." So that presented itself and we did it, but that was not in the long-form story arc.

Anyway, once we decided to do that story—and I forget what else went with that—we'd have A, B and C stories: a Tony story or two, a Carmela story, a Christopher story. It would be like, Story A has seventeen beats, Story B has eleven beats—something like that. We cut the pieces of paper together, so each beat was a strip of paper, and we'd rearrange them and tape them together. It was very primitive. Then, when we had all that, after we'd culled it all together so there was like a four-page outline—is this making sense to you?

M: Yes, it's very illuminating. Please continue. I'm learning a lot.

D: Okay, so we'd have the outline and then I'd say, "Terry, you take this one," or I'd say, "You want to take this one?" Usually people just stood up and did their job, so the script would get written. Sometimes I think we'd split, like when things were getting rough at the end of the season, but not often.

M: You mean split up an episode?

D: Yeah, "You take the first part, I'll take the second part." Like in "Whitecaps," Robin and Mitch started writing it, and I couldn't get to it until they were almost finished, because of problems in post-production. I wrote my part of it, and then I did a lot of rewriting on the first part that they had done. So, in that case, it had all of our names on it.

A: That's something I noticed in season four: there's a lot more scripts with five or six names on them, especially in the back half of the season. Were you just hitting a rough patch in terms of scheduling in that year more than others?

D: No. I tried a thing where everybody got credit, but it didn't really work out, because you have [Writers' Guild of America] rules, where there has to be a tribunal every time credit is shared, and the members read the script and say who deserves credit for this and that.

M: What are they trying to determine? What percentage was written by which person?

D: Yeah. It's important because of the residuals. If your name's not on it, you don't get any residuals. It becomes a real issue, and a not very pleasant one.

M: Are there particular kinds of material that certain people in the writer's room were known to be good at more than other things? With some people was it like, "Oh, this is hardcore Mob stuff, so it goes to this person," or, "This is family/kid stuff, this goes to that person"?

D: The only thing like that was that all hardcore Mob stuff and violence was Terry. He was really good at that. He's really got a knack for that. And he was really good with Christopher and Paulie stories.

M: And a lot of broad physical humor, like in "Pine Barrens"?

D: Exactly.

A: You'd already done three seasons of the show and been away for a while. Was the end of the series more on your mind at this point?

D: No. I didn't start to think about that until Chris Albrecht said to me, in season five, "You have to start thinking about how you want to end this." Don't forget, I come from an era of TV where, for drama shows, there were no finales. They were just cancelled and it was over. So I wasn't really thinking about that at all. Once he said that, I really got into it.

M: I'm always looking for foreshadowing, and there are a lot of things that feel like foreshadowing that may not be that.

D: I was always surprised at how many things could be taken as foreshadowing! If we're talking about something in episode two, or something in episode five that was foreshadowed in two, I was always amazed, with this particular show, at how much of that kind of thing there was! By the time you're at five, it could seem like a foreshadow, or a post-shadow, of two!

M: During my rewatch for this book, I noticed, as early as season three—I think it may even be in "University"—the first of several references to Ralphie "losing his head."

D: You know, it sounds kind of silly, but when stuff like that would happen, I would think, "This show is meant to be." I would feel like, "I'm not organizing this; someone else is, or a greater power, a muse, is organizing it. How could this fall into my lap like this?"

A: Were there thoughts of letting Ralphie keep his head through season five or six?

D: No. I think it was enough with him. I remember Joey did a great job in the scene where he goes to the priest . . . I don't mean just that scene, with the Rolling Stones lyric,[11] but also when his son got hit with the arrow. That was like a different guy. It was a different actor. There was a tremendous amount of talent shown there. And I kind of felt that was the apex for that character. You remember that?

A: Yeah. You feel great sympathy, and Tony's put in this position where he has to be nice to the person he hates most in all the world, and he resents him for it—and then Pie-O-My dies and things go downhill.

Going back to this idea of things being meant to be: when Tony's beating Ralphie to death, he says, "She was a beautiful creature," and later, in one of the final shots of the episode, Tony looking in the mirror, there's Tracee's photo taped to the mirror. How much of a clear line did you want to draw for the audience between "University" and this episode, and how much did you want them to think "This is about Tracee" versus "This is about the horse"?

D: I don't know, but I wanted to draw a line, and if people hadn't seen it, I would've felt that I failed. And probably a lot of people didn't see the line. If I really wanted, I would've [had Tony say], "Tracee was a beautiful creature," but I didn't do that, because I don't think Tony knew what he was doing at that point.

A: Did Ralphie burn down the stable?

---

11 "Were you there when Jesus Christ had his moment of doubt and pain?" Father Phil inadvertently paraphrasing "Sympathy for the Devil" to Ralphie in S4/E9, "Whoever Did This."

D: No.

M: Wow. I never even considered that he didn't burn it down.

D: What did I tell Joey? *Wait* . . . I take that back! I think he did burn it down. That was the intention.

A: That he did burn it down? Okay.

D: The goat was in there, right?

A: The goat made it out. When Tony looks at the corpse of Pie-O-My, you see the goat wandering around.

D: Because it's Joey and Satan, and Joey in the scene with the priest when he's quoting Satanic lyrics, and then the goat—so yes, Ralphie definitely did it.

M: Wow, this episode's like a devil festival!

D: You never got the devil thing with the goat?

M: I never put it all together like that, no!

D: The goat symbolism was definitely there in this episode, and Ralphie as Satan.

M: Are you a religious person? Do you think there's a God, a Heaven, a Hell, and all of that, like in the traditional Catholic way these characters would experience it?

D: No, I don't think there's a Heaven and a Hell. It's my hope that there's something else, but I'm not comfortable talking about this. However, I will say that I'm very interested in religion. I'm interested in the stories, in human behavior as depicted in the Bible, ways in and out of human predicaments. I'm interested in this idea that people bottom out, and that's when they go to God. It's the Fundamentalist idea of it: you'll come to Him when you're down and out.

A: The show features a number of clerical characters throughout the years: Father Phil, the immigrant priest Carmela goes to who tells her to "live on the good part" of what Tony earns, the Hasidic Jews in episode two, and when Christopher gets shot in season two, he has this vision of Hell.

M: Theology students find this show interesting, I've learned.

D: I didn't know that! Why?

M: Because they see strong religious and spiritual dimensions.

D: Well, before I even started writing the show, when HBO said they wanted to do it and I was thinking about it, I thought to myself, "Maybe Tony becomes a Buddhist." And I thought it was absurd, so I forgot about it. But I guess it kept pushing itself forward. The Ojibwe saying, "Sometimes I go about in pity for myself, and all the while, a great wind carries me across the sky" comes from a book I'd read, *The Snow Leopard*.[12] I had read it and that made a big impression on me for that season, whichever one it was. It's by Peter Matthiessen, who takes a trip to

---

12 1978 book by Peter Matthiessen, recounting his two-month search for the snow leopard in the Himalayas with naturalist George Schiller.

Nepal with a friend of his to look for the snow leopard, and it's really all about Zen Buddhism. The Ojibwe quote and the other quotes I think we used comes from there.

A: And then Kevin Finnerty gets slapped by a monk!

D: I read in some book about Buddhism that a monk slapped a disciple like, "Wake up. Be here now." That's what that moment was really about.

I'm searching for something. That's what's really going on here. That's all I can really say.

A: That episode is trailblazing in another way—you spend almost half of it dismembering and disposing of Ralphie, which has become a thing on TV now. What was interesting to you about showing the aftermath of his murder in that much detail in this particular case?

D: I just thought it was an interesting ride to be with those two guys at night. You know, we had to go all the way to Pennsylvania to find the quarry. Growing up in New Jersey, I remember going swimming in quarries, and there weren't any, but I just thought—look, I just loved Christopher, for one thing. I loved his scenes with Paulie, with Tony, and that was an extended Tony–Christopher thing, so I was just delighted by that.

A: You said you loved writing for Christopher. This season has a lot of him, and Adriana as well.

D: I also loved writing her, too.

A: That was a small role that we've talked about: she was just an extra in the pilot, then she came back in and you made the character Christopher's girlfriend. But I never anticipated Drea being able to do all the things she did over the course of seasons four and five. She goes from a small character who's eye candy for Christopher to one of the most tragic characters on the show.

D: And one of the most beloved.

A: How did you figure out that you could give her more?

D: I suppose we needed someone to deliver a line of exposition, and we'd think, "How are we going to get someone to deliver this line? Okay, well, Adriana's in the room, give it to her. It can't be this guy, because he's in Cleveland—give it to Adriana." Every little thing she did, she did really well. So her body of work, as it were, grew.

She was extraordinary. Drea was really good. Very professional. Could really take direction and modulate a performance. Terrific. In season one, "A Hit Is a Hit," that was the first one that she really featured heavily in, and I told her, "You're gonna be a star," and she was.

A: The idea of the FBI putting Adriana in a vise—do you recall how that came up in the first place?

D: It came from our research, that they approached wives and girlfriends and convinced them they're doing a good thing if they rat the boyfriend out, so they always did it for the guy.

A: Let's talk about the FBI on this show. They're not very competent over the run of the series. Most of their informants either die or just don't give them anything useful. Was it just a matter of plot convenience—like if the FBI was actually good at their job, it makes telling the stories harder? Or did you just have a feeling that this was actually how it would be for a guy like Tony?

D: Well, you know, we had FBI guys who were consultants. We got all that stuff from them, and they weren't shy about the agency's failings.

My feeling is that it's a never-ending battle against crime and corruption, and I was pointing that out. On and on it went, and they were both playing this strange game together. And then, when terrorism hit, that was a great thing for the Mob, because then Tony seemed like the best thing on earth compared to those guys!

M: Is the sheer number of informants on *The Sopranos* reflective of how things actually are in organized crime?

D: We were told they were all informants. I mean, obviously that's an exaggeration to say they're *all* informants, but a large percentage of them are. They're informing so they don't get busted, so they don't go to jail.

A: Let's talk about Paulie this season. There was going to be an arc where he was actively working against Tony with Johnny Sack, but then Tony Sirico had to have back surgery and you couldn't do it. Do you remember much about how the season would've gone if Sirico had been more available?

D: We hadn't gotten that far. He had to go do that pretty early on. I had written that entire story chart, and I remember it was devastating when I heard about the surgery, because first Nancy went, and then in very short order, Tony got sick and couldn't do what he was supposed to. So it was really tough.

A: The season builds as Johnny tries to get Tony to team up with him to take on Carmine because he's mad Carmine Jr. has returned and is usurping him—but nothing happens. Tony says that it's too much trouble, let's not do it. He pretty much comes out and says, "we're anticlimaxing." Why?

D: Failure of imagination. [*Laughs*] We were having troubles, too. I was off dealing with some kinds of problems when Robin and Mitch were off writing "Whitecaps," and it was taking a lot of attention and a lot of my thought process as we went into that episode. . . . By the time we got to "Calling All Cars," we were in a little bit of trouble. I think we were tired, and we'd written all the other episodes, and we didn't really have anything good for that one. It might've been one of the ones Paulie was supposed to be big in and then he wasn't. Doing dreams that much, I think, was a gamble—doing that much of a dream thing. And I think we were kind of written out, and people were tired, and I think I was already looking forward to "Whitecaps," because it was one I was supposed to write myself, and I wasn't focused as much on the others, although I wrote a lot of "Calling All Cars."

A: In that episode, the title comes from the fact that Tony's quit therapy and Melfi puts in the red alert call to Elliot. What was it like doing at least half a season of the show without that relationship?

D: I don't think the show suffered at all. I think it was interesting without it. I think the reason we stopped it is because that trope was getting to be a little bit tired: "How much longer is this gangster gonna keep going to this psychiatrist?"

A: Did you give any thought to her not coming back?

D: Yes.

A: What made you decide you didn't want to lose her?

D: An entanglement of personal feelings and the needs of the show.

M: What were the needs of the show? People just liked her and would have complained if she got cut? Or something else?

D: Maybe Tony was changing. Maybe that's what it was. And I needed to have somebody to take us through that.

See, I say that Tony was changing, and I agree with that. But I don't agree when people say, "Tony got darker and darker."

What do you guys think? Do you think Tony got darker and darker?

A: I think some of his behavior is worse at the end. He does things that he wouldn't have done early on. In "Irregular Around the Margins," I think he would've had sex with Adriana if Phil Leotardo hadn't knocked on the door, for instance, which is not something he might've done at the beginning of the show. In season six, the stuff with Hesh in "Chasing It"—there's a scene in season one where he goes out of his way to pay Hesh money he's owed and is so happy to do it, but by the end of the show, he's thinking about whacking Hesh just to get out of having to pay him.

M: And this is a big one for me: Do you think the Tony of season one would've casually murdered Christopher? I mean, I know there's obviously plot circumstances contributing to that, but to me, that was like—I thought I couldn't be shocked anymore, but that shocked me, because he was seizing an opportunity.

D: It wasn't just an opportunity, though; it was something he felt had to be done. It's true that the Tony of season one wouldn't have murdered Christopher. But was season six Christopher the same guy as he was in season one? He's an endless junkie with all his bullshit and all his sensitivities who knows a lot more about the Family business than he did in season one. By that point, Tony has a lot more to lose.

M: How do *you* think Tony changed over the course of the show?

D: He was sharper, smarter, more experienced. He was a better gang boss. I think raising his children had made things difficult. I think he'd learned a lot from raising them. I think Tony was getting a different view of human nature.

And I hate to say this, but maybe he was less good-humored, which does happen as life goes on, by and large. As I recall it, Tony seemed to have less fun. Jim brought a lot of fun to that character, a lot of teasing, ballbusting fun. That wicked smile. Tony was more serious, I think, as time went on.

A: Was that you making it more serious, or Jim?

D: Maybe both.

A: Physically, Jim got bigger. You watch the Tony in the credits versus the Tony who stumbles out of the woods like the bear—

D: Tony, in the pilot, is a kid. He was very young! You didn't question it at the time, I guess, because it was all right. But he was a much older man near the end.

A: One of the things I noticed that's much clearer in the sound design of later seasons—you hear Tony breathing a lot!

D: That wasn't intentional. That was just him breathing.

A: A casting question: at the end of season three, we first meet Agent Deborah Ciccerone, and she's played by Fairuza Balk. The show comes back and she's played by Lola Glaudini. Not only did you recast her, but you did something I don't think you did with any other instance of recasting: you went back and reshot the one scene with her in season three, so anyone who watches the show now only sees Lola. Why was this instance different than some of the others, like when Paul Schulze replaced Michael Santoro as Father Phil after the pilot?

D: Because by then we could afford to do it. I could make HBO pay for it.

A: Did you ever have the temptation to get some more HBO money go full George Lucas and be like, "Let's go back and reshoot all the things I didn't like, like CGI Livia"?

D: I wish we could've done that! We never did, though.

A: The one other thing we need to talk about in season four is "Christopher." How do you feel about that episode?

D: Not our strongest, but I have a lot of personal feelings attached to it. You know, from my days on *The Rockford Files*, I was stung by that stuff. We had to call gangsters "Mr. Anderson," you know? And "Joey Olsen." I was just really, really tired of the hypocrisy of all those anti-Italian anti-defamation [accusations], and I was tired of the fact that our people weren't allowed to march in Columbus Day parades[13] or be involved in various charities, which I thought was really the worst. So however "Christopher" went down, I felt I had accomplished my point.

---

13 During production, *Sopranos* cast and crew sometimes met opposition from anti-defamation groups when they were invited to participate in fundraisers, parades, ribbon-cuttings and the like. The highest-profile incident occurred in 2002, when then–New York City mayor Michael Bloomberg invited Lorraine Bracco and Dominic Chianese to march in the Columbus Day parade, and the Columbus Citizens Foundation, which organizes the event and was incensed by the "Christopher" episode, won a court injunction to keep the actors out. Bloomberg sat out the parade in protest, eating lunch at an Italian restaurant in the Bronx with Bracco and Chianese instead.

Do I think it's a good episode? There's funny stuff in it, good stuff.

A: The last scene with Tony and Silvio in the car arguing about Frankie Valli is great. I wonder what it would be like though, because Terry told me something which I assumed was the case, which was that it was going to be a Paulie episode, because he was always the one stuck up on cultural pride, but Tony Sirico was off having surgery so it became a Silvio episode.

D: Yeah, and it's really not a Silvio issue.

M: It doesn't seem like something he'd obsess over.

D: No, and when it blends in with what you know about Stevie Van Zandt, who was involved in South Africa and all that,[14] you can't help having that influence you.

M: If I say, "Season four of *The Sopranos*" to you, what's the first thing you think of?

D: What the hell is that? [*Laughs*]

Session Five: "There was no plan B."

Adriana goes into the woods, the Class of 2004 causes trouble, and Tony has a long dream.

[*Chase sits down and immediately wants to address the end of the prior interview*]

DAVID: There was an important thing that happened [at the end of season four], which is that I thought I had more to give *The Sopranos*. I wasn't ready to give up. I was feeling really good, and I wanted to keep doing it.

ALAN: Was it before, during, or after season five that Chris Albrecht said to start thinking about wrapping things up? And did his directive factor into the plotting of season five?

D: I think it did, yeah. We would do two more seasons. At the end of season four, I felt I had two more seasons in me.[15]

---

14 Van Zandt wrote the 1985 protest song "Sun City" to spotlight South Africa's policy of apartheid and persuade fellow musicians not to play the titular resort, located within the Bantustan of Bophuthatswana, where the indigenous black population had been relocated by the white minority government. Over forty prominent musicians and other celebrities participated in the recording of the song.

15 Chase is using the official season designations here, counting the final eighteen episodes as one season, because that was the way HBO officially wanted season six to be described. But as we've discussed elsewhere in this book, Chase ultimately considers them to be separate seasons, which means that in his mind, *The Sopranos* has seven seasons, total.

A: How was writing the show and telling these stories different without Carmela and Melfi in Tony's life as much? Did the show feel different to you?

D: No, it didn't feel different. Of course it was different having him not live in the house, but the work on the show wasn't different.

A: Did you ever consider a version where Carmela did not take him back?

D: I don't believe we did. They were just really good together, and that relationship just really interested me. And I wanted to see more of it. I wanted to see more of what it was like *after* the breakup. Turns out it wasn't that much different!

A: One of the things that has been common to a lot of the shows that have followed is this idea that there's a male antihero at the center of it, and there's a wife whose actions are not as objectionably bad as her husband's, but the wife turns into the audience's punching bag and they hate her for standing up to her husband. My recollection is that Edie and Carmela did not get nearly as much of that reaction as others.

D: No, they didn't.

A: What immunized Carmela?

D: Carmela was strong, she was tough. She seemed highly intelligent. Something also tells me it had something to do with Edie being a superb actress. So it was . . . all the little details.

A: Why did you make Mr. Wegler Carmela's first sex partner after Tony?

D: Well, I think she had this desire to be an intellectual. She had the book club and the movie club and all that. And Mr. Wegler was so different from Tony, who has read Sun Tzu, or claims to have.

A: Carmela thinks she's going to have this affair with this guy, but at a certain point he starts judging her as the Mob wife who's using him, and then she realizes, "No matter where I go, people will always assume this of me," and that starts her on the path back to Tony.

D: That's a bleak storyline. That she wouldn't be accepted as herself or as a regular person, she'd always be identified with this Mob thing, which has a lot to do with her finally reconciling to herself that she has no choice.

MATT: Wegler accuses Carmela of withholding sex to get him to intervene academically on AJ's behalf. Do you think there's any truth to the charge?

D: Yes.

M: Do you think the manipulation is intentional on her part?

D: I think she's been around that kind of behavior so much, where everything's a transaction, that it comes naturally to her. And that brings up a lot of questions: Why is she married to Tony? What did she see in him? It must've been stuff like that.

M: Periodically, throughout the show, it feels like the writers are speaking directly to the audience. One [point] I flagged is when Carmela is talking to Mr. Wegler about *Madame Bovary* and she says, "The story's really slow. Nothing really happens. I think he could've said what he has to say with a lot less words."

A: And then Wegler responds, "Outside, nothing happens. But inside, she has these extremes of boredom and exhilaration."

M: Is that you saying to the "Less yakking, more whacking" contingent in the audience, "What is wrong with you people?"

D: Yes! Me and Matt [Weiner], I mean. Matt wrote that episode.

M: What did Matthew Weiner bring to the show that wasn't there before? What did he amplify?

D: Humanity. There was humor in places you would not have expected, expressed in certain ways you wouldn't have expected.

A: This is also the episode where Tony B gives up on being a massage therapist and rejoins the Mob. What do you think the show has to say about the possibility of human beings to change both themselves and their circumstances?

D: I know a lot of people said the show was about how people never change, but that was never the intention. To me, people do change, but it's a long process. People always think, "Well, people have trauma and then they change." But I don't know if that's true.

A: Is there a character you could point to over the show who very significantly changed between when we met them or when the show either ended or they were written out?

D: Paulie's arc is kind of an interesting case. Paulie was not a religious person. In fact, he had his troubles with God. And yet Paulie's the one who saw the Virgin in the Bada Bing and reconciled with his mother, out of religious feelings. Tony and he discussed religion in the final episode. And I don't know if it changed Paulie's behavior, but Paulie was also getting older, too. I think Paulie was a softer character than when it started. He had a little more feeling, I think.

M: How loyal do you think Paulie really is to Tony? Is he loyal to him, or to the organization?

D: I don't believe those guys are loyal to anything, really. There must be some people who are, but I don't think it's a big feeling with them. I mean, the whole RICO system is based on mobsters ratting somebody out to avoid their own punishment.

I don't think Paulie is that loyal to Tony. I think he's loyal to the *idea* that he's loyal. He likes that *idea*. And as with anybody, it depends on what day you talk to him. I was thinking about "Remember When" and I thought that was really mean, what happened in the restaurant. When [Tony] said, "Remember when is the lowest form of conversation," it was meaner than what happened on the boat! And this was after Paulie had a picture painted of him. And you know, at the end of season six, in the last show, Paulie looked upon the promotion he was getting as a burden, not as a good thing. He told him Tony didn't want it. So I think Paulie's head was changing in certain ways.

A: Where did the idea for the bear come from?

D: Newspapers. At that time, there were a lot of bears in Jersey. They were crawling into people's cabinets and stuff like that, and busting their refrigerators open! I was like, "We have to do this!" [*Laughs*]

As I've said, there was a whole thing about *The Sopranos* and me with nature. Having grown up in North Caldwell, it was kind of distressing to see what had become of the place. When I lived there, there were not so many developments. There's a ridge of mountains that goes through that part of the state, and North Caldwell is on one side, and Cedar Grove is on the other side. Most of that mountain was wooded. We got back there to shoot in the year 2000 or so, and in the intervening years since I'd left, the housing had crept up, and there were no more woods. I found that very sad. There's a lot of natural imagery on the show, like trees, and the impulse of the bear came from that, and also hearing that the bears were on the rebound.

To me, the bear was about nature. It was about America, about the commercialization and monetization of America.

A: So you'd read a *Star-Ledger* article that inspired the Class of 2004, right?

D: Yeah. It talked about a number of guys getting out of prison, a bunch of pretty heavy-duty wiseguys getting back on the street.

A: One of your new ex-con characters was the legendary Feech LaManna. Why did you decide Robert Loggia was the guy to embody him?

D: What I remember was the movie with Jack Nicholson, *Prizzi's Honor*. Nicholson, in whatever he does, is really great, but Loggia was the only one who really felt Italian in that movie, and that's what I remembered.

I also remember watching Loggia in a show called *T.H.E. Cat* when I was a kid, in which he played a cat burglar who also solved crimes! [*Laughs*] And at the age of eleven or whatever, I thought he was great. He was still great when I worked with him.

M: Why did you send Feech back to prison instead of killing him?

D: I just thought we should do something different for a change.

M: All the stuff related to Feech and Paulie's battle over territory with the landscaping businesses reminded me of how almost every extremely violent scene in this show has an element of slapstick to it.

D: Absolutely! I was just going to say that.

M: Do you have a particular aesthetic when it comes to violence?

D: For this show I do.

M: Can you talk about it more detail? I think this is important, because there were accusations that you were getting off on the violence, that it was sadistic and cruel. But at the heart of it, you're saying it's more Three Stooges or Laurel and Hardy?

D: It's interesting you say that, because I am a huge Laurel and Hardy fan. They did a thing on *The Sopranos* at the Musum of Modern Art, and I was interviewed by Larry Kardish[16] and he asked me about my influences. I said Laurel and Hardy, and I guess it's probably still true! Terry Winter is a Three Stooges guy, and Terry is one of the best at depicting violence.

M: Even the emotionally intense violence that's not supposed to be funny has elements of slapstick, like the fight between Tony and Ralphie resulting in Ralphie's death. They use a frying pan and a can of bug spray, like a characters in a cartoon.

D: Ilene [Landress] used to tell me all the time that I should make a slapstick feature. But I don't know that they work anymore.

M: I can't deny that a lot of the violence is funny.

D: How did you feel about Lorraine Calluzzo being chased out of the living room with the towel snapping?

M: That was too much for me. It's hard to describe why that was too much for me.

D: That's why I asked you.

M: Maybe because I didn't find her humiliation funny, but I felt like you wanted me to. Whereas Richie Aprile running over Beansie is not funny, and seemed like you didn't want me to think it was.

A: About Lorraine Calluzzo: she's styled in a very particular way, and there's a scene outside Shea Stadium parking lot where Johnny complains to Tony, "All she ever wants is whack, whack this, whack that," and at the time, there was some speculation that she was specifically modeled off of Linda Stasi, the TV critic at the *New York Post* who had written a screed at the end of season four about how the show wasn't violent enough for her anymore.[17]

D: I remember being really angry at it. I thought it was a stupid comment.

What did happen before that was that [Stasi] came in to read for a part. I never should've agreed to it. She read, didn't get the part, and then she turned negative after that.[18]

---

16 Laurence Kardish, senior curator of the department of film at New York City's Museum of Modern Art. Retired in 2012.

17 From Stasi's *NY Post* column about the season four finale: "If that wasn't dopey enough, we waited a whole season to see chubbette Janice finally bag tubby Bobby? Who cares? If they had devoted one more episode to the frozen baked ziti, I would have gone over and killed them both with it, defrosted it, and eaten the evidence." And: "At the end of the day (or night, in this case), they should have whacked somebody important and put the rest of us out of our misery. Or maybe David Chase was right when we heard he wanted to end it all—the show I mean—a season ago."

18 According to *Sopranos* casting associate Meredith Tucker, Stasi auditioned for the Roma Maffia character in "Christopher," the woman who gives the speech at the church that offends all the Mob wives.

A: I found in some of the archival *Star-Ledger* material a quote you gave me at the start of season five: "There was one woman writer back then who was saying, 'Whack somebody! Whack somebody, for god's sake!' So this year, we decided to whack somebody who looks like her."

D: Right! I'm glad I said it!

M: I want to get back to this slapstick thing. Certain types of screen violence are acceptable and other kinds are not. Some kinds are controversial and problematic, and others are not. Why?

D: I'm not sure. All I know is none of us want to see violence against an animal. A dog, a cat, whatever. It's *outré*.

M: Why?

D: Because they're really innocent, I guess. Same as a baby or a child.

And . . . I guess maybe the reason a lot of the violence on this show seems funny is because of a notion that we've all done bad things, we're all jerks in some way or another, but here you see somebody get their comeuppance. Of course I can only talk about it in *The Sopranos*. For instance, Beansie had it coming in some way.

I don't mean just with the Mob. For example, if we'd had Mr. Wegler fall down some stairs and break his collarbone, we'd all be hooting about that right now.

M: Why, because he's a bit of a pretentious person?

D: He was.

M: That's an interesting idea—that, to quote Clint Eastwood in *Unforgiven*, "We've all got it coming."

D: Yeah, yeah. I don't mean in Mob-speak, either.

M: You think we've all got it coming? In what sense do you mean? Cosmically?

D: You know what it is? We all have this image we want to portray, that we're in control. Control is a big issue in human life. Falling down, or having violence arrayed against you, is a lack of control, and all your pretenses, your image—that all goes down the toilet, who you're trying to project yourself as.

A: But some characters don't suffer on camera. Arguably, the most memorable bit of violence in season five happens off-camera: Adriana crawls away from Silvio, he raises the gun, and you don't see her death. Why did we not get to see that, yet you were happy to show us other stuff in detail?

D: Part of it was, I liked the whole image of her crawling through the leaves, and the sound it makes, and how autumn is so cozy, and you don't see her killed for those reasons, aesthetic reasons having to do with the architecture of the shots. And then later on, when Carmela and Tony are sitting together in the woods, it's a callback to that.

But I really wonder why I didn't show Adriana getting it. I've thought about it a lot, the fact that you don't see her get shot.

I guess it just felt wrong. It's probably something that I didn't want to see. I liked that character too much. She'd suffered enough. And she wasn't pretentious. She was not a phony intellectual. She was just trusting, sobbing-prone. She was innocent.

M: She always wanted to believe the best of people.

D: She really did, and she fell into this trap of the FBI's that wasn't really her doing, and she didn't even really understand it.

A: You'd set the Adriana-FBI story up at the end of season three, and we followed it all through season four and most of five as well. Was that story always meant to end in her death?

D: No.

A: When did you realize the character had to die?

D: Well, at the beginning of the season, we started talking about what was going to happen to her and Christopher. That relationship had been up and down. "We're gonna get married/we're not gonna get married." And I guess at that point, I'd already had my conversation with Chris [Albrecht], maybe, and we started to think, "How are we going to deal with all these various people?" I don't know when I actually decided she had to go, I just knew it was going to be a great episode. There'd be a lot of emotion in it, and the audience would be really affected by it. I knew that her leaving was going to be hard.

A: In general, what was the atmosphere on the set like when someone got whacked and it was going to be their last scene?

D: I don't know what you'd call it. It wasn't nervousness. Those guys would bust people's balls. Jim would sometimes do that. In the end, they'd make it up to them, but that was their way of handling what was stress, I think.

M: What would they say to them?

D: Well, the one that I remember was the read-through for the show where Mikey Palmice dies. That actor campaigned vigorously to stay on the show: he really didn't want to go. We were gathering for the read-through and Sirico came in, and I forget what the comment was, but Al Sapienza said he just really didn't want to go, something like that, and he made some kind of wiseguy comment, and Sirico went [*finger guns*] *Dat dat dat dat dat*. Because he's the one who kills him! [*Laughs*]

A: How far in advance did people tend to find out they were going to be killed off? When did they get the scripts?

D: At the beginning of prep, right before the read-through. I'm sure they were frustrated by the secrecy, but there were too many people trying to find out what was going on!

A: You were the first HBO show to turn off the screener tap for critics before the show was over.

M: How would fans try to find out what was happening next?

D: They'd pile through garbage cans for script pages. People would circle around the set, find discarded pages and take those. That was mostly how it happened.

M: Were any plot twists spoiled by people doing that?

D: I don't remember any spoiler having an effect, but we were really paranoid about it. There was also suspicion about people within the crew that somebody was a quisling . . .

M: A rat?

D: Yeah! [*Laughs*] It was ugly.

M: Did anyone get fired for leaking stuff or for being sloppy?

D: You should ask my assistant, Jason Minter. He was very much involved with that. He was the security guy tracking down who said what.[19]

A: In "Irregular Around the Margins" it seems like something is about to happen between Tony and Adriana, but a car wreck prevents it. Do you think that if circumstances had been slightly different, they would've slept together?

D: I don't think that Adriana could betray Carmela. I don't think she'd allow that to happen to herself.

A: And it would be Carmela, not Christopher, whom she'd be primarily concerned about?

D: Well, that, too—but Christopher's not nice to her. People are unfaithful to each other. She would've felt terrible about Christopher if she'd [had sex with Tony], but I still think she might've done it. But I don't think she would allow herself to betray Carmela.

M: Do you remember what plan B would've been, if you decided not to kill Adriana?

D: There was no plan B.

A: What would you have done with Tony Blundetto if he'd lived into season six? You said to me one time that he was going to be an advisor to Tony, and at another time, you said he was going to be the major antagonist of the final season. Did you really have a specific plan?

D: No, no. I just knew that whatever we did, it would be really good. [Steve Buscemi] would carry it off and it would be terrific, because he's such a great actor. And I wanted to experience that and have it. But we just couldn't justify it.

---

19 Minter (who worked in a variety of jobs for the series in addition to being Chase's assistant) says no one ever got fired, but only because he couldn't catch them: "Somebody kept leaking things to the *Enquirer*, specifically Adriana's death, and I went on a quest to find out who that was, and I never could," he recalls. "There was a lot of information leaked, and Adriana was the most egregious. However, about two years ago, I learned who the person was in passing, and it was a senior crew member—like a department head. And they were making a fortune from selling stories to the *Enquirer*—thousands and thousands of dollars. There were photographs taken from production, so I would try to figure out who was there on that day, and I would always get derailed. I never in a million years suspected it would have been that person."

A: Frankie Valli and Tim Daly appear in this season after they'd been referred to by their real names earlier in the series. In "Christopher," Valli's the final punch line, and Noah Tannenbaum's father says he's the real Tim Daly's agent. In either case, did you think about that stuff when you were casting?

D: No. And you know, Frankie actually read for the pilot.

A: For who?

D: Uncle Junior, maybe? He reached out to us originally, before the show even debuted.

It turned out that, as we all know now, Frankie Valli is from that particular area in New Jersey, and Frankie Valli had a real-life experience which inspired the "How am I funny?" scene from *Goodfellas*. Frankie Valli told me that story.

M: What did Frank Vincent bring to the role of Phil Leotardo?

D: Tremendous verisimilitude. When Frank Vincent was in the movies he's famous for, and on *The Sopranos*, you felt you were looking at a real wiseguy at work. I think he's more intelligent than the majority of those guys. There's something about Frank that's scary. And also, in *The Sopranos*, he was foolish. There was a scene between him and one of his guys, Butchie, and another guy, where he's talking about the death of his brother, and he's saying, "I can't forget. I don't forget." His use of language was so preposterous. He could play the joke without *pointing* to the joke. That's very difficult.

M: I don't think he was ever given credit for how good an actor he was.

D: I think you're right, maybe because he was often typecast. But he was a terrific actor. I'm thinking now about the scene between him and Vito's kid, with the milkshake. Very unimportant scene, and not a very long scene, but he's terrific in it. A Matt Weiner scene—as only he can write.

M: There's also the moment where we get that silent close-up, no dialogue, of him remembering his brother's murder, right after "The Test Dream." I'd seen Frank Vincent in several films, but that was the first time I'd ever felt *bad* for a character played by Frank Vincent. It's a painful moment, and he doesn't even say anything.

D: No. He was a very, very great actor. He held that spot there on that show as an antagonist, foil, nemesis for what, three years?

A: We should talk about "The Test Dream." That type of dream is one that I, unfortunately, have a lot.

D: What's your test dream? How does it work?

A: Usually I'm back in college, late in the semester, I discover I'm still enrolled in a class I haven't been to once, the exam is about to start, and I'm trying to get the teacher to let me out of the class and he will not do it.

M: I tell a friend of mine, "Hey, we should hang out Friday." He says I can't hang out Friday. I ask why not. He says, "It's opening night." "Opening night of what?"

"*Hamlet*." "I'm involved in that?" "Yeah." "How?" "You're playing Hamlet!" Cut to me going into a bookstore to buy a copy of *Hamlet*.

D: Here's mine: I'm going to direct something, and people say to me, "Are you prepared to shoot scene forty-two?" and I say "Yeah, yeah." Have you storyboarded it? "No, I don't need to." "Do you have a shot list?" "It's not that big of a deal. I don't need to shot-list it," there's a lot of that. Then, the day comes when I'm supposed to shoot it, and the truth is I've never even *read* the scene! I'm on set, and I kind of know what's in the scene, it's the first time I've heard about it, and I have no idea, and I'm in no way prepared!

A: You'd used dreams before on the show, but you'd never done something on the level of "The Test Dream." Had you been itching to do something like that before?

D: There are a couple things I always wanted to do. One was to do an entire episode that was basically all dreams. It doesn't really have a Luis Buñuelian[20] feel to it at all, but Buñuel was one of my inspirations. The other thing I wanted to do was do an entire episode in the psychiatrist's office with Tony and Melfi, which I decided to never do. I just don't think it would have worked. People would've gotten bored.

A: The dreams ride a delicate line between abstract imagery you can interpret however you want, and literal imagery that has to tell Tony something important, and that the audience can understand enough of to justify the journey. How do you figure out where that line is, and how much info has to be comprehensible in each of these dreams?

D: You just go by what's an entertaining storyline. You just feel your way through it. If it feels thrilling to you, then you do it. There's ideas you get that are good, and some that are thrilling.

A lot of the questions you guys ask is, "Why'd you do this? How'd this come to be?" But often, the answer is, "Merely to try it." That's why I was very lucky to be a part of that show. I had a lab. I knew that I was in a fortunate position, and that was part of what made me want to stick with the show. I just knew that the particular place we held in the culture was enough, and HBO economically strong enough, that I was probably going to get to do whatever I wanted to do, and that just doesn't happen very often.

Now, I'm sure people in the audience go, "Fuck you! What are we, lab rats?" But nothing goes forward unless people try things!

Matt Weiner wrote that one. I don't think he was too happy about getting the assignment.

M: Why not?

---

20 Buñuel was a Spanish filmmaker whose work often had a surrealistic flavor and tended to be powered by dream logic and imagery. Collaborated with Salvador Dalí on one of the most influential experimental films, 1929's *Un Chien Andalou*.

D: It's hard! It's really hard not to know what's real and what isn't in the show, and to write stuff that feels real but isn't. Separating that is really difficult. What episode number was that, eleven?

A: Yes, right before "Long Term Parking."

D: I think it probably came about out of desperation. We were running out of ideas.

A: Meadow and Finn's argument about the suitcase in "Unidentified Black Males" doesn't consume as much of the episode as "Test Dream," but it's an argument that goes and goes and goes.

D: It became more difficult writing for Meadow as time went on. She wasn't a teenager anymore, and teenagers—you can hit tropes with them that always seem okay. But when she went to Columbia, I don't know. What was she really doing there? Did you really believe she was there? All those thoughts went through my mind.

The suitcase scene came about because Denise and I got married very young, and this was the way we used to fight. It was exactly like that: late at night, and I would be exhausted, all I wanted to do was go to bed, and I'd agree on anything. I just wanted to go to sleep! We never had a suitcase fight, but that was the kind of thing. "But you took out a suitcase!" "I know, but it doesn't mean . . ." and it would go on until five o'clock in the morning! And apologizing wasn't good enough.

M: I wanted to ask you about immigrants, the episode where Tony B is staked in his massage parlor venture by his Korean boss, Mr. Kim. There are a lot of immigrants in this show. Obviously, the Italian Americans, but you've also got Poles, Russians, Koreans . . . what's the fascination, and how does it tie in with these larger themes of people trying to change who they are?

D: Well, it's a show about America, and I was just overjoyed to be able to show that. It seemed to me at that time, if you wanted to do a garage mechanic, on a network show, that character would not be an Indian guy. Maybe I'm wrong, maybe they would've been fine with it, but I just never felt they would've been. And I just loved the diversity of New York and New Jersey, and being here, having Pakistani guys behind the gas pump, and auto mechanics, I just loved the diversity part of it. That simple. And *The Sopranos* itself is an immigrant story.

A: You didn't win the best drama series Emmy until season five. Do you feel like you should've gotten it sooner?

D: Yeah, I did. To tell you the truth, I think there was a lot of jealousy. I think there was a lot of moral posturing. I think there was a lot of anti–New York sentiment, you know—Writers Guild East and Writers Guild West, all that stuff. That tension doesn't exist anymore, as far as I know. But it was all those things.

They thought the DPs [directors of photography] from New York couldn't be as good as the ones from Los Angeles. Our DPs got screwed. They were so good, and they never got *anything*. I thought the fact that our title sequence never got anything—come on! At that time, it was really revolutionary! I've thought a lot about that.

I think there was probably a certain amount of . . . Puritanism, also. I mean, look what TV had been like. It was so vanilla. All of a sudden, the Academy is being asked to give an award to something that was not. At that time, I actually thought we never should have gotten the Emmy. I thought, "This show is an outlaw show and should stay an outlaw show."

One time I wasn't going to go, the year of 9/11. I wasn't going to go because of 9/11, but also this other thing, and I told [then–HBO CEO] Jeff Bewkes I wasn't going to go, and he gave me a lecture. He said, "Part of your job is showing up at these things!" [*Laughs*]

Session Six:
"Fuck you guys."

In which a conversation about the penultimate season
takes a very unexpected turn into Holsten's.

MATT: You see this batch of episodes, from "Members Only" through "Kaisha," as being a complete, stand-alone season?

DAVID: Yes.

ALAN: And the other nine are its own separate thing?

D: Yes. Seven seasons.

A: But contractually, it was considered one season to avoid giving too many people raises?

D: That's exactly right. The actors, specifically.

M: What did having Junior shoot Tony do for the story, for Tony, for Junior? What did that give you as a writer?

D: Well, it gave us a whole other look at Tony, and a whole bunch of different stories that we never would've had. I think the best thing to come out of it was the two shows about the alternate universe, or whatever you want to call it, though I shouldn't call it that. [*Laughs*] It's not a dream, but I guess you could actually say the alternate universe. . . . I was really proud of those two episodes. We never would've had anything like that, obviously. They also gave us a lot of Junior, which I always liked.

It came about because our friend and director John Patterson was sick with cancer, and he was dying. He told Denise and I, or his daughter told us, that he was brought to Cedars-Sinai hospital and he was making these big statements from the show: "Where am I? Who am I? Where am I going?" That's what brought the whole thing about. That's where we got the idea.

I'd read *The Snow Leopard*, so a lot of things from that book are in those episodes, like the monks and the Ojibwe saying.

A: If you look at the saying, it's almost a fancy way of saying "Poor you."

D: Yes, it is. [But] I took it as a very . . . inspiring, supportive statement, not so much "poor you," but the fact that there is some force carrying me across the sky. I really liked that thought. And in our house in France, when I was reading that book, we had a cliff on our property that was about, I don't know, 200 feet above the river. It was the top of a mountain or something, and all these nice breezes were coming back and forth. It was like country, the woods. The combination of those two things was very pungent for me.

A: You follow the arc of Tony being shot and recovering in the hospital with the wedding of Allegra Sacrimoni, which is maybe the most overtly *Godfather*-flavored episode you ever did.

D: Usually we did funerals, this time we did a wedding. Johnny breaking down and crying was very interesting to me. I like that character, and I thought Vince was very good. And just this image of power that he was trying to exert, spending all that money on the wedding; "half a rock," as Tony called it.

A: When Johnny Sack breaks down crying, that is essentially the end of Johnny as the boss of New York. Was it just you needing to move him out of the way because he and Tony got along a little too well and the war with New York had to happen, or did you feel you'd just used up the character?

D: We'd just used him up. Maybe they were too close, in a way? I thought it would be harder for Tony to have a warm relationship with Phil.

A: Before Junior shoots Tony, the bulk of the premiere is a Eugene Pontecorvo short story, which puts a spotlight on Robert Funaro. Here's someone who's been around since season three but you haven't done a whole lot with. Now you're building the premiere of your penultimate season around this guy.

D: It just seemed like a natural to me. He's a good actor, Bobby [Funaro].

M: Eugene and his wife come into this inheritance and have the chance to go to Florida, and he basically asks, "Hey, can I get out of this thing?" Would a mobster really ask that? Wouldn't he know the answer would be no? Or is he just going for broke?

D: I don't think so. I've heard since then that there are guys who have left, retired.

M: Then you have Vito, which is a more elaborate working-through of an idea of a guy who realizes this life is not for him anymore and wants out.

A: Vito's Dartford storyline really begins in "Unidentified Black Males," where we find out Vito is gay. That was Joe Gannascoli's idea. How often did actors pitch stories to you?

D: Never.

A: That was the only time that happened?

D: Probably not the only time, but it happened very seldom. I had read . . . maybe in the *Star-Ledger*, about a gangster who was potentially or probably gay, something like that, and it just interested me because gayness is not what they usually are projecting. And also, I often felt about that culture that there is something very feminine about it. These guys hang around all day cooking and playing cards, gossiping, like fifteen-year-old girls. I often felt that aspect was very strong, and I wondered what it meant. So when Joe came through with that, I thought, "Let's explore that."

A: It's so completely unlike anything the show had done before. How did you shape the story of Vito, and what was the response like from the writers, actors, everybody?

D: Well, I remember Tony Sirico wasn't crazy about it. [*Laughs*]

M: So, his distress in those scenes where he's complaining about Vito is not really acting?

D: Not really, no. It's a tough question to answer because, how can I put this . . . there were certain tensions on that set, and certain people were liked more than others. I don't think that character's arc helped Joe Gannascoli with his popularity on set, maybe also because he brought that story to us.

M: So, there was resentment of pulling him deep off the bench and giving him something to do?

D: Yeah, I think that had a lot to do with it.

A: There was a lot of negative response about the storyline set in Dartford. Do you think that's just a case of there being a certain flavor of *Sopranos* viewers who are just not going to be interested in that story no matter how you tell it?

D: I think that audiences didn't find Vito a compelling character, no matter what he did. They'd say like, "Who cares about this guy?" If we'd done it with Paulie or Silvio, it would've probably been a whole different thing.

M: Oh my God, if Paulie realized he was gay, Tony Sirico would have an Emmy! [*Laughter*]

D: He probably would've quit!

M: "I'm feeling strange feelings, T."

A: Did Tony ever object to stories you gave him?

D: Do you remember the one about three o'clock?

A: Yeah, "From Where to Eternity," when Christopher's in the hospital.

D: He was concerned about his hair being messed up. He didn't want to wake up and have his hair be all astray. That was the limit! [*Laughs*] I think Tony really grew. I think he really grew into the things he would and wouldn't do. And I think he grew about things in life, too, like, what was going on on the set, or in the story. What it took to play that, what it meant, I think all that was important to him. He wasn't saying as many things like, "I'm not gonna do that," or "I'm not gonna play that scene with that guy." He was all in.

A: Tell us about Robert Iler's growth as an actor, and what was interesting about this particular moment of AJ's life that you chronicled over these final two seasons.

D: He was becoming a man, but you can tell me, people just didn't like that kid, and I didn't know why. I didn't know why. He was not an empowered teenager like they're usually portrayed nowadays. They hated AJ, and I thought he was a really good, confused, young person.

A: He goes through such a transformation as he keeps trying on these identities and forgetting about them. Every couple episodes it's a new AJ. It's a very volatile time in his life.

D: Think about that kid's parenting, his upbringing! His father is a depressed gangster! That's not even to talk about the DNA part of it! I never understood why they were so down on him.

A: I think people didn't like that he seemed weak. As we've talked about, there was a part of the audience that liked Tony, and liked watching him go in and kick ass and take names, and he's got this son who's very realistically portrayed as confused and whiny.

D: I think Anthony takes after Tony more. If you talk about being weak, you could make the case that Tony Soprano is a big baby.

M: He certainly does assume an absolute worst-case scenario whenever he doesn't get what he wants, like his mom. They're both willing to climb up on the cross and nail themselves to it immediately.

D: Like his creator, actually. I always think of the worst-case scenario. [*Laughs*] I do!

A: Going back to the "Seven Souls" montage, it ends with Adriana in the spec house, and as we've talked about, there were all these people saying, "We didn't see her die on camera! Maybe she's still alive!" Was that inspired in any way—

D: By the fact that people refused to believe she was dead? No.

A: You've had ghosts visit characters before. Adriana comes in at the very beginning of the season, and then again when Roe and Carmela visit Paris.

M: She visits Carmela twice. It's interesting. Carmela obviously feels very guilty about her.

D: Carmela must know on some level, I think, what Tony did.

M: Where did the Paris trip come from? What was accomplished by doing that?

D: My favorite thing about that is when she sees the Eiffel Tower and it's like the thing Tony saw [in his coma]. I gotta be honest, I loved that. Why did she go to

Paris? Originally, she was going to go to Rome. I think she was going to go with somebody . . .

A: Back in season two.[21]

D: She's a suffering person, and how much fun did Carmela have? It just seemed like going to Paris was something she would want to do. She's seeing people who have no idea who Tony Soprano is, who she is, about where New Jersey is, about the Mafia. It's a whole other world.

M: What role has Paris played in your life?

D: My connection to Paris starts with *Casablanca*. I probably saw it for the first time when I was in my early twenties, and it was not the kind of movie I would've been interested in before then, because it was a romance. Denise's mother was French, and she spoke really good French. We used to go to French films all the time, like Claude Chabrol, Jean-Luc Godard, Francois Truffaut, all those guys, you name it. I just loved those movies. They were really special to us. And those guys loved Paris, so they made it look really lovable.

So, in 1977, we went to Paris for the first time, and it was the first time either of us had been out of this country. And I don't know about you, but when I got there, I said to myself, "I've been to this place before. I don't know this city, but I've been here before." It reminded me of New York, which it isn't like at all except maybe some of the architecture a little bit. We were just crazy about it. Then we wanted to buy a house in France, and people would ask, "Why not Italy?" and I'd say, "We love France more, her mother was French, and blah blah blah."

Carmela's feelings about Paris are my feelings about Paris. For Carmela to be in a place that goes back two thousand years would be a real eye-opener, and that's what it does for her. Travel expands your horizons. There's a reason Paris is, or was, the number one destination in the world. I also feel it's a very feminine city.

M: When Carm talks to Roe, there's a scene that really jumped out at me, which is when she talks about that sense of history. It was very moving to me when I watched the scene again for this book. I don't remember being so taken by it the first time. I guess maybe because I'm older now, her line about how all this just washes away . . . she's really torn up by this. I thought about the ending of the show, and this idea that life is precious and can be taken from us at any moment. I don't know if I'm reaching here—

D: I don't think you are. That's what she said, right? "But in the end it just gets washed away. All of it just—just gets washed away." And it washes away more here than it does there. I mean, you know what it's like in the United States, when a building gets too old, they knock it down. They don't do that in Paris.

What did you guys think of "Cold Stones"?

---

21 At the end of "The Knight in White Satin Armor."

M: When Vito is leaving New Hampshire and going back to New York I felt this dread in the pit of my stomach, because I knew the first time I watched the episode that he wouldn't make it out, but this time I knew how he died, and I felt so bad for him, knowing what was coming. I felt bad for everybody this season.

D: Really?

M: Yeah, because on some level, they all want out and they can't get out. Even Tony. I think that's what a lot of his coma stuff is about: his realizing he can't get out of this life he's in. Even Carmela's trip to Paris has a touch of that. None of these folks can escape.

D: Well, sadness is definitely a part of it for sure. Intentionally. It's not like I said, "Let's do something really sad," but that would be the feeling. There is something sad about Tony Soprano. For one thing, there's something sad about Jim, a big guy with those eyes. I think in real life, there was something sad going on there. I think that's maybe why people liked him so much—he was like a big child or a big puppy dog, in a way. There was something sad about him, period, and something sad about Tony Soprano because you knew he was a gangster, and an efficient gangster, and yet he wasn't happy. In fact, he was very unhappy. He was depressed. Of course it would be sad. The depression was also used for comedy. I think most Mafia movies would not have that be part of it.

A: In terms of what Matt's saying about people's inability to get out, the season opens with the Eugene story and his escape is at the end of a noose because it's the only way he can help his family. That informs everything that follows.

M: And Vito makes a physical escape, but then he comes back both because of his family and because the Mob is the only life he knows.

And Paris is a part of this idea, too. Carmela gets out of that life for a bit, and just for a moment, it gives her perspective.

I remember hearing from viewers who were really, really not happy about that whole Paris trip. They didn't understand what it was about.

D: I don't understand why that was. They didn't say that when Tony went to Italy, right? I always wonder, what did people want? [Do] people not understand it? Or is it that they just don't get it? People will accept that stuff in a horror movie, a ghost story, a supernatural thing. Some people who don't like it here, they don't like dreams. I don't know why they don't like that.

A: I think the show was so many different things in one show, but there was definitely a segment of the audience who just wanted a Mob show. They wanted whacking of the week, asshole *du jour*, just that. Any time you steered too far away from that, they said, "This is not okay. This is not what we signed up for," even though the very first scene of the show is him in a psychiatrist's office.

D: You know what it must be, about the audience's resistance to dreams and stuff like that? It's like, you're presenting to me a fictional world, and I buy into that fictional world. It's not real, and I know that. And you're now telling me that there's a world beyond *that*? If I buy into that fictional world, the *Sopranos* universe, now you're telling me I have to go to some other level? Then it means what's gone before is not real, and I want to think what's gone before is real. I've got to get to the verisimilitude portion of everything, otherwise what am I watching this for? I've got to believe it.

M: I hear that a lot. The fictional representation of the character is the reality that the audience decides to accept. When something is revealed to have been a dream, they think, "Oh, then it didn't really happen." And they feel like you wasted their time.

But I'm not sure I understand the resistance, considering how many scenes, sequences, and entire storylines on *The Sopranos* have a dreamlike quality—where, for a moment, you may question how real something is, and the show doesn't necessarily resolve it. Almost the entirety of "Pine Barrens," with the stuff in the woods, feels that way.

D: Dreamlike.

M: Right. Sometimes what's happening on the screen is not a dream, per se, but there are several points where you think, "Is this really happening to these characters, or is it somebody's dream?"

D: Yeah. I think if we didn't have dreams, as a species, we wouldn't bother with the movies. I think they're so related. And movies don't have to have dreams in them to be dreamlike. Movies *are* dreamlike! That's the great thing about them, and TV. *Citizen Kane*, if that's not a dream . . . like, Denise and I watched *Vertigo* the other night. Those movies aren't dreamlike? I mean. . . .

A: Speaking of dreamlike, when Tony B appears—or Steve Buscemi, if it's not meant to be Tony B—in the alternate reality at the end, why did you choose him to be the one who tries to get Tony to put down his briefcase and enter the house?

D: You say there were a whole bunch of deceased characters we could've used? Why not his cousin, his boyhood friend? We had a hard time settling on that and who it was going to be and why. I remember that was difficult. We knew it had to be somebody from the Land of the Dead, and Tony had killed him, for one thing. Also, Steve was one of the seriously better actors we were working with, a great actor.

Plus, I don't know. It's just like, if you're close to Heaven or the afterlife and you see Steve Buscemi coming toward your car . . .

A: It's not good!

D: No!

A: If Chris Albrecht had not come to you and said, "You need to start thinking about wrapping it up," would you have gone on a number of more years past what you did?

D: No, I probably would've ended it sooner.

A: Really?

D: I think so. Once he said that, in a way, I was being given an alternative: "Do you want to do this or not?" So I said "Yes." If he hadn't come to me and said that I probably would've ended it some other season and said, "Let me go off and make movies now, that's my dream." His statement kind of gave me a structure, an endpoint that I could see.

A: But you said you didn't try to plan too far ahead. When you said there was an endpoint, you don't mean Tony at Holsten's, you just meant, "I think I have two more years' worth of stories in me."

D: Yes. I think I had that death scene around two years before the end. I remember talking with Mitch Burgess about it, but it wasn't—it was slightly different. Tony was going to get called to a meeting with Johnny Sack in Manhattan, and he was going to go back through the Lincoln Tunnel for this meeting, and it was going to go black there and you never saw him again as he was heading back, the theory being that something bad happens to him at the meeting. But we didn't do that.

M: You realize, of course, that you just referred to that as a death scene.

[*A long pause follows.*]

D: Fuck you guys.

[*Matt and Alan explode with laughter. After a moment, Chase joins in for a good thirty seconds.*]

D: But I changed my mind over time. I didn't want to do a straight death scene. I didn't want you to feel like, "Oh, he's meeting with Johnny Sack and he's going to get killed." That's the truth of it.

M: I'm stunned. . . . my brain just blew up.

A: Well, in the Director's Guild of America magazine story you did a couple of years ago, you come almost to the point of saying that anyway. You talk about how the feeling of the scene is "death could be coming for us at any moment."

D: That's the truth. That's all I ever wanted to say.

A: So the point of the scene is not "they whacked him in the diner?" It's that he *could* have been whacked?

D: Yes, that he *could* have been whacked in the diner. We *all* could be whacked in a diner. That was the point of the scene. He could have been whacked.

M: Since we've gone down the rabbit hole here, I'm curious about what you meant to say in the ending, and what you were able to articulate.

D: What did I mean to say? I meant to say that time here is precious, and it could end at any moment, and somehow, love is the only defense against this very, very cold universe. That's what I meant to say.

M: You originally had him going through the tunnel, and if you'd shot it that way, the implication would've been that wherever he was going, he got killed. Clearly the diner is an extension of that idea in some way.

D: No, it's not, because I went *away* from that.

M: So the initial impulse was to kill him, but then you pulled away from that impulse?

D: If you were producing that [tunnel scene], you'd say, "Well, obviously he's a gangster, and his death means the end of the show, so he should die. Anyone would, so he should go through that." But in the end, I decided I *didn't* want to do that. Otherwise I would've filmed him going to the meeting with Johnny.

M: You know there are people who analyze the ending like it's the Kennedy assassination. If somebody sits looking at the last four minutes of the show, within the totality of the seven seasons of the show, and says, "Okay, Tony got killed in the diner, I'm going to show you the math that proves it," what do you say to that? Do you say they're wrong? Are they incorrect?

D: I don't know if that's my job. They've interpreted the scene that way. That should be a good thing, that there's different interpretations.

M: So, if somebody says Tony got killed in the diner, they're not wrong? They're not incorrect?

[*Chase doesn't answer that question*]

A: One of the reasons that I, for a long time, was very ardently, "Tony's obviously alive," is the idea that in the narrative of the show at that point, nobody wants him dead. Did you think through this idea much of, if Members Only Guy is actually there to kill him, who is he and why, or was that not a concern?

D: Not a concern. There's always someone out there who hates a guy like this.

M: So, in theory, somebody else could kill him. There's always somebody who could kill Tony.

D: There you go. There's always somebody who could kill us, any of us.

A: In hindsight, do you think the cut to black wound up being counterproductive to the larger point you were trying to make? Is there anything you could've done differently?

D: I don't think it was counterproductive. Of course I could've done things differently, but I don't think it was counterproductive, no.

But I will say this: it was not my intention to create a ten-year long puzzlement about this. I never thought it would create that much of a stir. I thought people would be excited like the rest of it: they like this show, they'll get excited by it, they'll like this. I never thought, "Oh, they'll be talking about it for ten years because I want them to talk about it for ten years." And the other thing about it is, as a corollary, no matter what I say about it, I always dig myself in deeper.

M: What does it feel like to have a show that runs eight years, and then you're watching the very last episode?

D: You become very aware of it, like, "Am I really going to miss this thing?" But at that time, I was never fed up with *The Sopranos*, but I'd had enough. So that's kind of what I was mostly fed up with—I just didn't want to do it again. And you're always just wondering what people are thinking as it's going on. But I wasn't there [in the United States], I was in Paris, six hours ahead.

A: When you and I spoke the day after the finale, you didn't want to explain anything.

D: You were the only guy I talked to.

A: Right, and you didn't want to do that interview, and you said, "I have no interest in explaining, defending, reinterpreting, or adding to what is there."

D: That's what I said and that's what I should've stuck to! But as people have continued to argue about this whole thing, I've tried to . . . they've asked me, "What did you mean by this?" and I've told them, but it's not enough! They ask me, "What did you mean by this?" and I tell them, and that doesn't satisfy them. I really realize they only want one answer: Did he die or not? I've had people say, "Come on, you can say that! Yes or no? It's really simple, that's all we're asking you. Did he die or not?"

A: But I think part of that is also because, with all due respect, it lingered for so long. You went quite a while without saying anything, and when you started saying things, it was in the wake of this whole Zapruder-ing of the final scene and all these obsessive analyses. People in a vacuum had developed these theories, and they were committed to them.

But reading that DGA article[22] was the first time I felt, "Okay, this is clearly what it is."

M: When Alan and I watched the finale again together, I said, "Oh, it's interesting that the two repeating sounds in that final scene are the Journey song and the ringing bell," and one of the most famous poems in the English language is John Donne saying, "Ask not for whom the bell tolls." I felt like it was saying, "You, the person watching this show, your number's going to come up sooner or later."

D: Well you know, the bell was introduced at the lake. And what is the purpose of a bell? In the Buddhist religion, the bell calls you back to being here now. "Bing!" Oh yeah, that's right. "Bing!" Here we are.

---

22 See page 323.

A: The first episode of season six is called "Members Only." Vito makes fun of the jacket that Eugene's wearing. Was it an explicit callback to have the guy in the diner wearing the same jacket, or did that just seem like a guy who could be in the Mob?

D: Yeah, a guy who could be in the Mob, or not.

A: I remember that guy we've talked about who wrote the 20,000-word essay which he insists proves once and for all Tony is dead and you cannot convince him otherwise.[23]

D: I never read the whole thing.

A: Well, he goes on to say that one of the key pieces of evidence is the way you break point-of-view in the scene. You see Tony in the doorway, he's looking at the diner, then he's in the booth.

But you break POV other times in that episode: when he goes to see Junior, and when he sees Janice. And, in "Employee of the Month," when Melfi has the dream, you break POV in the exact same way—she's standing in the doorway of her office, and then she's at the vending machine. And there's all these references to dreams in the finale itself, well before the song that's playing when he walks into the diner.

D: A lot. . . . The influence for that [filmmaking technique] was *2001: A Space Odyssey*. It's when Dave Bowman is in the pod, and then the pod lands in that hotel room or whatever, and you hear the whooshing sound, and he sees himself outside—then he's outside, and then he sees himself in the mirror. That just blew my mind. I was high on mescaline, but it still blew my mind!

What happens in *The Sopranos* is there's less and less time between Tony and his POV, and what I was trying to say was that we put ourselves in these positions. We put ourselves in these scenes. Nothing happens by accident. We are the engineers of our destiny.

Like, for example, when he came up the stairs and he saw Janice, it took a certain amount of time before he went over and walked to her. There's less walking with Junior, and then in the last scene, there's no walking at all. It was all supposed to be about, "We are responsible for our own destiny." That's what that was supposed to mean, what I was supposed to get to.

A: And you played a song about dreams, but then you get to—

D: "All That You Dream" by Little Feat.

A: Yes, it's playing as he walks into the diner for the first time. Then he starts looking through the jukebox and next to "Don't Stop Believin'" is "Any Way You Want It."

---

23 "Master of Sopranos," a pseudonym for a blogger whose real identity remains unknown, published a June 9, 2008 piece on WordPress titled "*The Sopranos*: The Definitive Explanation of 'The END,'" which attempts to demonstrate via detailed analysis of shots in the final scene that there's no question that Tony died.

D: Complete accident!

A: Okay! But given the argument over whether he's dead or alive, it's perfect!

You said you wrestled for a long time with what the song was going to be, and also considered Al Green's "Love and Happiness." Why one versus the other? What would the scene have been with that versus this?

D: God knows. I just felt that this was better. What is the thing? "Strangers waiting, up and down the boulevard." It kind of felt like the show, in a way. Even though a lot of people think that song's a piece of shit, I don't happen to agree.

For people who say, "*The Sopranos* just got darker and darker," I would say, "It ended with 'Don't Stop Believin'.'" I was just reading something from *The Atlantic* that said, "David Chase Just Ruined the Finale of *The Sopranos*," because I'd said some kind of thing about how what I was trying to say was that life is very short and love is the only defense, so don't stop believing. The guy in *The Atlantic* said I ruined everything and I was better off when I kept my mouth shut—which he's probably right about!

A: What was the last scene of "Made in America" that you shot?

D: Holsten's diner.[24]

A: What was the overall atmosphere on the set like as you said goodbye to people one by one over the course of that episode?

D: It was very emotional, and I remember Silvio didn't die of course, but he was comatose in bed, and I remember when we called a wrap on Stevie, Jim came to me and said, "Well, that's the end of you and me working with a rock 'n' roll star." [*Laughs*]

A: How was Jim doing throughout this?

D: He was pretty good. He knew he could smell the barn, or whatever you call it. He was okay. Who would remember that? Ilene would remember more than I would. Terry, too.[25]

A: Do you recall if anyone was particularly emotional?

D: Somebody was, but I can't remember who it was. It wasn't me. [*Laughs*] No, I was emotional. But somebody was emotional.

It was weird, when Michael left. That was a weird feeling for everybody. He was so much a part of the show, so there was a feeling of, "How can this be happen-

---

24 There was actually one more shooting day after Holsten's, a simple shot of James Gandolfini walking toward the Bada Bing. The shoot was announced beforehand as the last scene and drew a crowd of onlookers, and area media outlets covered it as such; but it was a decoy intended to keep fans and reporters from besieging the set of the actual final scene.

25 Terence Winter: "After the final read-through (9:30 A.M., February 26, 2007), there was a round of applause, then as we all sat there in silence, Edie Falco wept quietly while Jim Gandolfini put a supportive hand on her shoulder. After about ten minutes, David looked up and asked if anyone had anything to say. No one did—how could anyone put that incredible experience into words? Slowly, everyone started to drift off and go about their days."

ing?" Also, I think it was a beacon saying, "Okay boys, you're almost done here." Just the fact that Michael and Christopher wouldn't be around was a hard one to take.

A: And the atmosphere as you were filming at Holsten's?

D: It just felt like another average day. It was all about the work, you know? I missed one of the final days. I think I didn't direct Meadow with the car. I went back to LA to start work on the cutting. Like I said before, I'd had enough of *The Sopranos* by then. I wasn't "disgusted" with it like "I couldn't take anymore," but I'd had enough of it. I wasn't particularly sad, but when Jim said that thing about, "That's the end of you and me working with a rock and roll star," I felt it then. I felt it then, and I felt it about Jim, because I also felt, "That's the end of you and me working together."

M: That final close-up of Tony . . . do you think he's worried that he's going to die at that moment?

D: No. No, I don't think so.

M: I've watched that scene so many times and there's tremendous dread and suspense in the scene itself, but I don't sense any from him necessarily.

A: What direction did you give Jim?

D: I don't think I gave him any direction. I don't think he needed it.

A: We're paranoid, but he's not playing it as if Tony is paranoid.

D: Not at all.

M: It's just so fascinating to me, David, that originally there was this implication that you were going to kill Tony, and you backed away from that.

D: I said he was going to a fatal meeting. But you didn't *see* the meeting. In that scheme for the end, he was in the Lincoln Tunnel going to New York toward a meeting, but you never saw him at the meeting and never saw him get killed.

M: But again, I'm not trying to be Dr. Melfi here, but you just said, "fatal meeting!" It could have been a "fateful" meeting, but you said "fatal."

D: Maybe "fateful"'s the better word. I never thought of that.

M: That theoretical Lincoln Tunnel ending feels like a mirror image of the opening credits.

D: It is. It was supposed to be the credits turned around.

M: And there you have an image that anybody who was raised on a diet of gangster movies would interpret as, "Oh, Tony is going to his death—it's the light at the end of the tunnel. It's what happens when you die. It's a way of saying 'we killed him' even though you never show him being killed."

D: I don't see it that way. Light at the end of the tunnel means a solution to a problem.

A: Salvation. "I can see it at the end of the tunnel," his problems going away.

M: That's true, but people who have near-death experiences . . .

D: They describe the bright light?

M: Yeah, a tunnel of light, like the end of *All That Jazz*, where they literalize the idea and add music, you know?

D: Right, right. I mean, I never had an ending where you saw him dead or saw him get killed. It was never on the menu.

A: I remember one of the things I'd read all the time were these conspiracy theories from readers like, "This must've happened, that must've happened," and I'd say, "No, that's not how the show works. If something important is happening, we see it," which I think is one of the reasons I wound up getting so hung up on the last scene. The storytelling mode is pretty omniscient most of the time.

D: It was, you're right. I was a big believer that people should have all the facts. The audience should have all the facts.

M: Except when it's not important that they have them.

D: Right, right.

M: You said you had this original idea where Tony goes through the Lincoln Tunnel to meet Johnny in New York, and it's not explicitly intended as a death scene but some people might interpret it that way. You kind of Freudian-slipped it there when you described it, but you said you pulled back from the idea later. But I wonder, is it possible that the tendency of people to want to describe the Holsten's ending as a death scene is a product of you having grown up watching gangster movies where they kill the guy at the end?

D: Yeah.

M: In other words, even if you don't want to do the standard gangster movie ending, you're still subconsciously doing things that suggest, "We killed him"—you know what I mean?

D: It's possible! I do know I was always thinking about James Cagney on the steps of the cathedral in *The Roaring Twenties*, whenever I was thinking about what we were *not* going to do at the end. I thought about it a lot, so maybe the toxin was in there.

M: The end of this show is one of my favorite endings of anything, because it forces people to tell you who they are when they talk about it.

D: Like a Rorschach? Give me an example.

M: I think that my fascination with the formal properties of film and TV makes me inclined to think that that ending is about the relationship between the audience and the show, and that's something that may not have been foremost in your mind. That tells you something about me, that my mind would immediately go there.

D: And it could tell you something about me: that I wasn't thinking about that, and maybe I should have been.

The fact of the matter is, so much of this is just instinct. It's not forward-thinking. It's not like, "Oh, I'll plan this, and it will mean this, and it will do this." It's just instinctual. Maybe that's why art works!

Why is the *Mona Lisa* considered the greatest painting in the world?

A: Because people can't decide what her expression means.

M: Yeah. And the painting inspired one of the great pop songs, "Mona Lisa," which doesn't offer any answers, either.

D: No, it doesn't.

M: The lyrics to the song "Mona Lisa" are a series of questions with no answers.

D: Right, right. Interesting.

A: When you were editing the scene, did it ever end on a different point in the Journey song?

D: No.

A: It was important for it to stop on "Stop?"

D: "Don't stop." Yeah.

Session Seven:
"It was very emotional."

The end of the road for Christopher, Bobby,
and The Sopranos *itself; life after* "death."

ALAN: When you reconvened the writers for these last nine episodes, what did you think was still important to tell about the story?

DAVID: I felt it was a good idea to concentrate on characters other than Tony and Carmela: Paulie, Johnny Sack, AJ—and the last episode is really about Junior, in a way. They were all about a particular character.

A: You start the year with "Soprano Home Movies," which, like "Whitecaps," is another small and theatrical episode. Why did you want to kick things off that way?

D: I was thinking it wouldn't cost too much. [*Laughs*] We thought it was going to be a bottle show! It ended up costing us a fortune.

A: After the fight, Tony sends Bobby to kill the French Canadian guy, knowing Bobby's never killed anybody, and that his father never wanted this for him. Is Tony doing this to punish him because Bobby showed him up?

D: Partly that, and partly because in the Mafia, you're supposed to make your bones, have a killing to your credit. That's all good for security. If you've committed a murder, you'll be careful about what you say to who, what you tell the police and what you don't tell them, because it'll come back to bite you in the ass.

A: Was Bobby even a made guy?

D: I never thought about it. Probably not, no. He hadn't done any of that.

MATT: Can you talk a little about Steven Schirripa?

D: He came to casting, and I don't think he'd done much acting before. He managed a nightclub in Vegas, and maybe he'd done a few things before coming to us, but that was mainly what he was doing. He came in through casting, and he just had a great expression. He's very calm, but easily touchy as Bobby. Tony gave him a lot of shit. They made fun of him.

Having Janice and Bobby play off against each other was a great thing, because she was so different from him. I'm sure he was kind of scared of her, in a way. But he never appeared that way. He was a perfect husband for her: big and cuddly. They were great.

A: "Remember When" has Junior and Carter in the mental hospital as the subplot to Tony and Paulie.

D: That's one of my favorite episodes. Terry, again, wrote a magnificent script. All-time. It's the whole mental hospital aspect of it, and the story of Junior and that kid. It's so outlandish that he'd become a mentor to Ken Leung, that they'd pal around together and snicker at everybody else. It had this kind of piquancy to it that I just loved.

A: Junior is first diagnosed with dementia late in season four, then he goes rogue early in season five, and there's different points over the next few years where the meds are working or not working.

D: According to our needs.

A: How did you figure out when he'd be sharp and when he wouldn't be?

D: The stories all interlace anyway, so if he was in a thing and there was something going on with someone else, and he needed to be either opposed to it or unaware of it, it just came according to the needs of the rest of the script.

A: And then, the last scene of the finale before Holsten's is Tony and Junior at the mental hospital. It's so sad and so beautiful. Tony gets a lot of farewells in the finale: one final scene with Junior, one with Janice, one with Paulie, but that one in particular—how important was it to have a final reckoning between the two bosses?

D: Really important. More so than just two bosses, that was really a father-son relationship, so you really needed that.

A: In addition to killing off Johnny Sack, "Stage 5" has the premiere of *Cleaver*. How closely did you want it to resemble the show itself?

D: We did, quite a bit. . . . We were watching *Born Yesterday*, and with the bathrobe and the bellowing, I thought, "This is amazing." I thought there was a story to be told where they make fun of Tony about *Born Yesterday*.

M: There's a lot of what academics would call "intertextuality," where the text of the TV show talks to these other texts, particularly movies and TV shows that inspired it. . . . *Cleaver* is particularly fascinating because it's like a dream—

[A restaurant patron passes our table on the way to the bathroom door, which is located directly behind Matt's seat.]

PATRON: *[to David Chase]* I was just thinking, this reminds me of a scene from a movie—your movie!

[Everyone laughs. The patron enters the bathroom and closes the door.]

D: Talk about intertextuality.

A: That guy's going to come out and shoot Matt in the head.

M: My daughter's outside, parking the car.

A: There's a lot of Christopher this season up until "Kennedy and Heidi." At what point did you realize that death was where this was going for him?

D: Before the season started. Not every season, but there was a point where I was thinking, "What does Tony put up with this guy for?" We like him, and he's a great character on the show, but he's such a risky proposition.

A: How much money does Tony actually have?

D: We asked Dan Castleman, our technical advisor, and I think he figured $1.5 million or something like that.

M: That's less than I would've thought.

D: It is.

M: Are there any Mob guys who were known to be good at handling their money?

D: I think there were, yeah—like, they invested it well.

A: When Tony assures Carmela that there's money in overseas accounts to care for her if he dies, was there actual money for them?

D: Not much. Overseas accounts means like the Cayman Islands or something.

M: Did Tony always have a gambling problem, or was that something he developed late in the show's run?

D: All those guys have gambling problems. Well, I don't know about every one of them, but it's really, really common. John Gotti had a gambling problem.

M: How many of the Mob characters on the show do you think have a gambling problem?

D: Probably all of them.

A: Why did you kill Christopher off the way you did? He's trapped in the car in the ditch, and all Tony's got to do is reach out and pinch, and he does it, like it's almost too easy for him to do.

D: I'll say one thing about that: I was always surprised that most people didn't get the fact that Tony saw the baby chair in the back and he said to himself, "That's enough. This guy's gonna kill his own kid, or my daughter could be in the car with him and he's gonna kill her." It didn't just come from anger or enough already with this wacko.

But why the pinch? Because when we were on *Rockford* we talked about this all the time. Legally, there are three things that constitute murder evidence: motive, weapon, and opportunity. In that case, we had motive, no weapon because he could've shot him but didn't, and opportunity, and that opportunity was too great for him to pass up. He was dying anyway, so why not speed it up a little bit?

A: After Christopher's funeral, Tony goes to Vegas, hooks up with Christopher's girlfriend out there, they drop peyote. They wind up in the desert, and the episode ends with the two of them watching the sun rise and Tony screams out, "I GET IT!" What did he get?

D: He got the fact that Christopher was a negative influence in his life. Christopher spiritually corrupted him. He started to win after he was dead. That's what he "got." But it's psychedelics, so I'm sure there's a lot of other stuff he was getting at the same time.

M: That's fascinating, because one of these recurring motifs in the show is Tony being close to a breakthrough and the audience understanding what that could be, and Melfi not only understanding what that could be but pushing him toward it, but the epiphanies he comes to are smaller and much more self-centered ones. That even happens in the pilot.

D: It's all about him. It is, it's his therapy, but you'd think it would have something to do with him in relation to other people: his children, his wife, but it wasn't. It was just about, "I'm a victim."

M: And also, just from a moral, spiritual point of view, it's like, well, maybe one reason he's unhappy is that he makes his living killing and stealing.

D: Exactly.

M: Can you talk about the mechanism by which you got Melfi out of the show and severed the relationship with Tony?

D: When we were given an award by the Psychiatrists' Association at the Waldorf-Astoria, one of them had mentioned this study, or at least one phase of a study. I called him up and verified there'd been a thing like this. I forget the name of the researcher.[26]

M: Here's what I wonder about, though: Do you think that's true about Tony? When Melfi turns on him, what he's talking about in that scene, the way he's talking to her, is actually very open. He's not lying to her. It seems to me like it's one of the

---

26 The three-part study, called *The Criminal Personality*, was by Samuel Yochelson and Stanton Samenow.

only times on the show where someone's accusing Tony of a crime he's not actually guilty of.

A: Or at least, not guilty of in that scene. He lies to her all the time!

M: Does he, though?

D: Oh yeah.

M: He withholds certain facts . . . I don't know, it's interesting you think he's a liar, Alan. I think he's being as honest as a guy like him can be. That's my take.

D: That's probably why he kept coming there, so he could unburden himself.

A: There's a line [in "Chasing It"] where he says to her the only reason he keeps coming is that "this is an oasis in my week." Do you feel he was getting anything out of therapy by the time she kicked him out?

D: No, I don't think so. I think he did get some things out of therapy. But nobody else seems to think that.

A: Besides curing the panic attacks, or curbing them, what would you say were those positive things he got out of it?

D: He was primed for this, but I think he became a better parent because of therapy. I think he probably had more patience with AJ than he would've had otherwise. And even in marriage counseling, his relationship with Carmela was probably affected positively by therapy.

A: You've said you thought many times in the past about having her drop him as a patient, but it doesn't happen 'til the penultimate episode. Why did you decide that you finally wanted to do it?

D: Because I wanted to point out that she'd made a deal with the devil, that she wasn't blameless. I don't know if I succeeded in that.

A: You'd previously introduced the idea that AJ suffered from panic attacks, but where did the idea come from of him having the same depressive Soprano gene as Tony, and going into this big spiral after Blanca dumps him?

D: The sins of the father and all that. It was really pretty simple.

A: AJ's suicide attempt is a really elaborate thing that requires an almost superhuman effort by Tony to save him. What do you recall of everyone trying to come up with what AJ would do, what it would look like?

D: Nobody came up with it. Someone we knew—their son did this.

M: That exact thing? Wow. Did he live?

D: Yeah. The thing that was interesting to me about it was, if you're gonna jump in the water with a block on your foot to drown, why would you also put a plastic bag over your head? It makes no sense whatsoever.

A: I remember at the time there was a lot of commentary about how with the bag over his head and the cover over the bag, he looked like an Abu Ghraib photo. Was that in any way intentional, or did it just wind up looking like that?

D: Just wound up looking like that.

People hated AJ, and I just didn't get it. I wanted them to try to understand what his problem was. I still don't know why they hated him. Was it because he was entitled?

I worry about AJ getting a bum rap, that's all. They say if you're a writer, all the characters are you. I kind of believe that in the case of AJ. I think I see myself, as a teenager, as kind of a bumbling person. The king of most literary teenagers is Holden Caulfield, and I see a little of him in AJ. To me, Holden Caulfield was this voice going, "Why? What? Why?" That's the way I see AJ. I think I was probably like that when I was a kid, which is why I stick up for AJ.

A: How'd you figure out who lives, who dies, or in the case of Silvio, just winds up in a coma? How'd you decide how you wanted them to drop (or not) over the course of the last few episodes? Like, Paulie or Patsy could've died, and didn't.

D: This isn't to downplay anyone else, but Paulie . . . I don't know. He's like Junior. He's a character you love to write. He has a strange outlook on life, and you enjoy going there. He's very entertaining. That's why.

A: Three years after the show ends, you finally got to write and direct a theatrical feature film, *Not Fade Away* [a 1960s period drama about teenagers obsessed with rock 'n' roll]. Jim plays the hero's dad. Steve van Zandt is the music supervisor. Why this movie?

D: I just loved the music from that era, and I had what I felt were some interesting events that happened in my life that I wanted to show. Also, Stevie and I would talk a lot about the fact that bands in that day were like gangs in a certain sense. A band was something that was like a religion. They all thought the same, dressed the same, hated and loved the same things.

The experience of making the movie was great. The reception of the movie was not great. It was not by any means like the reception of *The Sopranos*. But the making of it was great. It was a great cast, they were wonderful to work with, young people. The crew was good. I learned a lot, and I think I finally got over my terror of directing.

M: For somebody with a terror of directing, you didn't make things easy on yourself with this project. For example, a lot of directors would've had the actors lip-sync to playback and pretend to play their instruments, but a lot of the music in this film is either performed live or staged in such a way that it could plausibly have been performed live. That's much harder.

D: Stevie put them through boot camp, so they actually learned to play. We were thinking of having them play at the wrap party and all that, but it never really happened. They did really, really well.

M: Were they musicians?

D: None of them. The bass player was, who wasn't one of the principals. He was quite a musician.

M: Why was it important to you that the actors all seem like they were musicians?

D: I care about all that stuff. I'm very, very obsessed with details, and I love that music so much. To have somebody climbing their way through it . . . was just not working. I think it shows, quite frankly. I just didn't want that. And Stevie would've quit.

M: You have numbers that play out at full length, or that stay in the moment longer than other films might. Why?

D: It was a musical. It was about that music, and I thought they were good. They sold it. And I found it interesting to watch, so if I did, I had to assume other people would, too. Steve was great. He did more than consult, he was executive producer. He taught the cast everything about playing. He taught them what to do on stage.

M: What about the fear some directors of musical numbers have, that when characters are performing, the drama is stopping? I think that's why in so many musical numbers, they cut out as fast as they can because they want to get to the next plot point.

D: Well, I think maybe we picked the right songs. It was dynamic. I just thought that those songs helped the plot, that they were *part* of the plot. It never occurred to me that the drama would stop if they kept playing. I just thought they were really good, and that if you liked rock 'n' roll, you'd like it because there's something interesting about watching people play. Everybody has their favorite band, but they always want to go see them live.

A: How did Jim end up playing the dad?

D: He was on a list, and either he called me or I called him. There weren't that many candidates for it. Maybe he called me to say he wouldn't be able to do it, I should go elsewhere, it wasn't his cup of tea, and I said, "All right, that's that." Then we hung up or something, and I still hadn't cast it. I think he called me and said, "How are you doing?" and I said, "We still haven't cast it yet, I haven't gotten to that role yet," and he said, "Who are you thinking of?" and I named an actor and he said, "Oh, I can't let you do *that!*" [*Laughs*] "I'll do it!"

A: The dad in the movie is not Tony, but he does have a couple of violent, angry outbursts at different points in the film. We've talked about how Jim struggled playing that on the show. Was that your experience in making the movie, too?

D: No, it wasn't. He didn't beat anyone up or kill anybody in that movie. But you'd have to ask him, and you can't. He was a pleasure to work with. He seemed happier. I think he was married at that point, he had a new wife and a baby on the way. Yeah, he seemed happier, more relaxed. He was rid of that cross he had to bear of playing Tony Soprano. So I think he was more mellow.

Nobody even knows about this movie. I got an email last week from the former head of Paramount, who was writing to me about another subject, but he said to me, "The movie business is funny these days. I talk to people all the time and they love your movie and they quote it and just think it was terrific. It's too bad. I wish it had been that way back when." I wrote back and said, "There's no mystery as to why it wasn't—nobody knew it was there."

A: Jim had played not exactly you, but a guy on the show who had a mother much like your mother. And now in this movie he's playing someone who's somewhat, I assume, like your father, or the father figure to a character based on you. What's that like for you seeing him in these two different roles that were so heavily influenced by your own life?

D: I don't know what to say. I mean, Jim can do no wrong. I thought he was just great. But that's not really an answer.

See, he reminded me of my father sometimes during the making of *The Sopranos,* too. So that wasn't a new experience. And the father's story in the movie—what was my father's story? He did have this disease, and he did get into this sort of affair in the hospital. That was his story, and . . . I don't know, they weren't separate to me.

My father would always make fun of me or say that I thought I was a big shot because of show business. I remember my parents coming out to see me in LA one time. I took them to my office at Universal. It was a brand-new building, I had a patio and all this stuff. I was a story editor in this brand-new building, and I had this great new office with all these antiques. I took my parents to lunch, I took their picture in Clint Eastwood's parking spot, we rode up in an elevator with Charlton Heston. My mother was completely flabbergasted. And then my relatives came out the same night and my dad said, "We saw David's pretentious office today."

My father had a hardware store, and people told me that he would raise me up and then he'd put me down. They'd walk in the store and ask, "How's your son doing?" and they could see that he was proud, but he couldn't give it up.

M: Was it a class resentment thing? The son exceeding the father in some way?

D: That's probably true . . . it was probably that. But if I had been a lawyer, he wouldn't have felt that way. This was moving away from them so much, even philosophically. Nobody in our family is an artist, let alone in show business. And show business—movies—*everybody* goes to the movies. It's Hollywood! It's really big! And for me to be part of that was too much of a threat. If I had been a lawyer, that would've been fine, because I could've been *their* lawyer.

M: Was your father as much of an influence on your art as your mother?

D: I can only say it must be the case, yes. I mean, there was a lot of him in Tony. But I guess he was not the same. My father thought he was funny, and he wasn't. My mother didn't think there was anything funny about anything she was saying, but it was always very funny!

A: Speaking of your interest in music: I remember only one time in talking to you over the years where you didn't seem happy with a musical cue you used: the doo-wop piece when Tony chases down Mahaffey in the pilot. Did you realize it when you were watching it, or was it only later on when you figured out what the sound was?

D: It was Stevie Van Zandt's suggestion. I like Stevie a lot, and of course, he's Stevie Van Zandt. At first it appealed to me, but as I kept listening to it over and over, it started to grate on me, and I thought, "This is just what I don't want to do." I don't want to do a lot of Italianate music at all. I wanted to leave it open. Stevie often didn't agree with my choices. My first thing I thought about was, I wanted the music to be the kind of music Tony would have listened to in high school—and that music is not that great! So I ventured out from that. But there was still quite a bit of it.

A: How long did it take you over the course of that first season, or longer, till you instinctively knew, "This is a song to be on *The Sopranos*," and "this isn't"?

D: That never happened. It was kind of like found objects. Toward the end, people were sending us music and I'd sometimes use it. Those decisions got made, I would pick out interesting jazz songs I thought would be good, or other songs I thought would be good, or remember a song I always wanted to use, and tried it out against the picture to see, time after time after time after time, what really worked well.

A: Carmela's aria, the Andrea Bocelli piece that recurs in season two: Do you recall why you decided to make that her theme for a while?

D: Oh yeah, it's because you just heard that all over the place. Any time you went to an Italian restaurant, you heard that song over and over and over again. I was just trying to make it lifelike, realistic, you know?

A: First episode ends, closing credits are "The Beast in Me," it's the first hour of the show you're doing where you lay things down, and that song is telling in a lot of ways about who Tony is. Did you know that song? How did it wind up in the show?

D: We're both Nick Lowe fans, and I think he wrote that song for Johnny Cash, actually. There's a Johnny Cash version. It just seemed perfect for him. Lyrically it was perfect for it.

A: When I asked you years ago about using "I'm Not Like Everybody Else" after Tony upset Janice in "Cold Cuts," you said that one was obvious enough you didn't need to explain it. In general, how did you figure out when a song was, lyrically, too on the nose? Was that not a concern of yours?

D: Of course it was, there were some songs I wouldn't use. And I didn't do that on-the-nose business very much. I tried not to, anyway. But the quality of the song came first. "I'm Not Like Everybody Else" is a really good song . . . and it seemed like a funny comment. "The Beast in Me" . . . I don't know, it just felt like nobody else in TV would use that song.

A: Another Kinks song, "Living on a Thin Line," sets such a tone of dread for that episode ["University"] in a way I'm not used to hearing from them. A lot of Kinks stuff I like is a little more playful. Was that one you knew pretty well?

D: No, it wasn't, and it was by Dave Davies, not Ray. Most of their hits are Ray Davies songs. That song is about England, of all things. Denise and I had a CD of some kind of amalgam of Kinks songs, and that was on there. We were living on 57th Street and listening to it, and I heard it and thought, "That's great." For some reason, I made the connection with that and "University." Don't ask me why, I just did.

I don't particularly believe that is a Bing song, but it was just too good to pass up. It worked really well.

M: You have a number of songs that you used more than once in an episode. "Living on a Thin Line," you've got "My Lover's Prayer"; Jefferson Airplane's "White Rabbit." Was there a particular reason why you wanted to do that in a certain episode as opposed to another?

D: I think usually what that was about was that I would be demo-ing the record. I'd let them hear it in the beginning because they may not have heard it, or may not have heard it enough. They may think it's just another song, but if you do it twice, they'll see it's thematic, remember it from the first time, and it'll be a callback. Usually we'd demo it first and play it later.

A: Were there any groups you couldn't get over the years either because of expenses or other reasons?

D: The Beatles.

A: What did you want to use and where?

D: "I'll Follow the Sun." I think it would've played when Tony wakes up in the hospital after the alternate-reality state he was in. I think it would've closed that episode. I didn't want to devote that much money to it.

A: The morning after the finale aired, I asked if you'd ever see yourself returning to the world of the show. You said maybe either something where it was an event earlier in the series, like something that happened between seasons three and four, or doing Johnny Boy and Junior in the 1960s. Were those things that you ever really seriously thought about?

D: Yes.

A: How seriously?

D: Real serious.

M: Like, to the point of writing a treatment or outline?

D: Yes.

M: Really? So these things are sitting in a drawer somewhere?

D: They're not in a drawer, they're out there.

M: Really? So did HBO or whoever say no?

D: They said no.

M: Really?

D: They did and then they didn't . . . it was a corporate complication. But HBO should not be blamed for this. Who knows? Maybe we'll get close.[27]

A: What do you feel is the legacy of *The Sopranos* at this point?

D: I don't think I'm the right person to answer that. I don't know if its legacy is the same now as it was even five years ago. The show's gonna be forgotten, like everything. It's not gonna have a legacy.

A: Do you think people's feelings about the show changed as it went on, or five years after it ended, as opposed to now?

D: I think it's gotten better. I think more people have embraced the show. I can't count the numbers up because we obviously had a huge audience, but I think there are people who've come to it late and really like it. I thought it would be the opposite. I thought people would say, "It didn't age well."

A: This is a show that's really obsessed, among other things, with mortality and legacy. With Jim dying so young, do you feel differently about the show in any way?

D: Yes, there is an extra dimension. There is.

And I should be the last person to say this, but that's also multiplied somehow because of how the show ended. Jim didn't have the death scene on the show, and yet he did have a real one, a surprising one where you thought, "What? Who the fuck died? You're kidding me!"

A: This whole idea of the last scene that we've talked about, that fragility, that it could happen to anyone . . .

D: And it did!

M: Where were you when you heard he had died?

D: France. His agent told me. I couldn't believe it. I never heard from those people, and he called me in France. When I heard it was the agent on the phone, I thought, because the show was over and we had no business with each other, knowing Jim I felt, "This doesn't bode well. Something's not good here." By the time I got on the phone and the guy told me, I wasn't as shocked as you might think. It was unbelievable, but I wasn't like, "That's impossible."

M: Why didn't you think it was unthinkable? Was it because he was a guy who lived a hard life?

---

27 Chase declined to elaborate further, but a few months after this interview, New Line announced that it had greenlit *The Many Saints of Newark*, a *Sopranos* prequel movie written by Chase and *Sopranos* vet Lawrence Konner and directed by another series vet in Alan Taylor. Chase has remained tight-lipped on exactly how much of a prequel this is—declining our requests for a follow-up interview about the movie at an early stage of development—other than that it's set in the same fictional universe of the show, but taking place in the late '60s, circa the Newark riots. Will it be a traditional sort of prequel, or perhaps a movie where young Johnny and Livia are briefly glimpsed arguing in the background of a scene about the main characters? We have no idea at this writing, though the title suggests the film could be about Dickie Moltisanti and his extended family (*Moltisanti* is Italian for "many saints").

D: Yeah. He was hard on his body.

The family asked me to speak at his memorial. I don't like speaking in front of people, so I wasn't happy about that, but I knew I had to do it. I felt it was part of the job description.

I couldn't face it. That's why I decided to make it a letter to him. I couldn't figure out how else to do it. Like I had to be in character or something. [28]

M: We're both rewatching every episode to write the critical exegesis portion of this book, and I'm finding it very hard to not have an involuntary emotional reaction to Jim. I always liked him, I always responded to him, in addition to, or apart from, the actual show, I wrote about his acting a lot. It's great. But beyond the performance itself, there was something about that guy that was very vulnerable.

D: He was extremely emotional. He couldn't shut off his emotions.

M: His son was born shortly before he came out for the [Television Critics Association] press tour. I bought him a copy of *The Very Hungry Caterpillar* to read to his son. I had it in my backpack and he was on his way back from a session, surrounded by reporters, and I said, "Wait a second!" and gave it to him. He looked at it, puzzled, and he took it, opened it up—and he fucking read it! He sat there and turned the pages, smiling, and read it! Not out loud or anything—but he wanted to know how the story ended.

D: Quite a guy. A wild man and also a very . . . very *quiet* in some way. I think I said in the speech that day that there was something boyish about him, in his eyes, in his expression.

A: Is there anything else you wanted to talk about?

D: Just to put it through my brain: people complained about that show as to how demeaning it was to Italians. . . . I think it did a lot to raise the profile of Italians. I know they were gangsters and killers, but I think for the right audience, they were very innocent. I think what people liked about that show was the humanity of it, they were human beings. "This guy's like my cousin Eddie!" I think it did a lot for Italians. That's my point of view.

A: Did the experience of making the show make you feel differently about TV?

D: Yeah! I think it's got all kinds of possibilities now. I always did, I just never saw them exercised. Yeah, it made me think differently about TV. It can be a great medium, and it is in so many cases. When I was a kid I loved TV, but as I got older, I went to school and read Byron and stuff like that, so I started to think, "What is this? What the hell is *Marcus Welby*? If you're gonna do a doctor thing, why not do something interesting?" I had plenty of those feelings, and I had to work with those people and listen to their bullshit and terrible ideas, as I used to say, "cooking the vitamins out of it."

---

28 See page 468.

But yeah, *The Sopranos* changed my mind about TV completely, as so many people have proved since then. *Mad Men* is a great work of art, I think.

A: When you look at what TV is now versus what it was twenty years ago, how does it make you feel?

D: I guess the only way I can answer is that I can say I'm really proud of the work I did. I'm proud of the chances we took. That's about it.

Bonus:
"Pine Barrens"

The following is an edited transcript of a conversation among Matt Zoller Seitz, David Chase, Terence Winter, and Steve Buscemi, held at the Split Screen Festival TV at IFC Center in June 2017. Chase was given the festival's first Vanguard Award, honoring individuals who changed television.

MATT: How cold was it?

STEVE: It wasn't as cold as we'd hoped! [*Laughter*] I mean, it was pretty cold, but I was thinking, the inside-the-van scenes were the problem. We were worried because the inside of the truck was shot in a studio and so it wouldn't look as cold. When I saw the episode, I was amazed that they actually had the condensation coming out of their mouth, and that was CGI!

TERENCE: It's one of those things that, if it wasn't there, you'd feel like something was wrong, but when it is there, you accept it for the reality. Actually, the very first shot of the Russian, Valery, being marched in the woods, if you see the snow, that was the last flakes of snow from the blizzard the morning we shot that. It had just stopped snowing for that shot, and then we shot the rest of the episode, so that blizzard had taken place over several days, I guess, December into January 2001.

S: And it wasn't written for snow.

DAVID: We were so lucky it snowed, and we thought at first it would be a disaster because we thought, "Oh, they'll just be able to follow their footsteps back."

S: And you thought you had to rewrite.

T: Yes, you said that, and I made the convincing case that you could take me a block away from here, spin me around, and I wouldn't be able to find my way back.

Footsteps or no, there's no way. You get that disoriented, you start to retrace, and we thought, "That seems logical, I buy that."

S: That happens all the time. You read stories in the news about people who get lost in the woods and then they die and then they find out they were like, a mile away from the road, you know?

M: So for Terry and David, do you recall what exact position in the story of season three this was supposed to occupy? What were you trying to do? As a moving part, what was this episode supposed to do? Where was it going to get you?

T: Well, originally it was pitched as a part of season two. I was sitting with Todd Kessler, one of our writers at the time who went on to create *Damages* for FX and *Bloodline* for Netflix. Todd and I . . . were kicking around story ideas, and Tim Van Patten, who's one of our regular directors, happened to show up and just sat down and asked, "What are you guys doing?" and we said, "Oh, we're just bullshitting, talking about ideas for stories." And Tim said, "Oh, I had an idea for a story, but it's really stupid." "Oh, it can't be any dumber than what we're talking about, what is it?" "Nah, I don't wanna tell you."

We finally cajoled it out of him, and he said, "I had a dream that Paulie and Christopher got lost in the woods after taking a guy out there to kill him." And I said, "Timmy, that's great! Go pitch that to David!" and he said, "Nah, I'm embarrassed." David was in his office and I said, "I'm gonna pitch it to him right now." I knocked on the door and said, "You gotta hear this! Timmy had a great idea!" I pitched it to him and he said, "Great, let's do it." I think we were somewhere in the middle of season two, and it just didn't fit anywhere, so David said, "Let's put a pin in it," and when we came back for season three, we said, "Let's do that."

I don't remember exactly why it made sense later in the year. I guess things were coming to a head in terms of Tony and Paulie going head-to-head, Tony and Gloria's relationship, so it just sort of fit there.

M: David, how did Steve come to be a part of the show as a director?

D: He came to be a part of the show as a director because he had done a movie—a great movie, I happen to think—called *Trees Lounge*. I loved that movie. I thought it was so well-directed and clear, and not baroque or anything like that. From that movie, we got our casting people, Georgianne Walken and Sheila Jaffe. They were the casting directors on his movie, and that's how come I hired them . . .

M: Everybody thinks of this as one of the funniest episodes of *The Sopranos*. How much of that humor, those jokes, those gags were on the page, and how much of those came about when you were on location?

S: They were on the page. The point I remember, reading the script and just laughing so hard, was, "He killed Czechoslovakians and he's an interior decorator!" [*Laughter*] At that point, I just laughed so hard and I went, "Oh my God, I'd better not fuck this up. This is the funniest thing." I don't know if anything was made up, it was all written.

T: Despite what was on the page, when you get those guys out there doing it, you can describe Steve Schirripa walking out in a hunting costume . . . [*Laughter*] Dickens couldn't describe that, it wouldn't be as funny as when you see it! And Michael Imperioli and Tony Sirico together are one of the legendary comedy teams. You were always lucky to get a scene of them together, and then to put those two guys in that circumstance, where they're at each other's throats—for me, that's the funniest situation you can put two people in, is when two people are under pressure, literally, in an enclosed space, and have them go at each other.

M: And I think that's maybe one of Tony's finest moments, is this episode, because of the madness in his eyes.

T: That was maybe the biggest negotiation we'd ever had in the middle of our lives. Tony Sirico is standing in the middle of the woods, and his character is so well put together. By design, the episode opens with him being manicured, in his pristine state, and then we were going to take him and destroy him by the end of the episode.

So when we shot the episode, we were out in the middle of the woods and the stuntman did the tumble down the bank of snow, and he had a wig but his hair was completely askew, so that was our opportunity. We got Tony Sirico in, and he never lets you touch his hair, ever. This is completely true. He does his own hair. We said, "Tony, you've got to mess up your hair." He said, "I'm not touching my hair." "But this is the reality. Look at the stuntman. His hair is sticking out!" So, he very reluctantly went like this [mimes *barely* touching his hair], put a couple of hairs out of place, and Steve got involved! We were like, "Tony, come on!" The one way to appeal to Tony as a performer was by saying, "It's so funny, it'll be so funny. We've never seen you like this."

Finally, after fifteen minutes of negotiating in three feet of snow, he was like, "Fucking cocksuckers!" and he messed up his hair and we were like, "Go, go! Get it on film!" It was great, and he was such a great sport about it. He stayed like that for the rest of the episode.

M: But the whole style of humor, you're really going in the Wayback Machine to the '30s and '40s. This is the Two Stooges, almost, lost in the woods.

T: Yeah, I'd be lying if I said we didn't reference the Three Stooges at least once a day in that writer's room in some way or another!

M: I also want to talk a bit about Annabella Sciorra. This is one of her big episodes in season three. Can you talk a bit about working with her, directing her, particularly the throwing the meat at the back of James Gandolfini's head, and then, I'd forgotten about this, the breaking of the vase after he leaves. Was that all scripted?

S: Well, that was something else that was written, and I think it was important to see with this character, how fragile and violent she is. You mentioned the steak hitting the back of the head: she couldn't quite get it, so she kept missing him. The prop guy tried, and he kept missing him—he'd hit the shoulder, or the top of the head. So I said, "Gimme that," and I took it, and—I'm sure [Gandolfini] looked at me and went, "Oh, you've been waiting to do this!"—I hit a bull's-eye!

M: How many takes did it require to get to the point where James Gandolfini laughed his ass off at Bobby in the hunting outfit?

T: I don't know if I'm talking out of school or not, but he had an apparatus on at one point that's usually used for sexual gratification, from what I hear. [*Laughter*] He'd walk in with different visuals, and Jim would look. Because after the first couple of times it's not as funny, Steve would walk in with a different thing protruding from various places—from what they tell me. I wasn't there that day.

But it's funny, when you got Jim laughing. I remember in a different episode, Uncle Junior had a CPAP mask for sleep apnea, and the line was, "How many MiGs you shoot down last week?" Jim Gandolfini could not look at Dominic with that mask on and say that line. It was the night before Thanksgiving when we shot it, and all Jim had to do was come in and say the line, and like, eighteen times in a row, he broke down. It was two in the morning, everyone wanted to go home.

I remember Tim Van Patten directing that and he was like, "Jimmy, enough already, let's do it." "All right, all right." And he came in, and ultimately, it had to be done in two separate shots. We had to send Dominic out of the room. It was the only time Jim could not physically do his job. Once you got him laughing, he really couldn't recover.

M: I think we need to talk about the Russian. . . . In summer of 2001, HBO did a *Sopranos* presentation at the Television Critics Association press tour, and everybody was asking about the Russian. What happened to the Russian? Are we going to see the Russian? Is there going to be a gang war between Tony's gang and the Russian's? And you [David] got increasingly . . . it was almost like a moment out of "Pine Barrens" because I could see you going, "What does it matter what happened?" You were dyspeptic. Have people ever stopped asking you about the Russian?

D: No. They never have. [*Laughs*] What do you want to know?

M: Why doesn't the Russian matter? Why is it not important to know what happened?

D: I don't know. I felt that was more in keeping with a Russian folktale or something, that the guy just disappears. Now, we didn't do folktales every week, but it seemed appropriate for this.

M: Terry, do you share that interpretation about why we don't care what happens to the Russian?

T: I do, but I have to confess that ultimately, it's hard for me. We all grew up watching TV and expecting closure. I think I fought for it. And even over the years, I lobbied for it, saying, "It'd be cool to finally pay it off." I think at one point, I almost had David agreeing with me, and I made the cardinal [mistake] of saying, "People will love it!" He said, "Fuck it! We shouldn't do it for *that* reason!" [*Laughter*]

This was absolutely the right way to go, and we never should have known what happened.

D: That was the other thing—we didn't want to do a thing where Tony fought the Russians. There just isn't any combat between the Italian and Russian Mobs. They just don't have any overlap.

M: When I wanted to do a *Sopranos*-related panel, my first thought was, of course, "We'll show the finale." And then I thought, "We can't do that, because David will never come out for that." You've explained what you were trying to do in that finale—generally, not specifically—so many times that I didn't want to inflict that on you again.

But I kind of feel like we got to do that here tonight, in a way, because this, for me, is the first blatant example in *The Sopranos* of that kind of thing—the thing that most people would fixate on, the obvious, linear narrative thing like, "What happened to the Russian?" or "What happened after the cut to black?" You said, "That's not what this is about. This is not important." You're not just being obstinate about it. There's actually a reason.

D: Yeah, there's a reason. [*Pause*] I should've had the Russian walk into Holsten's!

T: One thing we talked about was that at some point, Christopher, way late in the game in the series, would walk into Slava's club and the Russian guy would be there mopping the floor and they'd just meet eyes, and then the camera would come around to the back of the Russian's head and you just see that a big chunk of his head is missing and he can't communicate. They're like, "Yeah, kids found him, they sent him to Russia and nursed him back to health, but he can't really talk." All through the meeting, he's just kind of looking at Christopher, and you feel like he knows but he can't communicate it. That was it.

My proposed ending for *The Sopranos* was that a very elderly Nucky Thompson walks in and kills Tony Soprano! [*Laughs*] That was how we were going to end *Boardwalk Empire*, but it didn't work.

D: I'll tell you what Matt Weiner said: he wanted to end *Mad Men* with Don Draper at age ninety-two, he's watching the end of *The Sopranos*, and he takes his beer bottle and throws it at the TV!

S: We lost a location.

T: That's right, for this episode!

D: We were going to shoot "Pine Barrens" in Essex County and the commissioner—

T: Who was an Italian American, who was a staunch opponent of defamation—

D: Who later went to prison for corruption—[*Laughs*]

T: The greatest punch line ever! He said he wouldn't let us shoot there because this gave a black eye to Italian Americans, and then he himself went to jail for accepting bribes! [*Laughter*] You couldn't write this stuff! But yeah, we had that location scrapped so we had to scramble, and then we ended up in Harriman Park, up by West Point.

S: I can't tell you how intimidating it was—even though I knew, I'd worked with Michael and Tony before, but I hadn't worked with Jimmy, and it was really surreal walking onto that set the first day, because I felt like I was directing Tony Soprano, not Jimmy. And I didn't know how to do it! It's like, "How do I say to this guy?" But Jimmy's a sweet guy. He wanted direction. I just had to get over myself! It was so much fun, so much fun to do.

M: What was it like acting on the show after directing it for two seasons?

S: When I acted on the show, I was very nervous and intimidated again! But they just made me feel so welcome. I loved acting on the show. I mean, with directing, directing always makes me a little bit more anxious and nervous because there's so much that you have to keep in your head. But as a director, I also get to act every part in my head, you know? As an actor, I got to work with the other directors, and that was just great. It's hard to say which one I liked more.

M: You got a hell of a send-off. They played a nice, big piece of Van Morrison and Tony shoots you.

S: Yeah! To me, that was like the best way to go! To be shot in the face by Tony Soprano . . . and he did it out of love, you know? Yeah! He was saving me from a fate much worse!

D: He wasn't supposed to die, and we had a lot of discussion about it, because we'd hired Steve for two seasons. And then it became clear, the way the story had taken us, that he wasn't going to make it till the second season.

S: So I got a call. You left a voice message, I called you back, and I fully expected you to tell me [you were killing my character], and instead you said, "You want to have lunch tomorrow?" and I said, "Sure!" I convinced myself, "Oh, he wants to have lunch! Maybe he has a great story idea for the next season, or maybe he's got another idea that he wants to do!" I was sort of in denial because I couldn't accept it. They'd hired me for two seasons! We sat down at lunch and he told me.

D: It wasn't fun.

S: We still had a good lunch!

THE MORGUE

Selected writing from the *Star-Ledger*

1999–2006

*The following is a collection of features and criticism
published in the arts section of the* Star-Ledger,
*Tony's newspaper, by Matt Zoller Seitz,
who covered* The Sopranos *from 1999 to 2003,
and Alan Sepinwall, who covered it from 2004 to 2006.
Some pieces are presented in their entirety.
Others are represented by a section or fragment.*

Married to the Mob

**A HARRIED GODFATHER STRUGGLES TO BALANCE HIS PERSONAL
AND PROFESSIONAL LIVES | BY MATT ZOLLER SEITZ | 1/9/1999**

SHOT ON LOCATION in towns throughout northern New Jersey, *The Sopranos* is a bittersweet domestic fable that plays like *Everybody Loves Raymond* meets *Goodfellas*. It's an absurdist comedy about criminal behavior and suburban life that gently mocks its targets while taking its characters and their emotions seriously.

Says former E Street Band member Steve Van Zandt, who plays a nightclub owner and low-level mobster named Silvio Dante, "I like to call it 'The Gangster Honeymooners.'"

"It's not so much about the Mob as much as it is about the family," says Gandolfini, an Englewood native and graduate of Rutgers University who has had supporting parts in such films as *True Romance* (the assassin who beats up Patricia Arquette), *Get Shorty* (as Delroy Lindo's bearded right-hand man), and the current *A Civil Action* (as a whistle-blowing employee at a polluting tannery).

The Sopranos is also, Gandolfini says, an exaggerated comic tale of the children and grandchildren of immigrants trying to make it in so-called polite society. Tony and his pals hustle to make it in the Mob as if it were a legitimate business, complete with politicking, internal feuds over promotions, and sudden "layoffs," many of which end with the deposit of a large, canvas-wrapped package somewhere near the Meadowlands. These guys are thugs and killers, but they also worry about throwing parties and backyard barbecues, driving the right car, and getting their kids into the right college.

"I see the show as being about the pressure of being the first," Gandolfini continues. "Tony is the first guy to really rise high in his profession, to get out, to move into a nice suburban neighborhood, to have a shot at fitting in. But there's this conflict between that and what you might call the Old World way of doing things."

The show's creator, executive producer, writer, and sometime director, David Chase, knows a thing or two about these issues. Raised in North Caldwell, where the Sopranos' on-screen house is actually located, his family's name was originally DeCesare.

"All the time I was growing up, I knew of guys who, it was said, had ties to that kind of life—or who had ties to people who had ties," Chase says. "I grew up seeing representations of Mob life in the movies and on TV. Those characters didn't look much like the ones I was familiar with. The guys who were pointed out to me as having Mob ties were guys who lived in the suburbs after starting out in the city, in someplace like Newark. They wanted to get out, they wanted to get their families out. And now they had a whole different set of problems to deal with. Suburban life.

"The fact is, in some way, every single character on this show is trying to make it."

———

Lorraine Bracco, who plays Tony's therapist, Dr. Jennifer Melfi, knows this fictional terrain well. She got an Oscar nomination for playing a Mob wife in Martin Scorsese's 1990 epic *Goodfellas*. Like *The Godfather*, Scorsese's film treated Mob life as an exaggerated metaphor for life in general, and spotlighted its ambitious characters' attempts to be taken seriously by the rest of society—by force, if necessary.

"When I met David about being in this project, I was very unsure about committing for exactly those reasons,"

she says. "But he alleviated my fears. If you watch the show, you see that it really is dealing with a lot of family issues. Tony is a man who's lost and depressed. He feels life doesn't make sense anymore and everything is in a decline. Everything is changing for him. He's got troubles in his marriage, troubles in his job, with his mother, with his daughter who's going off to college."

Van Zandt, who immersed himself in books about mobsters to get in character, puts the gangster element in an even larger context.

"In the romantic version of the criminal lifestyle, there is always the suggestion that the gangster is the guy who breaks all the rules and gets away with it, at least for a while," Van Zandt says. "It's booze and broads and horses and dice and killing a guy if he gets in your way and not caring what anybody thinks of you. It's no wonder audiences love that kind of story.

"It's not just Italian American gangsters," he continues. "It's Cagney and Bogart movies, it's Westerns. American seems to have some kind of fascination with outlaws in general. Maybe it's because we were an outlaw nation to begin with. This nation was born of rebellion against authority, and in a weird way, that's what these characters represent. That image is very attractive to Americans. It's part of the national unconscious. It's practically in our genetic code."

The Godfather Meets Ralph Kramden

BY MATT ZOLLER SEITZ | 2/2/1999

IN AN ERA when television and movies prefer to fill leading roles with known quantities, it is a real thrill to watch a star being born. That star is James Gandolfini, the lead actor in HBO's drama series *The Sopranos*. His is the kind of excellence that doesn't announce itself. In scene after scene and episode after episode, he keeps sneaking up on you, pulling small miracles out of his hip pockets.

It's one of the richest roles in TV history—maybe as rich a role as any actor has ever had. Tony is like Michael Corleone as played by Ralph Kramden. He's pathetic and noble, fearsome and tragic, sweet and grand.

Yet Gandolfini inhabits the part with such ease and subtlety that you take the complexity of either the character or the performance for granted. He never suggests he is superior to Tony, or invites us to feel superior. He never implies, though voice or gesture, that Tony draws a distinction between lawful and unlawful business activities—or that he can imagine any life but the one he has.

There's a disconnect between Tony's business activity and his family life. There has to be, otherwise Tony couldn't function. But there is no disconnect between the character and Gandolfini. He talks like an average guy, not an actor pimping a role. Often the lines and situations are funny not because of the words themselves, but because of how Gandolfini plays them.

Watch the scene in tonight's episode where Tony visits his mother in the retirement home and offers her macaroons. "Oh, they're too sweet," she says coldly. Tony hides his hurt from his mother, but we sense it by the way he pauses, unmoving, before he speaks again. You want subtlety? In this particular shot, Gandolfini's back is turned and we can only see a sliver of his face. The man is acting with the back of his neck.

———

Gandolfini suggests Tony's brooding, yearning, troubled qualities with just a few choice bits of body language. He sometimes looks up at the sky after a violent act, as if to say, "Geez, I hope you didn't see that, God." When he's not getting through to somebody in conversation, he'll push the heel of his hand against his forehead as if trying to force his brain to work harder. When he's really feeling put upon, he'll slouch forward in a chair and peer up at the camera from beneath his broad brow; the image suggests that Tony really is carrying the world on his back.

Gandolfini: Star Quality, Not Attitude

BY MATT ZOLLER SEITZ | 2/14/1999

"IT'S LIKE SHOWING emotion has become a bad thing. Like there's something wrong with you and you're really in love or really angry and you show it. Like if you feel those powerful emotions and you express them, instead of keeping them inside or expressing yourself politely, then you must be someone who needs therapy, or Prozac. That's the world we're in right now."

The words would flow easily off the tongue of Tony Soprano, the North Jersey Mob capo who serves as the comic antihero of HBO's acclaimed new drama, *The Sopranos*. Nearly every episode contains a monologue by Tony—sometimes bitter, sometimes comic, sometimes poignant—about how difficult society makes life for guys like him.

Except this time, it's not Tony who's venting. It's James Gandolfini, the 37-year-old actor who plays him.

"The character is a good fit," says Gandolfini, who was raised in Park Ridge, NJ. He's sitting in a sunny window seat at the White Horse Tavern in Greenwich Village after a workout at a nearby gym. "Obviously, I'm not a mobster, and there's other aspects of the guy I'm not familiar with, like how comfortable he is with violence. But in most of the ways that count, I have to say, yeah—the guy is me."

Created by producer-writer David Chase, the thirteen-episode series is *The Godfather* meets *The Honeymooners*, about a mobster who feels disconnected from his wife and kids, feels guilty for putting his mother in a nursing home, is convinced the world is out of balance, and is even seeing a therapist to cope with stress. The guy can't win for losing.

With material this rich, it's no wonder Tony and *The Sopranos*, seen Sunday nights at 9, have become a lightning rod for media stories on a variety of topics: Italian Americans on film, the persistent allure of crime stories, images of suburban life in pop culture, even the malaise affecting some Baby Boomers as they enter middle age. Chase's show is a coast-to-coast critical favorite, a hit with pay cable viewers (posting the highest ratings for an original drama in HBO history) and, perhaps most importantly, a success with executives at the cable channel, who ordered up another thirteen episodes after airing only two.

The Sopranos has also cemented Gandolfini's stardom. For the first few years of his career as an actor, which started fourteen years ago, he has done mostly stage work at small theaters in New York and Los Angeles. His breakthrough film role was in 1993's *True Romance*, where he played the hired killer who perishes in a fight to the death with Patricia Arquette. "It was like a dance," Gandolfini says. "We kind of made it up as we went along."

Since then, he has been cast mostly as thugs, murderers, and sweet-natured palookas—in Gandolfini's words, "the roles you'd expect a guy who looks like me to get."

But these days, he's looking suspiciously like a leading man. In the current film *A Civil Action*, starring John Travolta as a crusading litigator, Gandolfini's scenes as a whistle-blowing worker at a tannery serve as the film's moral compass. Gandolfini also plays the heavy opposite Nicolas Cage in *8mm*, a bleak thriller from the writer of *Seven* that opens February 29. ("A dark, dark film," Gandolfini says.)

And of course, it's getting hard to walk the streets of any city without passing posters and bus billboards featuring Tony Soprano and his stare of death.

Filmmakers and actors who have worked with Gandolfini are rhapsodic in their praise.

"I don't think he has any idea how good he is, which may be one of the reasons he's as good as he is," says Edie Falco, a regular on HBO's *Oz*, who plays Tony Soprano's wife, Carmela.

"He has an extremely large emotional well that I guess he can draw from whenever he wants," says Michael Imperioli, a veteran of *Goodfellas* and several Spike Lee movies, who plays Chris, Tony's impulsive

young nephew. "It's quite powerful. The force of it sometimes can knock me out of any kind of complacency that I might fall into."

"He is a very serious actor," says Steven Zaillian, who directed Gandolfini in *A Civil Action*. "He was one of the very few actors in that film who would ask *me* to do another take. . . . He always thinks he can be better when what he has just done is perfect."

You might think such praise would excite an actor who has struggled so long for recognition. In one way, it does. But in another way, it makes Gandolfini uncomfortable. In interviews, he often chalks up his success to pure luck, makes self-deprecating remarks about his weight and his hair, and expresses astonishment at the notion that a guy who looks like him could suddenly have so much industry heat behind him.

"That's a genuine part of him," says Martha Coolidge, who directed Gandolfini in 1994's *Angie*, in which he played his first romantic role as Geena Davis' lover. "I'm not talking about looks, because I think he's an enormously attractive man. I'm talking about his own impression of how he looks. It's that [self-deprecating] attitude that makes him a character actor. In *Angie*, I got the best of both worlds. I wanted a guy who was very real but who also had leading man qualities to play opposite Geena. James is a real man, so he can be tough and sexy, but he also can be vulnerable and sensitive. He was ideal for that kind of part, and he's also ideal for *The Sopranos*.

"I feel like I'm being singled out for praise when it's an ensemble thing," Gandolfini explains. "It's not fair to the other actors on the show—Edie, Michael, Lorraine [Bracco], and all the rest. And David Chase, who is, let's face it, brilliant. Without the mind of David Chase behind this thing, we actors might as well just go home."

Endearing stories about Gandolfini's discomfort with fame have already begun circulating. HBO sources confirm a few of them—that he has been reluctant to do many interviews because he doesn't want to draw attention away from Chase and his fellow actors; he hates posing for publicity photographs of any sort; that he nearly came to the New York premiere party for *The Sopranos* in a yellow cab because he didn't want friends to see him get out of a limo and think he'd gone Hollywood.

He dislikes interviews for profile pieces. "I'm not trying to be difficult," he says. "It's not that I'm afraid to reveal personal stuff. . . . It's just that I really, genuinely don't see why people would find that sort of thing so interesting."

Asked about his youth, he will volunteer only that he was raised "middle class" or "blue collar." He says he always liked going to movies. ("John Wayne. You can't go wrong with John Wayne.") But he was never really star-struck, and to this day, he doesn't consider himself a film buff.

He doesn't like most big-budget genre movies, preferring *On the Waterfront*, tough domestic dramas like *Ordinary People*, and especially outdoor films like *Jeremiah Johnson* and *A River Runs Through It*.

"It's funny," he says. "All these city movies I do, and the ones that appeal to me are the outdoor movies."

He didn't take his first acting class until 1985, two years after he graduated from Rutgers University in New Brunswick, N.J. He isn't married and has no kids. He is seeing a woman and would prefer her name not be published. He has two sisters. His mother is dead. His father used to be a cement mason in New York City and now works as a janitor in a Catholic school in New Jersey. He doesn't want their names mentioned either because of the phone calls they've been getting at home from strangers. He lives in a Greenwich Village apartment but is thinking about selling it, moving back to New Jersey, and getting a smaller place in Manhattan. After the second season of *The Sopranos* wraps, he'll probably take a year off.

Asked what he majored in at Rutgers, he says, "I don't remember." (According to Rutgers, Gandolfini majored in communications. He graduated in 1983.)

Many actors claim to be ambivalent about fame. Gandolfini truly is ambivalent. He doesn't even like to use celebrity status as a soapbox—a favorite pastime of supposedly shy and serious performers. Many times during this interview, he would begin to express an opinion about a particular type of film that he likes or doesn't like, or the relative value of college acting programs versus real-world experience. Then he would trail off and say, "Scratch that" or "Never mind. Who cares what an actor has to say about anything?"

"If there's one thing I hate, it's an actor getting up on a soapbox," he says. Then he chuckles and makes a "scratch that" motion. "Hey, forget I said that. If you print me saying that, it's me getting up on a soapbox."

"You have to remember, he worked in a lot of films and theater before this stage in his career, so he is known to moviegoers but not quite recognizable," explains Imperioli. "Now he's Tony Soprano. He's in their house once a week. He likes that, but he wants to keep it real."

One thing Gandolfini is adamant about is sincerity in movies. His favorite recent film is *Shakespeare in Love*, which he says he found "very moving."

He hates advertising and films that look like advertising. He dislikes hipness and mean humor. He prefers films that are very emotional rather than sardonic, glib, or otherwise "cool."

"I like when you go to a movie or turn on a TV show that has people who, in one way or another, look like you, act like you, and feel some of the things you feel," he says. "I like stories about regular guys, not the cool guys. Cool makes me want to vomit."

Hearing Gandolfini's rare soapbox statement makes Coolidge laugh with delight.

"Notice how his own assessment of what he's interested in as a moviegoer points him toward the material he's best suited to play," she says. "By virtue of his look and his personality, James is well-suited to be in the kinds of movies he likes. That's a happy accident. Imagine if he looked like some male model. The kinds of movies he hates are the only kinds of movies they'd let him be in. It would be Purgatory."

Mob Fatigue

ITALIAN AMERICAN GROUPS FIND *THE SOPRANOS* TO BE JUST
ANOTHER NEGATIVE PORTRAYAL
BY MATT ZOLLER SEITZ | 3/5/1999

BY MOST ACCOUNTS, HBO's series *The Sopranos*, about a middle-class family in suburban New Jersey whose patriarch, Tony Soprano, is a mobster in therapy, is a success for the premium cable channel. It's a ratings hit, has already been renewed for a second season, and has won near-unanimous acclaim from critics.

Emanuele Alfano is not impressed. "I don't care how good it is as a drama," says the Bloomfield physician, a member of the anti-bias committee for UNICO National, an Italian American organization. "The fact is, it's just another Mob story, which Italian Americans do not need."

"So the show is well written, well acted," says Nicolas Addeo, chairman of Speranza, a New Jersey–based group that promotes positive images of ethnic, religious, and racial groups in Hollywood. "Whatever. It's a well-upholstered hell."

Since *The Sopranos* hit the air Jan. 10, it has been the object of public protest by UNICO National, Speranza, Sons of Italy, the Italian American One Voice Committee and other groups. They have targeted HBO with letters, faxes, and phone calls, and staged lectures and teach-ins about defamation.

Alfano, Addeo, and other anti-defamation activists claim *The Sopranos* is merely the latest salvo in a never-ending pop culture war against Italian Americans. In their view, since the release of *The Godfather* in 1972, Hollywood has served up an increasing number of problematic images, some blatant and grotesque (death-dealing gangsters); others comic and outwardly harmless (the crude, back-stabbing Dr. Romano on *ER*, Matt LeBlanc's dimwitted Joey Tribbiani on *Friends*).

When a show like *The Sopranos* comes along and earns acclaim for its artistry but little criticism for its subject matter, says Addeo, it makes the struggle for positive images harder.

"So you hear *The Sopranos* is a quality show, you turn it on to check it out, and it's the same old thing again—Italian Americans stealing, hitting, shooting, cheating, killing," Addeo says.

The show's creator, David Chase—an Italian American reared in North Caldwell whose family name was originally DeCesare—says the protesters overstate the damage done by gangster movies. "It has yet to be proven to me that a single Italian American has suffered in the past fifteen years because of this."[1]

He also notes the majority of the talent involved in the show is Italian American—including lead actors James Gandolfini, Edie Falco, and Michael Imperioli—and says if any of them thought the material was defamatory, they wouldn't have become involved.

Imperioli, who plays a low-level mobster named Chris on *The Sopranos*, echoes Chase's sentiments. "I honestly think Italian Americans are at a place right now where that type of thing is not defamation, or if it is stereotypical, it's not damaging. Italian Americans have assimilated in all aspects of the culture. They're in government, in law. They're corporate heads. If this were the '20s or '30s, which is when my grandfather came over here, a show like *The Sopranos* would be a lot more damaging to somebody like him."

"Those guys need a little consciousness-raising," says Addeo, on being informed of Chase's and Imperioli's statements. "That they think there's not a problem only proves to me that we have a long way to go."

Chase says there are so many gangster stories because criminality is a great subject for movies. "Taking money, power plays, shooting—that's the territory in American movies, by and large." And unfortunately, he adds, many newspaper headlines about organized crime in the past thirty years have concerned Italian American gangsters, who have had an impact on American society out of proportion to their numbers. "The man who was assassinated for control of the Gambino Crime Family in front of Sparks Steakhouse in New York City was not named Phil Van Hoovel, he was named Paul Castellano. . . . When the phenomenon to which I am referring ceases to be a demonstrable fact of life, we'll probably see these kinds of stories disappear, just as Westerns began to decline when the vast majority of Americans couldn't see a horse anymore."

---

1   Due to a bad phone connection, I misheard David saying "fifty years" rather than "fifteen years," which was close to the length of time elapsed between the release of *The Godfather Part II* and the debut of *The Sopranos*, so "fifty" is the number that made it into the paper, prompting a flood of angry mail from Italian Americans who wondered if he'd lost his mind. David subsequently wrote a Letter to the Editor saying he'd been misquoted and apologizing for that particular sentiment, as Italian Americans obviously had been discriminated against during the preceding half-century, and I ran a mea culpa. Fortunately, he continued to speak to me after that.

Uncle Junior is the Singing 'Soprano'

BY MATT ZOLLER SEITZ | 12/2/1999

DOMINIC CHIANESE HAS been acting and singing for more than four decades, culminating in his high-profile role on HBO's *The Sopranos* as the stoic, vengeful Mob boss Uncle Junior, and in two sold-out evenings of cabaret at Judy's Chelsea, a Manhattan nightclub, December 5 and 12. He has performed on and off Broadway, in movies, and on TV.

If he hadn't gotten off a bus in 1952, it's possible none of it would have happened.

Back then, Chianese was a wiry twenty-year-old, recently discharged from the Marine Reserves and working construction jobs with his father, Gaetano "Tony" Chianese, a bricklayer. He had been singing seriously since high school and wanted to become a professional musician. But he hesitated, partly because he wasn't sure his father would understand or approve.

On this important day, the two men were riding from their home in the Bronx to work on a garden apartment in Clifton, NJ. "We were on a bus full of bricklayers from the Bronx," recalls Chianese, sixty-eight, sitting in a coffee shop not far from his apartment on Manhattan's Upper East Side. "My father was sitting in the front of the bus. I was in back."

Chianese came across an audition ad in the *New York Herald Tribune* seeking singers for a musical company specializing in Gilbert and Sullivan operettas. He asked his father if he could skip bricklaying that day and get off the bus at 74th Street to audition.

"He said, 'An audition? For what?'"

"I said, 'Singing.'"

The elder Chianese waited about four or five seconds before answering. Finally, he said, "Okay."

Chianese auditioned and made the cut. Since then, he has performed more or less nonstop, in a surprising variety of settings.

In the mid- to late '60s, he was the master of ceremonies at the West Village coffee shop Gerde's—better known as Folk City because of the musical acts that played there, from Bob Dylan to Emmylou Harris and Arlo Guthrie. He also sang in *Jacques Brel Is Alive and Well and Living in Paris*, a late-'60s, off-Broadway revue of the composer's work. (Chianese will likely perform a couple of Brel songs in his cabaret act, with accompaniment by pianist David Lahm.)

He was noticed by casting agents as a supporting player in HBO's Mob docudrama *Gotti*.

Chianese isn't big on Method acting. He believes in studying the text, understanding the character, and saying his lines in as direct and unfussy a manner as possible. He thinks research and character identification are useful tools for an actor, but they are no substitute for poring over the dialogue and stage directions, especially if the script was written by someone with a brain in his head.

"The playwright's vision is the one you should aim for," he says. "Uncle Junior can only be played one way. That's because [series creator] David Chase was very specific in creating this character. He knows what this man is about, what he values. He protects his money, he hates the FBI, he loves his family.

"I believe that Shakespeare has to be played a certain way. I feel the same about any playwright of talent. The text tells you what to do—at least, it should. Even in a terrible piece of writing, you can bring yourself to the character and find something in there worth playing, but our job as actors isn't to try to make it interesting. That's the writer's job."

Chianese has six children and ten grandchildren. Three of his children are in the arts. Daughter Rebecca Scarpatti is a playwright. Another daughter, Sarah Francesca, programs film festivals. Son Dominic Chianese Jr. is an actor whose most recent screen credit is as one of the museum thieves in *The Thomas Crown Affair*.

———

He says that, although he has been singing since he was a kid, he didn't fixate on the notion of becoming a professional singer until he saw Frank Sinatra perform at the Paramount Theater in Manhattan in 1947. The bobby-soxers were screaming. Chianese sat tenth-row center. Sinatra was magnificent—a skinny god of music in a white shirt, a brown sports jacket, and a green tie.

"He hit me right where the heart was," Chianese remembers. "His first number was Harold Arlen's "I've Got the World on a String.' I don't remember any other song but that one. It's the first song in my act—my opener. I tell you, it made an impression. His voice! The singing. Back then, if you were an Italian American boy from the Bronx, that was your way into the dream world. If you weren't a boxer or a ballplayer, then it had to be performing, singing, something like that.

"I couldn't be a boxer. My father knew that. I couldn't follow in his footsteps, either, and he knew that, too. That's why he let me get off the bus."

SEASON TWO: 2000

Location, Location, Location

FEEL LIKE YOU'VE BEEN THERE? YOU PROBABLY HAVE

BY MATT ZOLLER SEITZ | 1/16/2000

WHEN YOU'RE EXPLORING fresh TV terrain, it helps to have a guide who knows the territory. On *The Sopranos,* that role is filled by locations manager Mark Kamine, an industry veteran who is New Jersey to the bone: born in Jersey City, raised in Wayne, and a resident of Montclair.

Kamine describes *The Sopranos* as "the most intense New Jersey experience I've ever had on a [project]." Currently, at least 75 percent of exteriors on *The Sopranos* are shot on location in New Jersey, with side trips into New York City and Long Island. Most interiors are filmed on soundstages at Silvercup Studios in Queens. Most of the cast and crew live and work in the New York–New Jersey area.

Kamine is careful to point out that few locations in *The Sopranos* have an exact real-world equivalent. . . . *The Sopranos* crew can shoot an exterior in, say, Verona, another interior in Montclair, and a couple of interiors at Silvercup Studios, then put the shots together in the editing room to create a convincing place.

Take episode four of the first season, in which Tony Soprano (James Gandolfini) takes his teenage daughter, Meadow (Jamie-Lynn Sigler) on a driving tour of colleges. While in Maine, they stay at a motel and tour a college; in the process, Tony randomly encounters a stool pigeon who's in witness protection, tracks him down, and kills him.

The *Sopranos* crew never set foot in Maine.

"The college they toured was actually Drew University in Madison," says Kamine. "The motel they stayed at was in Oakland, New Jersey. We filmed the scenes where they're driving around the roads, and the scene where Tony kills the guy, in New York state, up in Rockland County."

The opening credits sequence also takes a few liberties with geography, says Jason Minter, the assistant locations manager and New York City native who helped create it. But the ultimate goal is the same: to give viewers an abstract, almost poetic sense of New Jersey and its landscapes.

A couple of years ago, when Chase was looking for ideas on opening credits, he had Minter and first assistant director Henry Bronchtein drive around northern New Jersey with a camcorder, taping whatever they saw. Chase liked the jagged, staccato look of the raw footage so much that he wanted to duplicate it on film. So Minter, frequent *Sopranos* director Allen Coulter, and cinematographer Phil Abraham revisited the locations on the videotape twice with 35mm film cameras: the first time with a fully loaded camera car, the second time with a hand-held camera in a car driven by star James Gandolfini.

There were complications (the State Police don't permit camera cars on the Turnpike) and fakery (the World Trade Center is seen in Tony's rearview mirror coming out of the Lincoln Tunnel, which is not possible; the shot was taken from a road near the Liberty Science Center). But the result has the desired effect.

"One of the producers said, 'I don't know—I think you need Dramamine to watch it,'" says Minter. "But it works on you, especially if you're from New Jersey. It has all these things that stay in the back of your mind even if you move away."

Changing Direction

DIRECTOR PETER BOGDANOVICH TRIES A NEW ROLE—AS AN ACTOR

BY MATT ZOLLER SEITZ | 1/22/2000 (EXCERPT)

"**PEOPLE ARE OFTEN** afraid of the word 'ambiguity,' but this show really embraces it in the best '70s tradition. You would be hard-pressed to find someone in real life whose not laced with ambiguity. Not that the first goal of *The Sopranos* isn't to entertain, but the characters are written so well that they are rich with ambiguity."

———

Bogdanovich says although the *The Sopranos* is very specific in its settings and characters, its significance goes beyond that. He says it's the right show for this period in American history—the dawn of a new century when people aren't quite sure if the old rules still apply, and are concerned that the past and its values might be fading away.

"On this show, values aren't black and white. That reflects what's going on in the country at the moment. I get the sense that people aren't entirely sure what's right anymore. The whole Clinton thing brought this feeling to a boil," he says, referring to the Monica Lewinsky scandal.

"There is a tremendous unease right now with judgments of any kind, yet at the same time, as you watch the show, you make moral judgments anyway. You kind of go back and forth. That's also reflective of this moment in history. It's mordantly in tune with the way things are right now. *The Sopranos* is sort of a big moral question mark."

A Star of Stage and *Sopranos*, Nancy Marchand Dies of Cancer

BY MATT ZOLLER SEITZ | 6/20/2000

NANCY MARCHAND, who played a monstrous matriarch on HBO's *The Sopranos* and a blueblood newspaper publisher on CBS's long-running *Lou Grant*, died Sunday night at her home in Stratford, Connecticut, after a long battle with lung cancer.

Marchand's death came on the day before what would have been her seventy-second birthday. She was best known to contemporary audiences for her Emmy-nominated, Golden Globe-winning work on *The Sopranos*, a drama about suburban New Jersey gangsters that her character, Livia Soprano, ruled with a Roman senator's guile. Furious over being put in a nursing home by her son, crime boss Tony Soprano (James Gandolfini), Livia plotted to unseat Tony from power by any means necessary, including murder. Her nonstop nagging and frequent admissions of memory loss camouflaged a hitman's savagery and a monk's patience.

The role of Livia was merely the last in a fifty-year run of distinguished stage, screen, and TV characterizations. Born and raised in Buffalo, New York, Marchand played a startling variety of roles, appearing in everything from stage productions of Shakespeare and Tennessee Williams to movies (including the 1970 satire *The Hospital*, opposite George C. Scott) to primetime series (including *Cheers*, on which she played the mother of Kelsey Grammer's character, Dr. Frasier Crane).

"This is a great loss to American theater and film," said Dominic Chianese, who plays elderly crime boss Corrado "Uncle Junior" Soprano on the HBO series.

"This was someone who had enough range to play Mrs. Pynchon on *Lou Grant* and then do that extraordinary mother on *The Sopranos*," said Mason Adams, Marchand's costar on *Lou Grant* as well as numerous stage productions. "She was an amazingly versatile actress."

Marchand's breakthrough came on March 24, 1953, when she starred opposite Rod Steiger in the original live telecast of *Marty*, playwright Paddy Chayefsky's gritty drama about a meek Bronx butcher. One of the biggest ratings hits of the live TV era, *Marty* was remade two years later as a hit film that won four Academy Awards.

Marchand's lengthy list of Broadway and off-Broadway credits included Obie-winning parts in *The*

Cocktail Hour and *The Balcony* and a Tony-nominated role in *White Liars and Black Comedy.* Her motion picture work ranged from Paddy Chayefsky's 1970 *The Hospital*, a satirical expose of corruption and incompetence in American medicine, to slapstick roles in *The Naked Gun* and the Marx Bros.–style slapstick farce *Brain Donors.*

During her *Lou Grant* stint, Marchand won four consecutive Emmy awards as best supporting actress in a drama, from 1978 to 1982. Her character, Mrs. Pynchon, was a tough, smart, socially connected newspaper heiress partly modeled on Katharine Graham, the longtime publisher of the *Washington Post.*

"I first met her at the Stratford Shakespeare Festival in Stratford, Conn., back in 1959," said *Lou Grant* star Ed Asner. "She dazzled me with her acting, and with her legs as well. She was an experience. She was a learning experience. She was a joy experience. She was a regular guy, if you know what I mean. She was tough."

Asner fondly recalled the speed with which Marchand could size up a script and mine it for unexpected emotions.

"This woman would get a script and find the faults within it immediately. I was always dazzled by her incisiveness. Once we got on our feet and began acting a scene, she would just dazzle me with the depths she would pull out of a character, or from a single speech within the scene. I regarded

her as one of the premier actresses in America."

Victor Kemper, a Newark native and president of the American Society of Cinematographers, worked with Marchand on *The Hospital* and several commercials. "She really had a sense of what was going on around her, and was always receptive to comments by the director or the camera crew. She was a true collaborator, as opposed to some of these people who insist on only doing it their way."

The Sopranos creator David Chase said Marchand's passing left "a huge hole" in the show—not just because the issue of Livia's declining health was not resolved before Marchand's death, but also because Marchand was well-liked for her talent, professionalism, and "deadpan" sense of humor. "She could defeat any stupid or pompous situation with just one or two well-timed words. . . . When we used to rehearse the scenes between Livia and Tony, and we'd kind of unveil them for the first time so we could block them, she just had everybody in stitches the whole time."

Marchand's casting as a middle-class Italian American struck some observers as surprising, since most viewers knew her from her WASPy part on *Lou Grant.* Marchand, as always, confounded those would pigeonhole her, winning critical acclaim and numerous awards and nominations. She continued to act on *The Sopranos* even after it became known she was fighting a losing battle with lung cancer. (Marchand's husband of forty-seven years, actor Paul Sparer, died in November, also of cancer.)

Chase said he and Marchand had discussed what to do in the event the actress died—whether to film a death episode in advance or to have it happen offscreen. By mutual agreement, the matter was never resolved.

"We came to the conclusion that we would deal with it when it happened," Chase said. "I mean, what could you do? We really had no contingency plan."

Chase said the most surprising thing about Marchand's performance as Livia was her ability to make a monstrous character seem human, as sad and lonely as she was ruthless. "The most surprising thing, given what the character of Livia is like, is that so many people came up to me after the series debuted and said, 'My God, I hate to tell you this, but my mother is like that.' Or maybe they had a grandmother, or an aunt. I don't think

they meant these women took things as far as trying to have a son killed. They were talking about general long-suffering morbid attitude. A complete and utter selfishness."

Asner fondly remembered another side of Marchand: her driving. "I brought her home to dinner one time. She followed me on the freeway. You know these people who feel they have to leave 1,000 feet between you and them as you're leading them? Nancy was like that. . . . I'd practically have to come to a complete stop on the freeway and wait around for her to surface. It was the most unbelievable, mind-destroying trip I've ever taken. I hope somebody doesn't have to lead her to heaven."

Mason Adams said he last saw Marchand a few weeks ago, when she came to Westport, Connecticut, to see her son-in-law sing at a concert. "She was there in a wheelchair. She was obviously very weak. But she came to hear her son-in-law sing. She was really something."

SEASON THREE: 2001

Actor behind Artie Bucco
Shows Another Side

BY MATT ZOLLER SEITZ | 9/16/2000

ACTOR JOHN VENTIMIGLIA is best known for his work on *The Sopranos,* where he plays restaurateur Artie Bucco. The character is a kindhearted working man on a show full of violent misfits; a regular Joe who's proud of his own labor, yet tempted by the dark allure of Mob life, represented by childhood pal Tony Soprano (James Gandolfini). If you only associate Ventimiglia with Artie, his star turn in the low-budget independent picture *On the Run* might come as a bit of a shock. The film, which opened yesterday in a limited run in Manhattan, is a droll urban comedy that pairs him with longtime friend Michael Imperioli, who plays volatile young mobster Chris Moltisanti on *The Sopranos.*

In typecasting terms, they're playing each other's roles. This time, Imperioli is the law-abiding, responsible one, meek travel agent Albert DeSantis. Ventimiglia takes the showier role as Albert's childhood buddy Louie Salazar, a sexy, dangerous charmer who reenters Albert's life after busting out of prison. As Louie,

Ventimiglia, who is not a large man, somehow seems enormous—a charismatic, Jack Nicholson–style alpha male who has a good time at everyone else's expense.

"I'm a big fan of '70s films," said Ventimiglia, talking to a reporter over sandwiches and olives at his favorite Italian deli in the Cobble Hill neighborhood of Brooklyn, where he lives with his wife and two young children. "This is that kind of movie, with that kind of role—something like you'd get from Jack Nicholson or Al Pacino or Gene Hackman back then."

Ventimiglia isn't banking on this one role to prove his versatility as a leading man, but he thinks it's a step in the right direction. But since he plays a recurring role on a hit show, it'll be an uphill battle.

In the middle of the interview, a stranger walks into the deli, ducks around the seated Ventimiglia to get a Coke from the refrigerator, and delightedly exclaims, "Hey, Artie! How's the restaurant business?"

"It's doing fine, man, just fine," says Ventimiglia, smiling.

HBO Turns an Office Manager into a Mobster's Wife

BY MATT ZOLLER SEITZ | 2/22/2001

WHEN DENISE BORINO auditioned for a bit part on *The Sopranos*, she says she wasn't anxious. She had so much on her mind that winning a part was the least of her worries.

"My grandmother had just passed away," says the Roseland resident, who has a small role in three episodes this season as Ginny Sack, the wife of New York Mob captain Johnny Sack (Vincent Curatola). "On the Tuesday night when I went to read, I was missing the night-time part of her wake. With all of that going on, I never had the chance to think about being nervous."

Borino is an office manager and legal assistant for Coffey & Sullivan, a law firm in Morristown. Like seven other nonprofessionals—four from New Jersey, one from Philadelphia, two from New York—Borino attended an open casting call in Harrison last July seeking fresh faces for HBO's crime drama.

————

Borino says she came away from the experience impressed with the production—and very interested in acting again. "My first scene in my first episode was a scene with James Gandolfini. He was a very intelligent, nice guy. At the end of the shoot he made a point of coming over to tell me that I did a nice job. That made my day."

She insists she's not going to have a party the night her first episode premieres. But her friends may have other ideas.

"I said to my friends, 'Gee, I don't know if I'm gonna let you guys watch it with me.' They were gonna tie me to a chair."

Stopping by the Woods on a Snowy Evening

BY MATT ZOLLER SEITZ | 5/8/2001

SUNDAY'S *SOPRANOS,* titled "Pine Barrens" and built around a bizarre foot chase through snowy woods, was a brutal black comedy set in an icy white hell. It was also the finest hour the series has produced this season. As soon as it was over, I wanted to watch it again; though some episodes this year have been quite good, this was the first one that indisputably equaled or surpassed anything from Season 1.

The change of scenery probably had something to do with it. *The Sopranos* has two dominant colors, brown and green—brown for the whiskey-colored interiors where family business is conducted; green for the suburbs the title clan calls home. The bleached-out ivory tones of Sunday's hour commanded attention; you got the sense that you were watching an hour which, somewhere down the road, would turn out to be pivotal.

Written by a longtime *Sopranos* producer and director named Terence Winter (yes, that's his real name), "Pine Barrens" was directed by actor Steve Buscemi, who knows a thing or two about shooting in snow after starring in the Coen brothers' *Fargo*. (He's also a superb filmmaker in his own right; if you haven't seen his two

features, the barroom comedy *Trees Lounge* and the prison drama *Animal Factory*, rent them immediately.)

The main plot was delightfully strange: When regular bagman Silvio (Steve Van Zandt) falls ill with the flu, Tony (James Gandolfini) assigns Paulie (Tony Sirico) and Chris (Michael Imperioli) to collect money laundered by a Russian business associate. Unfortunately, the meeting with the Russian contact—a giant, loudmouthed drunk named Valery (Vitali Baganov)—degenerates into an argument, then a fight, whereupon Paulie strangles the guy with a floor lamp—to death, or so he thinks.

Turns out Valery's too tough to die. Paulie and Chris stuff Valery, referred to in cell phone conversations as "the package," in the trunk of Paulie's car and take him out to the Pine Barrens to bury him. When Valery turns out to be alive, they make him dig his own grave.

But the resourceful Valery, who was once an elite soldier in the Russian army, escapes ("The package hit Chrissie with an implement," Paulie tells the boss, proving he's not exactly the king of euphemisms). The baddest Russian since Ivan Drago in *Rocky IV*, Valery survives a wound to the head and leads the two hapless Jersey suburbanites on an increasingly weird and hopeless foot chase that resembles *The Blair Witch Project* by way of *Dr. Zhivago*. (Can a shooting war between two Jersey mobs be far off?)

Though the bickering desperation of Paulie and Chris occupied center stage this hour, there was plenty of interesting secondary action, including Tony's newly strained relationship with mistress Gloria Trillo (Annabella Sciorra), whom he keeps pushing away whenever work intrudes. "If I wanted to be treated like —, I'd get married," she complained, before beaning Tony in the back of the neck with a cold slab of London broil.

————

It's interesting that "University," the sickeningly violent episode of *The Sopranos* that aired earlier this year, was intended to evoke comparison to the first-season episode "College," which some fans still think is the drama's finest hour. Despite the lack of structural similarities, "Pine Barrens" is actually much closer in spirit to "College." While furthering some of the series' major plot strands, it's a stand-alone, one-hour mini-movie that can be enjoyed by anyone who likes rough-edged black comedy.

Can This Marriage Be Saved?

BY ALAN SEPINWALL | 9/15/2002

AS *THE SOPRANOS* enters a season of which creator David Chase says the dominant theme will be the state of Tony and Carmela's marriage, how healthy does Carmela's alter ego Edie Falco find the union?

"Who's to say what's healthy and unhealthy?" Falco asks. "It's hard to see from how close I am [to the role], but I look around in the world, and there are a lot of marriages very similar to it, minus the Mob aspect. A lot of marriages exist with compromises, spoken and unspoken. For Carmela, there's a sense of consistency: he does provide for his family, he does care for her and the children, and it gives her a place in society."

While Falco has never been married, she is frequently approached by female fans who explain how much Carmela inspires them in dealings with their own inconsiderate spouses, who may not be killers but nevertheless engage in plenty of hurtful behavior.

"These women come up to me and say, 'I just have to say I really find you

a role model,' which is really amazing to me," says Falco. "'He's just like my husband, I love the way you deal with him, you tell it how it is.'"

Which is not to say that Falco resents playing Carmela, who is now as comfortable as an old pair of shoes for her—literally. She noticed earlier this year that a pair she had been wearing as Carmela since the first season were completely worn out.

"I can't be more different from her, and on another level, I am her. She is this other corner of myself. It is an exceedingly fulfilling experience for an actor. I love that people know her."

And, of course, there's always her acting marriage with James Gandolfini.

"It is just perfect, the two of us," she says of the partnership. "It reminds me of when I was a little kid and you used to play House. It feels like playing. I have never been more comfortable opposite an actor. It is pure serendipity; they could have cast two people where it didn't happen."

"Joey Pants" Comes Home

BY ALAN SEPINWALL | 9/13/2002

"THIS IS WHERE I got my ass kicked by Rabies," says Joe Pantoliano, grinning in the courtyard of the Jackson Street housing projects in Hoboken.

"And right over there," he says, racing excitedly into the middle of the street, "is where my dad and cousin Florie got into a fistfight and the car started rolling backward while Mommy was still in it."

Pantoliano, who plays sociopathic mobster Ralphie Cifaretto on *The Sopranos*, isn't describing scenes from one of the dozens of movies and TV shows he's appeared in. On a drizzly afternoon in late August, he's taking a walk down his own personal Memory Lane.

Pantoliano—or Joey Pants, as he's known from Hudson County to Hollywood—spent the first fifteen years of his life growing up on the streets of Hoboken. Not the cleaned-up, yuppified Hoboken of today, but the rough-and-tumble, *On the Waterfront* Hoboken.

"Now right here," he says, pointing at a sewer grate a few blocks away from the projects, "is where Daddy dangled the kid who threw my ball down the sewer."

And, a few blocks north, he studies a forty-year-old dent left in the side of a brick apartment building when a car careened into it.

"We were living on the second floor at the time, and Daddy poked his head out the window to see what happened, and it was a guy he knew," says Pantoliano, amazed the brick hasn't been replaced in all this time.

Pantoliano has dozens of stories like these. As the son of two combative degenerate gamblers, growing up in a town where swag was the only acceptable merchandise at holiday time and budding juvenile delinquents like the aforementioned Rabies lurked around every corner, he would almost have to.

His parents, Monk and Mary Pantoliano, skirted the edge of indigence for most of Joe's childhood, preferring to change apartments instead of pay bills. Failing that, Mary used her powers of persuasion, which were legendary.

"One time, my cousin Mario worked for Sears and Roebuck and they sent him to take our furniture," he recalls. "She made him feel so bad, he lent her $200."

Mary loved her little Joey, but she had little patience for the other men in her life. (Pantoliano blames this attitude on his maternal grandfather, a terrifying brute who once shot a man in the leg for spitting on the sidewalk near Mary.) She would bully Monk every chance she got, verbally and physically. One night, a triumphant Monk returned home after bowling a

300 game. Mary accused him of cutting around, and when Monk pointed to his bowling trophy as a defense, she whacked him with it so hard that she broke his collarbone.

Pantoliano is as quick to defend his mother as he is to point out her missteps. "As nutty as she was, she was fun-loving," he says.

Cousin Florie, aka Florio Isabella, was a mobster who flitted in and out of young Joe's life, disappearing for a long stretch when he was convicted of robbing the Hoboken ferry.

"Florie went right up to the captain with a gun and said, "Captain, we have a mutiny,'" according to Pantoliano.

Movie and TV actors have a lot of downtime between takes, and Pantoliano has spent a lot of his career filling that time by telling these tales of the old neighborhood.

"Every time I tell the stories, people say, 'These are fictional characters. These characters can't be real.' And I go, 'No, I swear to Christ, they're real.'"

After toying for years with the idea of turning his family's story into a movie—he briefly held rehearsals for the project, with Diane Lane playing his mother Mary and Andy Garcia as Florie—he decided it would work better as a book. *Who's Sorry Now?*, cowritten by David Evanier, traces Pantoliano's story from his birth until the day he left New Jersey to study acting.

After living in southern California for the early part of his career, Panto-liano moved back to Hoboken a decade ago. Despite acting under a variety of toupees since losing his hair, he's still easily recognizable as That Guy from *The Matrix* or *Risky Business* or *The Sopranos*, and he spends much of this walk through his childhood politely signing autographs.

"I used to work with the real guys, down there," says one wiseguy wannabe, as Pantoliano tries to keep from rolling his eyes. Another calls from across the street, "Hey, Ralphie! When's the new season gonna start?"

"I'm like a melting pot kind of actor," he says. "People recognize me from everything. But I always know a *Sopranos* fan, because they always call me Ralphie. Every other movie people know me from, they go, 'Hey, Joe Pantoliano,' 'Hey, Joey Pants.'"

Despite its gritty urban feel, Hoboken is still only a mile square, and on this walk Pantoliano keeps bumping into people he knows or used to know: a local fire captain who helped him research portions of the book related to his grandfather, a grade school classmate he hasn't seen in forty years.

Pantoliano recognizes that the best he'll ever do is to become the second-most-famous person to ever come out of Hoboken, but he has a more personal connection to Frank Sinatra than most: his mother grew up down the street from the Chairman of the Board, while his father's family had an ongoing feud with the Sinatras.

Family legend has it that Dolly Sinatra offered Monk's father Pete $1,000 if he would recommend her husband to succeed him as Hoboken fire captain, but that Frank refused to fork over the cash after Pete held up his end of the deal. Monk Pantoliano's hatred for Sinatra ran so deep that he literally got up from his deathbed at a South Jersey hospital when his doctor wouldn't stop talking about Sinatra. (Monk died about an hour later at a different hospital.)

"One of the things I found out while researching this book is that my grandfather owed money to this local bookie, and we think that the bookie approached Frank directly and said, "This guy owes me money, so just give it to me instead of him,'" says Pantoliano. "So [the family] made it a bigger deal than it maybe should have been."

Pantoliano insists he never knew anyone like Ralphie while growing up—"Nobody that crazy exists," he says—but he did have Florie, who became his unofficial stepfather when Mary left Monk, as both a negative and positive influence. On the one hand, Florie took him to Mob hangouts and made the gangster lifestyle look incredibly glamorous. On the other, Florie did everything he could to keep Joe from getting into that life. While Mary was trying to keep her son close to home, Florie was encouraging his acting dreams and hooking him up with his first real acting teacher.

"All these groups talk about *The Sopranos* and negative stereotypes," says Pantoliano. "Well, I was raised by a negative stereotype that did an incredible thing for me. In me, I guess, he found a kid who had a chance that he never did."

The walk continues, as Pantoliano marvels over the life he's built for himself. A dyslexic who was held back in school three times by teachers who were convinced he was developmentally disabled, he has now coauthored a book. A child of poverty, he's one of the most sought-after character actors in Hollywood. And he owes it all to Hoboken.

"Broke as we were, I always had a lot of fun living here," he says. "It was a tough neighborhood. So what? You'd get smacked around every once in a while, but it helped me down the road. Getting rejected for an audition in a room, going in front of Bob Fosse and Martin Scorsese and having them say no is a lot easier than having Rabies hold you down and kick the [bleep] out of you. I was born to have somebody say no to me."

The grin that's been plastered across Pantoliano's face all day finally disappears as he approaches a building on Monroe Street, the second place he lived in and the location where the book's cover photo was shot. The stoop he used to run up and down was torn up and badly reconstructed a few months ago.

"Would you look at what they did to my stoop?" he sighs. "Who's sorry now?"

Best of Both Worlds: Michael Imperioli Shines as Actor and Writer on *The Sopranos*

BY ALAN SEPINWALL | 9/14/2002

FOR THIRTEEN WEEKS a year, Michael Imperioli gets to play impatient *Sopranos* wiseguy Christopher Moltisanti. For one or two weeks a year, he gets to play with everyone else on the show.

———

"Writing for the show came out of my love of the other characters and wanting to put myself into their shoes for a bit," says Imperioli, who also cowrote the screenplay for Spike Lee's *Summer of Sam*. "I loved the characters, particularly Paulie Walnuts, who for some reason I have an affinity for, and for Silvio, whose voice I really like getting into."

During the hiatus between the first two seasons, he sat down and wrote an uncommissioned script that featured Christopher overdosing on heroin and having an out-of-body experience.

He warily approached *Sopranos* creator David Chase, who explained that the writers were already planning to have Christopher get shot. The two ideas were combined for "From Where to Eternity," which became one of that season's highlights.

———

"Michael's just like any other writer on the show at this point," says writer/producer Terence Winter. "His stuff is really good."

Imperioli has written two of the upcoming season's thirteen episodes, including "Christopher" (the title refers to Columbus, not Moltisanti), a comic look at ethnic pride—and a not-so-thinly-veiled rebuttal to all the Italian American activists who claim that the *Sopranos* mobsters promote negative stereotypes.

"I don't buy this thing that we're supposed to represent demographics and ethnic groups of people," says Imperioli, who also appeared in *Goodfellas*. "It's drama. Were the Greeks upset because one of the first plays was *Oedipus*? Does that mean Greeks are these treacherous, crazy people? This show is not meant to represent the Italian American experience. It's about a specific group of people, a specific time and place.

"I think most people know it's a TV show and don't think every Italian person they meet is in the Mafia," he adds. "And the idea that Italians are held back by *The Sopranos*? We assimilated years ago, we're already senators and governors and lawyers on all levels of society. I just think [the activists are] crybabies."

'Sopranos' Cast Flourishes with Late-Blooming Actors

BY ALAN SEPINWALL | 9/5/2002

GROWN MEN DON'T up and quit their jobs to join the Mafia. They do, on occasion, quit their jobs to play Mafia bosses on TV.

———

The latest addition to the cast continues the *Sopranos* tradition of late-bloomers. Vincent Curatola, who becomes a full-time regular this year as New York underboss Johnny Sack, was a masonry contractor until the early '90s.

———

Until 1989, the closest Curatola came to acting was working the phones at his Bergen County contracting company.

"My wife, Maureen, said to me, "You're so good with customers, with people at banks, and you change gears so quickly from one phone call to the next, you really need to be an actor.'"

Curatola had grown up admiring the actors he saw on Channel 9's *Million Dollar Movie*, but he didn't think much of his wife's flattery until she showed him an ad in *Backstage*

magazine about an acting class being taught by Michael Moriarty. Moriarty was intrigued enough by Curatola's call to invite him to audit the class, and the contractor quickly became a classroom fixture.

"After about a month and a half, I was comfortable enough to begin actually working on a monologue, and that's how it began," he says. "I would go out and rent a space every couple of months to let the students come and do a showcase for agents. I took over the production end of the Michael Moriarty acting studio.

"Every time I walk into something, I wind up taking it over."

"None of us are kids," he says. "There are things that we've all experienced being businessmen or whatever we were before this that enhances what we do on-screen. It fits so well that we would be so adamant about a particular deal or a particular split on the money. The fact that a lot of us have come from other avenues just adds to the realism."

Buscemi Joins the Family

BY ALAN SEPINWALL | 3/4/2004

STEVE BUSCEMI WANTED to be on *The Sopranos* from the minute he first saw it. David Chase wanted Buscemi on the show from the minute he created it.

But both men were too afraid of rejection to approach the other about a role on the show—even when Buscemi was on set to direct the famous "Pine Barrens" episode.

"We never talked about it," recalls Chase, "because I was embarrassed to ask him to come on the show. He's Steve Buscemi, he's got a thriving feature career, and the TV life is very difficult for an actor."

"It's something that I thought about sometimes," says Buscemi, "but I was too shy to mention it."

———

Because Buscemi had been a *Sopranos* fan from the beginning—he had actually hoped to direct episodes in the first two seasons but couldn't because of schedule conflicts—he found himself a bit starstruck when it came time to step in front of the camera.

"All of a sudden being in a diner with Tony Soprano—there's this thing that I just go, 'I can't believe that I'm doing this,'" he says.

———

Buscemi is remaining mum on the overall plan for Tony Blundetto, but he did let one detail slip at a recent news conference: "I keep my head, if that's what you're asking."

Chase Follows His Inner Mobster

BY ALAN SEPINWALL | 3/2/2004

DAVID CHASE TRIES not to pay attention to the complaints. Really, he does. *The Sopranos* creator still remembers the blissful experience of making the first season, when every scene was written, shot, and edited long before anyone had any idea what the show would become. So every year, he encourages his fellow writers to seal themselves into soundproof cocoons and ignore what's being written and said about their work.

But occasionally, he lets the rising din get to him.

"There was one woman writer who said, 'Whack somebody! Whack somebody for God's sakes!'" says the Caldwell native. "So this year we decided to whack somebody who looks like her."

Whacking—or the lack thereof—was the hot-button issue surrounding the fourth season. After getting slammed the previous year for too much violence, suddenly Chase was being accused of not showing enough blood and guts.

"I'm somewhat mystified by a lot of those comparisons," he says. "I thought there was a fair amount of violence last year, and then people say there's not enough violence, too much violence."

Season five seems to have upped the potential for mayhem with a story arc inspired by an article Chase read in the *Star-Ledger* about mobsters convicted in the RICO trials of the '80s finally getting paroled. But Chase denies the arc is a reaction to any of the people who view *Sopranos* as a reality-style show where someone has to get whacked every week.

"We just try to do what interests us at the time," he says. "When people look at it as *Survivor* with bullets, I find that kind of galling."

———

All the "Where's the whacking?" carping might cause another writer to wish he was creating a less brutal world, but Chase understands the deal he made with the devil when he turned a show about his own family into a Family show.

"There wouldn't be the same show if Tony wasn't a mobster," he says. "That Mob spine intensifies everything. If Tony was selling medical replacement hips, it wouldn't be life and death. The little things of every day wouldn't have the same resonance. It intensifies the banal and mundane stuff."

Tony's winter will come at the end of next season (premiere date unknown), which will be the show's last. Previous seasons have been written largely in isolation from each other, but the fifth was crafted with an eye on the finish line.

"There are things that were laid down some time ago that have yet to play out," he says. "I'm talking about people's destiny—not so much crime plots, but how people are going to grow up or not grow up or how they're going to finish out their final years."

SEASON SIX: 2006

Until "Whacking Day" Do They Part

BY ALAN SEPINWALL | 3/7/2006

THE QUESTION OF who gets whacked and when can be a fun parlor game for *Sopranos* fans, but it's deadly serious business for the people who work on the show, from the actors who constantly have to fear for their employment to the writers who have to put them out of work.

"One of the things we agreed on early on was that we would not keep a character alive because we liked the actor," says writer/producer Terence Winter. "We've liked all the actors, from Vinny Pastore and before him on. We'd never kill anybody [otherwise]. The writers have to say, 'What makes the best sense for this story? What would Tony do? Pussy was a rat: gone.' But we work with these people for so long, and they're your friends. I'm sure for them it's hard, too, you're out of work. But it's sad, it feels like somebody is going."

"We realize that someone is going to be put out of work," says creator David Chase. "But the fact of the matter is, we're all here to tell a story, including the actors, and that's their part in it. And when you take a job in a Mob show, you have to understand that."

Chase's willingness to sacrifice other characters for the sake of Tony's story has created an understandable climate of paranoia on the set.

"We always ask each other, 'What have you heard?'" says Joseph Gannascoli, who plays capo Vito Spatafore.

"I race through the scripts every time I get one," says Tony Sirico, "just to make sure that it ain't my time. It's just the luck of the draw that I've made it up until now."

––––––––

"There are some people who come to me constantly," says Chase, "and tell me conditions under which they will and won't go: 'If I'm going out, I'm not going out as a rat. I told you that from day one!' 'If you're gonna kill me, you've gotta massacre me.' 'I gotta be in the movie.' 'I want to launch a spinoff. Don't do it!'"

––––––––

"When you're asked to dinner," deadpans Michael Imperioli, "it's not such a good thing."

The Stuff That Tony's Dreams Are Made of

BY ALAN SEPINWALL | 3/6/2006

THERE ARE GOING to be more dreams. Deal with it.

The only complaint more persistent among *Sopranos* fans than all the whining about whacking are those loud and long protests whenever Tony checks into a hotel and the viewers check into his unconscious mind.

"The Test Dream" seemed to especially anger the whacking crowd because it took place late in the season, just as the New York Mob civil war storyline was threatening to satisfy their bloodlust.

The Sopranos writers know a portion of their audience doesn't like the dreams. And they don't care.

"People complained to me about it," says writer/producer Terence Winter, "and I said, 'The opening shot of this series is a guy in a psychiatrist's office. You think maybe the show is going to deal with dreams and psychology?' That's how you've met Tony Soprano, so the show deals with that stuff. So if you're interested in Tony Soprano, aren't you interested in what he thinks about, what he dreams about? You would hope. Unfortunately, some people, all they're interested in is the Mob [stuff]. Everyone

has their own thing. You can't please everybody."

"I know people complain about them, but we come by them honestly," agrees creator David Chase. "This is the story of a therapy patient, and dreams form a lot of that."

Chase, who scripts most of the dream sequences, acknowledges that "because we do a psychiatric show, [the dreams] are interpretable." However, the symbolism doesn't always come out intentionally. Chase and the writers try to let the dream imagery "come from our subconscious," he said.

While he was writing "Funhouse," the image of Tony riding a bicycle to a fish market came into his head, and then he remembered the success he had on *Northern Exposure* using digital technology to create a talking dog. From there, he wound up with Pussy as a talking fish, which in turn evoked the old *Godfather* line about sleeping with the fishes.

"So you have to wonder why, in my mind, subconsciously, he rode up to a fish market. I wasn't thinking, 'Let's do it, it'll be cool because he sleeps with the fishes.' It just started with this guy, he's riding somewhere, he's on a bicycle, and it turned out to be a fish market. And to me, that's kind of like a real dream. And then I real- ized, 'Oh, he sleeps with the fishes.' And then that led to the whole thing where [Pussy really] went into the ocean at the end."

The Hits Keep on Coming: David Chase Talks about 10 Musical *Sopranos* Moments

BY ALAN SEPINWALL | 3/8/2006

I ASKED DAVID CHASE to talk about the origins of ten of the show's best musical moments. In chronological order:

The song: The classic lullaby "All Through the Night" (in season one's "Denial, Anger, Acceptance")

The scene: As Tony and Carmela beam at Meadow and her school choir's holiday performance, Mikey Palmice shoots Christopher's friend Brendan in the bathtub.

Chase: "If you look back on it, that's a *Godfather* move. I don't think I realized it at the time."

The song: Frank Sinatra's wistful "It Was A Very Good Year" (in season two's "Guy Walks into a Psychiatrist's Office")

The scene: The first of the season-opening montages, as we catch up on what all the characters have been up to (Livia doing physical therapy, Dr. Melfi working out of a motel room, Meadow learning to drive, Tony catting around, etc.) since the end of the surprisingly successful season one.

Chase: "It was a very good year. Our first year was a really good year."

The song: Sinatra's jaunty "Baubles, Bangles, and Beads" (in season two's "Funhouse").

The scene: Tony, Paulie, and Silvio confront Pussy about working with the FBI, then kill him.

Chase: "Musically, that song is so interesting and lilting and just floats, you know. It had nothing do with the fact of money or jewels. Sometimes, these lyrics kind of get in the way."

The song: A mash-up (in the days before most people knew what a mash-up was) of The Police's "Every Breath You Take" and the theme from the '50s private eye show *Peter Gunn* (in season three's "Mr. Ruggerio's Neighborhood")

The scene: FBI agents tail members of the Soprano family as they prepare to plant a listening device in Tony's basement.

Chase: "My wife said, 'You know that "Every Breath You Take" and the "Peter Gunn" theme are the same song?' And we played them and I said, 'Oh, they sort of are.' She has songwriting credit on that episode. 'Every Breath You Take' was interesting for that sequence, and *Peter Gunn* is the Feds' gangbuster music."

The song: The Kinks' dread-filled "Living on a Thin Line" (in season three's "University")

The scene: Used both as the dancing music for Tracee the stripper and a recurring theme to suggest her impending demise.

Chase: "There is this lyric about how there's no England now. I get chills thinking about that now, as we're talking about it." (Writer/producer Terence Winter adds, "I've got more emails and questions from friends about what that song was than anything else we've used in the show's history.")

The song: "Black Books," Nils Lofgren's ethereal ballad about a woman with a wandering eye (in season three's "Second Opinion")

The scene: Used twice, first as Carmela feels lonely and unwanted as she waits in the hall of Meadow's dorm; then, after debating whether to leave Tony, she gets him to donate a big chunk of money to Meadow's school, just so she can feel he did one nice thing for her lately.

Chase: "It's just a beautiful song. Nils's guitar playing is luminous."

The song: The relentless beat of "World Destruction," by Time Zone (in season four's "For All Debts Public and Private")

The scene: First heard as Tony waddles down the driveway to get his season-opening copy of the *Star-Ledger*, then again at the end as Christopher pins the $20 bill he took from the cop who allegedly killed his father to his mother's fridge.

Chase: "That episode was written the week of September 11, or

thereabouts. Very presciently, Afrika Bambaataa and John Lydon had sung about [being brainwashed by religion]. That song's from, what, 1985?

The song: "Dawn (Go Away)," by Frankie Valli and The Four Seasons (in season four's "Christopher")

The scene: On the way back from an Indian casino where they've just been blackmailed into booking Frankie Valli, Tony and Silvio have a debate about Italian American pride and harmful stereotypes. Tony replies to Sil's last opinion by barking, "Take it up with Frankie Valli when you talk to him" a split-second before the credits roll and the song cues up.

Chase: [*Laughing*] "You may not know this, but the Four Seasons are Italian American. . . . And that scene was about Italian Americans. It had to do with that whole thing Tony's telling Silvio about class differences."

The song: The Chi-Lites' soaring love song "Oh Girl" (in season four's "Watching Too Much Television")

The scene: After giving Assemblyman Zellman the okay to date his ex-mistress Irina, Tony hears "Oh Girl" on his car stereo and starts to cry. So he drives to Zellman's house, gives Irina a possessive, yearning look, and savagely beats Zellman with a belt.

Chase: "Just a great song. Certain people who really run from their emotions are very sentimental. It's hard for them to acknowledge true emotions, but they wallow in sentimentality. And that kind of a song, if you're driving along, late at night and that song comes on, it gets you."

The song: Another Kinks number, "I'm Not Like Everybody Else" (in season five's "Cold Cuts")

The scene: Tony is annoyed to see that Janice's anger management therapy is working much better for her than his sessions with Melfi ever have for him, so he so thoroughly humiliates her at dinner that she descends into a homicidal rage—at which point Tony triumphantly exits and walks home, accompanied by The Kinks.

Chase: [*Laughing*] "This one's pretty self-explanatory. . . . My favorite thing about that song is it's a live version, and Ray Davies is singing, and then he says, What are ya?' and 10,000 people say in unison, 'I'm not like everybody else!'"

Crimes of Fashion

BY ALAN SEPINWALL | 4/8/2007

SOPRANOS COSTUME DESIGNER Juliet Polcsa was recently at a fitting with Edie Falco when she had a disturbing epiphany.

"I went, 'Oh my God, is something wrong with me? I like this,'" Polcsa recalls with a laugh.

Since the pilot, Polcsa has been responsible for crafting or perfecting the look of virtually every character on the show, from Adriana's animal prints to Ralphie's ascots.

After Polcsa receives a script and meets with the writer and director, she figures out how many costume changes will be involved in the hour—100 to 120 is the average, though a recent show went up to 160—and then she and her team begin to shop. They visit stores all over the area, from department stores like Macy's to small men's shops in Bensonhurst and Howard Beach that outfit the real-life versions of Tony and Johnny Sack.

————

For the series regulars, the clothes they wear help define whom they're playing. Steve Van Zandt never feels in character until he's in full costume. As a sign of how much he values Silvio's clothes, he buys his full wardrobe at the end of every season, even though he would never wear most of it off-camera.

(Also buying old wardrobe, for a different reason: Tony Sirico, whose fashion sense is so close to Paulie Walnuts's that Polcsa once dressed him in a shirt identical to one in Sirico's closet at home. "A year later, he ripped his own shirt and he said, 'I need that shirt as a replacement.'")

Choreographing the Whack

BY ALAN SEPINWALL | 4/9/2007

WHEN TONY SOPRANO puts a hit out on someone, it's time to call Pete Bucossi.

The North Plainfield [New Jersey] native has been the stunt coordinator for *The Sopranos* from the very start, and over the course of nine years and seventy-seven episodes, he's helped orchestrate stabbings, shootings, car crashes, hangings, and other manners of death and dismemberment.

———

One of the series' longest, most brutal fight scenes was the season four kitchen brawl between Tony and Ralphie, which ended with Ralphie's death (and later beheading). Much of it, like Ralphie spraying Tony's eyes with Raid, was in the script, while other parts had to be negotiated in rehearsal.

"That was pretty complex," Bucossi explains. "You're working with props, there was some breakaway glass. You want to take it to a limit, almost where Ralphie's head is going through the floor. It's pretty detailed in the script, and for a major fight, we have the luxury of rehearsals."

The show's leading man also happens to be its most accomplished physical performer, which comes in handy, considering how often Tony is the one involved in a fight.

"Obviously, Jimmy [Gandolfini] can handle himself. He's a big and powerful-looking man already, but he's always concerned with not hurting anybody, making it look good. He's great."

A memorable scene in season three had Tony picking up mistress Gloria and hurling her to the floor. During rehearsal, there was debate over exactly how Tony should grab the much smaller woman, both for practical purposes and to make it look good.

"I don't remember if it was scripted as by the throat or her clothes, but she was in a nightgown, so we knew, obviously, if he grabbed her by the clothes, they would be ripped. He's got some big paws on him. I think Jim came up with the idea, 'I just grab her right by the throat.' So then we realized she could grab onto his hand with her hand and she could hold onto him and he could easily lift her. That was a happy marriage right there. And then we had a stunt double that took the fall."

Even the most basic stunt requires heavy preparation, sometimes just to reassure the actor. When Eugene Pontecorvo hung himself in last season's premiere, Bucossi made sure to put actor Robert Funaro into the two-piece harness a few days ahead of time, "just to know he's not going to hang himself." In the end, Funaro's relative comfort with the stunt allowed the director to linger for a long time on Eugene dangling from the end of the rope, turning a stock bit of movie magic into something unsettlingly different.

Setting the Scene

BY ALAN SEPINWALL | 4/8/2007

WHEN *SOPRANOS* PRODUCTION designer Bob Shaw and location manager Regina Heyman were tasked in season three with finding a home for Tony's new mistress, Gloria Trillo, both assumed they would put her in a high-rise apartment in Fort Lee or some other New York–adjacent location where a single career woman might live.

Then, they sat down with David Chase, who insisted, "No, no, she lives in some cabin in the woods! She's a witch!"

After picking her jaw up off the floor, Heyman sent her team of location scouts out to find just such a cabin. They looked and they looked, and every promising candidate was nixed because the location was too romote to get the entire production crew into. Finally, on a complete fluke, one of the scouts was driving past the Friar Tuck Inn on Route 23 in Cedar Grove and noticed a small cabin tucked right behind the inn.

And, after all that effort, the exterior of the cabin was glimpsed only briefly on-screen, while the interior of Gloria's home was built from scratch on the stages at Silvercup Studios in Long Island City.

Welcome to the world of Heyman and Shaw, who, since the start of season two, have been responsible for finding or building (or, in some cases, both) the places where Tony Soprano and company live, work and, occasionally, whack.

When Uncle Junior went under house arrest in season two, that meant he needed a house, and Shaw knew from his own childhood and the relatives from the Italian side of his family just what the place should look like.

"He was from an older generation. In those days, they didn't have aspirations to become part of the upper middle class, the way Tony and Carmela are. And older people, they just don't move, they say, 'This is my house.' We also assume that, never having been married, from that generation, he never moved out of his parents' home, so the last renovation that Junior's house had was in the '50s. People always wonder why, if he's the de facto Mob boss, does he live in such a crummy house, but it's actually a very accurate thing in terms of that generation of Italian Americans and the way the Mob used to be."

Chase has near-total recall of all the places he lived and visited while growing up in New Jersey and is very specific about what he wants and what he doesn't. While picking a location for Dr. Melfi's house, Shaw never noticed a hanging mirror in the foyer, and the way a scene was shot, the mirror was clearly showing a hat collection out of frame.

"David saw the scene," Shaw recalls, "and he was very upset and said, 'Melfi does not have a collection of hats!'"

Sopranos Creator's Last Word: End Speaks for Itself

BY ALAN SEPINWALL | 6/12/2007

WHAT DO YOU do when your TV world ends? You go to dinner, then keep quiet.

Sopranos creator David Chase took his wife out for dinner Sunday night in France, where he fled to avoid "all the Monday morning quarterbacking" about the show's finale. After this exclusive interview (agreed to before the season began), he intends to let the work—especially the controversial final scene—speak for itself.

"I have no interest in explaining, defending, reinterpreting, or adding to what is there," he says of the final scene.

"No one was trying to be audacious, honest to God," he adds. "We did what we thought we had to do. No one was trying to blow people's minds or thinking, 'Wow, this'll [tick] them off.'

"People get the impression that you're trying to [mess] with them, and it's not true. You're trying to entertain them."

———

"Anybody who wants to watch it, it's all there," says Chase.

Some fans have assumed the ambiguous ending was Chase setting up the oft-rumored *Sopranos* movie.

"I don't think about [a movie] much," he says. "I never say never. An idea could pop into my head where I would go, 'Wow, that would make a great movie,' but I doubt it.

"I'm not being coy," he adds. "If something appeared that really made a good *Sopranos* movie and you could invest in it and everybody else wanted to do it, I would do it. But I think we've kind of said it and done it."

Another problem: Over the last season, Chase killed so many key characters. He's toyed with the idea of "going back to a day in 2006 that you didn't see, but then [Tony's children] would be older than they were then and you would know that Tony doesn't get killed. It's got problems." (Earlier in the interview, Chase noted that often his favorite part of the show was the characters telling stories about the good ol' days of Tony's parents. Just a guess, but if Chase ever does a movie spinoff, it'll be set in Newark in the '60s.)[2]

Meanwhile, remember that twenty-one-month hiatus between seasons five and six? That was Chase thinking up the ending. HBO's then-chairman Chris Albrecht came to

---

2   Most of our predictions about the show during its run turned out very wrong; a decade later, *The Many Saints of Newark* is going to prove this one right.

him after season five and suggested thinking up a conclusion to the series; Chase agreed, on the condition he get "a long break" to decide an ending.

Originally, that ending was supposed to occur last year, but midway through production, the number of episodes was increased, and Chase stretched out certain plot elements while saving the major climaxes for this final batch of nine.

"If this had been one season, the Vito storyline would not have been so important," he says.

Much of this final season featured Tony bullying, killing, or otherwise alienating the members of his inner circle. After all those years of viewing him as "the sympathetic Mob boss," were we, like his therapist Dr. Melfi, supposed to finally wake up and smell the sociopath?

"From my perspective, there's nothing different about Tony in this season than there ever was," Chase says. "To me, that's Tony."

Chase has had an ambivalent relationship with his fans, particularly the bloodthirsty whacking crowd who seemed to tune in only for the chance to see someone's head get blown off (or run over by an SUV). So was he reluctant to fill last week's penultimate episode, "The Blue Comet," with so many vivid death scenes?

"I'm the number one fan of gangster movies," he says. "Martin Scors-

ese has no greater devotee than me. Like everyone else, I get off partly on the betrayals, the retributions, the swift justice. But what you come to realize when you do a series is, you could be killing straw men all day long. Those murders only have any meaning when you've invested story in them. Otherwise, you might as well watch *Cleaver*."

One detail about the final scene he'll discuss, however tentatively: the selection of Journey's "Don't Stop Believin'" as the song on the jukebox.

"It didn't take much time at all to pick it, but there was a lot of conversation after the fact. I did something I'd never done before: In the location van, with the crew, I was saying, 'What do you think?' When I said, 'Don't Stop Believin',' people went, 'What? Oh my God!'

"I said, 'I know, I know, just give a listen,' and little by little, people started coming around."

Whether viewers will have a similar time-delayed reaction to the finale as a whole, Chase doesn't know. ("I hear some people were very angry and others were not, which is what I expected.") He's relaxing in France, then he'll try to make movies.

"It's been the greatest career experience of my life," he says. "There's nothing more in TV that I could say or would want to say."

THE EULOGIES

A tribute to James Gandolfini: Matt Zoller Seitz's obituary and account from the funeral from Vulture.com, and David Chase's eulogy, as transcribed by Alan Sepinwall.

Seitz on James Gandolfini, 1961–2013: A Great Actor, A Better Man

BY MATT ZOLLER SEITZ | 6/20/2013

JAMES GANDOLFINI was real. He was special. You could feel it.

Friends felt it. Colleagues felt it. People who talked to him for five minutes and never saw him again felt it. People who never met him in person and knew him only through his performance on *The Sopranos* felt it.

It was real. It was deep. It was true. James Gandolfini had an authentic connection with viewers. Everyone who watched him perform, in a starring role or a bit part, came away feeling understood. You watched him act and you thought, "Yes. He gets it. He understands."

He wasn't one of them. He was one of us.

"I'm an actor," he once told a reporter. "I do a job and I go home. Why are you interested in me? You don't ask a truck driver about his job."

In the wake of James Gandolfini's death—of a heart attack, at the appallingly young age of fifty-one—I keep coming back to that realness, and the source of it, his goodness. I got to know him a bit as a reporter, and I can testify that what you've heard is true. He was a good man.

Gandolfini's goodness was, I believe, at the heart of the powerful connection he forged with viewers. You could sense the goodness in him, no matter how tortured and tormented his characters were. It was there in those sad eyes and that radiant smile.

I covered *The Sopranos* for the *Star-Ledger*, the paper Tony Soprano picks up at the end of his driveway. I kept in contact with members of the production staff after I handed the beat to my colleague Alan Sepinwall in 2004. I wasn't buddies with Gandolfini or anything. Not too many people in the press were, I don't think, except maybe people Gandolfini knew before he got famous.

I did one of the only one-on-one interviews with him, way back in late 1998, before *The Sopranos* premiered on HBO.

Two days before our scheduled interview, he called my house. My wife answered the phone.

"Yes?" she said.

Then her jaw dropped. She put her hand over the mouthpiece and whispered, "It's James Gandolfini!"

She loved Gandolfini. She'd had a crush on him ever since she saw him play Geena Davis's boyfriend in *Angie*.

Then she held up a silencing finger because Gandolfini was already talking, nervously. Stammering, practically.

"Okay," she said to him. "All right. Well, Okay. Well. Well . . . Well, I don't know about that. Are you sure?"

Long pause.

"It might not be so bad," she told him. "You never know. You know what? I think this is a conversation that you really should have with Matt. Hold on a second, he's right here."

When I picked up the receiver, Gandolfini said, "Hey, listen, I've been thinking about it, and I really think it's better if I don't do this interview."

"Why not?" I asked.

"I just don't see how I'd have anything interesting to say," he said. "Why would anybody care? I'm just not that interesting. Who cares what some actor has to say about anything? I'll just come off sounding like an idiot."

He was silent for an awkward moment.

Then he said, "I don't want to get you in trouble with your bosses, though. So I thought I should talk to you about it, and ask you if maybe there was some way we could not do this thing. And just . . . not do it. Without causing a problem for you. Or for me."

Somehow I managed to talk him into doing the interview anyhow.

My editor Mark Di Ionno asked if he could come along when I visited the set, because he'd gone to Rutgers with Gandolfini and claimed to be personally responsible for the distinctive dent in the actor's forehead. Appar-

ently a bunch of guys were tear-assing around the dorm shooting dart guns at one another, and Mark surprised Gandolfini by kicking a door open before he could burst through it. The door struck Gandolfini in the forehead and left that famous crease.

"I can't wait to see the look on his face," Mark said.

When we arrived on the set, Gandolfini saw Mark. His face lit up with one of the warmest smiles I've ever seen on anybody. He hugged Mark and clapped him on the back so hard you'd think he was trying to dislodge food lodged in Mark's gullet.

This is how James Gandolfini often greeted people: as if he was overjoyed to see them, and wanted to revel in their presence just in case he never saw them again.

We spent half a day together on the set of one of the *Sopranos* episodes. He was great. I wish I'd saved the cassette tape. He talked about coming up in Hollywood and in the New York theater scene. He talked about acting and bartending. I vividly remember him talking about how much he loved Mickey Rourke.

He said, "In the eighties, Mickey Rourke was the shit. If you were a young guy who loved movies and wanted to be an actor and [were] seeing a lot of movies in the eighties, there was nobody better than Mickey Rourke. De Niro, Pacino, Dustin Hoffman, they were all great, don't get me wrong. But Mickey Rourke was the man. I wanted to be Mickey Rourke."

I said, "You wanted to be like Mickey Rourke?"

He laughed and said, "No! I mean actually wanted to be Mickey Rourke. I wanted to be him. Like, steal his soul, like in *Angel Heart,* and actually be Mickey Rourke!"

In the summer of 1999, the Television Critics Association gave Gandolfini an award for his work on the show. Nobody warned him that the cocktail reception after the awards show was a press event and that he'd be swarmed by reporters with notepads and tape recorders. He thought it was an off-the-books type of deal, just one professional group appreciating another. I was already at the bar when he sidled up next to me, ordered a beer and said, "One of these days, you'll have to explain to me how this thing works," and waved his hand, indicating the media piling onto the hotel balcony where the bar was located. When the tape recorders and notepads came out, his eyes filled with panic.

When the cameras came out and the flashbulbs started going off, he stayed a couple more minutes, then fled. A friend later told me that the moment reminded him of the scene at the end of *King Kong,* right before the ape breaks his chains and goes berserk.

He got better about seeming comfortable talking to the press and in public forums. In time he was comfortable enough to do an hour-long conversation with James Lipton on *Inside the Actors Studio.*

But I think it's fair to say that none of this is proof that he'd "gone Hollywood." More likely he was just giving a different sort of performance, as convincing as his others.

Every time I spoke to him between 1998 and 2006—the last time I had any contact with him—he seemed like the same guy I'd met that first time, but with more money. I took my brother Richard, a big *Sopranos* fan, to the season six DVD release party. When Gandolfini saw me, he acted as if he'd never been happier to see anyone. He grabbed me in a headlock, gave me noogies, and crowed, "Hoah! What happened to all your hair?"

"What happened to all *your* hair?" I shot back lamely, pulling free of his grip.

"Look at this fuckin' guy, with the banter," he said to the room at large.

"When's the last time you saw him?" Richard asked me afterward.

"I don't know. Maybe three years?"

You wouldn't have known it.

You could tell he really got a kick out of people: experiencing their personalities, their idiosyncrasies; hearing their stories.

I think that's why, when he'd won some awards and made a ton of money and had enough clout to get his own projects made, the first thing he threw his weight behind was an oral history documentary about recently returned veterans. He was oncamera interviewing. He listened more than he talked. He had no political agenda. He just wanted to give the soldiers a platform to talk about what it was like to go through whatever they'd been through.

It wasn't about him. Even if he was the star of a TV show or a movie, it wasn't about him.

It was about them.

It was about you.

It was about us.

When my wife died suddenly of a heart attack in 2006, he sent me a condolence note. It read, "I am sorry for your loss. I remember talking to your wife on the phone that one time. She seemed like a nice lady."

It was signed, "Jim."

Anybody who had even the slightest contact with Gandolfini will testify to what a great guy he was, how full of life he was, how extraordinary he made other people feel. Yes, absolutely, he had problems—with drink, with drugs, with women, probably with lots of other things, for all we know—but so does everybody, to one degree or another. But whether he was feeling well or poorly, or living smartly or stupidly, there was always something about the guy that you wanted to embrace.

You could feel it shining through the screen, that warmth and vulnerability, that broken yet still-hopeful humanness.

That's what made Tony Soprano, a bully and killer and cheater and disgusting hypocrite, so likable. The decent part of Tony, the part that stood in for the tragically wasted human potential Dr. Melfi kept trying to tease out and embrace, came from Gandolfini. His humanity shone through Tony's rotten façade. When people said they sensed good in Tony, it was James Gandolfini they sensed.

He was Tony Soprano. He was James Gandolfini. He was us.

We lost a friend today.

Publicly Mourning a Private Man:
Seitz on the Funeral of James Gandolfini

BY MATT ZOLLER SEITZ | 6/27/2013

FUNERALS ARE FOR the living. James Gandolfini's was beautiful and wrenching and right. Given what an earthy guy he was, it seems appropriate that it was open to the public and that people started crowding the streets outside the Cathedral of Saint John the Divine in Harlem early in the morning to claim a seat and pay their respects.

I can't help thinking, though, that if he could have seen all the people in suits and dresses, the immense church with its vaulted ceiling and 1,800 pews, and the news vans and cameras and fans lining up at dawn, he might have thought, *This is silly. I'm just an actor* . . .

The James Gandolfini portrayed by eulogists this morning matched that perception of a man grateful for his talent and his opportunities, yet uncomfortable with the attention he got, as if he believed his contributions were too small in the greater scheme to bear mention. They weren't small—the outpouring of grief over his premature death of a heart attack at age fifty-one is proof. But the fact that his mind worked that way is one of the reasons people responded to his acting, and to Gandolfini the man.

A who's-who of actors, filmmakers, and media personalities were packed into the front section of the church. There were *Sopranos* producers and costars: David Chase, Michael Imperioli, Dominic Chianese, Lorraine Bracco, Tony Sirico, Edie Falco, Steve Buscemi, Annabella Sciorra, Aida Turturro, Vincent Pastore, Michael Rispoli, Vincent Curatola. There were performers and media personalities who knew or worked with Gandolfini: Alec Baldwin, Julianna Margulies, Brian Williams, Chris Noth, Dick Cavett, Marcia Gay Harden.

Jamie-Lynn Sigler, who played Tony Soprano's daughter Meadow on the show, was an especially poignant sight, very pregnant, and like so many other guests, red-eyed from crying. I overheard a guest saying of Gandolfini's thirteen-year-old son, Michael, "He's a really strong kid, but he looks so lost."

The actor's coffin was wheeled in as the Rev. James A. Kowalski intoned, "I am the resurrection, I am the life, says the Lord." The pallbearers tried to seem as calm and resolute as they could, as pallbearers always do, but you could see their inconsolable sadness. I will never forget the look on the face of the former *Sopranos* writer and producer Todd Kessler, the pallbearer near the end of Gandolfini's casket. A knot of anguish.

The eulogists drove home that there was a real kindness, empathy, and humility to Gandolfini. These qualities came through even when he was playing larger-than-life characters or succumbing to the darkness and turning into the wild man of early-aughts tabloid scandals—a side alluded to by Gandolfini's longtime friend Thomas Richardson and *Sopranos* creator David Chase.

Gandolfini's wife Deborah, the mother of his newborn daughter Liliana, remembered her husband as "an honest and loving man. Ironically," she said, indicating the crowd, "he was extremely private." She said that he was "always secretly helping someone," a trait confirmed in numerous obituaries and fleshed out in testimonials at the funeral.

Gandolfini's friend Richardson described him as "the most giving and generous person that everyone here has ever known." He talked about how Gandolfini's hugs were always a little bit tighter and went on a little bit longer than everyone else's. Then he asked everyone in the chapel to stand up and put their arms around the people next to them and hug them as tight as they could, "for it is in hugging that we are hugged."

There were anecdotes about Gandolfini randomly spending hours with fans he'd met on the street, hiring a sushi chef out of his own pocket to pamper the crew on film sets, and supporting people and organizations for years without anyone in the media knowing he was doing it.

The Rev. Kowalski remembered first meeting Gandolfini at a fundraiser for the Tannenbaum Center for Religious Understanding. He talked about how the actor used to keep a notepad and pen with him as he drove; if Gandolfini heard the name of a charitable organization on the radio that he wanted to get involved with, he'd pull over and write it down. "He'd say, 'I wanna do something to support what they're trying to do,'" Kowalski recalled.

Kowalski spoke movingly about Gandolfini's ability to tap universal fears and longings in such a direct way that it humanized an often monstrous character, Tony Soprano. He said that although he did not like the violence of *The Sopranos*, he watched the show anyway because he felt Gandolfini's performance gave him insight into where violence comes from.

"You can't pay someone enough to do a job like that," he said, of both Gandolfini's reaching into darkness as Tony Soprano and of the actor's personal generosity.

Gandolfini's old friend Susan Aston, credited as his "acting coach" on *The Sopranos*, spoke of the actor as someone who was fully aware of his flaws and worked as hard as he could to understand himself, control his demons, and be a better person. "In a small home office that he referred to as 'the cave,' where he and I worked late nights on the next day's scenes, this other thing he strove for was to be able to accept himself on the occasions when he fell short of his intentions," she said.

Chase's eulogy was presented in the form of a letter to his friend. "I tried to write a traditional eulogy, but it came out like bad TV," he joked. He said he'd thought about writing a few organizing thoughts on a piece of paper and then winging it, as Gandolfini used to do at awards shows, but decided against it, because "a lot of your speeches didn't make sense. But it didn't matter that it didn't make sense, because the feeling was real. The feeling was real. The feeling was real. I can't say that enough."

"When Jim focused his incredible gaze on you," Gandolfini's friend Richardson said, "you felt so important to him."

Absolutely.

We all felt that sense of importance, that feeling of being understood. Even if you never met the actor and knew him only by watching him as Tony Soprano, there was something about Gandolfini that felt knowable and reachable—a directness, a willingness to be vulnerable, to let himself be helpless or pathetic, to allow us to see through him, the better to see ourselves. Those qualities can't be taught, only harnessed. Gandolfini was born with them, and he worked like hell to transform them into tools that he could use to connect with us.

Connect he did.

After the funeral, I stopped off at a pizzeria for a slice. As I was sitting alone at a table, a man came over to me and asked if he could look at my program. He said, "Don't worry, I won't get anything on it."

This was Robert Sattinger, a fifty-two-year-old New Yorker who'd tried to get into the funeral but "arrived just a little bit too late." He told me he didn't see *The Sopranos* in its original run but caught up with it in reruns years later while recovering from "a medical situation," and ended up watching the entire run of the series twice.

"I've never done anything like this before," he said, of his attempt to attend the funeral of an actor he'd never met.

But Gandolfini's performance had moved him so much that when the actor died, he felt the need to go pay his respects.

As he watched Tony, Sattinger said, he knew that even at his most horrible, the character "had a human side to him, and he had weaknesses which he tried to get hold of. You could tell what was in his heart."

Eulogy for James Gandolfini

BY DAVID CHASE | 06/27/2013

Dear Jimmy,

Your family asked me to speak at your service, and I am so honored and touched. I'm also really scared, and I say that because you of all people will understand this. I'd like to run away and call in four days from now from the beauty parlor. I want to do a good job, because I love you, and because you always did a good job.

I think the deal is I'm supposed to speak about the actor/artist's work part of your life. Others will have spoken beautifully and magnificently about the other beautiful and magnificent parts of you: father, brother, friend. I guess what I was told is I'm also supposed to speak for your castmates whom you loved, for your crew that you loved so much, for the people at HBO, and Journey. I hope I can speak for all of them today and for you.

I asked around, and experts told me to start with a joke and a funny anecdote. "Ha ha ha." But as you yourself so often said, I'm not feelin' it. I'm too sad and full of despair. I'm writing to you partly because I would like to have had your advice. Because I remember how you did speeches. I saw you do a lot of them at awards shows and stuff, and invariably you would scratch two or three thoughts on a sheet of paper and put it in your pocket, and then not really refer to

it. And consequently, a lot of your speeches didn't make sense. I think that could happen in here, except in your case, it didn't matter that it didn't make sense, because the feeling was real. The feeling was real. The feeling was real. I can't say that enough.

I tried to write a traditional eulogy, but it came out like bad TV. So I'm writing you this letter, and now I'm reading that letter in front of you. But it is being done to and for an audience, so I'll give the funny opening a try. I hope that it's funny; it is to me and it is to you.

And that is, one day toward the end of the show—maybe season four or season five—we were on the set shooting a scene with Stevie Van Zandt, and I think the setup was that Tony had received news of the death of someone, and it was inconvenient for him. And it said, "Tony opens the refrigerator door, closes it, and he starts to speak." And the cameras rolled, and you opened the refrigerator door, and you slammed it really hard—you slammed it hard enough that it came open again. And so then you slammed it again, then it came open again. You kept slamming it and slamming it and slamming it and *slamming* it and went apeshit on that refrigerator.

And the funny part for me is I remember Steven Van Zandt—

because the cameras are going, we have to play this whole scene with a refrigerator door opening—I remember Steven Van Zandt standing there with his lip out, trying to figure out, "Well, what should I do? First, as Silvio, because he just ruined my refrigerator. And also as Steven the actor, because we're now going to play a scene with the refrigerator door open; people don't do that." And I remember him going over there and trying to tinker with the door and fix it, and it didn't work. And so we finally had to call cut, and we had to fix the refrigerator door, and it never really worked, because the gaffer tape showed on the refrigerator, and it was a problem all day long.

And I remember you saying, "Ah, this role, this role, the places it takes me to, the things I have to do, it's so dark."

And I remember telling you, "Did I tell you to destroy the refrigerator? Did it say anywhere in the script, 'Tony destroys a refrigerator'? It says 'Tony angrily shuts the refrigerator door.' That's what it says. You destroyed the fridge."

Another memory of you that comes to mind is from very early on—might have been the pilot, I don't know. We were shooting in that really hot and humid summer New Jersey heat. And I looked over, and you were sitting in an aluminum beach chair, with your slacks rolled up to your knees, in black socks and black shoes, and a wet handkerchief on your head.

And I remember looking over there and going, "Well, that's really not a cool look." But I was filled with love, and I knew then that I was in the right place. I said, "Wow, I haven't seen that done since my father used to do it, and my Italian uncles use to do it, and my Italian grandfather used to do it." And they were laborers in the same hot sun in New Jersey. They were stonemasons, and your father worked with concrete. I don't know what it is with Italians and cement. And I was so proud of our heritage—it made me so proud of our heritage to see you do that.

When I said before that you were my brother, this has a lot to do with that: Italian American, Italian worker, builder, that Jersey thing—whatever that means—the same social class. I really feel that, though I'm older than you, and always felt, that we are brothers. And it was really based on that day. I was filled with so much love for everything we were doing and about to embark on.

I also feel you're my brother in that we have different tastes, but there are things we both love, which was family, work, people in all their imperfection, food, alcohol, talking, rage, and a desire to bring the whole structure crashing down. We amused each other.

The image of my uncles and father reminded me of something that happened between us one time. Because these guys were such men—your father and these men from Italy. And you were going through a crisis of faith about yourself and acting, a lot of things, were very upset. I went to meet you on the banks of the Hudson River, and you told me, you said, "You know what I want to be? I want to be a man. That's all. I want to be a man." Now, this is so odd, because you are such a man. You're a man in many ways many males, including myself, wish they could be a man.

The paradox about you as a man is that I always felt personally, that with you, I was seeing a young boy. A boy about Michael's age right now. 'Cause you were very boyish. And about the age when humankind, and life on the planet are really opening up and putting on a show, really revealing themselves in all their beautiful and horrible glory. And I saw you as a boy— as a sad boy, amazed and confused and loving and amazed by all that. And that was all in your eyes.

And that was why, I think, you were a great actor: because of that boy who was inside. He was a child reacting. Of course you were intelligent, but it was a child reacting, and your reactions were often childish. And by that, I mean they were pre-school, they were pre-manners, they were pre-intellect. They were just simple emotions, straight and pure. And I think your talent is that you can take in the immensity of humankind and the universe, and shine it out to the rest of us like a huge bright light. And I believe that only a pure soul, like

a child, can do that really well. And that was you.

Now to talk about a third guy between us, there was you and me and this third guy. People always say, "Tony Soprano. Why did we love him so much when he was such a prick?" And my theory was, they saw the little boy. They felt and they loved the little boy, and they sensed his love and hurt. And you brought all of that to it. You were a good boy. Your work with the Wounded Warriors was just one example of this. And I'm going to say something because I know that you'd want me to say it in public: that no one should forget Tony Sirico's efforts with you in this. He was there with you all the way, and in fact you said to me just recently, "It's more Tony than me." And I know you, and I know you would want me to turn the spotlight on him, or you wouldn't be satisfied. So I've done that.

So Tony Soprano never changed, people say. He got darker. I don't know how they can misunderstand that. He tried and he tried and he tried. And you tried and you tried, more than most of us, and harder than most of us, and sometimes you tried too hard. That refrigerator is one example. Sometimes, your efforts were at cost to you and others, but you tried. And I'm thinking about the fact of how nice you were to strangers on the street, fans, photographers. You would be patient, loving, and personal, and then finally you would just do too much, and then you would snap. And that's of course what everybody read about, was the snapping.

I was asked to talk about the work part, and so I'll talk about the show we used to do and how we used to do it. You know, everybody knows that we always ended an episode with a song. That was kind of like me and the writers letting the real geniuses do the heavy lifting: Bruce, and Mick and Keith, and Howlin' Wolf and a bunch of them. So if this was an episode, it would end with a song. And the song, as far as I'm concerned, would be Joan Osborne's "(What If God Was) One Of Us?" And the set-up for this—we never did this, and you never even heard this—is that Tony was somehow lost in the Meadowlands. He didn't have his car, and his wallet, and his car keys. I forget how he got there— there was some kind of a scrape—but he had nothing in his pocket but some change. He didn't have his guys with him, he didn't have his gun. And so Mob boss Tony Soprano had to be one of the working stiffs, getting in line for the bus. And the way we were going to film it, he was going to get on the bus, and the lyric that would've run over that would've been—and we don't have Joan Osborne to sing it:

If God had a face
what would it look like?

And would you want to see
if seeing meant you had to believe?
And yeah, yeah, God is great.
Yeah, yeah, God is good.
Yeah, yeah, yeah.

So Tony would get on the bus, and he would sit there, and the bus would pull out in this big billow of diesel smoke. And then the key lyric would come on, and it was

What if God was one of us?
Just a slob like one of us?
Just a stranger on the bus
Trying to make his way home.

And that would've been playing over your face, Jimmy. But then—and this is where it gets kind of strange— now I would have to update, because of the events of the last week. And I would let the song play further, and the lyrics would be

Just trying to make his way home
Like a holy rollin' stone
Back up to Heaven all alone
Nobody callin' on the phone
'Cept for the Pope, maybe, in Rome.

Love,
David

Acknowledgments

Thanks to Terence Winter, Ilene Landress, Meredith Tucker, Tobe Becker, Diego Aldana, Angela Tarantino, and Cecile Cross-Plummer for helping fill in the gaps in both David Chase's memory and our own. Thanks to our many current and former bosses at the *Star-Ledger,* HitFix, Uproxx, *New York* magazine/Vulture.com, RogerEbert.com, and *Rolling Stone* for the support when the book's archival pieces were being written and/or for the flexibility they gave us to write the hundreds of thousands of words of new material. Thanks to David Chase for sitting down for these interviews, and to Denise Chase for tagging along on most of these marathon trips down memory lane.

Most importantly, thank you to our families for understanding all the times we disappeared down rabbit holes, or when we began talking about Artie Bucco in our sleep.

ABRAMS The Art of Books
195 Broadway, New York, NY 10007
abramsbooks.com